SRA ART Connections

D1194471

Arts Education for the 21st Century

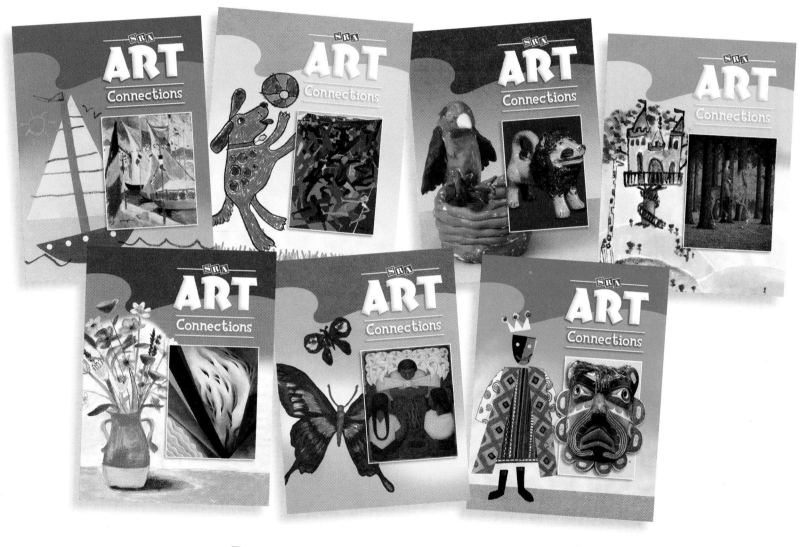

Culture

Personal Expression

Creativity

History

Beauty

Critical Thinking

Art encourages different ways of learning, knowing, and communicating.

i

All the Resources you Need for Great Art Teaching!

Art Connections provides everything teachers need to offer meaningful art education.

Student Edition K-6

Comprehensive student materials in two formats:

Student Edition

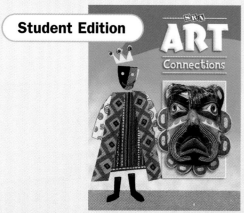

LEVEL 6

Big Book

LEVEL 6

Teacher Edition

Everything classroom and art teachers need to teach art effectively

LEVEL 4

- ■ Complete lesson plans to teach
  - ● elements and principles of art
  - ● art history and culture
  - ● art criticism
  - ● art production
- ■ Art background
- ■ Cross-curricular connections
- ■ Program resources guide

Technology Components

e-Presentation for students and teachers

LEVEL K

e-Presentation offers the complete Student Edition as a presentation tool for teachers, complete with multimedia experiences, assessments, teacher materials, and a gallery of all artworks in the entire program.

This electronic gallery allows immediate access to all the artwork in the **Art Connections** program.

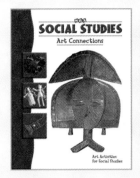
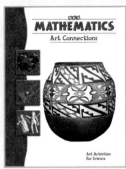

Cross-Curricular Art Connections

include practical art projects for the classroom to help meet subject-area guidelines in

- Social Studies
- Mathematics
- Language Arts and Reading
- Science

LEVEL 3

Reading and Writing Test Preparation

that reinforces art content

LEVEL 1

Home and After-School Connections

for every unit, in English and Spanish

Professional Development Guide

for both classroom teachers and art specialists

Assessment

with tests in English and Spanish for every lesson

LEVEL 5

Art Around the World CD-ROM

includes 150 works of art from the *Art Around the World Collection,* representing a variety of thought-provoking perspectives and activities.

The National Museum of Women in the Arts Collection CD-ROM

dynamically explores the 200-print collection to introduce students to key women artists.

Enrich students' lives with exposure to the great masters and cultures of the world.

Fine-Art Resources

Transparencies Overhead transparency study prints for all lesson artwork allow for up-close examination.

LEVEL 5

Large Prints for each unit provide exemplary artwork to develop unit concepts.

LEVEL 2

LEVEL 1

Artist Profiles Pictures, background information, and profiles for every artist in the program provide valuable historical and cultural information at your fingertips.

Literature and Art Videos and DVD develop art connections to literature.

The Polar Express

Art Around the World 150-print resource explores the art of the world's cultures.

ARTSOURCE logo

Artsource® Performing Arts Resource Package (Video and DVD) integrates the performing arts of dance, music, and theatre.

LEVEL 3

The National Museum of Women in the Arts Collection This 200-print resource provides famous artwork from famous women artists.

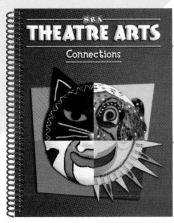

Theatre Arts Connections is a complete dramatic arts program that ties to *Art Connections*.

LEVEL 4

Elements and Principles of Art Teaching Resources

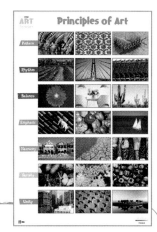

Elements of Art poster reinforces line, shape, color, value, form, space, and texture.

Principles of Art poster develops concepts of rhythm, balance, movement, harmony, variety, emphasis, and unity.

Use the *Color Wheel* to explore color concepts.

Flash Cards provide a quick review of the elements and principles of art.

v

SRA ART Connections

Build a foundation in the elements and principles of art.

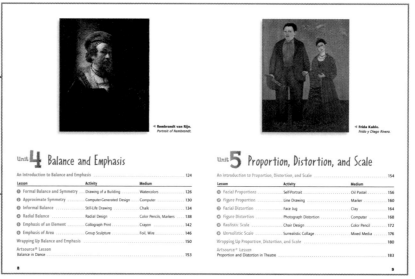

36 Lessons at every grade level develop the elements and principles of art in six-lesson units.

◄ **Rembrandt van Rijn.**
Portrait of Rembrandt.

◄ **Frida Kahlo.**
Frida y Diego Rivera.

Unit 4 Balance and Emphasis

An Introduction to Balance and Emphasis 124

Lesson	Activity	Medium	
❶ Formal Balance and Symmetry	Drawing of a Building	Watercolors	126
❷ Approximate Symmetry	Computer-Generated Design	Computer	130
❸ Informal Balance	Still-Life Drawing	Chalk	134
❹ Radial Balance	Radial Design	Color Pencils, Markers	138
❺ Emphasis of an Element	Collograph Print	Crayon	142
❻ Emphasis of Area	Group Sculpture	Foil, Wire	146

Wrapping Up Balance and Emphasis 150

Artsource® Lesson
Balance in Dance 153

8

Unit 5 Proportion, Distortion, and Scale

An Introduction to Proportion, Distortion, and Scale 154

Lesson	Activity	Medium	
❶ Facial Proportions	Self Portrait	Oil Pastel	156
❷ Figure Proportion	Line Drawing	Marker	160
❸ Facial Distortion	Face Jug	Clay	164
❹ Figure Distortion	Photograph Distortion	Computer	168
❺ Realistic Scale	Chair Design	Color Pencil	172
❻ Unrealistic Scale	Surrealistic Collage	Mixed Media	176

Wrapping Up Proportion, Distortion, and Scale 180

Artsource® Lesson
Proportion and Distortion in Theatre 183

9

LEVEL 6

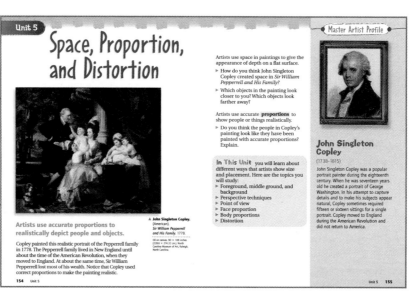

Unit 5

Space, Proportion, and Distortion

Artists use accurate proportions to realistically depict people and objects.

Copley painted this realistic portrait of the Pepperrell family in 1778. The Pepperrell family lived in New England until about the time of the American Revolution, when they moved to England. At about the same time, Sir William Pepperrell lost most of his wealth. Notice that Copley used correct proportions to make the painting realistic.

▲ **John Singleton Copley.** (American). *Sir William Pepperrell and His Family.* 1778.
Oil on canvas. 90 × 108 inches (228.6 × 274.32 cm.). North Carolina Museum of Art, Raleigh, North Carolina.

Artists use space in paintings to give the appearance of depth on a flat surface.
▶ How do you think John Singleton Copley created space in *Sir William Pepperrell and His Family?*
▶ Which objects in the painting look closer to you? Which objects look farther away?

Artists use accurate **proportions** to show people or things realistically.
▶ Do you think the people in Copley's painting look like they have been painted with accurate proportions? Explain.

In This Unit you will learn about different ways that artists show size and placement. Here are the topics you will study:
▶ Foreground, middle ground, and background
▶ Perspective techniques
▶ Point of view
▶ Face proportion
▶ Body proportions
▶ Distortion

Unit Openers introduce students to unit concepts and master artists.

● **Master Artist Profile** ●

John Singleton Copley
(1738–1815)

John Singleton Copley was a popular portrait painter during the eighteenth century. When he was seventeen years old he created a portrait of George Washington. In his attempt to capture details and to make his subjects appear natural, Copley sometimes required fifteen or sixteen sittings for a single portrait. Copley moved to England during the American Revolution and did not return to America.

154 Unit 5

Unit 5 155

LEVEL 4

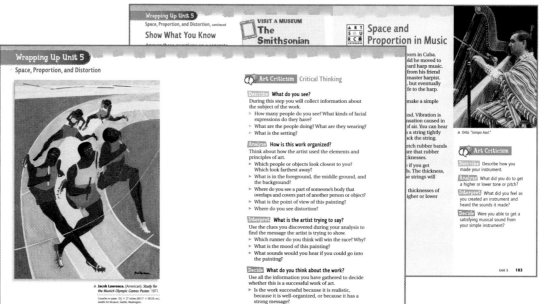

Wrapping Up Unit 5
Space, Proportion, and Distortion, *continued*
Show What You Know

VISIT A MUSEUM
The Smithsonian

Space and Proportion in Music

Unit Wrap-Ups review concepts, explore Art Museums or Art Careers and allow students to experience Artsource® connections to dance, theatre, and music.

Wrapping Up Unit 5
Space, Proportion, and Distortion

▲ **Jacob Lawrence.** (American). *Study for the Munich Olympic Games Poster.* 1971.
Gouache on paper. 35 × 27 inches (88.17 × 68.58 cm.). Seattle Art Museum, Seattle, Washington.

180 Unit 5

Art Criticism Critical Thinking

Describe What do you see?
During this step you will collect information about the subject of the work.
▶ How many people do you see? What kinds of facial expressions do they have?
▶ What are the people doing? What are they wearing?
▶ What is the setting?

Analyze How is this work organized?
Think about how the artist used the elements and principles of art.
▶ Which people or objects look closest to you? Which look farthest away?
▶ What is in the foreground, the middle ground, and the background?
▶ Where do you see a part of someone's body that overlaps and covers part of another person or object?
▶ What is the point of view of this painting?
▶ Where do you see distortion?

Interpret What is the artist trying to say?
Use the clues you discovered during your analysis to find the message the artist is trying to show.
▶ Which runner do you think will win the race? Why?
▶ What is the mood of this painting?
▶ What sounds would you hear if you could go into the painting?

Decide What do you think about the work?
Use all the information you have gathered to decide whether this is a successful work of art.
▶ Is the work successful because it is realistic, because it is well-organized, or because it has a strong message?

Unit 5 181

▲ Ortiz. "Joropo Azul."

Art Criticism

Describe Describe how you made your instrument.
Analyze What did you do to get a higher or lower tone or pitch?
Interpret What did you feel as you created an instrument and heard the sounds it made?
Decide Were you able to get a satisfying musical sound from your simple instrument?

Unit 5 183

LEVEL 4

Integrate the four disciplines of art into every lesson for well-rounded exposure to all the dimensions of art.

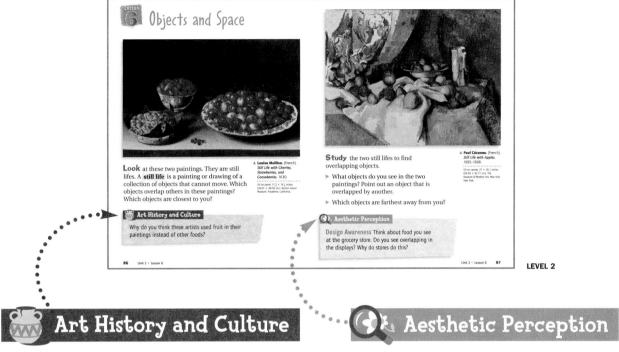

LEVEL 2

Art History and Culture

Explore the great art, artists, and cultures of the world.

Aesthetic Perception

Develop an understanding and appreciation for art.

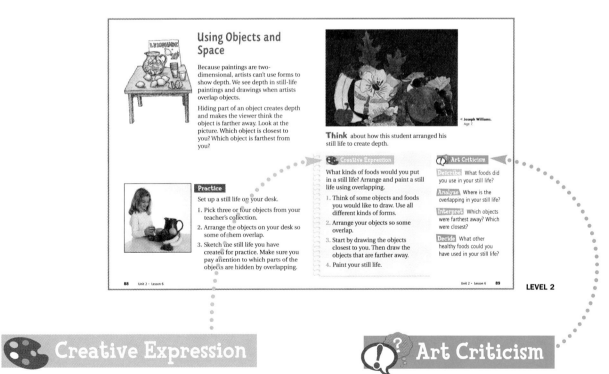

LEVEL 2

Creative Expression

Encounter a broad range of art media in a variety of hands-on art activities that give students an avenue for self-expression and self-esteem.

Art Criticism

Enrich critical-thinking skills as students learn about the elements and principles of art by examining their own and others' artwork.

Add dimension to all subjects with meaningful art connections.

Connect Art to Mathematics, Social Studies, Science, Language Arts and Reading.

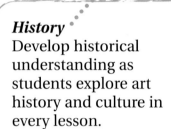

History
Develop historical understanding as students explore art history and culture in every lesson.

LEVEL 1

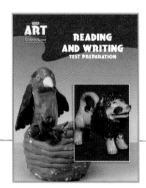

LEVEL 2

Reading and Writing Test Preparation
Use art content, information about artists, art concepts, and art history to practice reading and writing skills in every unit.

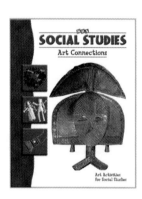

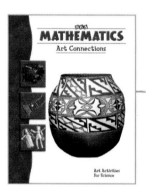

Cross-Curricular Art Connections
These books provide a wealth of exciting art activities designed specifically to support subject-area studies in Science, Mathematics, Social Studies, Language Arts and Reading as they reinforce art concepts.

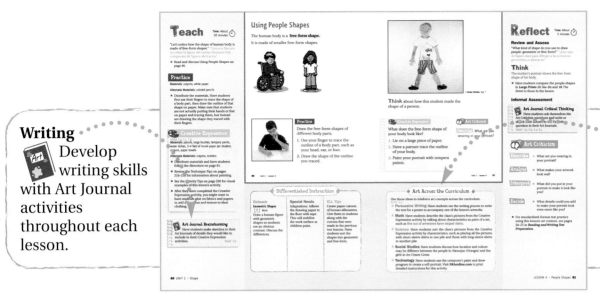

LEVEL 1

Writing
Develop writing skills with Art Journal activities throughout each lesson.

Cross-Curricular Ideas
Show students how artwork and concepts relate to science, mathematics, social studies, reading/language arts, and technology in every lesson.

LEVEL 2

LEVEL 4

LEVEL 3

Cross-Curricular Integration
Integrate language arts and reading, math, science, and social studies concepts naturally as students work through each art lesson.

Vocabulary Development
Key vocabulary terms are highlighted, defined, and reviewed to develop the language of art.

Literature Integration
Integrate literature with Illustrator Profiles and Literature and Art video experiences at the beginning of every unit.

Research has shown that incorporating the arts into core curriculum areas in a way that actively involves students in the learning process produces "significant positive effects on student achievement, motivation, and engagement in learning, and notable changes in classroom practices" ("Different Ways of Knowing: 1991-94 National Longitudinal Study Final Report" in Schools, Communities, and the Arts: A Research Compendium).

ART Connections

Integrate all the Performing Arts for a complete Art education.

Expose children to music, dance, and theatre as they explore the visual arts.

Music

LEVEL 2

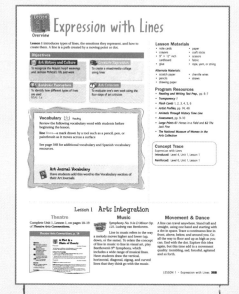

LEVEL 5

Music Connections in every Unit Opener translate the visual arts elements and principles into music.

Music Experiences in every lesson from Macmillan/McGraw-Hill's *Spotlight on Music* expand creativity and develop music appreciation.

Artsource® music performances on video and DVD explore the elements and principles of art through the performing arts.

LEVEL 4

Artsource®
LEVEL 3
dance performances on video and DVD explore the elements and principles of art through the performing arts.

Artsource®
LEVEL 5
theatre performances on video and DVD explore the elements and principles of art through the performing arts.

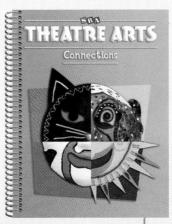

LEVEL 3

Theatre Arts Connections for grades K–6 lessons explore the elements and principles of theatre arts as students develop the elements and principles of visual arts.

Case studies have indicated that students perceive "that the arts facilitate their personal and social development." It also appears that to gain the full benefit of arts education, students should be exposed to all of the arts, including fine arts, dance, theatre, and music ("Arts Education in Secondary School: Effects and Effectiveness" in <u>Critical Links</u>, p. 76).

Meet Today's Standards for Art Education.

Art Connections exceeds the national standards for art education.

National Standards for Arts Education

Content Standard #1:

Understanding and applying media, techniques, and processes

The Creative Expression activity in every lesson of **Art Connections** develops understanding and experience with a wide variety of media, techniques, and processes. Practice activities in every lesson focus specifically on techniques.

Content Standard #2:

Using knowledge of structures and functions

Art Connections develops the elements and principles of art in every grade level, K–6. Units and lessons are organized to explore the elements and principles in exemplary art and then to practice techniques and create works of art that employ specific structures and functions of art.

Content Standard #3:

Choosing and evaluating a range of subject matter, symbols, and ideas

Art Connections introduces students to subject matter and symbols at the beginning of every grade level and then uses that knowledge throughout every lesson in the Aesthetic Perception questions and Creative Expression activities as students explore content to develop meaning in artwork.

Ali M. Forbes. Age 7.

Jasmine Krasel. Age 9.

Briana Kittle. Age 6.

Content Standard #4:

Understanding the visual arts in relation to history and cultures

Every lesson in ***Art Connections*** has a specific objective related to the understanding of art history and culture. These objectives are met as students analyze and interpret exemplary artwork and develop their own artwork.

Content Standard #5:

Reflecting upon and assessing the characteristics and merits of one's own work and the work of others

The four steps of art criticism are explored in every lesson throughout the program as students analyze their own artwork and the work of others.

Content Standard #6:

Making connections between visual arts and other disciplines

Theatre, Dance, and Music are integrated into every unit of ***Art Connections***. The elements and principles of visual art are translated into Dance, Theater, and Music through the Artsource® lessons and experiences. In addition, ***Theatre Arts Connections*** lessons and Music connections throughout the program develop a comprehensive understanding of the connections between visual arts and the performing arts.

Cross-curricular connections are built into every lesson through teaching strategies and ideas that integrate language arts and reading, math, science, and social studies concepts. Art Projects for each of the different subject areas are also included in the program.

Connections

Let the experts bring the best practices to your classroom.

Rosalind Ragans, Ph.D., Senior Author

Artist, Associate Professor Emerita

Georgia Southern University

Authors

Willis "Bing" Davis

Artist, Art Consultant

Associate Professor Emeritus,

Central State University, Ohio

Tina Farrell

Assisstant Superintendant, Curriculum and Instruction

Clear Creek Independent School District, Texas

Jane Rhoades Hudak, Ph.D.

Professor of Art

Georgia Southern University

Gloria McCoy

Former President, Texas Art Education Association

K–12 Art Director

Spring Branch Independent School District, Texas

Bunyan Morris

Art Teacher

Effingham County School System

Springfield, Georgia

Nan Yoshida

Art Education Consultant

Los Angeles, California

Contributors

Jackie Ellet

Elementary Art Teacher

Duncan Creek Elementary School

Georgia

Artsource® Music, Dance, and Theatre Lessons

Education Division

The Music Center of Los Angeles County

National Museum of Women in the Arts Collection

National Museum of Women in the Arts

Washington, D.C.

Your Fine-Arts Partner for K–12 Art, Theatre, Dance and Music

McGraw-Hill offers textbook programs to build, support, and extend an enriching fine-arts curriculum from kindergarten through high school.

**Senior Author
Rosalind Ragans**

Start with Art SRA

SRA/McGraw-Hill presents *Art Connections* for Grades K–6. *Art Connections* builds the foundations of the elements and principles of art across the grade levels as the program integrates art history and culture, aesthetic perception, creative expression in art production, and art criticism into every lesson.

Art Connections also develops strong cross-curricular connections and integrates the arts with literature, *Theatre Arts Connections* lessons, *Artsource*® experiences, and integrated music selections from Macmillan/McGraw-Hill's *Spotlight on Music*.

**Author
Rosalind Ragans
and Gene Mittler**

Integrate with Art Glencoe

Glencoe/McGraw-Hill offers comprehensive middle and high school art programs that encourage students to make art a part of their lifelong learning. All Glencoe art programs interweave the elements and principles of art to help students build perceptual skills, promote creative expression, explore historical and cultural heritage, and evaluate artwork.

- Introduce students to the many themes artists express.
- Explore the media, techniques, and processes of art.
- Understand the historical and cultural contexts of art.

ArtTalk offers high school students opportunities to perceive, create, appreciate, and evaluate art as it develops the elements and principles of art.

**Author
Rosalind Ragans**

Motivate with Music Macmillan McGraw-Hill

Macmillan/McGraw-Hill's *Spotlight on Music* offers an exiting and comprehensive exposure to music foundations and appreciation.

Sing with Style Glencoe

Glencoe/McGraw-Hill introduces *Experiencing Choral Music* for Grades 6–12. This multilevel choral music program includes instruction in the basic skills of vocal production and music literacy, and provides expertly recorded music selections in many different styles and from various periods of history.

Getting Started
The very basics...

Here are some tips for Getting Started with Art Connections.

Before School Begins

1. Explore the components you have (student materials, **Overhead Transparencies**, **Large Prints**, and so on). Consider uses and alternative uses for each of the components.

2. Plan your year.
   - Consider how often you meet with students.
   - Decide how many lessons you can present.
   - Examine your curriculum requirements.
   - Select the lessons that best meet your curriculum requirements.

3. Organize art materials.
   - Identify the *Creative Expression* activities you will have students develop.
   - Determine how you will budget materials to last the entire year.
   - Compile a list of materials and order them.
   - Arrange classroom space to store materials.

4. Arrange classroom space to create and store student artwork.

The First Day of School

1. Give an overview of your expectations, objectives, and what you want students to accomplish.

2. Introduce the artroom to students. Show them where things are kept.

3. Establish and communicate:
   - rules for behavior.
   - rules for handling art materials.
   - rules for cleaning up.

4. Begin the **Art Connections** introductory lessons, including *What Is Art?*, *About Art Criticism*, *About Aesthetic Perception*, and *About Art History and Culture*.

Planning a Lesson

1. Review the lesson in the *Teacher's Edition*, including lesson objectives, in-text questions, *Practice*, and *Creative Expression* activities.

2. Assemble program components, such as **Transparencies, Large Prints,** and the **Big Book**.

3. Make any copies of activities or assessments that will be needed for the lesson.

4. Assemble art materials.

5. Determine how you will assess the lesson.

TEACHER'S EDITION

SRA ART Connections

Level 2

Authors

Rosalind Ragans, Ph.D., Senior Author

Willis "Bing" Davis   Jane Rhoades Hudak, Ph.D.   Bunyan Morris
Tina Farrell   Gloria McCoy   Nan Yoshida

Contributing Author

Jackie Ellett

Education Division
The Music Center of Los Angeles County

Columbus, OH

The **McGraw·Hill** Companies

Authors

Senior Author
Dr. Rosalind Ragans, Ph.D.
Associate Professor Emerita
Georgia Southern University

Willis "Bing" Davis
Associate Professor Emeritus
Central State University - Ohio
President & Founder of SHANGO:
The Center for the Study of
African American
Art & Culture

Tina Farrell
Assistant Superintendent,
Curriculum and Instruction
Clear Creek Independent School
District,
League City, Texas

Jane Rhoades Hudak, Ph.D.
Professor of Art
Georgia Southern University

Gloria McCoy
Former President,
Texas Art Education Association
Spring Branch Independent
School District, Texas

Bunyan Morris
Art Teacher
Effingham County School System,
Springfield, Georgia

Nan Yoshida
Art Education Consultant
Retired Art Supervisor,
Los Angeles Unified School
District
Los Angeles, California

Photo Credit **Cover,** Attributed to John Bell, *Figure of a Lion.* Collection American Folk Art Museum, New York. Promised gift of Ralph Esmerian P1.2001.156. Photo ©2000 John Bigelow Taylor, New York.

SRAonline.com

Send all inquiries to:
SRA/McGraw-Hill
8787 Orion Place
Columbus, OH 43240-4027

Printed in the United States of America.

ISBN 0-07-600392-2

3 4 5 6 7 8 9 BCM 10 09 08 07 06

The **McGraw-Hill** Companies

Contributors

Contributing Author
Jackie Ellett, Ed.S
Elementary Art Teacher
Duncan Creek Elementary School
Hoschton, Georgia

Contributing Writer
Lynda Kerr, NBCT
Ed. D. Candidate, Art Teacher
Henry County, Georgia

 Artsource® Music, Dance, Theatre Lessons
Mark Slavkin, Vice President for Education
The Music Center of Los Angeles County
Michael Solomon, Managing Director
Music Center Education Division
Melinda Williams, Concept Originator and Project Director
Susan Cambigue-Tracey, Project Coordinator and Writer
Madeleine Dahm, Movement and Dance Connection Writer
Keith Wyffels, Staff Assistance
Maureen Erbe, Logo Design

Music Connections
Kathy Mitchell
Music Teacher
Eagan, Minnesota

More about Aesthetics
Richard W. Burrows, Executive Director
Institute for Arts Education
San Diego, California

Art History
Gene A. Mittler, Ph.D.
Professor Emeritus
Texas Tech University

Resources for Students with Disabilities
Mandy Yeager
Ph.D. Candidate
The University of North Texas
Denton, Texas

Brain-Based Learning in the Arts
Jamye Ivey
K-12 Art Supervisor
Dougherty County School System, Georgia

Safe Use of Art Materials
Mary Ann Boykin

Director, The Art School for Children and Young Adults
University of Houston–Clear Lake
Houston, Texas

Integrating the Four Art Forms
Susan Cambigue-Tracey
The Music Center of Los Angeles County

Using Writing to Enhance Your Art Curriculum
Mary Lazzari, EdS
Elementary Art Teacher
Clarke County School District
Athens, Georgia

Museum Education
Marilyn J. S. Goodman
Director of Education
Solomon R. Guggenheim Museum
New York, New York

Displaying Student Artwork
Jackie Ellett
Duncan Creek Elementary School
Hoschton, Georgia

Student Activities

Cassie Appleby
Glen Oaks Elementary School
McKinney, Texas

Maureen Banks
Kester Magnet School
Van Nuys, California

Christina Barnes
Webb Bridge Middle School
Alpharetta, Georgia

Beth Benning
Willis Jepson Middle School
Vacaville, California

Chad Buice
Craig Elementary School
Snellville, Georgia

Beverly Broughton
Gwinn Oaks Elementary School
Snellville, Georgia

Missy Burgess
Jefferson Elementary School
Jefferson, Georgia

Marcy Cincotta-Smith
Benefield Elementary School
Lawrenceville, Georgia

Joanne Cox
Kittredge Magnet School
Atlanta, Georgia

Carolyn Y. Craine
McCracken County Schools
Paducah, Kentucky

Jackie Ellett
Duncan Creek Elementary School
Hoschton, Georgia

Tracie Flynn
Home School
Rushville, Indiana

Phyllis Glenn
Malcom Bridge Elementary
Bogart, Georgia

Dallas Gillespie
Dacula Middle School
Dacula, Georgia

Dr. Donald Gruber
Clinton Junior High School
Clinton, Illinois

Karen Heid
Rock Springs Elementary School
Lawrenceville, Georgia

Alisa Hyde
Southwest Elementary
Savannah, Georgia

Kie Johnson
Oconee Primary School
Watkinsville, Georgia

Sallie Keith, NBCT
West Side Magnet School
LaGrange, Georgia

Letha Kelly
Grayson Elementary School
Grayson, Georgia

Diana Kimura
Amestoy Elementary School
Gardena, California

Desiree LaOrange
Barkley Elementary School
Fort Campbell, Kentucky

Deborah Lackey-Wilson
Roswell North Elementary
Roswell, Georgia

Dawn Laird
Goforth Elementary School
Clear Creek, Texas

Mary Lazzari
Timothy Road Elementary School
Athens, Georgia

Michelle Leonard
Webb Bridge Middle School
Alpharetta, Georgia

Lynn Ludlam
Spring Branch ISD
Houston, Texas

Mark Mitchell
Fort Daniel Elementary School
Dacula, Georgia

Martha Moore
Freeman's Mill Elementary School
Dacula, Georgia

Connie Niedenthal
Rushville Elementary
Rushville, Indiana

Barbara Patisaul
Oconee County Elementary School
Watkinsville, Georgia

Elizabeth Paulos-Krasle
Social Circle Elementary
Social Circle, Georgia

Jane Pinneau
Rocky Branch Elementary School
Watkinsville, Georgia

Marilyn Polin
Cutler Ridge Middle School
Miami, Florida

Michael Ramsey
Graves County Schools
Mayfield, Kentucky

Rosemarie Sells
Social Circle Elementary
Social Circle, Georgia

Jean Neelen-Siegel
Baldwin School
Alhambra, California

Debra Smith
McIntosh County School System
Darien, Georgia

Patricia Spencer
Harmony Elementary School
Buford, Georgia

Melanie Stokes
Smiley Elementary School
Ludowici, Georgia

Rosanne Stutts
Davidson Fine Arts School
Augusta, Georgia

Fran Sullivan
South Jackson Elementary School
Athens, Georgia

Kathy Valentine
Home School
Burkburnett, Texas

Debi West
Rock Springs Elementary School
Lawrenceville, Georgia

Sherry White
Bauerschlag Elementary School
League City, Texas

Patricia Wiesen
Cutler Ridge Middle School
Miami, Florida

Deayna Woodruff
Loveland Middle School
Loveland, Ohio

Gil Young
El Rodeo School
Beverly Hills, California

Larry A. Young
Dacula Elementary School
Dacula, Georgia

Table of Contents

What Is Art?

Introduction 12

Subject Matter 16

Elements of Art 22

Principles of Art 23

About Art

Art History and Culture 24

Aesthetic Perception 26

Art Criticism 28

Creative Expression 30

Safety 32

4

▲ **Jacob Lawrence.**
Street Scene (Boy with Kite).

Unit 1 Line and Shape

An Introduction to Line and Shape 34

Lesson	Activity	Medium	

●◆ ❶ Line Direction . . . . Paper Sculpture of a Playground . . . . . . Paper 36

❷ Types of Lines . . . . Dream Tree Line Collage . . . . Paper, Mixed Media 40

❸ Calm Lines . . . . Water Scene . . . . Watercolors 44

❹ Active Lines . . . . Abstract Painting . . . . Tempera 48

●◆ ❺ Geometric Shapes . . . . Construction Paper Picture . . . . Construction Paper 52

●◆ ❻ Free-Form Shapes . . . . Shadow Puppet . . . . Paper, Tagboard 56

Wrapping Up Line and Shape 60

Artsource® Lesson
Line and Shape in Theatre 63

●◆ indicates Core Lessons

5

Reading Comprehension Skills and Strategies
❶ Vocabulary, Using Literature
❷ Vocabulary, Using Literature, Thematic
   Connection: Imagination
❸ Vocabulary, Using Literature
❹ Vocabulary, Visualizing, Thematic Connection:
   Look Again
❺ Vocabulary, Using Literature
❻ Vocabulary, Using Literature

◀ **Henry Moore.**
Family Group.

Unit 2 Space and Form

An Introduction to Space and Form 64

Lesson	Activity	Medium	
❶ Geometric Forms	Sculpture	Cardboard Forms	66
❷ Free-Form Forms	Relief Describing the Student	Tagboard, Cardboard, Found Objects	70
❸ Body Forms	Body Form	Clay	74
❹ Animal Forms	Utilitarian Clay Animal Form	Clay	78
❺ People and Space	Paper People	Construction Paper	82
❻ Objects and Space	Still Life	Tempera, Chalk	86

Wrapping Up Space and Form 90

Artsource® Lesson
Space and Form in Theatre 93

6

➥ indicates Core Lessons

Reading Comprehension Skills and Strategies

❶ Vocabulary, Using Literature, Comparing and Contrasting
❷ Vocabulary, Using Literature

❸ Vocabulary, Using Literature
❹ Vocabulary, Using Literature

❺ Vocabulary, Using Literature, Main Idea and Details
❻ Vocabulary, Using Literature

▲ **Georgia O´Keeffe.**
The Red Poppy.

Unit 3 Color and Value

An Introduction to Color and Value 94

Lesson	Activity	Medium	
●◆ ❶ Color and Hue	Painting Hidden Under Rainbow Colors	Tempera	96
❷ Warm Hues	Resist	Tempera, Oil Pastel, Crayon	100
❸ Cool Hues	Landscape	Watercolors, Oil Pastel	104
●◆ ❹ Value	Value Painting	Tempera	108
❺ Light Values	Landscape	Tempera	112
❻ Dark Values	Feeling Painting	Tempera	116

Wrapping Up Color and Value 120

Artsource® Lesson
Color and Value in Dance 123

●◆ indicates Core Lessons

7

Reading Comprehension Skills and Strategies

❶ Vocabulary, Using Literature, Comparing and Contrasting
❷ Vocabulary, Using Literature

❸ Vocabulary, Using Literature
❹ Vocabulary, Using Literature

❺ Vocabulary, Using Literature
❻ Vocabulary, Using Literature, Comprehension Skills

◀ **Louise Nevelson.**
Dawn.

Unit 4 Pattern, Rhythm, and Movement

An Introduction to Pattern, Rhythm, and Movement 124

Lesson	Activity	Medium	
●◆ ❶ Patterns	Sponge Stamp	Tempera, Sponge	126
❷ Patterns in Nature	Glue Drawing	Tempera, Glue, Crayon	130
●◆ ❸ Rhythm	Still-Life	Tempera, Chalk	134
❹ Rhythm and Form	Storyteller Doll	Clay, Glaze	138
●◆ ❺ Diagonal Movement	Drawing of Dancing	Computer	142
❻ Curving Movement	Journey Picture	Crayon, Watercolors	146

Wrapping Up Pattern, Rhythm, and Movement 150

Artsource® Lesson
Pattern, Rhythm, and Movement in Storytelling 153

8

●◆ indicates Core Lessons

Reading Comprehension Skills and Strategies
❶ Vocabulary, Using Literature, Main Idea and Details
❷ Vocabulary, Using Literature
❸ Vocabulary, Using Literature
❹ Vocabulary, Using Literature, Thematic Connection: Storytelling
❺ Vocabulary, Using Literature
❻ Vocabulary, Using Literature

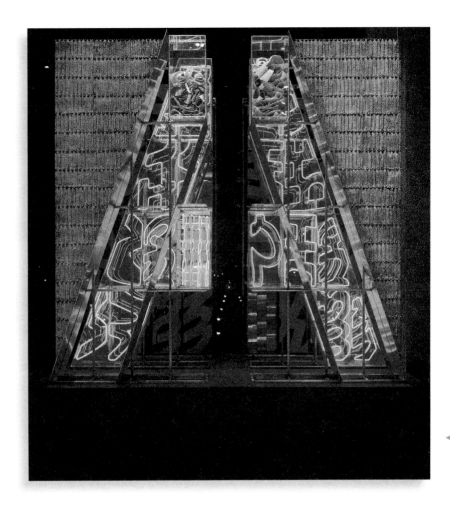

◀ **Chryssa.**
The Gates to Times Square.

Unit 5 Balance, Emphasis, and Texture

An Introduction to Balance, Emphasis, and Texture 154

Lesson	Activity	Medium	
●◆ ❶ Balance	Paper Jar	Construction Paper	156
❷ Balance in People	Hero Drawing	Crayon, Marker	160
●◆ ❸ Emphasis	Emphasis Drawing	Marker	164
❹ Emphasis Using Contrast	Night Scene	Oil Pastels	168
●◆ ❺ Tactile Texture	Stitched Design	Thread, Fabric	172
❻ Visual Texture	Texture Rubbings	Crayon, Marker, Paper	176

Wrapping Up Balance, Emphasis, and Texture 180

Artsource® Lesson
Balance, Emphasis, and Texture in Dance 183

●◆ indicates Core Lessons

9

Reading Comprehension Skills and Strategies
❶ Vocabulary, Using Literature
❷ Vocabulary, Using Literature

❸ Vocabulary, Using Literature, Author's Point of View
❹ Vocabulary, Using Literature, Making Connections

❺ Vocabulary, Using Literature
❻ Vocabulary, Using Literature

◀ **Diego Velázquez.**
Las Meninas (The Maids of Honor).

Unit 6 Harmony, Variety, and Unity

An Introduction to Harmony, Variety, and Unity 184

Lesson	Activity	Medium	
●◆ ❶ Harmony of Color	Tile Mural	Tiles, Paint	186
❷ Harmony of Shape and Form	Group of Animals	Computer	190
●◆ ❸ Variety of Color	Swimmy Print	Paint, Posterboard	194
❹ Variety of Shape and Form	Fantasy Bird	Colored Pencils, Watercolors	198
●◆ ❺ Unity in Sculpture	Stuffed Paper Animal	Paper, Cardboard Tubes	202
❻ Unity in Architecture	Building Design	Computer	206

Wrapping Up Harmony, Variety, and Unity 210

Artsource® Lesson
Harmony, Variety, and Unity in Dance 213

10

●◆ indicates Core Lessons

Reading Comprehension Skills and Strategies

❶ Vocabulary, Using Literature, Thematic Connection: Sharing Stories
❷ Vocabulary, Using Literature

❸ Vocabulary, Using Literature, Fact and Opinion
❹ Vocabulary, Using Literature

❺ Vocabulary, Using Literature, Making Connections
❻ Vocabulary, Using Literature

Technique Tips

Drawing 214
Painting 217
Collage 220
Printmaking 223
Sculpture 225
Needlework 230

Activity Tips

Unit 1 232
Unit 2 235
Unit 3 238
Unit 4 241
Unit 5 244
Unit 6 247

Visual Index 250
Glossary 260
Index 267

Teacher Handbook T1

Overview

The purpose of these pages is to open students' minds to the idea that visual arts include many components and take many forms. The arts satisfy the human needs for display, celebration, personal expression, and communication. We use the visual arts to enhance our innermost feelings and to communicate ideas. Art is made by people. Even people who are not professional artists can enjoy the creative process.

Activating Prior Knowledge

■ Ask students what they think art is. Encourage creative, divergent thinking. In visual art, there are many answers to a question.

Questions to Discuss

■ Have students look at the images on pages 12 and 13 and name the things that are visual art. Then ask the following questions.

▶ Which of these things could you hold in your hands?

▶ Which one could you walk inside?

▶ Which ones would you hang on a wall?

▶ Which ones could you wear?

■ Encourage students to think about things they have at home that fit the categories on these pages. The building they live in is architecture. They have dishes and other containers. Many of them have things hanging on the walls to enhance their visual environments. A few may have sculpture in the home. Many will have seen sculpture in and around public buildings.

What Is Art?

Art is . . .

Painting is color applied to a flat surface.

▲ **Edward Hopper.** (American). *Early Sunday Morning.* 1930.

Oil on canvas. $35\frac{3}{16} \times 60\frac{1}{4}$ inches (89.4 × 153 cm.). Whitney Museum of American Art, New York, New York.

Drawing is the process of making art with lines.

▲ **Pablo Picasso.** (Spanish). *Mother and Child.* 1922.

Oil on canvas. 40 × 32 inches (100 × 81 cm.). The Baltimore Museum of Art, Baltimore, Maryland.

Sculpture is art that fills up space.

▲ **Kiawak Ashoona.** (Inuit). *Seal Hunter.*

Serpentine. Home and Away Gallery, Kennebunkport, Maine.

Architecture is the art of designing and constructing buildings.

▲ **Artist Unknown.** (Roman), *Maison Carée.* 1st century B.C.

Nîmes, France.

Printmaking is the process of transferring an original image from one prepared surface to another.

◄ **Maria Sibylla Merian.** (German). *Plate 2 (from "Dissertation in Insect Generations and Metamorphosis in Surinam").* 1719.
Hand-colored engraving on paper. 18 × 13¾ inches (45.72 × 34.93 cm.). National Museum of Women in the Arts, Washington, D.C.

Photography is a technique of capturing an image of light on film.

▲ **Ansel Adams.** (American). *Early Sunday Morning, Merced River, Yosemite Valley, CA.* c. 1950, printed c. 1978.
9⅝ × 12⅞ inches (24.45 × 32.70 cm.). Museum of Modern Art, New York, New York.

Art is made by people

Pottery is an object made from clay.

▲ **Artist Unknown.** (China). *Covered Jar.* 1522–1566.
Porcelain painted with underglaze cobalt blue and overglaze enamels. 18½ inches high, 15¾ inches in diameter. (7 cm. high, 6 cm. in diameter). Asia Society of New York, New York.

A mask is a covering for the face to be used in ceremonies and other events.

◄ **Artist Unknown.** (Ivory Coast). *Senufo Face Mask.* Nineteenth to twentieth century.
Wood, horn, fiber, cloth, feather, metal. 14½ inches tall (35.56 cm.). The Metropolitan Museum of Art, New York, New York.

► to communicate ideas.

► to express feelings.

► to give us well-designed objects.

Using the Credit Line

The credit line is a list of important facts about the work of art that appears below or next to the work. For example, you can help students understand the size of an artwork and how it relates to their own size. Most credit lines contain the following information.

▪ Name of the artist.

▪ Title of the work. This always appears in italics. If the word *detail* follows the title, it means that the image is part of a larger work of art.

▪ Year the work was created. A *c* before the date indicates that the piece was made around the year given.

▪ Medium used by the artist.

▪ Size of the work. The first number is the height, the second is the width, and a third number indicates depth for three-dimensional works.

▪ Location of the work. This tells the museum, gallery, or collection in which the work is housed.

Art Studios, Galleries, and Museums

Works of art are created in **studios.** A studio is an artist's workplace, much like a classroom is a studio for students. Almost everything an artist needs to create an artwork will be found in his or her studio. It is possible for people to visit artist studios, but an invitation from the artist is usually required.

Art galleries are private businesses where art dealers display and sell works of art. Art galleries are typically open to the public and the works of art may be viewed even if the patrons do not intend to buy anything.

A *museum* is a public or private building where valuable and important works of art are cared for and displayed for the public to view. *Curators* are people who supervise the museum and organize exhibitions. *Docents* are special tour directors who help explain the art to visitors.

Overview

These pages introduce students to the three components that define a work of art: the subject, the composition, and the content.

Subject

The subject is the image that the viewer can easily identify in a work of art. The subject may be one person or many people. It may be a thing. It can be an event, such as a party. In recent years, some artists have chosen to create nonobjective art. This is art that has no recognizable subject matter, such as *The Voice of the City of New York Interpreted/The Great White Way Leaving the Subway (White Way I)*. In this work of art, the elements of art become the subject.

Composition

The composition is the way the principles of art are used to organize the elements of art. Notice how Henry Moore has organized line, form, and texture in space to create the feeling that we are looking at a seated family.

Content

The content is the message the work communicates to the viewer. The message may be an idea, such as family unity, or an emotion or feeling, such as joy or loneliness. If the work of art is functional, such as *Easy Chair,* then the function is the meaning. Does the work of art look like it could perform the function it is supposed to?

What Is Art?

Every work of art has three parts.

Subject

The subject is the object you can recognize in the artwork. If a work has no objects, the elements of art are the subject.

Composition

The composition is how the elements and principles are organized in the artwork.

Content

The content is the message or meaning of the artwork. When the work of art is functional, then the function of the work is the meaning.

▶ In which work of art do you think the subject matter is very important?

▶ In which artwork do you think composition is most important?

▶ Which work seems to have the strongest message? Explain.

▶ Which artwork's meaning relates to its function?

Lorenzo Scott. (American). *Ballet Dancers.*

Oil on canvas. 50 × 30 inches (127 × 76.2 cm.). Collection of Ann and Ted Oliver.

◀ **Joseph Stella.** (American). *The Voice of the City of New York Interpreted/ The Great White Way Leaving the Subway (White Way I).* c. 1920–1922.

Oil and tempera on canvas. 88½ × 54 inches (224.79 × 137.16 cm.). The Newark Museum, Newark, New Jersey.

▲ **Henry Moore.** (British). *Family Group.* 1948–1949.

Bronze (cast 1950), 59¼ × 46½ × 29⅞ inches (150.5 × 118.1 × 75.88 cm.). Museum of Modern Art, New York, New York.

▲ **Caleb Gardner.** (American). *Easy Chair.* 1758.

Walnut, maple, and hand stitched upholstery. 46⅜ × 32⅜ × 25⅞ inches (117.8 × 82.2 × 65.7 cm.). The Metropolitan Museum of Art, New York, New York.

What Is Art?   **15**

Activating Prior Knowledge

■ Ask students what is the first thing they look for when they look at a work of art. Students may say they look at color, size, or what it's about. Some may say they look for the feeling or message they get from it. Give students time to explore this question. It will provide a good context for the discussion on these pages.

Questions to Discuss

■ Read with students the text on page 14 and look at the images on page 15. Share with them some of the information above. Encourage students to think about their responses during the Activating Prior Knowledge discussion as they look at these images and think about the information you have shared with them.

▶ Read the questions on page 14, and discuss the answers. The subject matter is important in *Ballet Dancers* and *Family Group.* Composition is most important in *The Voice of the City of New York Interpreted/The Great White Way Leaving the Subway (White Way I).* *Easy Chair* is the work in which the meaning relates to its function. Most students will think that *Ballet Dancers* and *Family Group* have the strongest message. However, it is important to point out that the function of a work is an important message *(Easy Chair)* and that nonobjective work such as *The Voice of the City of New York Interpreted/The Great White Way Leaving the Subway (White Way I)* is communicating through the elements and principles of art.

Overview

In art, *subject* means something an artist has depicted or represented in an artwork. For example, the subject matter of Paul Cézanne's still life is fruit. Some subject matter, like the objects in Cézanne's still life, are easy to identify. Others are more difficult because the artwork may be symbolic or nonobjective. Artists create works of art on a variety of subjects: the natural world, literature, religion, the constructed world, history, and so on. These pages deal with several of the most common subject-matter topics—people, objects, everyday life, stories, things outside, colors and shapes, and things that have a deeper meaning.

Talk with students about each subject-matter topic description below. Encourage them to look for examples of different subject matter in the lessons. By helping them to look at each subject in greater detail and by asking thoughtful questions, your students will begin to develop an understanding for differences among subject matter in art.

Still Life

Artists create works of art that show a variety of objects. Traditional still lifes are bowls, vases, bottles, pitchers, fruit, flowers, food on a table, and/or musical instruments (among other things) that are artfully arranged.

▶ **Question:** What are the objects in this still life?

Subject Matter

Artists make art about many subjects. *Subject matter* is the content of an artist's work. For example, the subject of a painting can be a vase of flowers or a self-portrait. This subject matter is easy to see. The subject matter is harder to understand when the artwork stands for something beyond itself. Look at the artwork on these pages. Notice the different kinds of subject matter.

Still Life

▲ **Paul Cézanne.** (French). *Still Life with Apples. 1895–1898.*
Oil on canvas. 27 × 36½ inches (68.58 × 92.71 cm.). The Museum of Modern Art, New York, New York.

Landscape

▲ **Claude Monet.** (French). *Japanese Bridge over a Pool of Water Lilies.* 1899.
Oil on canvas. 36½ × 29 inches (93 × 74 cm.). The Metropolitan Museum of Art, New York, New York.

Landscape

This area includes the natural world—plants, animals, or other things outside. The suffix *scape* means "a view of." For example, a *cityscape* is buildings and city life in an artwork. A *seascape* is a scene of the sea.

▶ **Question:** What objects do you see in this landscape?

Genre

In art, the term *genre* is used to indicate subjects that have to do with ordinary people engaged in everyday activities.

▶ **Question:** What everyday activities are these people doing?

What Is Art?

Genre

▲ **Jacob Lawrence.** (American). *Street Scene (Boy with Kite).* 1962.
Egg tempera on hardboard. $23\frac{7}{8} \times 30$ inches (60.64 × 76.2 cm.). Conservation Center of the Institute of Fine Arts, New York, New York.

Nonobjective

▲ **Joseph Stella.** (American). *The Voice of the City of New York Interpreted/The Great White Way Leaving the Subway (White Way I).* c. 1920–22.

Oil and tempera on canvas. 88½ × 54 inches (224.79 × 137.16 cm.). The Newark Museum, Newark, New Jersey.

Nonobjective

Sometimes artwork is nonobjective. It does not have an identifiable subject matter—no familiar subjects are shown. People respond to the way the artwork has been organized and designed. Nonobjective art focuses specifically on the elements and principles of art: line, shape, color, and so on.

▶ **Question:** The artwork does not use a subject we can identify. What are some of the lines, shapes, and colors you see in this picture?

Portrait

This category includes portraits, self-portraits, and group portraits. Portraits are one of the oldest subjects in art history. An artist tries to present an accurate depiction and other aspects of a person's character in a portrait.

▶ **Question:** What do you think the artist is telling us about this person?

Portrait

▲ **Diego Rivera.** (Mexican). *Kneeling Child on Yellow Background.* 1927.
Oil on canvas. $25\frac{1}{2} \times 21$ inches (65 × 53 cm.). San Francisco Museum of Modern Art, San Francisco, California.

A Story Shown as Symbols

▲ **Artist Unknown.** (English). *The Five Senses: Hearing. (Detail.)* c. 1650–1675.

White satin embroidered in petit point and enriched with seed pearls and coral. The Metropolitan Museum of Art, New York.

Stories

A story is an account of an incident from a real person's life, a historic event, or from a myth, legend, or other piece of symbolic literature.

▶ **Question:** This antique needle-crafted artwork tells a story about one of the five senses. Which sense does it depict?

Overview

Each language has its own system of words and rules of grammar. To learn a new language, you need to learn new words and a new set of rules for putting the words together. The language of visual art also has its own system. The words of the language are the **elements** of art. They are the basic visual symbols in the language of art. Just as there are basic kinds of words such as nouns, verbs, adjectives, and adverbs, there are basic kinds of art elements. These are line, shape, color, value, space, form, and texture. These elements are the visual building blocks that the artist puts together to create a work of art. No matter what materials are used, the artwork will contain all of the visual elements. Sometimes one element will be more important than the others.

Visual images are organized according to rules. In language, these are the rules of grammar. In visual art, the rules for organizing the elements of art are called the **principles** of art. These principles include pattern, rhythm, balance, emphasis, harmony, variety, and unity.

Activating Prior Knowledge

- Ask students what they think of when they hear each of the following words: *line, shape, color.* Encourage them to look around the classroom for examples.

Questions to Discuss

- Have students examine the images on pages 22 and 23. Ask them what they can tell about each photo. What stands out in each image? How does each image help explain the element or principle?

Elements of Art

Art is a language. The words of the language are the elements of art.

Line

Shape

Form

Space

Color

Value

Texture

Principles of Art

Artists organize their works using the principles of art.

The Language of Art

The elements and principles of art are the concepts or ideas that artists use to organize their artwork. Artists use a variety of media and materials to make art. *Media* are types of art such as photography, watercolor, and so on. *Materials* are the things used to make the art, such as markers, paint, paper, clay, fabric, wood, metal, or glass.

There are specific techniques and processes that artists use to manipulate the materials. For example, the proper way to hold a brush to create a thin line with watercolor paint is a specific technique unique to watercolor painting. The process of creating a finished watercolor painting consists of many interwoven steps such as thinking about what to paint, sketching several ideas, deciding which elements and principles will enhance the work, choosing the best sketch, deciding which watercolor techniques to use, and finally producing the finished work.

Special techniques and procedures are used with each material. You will need to learn different techniques and follow different procedures for modeling clay than you will for creating paper sculpture. Drawing with crayons requires different techniques and procedures from drawing with oil pastels or chalk. Using the computer to make original art requires that you learn how to use specific computer hardware and software.

Overview

 Art History and Culture

Art history is the record of art from the past to the present. By looking at art from the past, we learn what the people who lived before us were like—their feelings and beliefs, clothes, food, houses, and how they viewed the world around them.

Questions to Discuss:

Knowledge

▶ Who created the artwork?

▶ When was the artwork created?

▶ What is the artwork's title?

▶ Have you ever seen an artwork like this? Where?

Comprehension

▶ Is this artwork useful? How is it used?

▶ Compare this artwork with another artwork from a similar time period. How are the works of art alike and different?

▶ What interests you most about this artwork?

▶ What is the major theme of this artwork?

Application

▶ What types of materials were used to create this artwork?

▶ Demonstrate how the artwork was created.

▶ Explain how this artwork could have a different use today.

Analysis

▶ What are the main elements in this artwork?

▶ Compare this painting with another painting in this book. How are they alike? How are they different?

▶ What does this artwork mean?

▲ **Horace Pippin.** (American). *Victorian Parlor II.*

1945. Oil on canvas. 25¼ × 30 inches (64.1 × 76.2 cm.). The Metropolitan Museum of Art, New York.

Art History and Culture

Look at the artwork.
▶ What people or objects do you see?
▶ Do they look like people and objects you see around you today? Explain.

Look at the caption.
▶ When was the artwork created?
▶ What can you learn about the artist?

Learn more.
▶ Do some research to find out more about the artist, the artwork, and the time period.

Synthesis
▶ How many titles can you create for this artwork? Name them.
▶ Name a person you would like to give this artwork to as a gift. Why?
▶ Imagine that two people in this room are having a conversation. What would they say to each other? Why?

Evaluation
▶ Do you think this artwork is interesting? Why?
▶ Summarize this artwork's unique qualities.

What to Do
▪ Have students research to find out information about the life and times of Horace Pippin. Students may write a biography of the artist or dress up as the artist and tell the artist's story to classmates.
▪ Have students research Pippin and another artist who lived at the same time. Students should research information about the media, styles, techniques, and procedures the artists used. Have pairs of students role-play a discussion between the two artists about media, style, and personal beliefs about art.
▪ Have students work in groups to act out this painting. They should write a script for what happened before, during, and after the moment shown in the painting.

Overview

Aesthetic Perception

Aesthetic perception encourages students to make choices rather than give "right answers." By understanding the process of aesthetic perception, students can see something from a new perspective and ultimately realize that art is all around them.

Journal writing is an integral part of aesthetic perception. It is an ongoing record of what a student does, notices, and thinks. Journals track the evolution of thoughts and experiences over time. Through this recorded journey, the student has the ability to reflect on where one has been and where one is going. Writing thoughts, reactions, perceptions, new information, and questions intensifies each student's life experiences.

Guidelines for Aesthetic Perception

Students like to know what is important about a work of art and what was important to the artist. They are fascinated with information, questions, and descriptions. There are some guiding principles in the development of aesthetic perception at this level that can profoundly influence teaching practice.

1. All aesthetic perception actively involves the learner.

2. All aesthetic perception involves reflection.

3. The works of art have substance. Their tools and a working vocabulary are vital to empower the learner.

4. Aesthetic perception is a process based upon examination of the artist's choices and the choices in response made by the viewer.

5. All responses are valid. Right and wrong are irrelevant issues when viewing works of art.

6. All works of art relate to each other, and each relates to all other areas of life.

▲ **Horace Pippin.** (American). *Victorian Parlor II.* 1945.
Oil on canvas. $25\frac{1}{4} \times 30$ inches (64.1 × 76.2 cm.). The Metropolitan Museum of Art, New York.

![icon](Aesthetic Perception)

Look

▶ Look at the work of art. What sounds and smells are in this work of art?

▶ What happened just before and just after in this work of art?

Look Inside

▶ Describe the rest of this house. What is in each room?

▶ Tell or write a story about this work of art with a beginning, a middle, and an end.

▶ How would it feel to sit in one of those chairs?

Look Outside

▶ How is this like or different from your own life?

▶ What does the artist want you to know or think about in this work of art?

▶ What will you remember about this work?

Questions to Discuss

▶ What is happening in this work of art?

▶ What is this work of art about?

▶ What is your favorite part of this work of art?

▶ What is most important in this artwork?

▶ What happened just before and just after in this work of art?

▶ If you were in this work of art, what would you be doing?

▶ What have you learned about the work of art?

▶ What does the artist want you to know or think about in this work of art?

▶ How do you feel about the work of art? What does it make you feel?

▶ What will you remember about this work of art?

▶ Has this work of art changed your thinking?

Things to Do

▪ Draw yourself into the work of art.

▪ Draw what you can't see in the work of art.

▪ Act out or show the story in the work of art.

▪ Collect objects that are similar to the objects in the work of art and make aesthetic judgments about them.

▪ Role-play an interview with the artist about how the work of art was made.

Overview

Art criticism is an organized system for looking at and talking about art. The purpose of art criticism is to get the viewer involved in a perception process that delays judgment until all aspects of the image have been studied. Learning art criticism also gives each viewer the confidence to discuss a work of art without worrying what other people might think.

Describe | What do I see?

During this step, the viewer lists all the obvious things in the artwork. Objectivity is important. For example, you do not know from looking at *Victorian Parlor II* that it is a room used by two people. All you can say is that you see a room with furniture.

Questions to Discuss

▶ List and describe everything you see in the artwork. Answers may include: There is a green rug with a design. There is a round, brown pedestal table with a lace doily and a large vase filled with flowers. On each side of the table is a black chair. Each chair has doilies to protect the head and arm areas. There is a brown footstool at the foot of each chair and a basket of yarn on the floor (and so on).

Analyze | How is the work organized?

During this step the viewer examines how the elements and principles of art are used in the artwork.

Questions to Discuss

▶ Describe the elements of art you see. Answers may include: **Line**—There are horizontal lines where the floor meets the wall, on the wall, and in the rug. **Shape**— The tabletops, bookcase, lamp, doilies, and picture frames are geometric. The chairs, vase, flowers, leaves, and pitchers are free-form shapes (and so on).

▶ How has the artist used the principles of design? Answers may include: **Balance**— The painting has formal balance, but it is not symmetrical. **Emphasis**—The area of emphasis is the center with the table and vase that are larger than the other objects, and the two matching black chairs (and so on).

About Art

▲ **Horace Pippin.** (American). *Victorian Parlor II.* 1945.

Oil on canvas. 25¼ × 30 inches (64.1 × 76.2 cm.). The Metropolitan Museum of Art, New York.

 **Art Criticism**

Describe

▶ List everything you see in this painting.

Analyze

▶ How has the artist used line, shape, color, value, space, and texture?

▶ How has the artist used rhythm, balance, and variety to organize this painting?

Interpret

▶ What is the artist telling you about the people who live in this room?

Decide

▶ Have you ever seen another artwork like this?

▶ Is it successful because it is realistic?

▶ Is it successful because it is well-organized?

▶ Is it successful because you have strong feelings when you study it?

More About Aesthetic Judging

You can use art criticism to make aesthetic judgments about functional objects such as cars or shoes. Follow the first two steps (**Describe** and **Analyze**) as described. During **Interpret,** consider the purpose of the object as its meaning. (Does a pitcher look like it will pour liquid without spilling?) As you **Decide,** consider whether the object works when it is used. (If a chair is not comfortable to sit in, it is not functioning properly and is not successful as a chair.)

Interpret **What is the artist saying to me?**

During interpretation, viewers will make inferences about the message in the work of art. Each interpretation can be different because each is based upon the feelings and life experiences of the viewer.

Questions to Discuss

▶ What do I think about this artwork?

▶ What is the artist trying to tell us about this room? This is a living room from a time before electricity. There is no cord for the lamp and no evidence of modern technology.

▶ Who lives here? What are they like? Answers will vary. They may be elderly because there is no sign of children. They are very neat. The large bouquet suggests that they like to garden.

Decide

This is when the viewer decides whether or not the work is successful. There are two levels of judgment to be made. The first is personal: do you like the work?

The second level is also subjective, but it uses aesthetic theories to help the viewer decide whether the work is successful. More than one theory may be used to judge a work.

▪ Some critics think that the most important thing about a work of art is the realistic presentation of the subject matter. This aesthetic theory is called **imitationalism** or **realism.**

▪ Other critics think that composition is the most important fact in a work of art. This aesthetic theory, called **formalism** or **composition,** emphasizes the design qualities and the arrangement of the elements of art by using the principles of art.

▪ Some critics claim that no object should be considered art if it fails to arouse an emotional response in the viewer. **Emotionalism** or **expressionism** is a theory concerned with the content or the meaning of the work of art.

Questions to Discuss

▶ Have you seen any works of art in this book that look similar to the style of this artist?

▶ Which aesthetic theories would you use to judge the success of this work? Even though objects have been simplified, it is still fairly realistic. The artist has used approximate symmetry to organize the work and has balanced harmony and variety to create unity. The painting evokes curiosity about the residents of this room.

Overview

Creative Expression

The creative process, like the writing process or the scientific method, is an organized approach to creative problem solving that can be used by professional artists and students alike. Throughout *Art Connections,* the Creative Expression activities are presented as problems to be solved. Remind students of the steps in the creative process as they work on the activities.

Get an idea.

▪ Inspiration can come from many places. In the *Art Connections* Creative Expression activities, the idea comes from the activity instructions. Professional artists may get ideas from a client who has commissioned a piece of art from nature, from a historical event, from everyday life, or from the available media and materials.

▪ Try the following to help students when they have trouble getting an idea.

1. As a class, brainstorm about where to get ideas for artwork: works by other artists, personal experiences, stories students have read, and so on.

2. Encourage students to write ideas in the Ideas section of their Art Journals. Remind students that they can make notes for ideas anytime, not just in art class.

3. Pair students who are having trouble thinking of ideas with students who have many ideas. One student can model getting ideas for the other student.

Plan your work.

▪ Once students have an idea, they must decide the best way to execute that idea. Would a two-dimensional or three-dimensional artwork best convey the idea that students are trying to show? Should students use watercolor or pencil?

Make a sketch.

▪ Just like professional writers, professional artists do not make a perfect work on the first try. They may make several sketches, evaluate those sketches, and revise them before deciding on a final vision for the artwork.

▪ Encourage students to make sketches in the Ideas section of their Art Journals.

About Art

▲ **Horace Pippin.** (American). *Victorian Parlor II.* 1945.
Oil on canvas. 25¼ × 30 inches (64.1 × 76.2 cm.). The Metropolitan Museum of Art, New York.

How does an artist create art? You can follow the same steps to create your own art.

1. Get an idea.
▶ Inspiration comes from many places. Look around you.

2. Plan your work.
▶ Decide what media you want to use. What materials will you need?

3. Make a sketch.
▶ Think about how you want your artwork to look. Sketch several ideas. Then choose the best idea.

4. Use the media.
▶ Make an artwork based on your best idea. You can practice using the materials first.

5. Share your final work.

Use the media.
■ In this stage of the creative process, students make their artwork based on their plans. Encourage students to practice using unfamiliar media, and to try out new techniques on a small practice piece before using those techniques on their artwork.

■ Even during this stage of the process, students may get new ideas. Encourage them to be flexible.

Share your final work.
■ Art is meant to be shared with and viewed by others. Encourage students to share their artwork with family or friends, display it in the classroom, or display it in the school display area. This is also a good time for students to self-evaluate their work using the four steps of art criticism.

More About Art Journals
■ Art Journals are a wonderful way to work through ideas. At the beginning of the school year, help students set up an Art Journal. This can be a spiral notebook or a three-ring binder with pages for writing and sketching. The Art Journal will be divided into sections for Concepts, Ideas, Critical Thinking (Art Criticism), Vocabulary, and Research (at Level 6 only).

1. Encourage students to use the Concepts section of their journals for summarizing unit and lesson concepts, writing questions they have, and listing other things they want to learn.

2. Students can use the Ideas section of their Art Journals for brainstorming, organizing, planning, and sketching. Remind students that they can write ideas in their journals any time; they do not need to wait until a designated time in art class.

3. Students can use the Critical Thinking section of their journals to self-evaluate their work using the four steps of Art Criticism. In *Art Connections* students are asked to self-evaluate after each Creative Expression activity. This can be a valuable tool to help students review art concepts and get ideas for their next work.

4. Encourage students to use the Vocabulary section of their Art Journals to record unfamiliar words, summarize or explain definitions, and so on. Developing vocabulary is an important step in being able to think about and communicate about art.

Overview

Elementary teachers are responsible for the safety of their students. Specific guidelines have been established by the Center for Safety in the Arts, and these guidelines should be followed to ensure that both students and teachers use art materials safely. Following are some general tips for using art materials safely. For more detailed information, see "Safe Use of Art Materials" on page T12 of this book.

Safe Art Materials

- Use only water-soluble AP- or CP-designated markers. Never use permanent or scented markers.

- Use only dustless chalk.

- Make sure that crayons have the AP or CP label to ensure that they do not contain lead.

- When using tempera paint, use only liquid tempera, not powdered tempera. Do not use any spray paints or fixatives.

- Use only water-soluble printers' inks.

- Use pencils to carve into soft surfaces for printing blocks. Do not use mat knives or other sharp instruments.

- Do not allow young children to use sharp scissors; blunt points are safe.

- Do not use rubber cement unless it bears the AP or CP label. Do not use solvent-based glues.

Safety

▶ Use art materials only on your artwork.

▶ Keep art materials out of your mouth, eyes and ears.

▶ Use scissors carefully. Keep your fingers away from the blades.

▶ Wash your hands after using the art materials.

▶ Wear an art shirt or smock to protect your clothes.

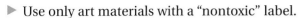

▶ Use only art materials with a "nontoxic" label.

▶ Keep fingers clear when using a stapler.

▶ Be careful not to breathe chalk or clay dust.

▶ Return art materials to their proper storage place.

▶ Always follow your teacher's directions when using art materials.

About Art **33**

General Safety Precautions for Art

▪ Read the labels on all materials used in the art room. Look carefully for the AP/CP labels. If these are not present, be suspicious. Imported art materials should be looked upon with extreme caution. Other countries have not developed the rigid safety codes adopted by the United States.

▪ Do not accept or use old art materials that may have been left in the school or donated by some well-meaning adult. If the materials do not bear the current safety codes, toss them out.

▪ Never allow food or drink in the room where art activities are being conducted. Dust and even fibers float freely in the air and can readily contaminate food or drink.

▪ Practice cleanliness. Have children wash their hands thoroughly with soap after using art materials.

▪ Use absolutely no permanent markers or solvent-based materials in the art room. If a material stains the clothes or hands and does not clean up with simple soap and water, it is not appropriate or safe for young children to use.

▪ Use plastic containers for washing paintbrushes; glass is dangerous in the hands of young children.

▪ Paper cutters should not be used by elementary school children. The paper cutter should be kept out of the students' reach, and left in a locked position always with the blade turned to the wall.

▪ Do not use commercial dyes around children; use vegetable or natural dyes (flowers, teas, onion skins).

▪ Do not allow children in a room where a kiln is firing; both the heat and the fumes are dangerous.

Unit 1 Planning Guide

	Lesson Title	Suggested Pacing	Creative Expression Activity
Lesson 1	Line Direction	55 minutes	Create a paper sculpture playground using different line directions.
Lesson 2	Types of Lines	55 minutes	Create a dream tree collage using different types of lines.
Lesson 3	Calm Lines	55 minutes	Create a water painting using calm lines.
Lesson 4	Active Lines	55 minutes	Create an abstract painting of an exciting event using active lines.
Lesson 5	Geometric Shapes	55 minutes	Create a cut paper picture using geometric shapes.
Lesson 6	Free-Form Shapes	55 minutes	Create a shadow puppet using free-form shapes.
ART SOURCE ARTSOURCE	Line and Space in Theatre	35 minutes	Create two-sided mask that shows opposite emotions.

Materials	Program Resources	Fine Art Resources	Literature Resources
12" × 12" black construction paper, ½" × 12" and ½" × 9" precut colored paper strips, glue, pencils	*Reading and Writing Test Preparation*, pp. 6–7 *Flash Cards*, 1–5 *Assessment*, pp. 9–10 *Home and After-School Connections*	*Transparency*, 1 *Artist Profiles*, pp. 37, 58 *Animals Time Line* *Large Prints*, 25 and 26 *Women in the Arts Collection*	*Madison Finds a Line* by Sunny Warner
9" × 12" paper, yarn, embroidery thread, thin precut paper strips, grasses, chenille stems, buttons, gel glue	*Reading and Writing Test Preparation*, pp. 8–9 *Flash Cards*, 1–6 *Assessment*, pp. 11–12	*Transparency*, 2 *Artist Profiles*, pp. 31, 53 *Large Prints*, 25 and 26 *Women in the Arts Collection*	*If the Dinosaurs Came Back* by Bernard Most
paper, medium and large brushes, watercolors, water containers, paper towels	*Reading and Writing Test Preparation*, pp. 10–11 *Flash Cards*, 1 and 2 *Assessment*, pp. 13–14	*Transparency*, 3 *Artist Profiles*, pp. 18, 40 *Large Prints*, 25 and 26 *Art Around the World Collection*	*Three by the Sea* by James Marshall
12" × 18" white construction paper, liquid tempera paint, brushes, water containers, paper towels, yarn	*Reading and Writing Test Preparation*, pp. 12–13 *Flash Cards*, 3–6 *Assessment*, pp. 15–16	*Transparency*, 4 *Artist Profiles*, pp. 28, 63 *Large Print*, 25 *Art Around the World Collection*	*Who's Hiding Here* by Yoshi *Prehistoric Pinkerton* by Steven Kellogg
white and colored construction paper, scissors, glue	*Reading and Writing Test Preparation*, pp. 14–15 *Flash Card*, 7 *Assessment*, pp. 17–18	*Transparency*, 5 *Artist Profiles*, pp. 23, 35 *Large Prints*, 25 and 26 *Art Around the World Collection*	*The Greedy Triangle* by Marilyn Burns
brads, tape, paper punch, markers, flashlight or light source, tagboard or colored paper, chopsticks or ⅛" dowels, ribbon, fabric scraps, yarn, scissors	*Reading and Writing Test Preparation*, pp. 16–17 *Flash Card*, 8 *Assessment*, pp. 19–20	*Transparency*, 6 *Artist Profiles*, pp. 74, 83 *Large Prints*, 25 and 26 *Art Around the World Collection*	*What Makes a Shadow* by Clyde Robert Bulla
"The Mask Messenger" by Faustwork Mask Theater, paper plates, glue, scissors, paper towel rolls, yarn, buttons, fabric scraps, crayons, markers, beans, rice, seeds			

Unit Overview

1 Line and Shape

Lesson 1: **Line Direction** describes in which direction a line is moving.

Lesson 2: **Types of Lines** describes what a line looks like, such as thick, thin, or broken.

Lesson 3: **Calm Lines** make artwork seem tranquil and peaceful.

Lesson 4: **Active Lines** make artwork seem alive and exciting.

Lesson 5: **Geometric Shapes** have special names and can be used to make pictures.

Lesson 6: **Free-Form Shapes** are irregular shapes.

Introduce Unit Concepts

"Artists use lines and shapes to express ideas and feelings in their artwork." *"Los artistas usan líneas y formas para expresar ideas y sentimientos en sus obras de arte".*

Lines

- Have students look around the room and describe the lines they see.

- Explain that different tools (pencils, pens, crayons, paintbrushes, and computer programs) make different lines. Have students make lines with several tools and compare the lines.

Shapes

- Have students find examples of geometric shapes in the room.

- Explain what a free-form shape is. Ask students to describe one.

Cross-Curricular Projects

- See the *Language Arts and Reading, Mathematics, Science* and *Social Studies Art Connections* books for activities that further develop line and shape.

Unit 1

Line and Shape

▲ **Jacob Lawrence.** (American). *Street Scene (Boy with Kite).* 1962.
Egg tempera on hardboard. $23\frac{7}{8} \times 30$ inches (60.64 × 76.2 cm). Conservation Center of the Institute of Fine Arts, New York, New York.

Artists use different kinds of lines to make people, objects, and places.

The lines and shapes make the painting more interesting.

Fine Art Prints

Display **Large Prints 25** *The Kitchen* and **26** *Le Fifre*. Refer to the prints throughout the unit as students learn about line and shape.

Large Print 25

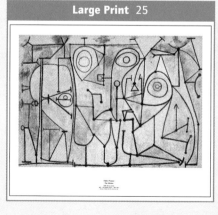

Large Print 26

By using different types of lines and shapes, artists can make many objects.

▶ Where do you see straight lines in this painting?

▶ Which objects in the painting are made using curved lines?

▶ Which objects in the painting are made using geometric shapes such as triangles or rectangles?

In This Unit you will learn how artists use lines and shapes to show ideas and feelings. You also will practice using lines and shapes to show your ideas and feelings. Here are the topics you will study:

▶ Line Direction
▶ Line Styles
▶ Calm Lines
▶ Active Lines
▶ Geometric Shapes
▶ Free-Form Shapes

Jacob Lawrence
(1917–2000)

Jacob Lawrence was born in New Jersey. His parents separated when he was seven years old. In 1930 Lawrence's mother brought the children to Harlem in New York City. Lawrence studied arts and crafts there in an after-school program. He painted pictures of his neighborhood and what he saw around him. Lawrence was a pioneer African American artist who also painted pictures about African American history.

Unit 1   **35**

Art History and Culture

Jacob Lawrence

Jacob Lawrence (jā´ kəb lär´ ənz) (1917–2000) was born in Atlantic City, New Jersey. His parents were originally from the South and moved north as part of the Great Migration. Lawrence started going to an after-school art program in Harlem; he also was working to help support his family. He eventually dropped out of high school. Lawrence began painting what he saw around him in his Harlem neighborhood during the Depression and Harlem Renaissance. He painted most of his art using tempera paints because they were inexpensive and vivid. Lawrence was one of the first African American artists to receive national mainstream recognition.

Artist Profiles, p. 32

● Artist Profile ●

Jacob Lawrence
1917–2000

Jacob Lawrence (jā´ kəb lär´ ənz) had parents who met on their migration to the North. His father was born in South Carolina, and his mother in Virginia. Lawrence was born in Atlantic City, New Jersey, in 1917. The family finally settled in Harlem in 1929 at the end of the Harlem Renaissance. Because his mother worked all day, she enrolled Lawrence in the Harlem Art Workshop after school to keep him out of trouble. He had many excellent teachers there, including Charles Alston. Lawrence won a scholarship to the American Artists School. He taught at New York's Pratt Institute from 1958 to 1965. From 1970, he taught at the University of Washington in Seattle, where he also served as head of the

Examine the Artwork

"Look for the lines and shapes Jacob Lawrence used in this painting." "Busquen las líneas y formas que Jacob Lawrence usó en esta pintura".

■ Have students look at *Street Scene (Boy with Kite)* and describe what they see.

■ Have students answer the questions about line and shape on page 35.

▶ The lines of the buildings and sidewalk are straight.

▶ The kite string, people, jumprope, and awnings are all made using curved lines.

▶ The pram has triangles in the wheel, which is a circle. The windows are rectangles.

■ Make sure students understand the differences between materials, techniques, and processes. Have students describe how different materials, techniques, and processes cause different viewer responses.

Unit Pretest

T Display **Transparency 43** as a pretest. Answers: 1. A, 2. C, 3. B, 4. B

Home Connection

■ See *Home and After-School Connections* for family newsletters and activities for this unit.

National Standards for Arts Education 1.a, 1.b

ILLUSTRATOR PROFILE

Theodore Seuss Geisel (Dr. Seuss)

(1904–1991)

Theodore Geisel was born into a family of brewmasters in Springfield, Massachusetts. When Geisel was a young child, his mother recited rhymes to get him to fall asleep. Geisel felt his mother gave him ability to rhyme. His father was a curator at the Forest Park Zoo and would send him animals' antlers and horns that he used to create fanciful animal sculptures.

Geisel attended Dartmouth and was the editor of the college's student magazine. After being forced to resign after throwing a party which violated prohibition laws, he contributed to the magazine using his mother's maiden name, and his pseudonym, "Seuss."

After Dartmouth, Geisel briefly attended Oxford with the intention of becoming a literature professor, but he soon tired of his studies and began a career in advertising and being a cartoonist. He became interested in children's literature and wrote and illustrated a book called *To Think that I Saw It on Mulberry Street*, using his pseudonym "Dr. Seuss." It was rejected 27 times by publishers before being printed. Geisel wrote his most famous book, *The Cat in the Hat*, after reading an article about the lack of interesting books for beginning readers. There are only 223 different words in the entire book.

Geisel was a private, quiet person who wrote and illustrated for children and adults throughout his life. He is among the most beloved and best known children's authors in the world. Throughout Unit 1, share Dr. Suess's illustrations with the class and discuss line and shape.

Music

In music, *line*, refers to the way the notes of a melody move higher or lower. Sing a song and have students show the higher/lower movement with their hands. Draw several shapes on the board and create sounds to correspond to them. Have the class decide which shape matches which sound.

Literature

Show the video or DVD *The Talking Eggs* by Robert San Souci to help introduce students to the concepts of line and shape.

Literature and Art

Performing Arts

 Show "The Mask Messenger." Point out the lines and shapes.

Artsource®

Lesson 1 Line Direction

Overview

Lesson 1 introduces line direction. Line direction describes the way a line is oriented or moving: vertically, horizontally, diagonally, zigzag, or curved.

Objectives

 Art History and Culture

To compare two works of art that feature structures and identify line direction

 Creative Expression

To create a paper sculpture playground that illustrates line direction

 Aesthetic Perception

To identify the five line directions—horizontal, vertical, diagonal, curved, and zigzag—in the classroom

Art Criticism

To evaluate own work using the four steps of art criticism

Vocabulary Vocabulary

Review the following vocabulary words with students before beginning the lesson.

line línea—mark made by a tool, such as a pen, pencil, or crayon as it moves across a surface

vertical vertical—oriented or moving up and down

horizontal horizontal—oriented or moving left to right

See page 59B for additional vocabulary and Spanish vocabulary resources.

Art Journal: Vocabulary

Have students add these words to the Vocabulary section of their Art Journals.

Lesson Materials
- 12" x 12" black construction paper, $\frac{1}{2}$" x 12" and $\frac{1}{2}$" x 9" precut colored paper strips
- scissors
- pencils
- glue

Alternate Materials:
- crayons, markers
- oil pastels

Program Resources
- *Reading and Writing Test Prep.*, p. 6–7
- *Transparency 1*
- *Flash Cards 1, 2, 3, 4, 5*
- *Artist Profiles*, pp. 37, 58
- *Animals Through History Time Line*
- *Assessment*, pp. 9–10
- *Large Prints 25* The Kitchen and *26* Le Fifre
- *The National Museum of Women in the Arts Collection*

Concept Trace

Line Direction
Introduced: Level 1, Unit 1, Lesson 2
Reinforced: Level 3, Unit 1, Lesson 1

Lesson 1 Arts Integration

Theatre

Complete Unit 1, Lesson 1 on pages 18–19 of *Theatre Arts Connections.*

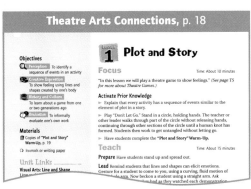

Music

 March from *the Nutcracker.* Piotr Illyich Tchaikovsky.

Line in music refers to the way a melody moves higher and lower (up, down, or the same). To relate the concept of line in music to line in visual art, play Tchaikovsky's *March* from *The Nutcracker.* Have students draw the vertical, horizontal, diagonal, zigzag, and curved lines that they think go with the music.

Movement & Dance

Have students walk freely to the beat of a drum or music. Direct their attention to the pathway they are making (probably curved); ask them to exaggerate it. Now ask students to change how they are traveling. Have them take bigger steps, walk backward or sideways, walk low to the ground and then try walking high. Explore skipping, sliding, and jumping.

Focus

Activate Prior Knowledge

"Have you ever seen a car moving down the road?" "¿Alguna vez han visto un carro moviéndose por la carretera?"

- Discuss student responses. Explain that the car is moving along a line in a certain direction.

Using Literature ⭐ Reading

- Read and discuss *Madison Finds a Line* by Sunny Warner. Talk to students about the line directions they see in the book.

Thematic Connection ⭐ Reading

- **Buildings:** Encourage students to discuss buildings. How do they think different buildings are made? How many different kinds of buildings can they think of?

Introduce the Art

Look

"Let's look closely at the sculpture and the painting." "Miremos de cerca la escultura y la pintura". NSAE 2.a

Human Settlement ⭐ Social Studies

- Have students discuss the ways buildings are constructed and how they think people decide where and when to build buildings. Where can they identify lines? What kinds of structures do they see in the artwork? The structures in *Church* are evident, but students may want to describe the buildings. The structures in the Stella piece are abstract, but read the title of the work to students and encourage them to use their imaginations when looking for buildings in the painting.
NSAE 4.a, 4.c, 5.a, 5.b

 Art History and Culture

Possible answer: Both buildings were important to the artists who made them, or the artists felt as though the buildings represented something special.

💻 **Web Connection**

Visit www.artsmia.org/ceramics to learn how ceramics have been used in different cultures throughout the world.

 Lesson 1 Line Direction

Look at the **lines** that are used in these two pieces of art. Trace the outlines of the doors, windows, and shapes on the sculpture with your finger. Trace the lines you see in the painting. Artists use different names to describe lines and the way they move. How many kinds of lines do you see?

◄ **Heron Martínez Mendoza.**
(Mexican). *Church*. c. 1960.
Painted earthenware. 24 inches high (60.96 cm.). Museum of International Folk Art, Santa Fe, New Mexico.

 Art History and Culture

These works of art are buildings. How did the artists feel about the buildings? Were they important to them?

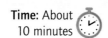 **Art History and Culture**

Herón Martínez Mendóza

Herón Martínez Mendóza (ā ron´ mär tē´ nez men dō´ zə) (1918–1989) was born in Acatlán de Osorio in Puebla, Mexico. His city is known for its ceramics. His mother was renowned locally for making small clay figures. Mendóza began making pots in 1941. His work is usually full of bright colors and contains imaginary creatures and animals. *Church* is part of a ceramic Mexican village that Mendóza was commissioned to create in the 1960s for the International Folk Art Museum in Santa Fe, New Mexico.

For more about art history and subject matter, see pages 24–25 and 16–21.

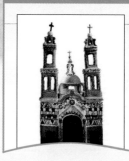

Artist Profiles, p. 37

◆ Artist Profile ◆
Herón Martínez Mendoza
1918–1989

Herón Martínez Mendoza (ā ron´ mär tē´ nez men dō´ zə) was born in Mexico. Like his parents, grandparents, and great-grandparents, he began his career by creating cooking pots. He had played with clay since childhood, but he did not want to become a potter. To support himself and his wife, he began making clay barrels, which sold well. Growing up, Mendoza listened to many myths and legends. These stories—and his own creativity—inspired him to create unique and beautiful pottery reflecting the myths and legends of his childhood. In his later years, he stayed busy filling orders for sculptures requested by

Study the **sculpture** and the **painting** to find examples of line direction.

▶ Where in the sculpture and painting do you see diagonal lines?

▶ Where in the sculpture and painting do you see vertical and horizontal lines?

▶ Do you see any other lines in the art?

◀ **Joseph Stella.** (American). *The Voice of the City of New York Interpreted/The Great White Way Leaving the Subway (White Way I).* c. 1920–22.

Oil and tempera on canvas. 88 ½ × 54 inches (224.79 × 137.16 cm.). The Newark Museum, Newark, New Jersey.

Aesthetic Perception

Seeing Like an Artist Look around your classroom and find objects that show lines. In what direction are the lines moving?

Study

▶ The rays and details in *The Voice of the City* are diagonal lines. The hatching detail and triangles in *Church* are also diagonal lines.

▶ The border and details in *The Voice of the City* and the lines of doors, windows, and decoration in *Church* are all horizontal lines. Vertical lines are in the grid frame and details in *The Voice of the City* and the lines of doors, windows, and decoration on *Church*.

▶ Curved lines are in the border, details, and steam in *The Voice of the City*, and the arches of doors, windows, domes, and decorations in *Church*. Zigzag lines are in the border and details of *The Voice of the City* and the decorations in *Church*.

■ For more examples of genre art, see *The National Museum of Women in the Arts Collection.*

Art Journal: Writing

Have students write their ideas about line direction in the Concepts section of their Art Journals.

Aesthetic Perception

Seeing Like an Artist Encourage students to identify variations in objects as they look for lines and line direction in the room. For example, the desks or tables may be arranged in rows of horizontal and vertical lines. The clock and doorknob are examples of curved lines. Can students find examples of line direction?   NSAE 2.b, 5.c

Developing Visual Literacy Have students discuss how these works of art make them feel about buildings and construction. Discuss architecture with the students and how architects pick a style when designing a building.

Art History and Culture

Joseph Stella

Joseph Stella (jō´sef ste´lə) (1877–1946) was born in Italy, but moved to New York as a young man. *The Voice of the City of New York Interpreted/The Great White Way Leaving the Subway (White Way I)* is one panel from a series of five that Stella painted. These paintings were made at a time when New York was gaining recognition all over the world as a testament to modern machinery and financial power. Stella used five panels and stained glass hues in these paintings to mimic Italian religious altarpieces. By doing this, he made a statement about technology and progress becoming a new religion in America.

For more about art history and subject matter, see pages 24–25 and 16–21.

Artist Profiles, p. 58

● Artist Profile ●
Joseph Stella
1877–1946

Joseph Stella (jō´ sef ste´ la) was born in Italy. He came to the United States as a young man and began painting portraits of immigrants living in New York City. A group that was concerned about immigrants was impressed with Stella's work. The group sent him to the coal mines and industrial regions of Pennsylvania and West Virginia. Stella painted the workers there so others would understand the terrible working conditions they faced. Stella saw how the growth of industry and the use of machines was affecting human lives. However, he was also impressed by the power and creativity of the American industrial age. In time, he turned from painting workers to painting symbolic pictures of technology and machines.

Web Connection

Visit **www.newarkmuseum.org/americanart/html/tour/galleries/labels/stella_panels.htm** to see the other paintings in the Stella series.

 **Teach**

"How can you use lines to show direction?"

"¿Cómo pueden usar las líneas para mostrar dirección?"

- Discuss the information about line direction on page 38.

Practice

Materials: a large open space

- Have students follow the directions on page 38.

- Help the students divide into groups and get into lines. Remind students to walk slowly and pay attention to where they are going. Assign each group a different line direction. You may want to have only one line move at a time.

- Have students identify and practice skills necessary for producing constructions using a variety of materials.

  NSAE 1.c, 1.d, 2.c, 3.b

Creative Expression

Materials: 12" x 12" black construction paper, $\frac{1}{2}$" x 12" and $\frac{1}{2}$" x 9" pre-cut colored paper strips, scissors, pencils, glue

Alternate Materials: crayons, markers, oil pastels

- Distribute materials and have students follow the directions on page 39.

- Encourage students to express ideas and feelings in their playgrounds using a variety of lines.

- Encourage students to create effective compositions using design elements.

- Review the Activity Tips on page 232 for visual examples of the activity if needed.

- Review the Technique Tips on page 227.

NSAE 3.a
Art Journal: Brainstorming

Have students brainstorm ideas for buildings and structures in the Ideas section of their Art Journals. Students may want to incorporate sketches or key adjectives to describe the structures they plan to make in the Creative Expression activity.

Vertical

Horizontal

Diagonal

Zigzag

Curved

Using Line Direction

A line is named for the direction in which it moves. To figure out which direction a line is moving, imagine drawing the line. Which way do you move your pencil to make the line?

Vertical lines move up and down.

Horizontal lines move side to side.

Diagonal lines move from one corner to the opposite corner.

Zigzag lines are made of **angles.**

Curved lines are made of **arcs** instead of straight lines.

Using lines that move in different directions makes artwork more interesting.

Practice

Walk around the room in a line direction.

1. Get into groups and form a line.

2. Walk around the room in the line direction your teacher gives you.

3. Look at how each line moves. Can you see the different line directions?

Differentiated Instruction

Reteach

Have students look for lines in the classroom or outside that fit into more than one line direction category.

Special Needs

Students with disabilities may need extra practice making the different types of paper strips mentioned in this lesson. To ensure success, provide examples of each type of paper strip and allow time for students to practice and master each technique before beginning the lesson.

ELL Tips

Students may be hesitant to answer interpretive questions about their artwork. You may wish to phrase questions as an *either/or* choice so the vocabulary needed to answer the question is contained in the question itself.

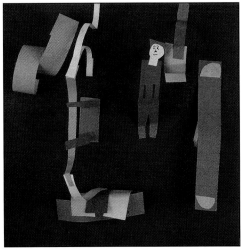

◄ **Anzlee Brock.**
Age 7.

Think about how this student used line direction when designing her playground.

 **Creative Expression**

What kind of buildings or structures would you put on a playground? Make a playground from paper using many lines.

1. Think of a playground you would like to create.
2. Twist, curl, and fold strips of paper to make different line directions.
3. Fold the ends of the strips for tabs and glue them onto the base paper to make your playground.

 **Art Criticism**

Describe What equipment is on your playground?

Analyze Which line directions did you use?

Interpret How would your playground look if you used a different line direction?

Decide Could builders construct your playground?

 **Reflect** **Time:** About 10 minutes

Review and Assess

"How would you explain what line direction is?" "¿Como pueden explicar lo que es dirección lineal?"

Think

This student used line direction when designing the structures for her playground.

- Use *Large Prints 25* The Kitchen and *26* Le Fifre to have students identify line direction.
- Have students identify stories and constructions in this lesson's artwork.
- Have students identify ideas in the art by this lesson's artists.

Informal Assessment

Art Journal: Critical Thinking
Have students answer the four art criticism questions—Describe, Analyze, Interpret, and Decide—in the Critical Thinking section of their Art Journals. In small groups, have the students discuss the use of line direction in their paper sculptures. Have them discuss reasons for preferences in their own works of art. Have them identify the ideas in their peers' works of art.

- For standardized-format test practice using this lesson's art content, see pages 6–7 in *Reading and Writing Test Preparation.*

Art Across the Curriculum   NSAE 6.a, 6.b

Use these simple ideas to reinforce art concepts across the curriculum.

★ **Poetry** Have students write a poem about buildings and lines.

★ **Math** Discuss how math problems can be written vertically or horizontally.

★ **Science** Have students use the scientific process to answer questions about why different line directions are used for different building parts.

★ **Social Studies** Discuss population with students and why most buildings in New York City are skyscrapers (vertical lines), and other buildings are low (horizontal lines).

★ **Technology Connection** Show students how they can make the cursor move in different line directions by using the mouse. Visit **SRAonline.com** to print detailed instructions for this activity.

For the Art Specialist

Time: About 45 minutes

Focus

Have students draw something that has straight, curved, and zigzag lines. Ask them to identify the lines and line directions in their pictures. Have students identify stories and constructions in this lesson's artworks.

Teach

Discuss with students what architecture is and explain that they will design a house or building using different line directions. Have students complete the Alternate Activity.

Reflect

Have students evaluate their artwork using the four steps of art criticism.

Alternate Activity

Materials:
- 9" × 12" black and white construction paper
- colored pencils (metallic if possible)
- images of different kinds of architecture

1. Look at the images of architecture and think of a structure you would like to design.

2. Using the colored pencils and either black or white paper, draw your buildings large and use different line directions.

3. Color in your buildings and add details.

Research
in Art Education

Research has shown that the "looking and reasoning skills" learned during visual art training can also be applied to scientific images ("Investigating the Educational Impact and Potential of the Museum of Modern Art's Visual Thinking Curriculum" in *Critical Links*, p. 142). Students involved in visual arts training showed less circular reasoning and more evidential reasoning when evaluating both fine art images and scientific images. As students learn to look for the lines and shapes in art, encourage them to look for the lines and shapes in their surroundings.

Assessment
Use the following rubric to evaluate the artwork students make in the Creative Expression activity and to assess students' understanding of line direction.

Have students complete page 9 or 10 in their *Assessment* books.

	Art History and Culture	Aesthetic Perception	Creative Expression	Art Criticism
3 POINTS	The student can compare two works of art featuring structures and identify the line directions.	The student accurately identifies line direction in the classroom.	The student's sculpture clearly illustrates a good use of line direction.	The student thoughtfully and honestly evaluates his or her own work using the four steps of art criticism.
2 POINTS	The student's identification or comparison is weak or incomplete.	The student shows emerging awareness of different types of line direction, but cannot consistently identify them.	The student's sculpture shows some awareness of line direction.	The student attempts to evaluate his or her own work, but shows an incomplete understanding of evaluation criteria.
1 POINT	The student cannot compare two works of art featuring structures and identify the line directions.	The student cannot identify line direction.	The student's sculpture shows no understanding of line direction.	The student makes no attempt to evaluate his or her own artwork.

Assessment, p. 9

Name _____ Date _____

Lesson 1 UNIT 1

Line Direction

A. Drawing
Draw each kind of line in the corresponding box.

| straight | curved | zigzag |
| horizontal | vertical | diagonal |

B. Cutting
Cut out the squares that contain curved and diagonal lines. Paste them in the box below.

Level 2   Unit 1 • Line and Shape   9

Types of Lines

Lesson 2 introduces the students to different types of lines. Lines have different qualities, such as thick, thin, smooth, rough, solid, and broken.

Objectives

Art History and Culture

To understand that artists use different types of lines and methods to express their imaginations

Creative Expression

To create a dream tree or line collage that illustrates the use of different types of lines and imagination

Aesthetic Perception

To identify different types of lines in an object in students' environments

Art Criticism

To evaluate own work using the four steps of art criticism

Vocabulary Vocabulary

Review the following vocabulary words with students before beginning the lesson.

thick gruesa—wide

thin fina—narrow

solid continua—has no breaks, gaps, or holes

See page 59B for additional vocabulary and Spanish vocabulary resources.

Art Journal: Vocabulary

Have students add these words to the Vocabulary section of their Art Journals.

Lesson Materials

- yarn, embroidery thread
- thin precut paper strips, grasses
- chenille stems
- buttons for broken lines
- 9" x 12" paper
- pencil
- gel glue

Alternate Materials:
- crayons, markers, colored pencils
- found objects

Program Resources

- *Reading and Writing Test Prep.,* pp. 8–9
- *Transparency 2*
- *Flash Cards 1, 2, 3, 4, 5, 6*
- *Artist Profiles,* pp. 31, 53
- *Animals Through History Time Line*
- *Assessment,* pp. 11–12
- *Large Prints 25* The Kitchen and *26* Le Fifre
- *The National Museum of Women in the Arts Collection*

Concept Trace
Types of Lines
Introduced: Level 1, Unit 1, Lesson 1

Reinforced: Level 3, Unit 1, Lesson 2

Lesson 2 Arts Integration

Theatre

Complete Unit 1, Lesson 2 on pages 20–21 of *Theatre Arts Connections.*

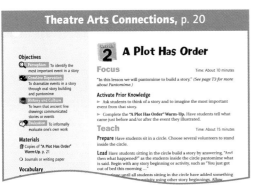

Music

Turkey in the Straw.

Lines can be thick, thin, smooth, rough, solid, or broken. To emphasize different types of lines, play *Turkey in the Straw* as students are creating different kinds of lines in the Practice activity in this lesson. Discuss what types of lines might go with the different animals in the song.

Movement & Dance

Discuss the following design motifs: circles, *C* curves, *S* curves, spirals, dots, zigzag lines, and straight lines. Explore each idea using axial (stationary) movement. For example, have students unfold the body in a spiral pattern.

Focus

Activate Prior Knowledge

"Have you ever seen an old tree planted next to a young tree?" "¿Alguna vez han visto un árbol viejo plantado al lado de uno joven?"

■ Discuss student responses. Explain that the older tree trunk is thick and the younger tree trunk is thin. Point out that these tree trunks are different types of lines.

Using Literature Reading

■ Read and discuss *If the Dinosaurs Came Back* by Bernard Most. Talk about how the author used his imagination to invent the story. Have students look for different kinds of lines.

Thematic Connection Reading

■ **Imagination:** Have students discuss what they think imagination is. How do they like to use their imaginations?

Introduce the Art

Look

"Let's take a close look at the two works of art." "Vamos a observar detalladamente las dos obras de arte".

■ Have students identify lines in the works of art and the environment.

Hypothesizing Science

■ Ask students to use their imaginations and describe what they see in *Alanda's Dream Tree* and *Blueberry Eyes*. Why do they think the artists named their pieces what they did? Explain how students are using their imaginations to form hypotheses.

NSAE 4.a, 4.c, 5.a, 5.b

Art History and Culture

Possible answer: Different artists like to use their imaginations to show things in different ways. Since every person's imagination is different, every person's art will be different.

💻 **Web Connection**

Visit www.arthurrogergallery.com/Artists/Scott/ to see more art by John T. Scott.

Types of Lines

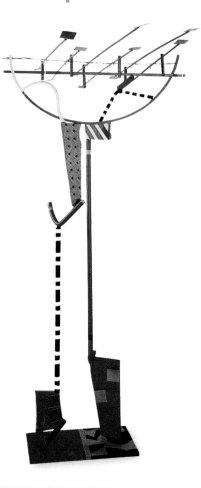

Look at these two pieces of art. *Alanda's Dream Tree* is a sculpture. *Blueberry Eyes* is an oil painting. Both of these works use different line styles. Where do you see a thick line? Where do you see a broken line?

◀ **John T. Scott.** (American). *Alanda's Dream Tree.* 1985.

Painted steel, brass, and stainless steel cable. 76 ½ × 36 × 78 inches (194.31 × 91.44 × 198.12 cm.). New Orleans Museum of Art, New Orleans, Louisiana.

Art History and Culture

Why do you think one artist used a sculpture and the other used a painting to show lines?

Art History and Culture

John T. Scott

John T. Scott (jän skät) (1940–) is a prominent artist, both in his home state of Louisiana and nationally. *Alanda's Dream Tree* is a sculpture made from painted steel, brass, and stainless steel cable. Scott carefully constructs and paints the abstract line sculptures for which he is well known. *Alanda's Dream Tree* does not really look like a tree, but it illustrates the imagination that Scott uses when he creates a piece. Like most abstract art, the real meaning in this piece is the viewer's interpretation.

For more about art history and subject matter, see pages 24–25 and 16–21.

Artist Profiles, p. 53

John Scott
b. 1940

John Scott (jän skät) was born in New Orleans, Louisiana. He received his bachelor of fine arts degree from Xavier University there. After earning his master of fine arts degree from Michigan State University, Scott returned to New Orleans. He spends his time creating artwork, working in the community, and teaching art at Xavier University.

Study the works of art to find different line styles.

▶ Do all the lines in the works of art look the same?

▶ What makes some lines look different from others?

▶ How do the different line styles make certain lines stand out?

◀ **Franz Kline.** (American).
Blueberry Eyes. 1959–1960.
Oil on paperboard. 40 ⅛ × 29 ¾ inches (101.7 × 75.5 cm.). Smithsonian American Art Museum, Washington, D.C.

 Aesthetic Perception

Design Awareness Look around the classroom and find an object with lots of lines in it. Can you name the line styles and directions you see?

Study

▶ No, some of the lines are thick, some are thin, some are rough, and some are broken.

▶ The lines look different because they are all made in different styles.

▶ Lines like thick lines attract your eye because they are bolder than the surrounding lines.

■ For more examples of abstract/non-objective art see *The National Museum of Women in the Arts Collection*.

Art Journal: Questioning
Encourage students to write any questions they have about types of lines in the Concepts section of their Art Journals.

Aesthetic Perception

Design Awareness Have students look around the classroom and find an object that is composed of several lines. Have them analyze and discuss the object to identify all the line styles and directions that are present. Encourage them to identify variations in the objects from the environments.   NSAE 2.b, 5.c

Developing Visual Literacy Discuss with students what they feel these works of art are "saying." What were the artists trying to convey by creating these works of art? Since these are both abstract works of art, the students will have many different interpretations. Discuss why an artist might choose to make an abstract work of art.

Art History and Culture

Franz Kline

Franz Kline (fräntz klīn) (1910–1962) was born in Wilkes-Barre, Pennsylvania. He studied in Boston and London before settling in New York. Kline painted traditionally at first, but soon began making large-scale abstract paintings in black and white. Kline began painting this way when he magnified one of his sketches and noticed how exciting the lines looked when they were large. He used large brushes and house paint in his work. Kline is famous for painting pictures of big, loose lines. In the late 1950s he began introducing strong colors into some of his work.

For more about art history and subject matter, see pages 24–25 and 16–21.

Artist Profiles, p. 31

◀ Artist Profile ●
Franz Kline
1910–1962
Franz Kline (fräntz klīn), was born in Wilkes-Barre, Pennsylvania, and is considered one of the most prominent twentieth century American abstract artists. He began his career as a landscape painter, and studied at the Art Department of Boston University and the Heatherly School of Art in London, England. During the early stages of his career Kline received awards in a number of National Academy of Design Annuals. After his schooling he lived in New York City, where he painted street and bohemian scenes until he began his exploration of abstract painting in 1946. When he enthusiastically committed himself to abstract expressionism in 1949, Kline was creating bold, large-scale works.

Web Connection
Visit **www.art54.com/franzkline** to see more art by Franz Kline.

 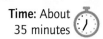

Teach

Time: About 35 minutes

"How can you show feelings using line styles?" "¿Cómo pueden mostrar sentimientos con estilos de líneas?"

- Discuss the information about types of lines on page 42.

Practice

Materials: paper and pencil

Alternate Materials: crayons, markers, or colored pencils

- Distribute the materials and have students follow the directions on page 42.

- Have students identify and practice skills necessary for producing constructions using a variety of materials.

NSAE 1.c, 1.d, 2.c, 3.b

Creative Expression

Materials: yarn, embroidery thread, thin precut paper strips, grasses, chenille stems, buttons for broken lines, 9" x 12" paper, pencil, gel glue.

Alternate Materials: found objects small enough to be used in a collage

- Distribute the materials and have students follow the directions on page 43.

- Encourage students to express their ideas and feelings in their dream trees using a variety of lines.

- Encourage students to create effective compositions using design elements.

- Review the Activity Tips on page 232 for visual examples of techniques if needed.

- Review the Technique Tips on pages 220–221.

Art Journal: Sketching

Have students sketch layouts for the lines of their dream trees in the Ideas section of their Art Journals.

Using Types of Lines

Lines can be **thick** or **thin, smooth,** or **rough, solid,** or **broken.** The way a line looks is its **style.** Using different line styles can make a work of art more interesting. Different line styles can also describe different moods. Can a line have more than one style?

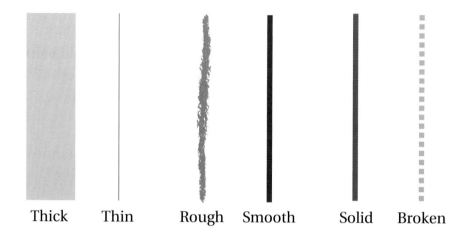

Thick   Thin   Rough   Smooth   Solid   Broken

Practice

Create different types of lines.

1. Think of the different types of lines.

2. Look around the classroom for different types of lines.

3. Practice drawing different types of lines on your paper.

Differentiated Instruction

Reteach

Let students experiment with differently sized brushes, markers, and crayons to vary the quality of lines.

Special Needs

Some students have difficulty gluing with traditional glue bottles. Glue sticks are usually easier to handle for students who lack fine motor skills.

ELL Tips

Introduce the concept of a broken line. Draw different kinds of lines, including broken, on the board. Have students identify each line.

◀ **James Ellis.**
Age 7.

Think about how this student used different types of lines in his dream tree.

 **Creative Expression**

How would you make a dream tree using your imagination? Make a line collage.

1. Draw the lines for your tree with a pencil. Fill the page.

2. Glue line collage materials over the lines.

3. Add objects you like to the branches of the tree. Name your piece.

 **Art Criticism**

Describe What did you put in your dream tree?

Analyze Which kinds of lines did you use the most?

Interpret How would your collage look if you had used only one color?

Decide How else could you arrange your lines?

● **Art Across the Curriculum** ●   NSAE 6.a, 6.b

Use these simple ideas to reinforce art concepts across the curriculum.

⭐ **Descriptive Writing** Have students write a paragraph describing the kinds of things they imagine.

⭐ **Math** Draw three lines of the same length using different line styles on the board. Then have students measure each line. Show them that line style does not affect the length of a line.

⭐ **Science** Discuss what a topographic map is and how different types of lines on the map mean different things.

⭐ **Social Studies** Show students a road map and have them find at least four different line styles on the map.

⭐ **Technology Connection** Tell students how to create different line styles using the computer's drawing program. Visit **SRAonline.com** to print detailed instructions for this activity.

eflect   **Time:** About 10 minutes

Review and Assess

"How would you explain the differences between types of lines?" ¿Cómo explicarían la diferencia entre los tipos de líneas?"

Think

This student used different materials to create different types of lines.

■ Use *Large Prints 25* The Kitchen and *26* Le Fifre to have students identify line styles.

■ Have students identify stories and constructions in this lesson's artwork.

■ Have students identify ideas in the art by this lesson's artists.

Informal Assessment

Art Journal: Critical Thinking
Have students answer the four art criticism questions—Describe, Analyze, Interpret, and Decide—in the Critical Thinking section of their Art Journals. In small groups, have students explain their dream tree line collages. Have students define reasons for preferences in their personal artwork. Then have them identify ideas in their peers' artwork.

■ For standardized-format test practice using this lesson's art content, see pages 8–9 in *Reading and Writing Test Preparation.*

Types of Lines

Focus

Study **Large Prints 25** and **26** and ask students to point out as many different types of lines as they can. How do these lines affect the way the image looks?

Teach

Tell students they will be designing a city using different types of lines and markers. They will be drawing a bird's eye view of the city. Have students complete the Alternate Activity.

Reflect

Have students evaluate their artwork using the four steps of art criticism.

Alternate Activity

Materials:

- 9" × 12" white drawing paper
- pencils
- colored markers (broad and fine points)
- rulers
- image of Mondrian's *Broadway Boogie-Woogie*

1. Look at the Mondrian image and point out the types of lines you see.

2. Use a pencil to draw a city from an overhead view using different types of lines.

3. Use markers to trace and color your city.

Research in Art Education

"The elementary classroom offers an environment that can foster creativity, independence, self-awareness, self-expression, and an understanding of the visual world. Education through art can provide opportunities for exploring one's creativity, for communicating ideas, and enabling students to express themselves through the use of materials, processes, and tools."
Andra Nyman, "Cultural Content, Identity, and Program Development: Approaches to Art Education for Elementary Educators," in *Contemporary Issues in Art Education*, edited by Y. Gaudelius and P. Speirs, 61–69. New Jersey: Prentice Hall, 2002

Assessment

Use the following rubric to evaluate the artwork students make in the Creative Expression activity and to assess students' understanding of types of lines.

Have students complete page 11 or 12 in their *Assessment* books.

	Art History and Culture	Aesthetic Perception	Creative Expression	Art Criticism
3 POINTS	The student can identify how artists use different techniques to express types of lines.	The student accurately identifies types of lines in an object from his or her environment.	The student's dream tree clearly illustrates a good use of types of lines.	The student thoughtfully and honestly evaluates his or her own work using the four steps of art criticism.
2 POINTS	The student's identification is weak or incomplete.	The student shows emerging awareness of types of lines, but cannot consistently identify them.	The student's dream tree shows some awareness of types of lines.	The student attempts to evaluate his or her own work, but shows an incomplete understanding of evaluation criteria.
1 POINT	The student cannot identify how artists use different techniques to express types of lines.	The student cannot identify types of lines.	The student's dream tree shows no understanding of types of lines.	The student makes no attempt to evaluate his or her own artwork.

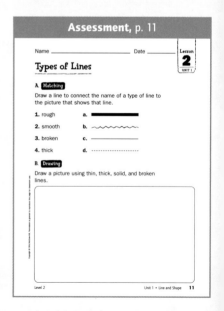

Lesson 3 Calm Lines

Overview

Lesson 3 introduces calm lines. Artists use horizontal and vertical lines to create stability and tranquil tones in their work.

Objectives

Art History and Culture

To compare and interpret styles of two water scenes

Creative Expression

To create a peaceful water scene using horizontal and vertical lines

Aesthetic Perception

To identify horizontal and vertical lines in the classroom

Art Criticism

To evaluate own work using the four steps of art criticism

Vocabulary Vocabulary

Review the following vocabulary words with students before beginning the lesson.

horizontal horizontal—oriented or moving left to right

vertical vertical—oriented or moving up and down

calm lines líneas tranquilas—lines that give a work of art a quiet and peaceful mood

See page 59B for additional Spanish vocabulary resources.

Art Journal: Vocabulary

Have students add these words to the Vocabulary section of their Art Journals.

Lesson Materials

- crayons, markers
- paper
- medium and large brushes
- tape
- water containers
- paper towels
- watercolors

Alternate Materials:
- oil pastels

Program Resources

- *Reading and Writing Test Prep.,* pp. 10–11
- *Transparency 3*
- *Flash Cards 1* and *2*
- *Artist Profiles,* pp. 18, 40
- *Animals Through History Time Line*
- *Assessment,* pp. 13–14
- *Large Prints 25* The Kitchen and *26* Le Fifre
- *Art Around the World Collection*

Concept Trace
Calm Lines
Introduced: Level 1, Unit 1, Lesson 2

Reinforced: Level 3, Unit 1, Lesson 2

Lesson 3 Arts Integration

Theatre

Complete Unit 1, Lesson 3 on pages 22–23 of *Theatre Arts Connections.*

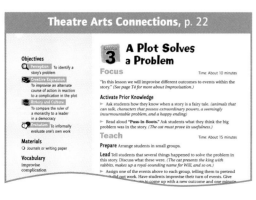

Theatre Arts Connections, p. 22

Music

What a Wonderful World. George Weiss and Bob Thiele.

Artists use vertical and horizontal lines to make a calm picture. To compare calm lines with calm music, play *What a Wonderful World.* Discuss the elements that make the music seem calm. Suggest other songs such as lullabies that have a calm feeling.

Movement & Dance

Look at photographs of natural scenes depicting calm landscapes. Look for specific shapes and colors that are soothing. Have students select one idea or object from the scene and show it in a pose. Have them teach this design to a partner. The partner copies the design and the original creator steps back to look at it. Does your design look how it feels?

Focus

Activate Prior Knowledge

"Have you ever stood and looked at a lake or ocean?" "¿Alguna vez han mirado un lago u océano?"

■ Discuss student responses. Explain that the shoreline is a horizontal line.

Using Literature 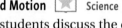 Reading

■ Read *Three by the Sea* by James Marshall and have the students look for calm lines.

Thematic Connection Reading

■ **By the Sea:** Have students discuss bodies of water. Does water make them feel calm? In what other situations have they encountered water?

Introduce the Art NSAE 2.a

Look

"Let's take a close look at the two works of art." "Vamos a observar detalladamente las dos obras de arte".

■ Have students identify lines in the artwork and environment.

Forces and Motion Science

■ Have students discuss the qualities of the water in these two paintings. Do they think the water is rough and moving or calm and still? What forces do they think would make water either rough or calm?

NSAE 4.a, 4.b, 4.c, 5.a, 5.b

Art History and Culture

Possible answer: The Monet because it is more realistic. Have students discuss why the artists chose to depict their scenes in such different ways.

Web Connection

Visit **www.sfmoma.org/anderson/index.html**, start the project, explore the artwork, and click the Diebenkorn painting to learn more about Diebenkorn. Or visit **www.pbs.org/wgbh/sisterwendy/works/oce.html** to see another *Ocean Park* painting.

Lesson 3 Calm Lines

◀ **Richard Diebenkorn.** (American). *Ocean Park #105.* 1978.
. . . .
Oil and charcoal on canvas. 99 $\frac{7}{8}$ × 93 inches (253.7 × 236.2 cm). Modern Art Museum of Fort Worth, Fort Worth, Texas.

Look at these two paintings. Artists use different kinds of lines in their art to show different feelings. These artists used horizontal and vertical lines to create a calm feeling.

Art History and Culture

Which painting reminds you more of water? Why?

Art History and Culture

Richard Diebenkorn

Richard Diebenkorn (riˊ chərd dēˊ bən korn) (1922–1993) was born in Portland, Oregon. He grew up in San Francisco, and took art classes at Stanford. Diebenkorn was stationed near Washington D.C. during World War II, and he later moved back to California with his wife. Diebenkorn is famous for his *Ocean Park* series, which shows an abstract view of the light and mood of his Santa Monica community. His use of light is often compared to Monet's.

For more about art history and subject matter, see pages 24–25 and 16–21.

Artist Profiles, p. 18

Artist Profile
Richard Diebenkorn
1922–1993

Richard Diebenkorn (riˊ chard dēˊ bən korn) was born in Portland, Oregon, to a middle-class family. When he was two years old he and his family moved to San Francisco where he grew up drawing and painting, planning to someday be an artist. Diebenkorn's father did not support his artistic talents and ridiculed him for wanting to be a painter. Only his grandmother understood and encouraged him. When Diebenkorn was in college his father hoped his son would study business, but the young artist had his own plans and continued to paint. This determination and individuality paved the way for Diebenkorn's long, prolific career as an abstract painter and one of contemporary art's leading

Study the two works of art to see how the artists used lines to create feelings.

▶ What colors are used in the two paintings?

▶ Where are there horizontal lines in the paintings? Where are there vertical lines?

▶ How do you think the use of horizontal and vertical lines affects the mood of each painting?

▲ **Claude Monet.** (French).
Palazzo da Mula, Venice.
1908.

Oil on canvas. 24 ½ × 31 ⅞ inches
(62 × 81.1 cm.). National Gallery of Art, Washington, D.C.

Aesthetic Perception

Design Awareness Look at the objects in your classroom. What objects have vertical lines? What objects have horizontal lines?

Study

▶ Mostly blues and greens, but also some yellows, reds, and blacks.

▶ There are many horizontal and vertical lines in the Diebenkorn. The water line, gondola, ripples, and windows are horizontal lines in the Monet. The columns and windows are the vertical lines in the Monet.

▶ They make the paintings seem calm and ordered. Student responses may vary.

■ For more examples of art from North America, see the **Art Around the World Collection**.

Aesthetic Perception

Design Awareness Discuss objects in the classroom with students. Objects may contain several different lines, such as diagonal, vertical, horizontal, or curved. Have students focus on the lines that are horizontal and vertical and objects that are primarily made of these lines. How do these objects strike the students? Have students identify variations in the objects from the environment.

NSAE 2.b, 5.c

Developing Visual Literacy Discuss what the main idea is in these two paintings. Are they just water scenes, or do they mean something else? Why are two water scenes so different?

Art History and Culture

Claude Monet

Claude Monet (klōd mō nā´) (1840–1926) was a founding member of the impressionist movement. He is one of the most recognized artists in the world. Monet's main focus was capturing the light variations in scenes. Instead of painting realistic images, impressionists painted blurry pictures of light and color. When critics first saw these works in a show organized by Monet, they gave them negative reviews. In fact, the term *impressionist* was taken from a Monet painting from that first show, *Impression: Sunrise, 1872.* When Monet died, the movement he had helped start had become accepted. Today his pieces are some of the most sought after in the world.

For more about art history and subject matter, see pages 24–25 and 16–21.

· **Artist Profiles,** p. 40

♦ Artist Profile ♦

Claude Monet
1840–1926

Claude Monet (klōd mō nā´) did not want to be a painter as a young man in France. He was already well paid for drawing caricatures of tourists. Painter Eugene Boudin saw talent in Monet's exaggerated drawings and encouraged him to paint. Although artists were "supposed" to paint in studios, Boudin urged Monet to paint outside in the open air. There Monet learned to capture his first impressions on canvas. He recorded these impressions during a long and productive life. His greatest wish was to "mingle more closely with nature."

 Web Connection

Visit **www.marmottan.com/uk/sommaire/index.htm** to see a collection of Monet's work.

 **each**

 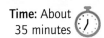

"How can you use calm lines to create a mood in a work of art?" "¿Cómo pueden usar líneas calmadas para crear un estado de ánimo en una obra de arte?"

- Discuss the information about calm lines on page 46.

Practice

Materials: crayons, paper

Alternate Materials: oil pastels

- Distribute materials and have students follow the directions on page 46.

- Have students identify and practice the skills necessary for producing paintings using a variety of materials.

NSAE 1.c, 1.d, 2.c, 3.b

Creative Expression

Materials: crayons, paper, medium and large brushes, tape, water containers, paper towels, watercolors, markers

Alternate Materials: oil pastels

- Distribute materials and have students follow the directions on page 47.

- Encourage students to express their feelings in their water scenes using lines. how have they also expressed their ideas?

- Encourage students to create effective compositions using design elements.

- Review the Activity Tips on page 233 for visual examples of techniques if needed.

- Review the Technique Tips on page 219.

NSAE 3.a

Art Journal: Making a List

Have students make a list of as many calm words they can think of in the Ideas section of their Art Journals. Encourage students to think of these words as they draw their water scene in the Creative Expression activity.

Using Calm Lines

Artists use different kinds of lines in their art to show different feelings. Horizontal and vertical lines are **calm lines** and give art a calm and quiet look. Can you find the horizontal and vertical lines in the picture below?

  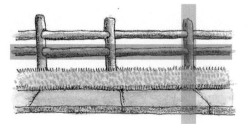

Horizontal   Vertical

Practice

Try drawing a water object and highlighting the calm lines.

1. Think about something you would find by the water.

2. Try drawing that object using only horizontal and vertical lines.

3. Add color or other line directions for details. Highlight the calm lines in your drawing.

Differentiated Instruction

Reteach

Cut a square hole in the center of dark paper. Ask students to look through the hole and observe only the vertical and horizontal lines of objects. Then have students draw those lines on paper.

Special Needs

For students who have difficulty grasping small paintbrushes, use tape or a rubber band to attach a foam rubber cylinder around the brush handle for the student to grasp.

ELL Tips

Discuss and demonstrate mood lines. Add *calm, stillness, quiet,* and *shoreline* to your vocabulary list. Give students several examples of calm places, and then contrast them with examples of busy places.

◄ **Zach Rearden.**
Age 7.

Think about how this student used calm lines in his water scene.

 Creative Expression

Make a peaceful water scene using horizontal and vertical lines.

1. Think of a calm water scene. What would you see there?
2. Paint your scene. Fill the paper using vertical and horizontal brush strokes.
3. Use markers to add details to your painting after it is dry.

 **Art Criticism**

Describe What kind of scene did you paint?

Analyze Which vertical and horizontal lines stand out the most?

Interpret How would your design be different if you had added other kinds of lines?

Decide If you wanted to paint another water scene, would you use calm lines?

Art Across the Curriculum

NSAE 6.a, 6.b

Use these simple ideas to reinforce art concepts across the curriculum.

★ **Personal Writing** Have students make a list of ten things that make them calm.

★ **Math** Discuss how to plot points on an *x*- and *y*-axis. Then discuss the relationship of horizontal and vertical lines on a graph.

★ **Science** Discuss how waves create sand by eroding rock.

★ **Social Studies** Show students a photograph of the Capitol building. Discuss where the horizontal and vertical lines are in the building.

★ **Technology** Have students open a word processing document and use the arrow keys to move the cursor in horizontal and vertical directions. Visit **SRAonline.com** to print detailed instructions for this activity.

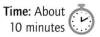 **Reflect**   **Time:** About 10 minutes

Review and Assess

"How would you explain the difference between calm lines and other lines?" "¿Cómo explicarían la diferencia entre las líneas calmadas y las otras líneas?"

Think

This student used mostly horizontal and vertical lines to give his water scene a calm mood.

■ Use *Large Prints 25 The Kitchen* and *26 Le Fifre* to have students identify calm lines.

■ Have students identify stories and constructions in this lesson's artwork.

■ Have students identify ideas of the artists in this lesson's art.

Informal Assessment

Art Journal: Critical Thinking
Have students answer the four art criticism questions—Describe, Analyze, Interpret, and Decide—in the Critical Thinking section of their Art Journals. Have students also write a small caption that explains their picture. Ask students to define their reasons for preferences in their art. Then have them identify ideas in their peers' art.

■ For standardized-format test practice using this lesson's art content, see pages 10–11 in *Reading and Writing Test Preparation.*

Lesson 3 Wrap-Up

Calm Lines

Extra! For the Art Specialist

Time: About 45 minutes

Focus

Study **Large Print 26** and ask students to point out and describe the line directions in it. Why are these lines calm? What mood does this work have?

Teach

Explain to students that they will be creating a sea creature and using horizontal and vertical lines in their designs. Have students complete the Alternate Activity.

Reflect

Have students evaluate their artwork using the four steps of art criticism.

Alternate Activity

Materials:
- white chalk
- 18" × 24" black construction paper
- white glue
- colored chalk

1. Using the white chalk, draw a large sea creature on your paper.

2. Fill in the sea creature with either vertical or horizontal lines. Use the opposite line direction in the background.

3. Outline your drawing and lines in glue and let it dry.

4. Color your art using the colored chalk.

Research in Art Education

Artistically talented students engage in more self-regulatory behavior in classes with arts integration than in classes without arts integration ("Using Art Processes to Enhance Academic Self-Regulation" in *Critical Links,* p. 64). These self-regulatory behaviors included paying attention, problem solving, asking questions, taking risks, being prepared, and so on. As students learn about calm lines, encourage them to think about behaviors and places that they find peaceful.

Assessment

Use the following rubric to evaluate the artwork students make in the Creative Expression activity and to assess students' understanding of calm lines.

	Art History and Culture	Aesthetic Perception	Creative Expression	Art Criticism
3 POINTS	The student can compare and interpret the styles of two works of art featuring water scenes.	The student accurately identifies calm lines in the classroom.	The student's water scene clearly illustrates a good use of calm lines.	The student thoughtfully and honestly evaluates his or her own work using the four steps of art criticism.
2 POINTS	The student's comparison or interpretation is weak or incomplete.	The student shows emerging awareness of calm lines, but cannot consistently identify them.	The student's water scene shows some awareness of calm lines.	The student attempts to evaluate his or her own work, but shows an incomplete understanding of evaluation criteria.
1 POINT	The student cannot compare and interpret styles of two works of art featuring water scenes.	The student cannot identify calm lines.	The student's water scene shows no understanding of calm lines.	The student makes no attempt to evaluate his or her own artwork.

Have students complete page 13 or 14 in their *Assessment* books.

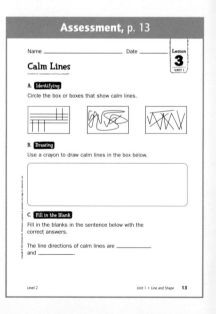

Assessment, p. 13

Name _____ Date _____ Lesson **3** UNIT 1

Calm Lines

A. Identifying
Circle the box or boxes that show calm lines.

B. Drawing
Use a crayon to draw calm lines in the box below.

C. Fill in the Blank
Fill in the blanks in the sentence below with the correct answers.

The line directions of calm lines are _____ and _____.

Level 2   Unit 1 • Line and Shape **13**

Lesson 4 Active Lines

Overview

Lesson 4 introduces the concept of active lines. Active lines show movement or add excitement to the art.

Objectives

 Art History and Culture

To recognize that some artists create abstract art and interpret their reasons

 Creative Expression

To paint active lines to make an exciting abstract painting of a scene

 Aesthetic Perception

To identify that diagonal, zigzag, and curving lines create and describe excitement

 Art Criticism

To evaluate own work using the four steps of art criticism

Vocabulary ⭐ Vocabulary

Review the following vocabulary words with students before beginning the lesson.

active lines líneas activas—lines that show action and add energy and movement to a work of art.

zigzag en zigzag—diagonal lines that connect at their ends and change direction sharply

See page 59B for additional vocabulary and Spanish vocabulary resources.

Art Journal: Vocabulary

Have students add these words to the Vocabulary section of their Art Journals.

Lesson Materials

- 12" x 18" white construction paper
- liquid tempera
- brushes
- newspaper
- water containers
- paper towels.
- 5' long pieces of differently colored yarn

Alternate Materials:
- crayons or markers

Program Resources

- *Reading and Writing Test Prep.*, pp. 12–13
- *Transparency 4*
- *Flash Cards 3, 4, 5, 6*
- *Artist Profiles*, pp. 28, 63
- *Animals Through History Time Line*
- *Assessment*, pp. 15–16
- *Large Print 25* The Kitchen
- *Art Around the World Collection*

Concept Trace

Active Lines

Introduced: Level 1, Unit 1, Lesson 6

Reinforced: Level 3, Unit 1, Lesson 1

Lesson 4 Arts Integration

Theatre

Complete Unit 2, Lesson 4 on pages 24–25 of *Theatre Arts Connections.*

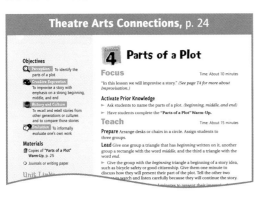

Theatre Arts Connections, p. 24

Music

 Dance Dance Dance!. Moses Hogan and Ava Hogan-Chapman.

Artists use active lines like diagonal, zigzag, and curved lines to create motion in a picture and give it a feeling of excitement. Have students pantomime to the words and music of *Dance Dance Dance!.* Have them identify movements of wiggling, jumping, and hopping and what types of lines might show those movements.

Movement & Dance

Select three design motifs. For example, spirals, straight lines, and dots. Have students create an axial (stationary) and locomotor (traveling) movement for each design. Organize them in a sequence, taking four counts for each idea. Some examples of axial movements are push, pull, swing, and reach. Some examples of locomotor movements are gallop, skip, and leap.

Focus

Time: About 10 minutes

Activate Prior Knowledge

"Have you ever seen someone doing a wild dance?" "¿Alguna vez han visto a alguien bailando un baile loco?"

■ Discuss student responses. Explain that the dancer was using active lines in his or her dance.

Using Literature ⭐ Reading

■ Read *Who's Hiding Here* by Yoshi. Have students look for active lines and hidden animals. Also read *Prehistoric Pinkerton* by Steven Kellogg and have students look for the active lines.

Thematic Connection ⭐ Reading

■ **Look Again:** Have students discuss how sometimes you have to look twice at things to see them well. Ask students to name times when they did not notice a detail until they looked at an object more closely.

Introduce the Art   NSAE 2.a

Look

"Let's take a close look at the two works of art." "Vamos a observar detalladamente las dos obras de arte".

■ Have students identify lines in the artwork and students' environment.

Visualizing ⭐ Reading

■ Read aloud the titles of *Composition VI* and *At Four and A Half.* Ask students to look closely at both works of art and explain what they are visualizing. Students may have many answers. This is dependent on what the student visualizes using his or her mind's eye.

NSAE 4.c, 5.a, 5.b

🏺 Art History and Culture

Possible answer: The artists wanted the viewers to be able to use their imaginations.

💻 Web Connection

Visit **www.hermitagemuseum.org/html_En/08/ hm88_0_2_75.html** to see the room in the Hermitage that houses *Composition VI* and for more information about Wassily Kandinsky. Visit **www.nga.gov/kids/kandinsky/kandinsky1.html** for an interactive look at a Kandinsky painting.

 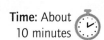

Look at the two works of art. The artists have used many different kinds of active lines to add excitement. Which lines look like they are moving?

▲ **Wassily Kandinsky.** (Russian). *Composition VI.* 1913.

Oil on canvas. 76 ¾ × 118 inches (195 × 300 cm.). The State Hermitage Museum, St. Petersburg, Russia.

🏺 Art History and Culture

Why did these artists make the viewer look closely to see their subjects? Why not paint a realistic picture?

🏺 Art History and Culture

Wassily Kandinsky

Wassily Kandinsky (va sēl´ ē kan din´ skē) (1866–1944) was born and raised in Moscow. He was a lawyer and did not become interested in painting until he saw the work of the French impressionists. Kandinsky then moved to Germany and began painting. After experimenting with many styles, he developed his own. He is considered one of the first abstract artists. Many of Kandinsky's paintings include not only bright colors and shapes, but also hidden images. For example, the subtitle of this piece is *The Flood.* If you look carefully, you can see rain and waves in the painting.

For more about art history and subject matter, see pages 24–25 and 16–21.

Artist Profiles, p. 28

◆ Artist Profile ◆

Wassily Kandinsky
1866–1944

Wassily Kandinsky (va sēl´ ē kan din´ skē) first tried painting as a teenager in his native Russia. Even then he felt that each color had a mysterious life of its own. He was still drawn to colors and painting while he studied law and economics in college, but he believed that art was "a luxury forbidden to a Russian." In time, he moved to Germany, studied art, and began his career. Throughout his life Kandinsky moved back and forth between Russia and Germany. In 1933 he settled in France after Nazi storm troopers labeled his painting style "degenerate."

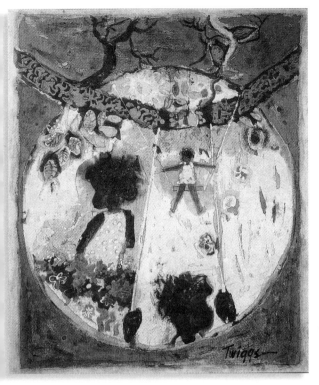

◀ **Leo Twiggs.** (American). *At Four and a Half.* 1972.
....
Batik on cotton. 40 × 38 inches (101.6 × 96.52 cm.). Private collection.

Study both works of art to find examples of active lines.

▶ Which lines give a feeling of movement?

▶ Do any lines seem to be standing still?

▶ How do the active lines make the art feel more exciting?

 Aesthetic Perception

Seeing Like an Artist Think of the kinds of lines you could use to describe a ringing telephone.

Unit 1 • Lesson 4   **49**

Study

▶ Almost every line in *Composition VI* is an active line. In *Four and a Half,* the active lines are primarily concentrated in the branches that contain leaves, the lines of the swing, and the legs and body of the children

▶ *Composition VI* does not have any stationary lines. In *Four and a Half,* the main branch seems to be stationary.

▶ The active lines in these works make the observer feel as though the painting is busy and moving.

■ For more examples of art from Europe, see the ***Art Around the World Collection.***

Art Journal: Writing
Encourage students to write a paragraph about how active lines make them feel in the Concepts section of their Art Journals.

Aesthetic Perception

Seeing Like an Artist Discuss with students how active lines can relate to all kinds of activities. Have students identify variations in objects from the environment. Ask students to think of some loud and busy scenes and active lines to describe them. For example, a birthday party, cars on a highway, or a ringing telephone. How do those lines make students feel? NSAE 2.b, 5.c

Developing Visual Literacy Discuss with students how the artists choice of style and subject matter helps give more meaning to these works of art. How effective would active lines be if they were used to describe a less exciting scene?

Art History and Culture

Leo Twiggs

Leo Twiggs (lē´ō twigs)(1934–) often draws from his experiences as a youth in South Carolina to produce his artwork. Twiggs's accomplishments in teaching art to disadvantaged African American students earned him the title "Outstanding Young Man of America" in 1970. He is also the first visual artist to receive the Governor's Trophy for outstanding contribution to the arts in South Carolina. Leo Twiggs began experimenting with the traditional batik process in 1965, and he eventually created his own personalized technique.
Instead of having only flat, defined areas of color, Twiggs manipulates the wax and dyes to overlap in some areas.

For more about art history and subject matter, see pages 24–25 and 16–21.

Artist Profiles, p. 63

● Artist Profile ●
Leo Twiggs
b. 1934

Leo Twiggs (lē´ō twigs) often draws from his experiences as a youth in South Carolina to produce his artwork. He has a doctorate of art from the University of Georgia and has won numerous awards and recognitions from organizations around the United States. Twiggs's accomplishments in teaching art to disadvantaged African American students earned him the title "Outstanding Young Man of America" in 1970. He is also the first visual artist to receive the Governor's Trophy for outstanding contribution to the arts in South Carolina.

Web Connection
Visit **www.scafam-hist.org/** to learn more about Leo Twiggs.

LESSON 4 • Active Lines   **49**

each

Time: About 35 minutes

"Can you think of an exciting event or action that you could draw?" *"¿Pueden pensar en un evento emocionante o una acción que podrían dibujar?"*

- Discuss the information about active lines on page 50.

Practice

Materials: 5' pieces of differently colored yarn

- Distribute the materials and have students follow the directions on page 51.
- Have students identify and practice skills necessary for producing paintings using a variety of materials.

NSAE 1.c, 1.d, 2.c, 3.b

 Creative Expression

Materials: 12" x 18" white construction paper, liquid tempera, brushes, newspaper, water containers, paper towels

Alternate Materials: crayons or markers

- Distribute materials and have students follow the directions on page 51.
- Encourage students to express feelings and ideas in their paintings using a variety of lines.
- Encourage students to create effective compositions using design elements.
- Review the Activity Tips on page 233 for visual examples of techniques if needed.
- Review the Technique Tips on page 218.

NSAE 3.a

Art Journal: Brainstorming

Have students break up into small groups and brainstorm ideas for active line abstract scenes that they could make in the Creative Expression activity. Have them write their ideas in the Ideas section of their Art Journals.

Using Active Lines

Artists use **active lines** to create motion in a picture and give it a feeling of excitement. They also use active lines when they want the viewer to feel like the art is animated. Diagonal, zigzag, and curved lines are examples of active lines.

Diagonal   Zigzag   Curved

Practice

Walk along an active line.

1. Take the piece of yarn your teacher gives you. Remember what color yarn is yours.

2. Lay your yarn on the ground so it forms an active line.

3. Walk back and forth, following the path of your yarn. Look at the paths your classmates are making.

Differentiated Instruction

Reteach
Play "Guess My Line" with students. Have volunteers role-play line movements that you whisper in their ears. Encourage the class to guess the lines.

Special Needs
Show students how to create an abstract painting from a real event. Provide pictures of exciting events and have students find the lines in the pictures. Complete a quick painting that uses the lines that students have identified.

ELL Tips
Add *action* and *excitement* to your vocabulary list. Define the new words and use them in a sentence strip exercise. Draw examples of action lines and other lines on the board, and have the students pick out the action lines.

◄ **Kendall Whittlesey.** Age 7.

Think about what kind of event this student could be describing in her abstract painting.

 Creative Expression

Can you create an abstract painting of an exciting event using active lines?

1. Think about which lines could describe an exciting event.

2. Draw different active lines with black paint to show the activity in your event.

3. Choose some bright colors and paint the spaces between the black lines.

 **Art Criticism**

Describe Where are the active lines in your picture? Explain your scene.

Analyze Which active lines did you use more than others?

Interpret How would you paint a different event? Would you use different lines?

Decide Could you have painted your event with calm lines?

Unit 1 • Lesson 4   **51**

Time: About 10 minutes

Review and Assess

"How would you explain the difference between active and calm lines?" ¿Cómo explicarían la diferencia entre líneas activas y calmadas?"

Think

Some examples of what she could be describing are a party, a sports game, or a circus.

■ Use *Large Print 25 The Kitchen* to have students identify active lines.

■ Have students search for and identify stories and constructions in this lesson's artwork.

■ Have students identify ideas of the artists in this lesson's art.

Informal Assessment

Art Journal: Critical Thinking
Have students answer the four art criticism questions—Describe, Analyze, Interpret, and Decide—in the Critical Thinking section of their Art Journals. Ask students to think about how their abstract scene shows active lines. Ask students to define their reasons for preferences in their art. Then have them identify ideas in their peers' art.

■ For standardized-format test practice using this lesson's art content, see page 12–13 in *Reading and Writing Test Preparation.*

Art Across the Curriculum

NSAE 6.a, 6.b

Use these simple ideas to reinforce art concepts across the curriculum.

★ **Expository Writing** Have students write a paragraph explaining how to create active lines.

★ **Math** Discuss how to plot and connect points on an *x*- and *y*-axis to form zigzag, curved, and diagonal lines.

★ **Science** Show students a chart illustrating the global population growth for the past 300 years. Discuss how the upward curve is an active line that indicates a rise in global population.

★ **Social Studies** Show students a picture of a person who is relevant to your local history doing something. Have students look for active lines in the picture. Encourage students to discuss why the person was important to the history of your area.

★ **Technology Connection** Show students how to use presentation software to key their names on a slide. Then show students how to use an animation scheme to make their names move on the slide. Discuss what effect the action line has on the text. Visit **SRAonline.com** to print detailed instructions for this activity.

Lesson 4

Active Lines

Wrap-Up

Extra! For the Art Specialist

Time: About 45 minutes

Focus

Study **Large Print 25** and ask students to point out the line directions. Are these lines calm or energetic? Why? What happens to your eyes when you look at a work of art full of active lines?

Teach

After students complete their paintings, play a fast song for them. (For example, rock and roll, a march, a waltz, or bluegrass music.) As students are listening to the music, have them sketch an idea for a new drawing using the music. Have students complete the Alternate Activity.

Reflect

Have students evaluate their artwork using the four steps of art criticism. Have them compare the active lines in their two works to see how different inspiration influenced their drawings.

Alternate Activity

Materials:
- 6" × 9" colored construction paper
- markers
- pencils
- oil pastels
- crayons
- radio with music samples

1. Talk about different instruments and music styles.

2. Select a color of paper and medium to work with. Listen to the music that your teacher plays.

3. Repeat the project for the different music styles your teacher plays.

Research in Art Education

"The arts help students develop their abilities to appreciate and interpret art of other cultures and to learn about people of the past through exposure to reproductions, to art works in museums and galleries, or through discussions about contemporary artists and art woks." Andra Nyman, "Cultural Content, Identity, and Program Development: Approaches to Art Education for Elementary Educators," in *Contemporary Issues in Art Education*, edited by Y. Gaudelius and P. Speirs, 61–69. New Jersey: Prentice Hall, 2002

Assessment

Use the following rubric to evaluate the artwork students make in the Creative Expression activity and to assess students' understanding of active lines.

Have students complete page 15 or 16 in their *Assessment* books.

	Art History and Culture	Aesthetic Perception	Creative Expression	Art Criticism
3 POINTS	The student can identify and make an interpretation of abstract art.	The student identifies that diagonal, zigzag, and curving lines create and describe excitement in a work of art.	The student's abstract painting clearly illustrates a good use of active lines.	The student thoughtfully and honestly evaluates his or her own work using the four steps of art criticism.
2 POINTS	The student's identification or interpretation is weak or incomplete.	The student shows an emerging awareness of active lines, but cannot consistently identify them or their purpose in a work of art.	The student's abstract painting shows some awareness of active lines.	The student attempts to evaluate his or her own work, but shows an incomplete understanding of evaluation criteria.
1 POINT	The student cannot identify or interpret abstract art.	The students can not identify active lines or their purpose.	The student's abstract painting shows no understanding of active lines.	The student makes no attempt to evaluate his or her own artwork.

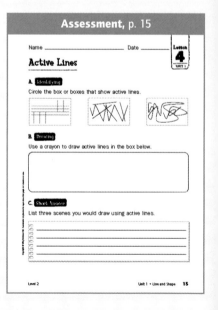

Lesson 5 Geometric Shapes

Lesson 5 introduces geometric shapes. Geometric shapes are defined and created according to specific mathematical formulas. Since the principle of geometric shapes is complicated for a second grader, geometric shapes are defined here as commonly used shapes that have names.

Objectives

Art History and Culture
To recognize that artists use geometric shapes in different ways in their art

Creative Expression
To create a picture using a variety of geometric shapes

Aesthetic Perception
To recognize geometric shapes in students' environments

Art Criticism
To evaluate own work using the fours steps of art criticism

Vocabulary Vocabulary

Review the following vocabulary words with students before beginning the lesson.

geometric shapes figuras geométricas—common shapes that are regular, have specific names, and can be defined according to mathematical formulas.

circle círculo—A round geometric shape made when all points are placed the same distance from a center point.

See page 59B for additional vocabulary and Spanish vocabulary resources.

Art Journal: Vocabulary

Have students add these words to the Vocabulary section of their Art Journals.

Lesson Materials
- white and colored construction paper
- scissors
- glue

Alternate Materials:
- oil pastels

Program Resources
- *Reading and Writing Test Prep.,* p. 14–15
- *Transparency 5*
- *Flash Card 7*
- *Artist Profiles,* pp. 23, 25
- *Animals Through History Time Line*
- *Assessment,* pp. 17–18
- *Large Print 25* The Kitchen and *26* Le Fifre
- *Art Around the World Collection*

Concept Trace
Geometric Shapes
Introduced: Level 1, Unit 2, Lesson 2
Reinforced: Level 3, Unit 1, Lesson 4

Lesson 5 Arts Integration

Theatre

Complete Unit 1, Lesson 5 on pages 26–27 of *Theatre Arts Connections.*

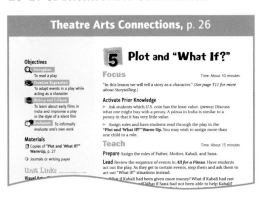

Music

Pata Pata. Miriam Makeba.

Many objects in paintings are made of geometric shapes like triangles, squares, circles, and rectangles. Play Miriam Makeba's *Pata Pata* and have students draw different shapes they visualize as they listen to the music.

Movement & Dance

Divide students into groups of three. Have each person stand on the point of a triangle. Number them 1, 2, and 3. 1 takes eight counts to travel along the pathway of the triangle to 2, who then takes eight counts to travel to 3 (similar to a domino effect). 3 then moves to 1's spot. Each person creates their own locomotor (traveling) movement to get them to the next point.

Focus

Activate Prior Knowledge

"Have you ever noticed the shape of street signs?" "¿Alguna vez han notado la forma de las señales de la calle?"

■ Discuss student responses. Explain that most signs are geometric shapes, and the shapes make the signs easy to recognize.

Using Literature 🟊 Reading

■ Have students read *The Greedy Triangle* by Marilyn Burns. Have students look for geometric shapes and discuss their differences.

Thematic Connection 🟊 Reading

■ **Shapes:** Have students discuss what they think shapes are. How many shapes can they name?

Introduce the Art

Look NSAE 2.a

"Let's look at these two works of art."
"Veamos estas dos obras de arte".

■ Have students identify shapes in the works of art and the environment.

Similar Figures 🟊 Math

■ Ask students to find similar geometric shapes in *Amour* and *Early Sunday Morning*. Is it easy to recognize similar shapes, or difficult?

NSAE 4.a, 4.b, 4.c, 5.a, 5.b

🏺 Art History and Culture

Possible answer: Both of these artists liked geometric shapes because it made their art appear neat and created a mood.

 Web Connection

Visit www.sanford-artedventures.com/play/lineshape/shapes.html to review information about geometric shapes.

52 UNIT 1 • Line and Shape

Geometric Shapes

◀ **Auguste Herbin.** (French). *Amour.* 1948.

Oil on canvas. Musée Matisse, Le Cateau-Cambresis, France.

Look at the artwork on these pages. These paintings are made of many shapes. Artists often use **geometric shapes** in their artwork. Can you name all the shapes you see?

🏺 Art History and Culture

Why do you think these artists used so many geometric shapes in their paintings?

🏺 Art History and Culture

Auguste Herbin

Auguste Herbin (ō gōōst´ âr ban´) (1882–1960) was raised in France. He showed a talent for art when he was young. In 1899 he went to art school in Lille, France. He then moved to Paris, where he started painting in the impressionist style. He soon became interested in cubism, and his paintings became more angular and abstract. During World War I, Herbin worked in a fabric factory designing camouflage patterns. By 1926 he was painting purely geometrical abstract paintings. Herbin developed a "plastic alphabet," a code of the correspondence between letter, colors, shapes, and sounds.

For more about art history and subject matter, see pages 24–25 and 16–21.

Artist Profiles, p. 23

♦ Artist Profile ♦

Auguste Herbin
1882–1960

Auguste Herbin (ō gŭst´ âr´ ban) was born in France and studied at the École des Beaux-Arts. Later he went to other countries to paint. In Italy, he noticed how different kinds of light changed the way things look. From then on he tried to ignore little details and paint only the main part of his subject. Herbin was enthusiastic and curious and loved his work. During the last years of his life Herbin created tapestry designs.

Study both works to find geometric shapes.

▶ What shapes do you see in each work? What colors are they?

▶ Where are the smallest shapes? Where are the largest shapes?

▶ How does the color of some shapes help them stand out?

▲ **Edward Hopper.**
(American). *Early Sunday Morning.* 1930.
Oil on canvas. 35 $\frac{3}{16}$ × 60 $\frac{1}{4}$ inches (89.4 × 153 cm.). Whitney Museum of American Art, New York, New York.

🔍 Aesthetic Perception

Design Awareness Look outside at a car or truck. Name the geometric shapes that make up the car or truck.

🏺 Art History and Culture

Edward Hopper

Edward Hopper (ed´ wərd hä´ pər) (1882–1967) was born into a middle-class family in Nyack, New York. At 17, he decided to be an artist. His parents pushed him toward a career in commercial illustration because of job stability. Hopper had small successes as an artist until he had a solo show in 1924, which sold out. He enjoyed a period of prosperity, during which he developed a strong style of using ambient light and nearly deserted buildings to create a mood of isolation. After Hopper found his style, he did not change it. He became increasingly alienated from painting because of the surge in popularity of styles such as abstract expressionism.

For more about art history and subject matter, see pages 24–25 and 16–21.

Artist Profiles, p. 25

◆ Artist Profile ◆

Edward Hopper
1882-1967

Edward Hopper (ed´ ward hä´ pər) was born in Nyack, New York. He attended the New York School of Art and made three trips to Europe to study art. He worked as an illustrator in New York City and eventually opened a studio in Greenwich Village. Hopper married another painter, Josephine Nivison, who helped arrange his first exhibition. They spent their summers on an island off the Maine coast, on Cape Cod, and at other East Coast locations. These spots became the settings of many of Hopper's paintings.

Study

▶ There are many different shapes and colors in these works, depending on the viewer's perspective.

▶ The smallest shapes in the Herbin work are the little circles. The smallest shape in the Hopper is the circle on the barber's pole.

▶ When the artist uses bright shapes on a dark background, the shape stands out more. Also, when little shapes are making up big shapes, the shapes that are the same color stand out.

■ For more examples of art from Europe, see the *Art Around the World Collection*.

📓 Art Journal: Writing

Have students write three sentences about geometric shapes in the Concepts section of their Art Journals.

🔍 Aesthetic Perception

Design Awareness Discuss cars and trucks with the students. Encourage students to identify variations in geometric shapes from the environment. Have them think about all the geometric shapes that they see both in and out of a car. Can they think of other modes of transportation that use geometric shapes?

NSAE 2.b, 5.c

Developing Visual Literacy Discuss with students what the main ideas in these two pictures might be. Then ask students to elaborate on these main ideas with examples of personal experiences they have had. For example, have they ever been in a place as quiet as the place in Hopper's *Early Sunday Morning*?

💻 Web Connection

Visit **www.whitney.org/american_voices/572/index.html** to hear and read about *Early Sunday Morning*.

 **each**

"How can you use geometric shapes in art?"
"¿Cómo pueden usar las figuras geométricas en arte?"

■ Discuss the information about geometric shapes on page 54.

Practice

Materials: empty space, classmates

■ Have students follow the directions on page 54.

■ Have students identify and practice skills necessary for producing constructions using a variety of materials.

NSAE 1.c, 1.d, 2.c, 3.b

 Creative Expression

Materials: white construction paper, colored construction paper, scissors, glue

Alternate Materials: oil pastels

■ Distribute materials and have students follow the directions on page 55.

■ Encourage students to create effective compositions using design elements.

■ Review the Activity Tips on page 234 for visual examples of techniques if needed.

■ Review the Technique Tips on page 221.

NSAE 3.a

Art Journal: Brainstorming
Have students brainstorm different ways to incorporate geometric shapes into a picture. Have them add their ideas to the Ideas section in their Art Journals.

Using Geometric Shapes

Many objects in paintings are made of shapes. These shapes are often geometric shapes. Geometric shapes can be made using special math rules. Not all shapes are geometric, but many common shapes are. Most geometric shapes have names. **Triangles**, **squares**, **circles**, and **rectangles** are all geometric shapes.

Triangle   Square   Circle   Rectangle

Practice

Make a geometric shape with your classmates.

1. Get into groups. Your teacher will assign your group a shape.

2. Lie on the floor and make that shape.

3. Can you name the shapes other groups made? Can you find something in your room that is your shape?

54   Unit 1 • Lesson 5

Differentiated Instruction

Reteach
Have students look at the alphabet and find geometric shapes in the letters. Are there ways they could change the letters to make them look like geometric shapes?

Special Needs
Students who have difficulty cutting may benefit from the use of adaptive scissors for this lesson activity.

ELL Tips
Bring in examples of geometric shapes, some colored and some not, some large and some small. Have students identify each shape.

Think about how this student used geometric shapes in her picture.

Creative Expression

Create a picture using a variety of geometric shapes.

1. Think of a picture you would like to make.
2. Cut out geometric shapes using the colored construction paper.
3. Glue them onto the white paper to create your picture.

Art Criticism

Describe Explain the subject of your picture.

Analyze How did you use geometric shapes to make other shapes?

Interpret What would your picture look like if you had used other shapes?

Decide Do you like the way things look when they are made of only geometric shapes?

NSAE 6.a, 6.b

Art Across the Curriculum

Use these simple ideas to reinforce art concepts across the curriculum.

★ **Descriptive Writing** Have students write a sentence describing each geometric shape they learned about in this lesson.

★ **Math** Show students other geometric shapes, such as hexagons, octagons, and dodecahedrons.

★ **Science** Show students salt crystals under a magnifying glass. Discuss that the crystals are cubes and that a cube is a geometric shape.

★ **Social Studies** Show students a map and have them find geometric shapes that are used as symbols. Then have students look at the legend to see what those shapes represent.

★ **Technology** Show students how to use the computer's paint or drawing program to make geometric shapes using the shape tools. Visit **SRAonline.com** to print detailed instructions for this activity.

Reflect

Time: About 10 minutes

Review and Assess

"Can you name some geometric shapes?"
"¿Pueden nombrar algunas figuras geométricas?"

Think

This student used geometric shapes to make a carnival ride.

- Use *Large Print 25 The Kitchen* and *26 Le Fifre* to have students identify geometric shapes.

- Have students identify stories and constructions in this lesson's artwork.

- Have students identify ideas of the artists in this lesson's art.

Informal Assessment

Art Journal: Critical Thinking
Have students answer the four art criticism questions—Describe, Analyze, Interpret, and Decide—in the Critical Thinking section of their Art Journals. Have students explain how they adapted the geometric shapes for use in their paper collages. Ask students to define their reasons for preferences in their art. Then have them identify ideas in their peers' art.

- For standardized-format test practice using this lesson's art content, see pages 14–15 in *Reading and Writing Test Preparation.*

Geometric Shapes

 For the Art Specialist

Time: About 45 minutes

Focus

Study *Large Print 25* and *26* and point out the various geometric shapes. Do these shapes have names? Name as many as you can.

Teach

Tell students that they will be creating an insect using geometric shapes. They will cut these shapes from poster board and do a crayon rubbing. Have students complete the Alternate Activity.

Reflect

Have students evaluate their artwork using the four steps of art criticism.

Alternate Activity

Materials:
- scissors
- white drawing paper
- posterboard scraps
- crayons
- images of insects

1. Look at the insect pictures and discuss geometric shapes. Plan your insect.

2. Cut out geometric shapes for your insect using the posterboard.

3. Using one shape at a time, place your drawing paper on top of the shape and make a rubbing of the shape.

4. Repeat step 3 while moving your drawing paper and arranging your shapes until you have finished your insect.

Research
in Art Education

Research continues to try to answer the questions of if and how the arts impacts student learning in other subject areas. Some researchers suggest that the relationship between the arts and other subject areas "may not be as unidirectional —from the arts to other disciplines—as other studies have implied. Rather, the relationship may be more dynamic and interactive" ("Learning in and Through the Arts: Curriculum Implications" in *Champions of Change*, p. 43). As students learn about geometric shapes, draw parallels to their math studies.

Assessment
Use the following rubric to evaluate the artwork students make in the Creative Expression activity and to assess students' understanding of geometric shapes.

Have students complete Page 17 or 18 in their *Assessment* books.

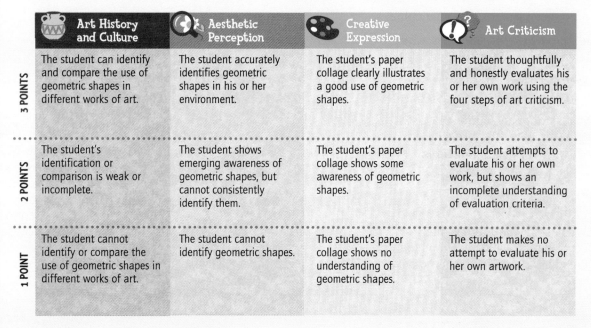

	Art History and Culture	Aesthetic Perception	Creative Expression	Art Criticism
3 POINTS	The student can identify and compare the use of geometric shapes in different works of art.	The student accurately identifies geometric shapes in his or her environment.	The student's paper collage clearly illustrates a good use of geometric shapes.	The student thoughtfully and honestly evaluates his or her own work using the four steps of art criticism.
2 POINTS	The student's identification or comparison is weak or incomplete.	The student shows emerging awareness of geometric shapes, but cannot consistently identify them.	The student's paper collage shows some awareness of geometric shapes.	The student attempts to evaluate his or her own work, but shows an incomplete understanding of evaluation criteria.
1 POINT	The student cannot identify or compare the use of geometric shapes in different works of art.	The student cannot identify geometric shapes.	The student's paper collage shows no understanding of geometric shapes.	The student makes no attempt to evaluate his or her own artwork.

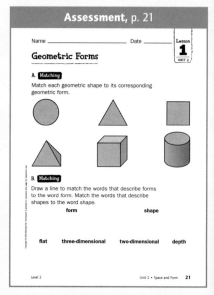

Lesson 6 Overview

Free-Form Shapes

Lesson 6 introduces students to free-form shapes. Free-form shapes differ from geometric shapes because free-form shapes have no set standards.

Objectives

 Art History and Culture

To identify and compare the use of free-form shapes in two Pacific shadow puppets

 Creative Expression

To create a free-form shadow puppet

 Aesthetic Perception

To identify free-form shapes in students' environments

 Art Criticism

To evaluate own work using the four steps of art criticism

Vocabulary Vocabulary

Review the following vocabulary words with students before beginning the lesson.

free-form shape forma abstracta—an irregular shape, not geometrical

irregular irregular—not ordered

splash salpicadura—a shape that looks like it was made from water hitting the paper

See page 59B for additional vocabulary and Spanish vocabulary resources.

 Art Journal: Vocabulary

Have students add these words to the Vocabulary section of their Art Journals.

Lesson Materials
- brads
- tape
- paper punch
- markers
- flashlight or light source
- tagboard or colored paper
- chopsticks, $\frac{1}{8}$" dowels, or drinking straws
- ribbon
- fabric scraps
- yarn

Alternate Materials:
- construction paper

Program Resources
- *Reading and Writing Test Prep.*, p. 16–17
- *Transparency 6*
- *Flash Card 8*
- *Artist Profiles*, pp. 74, 83
- *Animals Through History Time Line*
- *Assessment*, pp. 19–20
- *Large Prints 25* The Kitchen and *26* Le Fifre
- *Art Around the World Collection*

Concept Trace
Free-Form Shapes
Introduced: Level 1, Unit 2, Lesson 2

Reinforced: Level 3, Unit 1, Lesson 6

Lesson 6 Arts Integration

Theatre

Complete Unit 1, Lesson 6 on pages 28–33 of *Theatre Arts Connections.*

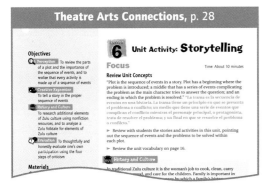

Theatre Arts Connections, p. 28

Music

 Variations and Fugue on a Theme of Purcell. Benjamin Britten.

Free-form shapes in visual art are irregular. Music can be rhythmic or irregular as well. Play *Variations and Fugue on a Theme of Purcell* as students plan the Practice activity in which they draw and cut out a free-form shape. Discuss the different shapes inspired by the music.

Movement & Dance

Divide students into groups of three. Have each person stand on the point of a triangle. Number them 1, 2, and 3. 1 takes 8 counts to travel along the pathway of the triangle to 2, as 2 leaves 1 creates a free-form shape. 2 travels for 8 counts to 3, creates a shape, and 3 travels to the empty point of the triangle and creates a shape. Each person creates their own locomotor (traveling) movement to get them to the next point.

Focus

Time: About 10 minutes

Activate Prior Knowledge

"Have you ever seen an unusual shadow on the wall?" "¿Alguna vez han visto una sombra rara en la pared?"

■ Discuss student responses. Explain that the shape was most likely a free-form shape.

Using Literature 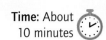 Reading

■ Read *What Makes a Shadow* by Clyde Robert Bulla and have students look for free-form shapes.

Thematic Connection ⭐ Reading

■ **Shadows:** Have students discuss shadows. How do they think shadows are made?

Introduce the Art

Look NSAE 2.a

"Let's look at *Indonesian Shadow Puppet* and *Thai Shadow Puppet*." "Veamos *Indonesian Shadow Puppet* y *Thai Shadow Puppet*".

■ Have students identify shapes in the works of art and the environment.

Perimeter ⭐ Math

■ Explain what *perimeter* is. Ask students to look at the silhouettes of the two puppets and compare them. Have students describe what they see. Explain that when the puppets are used in a shadow theatre, the silhouette, or perimeter is all the audience sees. The most important concept to grasp is that by looking at the perimeters or edges of these puppets, students understand that they are looking at free-form shapes.

NSAE 4.a, 4.b, 4.c, 5.a, 5.b

🏺 Art History and Culture

Possible answer: Because these puppets are important to the people that make them and the culture that uses them.

 Web Connection

Visit **www.getty.edu/art/exhibitions/devices/flash** and click on the shadow puppet on the upper left-hand side of the screen for an interactive look at Indonesian shadow puppets.

56 UNIT 1 • Line and Shape

Lesson 6 Free-Form Shapes

Look at both works of art on these pages. Artists often use **free-form shapes** in works of art. Both of these pieces of art are shadow puppets and were made using free-form shapes.

◀ **Artist Unknown.** (Indonesia). *Indonesian Shadow Puppet.* c. 1950.

Cut, painted leather. 31½ inches high (80.01 cm.). Private Collection.

🏺 Art History and Culture

Why do you think the artists decorated the puppets when audiences see only the puppets' shadows?

56 Unit 1 • Lesson 6

🏺 Art History and Culture

Indonesian Shadow Puppets (Wayang Kulit)

Wayang Kulit is an ancient tradition in Indonesian culture and one of the oldest storytelling techniques in the world. *Wayang* means *shadow*, and *Kulit* means *leather*. The stories acted out by the puppets are usually long-established tales from the Ramayana and Mahabarata, which are Indian epic poems. An oil lamp lights the screen for these productions. The good characters are kept on the right side of the stage, and the bad characters on the left. The person who manipulates the puppets is called a *dalang*.

For more about art history and subject matter, see pages 24–25 and 16–21.

Artist Profiles, p. 74

⟩ Artist Profile ⟨

Indonesian Shadow Puppet

Indonesia is a country in southeast Asia that consists of more than 13,600 islands. The islands lie along the equator and extend more than 3,000 miles. Indonesia ranks fifth in population among all countries. The most famous art forms of Indonesia include dances of the old royal courts of Java and the dramatic folk dances of Bali. Puppet dramas are a major part of Javanese and Balinese cultures. The most popular puppets are flat and made of leather.

Study both works of art to find examples of free-form shapes.

Study both works of art to find examples of free-form shapes.

► What shapes do you see in both works?

► Do you see any geometric shapes?

► Can you think of any names to describe the free-form shapes that you see?

◄ **Artist Unknown.** (Thailand). *Thai Shadow Puppet.* c. 1965.
....
Cut and painted leather. 25 inches tall (63.5 cm.). The Yoshida Collection.

 Aesthetic Perception

Seeing Like an Artist Look at free-form shadows in the classroom. Can you identify objects by looking at only the shadows?

Art History and Culture

Thai Shadow Puppets (Nang Talung)

Nang Talung is an ancient form of entertainment in Thailand. It is thought to have been inspired by the Indosesian Wayang Kulit. *Nang* is the Thai word for *leather*. However, the word *nang* is also a colloquialism for *movie*. *Talung* loosely means *spirit* or *shadow*. It is also indicative of the southern province in which this type of shadow Theatre is popular. Nang Yai is another type of shadow Theatre performed in Thailand. However, in Nang Yai, the puppets are almost a foot tall and include intricate cutwork backgrounds and no moveable parts. Nang Talung puppets, like the one in the *Student Edition*, are usually one-fifth that size and do have moving parts.

For more about art history and subject matter, see pages 24–25 and 16–21.

Artist Profiles, p. 83

› Artist Profile ›
Shadow Puppet
It is not known exactly who created this puppet, but the quality and care with which was made indicate that it was skillfully designed and crafted using traditional methods.

Study

► Most of the shapes are free-form, but students may have answers like fingers, legs, etc.

► The Indonesian puppet's eyes are circles. There are circles in the headdress of the Thai puppet. The Thai puppet is also standing on a rectangle.

► This is an open question. Allow the students to brainstorm names.

■ For more examples of art from Asia, see the *Art Around the World Collection*.

Art Journal: Storytelling
Encourage students to write a story for a shadow puppet show in the Concepts section of their Art Journals. Have volunteers share their stories with the class.

Aesthetic Perception

Seeing Like an Artist Discuss shadows with the students. Most objects are free-form shapes, so they will cast free-form shadows. Encourage students to identify variations in the free-form shapes from the environments. Discuss how shadows lengthen during the day with students. Ask students if they can think of a way that they could make their own shadow theatre. Which shadows are more interesting to look at, free-form or geometric?   NSAE 2.b, 5.c

Developing Visual Literacy Have students discuss how these two puppets contribute to the puppet show as a whole. Ask them to think about how the different mediums combine to create an effect. For example, watching the puppets combined with music would be more influential on one's feelings than watching the puppets alone.

Web Connection
Visit **coas.missouri.edu/anthromuseum/minigalleries/thaipuppets/charactersgallery.html** to learn about the characters in Nang Talung.

 **each**   **Time:** About 35 minutes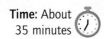

"Can you think of different ways to make free-form shapes?" "¿Pueden pensar en diferentes maneras de hacer formas abstractas?"

- Discuss the information about free-form shapes on page 58.

Practice

Materials: brads, tape, paper punch, flashlight or light source, tagboard or colored paper, chopsticks, $\frac{1}{8}$" dowels, or drinking straws

Alternate Materials: construction paper

- Distribute materials and have students follow the directions on page 58.

- Have students identify and practice skills necessary for producing constructions using a variety of materials.

NSAE 1.c, 1.d, 2.c, 3.b

Creative Expression

Materials: brads, tape, paper punch, flashlight or light source, tagboard or colored paper, chopsticks, $\frac{1}{8}$" dowels, or plastic drinking straws

Alternate Materials: construction paper

- Distribute materials and have students follow the directions on page 59.

- Encourage students to express their ideas and feelings in their puppets using a variety of lines.

- Encourage students to create effective compositions using design elements.

- Review the Activity Tips on page 234 for visual examples of techniques if needed.

- Review the Technique Tips on page 229.

NSAE 3.a

Art Journal: Planning

Have students plan their puppets for the Creative Expression activity. Plans could include a list, a sketch, or a description of what students plan to make. Have students add their plans to the Ideas section of their Art Journals.

Using Free-Form Shapes

Not all shapes in works of art are geometric shapes. Some shapes are free-form shapes. Free-form shapes are **irregular,** and they look different every time they are drawn. Free-form shapes do not have specific names. Some examples of free-form shapes are **splashes, blobs,** and **sails.**

Practice

Create a free-form shape for a shadow puppet.

1. Draw and cut out a free-form shape.

2. Attach it to a stick using a hole punch and a brad.

3. Use your shape to cast a shadow. What does the shadow look like?

Differentiated Instruction

Reteach

Have students tear shapes out of construction paper to make a second puppet. Compare students' torn shapes to the shapes they cut with scissors.

Special Needs

Students with disabilities will experience more success in this activity if they are able to understand the shape and proportion of their own body parts before beginning the shadow puppet activity.

ELL Tips

Add *free-form, shadow,* and *puppet* to your vocabulary list. Define the new words and use them each in a sentence strip exercise. Let students take turns standing in the path of a light while another student points out the shadows made.

Think about where the free-form shapes are in this student's shadow puppet.

◀ **Mandeep Kaur.** Age 7.

What kind of shapes could you use to make people? Make a person shadow puppet using body parts.

1. Think of a puppet you would like to create.

2. Draw it and cut out the parts. Add any details to the parts that you wish.

3. Attach moving parts. Tape the puppet to a stick. Add a costume to the puppet using fabric and ribbon.

4. Hold the puppet in front of a light to make a shadow.

Describe What kind of puppet did you make?

Analyze Which shapes are free-form? Which shapes are geometric?

Interpret How would your design be different if you used only geometric shapes?

Decide If you make another puppet, what will you do differently?

 **Time:** About 10 minutes

Review and Assess

"How would you explain what a free-form shape is?" "¿Cómo explicarían lo que es una forma abstracta?"

Think

This student used free-form shapes in the body of the puppet.

■ Use *Large Prints 25* The Kitchen and *26 Le Fifre* to have students identify free-form shapes.

■ Have students identify stories and constructions in this lesson's artwork.

■ Have students identify ideas in the art by this lesson's artists.

Informal Assessment

Art Journal: Critical Thinking
Have students answer the four art criticism questions—Describe, Analyze, Interpret, and Decide—in the Critical Thinking section of their Art Journals. In small groups, have students share the stories behind their puppets. Have students define reasons for preferences in their personal artwork. Then have them identify ideas in their peers' artwork.

■ For standardized-format test practice using this lesson's art content, see pages 16–17 in *Reading and Writing Test Preparation.*

● **Art Across the Curriculum** ●   NSAE 6.a, 6.b

Use these simple ideas to reinforce art concepts across the curriculum.

★ **Narrative Writing** Have students write a make-believe story for a shadow puppet theatre show.

★ **Math** Show students symmetrical and nonsymmetrical free-form shapes. Then discuss symmetry with students.

★ **Science** Show students how drops of food coloring diffuse through a beaker of water. Have students look for free-form shapes in the colored water. Discuss properties of matter with the students.

★ **Social Studies** Have students look at the borders of countries on a map. Are there more free-form or geometric shapes?

★ **Technology Connection** Run the Bezier screen saver on a computer and have the class look at the free-form shapes. Visit **SRAonline.com** to print detailed instructions for this activity.

Lesson 6 Wrap-Up
Free-Form Shapes

Extra! ## For the Art Specialist

Time: About 45 minutes

Focus

Study *Large Print 25* and *26* and point out the shapes that you see. Do these shapes have names? Why or why not?

Teach

Tell students that they will be making a crayon resist with a theatre theme. Using free-form shapes, they will create a theatre and stage. Have students complete the Alternate Activity.

Reflect

Have students evaluate their work using the four steps of art criticism.

Alternate Activity

Materials:
- 12 × 18" white drawing paper
- pencils
- crayons
- black watercolor paints
- brushes
- water dishes
- paper towels
- newspaper

1. Discuss free-form shapes and theatre. If you were going to design a stage, what would it look like?

2. Use the crayons to draw your theatre scene. Color the scene well, so that it looks waxy. Use free-form shapes.

3. Paint over the scene with black watercolor paints to see what your stage would look like in the dark.

Research in Art Education

Case studies have indicated that students perceive "that the arts facilitate their personal and social development." It also appeared that to gain the full benefit of arts education, students should be exposed to all of the arts, including fine arts, dance, theatre, and music ("Arts Education in Secondary School: Effects and Effectiveness" in *Critical Links*, p. 76). Now that students have learned about puppet theatre, encourage them to learn about other cultures' performing arts.

Assessment
Use the following rubric to evaluate the artwork students make in the Creative Expression activity and to assess students' understanding of free-form shapes.

Have students complete page 19 or 20 in their *Assessment* books.

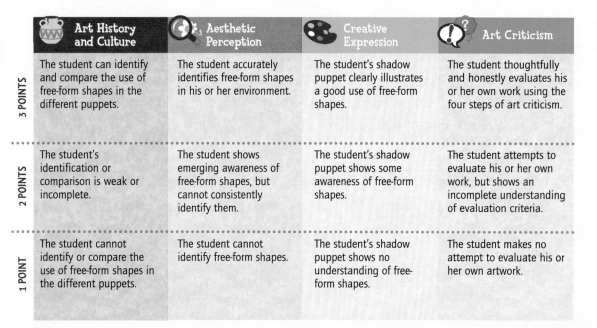

	Art History and Culture	Aesthetic Perception	Creative Expression	Art Criticism
3 POINTS	The student can identify and compare the use of free-form shapes in the different puppets.	The student accurately identifies free-form shapes in his or her environment.	The student's shadow puppet clearly illustrates a good use of free-form shapes.	The student thoughtfully and honestly evaluates his or her own work using the four steps of art criticism.
2 POINTS	The student's identification or comparison is weak or incomplete.	The student shows emerging awareness of free-form shapes, but cannot consistently identify them.	The student's shadow puppet shows some awareness of free-form shapes.	The student attempts to evaluate his or her own work, but shows an incomplete understanding of evaluation criteria.
1 POINT	The student cannot identify or compare the use of free-form shapes in the different puppets.	The student cannot identify free-form shapes.	The student's shadow puppet shows no understanding of free-form shapes.	The student makes no attempt to evaluate his or her own artwork.

Unit 1 Vocabulary Review

active lines—lines that show action and add energy and movement to a work of art *líneas activas*—*líneas que muestran acción y agregan energía y movimiento a una obra de arte*

angle—a shape formed when two lines extend in different directions from the same point *ángulo*—*una figura formada cuando dos líneas se extienden en diferentes direcciones a partir del mismo punto*

arc—a portion of a curved line from a circle *arco*—*porción de una línea curva de un círculo*

blob—a type of free-form shape *mancha*—*un tipo de figura abstracta*

broken—interrupted by areas of space *entrecortada*—*hecho de una serie de rayas que no son continuas*

calm lines—lines that give a work of art a quiet and peaceful mood *líneas tranquilas*—*líneas que dan a una obra de arte un ánimo tranquilo y sereno*

circle—a round geometric shape made when all points are placed the same distance from a center point *círculo*—*una figura geométrica redonda que se forma cuando todos los puntos se colocan en la misma dirección a partir del punto central*

free-form shape—an irregular shape *figura abstracta*—*una figura irregular*

geometric shapes—common shapes that are regular, have specific names, and can be created using mathematical formulas *figuras geométricas*—*figuras comunes que son regulares, tienen nombres específicos*

diagonal—oriented or moving on a slant *diagonal*—*orientada hacia o que se mueve en forma inclinada*

irregular—does not follow a rule or pattern *irregular*—*no sigue una regla o un patrón*

painting—a picture or scene that an artist has created on canvas or another surface using paint. *pintura*—*un dibujo o una escena que un artista crea sobre un lienzo u otra superficie usando pintura*

rectangle—a four-sided geometric shape made of all right angles and whose opposite sides are equal in length *rectángulo*—*una figura geométrica de cuatro lados donde todos los ángulos son rectos y cuyos lados tienen el mismo largo*

rough—has jagged, uneven edges *áspera*—*que tiene bordes dentados e irregulares*

sail—a type of free-form shape *vela*—*un tipo de figura abstracta*

sculpture—three-dimensional art that is not a body form *escultura*—*arte tridimensional que no es una forma de un cuerpo*

smooth—has even edges *suave*—*que tiene bordes regulares*

solid—has no breaks, gaps, or holes *continua*—*que no tiene cortes ni separaciones ni huecos*

splash—a type of free-form shape *salpicadura*—*un tipo de figura abstracta*

square—a four-sided geometric shape where all the sides are the same length and all the angles are the same. *cuadrado*—*una figura geométrica de cuatro lados en la cual todos los lados tienen el mismo largo y todos los ángulos son iguales*

style—the unique quality of an object *estilo*—*la cualidad única de un objeto*

thick—wide *gruesa*—*ancha*

thin—narrow *fina*—*estrecha*

triangle—a three-sided geometric shape *triángulo*—*una figura geométrica de tres lados*

vertical—oriented or moving up and down *vertical*—*orientada hacia o que se mueve de arriba a abajo*

zigzag—diagonal lines that connect at their ends and change direction sharply. *en zigzag*—*líneas diagonales que se conectan en sus puntas y cambian abruptamente de dirección*

Vocabulary Practice

T Display Transparency 37 to review unit vocabulary words.

Definitions:
Demonstrate Meanings ⭐ Vocabulary
Have volunteers select a vocabulary word and draw a picture on the board to explain that word.

Alphabetizing ⭐ Vocabulary
Have students select five words from the unit vocabulary and put them in alphabetical order.

Other References ⭐ Vocabulary
Have students select three unit vocabulary words and look them up in a rhyming dictionary.

Art Criticism

Critical Thinking Art criticism is an organized system for looking at and talking about art. You can criticize art without being an expert. The purpose of art criticism is to get the viewer involved in a perception process that delays judgment until all aspects of the artwork have been studied.

- See pages 28–29 for more about art criticism.

Describe

▶ Possible answer: There are two people. They are dancing.

▶ Possible answer: The man wears a plaid suit. The woman wears a red hat, yellow dress, and blue shoes.

▶ Possible answer: A piano, a saxophone, a trumpet, and a clarinet are in the background.

▶ Possible answer: The floor is striped. The wall is partly striped and partly solid blue.

Analyze

▶ Possible answer: Vertical lines appear on the wall and floor. The place where the wall meets the floor forms a horizontal line.

▶ Possible answer: Most of the outlines of the people, except for the heads, are diagonal. The piano and the other instruments are also outlines with diagonal lines. The top of the man's head forms a curve, and some of his fingers are curved. The woman's hat and feet have curved outlines. The ends of the horns have curved outlines.

▶ Possible answer: The stripes on the floor are thick lines. The pattern on the man's suit is formed of lines that look rough.

▶ Possible answer: The brass instruments.

◀ **William H. Johnson.** (American). *Jitterbugs (II).* c. 1941.
....
Tempera, pen, and ink with pencil on paper. 17 $\frac{15}{16}$ × 12 $\frac{3}{16}$ inches (40.48 × 30.96 cm). Smithsonian American Art Museum, Washington, D.C.

60 Unit 1

Art History and Culture

William H. Johnson

William Johnson (wilʹ yəm jänʹ sən) (1901–1970) was born in South Carolina. When he was young, a teacher saw him drawing in the dirt with a stick. She gave him pencils and encouraged him to draw more pictures. Johnson went to New York to study art. A teacher collected money so that Johnson could go to Paris, France, in 1926 to study art. In the late 1930s, Johnson and his wife returned to the United States to escape the beginning of World War II. In the early 1940s he worked for the Works Progress Administration (WPA). Johnson was part of the Harlem Renaissance of the 1920s.

Artist Profiles, p. 27

● Artist Profile ●
William H. Johnson
1901–1970
William Johnson (wilʹ yəm jän[t]ʹ sən) was born in Florence, South Carolina. When he was young, a teacher saw him drawing in the dirt with a stick. She gave him pencils and encouraged him to draw more pictures. At age 17, Johnson went to New York to study art. While there he won many prizes. A teacher collected money so that Johnson could go to Paris, France, in 1926 to study art.

In the late 1930s, Johnson and his wife returned to the United States to escape the beginning of World War II. For a time he worked as a teacher, and in the early 1940s, he worked for the Works Progress Administration (WPA). The WPA was a

 **Art Criticism** Critical Thinking

Describe **What do you see?**

▶ How many people do you see? What are they doing? Describe the room.

Analyze **How is this work organized?**

▶ Where do you see vertical lines? Can you find a horizontal line? Where?

▶ Where do you see diagonal lines? Do you see any curved lines? Where?

▶ Where do you see thick lines? Where do you see rough lines?

▶ Where do you see geometric shapes? Where do you see free-form shapes?

Interpret **What is the artist trying to say?**

▶ Do the lines in this picture make it active or calm?

▶ Is this a happy or sad picture?

▶ What kind of music do you think the people are dancing to?

▶ If you were in this room, what sounds, other than music, would you hear?

Decide **What do you think about the work?**

▶ Is this painting successful because it is realistic, because it is well organized, or because it has a strong message?

Unit 1   **61**

▶ Possible answer: The woman's hat is a circle. The end of the saxophone is made with circles and the end of the trumpet is painted with ovals. The piano has slanting rectangles. The end of the clarinet is a triangle. The people and the horns are free-form shapes. (Free-form shapes can be jagged.)

Interpret

▶ Possible answer: Even though the background is made with calm lines, the people are made with diagonal lines and they dominate the picture, so the feeling is active.

▶ Possible answer: Students will probably say this picture looks happy because of the smiles on the faces and the brightly colored clothing.

▶ Answers will vary. They may not know that there is a specific dance called the *jitterbug*. Students may list types of music they know, such as jazz, rock, or rap. They may list the names of songs they know.

▶ Possible answer: Other sounds might be people talking, dishes rattling, or the sounds of feet on the floor.

Decide

▶ Answers will vary. Many will get a message from this about dance. Some may say it is well organized.

Art Journal: Writing
Have students write answers to Aesthetic Perception in their Art Journals.

Aesthetic Perception

Seeing Like an Artist Have students think of other dances they have seen or kinds of dances they know. How do these dances compare with *Jitterbugs (II)*?

Describe ▶ List everything you can about the other dances you know.

Analyze ▶ What lines and shapes do you see in the bodies of the dancers?

Interpret ▶ How do the other dances make you feel? Are they calm or active?

Decide ▶ Do you like the other dances?

"What kinds of lines and shapes do artists use to show feelings and how things look?"
"¿Qué tipos de líneas y formas usan los artistas para demostrar sensación y cómo lucen las cosas?"

T Review unit vocabulary with students using *Transparency 37*.

> **Art Journal: Writing**
> Have students answer the questions on page 62 in their Art Journals or on a separate sheet of paper. Answers: 1. C, 2. B, 3. A, 4. C

T For further assessment, have student complete the unit test on *Transparency 43*.

VISIT A MUSEUM
The Smithsonian American Art Museum

► Encourage students to discuss the many functions of a museum (to inform, entertain, preserve, and so on) and why people visit them.

■ Have students put on an exhibition of their work in this unit. What ideas can they identify in their peers' exhibitions?

■ Ask a local artist to share his or her portfolio with the class. What ideas can students identify in the portfolio?

To draw you must close
your eyes and sing
                    —Pablo Picasso

Show What You Know

Choose the best answers and write them on a separate sheet of paper.

 Diagonal, zigzag, and curved lines are all _____.
 A. calm lines
 B. rough lines
 C. active lines

❷ _____ can be made using special math rules.
 A. Free-form shapes
 B. Geometric shapes
 C. Active lines

 _____ and _____ lines are calm lines.
 A. Horizontal, vertical
 B. Curved, smooth
 C. Zigzag, diagonal

 Two examples of line styles are _____ and _____ .
 A. curved, zigzag
 B. horizontal, vertical
 C. thick, broken

62   Unit 1

VISIT A MUSEUM
The Smithsonian American Art Museum

The Smithsonian American Art Museum is the largest collection of American art in the world. It is the first national art collection and was started in 1829.

The museum is in the Old Patent Office Building in Washington, D.C. The building was once used as a hospital for soldiers during the Civil War. In 1957 Congress almost tore down the Old Patent Office Building. Instead, they gave the building to the Smithsonian.

Unit Assessment Options

Aesthetic Perception

Practice Have students list two of the concepts found on page 62, then find examples of each in the classroom.

Creative Expression

Student Portfolio Have students review all the artwork they have created during this unit and select the pieces they wish to keep in their portfolios. Have students examine classmates' portfolios and identify original ideas.

Art Criticism

Activity Have students select an artwork from this unit and study it using the four steps of art criticism. (See pages 28–29 for more about art criticism). Have students work alone or in pairs and present their findings orally or in writing.

Line and Shape in Theatre

By wearing masks, Robert Faust can become many characters. In many cultures, masks are worn at festivals and celebrations. Masks help a person to pretend to be someone or something else. The lines and shapes used on a mask tell the viewer about the emotions.

What to Do Use lines and shapes to create masks that show two feelings.

1. Discuss opposite feelings such as happy and sad.

2. Create two masks, one for each opposite feeling. Sketch each face on a paper plate. Decorate your masks with shapes and lines. Fasten the two masks to each other so both faces are showing.

3. Cut a slit in the end of a cardboard tube. Put the masks in the slit. Use the tube as a handle.

4. Invent movements to express the feelings on each mask. Perform your expression of opposite feelings for the class.

▲ Robert Faust. "The Mask Messenger"

Art Criticism

Describe Describe your two-sided mask.

Analyze Explain how you used lines and shapes when creating your masks.

Interpret What opposite feelings did you create with your masks and your body?

Decide How well did you express two different emotions in both your mask and movements?

Unit 1 **63**

Art History and Culture

Masks and Theatre

Masks have been an important aspect of religious and social life in many cultures. The theatrical use of masks evolved from religious practices of ancient Greece. They were used to imitate a god and were made primarily of animal skins. As these ceremonies became more theatrical, the masks became more elaborate. Traditional masks depicting tragedy and comedy are derived from Greek theatrical traditions. Masks are effective in a performance because they can be seen from a distance. An actor must be well trained to use a mask because the actions must be large and clear and complement the character. Vocal projection within a mask also requires great skill and the ability to express a range and depth of emotions.

Line and Shape in Theatre

Objective: to express two opposing emotions using masks and movement

Materials: *"The Mask Messenger,"* Faustwork Mask Theater performed by Robert Faust. Running Time: 4:40, paper plates, glue, scissors, paper towel rolls, yarn, buttons, fabric scraps, crayons, markers, beans, rice, seeds or other natural materials

Focus
Time: About 5 minutes

- Discuss the information on page 63.

Art History and Culture

- Have students brainstorm and list emotions they can use in creating their masks and movement interpretations.

Teach
Time: About 20 minutes

Aesthetic Perception

- Point out to students that shape and lines can be used both on their masks and in their bodies.

Creative Expression

- Have students brainstorm different emotions, list them, and pair them into opposite groupings.

- Direct students to use facial expressions and hand gestures to show appropriate, opposing feelings.

- Have students use movements that express these opposing feelings.

- Have students hold their masks and show the feelings on each side with their body.

- **Informal Assessment** Comment positively on the physical interpretations of feelings the students invent.

Reflect
Time: About 10 minutes

Art Criticism

- Have students answer the four art criticism questions on page 63 orally.

- Did students effectively create shapes and lines through movement?

Unit 2 Planning Guide

	Lesson Title	Suggested Pacing	Creative Expression Activity
Lesson 1	**Geometric Forms**	55 minutes	Create a sculpture by taping geometric forms together.
Lesson 2	**Free-Form Forms**	55 minutes	Create a cardboard relief describing the students using free-form forms.
Lesson 3	**Body Forms**	55 minutes	Create a clay figure that describes students' cultures.
Lesson 4	**Animal Forms**	55 minutes	Create a utilitarian clay figure that illustrates animal forms.
Lesson 5	**People and Space**	55 minutes	Create a cut paper collage of a family playing to illustrate overlapping.
Lesson 6	**Objects and Space**	55 minutes	Create a still life that illustrates overlapping shapes to create depth.
ART SOURCE	**Space and Form in Theatre**	30 minutes	Create a tableau to illustrate a scene from a story.

Materials	Program Resources	Fine Art Resources	Literature Resources
various cardboard geometric forms, glue gun, spray paint, masking tape	*Reading and Writing Test Preparation*, pp. 18–19 *Assessment*, pp. 21–22 *Home and After-School Connections*	*Transparency*, 7 *Artist Profiles*, pp. 42, 56 *Animals Time Line* *Large Print*, 27 *Women in the Arts Collection*	*Cubes, Cones, Cylinders, and Spheres* by Tana Hoban
aluminum foil, tagboard, tempera paints, water colors, water dishes, brushes, paper towels, cardboard, scissors, markers, found objects	*Reading and Writing Test Preparation*, pp. 20–21 *Assessment*, pp. 23–24	*Transparency*, 8 *Artist Profiles*, pp. 79, 80 *Large Prints*, 27 and 28 *Art Around the World Collection*	*Ancient Egyptians and Their Neighbors* by Marian Broida
white or red clay, wooden ice-cream sticks, clay tools, slip, fabric to cover table, kiln	*Reading and Writing Test Preparation*, pp. 22–23 *Assessment*, pp. 25–26	*Transparency*, 9 *Artist Profiles*, pp. 4, 59 *Large Print*, 27 *Art Around the World Collection*	*Children of the Midnight Sun* by Tricia Brown
red or white clay, clay tools, fabric to cover work area, slip, kiln	*Reading and Writing Test Preparation*, pp. 24–25 *Assessment*, pp. 27–28	*Transparency*, 10 *Artist Profiles*, pp. 7, 75 *Large Print*, 28 *Women in the Arts Collection*	*Hiding Out* by James Martin
construction paper, white paper, crayons, markers, glue, scissors	*Reading and Writing Test Preparation*, pp. 26–27 *Assessment*, pp. 29–30	*Transparency*, 11 *Artist Profiles*, pp. 49, 55 *Large Print*, 27 *Women in the Arts Collection*	*Dumpling Soup* by Jama Kim Rattigan
construction paper, colored dustless chalk, liquid tempera, palettes, brushes, newspaper, food and still life objects, water dishes, paper towels *"The Long-Haired Girl"* by Eth-Noh-Tec, a short story divided into scenes with each scene summarized on a card	*Reading and Writing Test Preparation*, pp. 28–29 *Assessment*, pp. 31–32	*Transparency*, 12 *Artist Profiles*, pp. 11, 39 *Large Prints*, 27 and 28 *Women in the Arts Collection*	*Uncle Willie and the Soup Kitchen* by DyAnne DiSalvo-Ryan

2 Space and Form

Lesson 1: Geometric Forms are three-dimensional geometric shapes.

Lesson 2: Free-Form Forms are three-dimensional free-form shapes.

Lesson 3: Body Forms are three-dimensional body shapes.

Lesson 4: Animal Forms are three-dimensional animal shapes.

Lesson 5: People and Space shows how artists overlap people shapes to create depth in paintings.

Lesson 6: Objects and Space shows how artists overlap other shapes to create depth in paintings.

Introduce Unit Concepts

"Artists use space and form to show depth in their work." "Los artistas usan el espacio y la forma para mostrar profundidad en sus obras".

Space
- Ask students to think about what space is. Discuss with students how space is all around them. Discuss how the space around an object defines that object.

Form
- Show students different geometric and free-form shapes drawn on sheets of paper. Show students forms made out of clay that correspond to the shapes.

- Discuss with students how forms and shapes have height and width. Point out those dimensions on your models. Explain that forms also have depth. Show them the depth on the form.

Cross-Curricular Projects
- See the *Language Arts and Reading, Mathematics, Science,* and *Social Studies Art Connections* books for activities that further develop space and form.

Space and Form

◀ **Henry Moore.** (British). *Family Group.* 1948–1949.
Bronze (cast 1950). 59 $\frac{1}{4}$ × 46 $\frac{1}{2}$ × 29 $\frac{7}{8}$ inches (150.5 × 118.1 × 75.88 cm.). Museum of Modern Art, New York, New York.

Artists use forms to add dimension to their artwork.

Forms are objects that have height, width, and depth. Henry Moore's *Family Group* is a form because it is a statue and has depth.

64 Unit 2

Fine Art Prints
Display **Large Prints 27** *Canteleve* and **28** *Howl.* Refer to the prints as students learn about space and form.

Large Print 27

Large Print 28

Forms are like shapes, but forms are three-dimensional. Every shape can be paired with a form.

▶ Why is *Family Group* a form?

▶ Do the forms in *Family Group* match geometric or free-form shapes?

Space is the area around shapes and forms. By using space, artists can make some objects seem closer than others.

▶ Who is closer to you, the mother or the child?

In This Unit you will learn about and make forms. You will also learn how to use space to create depth on a flat surface. Here are the topics you will study:

▶ Geometric Forms

▶ Free-Form Forms

▶ Body Forms

▶ Animal Forms

▶ People and Space

▶ Objects and Space

Henry Moore
(1898–1986)

Henry Moore was born in England. When he was young, he decided he wanted to be a sculptor, but he became a teacher instead. Moore was a soldier in World War I. When he returned home, he went to art school. Moore made abstract figures based on the natural qualities of the materials he used. He was inspired by things he saw during his walks in the fields.

Unit 2 **65**

NSAE 1.a, 1.b

Examine the Artwork

"Look carefully at the statue." "Miren la estatua cuidadosamente".

■ Have students look at *Family Group* and describe what they see.

■ Have students answer the questions about space and form on page 65.

▶ *Family Group* is a form because it is three-dimensional and has depth.

▶ The base is a geometric form; the other forms would correspond with free-form shapes.

▶ The child is closer to the viewer.

■ Discuss the differences between materials, techniques, and processes and how they cause different responses.

Unit Pretest

T Display *Transparency 44* as a pretest. Answers: 1. B, 2. A, 3. C, 4. A

Home Connection

■ See *Home and After-School Connections* for family newsletters and activities for this unit.

 Art History and Culture

Henry Moore

Henry Moore (hen´ rē mor) (1898–1986) was born in a small coal mining town in Yorkshire, England. Moore decided at a young age that he wanted to be a sculptor. However, his father (who was well educated and adamantly against his son becoming a miner like himself) pushed Moore into teaching. After serving in World War I, Moore returned home and enrolled in the Leeds School of Art where his talents developed. Moore's unique style was a combination of surrealism and allowing the natural properties of his medium to influence his work.

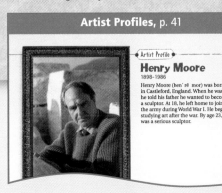

Artist Profiles, p. 41

Artist Profile

Henry Moore
1898–1986

Henry Moore (hen´ rē mor) was born in Castleford, England. When he was ten, he told his father he wanted to become a sculptor. At 18, he left home to join the army during World War I. He began studying art after the war. By age 23, he was a serious sculptor.

UNIT 2 • Space and Form **65**

ILLUSTRATOR PROFILE

Stan and Jan Berenstain

(1923–)(1923–)

Both Stan and Jan Berenstain (née Grant) were born in Philadelphia, Pennsylvania. They met while studying at the Philadelphia College of Art and later married. The Berenstains started their career by writing and illustrating an adult comic strip called *It's All in the Family*.

It wasn't until Theodore Geisel (Dr. Seuss) asked the Berenstains to write a book for a line of his beginning reader books that they really began to delve into children's books. Their first book, *The Big Honey Hunt*, was published in 1962.

Most of the books that the Berenstains write are based on events that actually happened when raising their two sons, Michael and Leo. Now that the boys are adults, the Berenstains base their stories on things that happen to their four grandchildren.

When teaching Unit 2, share the Berenstains' illustrations with the class and discuss the use of space in the art. Where do characters and objects overlap? What parts of characters and objects are hidden?

Music

In music, form is the way a composition is organized. For example, A-B-A form is one in which the first and last sections of a piece are the same, and the middle section is contrasting (as in the song *Twinkle, Twinkle, Little Star.*) Have students find examples of A-B-A form in the arrangements of physical objects in the classroom.

Literature

Have students watch the video or DVD *Heckedy Peg* by Audrey Wood and discuss how the illustrator used space and form.

Literature and Art

Performing Arts

Show students "Long Haired Girl," and have them look for space and forms in the dance.

Artsource®

Geometric Forms

Overview

Lesson 1 introduces the students to geometric forms and teaches the differences between geometric forms and geometric shapes. Students will learn how geometric forms occupy space in a different way than geometric shapes.

Objectives

 **Art History and Culture**

Compare the ways David Smith and Jesús Moroles used materials in their sculptures

 Creative Expression

To stack and tape geometric forms to create a sculpture

 Aesthetic Perception

To recognize and identify geometric forms

 Art Criticism

To evaluate own work using the four steps of art criticism

Vocabulary ⭐ Vocabulary

Review the following vocabulary words with students before beginning the lesson.

geometric form forma geométrica—a form whose corresponding shape is geometric

three-dimensional tridimensional—has measurements in three directions: height, width, and depth

See page 89B for additional vocabulary and Spanish vocabulary resources.

 Art Journal: Vocabulary

Have students add these words to the Vocabulary section of their Art Journals.

Lesson Materials
- various cardboard geometric forms, such as shoe boxes, cardboard tubes, etc.
- glue gun
- spray paint
- masking tape

Alternate Materials:
- markers

Program Resources
- *Reading and Writing Test Prep.*, pp. 18–19
- *Transparency 7*
- *Artist Profiles*, pp. 42, 56
- *Animals Through History Time Line*
- *Assessment*, pp. 21–22
- *Large Prints 27* Canteleve
- *The National Museum of Women in the Arts Collection*

Concept Trace
Geometric Forms
Introduced: Level 1, Unit 4, Lesson 1
Reinforced: Level 3, Unit 2, Lesson 4

Lesson 1 Arts Integration

Theatre

Complete Unit 2, Lesson 1 on pages 36–37 of *Theatre Arts Connections.*

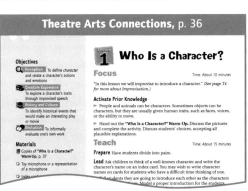

Music

 Listen to "March" from *The Nutcracker.* Determine that it is in A-B-A form. Another way to illustrate form without using letters is with geometric shapes. "March" would be triangle-circle-triangle. How many repeats of triangle-circle-triangle would you need to illustrate the song *Tinga Layo? Going over the Sea?*

Movement & Dance

Have students form a large circle, and then have them enter the circle in groups of three. Within each group of three, have one student create a geometric shape on a low level, one student create a geometric shape on a middle level, and one student create a geometric shape on a high level. Have all three students take eight counts to move the shape they created in a circular path without losing their relationship to each other.

 **ocus** Time: About 10 minutes

Activate Prior Knowledge

"Describe what it feels like to hold a ball."

"Describan cómo se siente agarrar una pelota".

■ Discuss student responses. Explain to students that a ball is a geometric form because it is a sphere.

Using Literature ⭐ Reading

■ Read *Cubes, Cones, Cylinders, and Spheres* by Tana Hoban. Discuss the geometric forms that students see in the book.

Thematic Connection ⭐ Reading

■ **Materials:** Have students discuss material properties and how they influence how materials are used. For example, would students want a blanket made of metal? Why not?

Introduce the Art

Look NSAE 2.a

"Let's look at these two works of art." "Vamos a ver estas dos obras de arte".

■ Have students identify geometric forms in the statues and the environment.

Comparing and Contrasting ⭐ Reading

■ Ask students to name similarities and differences in the two sculptures. Both sculptures are large and gray. Both use geometric forms. *Cubi XVIII* is made of steel and *Georgia Stele* is made of granite. *Georgia Stele* is much more balanced than the Smith piece.

NSAE 4.c, 5.b, 4.a

 Art History and Culture

Possible answer: These materials work well because they are hard and can be molded into very precise shapes. Encourage students to discuss how the artists' cultures influence material choices. Why do they think Moroles works with stone and Smith worked with steel?

🖥 **Web Connection**

Visit **http://www.sfmoma.org/anderson/ index.html** and click **Start Project**. Select **Explore 15 Works** and select the David Smith work for a detailed, interactive look at David Smith and several of his sculptures.

66 UNIT 2 • Space and Form

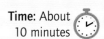 **Lesson 1** # Geometric Forms

Look at both **sculptures.** These sculptures were made using **geometric forms.** Using **forms** adds **depth** and **dimension** to artwork. If you saw these sculptures in a museum, you would be able to walk around them and see every side of the art.

◄ **David Smith.** (American). *Cubi XVIII.* 1964.

Polished stainless steel. 115 ¾ × 60 × 21 ¾ inches (294 × 152.4 × 55.2 cm.). Museum of Fine Arts Boston, Boston, Massachusetts.

 Art History and Culture

Look at the materials these artists used. Why do you think these materials work well for geometric forms?

 Art History and Culture

David Smith

David Smith (dā´ vəd smith) (1906–1965) was never formally trained as a sculptor. He learned about metalworking through jobs as a welder and riveter at an automobile factory. Smith, who was born in Decatur, Indiana, moved to Ohio with his family in 1921. In 1926 he moved to New York and began taking art classes. In the 1930s, Smith began creating welded metal sculptures, which is the style that he became known for. Smith's work was usually abstract and often involved principles of balance and space. Smith's career was cut short when he was killed in a car accident in 1965 at age 59.

See pages 24–25 and 16–21 for more about art history and subject matter.

Artist Profiles, p 56

Artist Profile

David Smith
1906-1965

David Smith (dā´ vəd smith) was born in Decatur, Indiana. He studied art during high school through a correspondence course with the Cleveland Art School in Cleveland, Ohio. He then attended Ohio University in Athens, Ohio, and the University of Notre Dame in South Bend, Indiana. In 1926, Smith studied at the Art Students League in New York. He taught art at many colleges, including Sarah Lawrence College in New York, and Bennington College in Vermont. Smith became interested in the welded-steel sculptures of Picasso while studying in New York. Drawing on skills learned while employed in a car factory one summer, he used his welding experience to construct welded-steel sculptures. He was the first

Study the two sculptures. Think about how the artists used geometric forms.

► What forms do you see in the two sculptures? What shapes would they be paired with?

► What do you think you would see if you looked at the backs of the sculptures?

◄ **Jesús Moroles.** (American). *Georgia Stele.* 1999.
Georgia gray granite. 82 × 12 ¼ × 8 inches (208.28 × 31.12 × 20.32 cm.). Smithsonian American Art Museum, Washington, D.C.

 Aesthetic Perception

Design Awareness Can you think of a time you have seen a geometric form? Can you find a geometric form in your classroom now?

Art History and Culture

Jesús Moroles

Jesús Moroles (hā sōōs´ mo rō´ lēz) (1950–) is a famous Hispanic sculptor who was born in Corpus Christi, Texas. Moroles was drafted into the Air Force immediately after high school which enabled him to travel the world. After returning home, Moroles enrolled in North Texas University where he majored in art. Upon graduation, he went to Italy for a year where he reflected on art and refined his artistic voice. He also spent a great deal of time studying the qualities of stone there, which is his medium. The central theme in Moroles's work is the balance of the human race with nature.

See pages 24–25 and 16–21 for more about art history and subject matter.

Artist Profiles, p. 42

◄ Artist Profile ►
Jesús Moroles
b. 1950
Born in Texas to Mexican immigrant parents, Jesús Moroles (hā sōōs´ mo rō´ lēz) creates monumental sculptures from granite, or "living stone." He has been working with granite since 1980 and now has his own successful studio headquarters—Moroles, Inc.—in Rockport, Texas. Moroles's sculptures have been exhibited all over the world, and he has had great success from the very beginning of his career. Often more than 20 feet tall, his massive creations can be found in numerous museums, as well as in outdoor environments such as the CBS Plaza in New York City, the White House sculpture gardens, the Edwin A. Ulrich Museum in Kansas, and the Albuquerque Museum in

Study

► Both statues are made of cubes and rectangular prisms or boxes. Some students may see the cylinder in *Cubi XVIII.* The matching shapes are squares, rectangles, and circles.

► Student answers will vary. However, it is important that the answers show a grasp of the fact that these are three-dimensional works of art.

■ For more examples of abstract/non-objective art, see the ***The National Museum of Women in the Arts Collection.***

Art Journal: Brainstorming
Have students brainstorm geometric forms that they have seen and make a list of their ideas. Have students add this list to the Concepts section of their Art Journals.

 Aesthetic Perception

Design Awareness Have students discuss the geometric forms that they see every day, such as buildings, balls, and doors. Ask them about other geometric forms they see in the classroom. Encourage them to identify the variations in the objects from the environments.
NSAE 2.b, 5.c

Developing Visual Literacy How do these geometric forms make students feel? What emotions do these works of art evoke in the students?

Web Connection
Visit **www.moroles.com** for more information about Jesús Moroles.

Teach

"When would it be better to use a geometric form instead of a geometric shape?"

"¿Cuándo sería mejor usar una forma geométrica en vez de una figura geométrica?"

- Read the information about geometric forms on page 68 and discuss it.

Practice

Materials: students, open space

- Have students follow the directions on page 68.

- Have students identify and practice skills necessary for producing constructions using a variety of materials. NSAE 1.c, 1.d, 2.c, 3.b

Creative Expression

Materials: various cardboard geometric forms, such as shoe boxes, cardboard tubes, etc., spray paint (teacher only), masking tape, glue gun (teacher only)

Alternate Materials: markers

- Have students begin gathering geometric forms several weeks prior to starting this lesson.

- Distribute materials and have students follow the directions on page 69.

- After the students assemble their forms with masking tape, use the glue gun to attach their sculptures to a cereal box base. Spray paint sculptures when students are done.

- Review the Activity Tips on page 235 for visual examples of the activity if needed.

- Review the Technique Tips on page 228.

- Encourage students to express ideas and feelings in their sculptures using a variety of forms.

- Encourage students to create effective compositions using design elements.

Art Journal: Sketching NSAE 3.a
Have students sketch ideas for their sculpture layouts in the Ideas section of their Art Journals.

Using Geometric Forms

circle

cylinder

square

cube

triangle

pyramid

Geometric forms are similar to geometric shapes. Geometric forms are different because they are **three-dimensional.** A dimension is a measurement. Shapes are **two-dimensional** because they have **height** and **width.** Forms have height, width, and depth. Look at these geometric shapes and forms. Can you see how they match? Can you see how they are different?

Practice

Create a geometric form with your classmates.

1. Stand in a horizontal line with one other classmate.

2. Have one classmate line up behind each of you.

3. What geometric form have you made? How many people high is your form? How many people wide is your form? How many people deep is your form?

Differentiated Instruction

Reteach
Take students outside and have them look at the school building. Ask them if they can find any geometric forms.

Special Needs
Help students understand the differences between shapes and forms by providing wire shapes and their related sculptural forms for students to compare.

ELL Tips
Hold up geometric forms such as balls, dice, and books along with their corresponding shapes. Ask students to tell you which is the shape and which is the form.

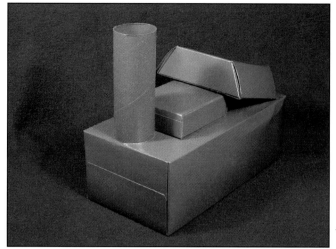

◀ **Matthew Ellett.**
Age 6.

Think about how this student used geometric forms in his sculpture.

 Creative Expression

How could you stack geometric forms to create a sculpture? Make a sculpture by stacking and taping geometric forms.

1. Look at your teacher's selection of geometric forms. Think about how you would stack the forms. Plan your design.
2. Select three forms you want to work with. Stack and tape the forms.

Art Criticism

Describe How did you create your sculpture?

Analyze Which geometric forms did you use?

Interpret How would your art be different if you had used shapes instead of forms?

Decide If you made another sculpture to create a series, what would it look like?

Art Across the Curriculum   NSAE 6.a, 6.b

Use these simple ideas to reinforce art concepts across the curriculum.

★ **Poetry** Have students use the writing process to write a poem about a material.

★ **Math** Review the names of geometric solids with students.

★ **Science** Have students use sugar cubes to identify, predict, and test uses of heat to cause change such as melting and evaporation.

★ **Social Studies** Have students use symbols, find locations, and determine directions on maps and globes. Point out that globes are geometric forms and maps are geometric shapes.

★ **Technology** Show students how a traditional mouse works. Take out the track ball so students can see that it is a geometric form. Does a computer have other geometric forms? Visit **SRAonline.com** to print detailed instructions for this activity.

 **Reflect** **Time:** About 10 minutes

Review and Assess

"What is the difference between a geometric shape and a geometric form?" "¿Cuál es la diferencia entre una figura geométrica y una forma geométrica?"

Think

This student's entire sculpture is geometric forms. Ask students to identify which forms he used.

■ Use *Large Print 27 Canteleve* to have students identify geometric forms.

■ Have students identify stories and constructions in this lesson's artwork.

■ Have students identify ideas in the art by this lesson's artists.

Informal Assessment

Art Journal: Critical Thinking
Have students answer the four art criticism questions—Describe, Analyze, Interpret, and Decide—in the Critical Thinking section of their Art Journals. In small groups, have students discuss the geometric forms in their sculptures. Have students define reasons for preferences in their personal artwork. Then have them identify ideas in their peers' artwork.

■ For standardized-format test practice using this lesson's art content, see pages 18–19 in *Reading and Writing Test Preparation*.

Geometric Forms

Extra! For the Art Specialist

Time: About 45 minutes

Focus

Study **Large Print 27** and ask students what forms they see. Can they find any geometric forms?

Teach

Discuss geometric forms with the students. Explain that they will be creating geometric forms using clay. Demonstrate clay techniques. Have students complete the Alternate Activity.

Reflect

Have students evaluate their work using the four steps of art criticism.

Alternate Activity

Materials:
- clay
- clay tools
- mats
- glazes and paints
- brushes
- kiln

1. Discuss geometric forms. Most forms can be made by starting from a simple oval and gently tapping the clay into the desired form.

2. Think of a form to make before starting. Create your form.

3. Use the clay tools to add details to your form.

4. Paint or glaze your form after it has been fired.

Research in Art Education

Research has indicated that one important outcome of integrating arts into other curriculum areas is an increased level of classroom discussions and more time spent on problem solving. The level of teacher dedication and experience seems to influence these outcomes (Different Ways of Knowing: 1991–94 National Longitudinal Study Final Report" in *Schools, Communities, and the Arts: A Research Compendium*).

Assessment
 Use the following rubric to evaluate the artwork students make in the Creative Expression activity and to assess students' understanding of geometric forms.

Have students complete page 21 or 22 in their *Assessment* books.

	Art History and Culture	Aesthetic Perception	Creative Expression	Art Criticism
3 POINTS	The student can identify and compare how Moroles and Smith selected and used materials to create geometric forms in works of art.	The student accurately recognizes and identifies geometric forms in his or her environment.	The student's sculpture clearly illustrates a good use of geometric forms.	The student thoughtfully and honestly evaluates his or her own work using the four steps of art criticism.
2 POINTS	The student's identification or comparison is weak or incomplete.	The student shows emerging awareness of geometric forms but cannot consistently identify them.	The student's sculpture shows some geometric forms.	The student attempts to evaluate his or her own work but shows an incomplete understanding of evaluation criteria.
1 POINT	The student cannot identify or compare how materials are selected and used to create geometric forms in different works of art.	The student cannot identify geometric forms.	The student's sculpture shows no geometric forms.	The student does not attempt to evaluate his or her own artwork.

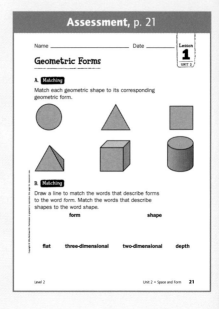

Assessment, p. 21

Name _____ Date _____

Geometric Forms

Lesson **1** UNIT 2

A. **Matching**
Match each geometric shape to its corresponding geometric form.

B. **Matching**
Draw a line to match the words that describe forms to the word *form*. Match the words that describe shapes to the word *shape*.

form   shape

flat   three-dimensional   two-dimensional   depth

Level 2   Unit 2 • Space and Form   **21**

Lesson 2 Free-Form Forms

Overview

Lesson 2 introduces free-form forms. Free-form forms are three-dimensional free-form shapes.

Objectives

 Art History and Culture

To identify the role of kings in ancient Iranian and Egyptian society and compare ancient art honoring kings

 Creative Expression

To create a cardboard relief using free-form forms that describes the student

 Aesthetic Perception

To identify free-form forms in students' environments

Art Criticism

To evaluate own work using the four steps of art criticism

Vocabulary ⭐ Vocabulary

Review the following vocabulary words with students before beginning the lesson.

free–form form *forma abstracta*—an irregular, three-dimensional object

relief *relieve*—a sculpture where forms project from a flat background

See page 89B for additional Spanish vocabulary resources.

 Art Journal: Vocabulary

Have students add these words to the Vocabulary section of their Art Journals.

Lesson Materials

- aluminum foil
- tagboard
- tempera paints
- water colors
- water dishes
- brushes
- paper towels
- cardboard
- scissors
- markers
- found objects

Program Resources

- *Reading and Writing Test Prep.*, pp. 20–21
- *Transparency 8*
- *Artist Profiles*, pp. 79, 80
- *Animals Through History Time Line*
- *Assessment*, pp. 23–24
- *Large Prints 27 Canteleve* and *28 Howl*
- *Art Around the World Collection*

Concept Trace
Free-Form Forms
Introduced: Level 1, Unit 4, Lesson 3

Reinforced: Level 3, Unit 2, Lesson 4

Lesson 2 Arts Integration

Theatre

Complete Unit 2, Lesson 2 on pages 38–39 of *Theatre Arts Connections* book.

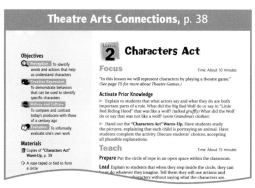

Music

 Listen to "Royal March of the Lions" from *The Carnival of the Animals* by Camille Saint-Saens. This piece is a light hearted tribute to a royal animal. How does the music contrast with the sculptures in this lesson that honor kings?

Movement & Dance

Have students form a large circle and then have them enter the circle in groups of three. Within each group of three, have one student create a free-form shape on a low level, one student create a free-form shape on a middle level, and one student create a free-form shape on a high level. Have all three students take eight counts to move the shape they created in a circular path without losing their relationship to each other.

Focus

Time: About 10 minutes

Activate Prior Knowledge

"Have you ever seen a picture of the Sphinx in Egypt?" "¿Alguna vez han visto una fotografía de la Esfinge de Egipto?"

■ Discuss student responses. Explain to students that the Sphinx is a free-form form. It is three-dimensional, but does not have geometric forms.

Using Literature ☆ Reading

■ Read and discuss selections from *Ancient Egyptians and Their Neighbors* by Marian Broida. Have students look for free-form forms.

Theme Connection ☆ Reading

■ **Ancient Civilizations:** Ask students to think about what tools people in ancient civilizations would have used to make free-form forms.

Introduce the Art   NSAE 2.a

Look

"Let's examine these two works of ancient art." "Vamos a examinar estas dos obras de arte antiguas".

■ Have students identify free-form forms in the artwork and environment.

■ Have students compare the ways individuals are depicted in these works of art.

Similarity ☆ Math

■ Have students discuss the similarities between free-form shapes and free-form forms. Then have students discuss the similarities between free-form forms and geometric forms. Free-form shapes and free-form forms are both irregular. Free-form forms and geometric forms are both three-dimensional.

NSAE 4.a, 4.b, 4.c, 5.a, 5.b

 Art History and Culture

Possible answer: Kings were very important to people in ancient cultures, which is why there was so much art created to honor them.

💻 **Web Connection**

Visit www.metmuseum.org/explore/First_Cities/ firstcities_splash.htm for interactive lessons on ancient art from Mesopotamia and the Indus Valley.

Free-Form Forms

◄ **Artist Unknown.** (Iran). *Plate with King Hunting Rams.* Late fifth century A.D. Sasanian period.
....
Silver with mercury gilding and niello inlay. Diameter 8⅝ inches (21.9 cm.). The Metropolitan Museum of Art, New York, New York.

Look at the two works of art. Both use free-form forms in their designs. The designs are made using reliefs. A **relief** is a type of sculpture that is made from forms sticking out from a flat background.

 Art History and Culture

Both works of art were made to honor kings. What does this tell you about kings in ancient civilizations?

 Art History and Culture

Iranian Artisans

This plate was made during the Sasanian Empire in Iran. The hunting scene on this plate represents the skill and power of the king. Plates like these would not be used for meals but instead would be given to nearby kingdoms as gifts. Sasanians made their bowls and plates by hammering the shape they wanted and then decorating the plates. The relief on this plate was achieved by making cuts and inserting pieces of silver in the plate. Then the artist decorated the plate by painting and inlaying it with alloys of mercury and gold and sulfur and silver.

See pages 24–25 and 16–21 for more about art history and subject matter.

Artist Profiles, p. 80

◦ Artist Profile ◦

Plate with King Hunting Rams

Many artists were skilled in metalwork in fifth- and sixth-century Persia, located in what is modern-day Iran. The name of the metalsmith who created this dish is not known. Because the style and techniques used to make this plate were widely practiced during this time period in Persia, the work of this particular artist cannot be isolated as a means of identifying him.

◄ **Artist unknown.** (Iran). *Plate with King Hunting Rams.* Late fifth century A.D.

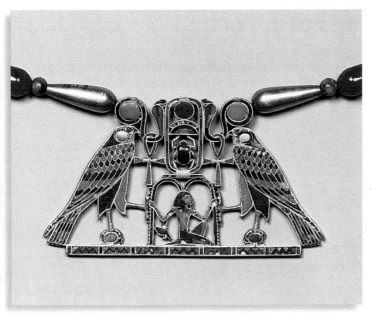

◄ **Artist unknown.**
(Egypt). *Pectoral
with the Name of
Senwosret II.*
c. 1897–1878 B.C.E.
. . . .
Gold, carnelian, feldspar,
garnet, turquoise. Length
of pectoral 3¼ inches
(8.25 cm.). The
Metropolitan Museum of
Art, New York, New York.

Study the two works of art to look for free-form
forms.

▶ What forms are most noticeable?

▶ What shapes do you think match the forms
you see?

▶ Do you see any geometric forms?

Aesthetic Perception

Design Awareness Look at the supplies on your desk.
Can you find free-form forms in any of the supplies?

 ### Art History and Culture

Ancient Egyptian Jewelry

This pectoral was made in honor of King Senwosret II. It was found
in the tomb of Princess Sit-hathor-yunet, who researchers think
was the king's daughter. All the hieroglyphics on the piece praise
Senwosret. The falcons are symbols of the sun god. The cartouche
is the name of Senwosret II. The snakes represent Nekhbet and
Udjo, the guardian goddesses of the king. Ancient Egyptians wore
jewelry to show status, but they also believed that wearing jewelry
in praise of a king would help protect that king. This pectoral was
made using gold and semi-
precious stones.

See pages 24–25 and 16–21
for more about art history
and subject matter.

Artist Profiles, p. 79

◇ Artist Profile ◇

**Pectoral with
the Name of
Senwosret II**

Artists of the Middle Kingdom of ancient
Egypt are known for their skilled attention
to even the smallest detail. Artists of this
period demonstrated more freedom of
creative expression than those of earlier
periods, creating ornately beautiful works
of precious metals, stone, granite, wood,
plaster, gesso, and ceramics. Middle
Kingdom jewelers created spectacular
ornaments for the royalty who wore them.

▲ **Artist unknown** (Egypt). *Pectoral with the Name
of Se...*

Study

▶ Answers will vary, but some obvious free-
form forms on the plate are the king, the
horse, and the ram. The falcons and the
Egyptian deity are most noticeable on
the pectoral.

▶ The students will have different answers
since these are mostly free-form forms,
but the important distinction that
students should make is that shapes are
two-dimensional and forms are three-
dimensional.

▶ On the plate, the quill is a box and the
crown contains a sphere. On the pectoral,
the bottom is a box and there are several
spheres.

■ For more examples of art from the Middle
East, see the ***Art Around the World
Collection.***

Art Journal: Writing
Ask students to write their own
explanations of free-form forms in the
Concepts section of their Art Journals.
Have them name some examples of free-
form forms.

Aesthetic Perception

Design Awareness Have students pick up and
examine the objects on their desks. Discuss
free-form forms and encourage students to
think why free-form forms were selected for
the supply designs. What would the supplies
look and feel like if they were made using
only geometric forms? Have students identify
variations in the objects from the
environment. NSAE 2.b, 5.c

Developing Visual Literacy Discuss the
message of each piece of art. What were the
artists saying about their respective kings?
Do students think that these opinions would
have been popular in ancient civilizations?

Web Connection
Visit **www.metmuesum.org/explore/newegypt/
htm/a_index.htm** for interactive lessons in Ancient
Egyptian art.

Teach

Time: About 35 minutes

"How are free-form forms different from free-form shapes?" "¿En qué se diferencian las formas abstractas de las figuras abstractas?"

- Read and discuss the information about free-form forms on page 72.

Practice

Materials: aluminum foil

- Distribute the materials and have students follow the directions page 72.

- Have students identify and practice the skills necessary for producing constructions by using a variety of materials.

Creative Expression

NSAE 1.c, 1.d, 2.c, 3.b

Materials: tagboard, tempera paints, water colors, water dishes, brushes, paper towels, cardboard, scissors, markers, glue, found objects

Alternate Materials: oil pastels, crayons

- Distribute materials and have students follow the directions on page 73.

- Encourage students to express their ideas and feelings in their reliefs by using a variety of forms.

- Encourage students to create effective compositions by using design elements.

- Review the Activity Tips on page 235 for visual examples of techniques if needed.

Art Journal: Listing NSAE 3.a

Have students make a list of personal traits they want to illustrate in their relief in the Ideas section of their Art Journals. Then have students pick their favorite ideas from the list to implement in their reliefs.

Using Free-Form Forms

Free-form forms are also three-dimensional. Like free-form shapes, free-form forms do not have set shapes. Artists use free-form forms to show things like trees and abstract objects in sculptures.

Practice

Can you make a free-form form? Use aluminum foil to practice.

1. Pinch and shape aluminum foil into a free-form form.

2. Does your form look the same as your classmates' forms or is it different?

Differentiated Instruction

Reteach

Hold up geometric and free-form forms for the students and ask them to tell you if the forms you are displaying are geometric or free-form.

Special Needs

Help students achieve the objectives of this lesson by discussing how artists use symbols to represent ideas or objects. Show and discuss examples of symbols such as hearts or stars.

ELL Tips

Review the definition of *free-form form* and have students find free-form forms in the room.

◀ **Matia Rujiraviriyapinyo.** Age 8.

Think about how this student showed free-form forms in her relief.

 **Creative Expression**

How would you use a relief to describe yourself? Create a relief using free-form forms.

1. Think about things you like or that describe you. What free-form forms will you use to show these things?
2. Paint a background on tagboard.
3. Draw your forms on cardboard, decorate them, and cut them out.
4. Glue your free-form forms onto the background.

 Art Criticism

Describe How does your relief describe you?

Analyze What free-form forms did you use?

Interpret How would your design look if you had used shapes?

Decide Are there times when you think it is better to use forms instead of shapes?

Art Across the Curriculum

Use these simple ideas to reinforce art concepts across the curriculum.

★ **Narrative Writing** Have students imagine that they are ancient artisans commissioned to make something for their king. Have them write a paragraph about what they will make.

★ **Math** Show students two free-form forms and have them use the attributes to describe how the two solids are alike or different.

★ **Science** Discuss how students could classify and sequence organisms, objects, and events based on properties and patterns, such as free-form forms.

★ **Social Studies** Discuss the roles of kings in ancient art.

★ **Technology** Show the students a mouse and point out that the ergonomic design is a free-form form. Visit **SRAonline.com** to print detailed instructions for this activity.

Reflect

Time: About 10 minutes

Review and Assess

"Explain the difference between free-form forms and free-form shapes." "Expliquen la diferencia entre las formas abstractas y las figuras abstractas".

Think

This student used free-form forms when she made her deer.

■ Use *Large Prints 27 Canteleve* and *28 Howl* to have students identify free-form forms.

■ Have students identify stories and constructions in this lesson's artwork.

■ Have students identify ideas of the artists in this lesson's art.

Informal Assessment

Art Journal: Critical Thinking
Have students answer the four art criticism questions—Describe, Analyze, Interpret, and Decide—in the Critical Thinking section of their Art Journals. In small groups, have students explain how their reliefs describe them. Ask students to define their reasons for preferences in their art. Then have them identify ideas in their peers' art.

■ For standardized-format test practice using this lesson's art content, see pages 20–21 in *Reading and Writing Test Preparation.*

Free-Form Forms

Extra! For the Art Specialist

Time: About 45 minutes

Focus

Study **Large Print 27** and ask students to find free-form forms. Can they think of other things that are free-form forms?

Teach

Explain to students that they will create a free-form form from clay. Demonstrate clay techniques for the students. Encourage them to create free-form forms that are not animals or people, but rather abstract forms. Have students complete the Alternate Activity.

Reflect

Have students evaluate their artwork using the four steps of art criticism.

Alternate Activity

Materials:
- clay
- clay tools
- mats
- brushes, water dishes, and watercolor paints

1. Discuss free-form forms and what an abstract object looks like.

2. Form a ball with the clay and pinch out an abstract form.

3. Add details to your form using the clay tools.

4. After your form has been fired, paint it using the watercolor paints.

Research

A pilot project evaluation of the effects of arts education showed that "when students spend additional time in arts programs their performance in other school subjects does not decline." Teachers do not need to be afraid that devoting class time to arts education will hurt students' studies in other curricula areas ("The Arts in Basic Curriculum Project: Looking at the Past and Preparing for the Future" in *Critical Links,* p. 90).

Assessment

Use the following rubric to evaluate the artwork students make in the Creative Expression activity and to assess students' understanding of free-form forms.

Have students complete page 23 or 24 in their *Assessment* books.

	Art History and Culture	Aesthetic Perception	Creative Expression	Art Criticism
3 POINTS	The student can identify the role of kings in ancient cultures and compare how kings are depicted in two works of art.	The student accurately identifies free-form forms in his or her environment.	The student's relief clearly illustrates a good use of free-form forms.	The student thoughtfully and honestly evaluates his or her own work using the four steps of art criticism.
2 POINTS	The student's identification or comparison is weak or incomplete.	The student shows emerging awareness of free-form forms but cannot consistently identify them.	The student's relief clearly illustrates a good use of free-form forms.	The student attempts to evaluate his or her own work but shows an incomplete understanding of evaluation criteria.
1 POINT	The student cannot identify the role of kings or compare the depiction of kings in different works of art.	The student cannot identify free-form forms.	The student's relief shows some awareness of free-form forms.	The student does not attempt to evaluate his or her own artwork.

Assessment, p. 23

Name _____ Date _____

Lesson **2** UNIT 2

Free-Form Forms

A Matching
Match each picture to the correct word.
form   shape

B Writing
Explain the difference between a free-form form and a free-form shape.

Level 2   Unit 2 • Space and Form   **23**

Lesson

3 Body Forms

Overview

Lesson 3 introduces students to body forms. Body forms are a special type of free-form forms.

Objectives

 Art History and Culture

To compare the roles of clowns and hunters in art created by a Pueblo artist and an Inuit artist

 Creative Expression

To make clay figures that describe the students' cultures

 Aesthetic Perception

To recognize and describe body forms in people in students' environments

Art Criticism

To evaluate own work using the four steps of art criticism

Vocabulary Vocabulary

Review the following vocabulary words with students before beginning the lesson.

body form *forma corporal*—a three-dimensional representation of a person

statue *estatua*—three-dimensional art that is a body form

See page 89B for additional vocabulary and Spanish vocabulary resources.

Art Journal: Vocabulary

Have students add these words to the Vocabulary section of their Art Journals.

Lesson Materials
- white or red clay
- wooden ice-cream sticks
- clay tools
- pencil
- fabric to cover table
- slip
- kiln

Alternate Materials
- air dry clay

Program Resources
- *Reading and Writing Test Prep.*, pp. 22–23
- *Transparency 9*
- *Artist Profiles*, pp. 4, 59
- *Animals Through History Time Line*
- *Assessment*, pp. 25–26
- *Large Prints 27 Canteleve*
- *Art Around the World Collection*

Concept Trace
Body Forms
Introduced: Level 1, Unit 4, Lesson 4
Reinforced: Level 3, Unit 2, Lesson 4

Lesson 3 Arts Integration

Theatre

Complete Unit 2, Lesson 3 on pages 40–41 of the *Theatre Arts Connections* book.

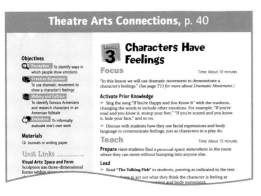

Music

Listen to "Minuet" from *Eine Kleine Nachtmusik*. Determine that this is in A-B-A form. Use scarves to move to the music. How do the students' body forms change in the middle section? Does the melodic line correspond to the shapes of the movements?

Movement & Dance

In many cultures, dance, music, and storytelling are used to relay information and pass on tales. Gestures are often used to show actions, express emotions, and imitate. Select a short story, and identify the action words in it. As the story is read, have students respond to selected words, phrases, or parts by depicting them through gesture and movement.

Focus

Activate Prior Knowledge

"Do you know what a paper doll is?" "¿Saben lo que es un muñeco de papel?"

- Discuss student responses. Explain that a paper doll is a body shape and a regular doll is a body form.

Using Literature ⭐ Reading

- Have students read selections from *Children of the Midnight Sun* by Tricia Brown. Discuss where they see body forms in the book.

Thematic Connection ⭐ Reading

- **Native Americans:** Discuss the significance of art in Native American cultures.

Introduce the Art NSAE 2.a

Look

"Look closely at the two statues." "Observen detalladamente las dos estatuas".

- Have students identify body forms in the artwork and their environments.

- Have students compare the ways individuals are depicted in these works of art.

Diversity ⭐ Social Studies

- Have students discuss the cultural context in which they think these two statues were created. Can they learn things about the two different cultures from looking at the statues? Answers will vary. Students may deduce that the clowns and stripes are important in Pueblo culture. When looking at *Seal Hunter*, students may guess that the person who created it lives in a cold climate.

NSAE 4.a, 4.b, 4.c, 5.b

🏺 Art History and Culture

Possible answer: Clowns and hunters are very important in both cultures. Hunters provide food for a society and the clowns are part of the culture's rituals.

💻 Web Connection

Visit www.eggsplore.com/rox.html for an explanation of how Swentzell makes her statues.

Body Forms

◄ **Roxanne Swentzell.** (Pueblo). *The Emergence of the Clowns.* 1988.

Coiled and scraped clay. Approx. 22 × 50 × 44 inches (55.88 × 127 × 111.76 cm.). Heard Museum, Phoenix, Arizona.

Look at the **statues** on these pages. *The Emergence of the Clowns* was made by layering **coils** of clay and then scraping them so they look smooth. *Seal Hunter* was carved from one piece of stone using **hand tools**. Both artists made **body forms**.

🏺 Art History and Culture

What role do you think clowns and hunters played in the societies these statues were created in?

🏺 Art History and Culture

Roxanne Swentzell

Roxanne Swentzell (rokz´ an swent´ zəl)(1962–) is an artist from the Santa Clara Pueblo in New Mexico and is one of the most respected Native American potters. The word *nung* means both "clay" and "people" in the Pueblo language. Clay is important to the traditional Pueblo people for pottery making and religious reasons. *The Emergence of the Clowns* shows the Koshares, a clan of Pueblo sacred clowns. The Koshares are funny tricksters, but they are also important people in Pueblo society. By using her culture's symbols of Koshares and clay, Swentzell is explaining her beliefs in a story of how the Pueblo came into existence.

See pages 24–25 and 16–21 for more about art history and subject matter.

Artist Profiles, p. 59

Artist Profile

Roxanne Swentzell
b. 1962

Roxanne Swentzell (rokz´ an swent´ zal) was born in Taos, New Mexico. She is half Native American. When she was a little girl she watched her mother make pots out of the clay surrounding their home. Swentzell liked to shape clay into figures. She had a hard time talking to other people, and tried to express her feelings through the figurines she made from clay. Her family saw that she was very talented. As a teenager she attended the Institute of American Indian Arts and the Portland Museum Art School. She went to college at the Pacific Northwest College of Art. She currently works and lives in Santa Clara, New Mexico.

Study the two statues to learn more about body forms.

▶ What do you think the people in the statues are doing?

▶ How do the artists use forms to make the statues seem alive?

Aesthetic Perception

Seeing Like an Artist Look closely at the people you see every day. Every person has a different body form. Describe some of the forms using art terms.

Unit 2 • Lesson 3   **75**

Art History and Culture

Kiawak Ashoona

Kiawak Ashoona (kē ə wak ə shōō nə) (1933–) was born in Canada. He taught himself how to carve and has been exhibiting art on a regular basis since 1953. Ashoona is a pioneer of Inuit art and has inspired the younger generation of Inuit artists. Most Inuit art depicts traditional scenes, such as family life, everyday people, arctic wildlife, or religious icons. Many Inuit carvers use stone that is native to their regions. Ashoona is known for his attention to detail in his sculptures, which are all done by hand.

See pages 24–25 and 16–21 for more about art history and subject matter.

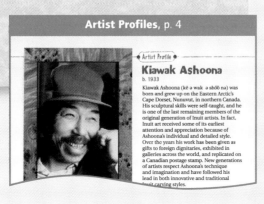

Artist Profiles, p. 4

Artist Profile
Kiawak Ashoona
b. 1933

Kiawak Ashoona (kē ə wak ə shōō nə) was born and grew up on the Eastern Arctic's Cape Dorset, Nunuvut, in northern Canada. His sculptural skills were self-taught, and he is one of the last remaining members of the original generation of Inuit artists. In fact, Inuit art received some of its earliest attention and appreciation because of Ashoona's individual and detailed style. Over the years his work has been given as gifts to foreign dignitaries, exhibited in galleries across the world, and replicated on a Canadian postage stamp. New generations of artists respect Ashoona's technique and imagination and have followed his lead in both innovative and traditional Inuit carving styles.

Study

▶ Answers may vary. The clowns are coming out of the ground. The figure of the man looks as if he is getting ready to go out and hunt.

▶ Both of these artists used forms of people who were in the middle of doing something. This makes the people look more alive, since they appear to be mid-action.

▪ For more examples of art from North America see the *Art Around the World Collection.*

Art Journal: Comparing
Have students compare body shapes and body forms in the Concepts section of their Art Journals. How are they alike and different?

Aesthetic Perception

Seeing Like an Artist Discuss how no two people are exactly alike, so no two people have the same body form. Encourage students to think about the body forms of the people in their families and have them use art terminology when describing the forms. Have students identify variations in subjects from the environment.
NSAE 2.b, 5.c

Developing Visual Literacy Discuss what each artwork means to the artist and what the artists are trying to say with their art. What are the main ideas of these works of art?

Web Connection
Visit **http://cybermuse.gallery.ca/cybermuse/search/artist_work_e.jsp?iartistid=2904** to see a gallery of Ashoona's artwork and hear an audio clip about one of his sculptures.

 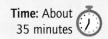

Teach

Time: About 35 minutes

"How can you use body forms to show an action?" "¿Cómo pueden usar las formas corporales para mostrar una acción?"

- Read and discuss the information about body forms on page 76.

Practice

Materials: red or white clay, wooden ice-cream sticks, clay tools, pencils, fabric to cover table

Alternate Materials: air-dry clay

- Distribute the materials and have students follow the directions on page 76.

- Have students identify and practice skills necessary for producing modeled forms by using a variety of materials.

Creative Expression

NSAE 1.c, 1.d, 2.c, 3.b
Materials: red or white clay, wooden ice-cream sticks, clay tools, pencils, fabric to cover table, kiln

Alternate Materials: air-dry clay

- Distribute materials and have students follow the directions on page 77.

- Encourage students to express feelings and ideas in their clay figures by using a variety of forms.

- Encourage students to create effective compositions by using design elements.

- Review the Activity Tips on page 236 for visual examples of the activity if needed.

- Review the Technique Tips on pages 225–226 for instructions on working with clay.

Art Journal: Planning NSAE 3.a

Have students think of ways they can describe their culture in their sculptures. Then have them write their plans in the Ideas section of their Art Journals.

Using Body Forms

Body forms are three-dimensional versions of body shapes.

Body forms can be shown in many different positions, just like real bodies. Bodies are forms because they have height, width, and depth.

Practice

Make a hand or foot out of clay.

1. Use the clay your teacher gives you to make a hand or foot.

2. Pinch apart the clay to make fingers or toes. Think about how hands and feet work.

3. Look around at other students' work. Can you see what they created?

Differentiated Instruction

Reteach	Special Needs	ELL Tips
Point to different body parts and have the students call out the names of those parts.	Some students may find it helpful to look at themselves from different vantage points in a mirror so they can successfully render their form in clay.	Review free-form shapes, free form forms, and lines that show movement. Play "Freeze" and when a students freezes, model clay to represent his or her action.

◀ **Sarah Leggett.**
Age 7.

Think about how this student described herself using body forms.

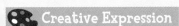 **Creative Expression**

Can you make a body form to describe your culture?

1. Decide how your body form will represent your culture.

2. Make the parts of your body form from the clay your teacher gives you. Join the pieces together using slip and scoring.

3. Add details to your body form by using a pencil to etch lines and shapes.

 **Art Criticism**

Describe How did you illustrate your culture in your body form?

Analyze Where are the three dimensions in your form?

Interpret What would you title your body form?

Decide What other forms could you make to illustrate your culture?

 **Reflect** **Time:** About 10 minutes

Review and Assess

Can you explain the difference between a body form and a body shape? "¿Pueden explicar la diferencia entre una forma corporal y una figura corporal?"

Think

This student used body forms to show herself in a hammock.

■ Use *Large Print 27 Canteleve* to have students find an abstract body form.

■ Have students search for and identify stories and constructions in this lesson's artwork.

■ Have students identify the ideas of the artists in this lesson's art.

Informal Assessment

> **Art Journal: Critical Thinking**
> Have students answer the four art criticism questions—Describe, Analyze, Interpret, and Decide—in the Critical Thinking section of their Art Journals. Have students break into small groups and describe how their sculptures describe their cultures. Ask students to define their reasons for preferences in their art. Then have them identify ideas in their peers' art.

■ For standardized-format test practice using this lesson's art content, see pages 22–23 in *Reading and Writing Test Preparation.*

Art Across the Curriculum   NSAE 6.a, 6.b

Use these simple ideas to reinforce art concepts across the curriculum.

★ **Expository Writing** Have students write an expository paragraph about how Inuits and Roxanne Swentzell create their sculptures.

★ **Math** Discuss the golden ratio with students and its place in ancient sculpture.

★ **Science** Discuss the properties of clay and serpentine. For example, how hard they are, how porous they are, and so on.

★ **Social Studies** Investigate how the Santa Clara Pueblo and the Inuit cultures came to settle where they did.

★ **Technology** Discuss how CGI animation can be used to create body forms. Visit **SRAonline.com** to print out detailed instructions for this activity.

Body Forms

Wrap-Up

Extra! For the Art Specialist

Time: About 45 minutes

Focus

Have students look in a mirror and describe their body forms using art words.

Teach

Explain to students that they will create a body form using papier-mâché. Students will cover several differently shaped balloons using newspaper and papier-mâché. Each student will need one round balloon for the head, one long balloon for the torso, and four smaller long balloons for the arms and legs. After the pieces are dry, student will paint them using tempera. Then the teacher should pop the balloons and sew the various pieces together using leather cord or twine. Demonstrate the papier-mâché process and have students complete the Alternate Activity.

Reflect

Have students evaluate their body forms using the four steps of art criticism.

Alternate Activity

Materials:

- balloons of various shapes and sizes, blown up
- newspaper, torn into strips
- wheat paste
- tempera paints
- brushes, water dishes
- cord or twine
- hole punch

1. Select the forms you will use to make your body form. Cover them carefully with the newspaper strips and wheat paste the way your teacher showed you.

2. Once your forms are dry, decorate them by painting them with the tempera paints.

3. Give your forms to your teacher so he or she can assemble them.

Research in Art Education

"Children respond to art in a holistic manner; their reactions are immediate, subjective, and rarely go beyond the 'like/don't like' stage . . . It takes a sensitive teacher to help educate the vision of the child so that appreciation may occur" (Hurwitz, Al, and Stanley Madeja. *The Joyous Vision.* New Jersey: Prentice Hall, 1997).

Assessment

Use the following rubric to evaluate the artwork students make in the Creative Expression activity and to assess students' understanding of body forms.

Have students complete page 25 or 26 in their *Assessment* books.

	Art History and Culture	Aesthetic Perception	Creative Expression	Art Criticism
3 POINTS	The student can identify the roles of clowns and kings in Pueblo and Inuit cultures and compare how they are depicted in two works of art.	The student accurately identifies body forms in his or her environment.	The student's sculpture clearly illustrates a good use of body forms.	The student thoughtfully and honestly evaluates his or her own work using the four steps of art criticism.
2 POINTS	The student's identification or comparison is weak or incomplete.	The student shows emerging awareness of body forms but cannot consistently identify them.	The student's sculpture shows some awareness of body forms.	The student attempts to evaluate his or her own work but shows an incomplete understanding of evaluation criteria.
1 POINT	The student cannot identify the roles of clowns or kings in Pueblo and Inuit culture or compare their depiction in different works of art.	The student cannot identify body forms.	The student's sculpture shows no understanding of body forms.	The student does not attempt to evaluate his or her own artwork.

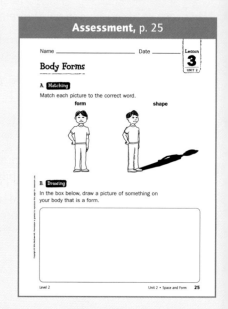

Assessment, p. 25

Name _____ Date _____ Lesson **3** UNIT 2

Body Forms

A. Matching

Match each picture to the correct word.

form   shape

B. Drawing

In the box below, draw a picture of something on your body that is a form.

Level 2   Unit 2 • Space and Form **25**

Animal Forms

Lesson 4 explains what animal forms are. Animal forms are a kind of free-form form.

Objectives

 Art History and Culture

To identify and compare the use of animal forms in early American and African utilitarian works of art.

Creative Expression

To create a clay figure that illustrates animal forms

 **Aesthetic Perception**

To identify animal forms in students' environments

Art Criticism

To evaluate own work using the four steps of art criticism

Vocabulary Vocabulary

Review the following vocabulary words with students before beginning the lesson.

earthenware loza de barro—ceramics made of porous clay and fired at a low heat

brass latón—a metal made by combining copper and zinc

animal form forma animal—a three-dimensional representation of an animal

See page 89B for additional Spanish vocabulary resources.

Art Journal: Vocabulary

Have students add these words to the Vocabulary section of their Art Journals.

Lesson Materials

- red or white clay, rolled into small balls for each student
- clay tools
- fabric to cover work area
- slip made from water and clay, mixed and softened to a milkshake consistency
- kiln

Alternate Materials:
- Glaze or acrylics to paint animal form
- air dry clay

Program Resources

- *Reading and Writing Test Prep.*, pp. 24–25
- *Transparency 10*
- *Artist Profiles*, pp. 7, 75
- *Animals Through History Time Line*
- *Assessment*, pp. 27–28
- *Large Print 28* Howl
- *National Museum of Women in the Arts Collection*

Concept Trace

Animal Forms

Introduced: Level K, Unit 4, Lesson 5

Reinforced: Level 3, Unit 2, Lesson 4

Lesson 4 Arts Integration

Theatre

Complete Unit 2, Lesson 4 on pages 42–43 of the *Theatre Arts Connections* book.

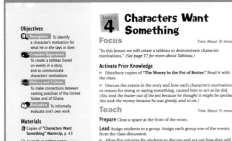

Theatre Arts Connections, p. 42

Music

 Sometimes you can recognize an animal in music by the composer's melodies, dynamics, and rhythm. If you have knowledge of the animal, and perhaps its sound and body shape, you can enjoy guessing the animals represented in each section of *The Carnival of the Animals*. Contrast the music of "The Elephant" and Modest Mussorgsky's "Ballet of the Unhatched Chicks." Discuss why you would identify the music with the animal.

Movement & Dance

Identify the five categories of vertebrae animals: mammals, reptiles, amphibians, birds, and fish. Look at pictures of the animals, and discuss the similarities and differences among their forms and how they move. Explore the movements of each type of vertebrae animal. Give attention to the energy, weight, size, and motion of each.

 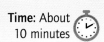

Activate Prior Knowledge

"What kind of animal shapes can you think of?" "¿En qué formas animales pueden pensar?"

■ Discuss student responses. Explain that artists often use animal forms in art or when designing household tools.

Using Literature ⭐ Reading

■ Read *Hiding Out* by James Martin. Discuss the animal forms students see in the book.

Thematic Connection ⭐ Reading

■ **Useful Objects:** Encourage students to discuss tools or objects that are useful in everyday life. How might animals be useful in everyday life?

Introduce the Art NSAE 2.a

Look

"Let's take a close look at the two animal forms." "Vamos a obervar detalladamente las dos formas animales".

■ Have students identify forms in the artwork and students' environments.

Hypothesizing ⭐ Science

■ Tell students that when *Figure of a Lion* and *Leopard Aquamanile* were made, they were both used to help with common chores. Ask students to hypothesize what these animal forms were used for. Student answers will vary. Some answers might center on the fact that both works of art look as though they are heavy.

NSAE 4.a, 4.b, 4.c, 5.a, 5.b

 Art History and Culture

Possible answer: The animals represented something significant to the artists, either because of their culture, or because of the jobs the tools were used for.

 Web Connection

Visit **http://www.folkartmuseum.org/afam_ frames.asp?platform=win&browser=ie&ver=6** to view selections from the American Folk Art Museum's permanent collection.

◀ **Attributed to John Bell.** (American). *Figure of a Lion.* c. 1850–1860.
....
Glazed red earthenware. 8 x 8 $\frac{1}{2}$ × 4 $\frac{1}{2}$ inches (20.32 × 21.59 × 11.43 cm). American Folk Art Museum, New York, New York.

Look at these two animals. The lion was used as a doorstop and is **earthenware.** The leopard is a special type of pitcher and is **brass.** Both of these are **animal forms.**

 Art History and Culture

Why do you think the artists chose to use animal forms for these household tools?

Art History and Culture

John Bell

John Bell (jän bel) (1800–1880) was born in Pennsylvania and was the son of a master potter. Bell established his pottery in Waynesboro, Pennsylvania. He produced many unique pieces of pottery because he liked experimenting with glazes and clay. When Confederate troops marched through Pennsylvania during the Civil War, they used the rooster weather vane on Bell's pottery for target practice. Bell liked making animal forms. He would often make small animals from balls of clay for school children. *Figure of a Lion* was most likely used as a doorstop in a home.

See pages 24–25 and 16–21 for more about art history and subject matter.

Artist Profiles, p. 7

⊹ Artist Profile ⊹

John Bell

John Bell (jän bel) was born in 1800 in Hagerstown, Pennsylvania. From a very young age he was fascinated with creating clay objects. As a young adult, Bell opened his own pottery studio in Waynesboro, Pennsylvania. He and his wife, Mary Elisabeth, had nine children and enjoyed a comfortable lifestyle, thanks to the successful sales of his pottery. Bell died in Waynesboro in 1880. His five sons all became ceramic artists. They followed in their father's artistic footsteps and continued the family's pottery business.

▲ **Attributed to John Bell.** (American). *Figure of a Lion.* 1850–1860.

◀ **Artist Unknown, Court of Benin.** (Nigeria). *Leopard Aquamanile.* 16th–19th century.

Brass. 7 $\frac{7}{8}$ inches (20 cm.). The Metropolitan Museum of Art, New York, New York.

Study the two animals and look at their forms.

▶ Do the animals look like they are moving or like they are standing still?

▶ Are the animals realistic?

▶ What do you think these animal forms were used for?

Aesthetic Perception

Seeing Like an Artist Look at your pet or favorite stuffed animal. Can you see the animal form?

Study

▶ The two animals look like they are standing still.

▶ The lion is more realistic than the leopard, but both are stylized.

▶ Answers will vary. Students should use their imaginations.

■ For more example of utilitarian art see *The National Museum of Women in the Arts Collection.*

Art Journal: Questioning

Ask students to write questions they have about body shapes in the Concepts section of their Art Journals. Have them reflect on their questions and try to answer them.

Aesthetic Perception

Seeing Like an Artist Have students think about stuffed animals and pets. These are common animal forms that most students have seen at some point in time. How would they describe these animal forms? Have students identify variations in the subjects from the environment. NSAE 2.b, 5.c

Developing Visual Literacy Ask the students to imagine what the artists were saying when they chose to use leopards and lions for the everyday tools. What might the animals symbolize to the people who made and used them?

Art History and Culture

Court of Benin

Although there is a present day Benin, the art in this lesson is from the ancient Court of Benin (1300?–1897). Benin art gained attention in 1897 when British soldiers brought it back as plunder from a military expedition. Although the British had burnt the wooden city of Benin, most of the art was brass, bronze, and ivory and survived the destruction. Aquamanile were used for hand washing in palace rituals and in day-to-day life. They are pitchers with hinged openings that were filled with water. The leopard was a common animal aquamanile, as the leopard is a symbol of the Oba, or divine king. Because of its resistance to corrosion, the people of Benin, saw brass as a symbol of the stability of their monarchy.

See pp. 24–25 and 16–21 for more about art history and subject matter.

Artist Profiles, p. 75

⌐ Artist Profile ⌐

Leopard Aquamanile

This aquamanile was made by an unknown artist of the Edo people of the Court of Benin. The majority of Edo people today live in the neighboring nations of Benin and Nigeria in west Africa. The artistic and cultural traditions of these people have been well maintained through the years to the present day. The word *aquamanile* refers to a hollow vessel used to pour water for washing the hands.

◀ **Artist unknown,** Court of Benin. (Nigeria). *Leopard Aquamanile.* 16th–19th century.

Web Connection

Visit **www.artsmia.org/animals/leopard/art_6.html** to see another example of a leopard aquamanile.

each **Time:** About 35 minutes

"How can you use animal forms to describe animals?" "¿Cómo pueden usar formas animales para describir animales?"

- Read and discuss the information about animal forms on page 80.

Practice

Materials: red or white clay, clay tools, slip, fabric to cover work area, kiln

Alternate Materials: air-dry clay

- Distribute materials and have students follow the directions on page 80.

- Have students identify and practice skills necessary for producing modeled forms by using a variety of materials.

- Fire students' pieces once they are dry.

Creative Expression

NSAE 1.c, 1.d, 2.c, 3.b
Materials: red or white clay, clay tools, fabric to cover work area, slip, kiln

Alternate Materials: glaze or school acrylics

- Distribute the materials and have students follow the directions on page 81.

- Encourage students to express feelings and ideas in their clay animals by using a variety of forms.

- Encourage students to create effective compositions by using design elements.

- Review the Activity Tips on page 236 for visual example of techniques if needed.

- Fire the students' pieces once they are dry. Allow students to glaze their pieces if time permits.

Art Journal: Sketching NSAE 3.a
Have students sketch ideas for animal form tools they could make and write a brief description of how each would be a useful object. Have them pick their favorite idea and implement that idea in the Creative Expression activity.

Using Animal Forms

Artists use animal forms to show viewers all parts of an animal. Like people, animals have height, width, and depth. When an artist uses an animal form, we can see what the animal looks like from all angles.

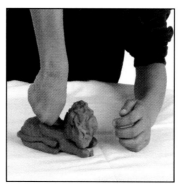

Practice

Can you make a form that can also be used as a bowl? Practice making forms.

1. Think about your favorite animal.

2. Mold your animal form out of clay.

3. Make a depression in your animal form so it can be used as a bowl.

Differentiated Instruction

Reteach
Ask students to find pictures of animals in magazines. Have students compare the pictures they find to the clay animals they created.

Special Needs
If using Plasticine clay, ensure that it has been heated so that it is not difficult for students with limited upper-body strength to manipulate.

ELL Tips
Reinforce the concepts of *two-dimensional* and *three-dimensional*. Ask which animals students think have the most interesting forms. Discuss each animal.

◀ **J. T. Larrison.**
Age 8.

Think about how this student created an animal form. How could it be used as a tool?

 **Creative Expression**

How would you make an animal form tool? Construct an animal form using clay.

1. Think about a four-legged animal form you would like to make.

2. Create your animal form. Score your clay and use slip when joining two pieces.

3. Carve details in the clay.

 **Art Criticism**

Describe How did you create your animal form?

Analyze Where is the depth on your animal form?

Interpret How is your animal form different from an animal shape?

Decide How could you use your animal form as a tool?

Art Across the Curriculum

NSAE 6.a, 6.b

Use these simple ideas to reinforce art concepts across the curriculum.

★ **Personal Writing** Have students write a letter to a friend to describe an animal form they have seen.

★ **Math** Discuss how to figure out how long ago John Bell lived.

★ **Science** Discuss the habitats of lions and leopards.

★ **Social Studies** Discuss colonization and its impact on the world. Explain what colonization is.

★ **Technology** Ask students to think of ways in which a computer is a useful everyday object. Visit **SRAonline.com** to print detailed instructions for this activity.

 **Reflect**

Time: About 10 minutes

Review and Assess

"Can you explain the differences between an animal form and an animal shape?" "¿Pueden explicar las diferencias entre una forma animal y una figura animal?"

Think

This student's animal form could be used to hold an eraser.

■ Use *Large Print 28 Howl* to have students identify animal forms.

■ Have students search for and identify stories and constructions in this lesson's artwork.

■ Have students identify the ideas of the artists in this lesson's art.

Informal Assessment

Art Journal: Critical Thinking

Have students answer the four art criticism questions—Describe, Analyze, Interpret, and Decide—in the Critical Thinking section of their Art Journals. Have students discuss how their animal form could be used to help with an everyday task. Ask students to define their reasons for preferences in their art. Then have them identify ideas in their peers' art.

■ For standardized-format test practice using this lesson's art content, see pages 24–25 in *Reading and Writing Test Preparation.*

Animal Forms

Extra! For the Art Specialist

Time: About 45 minutes

Focus

Study *Large Print 28* and ask the students to describe the animal form they see.

Teach

Explain to students that they will create an animal form out of construction paper. They will use folding and cutting techniques to form their animals and make them stand upright. Demonstrate how to start an animal by folding a piece of paper in half and cutting out the negative space between the legs. Feet can be folded so that the animal stands, and other parts can be added by gluing. Have the students complete the Alternate Activity.

Reflect

Have students evaluate their artwork using the four steps of art criticism.

Alternate Activity

Materials:
• colored construction paper
• pencils
• scissors
• colored markers

1. Discuss animal forms. Select a piece of construction paper for the body. Fold it in half and draw a side view of your animal.

2. Cut out the animal. Make sure you do not cut out the entire folded edge, or your animal will not stand up.

3. Add parts to your animal using paper and glue. Add other details using markers. Stand your animal up.

Research in Art Education

It is important that arts education not only be present, but also "rich and continuous" in order to receive the full benefits it can add to "learning and instruction that is critical to health development." These benefits include higher levels of cooperation, creativity, and problem-solving skills ("Learning in and Through the Arts: Curriculum Implications" in *Champions of Change*, p. 36).

Assessment

Use the following rubric to evaluate the artwork students make in the Creative Expression activity and to assess students' understanding of animal forms.

Have students complete page 27 or 28 in their *Assessment* books.

	Art History and Culture	Aesthetic Perception	Creative Expression	Art Criticism
3 POINTS	The student can identify and compare the use of animal forms in utilitarian art.	The student accurately identifies animal forms in his or her environment.	The student's sculpture clearly illustrates a good use of animal forms.	The student thoughtfully and honestly evaluates his or her own work using the four steps of art criticism.
2 POINTS	The student's identification or comparison is weak or incomplete.	The student shows emerging awareness of animal forms but cannot consistently identify them.	The student's sculpture shows some awareness of animal forms.	The student attempts to evaluate his or her own work but shows an incomplete understanding of evaluation criteria.
1 POINT	The student cannot identify or compare the use of animal forms in different works of art.	The student cannot identify animal forms.	The student's sculpture shows no understanding of animal forms.	The student makes no attempt to evaluate his or her own artwork.

Assessment, p. 27

Name _____ Date _____

Animal Forms

Lesson 4 UNIT 2

A. Matching
Match each picture to the correct word.

shape   form

B. Short Answer
List three animal forms that you have seen.

_____

_____

Level 2   Unit 2 • Space and Form   **27**

Lesson 5 Overview

People and Space

Lesson 5 explains how artists create depth in paintings by overlapping body shapes.

Objectives

 Art History and Culture

To compare the portrayal of women in families in two paintings

 Creative Expression

To create a paper cutout that illustrates overlapping body shapes to create depth

 Aesthetic Perception

To identify overlapping body shapes in students' environments

 Art Criticism

To evaluate own work using the four steps of art criticism

Lesson Materials
- construction paper, white paper
- crayons, markers
- glue
- scissors

Alternate Materials:
- scrap paper

Program Resources
- *Reading and Writing Test Prep.*, p. 26–27
- *Transparency 11*
- *Artist Profiles*, pp. 49, 55
- *Animals Through History Time Line*
- *Assessment*, pp. 29–30
- *Large Prints 27* Canteleve
- *The National Museum of Women in the Arts Collection*

Concept Trace
People and Space
Introduced: Level 1, Unit 4, Lesson 6

Reinforced: Level 3, Unit 2, Lessons 2–3

Vocabulary ⭐ Vocabulary

Review the following vocabulary word with students before beginning the lesson.

overlap superponer—to rest on top of and partly cover something

See page 89B for additional Spanish vocabulary resources.

Art Journal: Vocabulary

Have students add this word to the Vocabulary section of their Art Journals.

Lesson 5 Arts Integration

Theatre

Complete Unit 2, Lesson 5 on pages 44–45 of *Theatre Arts Connections* book.

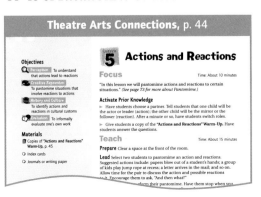

Music

When children sing a round, or canon, the melody overlaps. *Frere Jacque* and *Row, Row, Row, Your Boat* can be sung to illustrate this. Divide the class into two groups. One group begins singing. Four beats later, the second group begins, starting at the beginning of the song while the first section continues. At the end of the song, the first group will end first, and the second group will end four beats later.

Movement & Dance

Have students walk freely to the beat of a drum. When the drum stops, have students take four counts to create a shape that connects to two or three people closest to them. Have students try overlapping shapes, reaching through empty space, and exploring different levels. Have students repeat the sequence, finding new people to connect to.

 **ocus**

Time: About 10 minutes

Activate Prior Knowledge

"What does a family standing together in a cluster look like?" "¿A qué se parece una familia parada en grupo?"

- Discuss student responses. Explain that usually when a group of people stands or sits together, one person is closer to you than the others. The people who are closer overlap the people who are farther away.

Using Literature ★ Reading

- Read *Dumpling Soup* by Jama Kim Rattigan and discuss families. Have students look for overlapping in the families in the book.

Thematic Connection ★ Reading

- **Families:** Discuss the different kinds of families that exist. For example: nuclear families and extended families.

Introduce the Art   NSAE 2.a

Look

"Look closely at *Jungle Tales* and *Two Sisters*." "Miren detalladamente *Jungle Tales* y *Two Sisters*".

- Have students identify space and overlapping in the works of art and the environment.

- Have students compare the ways families are depicted in these works of art.

Main Idea and Details ★ Reading

- Have students discuss where they think the families in these pictures are. Can they learn things about the two families by looking at the details? What kind of details do they see? Answers may vary. Students will probably point out that the girls in *Jungle Tales* are ready for bed and that the sisters in *Two Sisters* are outdoors.

NSAE 4.a, 4.b, 4.c, 5.b

 Art History and Culture

Possible answer: None of the women in these paintings are working. They are reading or doing other relaxing things.

 Web Connection

Visit http://americanart.si.edu/t2go/1ga/index-frame.html and select artwork 46 to see a portrait Shannon painted of his wife and daughter.

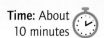 **Lesson 5** People and Space

Look at the girls in these paintings. You cannot see the entire girl in the center of *Jungle Tales*. Other bodies **overlap** the girl and hide her. In *Two Sisters,* the younger sister overlaps the older sister. Overlapping creates depth in a painting.

▲ **James J. Shannon.** (American). *Jungle Tales.* 1895.

Oil on canvas. 34 ½ × 44 ¾ inches (86.99 × 113.67 cm.). The Metropolitan Museum of Art, New York, New York.

 Art History and Culture

What do these paintings tell you about the role of women in families at this time?

 Art History and Culture

Sir James J. Shannon

James Shannon (jāmz sha´ nən) (1862–1923) was born in New York to Irish parents. He was interested in art at a young age and moved to England in 1878 to study art. Shannon would end up living in England for the rest of his life. He was a famous portrait painter, but Shannon also enjoyed painting every day scenes using his wife and daughter as models. *Jungle Tales* was created in 1895; the year after Rudyard Kipling published *The Jungle Book.*

See pages 24–25 and 16–21 for more about art history and subject matter.

Artist Profiles, p. 55

♦ Artist Profile ♦

James J. Shannon
1862-1923

Known as J. J., James Jebusa Shannon (jāmz sha´ nən) was born in New York to Irish parents. Even as a boy, he showed drawing talent, so he was sent to England in 1878 to study at the Royal College of Art. Several of his instructors at the college were French artists. A promising student, Shannon was asked to paint a portrait of a female staff member of the queen. This picture marked the beginning of his career as a portrait painter.

◄ **Orlando Rouland.** (American). *J. J. Shannon, R. A.* c. 1910.

Oil on fabric canvas mounted on fiberboard. 45 ¼ × 34¼ inches (115.4 × 87 cm.).

Study the two works of art to find overlapping people.

▶ What are the people doing in these two works of art?

▶ What parts of people are covered up by overlapping?

▶ Which people are farther away from you?

◀ **Auguste Renoir.** (French). *Two Sisters (On the Terrace).* 1881.

Oil on canvas. 40 × 32 inches (100.5 × 81 cm.). The Art Institute of Chicago, Chicago, Illinois.

Aesthetic Perception

Seeing Like an Artist Think about what your family looks like when you sit or stand together. Do any of you overlap?

Art History and Culture

Pierre Auguste Renoir

Pierre Auguste Renoir (pyâr ō gōōst ren wär´) (1841–1919) was born in Limoges, France. As a child, he worked in a Parisian porcelain factory painting designs on china. Renoir was heavily influenced by other impressionists, namely Claude Monet. However, Renoir enjoyed painting portraits and families as much as he did landscapes. He was renowned for his depiction of light and human skin. In the last 20 years of his life, Renoir's arthritis was so advanced he had to strap a brush onto his arm in order to paint.

See pages 24–25 and 16–21 for more about art history and subject matter.

Artist Profiles, p. 49

Artist Profile
Pierre-Auguste Renoir
1841–1919
Pierre-Auguste Renoir (pyâr ō gōōst ren wär´) was one of the most widely known and best-loved European painters. The sixth of seven children, Renoir was born into a poor family in Limoges, France. His father was a tailor, and the family had to live in a slum, with few luxuries or comforts. Renoir showed signs of talent at an early age in many artistic fields. Although he was a talented singer, he became an apprentice at a porcelain factory, where for five years he copied French masterpieces onto plates and soup tureens. During this apprenticeship Renoir developed his brushwork and his passion for the eighteenth century French

Study

▶ Answers may vary. The girls are being read to before bed in *Jungle Tales* and the girls in *Two Sisters* look as though they just finished picking flowers.

▶ The girl farthest away in *Jungle Tales* only has her face and part of her neck showing. In *Two Sisters* the left arm of the older sister is covered.

▶ The girl looking straight ahead in *Jungle Tales* and the older sister in *Two Sisters* are farthest away.

■ For more examples of portraits see *The National Museum of Women in the Arts Collection.*

 Art Journal: Defining
Have students write their own definitions of space and overlapping in the Concepts section of their Art Journals. Encourage them to use sketches if they need to.

Aesthetic Perception

Seeing Like an Artist Encourage students to pay attention to what their families look like when they are together. How do people stand? Do they overlap? Have students identify variations in subjects from the environment.

NSAE 2.b, 5.c

Developing Visual Literacy What do you think the artists were saying about families when they painted these pictures?

 Web Connection
Visit www.mfa.org/handbook/portrait.asp?id= 267&s=6 to see and hear about another Renoir painting.

each

Time: About 35 minutes

"How can you use body shapes to show a group of people?" "¿Cómo pueden usar figuras corporales para mostrar a un grupo de personas?"

■ Read and discuss the information about people and space on page 84.

Practice

Materials: students, open space

■ Have students follow the directions on page 84.

■ Have students identify and practice techniques necessary for producing constructions by using a variety of materials.

Creative Expression

NSAE 1.c, 1.d, 2.c, 3.b
Materials: construction paper, white paper, crayons, markers, glue, scissors

Alternate Materials: scrap paper

■ Distribute the materials and have students follow the directions on page 85.

■ Encourage students to create effective compositions by using design elements.

■ Review the Activity Tips on page 237 for visual examples of the activity if needed.

NSAE 3.a
Art Journal: Brainstorming

Have students brainstorm to think of times when they have seen people standing in groups. Ask them to try and think of circumstances were they would see groups of people and write them in the Ideas section of their Art Journals.

Using People and Space

Because paintings are two-dimensional, artists can't use forms. To show depth, artists use overlapping.

By hiding part of a person, artists make it seem as if the person is behind something. That makes the viewer think the person is farther away and creates depth. Look at the picture. Which person is closest to you? Which person is farthest away?

Practice

Assemble in a group of classmates so that you overlap and create depth.

1. Break up into small groups.
2. Position yourselves so you are all overlapping.
3. Look at your group. Do you see that the person in front is overlapped by no one? Do you see that the person in back is overlapped by several people?

Differentiated Instruction

Reteach
Have students practice overlapping techniques by making a collage with people cut from magazines.

Special Needs
To check for understanding, have students identify who in their picture is the farthest away and who is the closest.

ELL Tips
Using demonstration, define *overlapping* for students. Hide different papers and books by overlapping them to create the concept of depth.

Think about how this student used overlapping to show her family playing.

 **Creative Expression**

What does a family on a playground look like from far away? Overlap shapes of people playing.

1. Think about the way your body moves when you play.

2. Use construction paper and draw a family playing. Cut out the shapes.

3. Arrange and overlap your family on white paper. Move them around until you like the way they look. Glue the shapes onto the paper.

Art Criticism

Describe What is the family in your picture doing?

Analyze Find the places in your design where figures overlap.

Interpret How would your design look different if none of the figures overlapped?

Decide What other kinds of activities could you use to show a family overlapping?

 **Reflect** Time: About 10 minutes

Review and Assess

"Can you explain how overlapping body shapes creates depth in a painting?" *"Pueden explicar cómo al sobreponer figuras corporales se crea profundidad en una pintura?"*

Think

This student used overlapping to make some members of her family look farther away.

- Use *Large Print 27* Canteleve to have students identify overlapping objects in the abstract body form.

- Have students identify ideas and constructions in this lesson's artwork.

- Have students identify the ideas of the artists in this lesson's art.

Informal Assessment

Art Journal: Critical Thinking

Have students answer the four art criticism questions—Describe, Analyze, Interpret, and Decide—in the Critical Thinking section of their Art Journals. Have each student explain to the class what his or her family is doing on the playground. Have students define their reasons for preferences in their art. Then have them identify ideas in their peers' art.

- For standardized-format test practice using this lesson's art content, see pages 26–27 in *Reading and Writing Test Preparation.*

Art Across the Curriculum NSAE 6.a, 6.b

Use these simple ideas to reinforce art concepts across the curriculum.

★ **Poetry** Have students write a poem about being in a group of people.

★ **Math** Discuss fractions in relationship to overlapping. For example, with overlapping, you may only be able to see half of a person.

★ **Science** Discuss heredity and how we inherit traits from our parents.

★ **Social Studies** Discuss how to describe the order of events by using labels of time periods such as ancient times and modern times. Discuss how time periods can overlap.

★ **Technology** Show students how to arrange clip art of people so that they are overlapping. Visit **SRAonline.com** to print detailed instructions for this activity.

People and Space

Extra! For the Art Specialist

Time: About 45 minutes

Focus

Have students look through the *Large Prints* and *Student Edition* to find other examples of body shapes overlapping.

Teach

Discuss overlapping with students. Explain to students that they will work as a class to build a city full of people using overlapping. Students will draw a cityscape on large paper. Students will then cut out photos of people in magazines. Students will arrange and glue the "citizens" of their city as a class and use overlapping. Have students complete the Alternate Activity.

Reflect

Have students evaluate their artwork using the four steps of art criticism.

Alternate Activity

Materials:
- brushes, water containers, newspaper
- roll of butcher or drawing paper
- tempera paints
- pencils
- chalk
- scissors
- glue
- construction paper
- magazines

1. As a class, brainstorm and plan the background of your city. What buildings should be in it? Paint your city on the roll of paper.

2. Look through the magazines and find photos of people to put in your cityscape. Cut the people out.

3. Work as a class to arrange and glue down the people in your cityscape. Be sure to use overlapping to show people who are farther away.

Research in Art Education

"Talk about art, or art criticism, is probably one of the ways we share the contents of our inner lives without embarrassment. Art criticism is very much like teaching: it is the sharing of discoveries about art, or in some cases about life, where art has its ultimate source" (Hurwitz, Al, and Stanley Madeja. *The Joyous Vision.* New Jersey: Prentice Hall, 1997).

Assessment

Use the following rubric to evaluate the artwork students make in the Creative Expression activity and to assess students' understanding of body shapes and space.

Have students complete page 29 or 30 in their *Assessment* books.

	Art History and Culture	Aesthetic Perception	Creative Expression	Art Criticism
3 POINTS	The student can compare how families are depicted in two works of art.	The student accurately identifies overlapping body shapes in students' environments.	The student's collage clearly illustrates a good use of people and space.	The student thoughtfully and honestly evaluates his or her own work using the four steps of art criticism.
2 POINTS	The student's comparison is weak or incomplete.	The student shows emerging awareness of people and space but cannot consistently identify them.	The student's collage shows some awareness of people and space.	The student attempts to evaluate his or her own work but shows an incomplete understanding of evaluation criteria.
1 POINT	The student cannot compare how families are depicted in two works of art.	The student cannot identify overlapping body shapes.	The student's collage shows no understanding of people and space.	The student does not attempt to evaluate his or her own artwork.

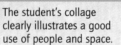

Assessment, p. 29

Name _____ Date _____ **Lesson 5** UNIT 2

People and Space

A. Drawing
Draw three overlapping people in the box below. Circle the one who is farthest away.

B. Writing
Explain what overlapping is.

Level 2   Unit 2 • Space and Form   **29**

Objects and Space

Lesson 6 explains how artists create depth in paintings by overlapping object shapes.

Objectives

 Art History and Culture

To compare the use of food in two paintings from different time periods

 Creative Expression

To create a still life that illustrates overlapping shapes to create depth

 Aesthetic Perception

To identify overlapping objects in students' environments

 Art Criticism

To evaluate own work using the four steps of art criticism

Vocabulary ⭐ Vocabulary

Review the following vocabulary word with students before beginning the lesson.

still life *naturaleza muerta*—a painting or drawing of a collection of objects that cannot move.

See page 89B for additional Spanish vocabulary resources.

 Art Journal: Vocabulary

Have students add this word to the Vocabulary section of their Art Journals.

Lesson Materials
- construction paper
- colored dustless chalk
- liquid tempera
- palettes, brushes
- newspaper
- food and other objects for still lifes
- water dishes
- paper towels

Alternate Materials:
- crayons and markers

Program Resources
- *Reading and Writing Test Prep.,* pp. 28–29
- *Transparency 12*
- *Artist Profiles,* pp. 11, 39
- *Animals Through History Time Line*
- *Assessment,* pp. 31–32
- *Large Prints 27* Canteleve and *28* Howl
- *The National Museum of Women in the Arts Collection*

Concept Trace
Objects and Space
Introduced: Level 1, Unit 4, Lesson 6
Reinforced: Level 3, Unit 2, Lessons 2–3

Lesson 6 Arts Integration

Theatre

Complete Unit 2, Lesson 6 on pages 46–51 of *Theatre Arts Connections* book.

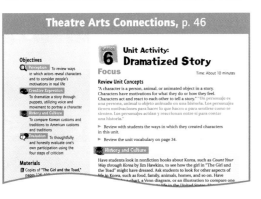

Music

 Listen to *Serenade op. 29 for Piano* by Cecile Chaminade. Just as you would sit and enjoy looking at Cezanne's *Still Life,* listen and enjoy the piano music. It is music for its own sake, it doesn't need to describe anything.

Movement & Dance

A tableau is a frozen, living picture made up of shapes that connect and overlap on different levels. Working in small groups, create three different tableaux that use curved lines, straight lines, different levels, and overlapping.

 **ocus**

Time: About 10 minutes

Activate Prior Knowledge

Ask students, "Have you ever seen a group of groceries out on the table before they are put away?" "¿Alguna vez han visto un grupo de comestibles en la mesa antes de ser guardados?"

- Discuss student responses. Explain that when the groceries are on the table, certain items are closer to you than others. The closer items overlap the others.

Using Literature 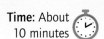 Reading

- Read *Uncle Willie and the Soup Kitchen* by DyAnne DiSalvo-Ryan. Have students look for overlapping shapes.

Thematic Connection [★] Reading

- **Food and Nutrition:** Discuss the different kinds of foods students like to eat. Talk about the food pyramid.

Introduce the Art NSAE 2.a

Look

"Look closely at the two paintings." "Miren detalladamente las dos pinturas".

- Have students identify space and overlapping in the works of art and the environment.

Classifying [★] Math

- Have students discuss what kinds of food they see in the paintings. To which food group do the foods belong? Both paintings are of fruit. When looking at the Moillon painting, students will most likely not know what gooseberries are. They may think the pitcher in the Cezanne work is filled with milk.

NSAE 4.a, 4.c, 5.a, 5.b

 Art History and Culture

Possible answer: Fruits have many different interesting textures and colors that would be good to paint or draw.

 Web Connection

Visit http://www.nortonsimon.org/collections/ browse_artist.asp?name=Louise+Moillon to see another still life by Moillon.

86 UNIT 2 • Space and Form

 Lesson 6 Objects and Space

▲ **Louise Moillon.** (French). *Still Life with Cherries, Strawberries, and Gooseberries.* 1630.

Oil on panel. 12 $\frac{5}{8}$ × 19 $\frac{1}{4}$ inches (30.07 × 48.58 cm.). Norton Simon Museum, Pasadena, California.

Look at these two paintings. They are still lifes. A **still life** is a painting or drawing of a collection of objects that cannot move. Which objects overlap others in these paintings? Which objects are closest to you?

 Art History and Culture

Why do you think these artists used fruit in their paintings instead of other foods?

86 Unit 2 • Lesson 6

 Art History and Culture

Louise Moillon

Louise Moillon (lü´ ēz mwä lôn´) (1610–1696) was a famous French Baroque artist. Her father, a painter and art dealer, died when she was a child and her mother remarried a man who was also a painter and art dealer. As a result, Moillon was exposed to art at a very young age. She specialized in still lifes and her refined work was often compared to Flemish styles. Her work is known for its painstaking attention to detail.

See pages 24–25 and 16–21 for more about art history and subject matter.

Artist Profiles, p. 39

Artist Profile

Louise Moillon
1610-1696

Louise Moillon (lü ēz´ mwä lôn´) was one of the earliest French artists to specialize in still-life painting. Her father was a painter and picture dealer, and most likely her teacher. By the time she was 11, her artistic talent was evident. Most of her dated work was produced between 1629 and 1641. She married in 1640 and had three children. Later in her life she again produced paintings with dates, perhaps because of financial need. As a Calvinist, she and her family suffered persecution after the 1685 repeal of the Edict of Nantes, which granted religious freedom to Protestants in France.

Study the two still lifes to find overlapping objects.

▶ What objects do you see in the two paintings? Point out an object that is overlapped by another.

▶ Which objects are farthest away from you?

▲ **Paul Cézanne.** (French).
Still Life with Apples.
1895–1898.

Oil on canvas. 27 × 36 ½ inches (68.58 × 92.71 cm.). The Museum of Modern Art, New York, New York.

Aesthetic Perception

Design Awareness Think about food you see at the grocery store. Do you see overlapping in the displays? Why do stores do this?

Art History and Culture

Paul Cézanne

Paul Cézanne (pôl sā zan´) (1839–1906) was born in the south of France. Under pressure from his father, he studied law in his youth, but eventually dedicated himself fully to art. Cézanne is considered to be one of the founders of modern painting. He was a contemporary of the impressionists but chose to paint with more substance. Cézanne painted many still lifes using bold colors and brush strokes.

See pp. 24–25 and 16–21 for more about art history and subject matter.

Artist Profiles, p. 11

Study

▶ Answers may vary. Students will see many different kinds of fruit. One example of an overlapping object is the white cloth in the Cezanne painting.

▶ The bowl of green pears in the Cezanne is farthest away. The bowl of strawberries is farthest away in the Moillon.

■ For more examples of still lifes see *The National Museum of Women in the Arts Collection.*

Art Journal: Planning

Encourage students to think about what items they could put in a still life. Ask them to make a list planning what items they would like to use in the Concepts section of their Art Journals.

Aesthetic Perception

Design Awareness Possible answer: To make the food look more appealing and natural so that people will buy it. Have students identify variations in the objects from their environments.

NSAE 2.b, 5.c

Developing Visual Literacy What details do you see when you are looking at these still lifes of fruit? Why do you think the artists used such different styles?

Web Connection

Visit **http://www.mfa.org/handbook/portrait. asp?id+268&s=6** to view a portrait painted by Cézanne.

Teach

"How can you use overlapping shapes to show a group of objects?" "¿Cómo pueden usar figuras sobre puestas para mostrar un grupo de objetos?"

- Read and discuss the information about objects and space on page 88.

Practice

Materials: paper, pencil, food and other objects for still lifes

Alternate Materials: oil pastels

- Have students identify and practice skills necessary for producing drawings and paintings by using a variety of materials.

- Distribute materials and have students follow the directions on page 88.

Creative Expression

NSAE 1.c, 1.d, 2.c, 3.b

Materials: construction paper, colored dustless chalk, liquid tempera, palettes, brushes, newspaper, food and other objects for still lifes, water dishes, paper towels

Alternate Materials: crayons, markers

- Distribute the materials and have students follow the directions on page 89.

- Encourage students to create effective compositions by using design elements

- Review the Activity Tips on page 237 for visual examples of the activity if needed.

Art Journal: Sketching NSAE 3.a

Have students sketch layout for their still lifes in the Ideas section of their Art Journals.

Using Objects and Space

Because paintings are two-dimensional, artists can't use forms to show depth. We see depth in still-life paintings and drawings when artists overlap objects.

Hiding part of an object creates depth and makes the viewer think the object is farther away. Look at the picture. Which object is closest to you? Which object is farthest from you?

Practice

Set up a still life on your desk.

1. Pick three or four objects from your teacher's collection.

2. Arrange the objects on your desk so some of them overlap.

3. Sketch the still life you have created for practice. Make sure you pay attention to which parts of the objects are hidden by overlapping.

Differentiated Instruction

Reteach
Hold up several two-dimensional shapes and overlap them. Ask students which shapes overlap the others and what parts of the shapes they cannot see.

Special Needs
To reinforce past lesson objectives and increase learning, have students identify the forms they see in their still-life arrangement.

ELL Tips
Have students arrange pieces of colored paper in an overlapping pattern, then plan a still life with students using classroom objects. Overlap to convey the concept of nearness.

◄ **Joseph Williams.**
Age 7.

Think about how this student arranged his still life to create depth.

 Creative Expression

What kinds of foods would you put in a still life? Arrange and paint a still life using overlapping.

1. Think of some objects and foods you would like to draw. Use all different kinds of forms.

2. Arrange your objects so some overlap.

3. Start by drawing the objects closest to you. Then draw the objects that are farther away.

4. Paint your still life.

Art Criticism

Describe What foods did you use in your still life?

Analyze Where is the overlapping in your still life?

Interpret Which objects were farthest away? Which were closest?

Decide What other healthy foods could you have used in your still life?

Unit 2 • Lesson 6 **89**

NSAE 6.a, 6.b

Art Across the Curriculum

Use these simple ideas to reinforce art concepts across the curriculum.

★ **Descriptive Writing** Have students write a description of objects sitting on a table.

★ **Math** Have students name fractional parts covered by overlapping of a set of objects in a still life while looking at a concrete representation.

★ **Science** Have students discuss, describe, and illustrate the water cycle. Discuss overlapping in the water cycle.

★ **Social Studies** Have students compare various interpretations of the same time period using evidence such as photographs and interviews. Discuss how these interpretations overlap.

★ **Technology** Show students how to create shapes that overlap in a drawing program. Visit **SRAonline.com** to print detailed instructions for this activity.

 **Reflect** Time: About 10 minutes

Review and Assess

"Can you explain how overlapping objects creates depth in a painting?" "¿Pueden explicar cómo al sobreponer objetos se crea profundidad en una pintura?"

Think

This student created depth by overlapping objects in his still life.

■ Use *Large Prints 27 Canteleve* and *28 Howl* to have students identify overlapping objects.

■ Have students identify stories and constructions in this lesson's artwork.

■ Have students identify ideas in the art by this lesson's artists.

Informal Assessment

Art Journal: Critical Thinking
Have students answer the four art criticism questions—Describe, Analyze, Interpret, and Decide—in the Critical Thinking section of their Art Journals. Then have students break into small groups and talk about the healthy foods in their still lifes. Have students define reasons for preferences in their personal artwork. Then have them identify ideas in their peers' artwork.

■ For standardized-format test practice using this lesson's art content, see pages 28–29 in *Reading and Writing Test Preparation.*

Lesson 6 Wrap-Up
Objects and Space

Extra! For the Art Specialist

Time: About 45 minutes

Focus

Study **Large Prints 27** and **28** and ask students to point out and discuss the objects they see. Are any of the objects touching or in front of others? Discuss what a still life is. How do artists paint something to make it look far away? Explain.

Teach

Explain to students they will be creating a still life by joining several drawn and painted objects together and gluing them on a background. Line up the objects for the still life so the students can see them all.

Reflect

Have students evaluate their work using the four steps of art criticism.

Alternate Activity

Materials:
- a variety of still life objects
- pencils
- 12" × 18" black or white drawing paper and 9" × 12" white drawing paper
- crayons
- brushes, water dishes, newspapers
- watercolors
- scissors
- glue

1. Sketch the still life objects on your 9" × 12" paper. Trace the outline of the objects with crayons and paint them with watercolors.

2. When the objects are dry, cut them out and arrange them on the larger paper.

3. Arrange your objects and create your own still life. Be sure to use overlapping to show depth. Glue the objects down.

Research in Art Education

Research has show that "looking and reasoning skills" learned during visual art training can also be applied to scientific images ("Investigating the Educational Impact and Potential of the Museum of Modern Art's Visual Thinking Curriculum" in *Critical Links*, p. 142). Students involved in visual-arts training showed less circular reasoning and more evidential reasoning when evaluating both fine art images and scientific images.

Assessment

Use the following rubric to evaluate the artwork students make in the Creative Expression activity and to assess students' understanding of objects and space.

Have students complete page 31 or 32 in their **Assessment** books.

	Art History and Culture	Aesthetic Perception	Creative Expression	Art Criticism
3 POINTS	The student can identify and compare the use of fruit in two works of art.	The student accurately identifies overlapping objects in their environments.	The student's still life clearly illustrates a good use of objects and space.	The student thoughtfully and honestly evaluates his or her own work using the four steps of art criticism.
2 POINTS	The student's identification or comparison is weak or incomplete.	The student shows emerging awareness of objects and space but cannot consistently identify them.	The student's still life shows some awareness of objects and space.	The student attempts to evaluate his or her own work but shows an incomplete understanding of evaluation criteria.
1 POINT	The student cannot identify or compare the use of fruit in different works of art.	The student cannot identify overlapping objects.	The student's still life shows no understanding of objects and space.	The student does not attempt to evaluate his or her own artwork.

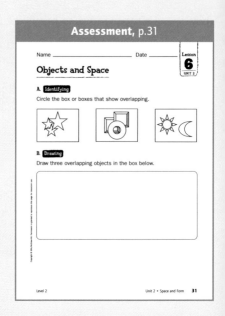

Assessment, p.31

Name _____ Date _____ Lesson **6** UNIT 2

Objects and Space

A. Identifying
Circle the box or boxes that show overlapping.

B. Drawing
Draw three overlapping objects in the box below.

Level 2   Unit 2 • Space and Form **31**

animal form—a three-dimensional representation of an animal forma animal—una representación tridimensional de un animal

body form—three-dimensional representations of a person forma corporal—una representación tridimensional de una persona

brass—a metal made by combining copper and zinc latón—una metal hecho combinando cobre y cinc

coil—A long roll of clay joined into a circle or spiral. Clay coils are used to make pottery. rollo—un rollo largo de arcilla unido en un circulo o espiral. Rollos de arcilla son usados para hacer cerámicas

depth—a front to back measurement, or how far back something goes profundidad—una medida de frente hacia detrás, o que detrás algo va

dimension—a measurement of the amount of space an object takes up in one direction dimensión—una medida del tamaño de espacio que un objeto toma en una dirección

earthenware—ceramics made out of clay and fired at a low heat loza de barro—cerámicas hecha de arcillo en fuego de baja intensidad

form—any object that has three dimensions: height, width, and depth forma—cual quier objeto que tiene tres dimensiones: altura, anchura y profundidad

free-form form—an irregular, three-dimensional object forma abstracta—una irregular, objeto tridimensional

geometric form—a three-dimensional object whose corresponding shape is geometric forma geométrica—un objeto tridimensional que su forma correspondiente es geométrica

hand tools—simple instruments for carving or sculpting herramientas de mano—instrumentos simples para entalladura y escultura

height—a vertical measurement, or how tall something is altura—una medida vertical o que alto es algo

overlap— to place one object on top of another object and partially cover the first object up superponer—poner un objeto encima de otro y cubrir parcialmente el primero

relief—a type of sculpture where forms project from a flat background relieve—un tipo de escultura por donde formas proyectan de una fondo plano

sculpture—three-dimensional art that is not a body form. escultura—arte tridimensional que no es de forma corporal

statue—three-dimensional art that is a body form estatua—arte tridimensional que es de forma corporal

still life—a painting or drawing of a collection of objects that cannot move naturaleza muerta—una pintura o dibujo de una colección de objetos que no se mueven

three-dimensional—has measurements in three directions: height, width, and depth tridimensional—tiene medidas en tres direcciones: altura, anchura y profundidad

two-dimensional—has measurements in two directions: height and width bidimensional—tiene medidas en dos direcciones: altura y anchura

width—a horizontal measurement, or how long across something is anchura—una medida horizontal o de que tamaño a través es algo

Vocabulary Practice

T Display *Transparency 38* to review unit vocabulary words.

Examples [★] Vocabulary
Have students provide descriptions to illustrate the meaning of five unit vocabulary words.

Silly Words and Sentences [★] Vocabulary
Ask students to select three unit vocabulary words and invent nonsense rhymes using those words.

Words and Sounds: Alliteration [★]
Vocabulary
Have students select four unit vocabulary words and invent alliterations for those words.

Wrapping Up Unit 2
Space and Form

Art Criticism

Critical Thinking Art criticism is an organized system for looking at and talking about art. You can criticize art without being an expert. The purpose of art criticism is to get the viewer involved in a perception process that delays judgment until all aspects of the artwork have been studied.

■ See pages 28–29 for more about art criticism.

Describe

▶ Possible answer: This is a headdress from the Yoruba people of Nigeria. It is made of carved wood and painted with pigment. It is 50 inches tall. It is probably taller than most second graders.

▶ Possible answer: The bottom looks like a head with an eye, a nose and a mouth. Above that is a round platform. A small horse and a rider sit on the platform. The man sits on a decorated blanket on the horse. His clothes are covered with designs. He has bracelets on his wrist. He has three rings around his long neck. He has a large eye with a thick white line around it like the face at the bottom of the headdress. There are three stripes painted on the cheek we can see. His head is as large as his body, and his arms are larger than his legs. He has a long stocking hat on his head that is decorated to match his shirt and the blanket. There are many decorations on the horse's reins.

Analyze

▶ Possible answer: The platform is a very flat cylinder. The supports for the platform are 3D rectangles. The ear on the bottom head is a short cylinder. The negative space for the mouth is a rectangle. Cylinders also make the horse's legs, the man's arms, and his neck. The man, the horse, and the bottom head are free-form forms.

▶ Possible answer: The man and the horse

▲ **Yoruba People.** (Nigerian). *Headdress for Epa Masquerade.* c. 20th century.
Carved wood and pigment. 50 × 20 × 18 inches (127 × 50.8 × 45.72 cm.). Birmingham Museum of Art, Birmingham, Alabama.

90 Unit 2

Art History and Culture

Yoruba People

This headdress was made by an artist of the Yoruba people of Nigeria. The majority of Yoruba people today live in the west African countries of Nigeria and Benin. This Yoruba headdress was worn by a male dancer during the climax of the annual Epa festival. The tall, heavy, wooden masquerade masks are placed over the dancers' heads, with the bottom portion of the mask partially covering the wearer's face. The dancer then covers his body with long leaves. Pottery, textiles, weaving, beadwork, metalwork, masks, and wood carvings are some of the types of art for which the Yoruba are known. Yoruba works of art often have spiritual significance.

Artist Profiles, p. 70

Artist Profile

Headdress for Epa Masquerade

This headdress was made by an artist of the Yoruban people of Nigeria. The majority of Yoruban people today live in the west African countries of Nigeria and Benin. The exact date the headdress was created is not known, but it is estimated that it was made during the early twentieth century.

◀ **Artist unknown.** (Nigeria). *Headdress for Epa Masquerade.* c. 20th century.

 **Art Criticism** Critical Thinking

Describe **What do you see?**

► Read the credit line to find out what this object is, what it is made of, and how big it is. Is it taller or shorter than you?

► Describe the parts of this object.

Analyze **How is this work organized?**

► Where do you see geometric and free-form forms on this headdress?

► Where do you see a body form and an animal form?

Interpret **What is the artist trying to say?**

► What do you think this headdress is used for?

► How do you think it would feel to cover your body with long leaves and put this on your head?

► How would you move when wearing this?

► Write a short poem to say while wearing this headdress.

Decide **What do you think about the work?**

► Is this headdress successful because it is realistic, because it is well organized, or because it has a strong message? Explain.

Unit 2 **91**

---

are body and animal forms. Both body and animal forms are special kinds of free-form forms.

Interpret

► Possible answer: Answers will vary. Some may suggest a religious ceremony, others may think about theatre performances

► Possible answer: Answers will vary. Some will say it would make them feel important or powerful. Some might imagine it would make them feel like super heroes.

► Possible answer: Answers will vary. Some may say very slowly because of the weight.

► Possible answer: Answers will vary. Ask volunteers to read what they have written aloud to the class.

Decide

► Possible answer: Answers will vary. Some will say it is well organized. Most will probably talk about the message of the work.

 Art Journal: Writing
Have students write answers to Aesthetic Perception in their Art Journals.

Aesthetic Perception

Design Awareness Have students think of other hats they have worn or have seen people wear. How do these things compare with the headdress in the *Student Edition?*

Describe ► List the other hats you have worn or have seen people wear.

Analyze ► What kind of forms were the other hats made of?

Interpret ► How do the other hats make you feel?

Decide ► Why do you think people wear the hats they do?

"Artists show depth by overlapping objects when working on two-dimensional surfaces like paintings or drawings. Artists can also use three-dimensional forms to show depth."

"Los artistas muestran profundidad al sobreponer objetos cuando trabajan en superficies bidimensionales como pinturas o dibujos. Los artistas también pueden usar formas tridimensionales para mostrar profundidad".

T Review unit vocabulary with students using *Transparency 38.*

 Art Journal: Writing
Have students answer the questions on page 92 in their Art Journals or on a separate sheet of paper. Answers: 1. B, 2. A, 3. B, 4. B

T For further assessment, have students complete the unit test on *Transparency 44.*

CAREERS IN ART
Horticulture

► Encourage students to discuss flower arrangements they have seen. In what kinds of environments do they see flower arrangements?

"True art is characterized by an irresistible urge in the creative artist."

—Albert Einstein

Show What You Know

Select the best answers to these questions. Write your answers on a separate sheet of paper.

❶ Forms have height, width, and _____.
A. space
B. depth
C. lines

❷ The difference between shapes and forms is that forms are _____.
A. three-dimensional
B. large
C. smooth

❸ Artists use _____ to create depth in a painting.
A. glitter
B. overlapping
C. still lifes

❹ A _____ is a painting or drawing of a collection of objects that cannot move.
A. portrait
B. still life
C. relief

92   Unit 2

CAREERS IN ART
Florist

Have you ever seen flower arrangements in a vase or park? These flowers were arranged by someone who made careful decisions about space and form when putting together the design.

Florists must be able to plan a design based on the forms and colors of the flowers they are using.

Botanical curators design where to place outdoor plant exhibits in botanical gardens based on space so the plants look their best.

▲ **Florist**

Unit Assessment Options

 **Aesthetic Perception**

Practice Have students find examples of each lesson concept in the classroom.

Creative Expression

Student Portfolio Have students review all the artwork they have created during this unit and select the pieces they wish to keep in their portfolios. Have them look through peers' portfolios and identify ideas in the portfolios.

Art Criticism

Activity Have students select a work of art from this unit and study it using the four steps of art criticism (See pages 28–29 for more information about Art Criticism.) Have students work alone or in pairs and present their findings orally or in writing.

Space and Form in Theatre

Eth-Noh-Tec, an Asian American Company, combines music, movement, and words in their performances. They use dialogue, body poses, comic facial expressions, and hand gestures. This is based on ancient Asian theatre styles from Chinese and Japanese traditions. They perform Asian stories that have a moral at the end.

▲ Eth-Noh-Tec. "Long Haired Girl."

What to Do Create a frozen picture of a scene from a class story.

1. Divide into groups and take a card that describes one event from the story.

2. Work together to create your frozen scene of that event. One person should be the director.

3. Decide which things will overlap to create depth in your scene. Think about what forms you are making.

4. Have each group present their frozen scene to the class in story order.

 **Art Criticism**

Describe How did you create depth in your frozen scene?

Analyze Explain the decisions you made to create your frozen scene.

Interpret How does your frozen scene express the main idea of your scene.

Decide How well did you capture the mood of your scene?

Unit 2   **93**

 Art History and Culture

Asian American Theatre

The Eth-Noh-Tec performance style reflects ancient Asian theatre styles. These include Chinese opera which has highly moral stories about the lives of common people; and Japanese Kyogen which are comic plays written in everyday language. They also incorporate musical sounds of the *ditze,* a Chinese flute, and *taiko,* Japanese drums.

Eth-Noh-Tec combines three different types of performing arts: theatre, movement, and music. They can each be used separately to tell stories, but when combined they touch all of the senses. Dance tells a story primarily through movement, although it is often accompanied by music. Theatre tells a story through spoken words and staged images. Music tells a story through sound and rhythm.

Space and Form in Dance

Objective: To create a tableau using lines that illustrates a specific scene from a story.

Materials: The Long Haired Girl, performed by Eth-Noh-Tec Running time: 9:03; A short, simple story, divided into scenes, with each scene summarized on a card.

Focus

Time: About 5 minutes

- Discuss the information on page 93.

Art History and Culture

- Have students review the selected story as a class; have them discuss their scene with their group. Why do they think this story is important to the culture that created it?

Teach

Time: About 20 minutes

- Explain what a tableau, or frozen scene is and demonstrate.

Aesthetic Perception

- Have students think of scenes they have seen in their community that would make a good tableau.

Creative Expression

- Select a story for the class to interpret. Divide the story into 4–5 scenes. Divide students in small groups and assign each group a scene.

- Ask students to brainstorm ideas for a tableau. Have them create a tableau and share them in story sequence.

- **Informal Assessment** Comment positively on any physical interpretation of the story.

Reflect

Time: About 5 minutes

Art Criticism

- Have students answer the four art criticism questions on page 93 orally or in writing.

- Did students effectively create tableaux that showed a specific scene and used space and form?

Unit 3 Planning Guide

	Lesson Title	Suggested Pacing	Creative Expression Activity
Lesson 1	Color and Hue	55 minutes	Create a painting using the spectral colors in their correct order.
Lesson 2	Warm Hues	55 minutes	Create a watercolor resist using warm hues and a warm object.
Lesson 3	Cool Hues	55 minutes	Create a painting of an imaginary backyard using cool hues.
Lesson 4	Value	55 minutes	Create an abstract value painting of an object from students' neighborhoods.
Lesson 5	Light Values	55 minutes	Create a landscape painting utilizing light values.
Lesson 6	Dark Values	55 minutes	Create a painting to express a feeling using dark values.
ARTSOURCE	Color and Value in Dance	35 minutes	Create original gestures to express ideas and feelings.

Materials	Program Resources	Fine Art Resources	Literature Resources
large white construction paper, black markers, tempera paints, brushes, water dishes, paper towels	*Reading and Writing Test Preparation,* pp. 30–31 *Flash Cards,* 7–8 *Assessment,* pp. 33–34 *Home and After-School Connections*	*Transparency,* 13 *Artist Profiles,* pp. 34, 15 *Animals Time Line* *Large Print,* 30 *Women in the Arts Collection*	*A Color of His Own* by Leo Lionni
warm oil pastels, water containers, watered-down black tempera paint, paper towels, paintbrushes, newspaper, 18" × 18" white paper	*Reading and Writing Test Preparation,* pp. 32–33 *Flash Cards,* 1–3, 19 *Assessment,* pp. 35–36	*Transparency,* 14 *Artist Profiles,* pp. 17, 65 *Large Print,* 30 *Art Around the World Collection*	*The Year at Maple Hill Farm* by Alice Provensen
paper, cool oil pastels, cool watercolors, water dishes, brushes, cool crayons, cool markers, tempera paints	*Reading and Writing Test Preparation,* pp. 34–35 *Flash Cards,* 4–6, 19 *Assessment,* pp. 37–38	*Transparency,* 15 *Artist Profiles,* pp. 29, 61 *Large Print,* 30 *Women in the Arts Collection*	*Houses and Homes* by Ann Morris
white paper, white and black tempera paint, water dishes, paper plates, brushes	*Reading and Writing Test Preparation,* pp. 36–37 *Flash Card,* 11 *Assessment,* pp. 39–40	*Transparency,* 16 *Artist Profiles,* pp. 3, 57 *Large Prints,* 29 and 30 *Art Around the World Collection*	*What Zeesie Saw on Delancey Street* by Marjorie Priceman
paper, crayons, oil pastels, white tempera paint, brushes, water dishes, colored tempera paint, paper plates	*Reading and Writing Test Preparation,* pp. 38–39 *Flash Card,* 9 *Assessment,* pp. 41–42	*Transparency,* 17 *Artist Profiles,* pp. 60, 69 *Large Prints,* 29 and 30 *Women in the Arts Collection*	*White Dynamite and Curly Kidd* by Bill Martin Jr. and John Archambault
dark paper, tempera paints, black tempera paint, brushes, water dishes, paper plates, white drawing paper	*Reading and Writing Test Preparation,* pp. 40–41 *Flash Card,* 10 *Assessment,* pp. 42–43	*Transparency,* 18 *Artist Profiles,* pp. 21, 62 *Large Print,* 29 *Women in the Arts Collection*	*Alexander and the Terrible, Horrible, No Good, Very Bad Day* by Judith Viorst
"Lai Haraoba" by Ranganiketan Manipuri Cultural Arts troupe			

Color and Value

Lesson 1: Color and Hue are the hues of the spectrum and the colors black and white.

Lesson 2: Warm Hues are red, orange, and yellow.

Lesson 3: Cool Hues are green, blue, and purple.

Lesson 4: Value is the principle of art that determines how dark or light a hue is.

Lesson 5: Light Values are hues that have white added to them.

Lesson 6: Dark Values are hues that have black added to them.

Introduce Unit Concepts

"Artists use color and value to show variety in their work." *"Los artistas usan el color y el valor para mostrar variedad en sus obras".*

Color
- Ask students to think about color. Discuss the difference between a color and a hue.
- Discuss why we see different colors and teach students about the spectrum.

Value
- Show students different values of the same hue.
- Discuss with students that all colors have values and there are many different dark and light values for the same color.

Cross Curricular Projects
- See the *Language Arts and Reading, Mathematics, Science,* and *Social Studies Art Connections* books for activities that further develop color and value.

Color and Value

Artists use color and value to add variety to their artwork.

▲ **Georgia O'Keeffe.** (American). *The Red Poppy.* 1927.
Oil on canvas. Private collection.

Georgia O'Keeffe used both **color** and **value** when she painted *The Red Poppy.* In art, color is every color in the **spectrum,** or rainbow, as well as black and white. Only the **spectral colors** are called **hues.** Value is how dark or light a color is.

94 Unit 3

Fine Art Prints

Display **Large Prints 29** *Thunderstorm Over Narrangansett Bay* and **30** *Exuberance.* Refer to the prints as students learn about color and value.

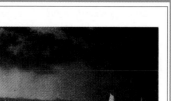

Large Print 29

Large Print 30

Artists use color to express an idea or feeling.

▶ What color did O'Keeffe use most in this painting?

Artists use value when they want to change how light or dark a color appears.

▶ Where is the red darker and lighter in this painting?

▶ Where are the darkest and lightest areas in the painting?

In This Unit you will learn about and practice mixing colors and creating values. Here are the topics you will study:

▶ Color and Hue
▶ Warm Hues
▶ Cool Hues
▶ Value
▶ Light Values
▶ Dark Values

Georgia O'Keeffe
(1887–1986)

Georgia O'Keeffe decided at a young age to be an artist and studied at the Art Institute of Chicago. She became frustrated with the painting style of her teachers and quit making art. Alfred Stieglitz, a famous photographer and gallery owner, noticed her art and pushed O'Keeffe to paint more. She soon created her own style of painting. O'Keeffe was most famous for painting close-up views of flowers and desert life.

Unit 3 **95**

NSAE 1.a, 1.b

Examine the Artwork

"Look carefully at the painting of the flower."
"Miren cuidadosamente la pintura de la flor".

■ Have students look at *The Red Poppy* and describe what they see.

■ Have students answer the questions about color and value on page 95.

▶ Red

▶ Students may also see black, blue, gray, white, and green.

▶ The petals are darker closer to the center and the left petals are darker than the edges of the right petals.

▶ The background color is darker and lighter in areas. Also, the center of the poppy has values of black.

■ Discuss the differences between materials, techniques, and processes. Have students describe how different materials, techniques, and processes cause different responses.

Unit Pretest

[T] Display *Transparency 45* as a pretest. Answers: 1. C, 2. A, 3. B, 4. B

Home Connection

■ See *Home and After-School Connections* for family newsletters and activities for this unit.

Art History and Culture

Georgia O'Keeffe

Georgia O'Keeffe (jorˈjə ōˈkēfˈ) (1887–1986) decided when she was young that she wanted to be an artist. She studied in both Chicago and New York. Despite early acclaim, in 1908 she quit painting, feeling that she could never achieve the results she wanted. Later, her friend mailed some charcoal drawings that Georgia did to Alfred Stieglitz, owner of the famous gallery 291. Stieglitz began a correspondence with O'Keeffe that led to her exhibition in his gallery and their eventual marriage. O'Keeffe was renowned for painting close-up views of flowers and later, after moving to New Mexico, for painting desert objects.

Artist Profiles, p. 46

Artist Profile
Georgia O'Keeffe
1887–1986
Georgia O'Keeffe (jorˈjə ōˈkēfˈ) was born in Sun Prairie, Wisconsin. At the age of ten she began taking private art lessons, but the thing she liked most was experimenting with art at home. By 13, she had decided to become an artist. She trained under experts and won many prizes for her art. For years she challenged the art world with her unique vision. She eventually became famous for her spectacular, larger-than-life paintings of natural objects, including flowers, animal skulls, and shells. She loved nature, especially the desert of New Mexico, where she spent the last half of her life. O'Keeffe was married to the famous American photographer Alfred Stieglitz and appears in many of his photographs.

UNIT 3 • Color and Value **95**

ILLUSTRATOR PROFILE

Virginia Lee Burton
(1909–1968)

Virginia Burton was born and raised in Massachusetts. She studied art and dance in college and combined these interests in her work for the newspaper the *Boston Transcript*. Burton attended music, dance, and theater events, then sketched the performers to provide illustrations for the paper.

Later Burton and her husband moved from Boston to Folly Cove, Massachusetts, and had two sons. Her boys inspired and guided her efforts as an author and illustrator of children's books. One son's unfavorable review of her story about a dust particle (he fell asleep while she read it) caused her to abandon that manuscript and move on to topics that her children found more appealing. *Choo Choo: The Runaway Engine* became her first published book, which was followed by the classic *Mike Mulligan and His Steam Shovel*.

Burton had a unique talent for, and unusual approach to, merging the text and illustrations in her books. She would complete all of the drawings for a book before she began to write the story.

Throughout Unit 3, share Burton's illustrations with the class and discuss her use of color and value.

Music

Color in music refers to the distinctive tone qualities (timbre), of different instruments and voices. Value in music is the ability of performers to create subtle differences in tone, which are characterized as dark and light.

Literature

Show the video or DVD *The Polar Express* by Chris Van Allsburg to introduce the concepts of color and value. Pause the program and have students describe the color and values they see.

Literature and Art

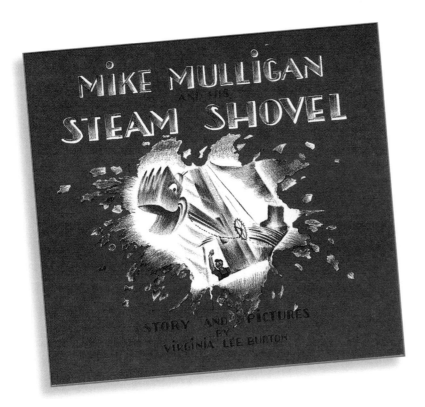

Performing Arts

 Show "Lai Haraoba" and have students look for color and value in the costumes.

Artsource®

Lesson 1 Color and Hue

Lesson 1 introduces students to color and hue and teaches basic vocabulary for discussing color. Students will learn about the spectrum and the difference between a color and hue. Students will also learn about primary and secondary hues.

Objectives

Art History and Culture
To identify two paintings as modern art

Creative Expression
To paint a picture putting the spectral colors in the correct order

Aesthetic Perception
To identify hues and colors in students' environments

Art Criticism
To evaluate own work using the four steps of art criticism

Vocabulary Vocabulary

Review the following vocabulary words with students before beginning the lesson.

hue *matiz*—the colors of the spectrum, or rainbow. All colors excluding black and white.

primary hues *matices primarios*—cannot be made by mixing other hues. red, blue, and yellow

See page 119B for additional vocabulary and Spanish vocabulary resources.

Art Journal: Vocabulary
Have students add these words to the Vocabulary section of their Art Journals.

Lesson Materials
- large white construction paper
- black markers
- tempera paints
- brushes
- water dishes
- paper towels
- newspaper

Alternate Materials
- watercolors
- oil pastels

Program Resources
- *Reading and Writing Test Prep.*, pp. 30–31
- *Transparency 13*
- *Flash Cards 7* and *8*
- *Artist Profiles*, pp. 34, 15
- *Animals Through History Time Line*
- *Assessment*, pp. 33–34
- *Large Print 30 Exuberance*
- *The National Museum of Women in the Arts Collection*

Concept Trace
Color and Hue
Introduced: Level 1, Unit 3
Reinforced: Level 3, Unit 3, Lesson 1

Lesson 1 Arts Integration

Theatre
Complete Unit 3, Lesson 1 on pages 54 and 55 of *Theatre Arts Connections.*

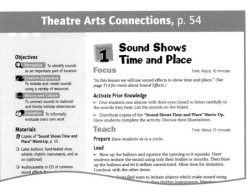

Music
 Some music research has found that people associate certain colors with the same musical instruments. Listen to *Mars*, from "The Planets" by Gustav Holst. Mars is nicknamed The Red Planet. Would you use the same instruments Holst did to portray the color red?

Movement and Dance
Using colored scarves, arrange the students in a circle. Place those with the primary-hued scarves on one side. Place students with secondary-hued scarves on the other side. Call two of the primary hues into the circle. Have students take eight counts to dance in and around each other, then freeze; the secondary hue made by these two primary hues enters and moves around the primary hues for eight counts.

Focus

Time: About 10 minutes

Activate Prior Knowledge

"What color are your clothes?" "¿De qué color están vestidos?"

- Discuss student responses. Explain to students that there are many different colors.

Using Literature ⭐ Reading

- Read *A Color of His Own* by Leo Lionni. Discuss the use of color and hue in the book.

Thematic Connection ⭐ Science

- **Underneath:** Have students discuss what *under* means. What is the opposite of *under*?

Introduce the Art

Look NSAE 2.a

"Let's look at these two works of art." "Vamos a observar estas dos obras de arte".

- Have students identify color in the works of art and the environment.

- Have students compare the ways individuals are depicted in this and other art.

Comparing and Contrasting ⭐ Reading

- Ask students to name similarities and differences in the two paintings. Students may have many answers. Both paintings use lots of color. In *Baird Trogon*, the subject is clear but in *Simultaneous Contrasts: Sun and Moon*, the subject is abstract. Both paintings use color to help convey a message about their subjects. The man is hidden under bright feathers and the abstract sun and moon are described using layers of color.

NSAE 4.a, 4.b, 4.c, 5.a, 5.b

🏺 Art History and Culture

Possible answer: These paintings look like modern art because of the way the artists used color and hue and the choice of subject matter. Both artists experimented with color and layers to express themselves.

💻 **Web Connection**

Visit **www.toryfolliard.com/profiles.asp?artist= Lostutter** to see more art by Robert Lostutter.

 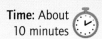

1 Color and Hue

Look at these two works of art. Artists use color to express themselves. Both artists used spectral colors to make this art.

▲ **Robert Lostutter.** (American). *Baird Trogon.* 1985.

Watercolor over graphite on paper. 24 ¼ × 34 ⅝ inches (61.5 × 88 cm.). The Art Institute of Chicago, Chicago, Illinois.

🏺 Art History and Culture

Do you think these paintings are modern art? Why?

🏺 Art History and Culture

Robert Lostutter

Robert Lostutter (räb´ ərt lō stut´ ər)(1939–) was born in Kansas and trained in Chicago. Lostutter is a well-known Chicago artist. He is known for mixing both reality and fantasy in his work. Many of his paintings are of men with bird faces or men with plant faces. *Baird Trogon* is a reference to the bird Baird's Trogon. The Baird's Trogon is a tropical bird that lives in forests and woodlands. They have short bills and eat mostly insects and fruit.

See pages 24–25 and 16–21 for more about art history and subject matter.

Artist Profiles, p. 34

◆ Artist Profile ◆

Robert Lostutter
b. 1939

Robert Lostutter (räb´ art lō stut´ ar) was born in Kansas. He attended the School of the Art Institute of Chicago, and has been a participant in many exhibitions. His work has won three Logan Prizes and a Tuthill Prize, among others. Lostutter has made many trips to Mexico, and the influence of Mexican culture and geography can be seen in his work.

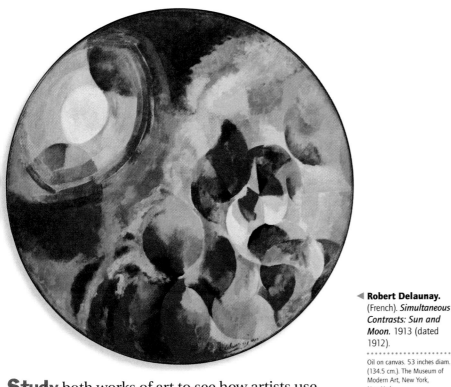

Study both works of art to see how artists use color.

▶ What do you see in these two works of art? Can you find any hidden pictures?

▶ Where do you see colors in these paintings that are not hues?

 Aesthetic Perception

Design Awareness Open your crayon or marker box and look at the colors. Where else in the room do you see those colors?

◀ **Robert Delaunay.** (French). *Simultaneous Contrasts: Sun and Moon.* 1913 (dated 1912).
. . . .
Oil on canvas. 53 inches diam. (134.5 cm.). The Museum of Modern Art, New York, New York.

Study

▶ Both paintings use many hues. There is a man's face underneath bird features in the Lostutter painting. The Delaunay is an abstract picture of the sun and moon. The hues on the right side of the canvas represent the sun and the hues on the left side of the canvas represent the moon.

▶ The facial features, ear, and feathers are detailed using black in the Lostutter painting. In the Delaunay, there are areas of black on the sun side of the canvas. White can be found in the eye on the Lostutter and the moon and sun areas on the Delaunay.

■ For more examples of abstract/ nonobjective art, see *The National Museum of Women in the Arts Collection.*

Art Journal: Defining
Have students use their own words to write definitions of hue, color, spectrum, and spectral colors in the Concepts section of their Art Journals.

Aesthetic Perception

Design Awareness Have students discuss the colors and hues that they see in their crayon and marker boxes. Encourage them to find these colors in the room. Ask students where else in their school or community they see these colors. Why do they think designers make things the colors that they do? Encourage students to identify variations in objects from the environment.
NSAE 2.b, 5.c

Developing Visual Literacy Discuss *underneath* with the students and the way the artists have layered their subjects in the works of art. Can students think of other things that are commonly placed underneath other objects? For example, socks are put on under shoes.

Art History and Culture

Robert Delaunay

Robert Delaunay (rō´ bâr dā län´ ā) (1885–1941) was born in Paris. Delaunay began his art career with an apprenticeship as a Theatre set designer. Aside from that, Delaunay never had any formal training as an artist. He developed his own style after being influenced by Cézanne and the cubists. During his life, Delaunay formed friendships with Wassily Kandinsky, Diego Rivera, and Igor Stravinsky. Delaunay was intrigued by the idea of "pure color." Many of his paintings focus on color and light. The term *Orphism,* derived from "Orphic Cubism" was coined by Guillaume Apollinaire, the poet, to describe Delaunay's paintings.

See pages 24–25 and 16–21 for more about art history and subject matter.

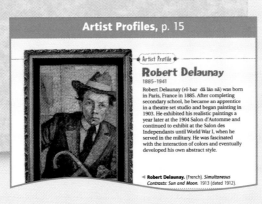

Artist Profiles, p. 15

◆ Artist Profile ◆
Robert Delaunay
1885–1941
Robert Delaunay (rô bar dä län nä) was born in Paris, France in 1885. After completing secondary school, he became an apprentice in a theatre set studio and began painting in 1903. He exhibited his realistic paintings a year later at the 1904 Salon d'Automne and continued to exhibit at the Salon des Independants until World War I, when he served in the military. He was fascinated with the interaction of colors and eventually developed his own abstract style.

◀ **Robert Delaunay.** (French). *Simultaneous Contrasts: Sun and Moon.* 1913 (dated 1912).

Web Connection
Visit **www.albrightknox.org/artgames/html/ Delaunay/delaunay01.html** to play a game with a Robert Delaunay painting.

LESSON 1 • Color and Hue 97

 **each**

Time: About 35 minutes

"Why would you use color and hue in a work of art?" "Por qué usarían el color y el matiz en una obra de arte".

■ Read the information about color and hue on page 98 and discuss it with the class.

Practice

Materials: students, open space

■ Have students follow the directions on page 98.

■ The object of this practice is for students to group together according to what color or hue they are wearing.

■ Have students identify and practice skills necessary for producing paintings using a variety of materials.

NSAE 1.c, 1.d, 2.c, 3.b

Creative Expression

Materials: large white construction paper, black markers, tempera paints, brushes, water dishes, paper towels, newspapers

Alternate Materials: watercolors

■ Distribute the materials and have students follow the directions on page 99.

■ Encourage students to express their ideas and feelings in their paintings using a variety of colors.

■ Encourage students to create effective compositions using design elements.

■ Review the Activity Tips on page 238 for visual examples of techniques if needed.

■ Make sure students add paint to their drawing using the order of the spectrum.

NSAE 3.a

Art Journal: Brainstorming

Have students brainstorm ideas for the subjects of their drawings and write their lists in the Ideas section of their Art Journals.

Using Color and Hue

A **color wheel** is a way of organizing the spectral colors, or hues. Red, blue, and yellow are **primary hues.** Orange, green, and violet are **secondary hues.**

Two primary hues mixed together make a secondary hue. No two colors can be mixed to make a primary hue.

Practice

Make groups according to the color of your clothing.

1. Look at the colors that your classmates are wearing.

2. Group yourself with other classmates who are wearing the same color shirt.

3. Can you name the colors of the other groups? Are they primary or secondary?

Differentiated Instruction

Reteach

Review colors by holding up objects and asking the class to identify if they are primary or secondary hues. Have students mix paints to create secondary hues. Have them try to make primary hues.

Special Needs

Students who have a lack of fine motor skills may benefit from a thicker tipped water-soluble marker for this activity.

ELL Tips

Discuss *hue* with students. Have students name each primary hue.

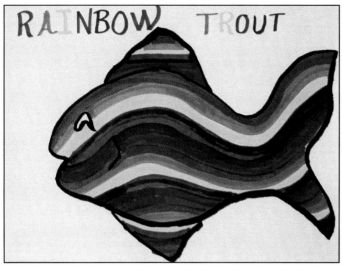

RAINBOW TROUT

◄ **Avery Runnels.**
Age 8.

Think about how this student used color and hue.

 **Creative Expression**

Can you hide an object underneath color? Use color to hide a drawing you make.

1. Think of a scene or picture that you would like to draw.
2. Draw the scene on your paper using a black marker. Make your lines very bold.
3. Paint your picture using spectral colors in the correct order.

Art Criticism

Describe Where is the hidden drawing in your picture?

Analyze What colors did you use to hide your drawing?

Interpret How would your picture look different if you had used other colors to hide your drawing?

Decide Which works better for this project, dark or light colors?

Unit 3 • Lesson 1 **99**

◀ **Art Across the Curriculum** ▶   NSAE 6.a, 6.b

Use these simple ideas to reinforce art concepts across the curriculum.

★ **Descriptive** Have students use the writing process to write a paragraph about being underneath a colored blanket.

★ **Math** Review fractions with the students. Talk about how the numerator is above the fraction bar and the denominator is underneath.

★ **Science** Discuss the things that live underneath rocks. Talk about how those creatures have adapted to that environment.

★ **Social Studies** Discuss the colors in the national and state flags. Talk to students about flag etiquette, such as flying all flags below the national flag.

★ **Technology** Show students how to change the color of the Desktop. Visit **SRAonline.com** to print detailed instructions for this activity.

Reflect   Time: About 10 minutes

Review and Assess

"What is the difference between a color and a hue?" "¿Cuál es la diferencia entre un color y un matiz?"

Think

This artist used color to create the outline of her fish and hues to fill in or cover her fish. Notice that the student applied the hues in the order that the hues fall in the spectrum.

- Use *Large Print 30 Exuberance* to have students identify colors and hues.

- Have students identify stories and constructions in this lesson's artwork.

- Have students identify ideas of the artists in this lesson's art.

Informal Assessment

Art Journal: Critical Thinking
Have students answer the four art criticism questions—Describe, Analyze, Interpret, and Decide—in the Critical Thinking section of their Art Journals. Have students discuss their thoughts on color and hue in small groups. Ask students to define their reasons for preferences in their own art. Then have them identify ideas in their peers' art.

- For standardized-format test practice using this lesson's art content, see pages 30–31 in *Reading and Writing Test Preparation*.

LESSON 1 • Color and Hue **99**

Color and Hue

Extra! For the Art Specialist

Time: About 45 minutes

Focus

Study **Large Print 30** *Exuberance* and ask students if this image has more of some hues than others. Which ones? Does anyone know the primary hues? How many secondary hues are there?

Teach

Explain to student that they will be creating new colors today and using them to paint a snail picture. Have students complete the Alternate Activity.

Reflect

Have students evaluate their work using the four steps of art criticism.

Alternate Activity

Materials:

- 12" × 18" white drawing paper
- mixing trays or paper plates
- small brushes
- water dishes
- newspaper
- red, yellow, and blue tempera paint
- a snail image

1. Paint three pairs of snails, leaving space to add a third snail to each group. Paint the snail pairs using the following colors:

   a yellow snail with a blue snail

   a blue snail with a red snail

   a red snail with a yellow snail

2. Mix the primary colors to create the secondary colors. Paint a third snail in each group. Match the secondary snail color with the primary snail color group it belongs to.

Research in Art Education

"The general goal of art criticism is to try to understand mankind and the human condition. But beyond that, it seeks to discover and communicate the 'meaning' of art—usually of modern or contemporary art because it can be examined in the context of the present." Risatti, H. "Art Criticism in Discipline–Based Art Education." *Journal of Aesthetic Education* 21 (2), (Summer 1987): 217–225.

Assessment

Use the following rubric to evaluate the artwork students make in the Creative Expression activity and to assess students' understanding of color and hue.

Have students complete page 33 or 34 in their **Assessment** books.

	Art History and Culture	Aesthetic Perception	Creative Expression	Art Criticism
3 POINTS	The student can identify and compare two modern art paintings.	The student accurately identifies color and hue in his or her environment.	The student's painting clearly illustrates a good use of color and hue.	The student thoughtfully and honestly evaluates his or her own work using the four steps of art criticism.
2 POINTS	The student's identification or comparison is weak or incomplete.	The student shows emerging awareness of color and hue, but cannot consistently identify them.	The student's painting shows some awareness of color and hue.	The student attempts to evaluate his or her own work, but shows an incomplete understanding of evaluation criteria.
1 POINT	The student cannot identify or compare two modern art paintings.	The student cannot identify color and hue.	The student's painting shows no understanding of color and hue	The student makes no attempt to evaluate his or her own artwork.

Assessment, p. 33

Name _____ Date _____ Lesson **1** UNIT 3

Color and Hue

A. Short Answer
Write the names of the primary hues.

a. _____
b. _____
c. _____

Write the names of the secondary hues.

a. _____
b. _____
c. _____

B. Coloring
Use crayons to color each box. Show which two primary hues are mixed to create each secondary hue.

☐ + ☐ = ☐ orange

☐ + ☐ = ☐ green

☐ + ☐ = ☐ violet

Level 2   Unit 3 • Color and Value **33**

Lesson 2 Warm Hues

Overview

Lesson 2 introduces warm hues: red, orange, and yellow. These hues are next to each other on the color wheel.

Objectives

 Art History and Culture

To identify and compare the use of warm hues and seasons in two paintings

Creative Expression

To express a warm object in a resist using warm hues

 Aesthetic Perception

To identify warm hues in students' environments and know what the warm hues are

Art Criticism

To evaluate own work using the four steps of art criticism

Vocabulary Vocabulary

Review the following vocabulary word with students before beginning the lesson.

warm hues matices cálidos—red, orange, and yellow. Warm hues are associated with warm things such as fire or sunshine.

See page 119B for additional Spanish vocabulary resources.

 Art Journal: Vocabulary

Have students add this word to the Vocabulary section of their Art Journals.

Lesson Materials
- warm oil pastels
- water container
- watered down black tempera paint
- paper towels
- paintbrushes
- newspaper
- 18" × 18" white paper
- drawing paper
- warm markers

Alternate Materials
- warm crayons

Program Resources
- *Reading and Writing Test Prep.*, pp. 32–33
- *Transparency 14*
- *Flash Cards 1, 2, 3, 19*
- *Artist Profiles*, pp. 17, 65
- *Animals Through History Time Line*
- *Assessment*, pp. 35–36
- *Large Print 30 Exuberance*
- *Art Around the World Collection*

Concept Trace
Warm Hues
Introduced: Level 1, Unit 3, Lesson 3
Reinforced: Level 3, Unit 3, Lesson 5

Lesson 2 Arts Integration

Theatre
Complete Unit 3, Lesson 2 on pages 56–57 of *Theatre Arts Connections.*

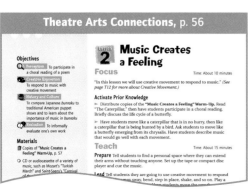

Theatre Arts Connections, p. 56

Music
 Listen to *Humming Chorus* from "Madame Butterfly" by Giacomo Puccini. This music was used in the opera when Madame Butterfly was waiting for a loved one. What emotions do you think she was having at this time?

Movement & Dance
Have students explore movements that go forward in space, for example, pushing, diving, reaching, and grasping. Have students find different ways to do each of the actions. Have students change the level, speed, and force behind each movement, then organize the movements in a sequence, taking four counts for each one.

Focus

Time: About 10 minutes

Activate Prior Knowledge

"Have you ever seen a fire burning?" "Alguna vez han visto un fuego ardiente?"

- Discuss student responses. Explain to students that a fire has many warm hues in it, usually red, yellow, and orange.

Using Literature Reading

- Read *The Year at Maple Hill Farm* by Alice Provensen. Have students find warm hues in the book.

Thematic Connection ★ Science

- **Weather and Seasons:** Ask students to think about the weather in different seasons. Which seasons make them think of warm hues? Answers will vary depending on what your local weather is like.

Introduce the Art

Look NSAE 2.a

"Let's examine these two paintings." "Vamos a examinar estas dos pinturas".

- Have students identify color in the artwork and environment.

- Have students compare the ways families and individuals are depicted in the artwork.

Logical Reasoning ★ Math

- Have students discuss how they can classify the seasons as well as hues. Can they deduce why warm hues are called warm? Some students may deduce that the hues are associated with many warm things, which makes them warm hues.

NSAE 4.a, 4.b, 4.c, 5.a, 5.b

 Art History and Culture

Possible answer: *Gathering Wild Rice* takes place in the late summer or early fall, since that is when crops are harvested. *Summer's Sunlight* takes place in the summer since people are out on a boat in hot weather clothes.

 Web Connection

Visit **http://www.statemuseum.arizona.edu/ exhibits/avery/poetry/corn_harvest.shtml** to see another DesJarlait work and read a poem a student wrote about it.

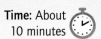

100 UNIT 3 • Color and Value

Lesson 2 Warm Hues

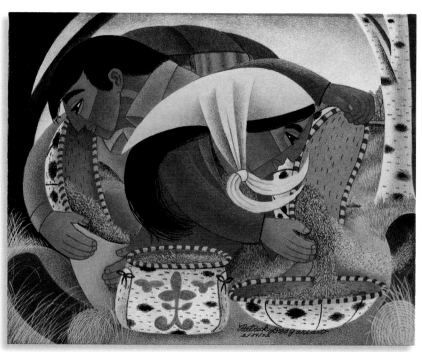

▲ Patrick Des Jarlait.
(Ojibwe/Chippewa).
Gathering Wild Rice.
1972.
....
Watercolor on paper. 10 $\frac{9}{10}$ × 15 $\frac{1}{2}$ inches (27.69 × 39.5 cm.).
Heard Museum, Phoenix, Arizona.

Look at the hues used in these paintings. Both *Gathering Wild Rice* and *Summer's Sunlight* were painted using many yellows, oranges, and reds. These are **warm hues.**

 Art History and Culture

In which seasons do you think these scenes take place? Why?

 Art History and Culture

Patrick Des Jarlait

Patrick DesJarlait (pa´ trik dā zhär lā´)(1921–1973) was an Ojibwe/ Chippewa artist who lived in Minnesota. He grew up on the Red Lake Indian Reservation, and enjoyed sketching as a child. His father was a woodcutter and DesJarlait's mother died when he was seven. After his mother's death, he lived primarily in boarding schools. DesJarlait was encouraged in high school to develop his art talents. After school, DesJarlait studied at Arizona State College. During World War II, he taught art in a Japanese Relocation Camp.

After World War II, DesJarlait returned home to the reservation where he continued to paint Native American life.

See pages 24–25 and 16–21 for more about art history and subject matter.

Artist Profiles, p. 17

Artist Profile

Patrick Des Jarlait
1921-1973

Patrick Des Jarlait (pa´ trik dā zhär lā´) was born at Red Lake Indian Reservation in Minnesota. Growing up, he learned the traditions of the Chippewa, also called *Anishinabe* and *Ojibwe*. From the age of five, Des Jarlait loved to paint, sketch, and draw. He studied art in high school and at Arizona State, then served in the U.S. Navy during World War II. When he returned home, he continued to paint. He frequently gave talks to students about his Native American heritage.

Study the two paintings to find the warm hues.

▶ What items do you see that were painted using warm hues?

▶ How do the warm hues used in these paintings make you feel?

▲ **Beatrice Whitney Van Ness.** (American). *Summer's Sunlight.* c. 1932–1934.

Oil on canvas. 40 × 50 inches (101.6 × 127 cm). National Museum of Women in the Arts, Washington, D.C.

Aesthetic Perception

Seeing Like an Artist When you look through the window, what things do you see that are warm hues?

Art History and Culture

Beatrice Whitney Van Ness

Beatrice Whitney Van Ness (bē´ ə tris hwit´ nē van nes) (1888–1981) was born and raised in the suburbs of Boston. Her work was so highly respected that the art school she attended hired her as a painting professor before she had even graduated. Van Ness was commissioned to paint portraits, still lifes, and interiors, but she was best known for her brightly-colored outdoor scenes. The subjects of these compositions were often her family and friends, and her summer vacation home.

See pages 24–25 and 16–21 for more about art history and subject matter.

Artist Profiles, p. 65

● Artist Profile ●

Beatrice Whitney Van Ness
1888–1981

Beatrice Whitney Van Ness (bē´ ə tris hwit´ nē van nes´) was born and raised in the suburbs of Boston, Massachusetts. When she first began painting in art school she was regarded as a prodigy. Her work was so respected that the school hired her as a professor before she had even graduated. In addition to her own artwork, teaching was important to her, and she published a number of articles on art education.

Study

▶ Some obvious warm hues in *Gathering Wild Rice* are the woman's scarf, the rice, the skin tones and the man's shirt. The woman's hat, the umbrella, skin tones and the woman's necklace are most noticeable in *Summer's Sunlight.*

▶ Answers will vary. Most students will describe warm feelings.

■ For more examples of art from North America, see the ***Art Around the World Collection.***

Art Journal: Writing

Encourage students to write their own definitions of warm hues and any questions they have about warm hues in the Concepts section of their Art Journals.

Aesthetic Perception

Seeing Like an Artist Have students find things outside that are warm hues. Have them share what they find with the class. Encourage students to identify variations in the objects from the environment.

NSAE 2.b, 5.c

Developing Visual Literacy Discuss the message of the two pieces of art. What were the artists saying about the seasons and how different cultures celebrate the seasons? Do students think that these pictures are still true for today's people?

Web Connection

Visit **http://www.childsgallery.com/publication. php?publication_id=10&start_ndx=9** to see more paintings by Beatrice Whitney Van Ness.

 **each**

Time: About 35 minutes

"How are warm hues different from other colors?" "¿En qué se diferencian los matices cálidos de otros colores?"

- Read and discuss the information about warm hues on page 102.

Practice

Materials: drawing paper, warm markers

Alternate Materials: warm crayons

- Distribute the materials and have students follow the directions on page 102.

- Have students identify and practice skills necessary for producing paintings using a variety of materials.

NSAE 1.c, 1.d, 2.c, 3.b

 Creative Expression

Materials: warm oil pastels, water container, watered down black tempera paint, paper towels, paintbrushes, newspaper, 18" × 18" white paper.

Alternate Materials: warm crayons

- Distribute the materials and have students follow the directions on page 103.

- Encourage students to express their ideas and feelings in their artwork using a variety of colors.

- Encourage students to create effective compositions using design elements.

- Review the Activity Tips on page 238 for visual examples of the activity if needed.

- Review the Technique Tips on pages 219–220 for examples of techniques if needed.

NSAE 3.a

 Art Journal: Brainstorming

Have students brainstorm ideas for other warm objects to make a resist of and write their lists in the Ideas section of their Art Journals.

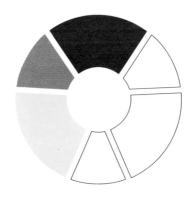

Using Warm Hues

Hues can be divided into two groups. The warm hues are red, orange, and yellow. Warm hues are next to each other on the color wheel. These hues are associated with warm things such as fire or sunshine.

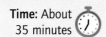

sun
oven
fire

Practice

Use warm hues to write words.

1. Think of words that you associate with the word *warm*.

2. Pick out warm-colored markers or crayons.

3. Make a list of your warm words using warm hues.

Differentiated Instruction

Reteach

Hold up different objects and have students tell you if they are warm hues or not.

Special Needs

Increase students' expressive language skills by giving the entire class and opportunity to list a word that they associate with warm. Repeat each word and write it on the board.

ELL Tips

Create a color wheel and label the warm hues. Have students pick out the warm hues in the room.

◀ **Stefani Brogdan.**
Age 7.

Think about how this student used warm hues for a warm object.

 Creative Expression

How can you express a warm object in a piece of art? Make a resist that uses warm hues.

1. Think of an object that reminds you of summer.
2. Draw that item with warm oil pastels.
3. Paint over the drawing using black tempera.

 Art Criticism

Describe What warm object did you draw?

Analyze What hues did you use to express your object?

Interpret How do the hues that you used tell a viewer how your object makes you feel?

Decide If you were going to do the same thing with a cold object, what hues would you use?

Unit 3 • Lesson 2   **103**

Review and Assess

"How would you explain the difference between warm hues and other colors?"
"¿Cómo explicarían la diferencia entre los matices cálidos y otros colores?"

Think

This student used warm hues to draw a sun.

- Use *Large Prints 30 Exuberance* to have students identify warm hues.

- Have students identify stories and constructions in this lesson's artwork.

- Have students identify ideas of the artists in this lesson's art.

Informal Assessment

Art Journal: Critical Thinking
Have students answer the four art criticism questions—Describe, Analyze, Interpret, and Decide—in the Critical Thinking section of their Art Journals. Have them describe the warm hues in their resists. Have students define reasons for preferences in their own artwork. Then have them identify ideas in their peers' artwork.

- For standardized-format test practice using this lesson's art content, see pages 32–33 in *Reading and Writing Test Preparation.*

Art Across the Curriculum   NSAE 6.a, 6.b

Use these simple ideas to reinforce art concepts across the curriculum.

★ **Narrative Writing** Have students write a story about a hot summer day.

★ **Math** Have students perform basic math functions with the number of warm hues and the number of seasons.

★ **Science** Discuss with students what causes the seasons.

★ **Social Studies** Discuss how different parts of the world have less severe seasons than others. Talk about how people adjust to different climates.

★ **Technology** Show students how to change their desktop color scheme to warm hues. Visit **SRAonline.com** to print detailed instructions for this activity.

Warm Hues

Extra! For the Art Specialist

Time: About 45 minutes

Focus

Study *Large Print 30* and ask students to point out and describe the hues they see. Do the hues remind you of something hot or cold? Explain.

Teach

Explain to students that they will be creating an edition of 3 prints using the warm hues. They will create a layered printing plate using cardboard pieces. Discuss the process of printmaking. Have students identify and practice skills necessary for printmaking using a variety of materials. Have the students complete the Alternate Activity.

Reflect

Have students evaluate their work using the four steps of art criticism.

Alternate Activity

Materials:
- cardboard scraps
- 9" × 12" cardboard pieces for the plates
- scissors
- glue
- black and white paper for printing
- brushes or brayers for inking plates
- red, orange, and yellow tempera paints
- newspapers

1. Cut out shapes and objects from the cardboard scraps and glue them onto the 9" × 12" plates. Be sure to let pieces overlap. Let the plate dry.

2. Ink the printing plate with a warm hue. Watch as your teacher pulls a print on your choice of black or white paper.

3. Repeat step 2 for the other two warm hues.

Research
in Art Education

Students in after-school arts-based programs gain practice in working with adults to plan, develop and execute ideas, and assess "next steps from a current situation" that they rarely receive in any other context ("Imaginative Actuality" in *Champions of Change*, p. 27). These are valuable workplace skills.

Assessment
Use the following rubric to evaluate the artwork students make in the Creative Expression activity and to assess students' understanding of warm hues.

Have students complete page 35 or 36 in their *Assessment* books.

	Art History and Culture	Aesthetic Perception	Creative Expression	Art Criticism
3 POINTS	The student can identify and compare the use of warm hues and seasons in works of art.	The student accurately identifies warm hues in his or her environment.	The student's resist clearly illustrates a good use of warm hues.	The student thoughtfully and honestly evaluates his or her own work using the four steps of art criticism.
2 POINTS	The student's identification or comparison is weak or incomplete.	The student shows emerging awareness of warm hues, but cannot consistently identify them.	The student's resist shows some awareness of warm hues.	The student attempts to evaluate his or her own work, but shows an incomplete understanding of evaluation criteria.
1 POINT	The student cannot identify or compare the use of warm hues and seasons in different works of art.	The student cannot identify warm hues.	The student's resist shows no understanding of warm hues.	The student makes no attempt to evaluate his or her own artwork.

Assessment, p. 35

Name _____ Date _____

Warm Hues

A. Coloring
Use crayons to fill in the circles with warm hues.

○ ○ ○ ○ ○ ○

B. Drawing
Draw a picture using warm hues.

Level 2   Unit 3 • Color and Value   **35**

Lesson 3 Cool Hues

Overview

Lesson 3 introduces cool hues: blue, green, and violet. These hues are next to each other on the color wheel.

Objectives

Art History and Culture

To know that both Thomson and Kensett painted many landscapes of the areas around their homes

Creative Expression

To paint an imaginary backyard landscape using cool hues

Aesthetic Perception

To recognize cool hues in students' environments

Art Criticism

To evaluate own work using the four steps of art criticism

Vocabulary Vocabulary

Review the following vocabulary word with students before beginning the lesson.

cool hues matices fríos—blue, green, and violet. Cool hues are associated with cool things like snow, water, and grass.

See page 119 B for additional Spanish vocabulary resources.

Art Journal: Vocabulary

Have students add this word to the Vocabulary section of their Art Journals.

Lesson Materials

- paper
- cool oil pastels
- cool watercolors
- water dishes
- brushes
- cool crayons
- cool markers
- tempera paints

Alternate Materials:
- cool colored pencils

Program Resources

- *Reading and Writing Test Prep.,* pp. 34–35
- *Transparency 15*
- *Flash Cards 4, 5, 6, 19*
- *Artist Profiles,* pp. 29, 61
- *Assessment,* pp. 37–38
- *Large Print 30 Exuberance*
- *The National Museum of Women in the Arts Collection*

Concept Trace

Cool Hues

Introduced: Level 1, Unit 3, Lessons 4–5

Reinforced: Level 3, Unit 3, Lesson 4

Lesson 3 Arts Integration

Theatre

Complete Unit 3, Lesson 3 on pages 58–59 of *Theatre Arts Connections.*

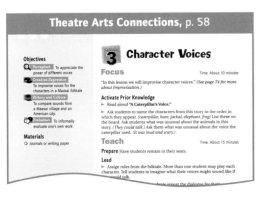

Theatre Arts Connections, p. 58

Music

 Listen to *Suoni la Tromba* theme from "I Puritani" by Vincenzo Bellini. In your opinion, do brass instruments successfully portray cool colors? Do you think brass instruments can play quietly?

Movement & Dance

Have students explore movements that recede in space, for example, contracting, dropping, wrapping, and pulling. Find different ways to do each of the actions. Change the level, speed, and force behind each movement. Organize them in a sequence taking four counts for each one.

Focus

 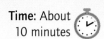

Time: About 10 minutes

Activate Prior Knowledge

"Name some cool or cold objects." "Nombren algunos objetos frescos o fríos".

- Discuss student responses. Ask them what hue the objects they named are. Point out that many of these objects are cool hues.

Using Literature ⭐ Reading

- Read *Houses and Homes* by Ann Morris. Have students find cool hues.

Thematic Connection ⭐ Social Studies

- **Homes:** Discuss the significance of location when it comes to painting a landscape. Both of these artists painted landscapes of their home areas.

Introduce the Art

Look NSAE 2.a

"Look closely at the two paintings." "Miren detalladamente las dos pinturas".

- Have students identify colors in the artwork and the environment.

Environment and Society ⭐ Social Studies

- Both of these artists painted many landscapes of the same areas. Have students discuss the cultural context in which these two paintings were created. Can they tell what kind of life these artists lived by looking at the landscapes of their homes? Answers may vary. Both of these artists painted pictures of these environments because they were personally important to the artists. The Thomson painting shows the Canadian wilderness, while the Kensett painting shows a much more settled, manicured landscape.

NSAE 4.a, 4.b, 4.c, 5.a, 5.b, 5.c

 Art History and Culture

Possible answer: Both of these places were places from the artists' homes, so they were very special places to them. They have happy memories of these places.

🖥 **Web Connection**

Visit **www.gallery.ca/exhibitions/exhibitions/ tom_thomson/index_e.html** to learn more about Tom Thomson.

Lesson 3 — Cool Hues

▲ **Tom Thomson.** (Canadian). *Spring Ice.* 1916.
••••••••••••••••••••
Oil on canvas. 28 $\frac{1}{3}$ × 40 $\frac{3}{10}$ inches (72 × 102.3 cm.). National Gallery of Canada, Ottawa, Ontario, Canada.

Look at the hues used in these works of art. *Spring Ice* and *A View of Mansfield Mountain* were painted using blues, greens, and violets. These hues are known as **cool hues.**

 Art History and Culture

Both artists painted many landscapes throughout their careers. What do you think these places meant to them?

 Art History and Culture

Tom Thomson

Tom Thomson (tom tom´ sən) (1877–1917) was born in Canada and lived the life of an outdoorsman. He was close friends with the Group of Seven, a society of famous Canadian artists. Thomson started his art career by working as a commercial artist. He became fascinated by Canada's Far North and decided to make a series of trips to paint it. He lived in a cabin in the Canadian wilderness and took many trips by canoe. Thomson died when he was out on a canoe trip sketching the wilderness. The sketches he made on that trip were lost and never recovered. He was somewhat successful when he was alive, but his artistic brilliance was not recognized until after his death.

See pages 24–25 and 16–21 for more about art history and subject matter.

Artist Profiles, p. 61

◆ Artist Profile ◆

Tom Thomson
1877–1917

Tom Thomson (tom tom´ san) was born in Claremont, Ontario, Canada, to a Scottish family. He was a quiet, modest man who lived a simple life. He began his art career by working as a commercial artist. He was very interested in Canada's Far North. At the age of 35, he decided to try to paint landscapes, so he quit his job. In only three and a half years, Thomson finished nearly 300 sketches and two dozen of paintings. At first, not many people respected his artwork. Lumberjacks and trappers who knew the Far North were among the few who did. Thomson did not have much money. However, after his death, his paintings became popular. Now they hang in many Canadian galleries. Small sketches

Study the two works of art to find cool hues.

▶ What objects in the painting were made using cool hues?

▶ How do the cool hues in the paintings make you feel?

▶ Do you see any warm hues in the paintings?

◀ **John Frederick Kensett.**
(American). *A View of Mansfield Mountain.* 1849.
....
Oil on canvas. 48 × 39 ⅝ inches (121.92 × 100.7 cm.). Museum of Fine Arts Houston, Houston, Texas.

Aesthetic Perception

Design Awareness Look around your classroom. Can you find three things that are cool hues? Can you think of things in your school that are cool hues?

Study

▶ Answers may vary. The sky, water, and grass in both paintings were made using cool hues.

▶ Students will have their own responses, but calm might be a common answer.

▶ Yes, the rocks and ground both contain warm hues.

■ For more examples of landscapes, see *The National Museum of Women in the Arts Collection.*

Art Journal: Listing
Have students make a list of objects they associate with cool hues in the Concepts section of their Art Journals.

Aesthetic Perception

Design Awareness Give students time to look around the classroom to find cool hues. Ask students to share the cool colored items that they find or can think of with the rest of the class. Encourage students to identify variations in objects from their environments.
NSAE 2.b, 5.c
Developing Visual Literacy Discuss what each artwork means to the artist and what the artists are trying to say with their artwork. What are the main ideas of these works of art?

Art History and Culture

John Frederick Kensett

John Kensett (jän fre´drik ken´sət)(1816–1872) began his career as a commercial artist. He was born in 1816 in Connecticut. He studied engraving with his father and his uncle and soon was engraving bank notes for a living. Shortly afterwards, he began experimenting with landscapes. Kensett was considered to be one of the best landscape artists of his time, and preferred to work on small- to medium-sized canvases. Instead of painting exotic locations, Kensett preferred to depict the landscapes around his home of New York. Kensett died in New York City after contracting pneumonia and heart disease. He was a well-respected artist whose loss was mourned by the entire nation.

See pp. 24–25 and 16–21 for more about art history and subject matter.

Artist Profiles, p. 29

● Artist Profile ●
John Frederick Kensett
1816–1872

John Frederick Kensett (jän fre´drik ken´sət) was born in Cheshire, Connecticut, in 1816. His father was an immigrant engraver, and Kensett first learned how to draw by working in his father's firm. As he spent more and more time with other artists, Kensett was persuaded to teach himself to paint, and this self-education led to further schooling in Europe. The mountainous regions of the American northeast were some of Kensett's favorite landscapes to paint, and he spent the later part of his artistic career painting landscapes of the Long Island Sound in his native Connecticut.

Web Connection
Visit **http://www.metmuseum.org/collections/view1.asp?dep=2&full=0&item=15%2E30%2E61** to see another Kensett landscape.

each

Time: About 35 minutes

"How can you use cool hues to show a feeling?" "¿Cómo pueden usar matices fríos para mostrar un sentimiento?"

- Read and discuss the information about cool hues on page 106.

Practice

Materials: paper, cool crayons, cool markers, cool watercolors, water dishes, brushes

Alternate Materials: cool colored pencils

- Distribute the materials and have students follow the directions on page 106.

- Have students identify and practice skills necessary for producing paintings using a variety of materials.

 **Creative Expression**

Materials: paper, cool oil pastels, cool watercolors, water dishes, brushes, tempera paints

Alternate Materials: cool-colored pencils

- Distribute the materials and have students follow the directions on page 107.

- Encourage students to express their ideas and feelings in their landscapes using a variety of colors.

- Encourage students to create effective compositions using design elements.

- Review the Activity Tips on page 239 for visual examples of the activity if needed.

NSAE 3.a

Art Journal: Writing
Have students write descriptions of things they want to put in their backyard in the Ideas section of their Art Journals.

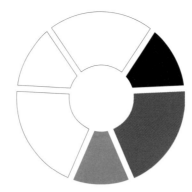

Using Cool Hues

Cool hues are the opposite of warm hues. The cool hues are blue, green, and violet. Cool hues are also next to each other on the color wheel. These hues are associated with cool things such as snow, water, and grass.

Practice

Create an imaginary plant using cool hues.

1. Use your imagination and think of a plant that would be in your perfect backyard.

2. Draw the plant using crayons or markers.

3. Use cool watercolors to paint the plant.

Differentiated Instruction

Reteach
Hold up pictures of landscapes from magazines, calendars, or books and have students tell you which are cool-hued landscapes.

Special Needs
To reinforce the concept of cool colors, bring in advertisements for products such as ice cream, breath mints, or fans which use cool colors in their design.

ELL Tips
Have students describe a cold day. Ask them to think of words that remind them of cold.

◄ **Xavier Andrews.**
Age 7.

Think about how this student painted his perfect backyard using cool hues.

 Creative Expression

What would your perfect backyard look like? Make a painting of your landscape using cool hues.

1. Think about your perfect backyard. What would it look like? What would be there?

2. Paint the background for your landscape using cool watercolors.

3. Add details to your painting using cool oil pastels or tempera paints.

 **Art Criticism**

Describe What did you choose to put in your landscape?

Analyze Which cool hues did you choose?

Interpret How would your landscape be different if you had used only warm hues?

Decide If you added accents of warm hues, what effect would they have on your landscape?

 **Reflect**   Time: About 10 minutes

Review and Assess

"Can you explain the difference between cool hues and warm hues?" "¿Pueden explicar la diferencia entre los matices fríos y los cálidos?"

Think

This student used cool hues in the water of his ocean-view backyard.

■ Use *Large Print 30 Exuberance* to have students identify cool hues.

■ Have students identify stories and constructions in this lesson's artwork.

■ Have students identify ideas of the artists in this lesson's art.

Informal Assessment

Art Journal: Critical Thinking
Have students answer the four art criticism questions—Describe, Analyze, Interpret, and Decide—in the Critical Thinking section of their Art Journals. Ask students to define their reasons for preferences in their own art. Then have them identify ideas in their peers' art.

■ For standardized-format test practice using this lesson's art content, see pages 34–35 in *Reading and Writing Test Preparation.*

● **Art Across the Curriculum** ●   NSAE 6.a, 6.b

Use these simple ideas to reinforce art concepts across the curriculum.

★ **Expository Writing** Have students write an expository paragraph comparing the lives of Tom Thomson and John Frederick Kensett.

★ **Math** Show students how to measure the area of shapes so they can measure their backyards.

★ **Science** Discuss how thermometers work and the different units of measurement (Fahrenheit, Centigrade, Kelvin).

★ **Social Studies** Discuss where Canada is located in relation to New York State. Find where Thomson and Kensett lived on a map.

★ **Technology** Show students how they can create their own custom cool hues to use in the drawing program. Visit **SRAonline.com** to print detailed instructions for this activity.

 ## For the Art Specialist

Time: About 45 minutes

Focus

Study **Large Print 30** *Exuberance* and ask the students to describe the hues they see. Do they see any cool hues? Where?

Teach

Explain to students that they will be creating a rain forest scene using cool colors. They will use oil pastels for this project. Demonstrate blending with the pastels to get new, tertiary colors. Have the students complete the alternate activity.

Reflect

Have students evaluate their work using the four steps of art criticism.

Alternate Activity

Materials:
- oil pastels
- white drawing paper
- pencils
- images of rain forests.

1. Discuss the cool hues you see in the rain forest pictures.

2. Sketch a simple rain forest scene using your pencil.

3. Color your picture using cool-hued pastels and blend the pastels to get a variety of cool hues.

4. Add small portions of black and warm hues for details.

Research in Art Education

"The child's artistic responses in the early primary grades, reflecting the nuances of their world, are usually wonderfully fresh and disarmingly naive." Kent, Robert, and Mark Luca, *Art Education: Strategies of Teaching.* New Jersey: Prentice Hall, 1968.

Assessment
Use the following rubric to evaluate the artwork students make in the Creative Expression activity and to assess students' understanding of cool hues.

Have students complete page 37 or 38 in their *Assessment* books.

	Art History and Culture	Aesthetic Perception	Creative Expression	Art Criticism
3 POINTS	The student can identify that setting was important to Thomson and Kensett.	The student accurately identifies cool hues in his or her environment.	The student's landscape clearly illustrates a good use of cool hues.	The student thoughtfully and honestly evaluates his or her own work using the four steps of art criticism.
2 POINTS	The student's identification or comparison is weak or incomplete.	The student shows emerging awareness of cool hues, but cannot consistently identify them.	The student's landscape shows some awareness of cool hues.	The student attempts to evaluate his or her own work, but shows an incomplete understanding of evaluation criteria.
1 POINT	The student cannot identify that setting was important to Thomson and Kensett.	The student cannot identify cool hues.	The student's landscape shows no understanding of cool hues.	The student makes no attempt to evaluate his or her own artwork.

Assessment, p. 37

Name _____ Date _____

Cool Hues

Lesson **3** UNIT 3

A. Short Answer
Name three cool hues.

_____
_____

B. Drawing
Draw a picture using only cool hues.

Level 2   Unit 3 • Color and Value **37**

107A UNIT 3 • Color and Value

Lesson 4 Value

Overview

Lesson 4 explains what *value* is. Value is the element of art that deals with darkness and lightness. The three properties of color are value, hue, and intensity. Only value and hue are taught in second grade.

Objectives

 Art History and Culture

To know that artists can depict similar objects in different settings and provide contextual clues

 Creative Expression

To create a value painting of an object from students' neighborhoods

 Aesthetic Perception

To recognize values in students' environments

 Art Criticism

To evaluate own work using the four steps of art criticism

Vocabulary Vocabulary

Review the following vocabulary words with students before beginning the lesson.

photograph fotografía—a picture taken using light-sensitive film and a camera

value valor—the element of art that describes how light or dark a color is

See page 119B for additional Spanish vocabulary resources.

Art Journal: Vocabulary

Have students add these words to the Vocabulary section of their Art Journals.

Lesson Materials
- white paper
- white and black tempera paint
- water dishes
- paper plates
- brushes
- index cards with different values of gray on them

Alternate Materials:
- manila paper

Program Resources
- *Reading and Writing Test Prep.*, pp. 36–37
- *Transparency 16*
- *Flash Card 11*
- *Artist Profiles*, pp. 3, 57
- *Assessment*, pp. 39–40
- *Large Prints 29* Thunderstorm Over Narrangansett Bay and *30* Exuberance
- *Art Around the World Collection*

Concept Trace
Value
Introduced: Level K, Unit 3, Lesson 6
Reinforced: Level 3, Unit 3, Lesson 1

Lesson 4 Arts Integration

Theatre

Complete Unit 3, Lesson 4, on pages 60–61 of *Theatre Arts Connections.*

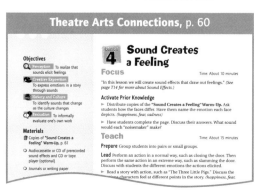
Theatre Arts Connections, p. 60

Music

 Value in music can refer to a low pitch being darker than a higher pitch. The woodwind family has a very wide pitch range. The highest instruments (the piccolo, flute and oboe) have a large contrast to the bassoon and bass clarinet.

Movement and Dance

Have students explore going from light to dark in small groups in a large circle. Have one person move for eight counts, then take and hold a shape; two people then enter, move for eight counts and add on to the first person's shape. Then three people enter and repeat the above. Darkness is dense; by adding groups of people to a movement sequence you create a feeling of density.

Focus

Time: About 10 minutes

Activate Prior Knowledge

"Have you ever seen a black and white movie or television show?" "¿Alguna vez han visto una película o un programa de televisión en blanco y negro?"

- Discuss student responses. Explain that black and white pictures show value.

Using Literature Reading

- Read *What Zeesie Saw on Delancey Street* by Marjorie Priceman. Have students find value in the book.

Thematic Connection ⭐ Social Studies

- **Neighborhoods:** Encourage students to discuss their neighborhoods or different neighborhoods they have seen. What kinds of plants grow in those neighborhoods?

Introduce the Art

Look NSAE 2.a

"Let's take a close look at the two photographs." "Vamos a mirar detalladamente las dos fotografías".

- Have students identify value in the artwork and environment.

Draw Conclusions ⭐ Science

- Tell students that these two photos were taken in very different parts of the country. Ask students to look at the clues in the photos and draw conclusions about what kind of people they think took these photos. Ask them where they think these photos were taken. Students will have many different answers, depending on what they imagine. They should all draw the conclusion that the Steichen photo is an urban tree and the Adams photo is in the woods.

NSAE 4.a, 4.b, 4.c, 5.a, 5.b

🏺 Art History and Culture

Possible answer: The Adams tree is in the forest because there are lots of other trees around it. The Steichen tree is in the city because there is a building and street lights.

 Web Connection

Visit http://www.getty.edu/art/collections/bio/a1816-1.html to learn more about Steichen and see a self-portrait.

108 UNIT 3 • Color and Value

Look at these two **photographs.** Both *The Flatiron* and *Early Sunday Morning, Merced River, Yosemite Valley, CA* were taken using black and white film. Instead of using color, the artists have chosen to express what they see by using value.

◀ **Edward Steichen.** (American). *The Flatiron.* 1904, printed 1909.
....
Gum bichromate over platinum print. 18 $\frac{13}{16}$ × 15 $\frac{1}{8}$ inches (47.78 × 38.42 cm.). The Metropolitan Museum of Art, New York, New York.

🏺 Art History and Culture

These photos show trees in different areas. What can you tell about the neighborhoods from the photographs?

🏺 Art History and Culture

Edward Steichen

Edward Steichen (ed´ wərd stī´ kən)(1879–1973) was born in Luxembourg and came to the United States when he was a baby. His mother fostered his interest in art and he became an apprentice in a lithography office. He was introduced to Alfred Stieglitz, who was a famous photographer. Steichen spent time before World War I painting and taking photographs in Europe. He later destroyed almost all the paintings. During World War I, Steichen was an aerial photographer and began experimenting with different photographic techniques. He became the Director of Photography for the Museum of Modern Art.

See pages 24–25 and 16–21 for more about art history and subject matter.

Artist Profiles, p. 57

Artist Profile

Edward Steichen
1879-1973
Edward Steichen (ed´ wərd stī´ kən) was born in Luxembourg and immigrated to the United States with his family when he was still a child. Steichen initially trained as a painter and took up photography to aid in making drawings for a lithographic firm. Steichen met the photographer Alfred Stieglitz while passing through New York on his way to Paris. Stieglitz not only purchased many of Steichen's photographs, he encouraged him to continue experimenting with the camera. During World War I, Steichen was chief of the photographic division of the Army Air Corps, and in World War II he directed a U.S. Navy combat photography team. Steichen is also known for his photographs of noteworthy

Study the two photographs to find examples of value.

▲ **Ansel Adams.** (American). *Early Sunday Morning, Merced River, Yosemite Valley, CA.* c. 1950, printed c. 1978.

$9\frac{5}{8} \times 12\frac{7}{8}$ inches (24.45 × 32.70 cm.). The Museum of Modern Art, New York, New York.

▶ What is the darkest area in each photograph?

▶ What is the lightest area in each photograph?

▶ What colors do you see in the photographs?

Aesthetic Perception

Design Awareness Look in your crayon or marker box. Can you find three crayons or markers that are different values of the same color?

Art History and Culture

Ansel Adams

Ansel Adams (än´ səl ad´ əms)(1902–1984) is perhaps the most well known and respected American photographer. By age twelve, Adams was being homeschooled due to his disruptive nature during class. In 1916, he went with his parents to visit Yosemite National Park and they gave him a camera as a gift. Adams soon became obsessed with trying to capture the pristine beauty of nature on film. He was most famous for his photographs of the Sierra Nevada mountain range, which includes spectacular national parks. Adams was a wildly successful photographer whose name is now synonymous with the national park system and the conservation of nature.

See pp. 24–25 and 16–21 for more about art history and subject matter.

Artist Profiles, p. 3

◀ Artist Profile ▶

Ansel Adams
1902–1984

Ansel Adams (an´ sal ad´ ams) was born in San Francisco. In 1903, his family moved to a house amid the sand dunes near the ocean. Adams always believed that the sights, sounds, and smells of the ocean shaped the way he thought. Adams had a difficult time at school. With his father's approval, he quit early, intending to become a classical pianist. He became fascinated with the beauty of places such as the Yosemite valley, but was frustrated that his photography did not catch its inherent grandeur. As he pursued perfecting his photographic and development processes his talent became evident to others, and books containing his photographs began to sell. His popularity continued to increase

Study

▶ The branch and carriage are the darkest in the Steichen photo. The background is the darkest value in the Adams.

▶ The lights are the lightest object in the Steichen photo. The rocks, trunk of the tree, and fir are the lightest objects in the Adams.

▶ Students will see black, white, and shades of gray.

■ For more examples of art from North America, see the *Art Around the World Collection.*

Art Journal: Definitions

Encourage students to write their own definitions of value in the Concept section of their Art Journals. What do they want to learn about value?

Aesthetic Perception

Design Awareness Students initially may need help choosing three values of the same color from their crayon or marker box. Once students have chosen their colors, ask them to tell you which is the lightest value and which is the darkest value. Have students identify variations in objects from the environment. NSAE 2.b, 5.c

Developing Visual Literacy Ask the students to think about why the artists chose to make these photos black and white when color film was available.

Web Connection

Visit **http://www.pbs.org/wgbh/amex/ansel/** to learn more about Ansel Adams.

Teach

 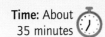

Time: About 35 minutes

"How can you use value to show a tree?"
"¿Cómo pueden usar el valor para mostrar un árbol?"

- Read and discuss the information about value on page 110.

Practice

Materials: index cards with different values of gray on them (one per student)

- For this activity, you may wish to break students up into groups of five and give each group the same value scale.

- Distribute materials and have students follow the directions on page 110.

- Have students identify and practice the skills necessary for producing paintings using a variety of materials.

NSAE 1.c, 1.d, 2.c, 3.b

 Creative Expression

Materials: white paper, white and black tempera paint, water dishes, brushes, paper plates

Alternate Materials: manila paper

- Distribute the materials and have students follow the directions on page 111.

- Encourage students to express their ideas and feelings in their paintings using a variety of colors.

- Encourage students to create effective compositions using design elements.

- Review the Activity Tips on page 239 for visual examples of this activity if needed.

NSAE 3.a

Art Journal: Brainstorming

Have students list different neighborhood objects whose shapes would make good outlines for abstract paintings. Students should write their list in the Ideas section of their Art Journals.

Using Value

Value describes how light or dark a color is. If the value is darker, then there is more black mixed in with the color. If the value is lighter, then there is more white mixed in with the color.

Practice

Make a line with your classmates that shows value.

1. Look at the value on the card your teacher hands you. Is your value dark or light?

2. Hold up your color so people can see it. Compare your value with your classmates' values.

3. Stand in a horizontal line according to your value.

Differentiated Instruction

Reteach	Special Needs	ELL Tips
Have students organize paint samples from a paint store that are shades of gray to create a value scale.	Some students with cognitive disabilities may benefit from having actual objects to observe and paint. Ask students to identify the object and then find values that range from darkest to lightest. Do a painting demonstration showing students how to create different values.	Define *value* for the students and use the word in a sentence. Show students a gray scale on a computer program.

◄ **Brian Magelsson.**
Age 7.

Think about how this student used value in his art.

Creative Expression

Can you paint an object from your neighborhood using dark and light values? Paint a picture using black and white values.

1. Think of an object that you see often in your neighborhood. Paint that object using white paint.

2. Mix black and white paint to create a gray value. Make a gray outline around your object.

3. Mix darker values and continue outlining your object until you make a black line.

Art Criticism

Describe What object did you draw?

Analyze How did you create the darker values? The lighter values?

Interpret How would the painting look if you had started with dark values and worked to light?

Decide What other kinds of drawings would make good designs using values?

Reflect

Time: About 10 minutes

Review and Assess

"Can you explain the difference between value and color?" "¿Pueden explicar la diferencia entre el valor y el color?"

Think

This student created value by adding more black to each color that he used.

■ Use *Large Prints 29 Thunderstorm Over Narrangansett Bay* and *30 Exuberance* to have students look for values.

■ Have students identify stories and constructions in this lesson's artwork.

■ Have students identify ideas of the artists in this lesson's art.

Informal Assessment

Art Journal: Critical Thinking

Have students answer the four art criticism questions—Describe, Analyze, Interpret, and Decide—in the Critical Thinking section of their Art Journals. Ask students to define their reasons for preferences in their own art. Then have them identify ideas in their peers' art.

■ For standardized-format test practice using this lesson's art content, see pages 36–37 in *Reading and Writing Test Preparation.*

● Art Across the Curriculum ●

NSAE 6.a, 6.b

Use these simple ideas to reinforce art concepts across the curriculum

★ **Personal Writing** Have students write a letter to a friend to describe their neighborhoods.

★ **Math** Discuss percentages and how values are a certain percentage of a color and a certain percentage of either black or white.

★ **Science** Discuss how specific trees are planted in cities because of how they grow. Discuss how when a tree's roots get too big, the force pushes up the pavement.

★ **Social Studies** Discuss the national park system and the parks that are located in the Sierra Nevada range. These are Yosemite, Sequoia, Mount Rainier, and Glacier.

★ **Technology** Show students how to print an object in grayscale. Visit **SRAonline.com** to print detailed instructions for this activity.

Value

Extra! For the Art Specialist

Time: About 45 minutes

Focus

Study *Large Prints 29* and *30* and ask students to look for values. What do they think makes a color lighter or darker?

Teach

Explain to students that they will be creating a landscape, cityscape, or seascape using different values. Have students complete the alternate activity.

Reflect

Have students evaluate their work using the four steps of art criticism.

Alternate Activity

Materials:
- white drawing paper
- paper plates
- brushes, water dishes, newspaper
- pencils
- black and white tempera paint

1. Discuss value. Think of a landscape, cityscape, or seascape you would like to draw and sketch it on your paper.

2. Using white, and adding different amounts of black each time, mix different values to paint your scene with. Paint your entire scene.

Research
in Art Education

"Since the matter of aesthetic criticism is the perception of aesthetic objects, natural and artistic criticism is always determined by the quality of firsthand perception; obtuseness in perception can never be made good by any amount of learning, however extensive, nor any command of abstract theory however correct." John Dewey, *Art As Experience* (1934).

Assessment
Use the following rubric to evaluate the artwork students make in the Creative Expression activity and to assess students' understanding of value.

Have students complete page 39 or 40 in their *Assessment* books.

	Art History and Culture	Aesthetic Perception	Creative Expression	Art Criticism
3 POINTS	The student can identify and compare the use of objects and contextual clues in two works of art.	The student accurately identifies value in his or her environment.	The student's value painting clearly illustrates a good use of value.	The student thoughtfully and honestly evaluates his or her own work using the four steps of art criticism.
2 POINTS	The student's identification or comparison is weak or incomplete.	The student shows emerging awareness of value, but cannot consistently identify them.	The student's value painting shows some awareness of value.	The student attempts to evaluate his or her own work, but shows an incomplete understanding of evaluation criteria.
1 POINT	The student cannot identify or compare the use of objects and contextual clues in different works of art.	The student cannot identify value.	The student's value painting shows no understanding of value.	The student makes no attempt to evaluate his or her own artwork.

Assessment, p. 39

Name _____ Date _____

Lesson 4 UNIT 3

Value

A. Ordering
Number the squares in order of value from light to dark, one being the lightest value and three being the darkest value.

B. Coloring
Create seven different values from light (white) to dark (black).

C. Drawing
Draw a picture using three different values of gray.

Level 2 · Unit 3 · Color and Value **39**

 **Light Values**

Lesson 5 explains how artists use light values in paintings to create mood. Light values are created by adding white to a color.

Objectives

 **Art History and Culture**

To identify and compare the use of light values and mood in two paintings of the American west

Creative Expression

To create a landscape painting of the American west that uses light values

 Aesthetic Perception

To recognize tints in students' environments

Art Criticism

To evaluate own work using the four steps of art criticism

Vocabulary ⭐ Vocabulary

Review the following vocabulary words with students before beginning the lesson.

light value *valor claro*—a value that has more white added to it

tint *tinte*—a light value of a hue

See page 119B for additional Spanish vocabulary resources.

 Art Journal: Vocabulary

Have students add these words to the Vocabulary section of their Art Journals.

Lesson Materials
- paper
- crayons
- oil pastels
- white tempera paint
- brushes
- water dishes
- colored tempera paint
- paper plates

Alternate Materials:
- markers

Program Resources
- *Reading and Writing Test Prep.,* pp. 38–39
- *Transparency 17*
- *Flash Card 9*
- *Artist Profiles,* pp. 60, 69
- *Assessment,* pp. 41–42
- *Large Prints 29 Thunderstorm Over Narrangansett Bay* and *30 Exuberance*
- *The National Museum of Women in the Arts Collection*

Concept Trace
Light Values
Introduced: Lesson K, Unit 3, Lesson 6

Reinforced: Lesson 3, Unit 3, Lesson 1

Lesson 5 Arts Integration

Theatre

Complete Unit 3, Lesson 5, on pages 62–63 of *Theatre Arts Connections.*

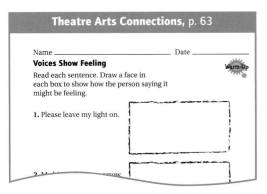

Theatre Arts Connections, p. 63

Name _____ Date _____

Voices Show Feeling

Read each sentence. Draw a face in each box to show how the person saying it might be feeling.

1. Please leave my light on.

Music

The highest woodwinds play along with strings in *Tuileries* from "Pictures at an Exhibition" by Modest Mussorgsky. The woodwind sounds are used to portray small active animals. Sounds of this type are often called *light* or *bright*. What animals do you think live in Tuileries?

Movement and Dance

Ask students to explore creating shapes that have a light quality and an open feeling. Explore movements that are like rays of light reaching up and out. Use the imagery of the sun rising. Move for eight counts then freeze in a light, open shape for four counts. Have half of the class move and the other half observe.

 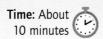

Lesson 5 Light Values

F**ocus**

Time: About 10 minutes

Activate Prior Knowledge

"Do you know what a pastel hue is?" "¿Saben lo que es un matiz pastel?"

■ Discuss student responses. Explain to students that a pastel hue is a light value.

Using Literature [★] Reading

■ Read *White Dynamite and Curly Kidd* by Bill Martin Jr. and John Archambault. Have students look for light values.

Thematic Connection [★] Social Studies

■ **Going West:** Discuss the different groups of people that settled or lived in the early American West.

Introduce the Art

Look NSAE 2.a

"Look closely at the two paintings." "Miren detalladamente las dos pinturas".

■ Have students identify value in the works of art and the environment.

■ Have students compare the ways individuals are depicted in art using art from this lesson.

Expansion [★] Social Studies

■ Have students discuss what they know about the history of the American West. Can they learn things about the west by looking at these paintings? What kind of details do they see? Answers may vary. Students will probably say something about the wide, open spaces presented in the Wilson painting and the depiction of the Native American in the Teichert painting.

NSAE 4.a, 4.b, 4.c, 5.a, 5.b

 Art History and Culture

Possible answer: Both artists feel like the American West is a wide, open, untamed space.

 Web Connection

Visit http://www.varoregistry.com/wilson/ to see more paintings by Jane Wilson.

◄ **Jane Wilson.** (American). *Solstice.* 1991.
....
Oil on linen. 60 × 70 inches (152.4 × 177.8 cm.). Fishbach Gallery, New York, New York.

Look at these two paintings of the American West. People who lived in the early American West were surrounded by wide, empty spaces. Both paintings were made using **light values.** Could you tell what time of day these paintings represent by looking at only the colors and values?

 Art History and Culture

Can you tell how the artists feel about the West by looking at their paintings?

Art History and Culture

Jane Wilson

Jane Wilson (jān wil´ sən)(1924–) grew up in Iowa. She was heavily influenced by the wide vistas that she saw growing up. When Wilson got married, she moved to New York City where she lives today. However, she continues to paint the wide skies of Iowa that she saw growing up. Wilson paints mostly from memory, but sometimes she will paint from a photograph. Before she was a famous artist, she was a fashion model in the 1950s. Her art career began to flourish when the Museum of Modern Art bought one of her paintings in 1960. Wilson uses a limited number of colors when she paints and instead relies on value to express her vision.

See pages 24–25 and 16–21 for more about art history and subject matter.

Artist Profiles, p. 69

Artist Profile

Jane Wilson
b. 1924

Jane Wilson (jān wil´ sən) was born on a small farm outside Seymour, Iowa, and earned degrees from the University of Iowa in Iowa City. Regarded as one of the leaders of American landscape painting, Wilson works in an abstract style that often focuses on recalling place-oriented memories and depictions of landscapes and seascapes.

Study the two paintings to find light values.

▶ Where are the lightest values in these paintings?

▶ What kind of mood is created by using the light values?

▲ **Minerva Teichert.**
(American). *Night Raid.*
c. 1935.

Oil on canvas. 45 $\frac{15}{16}$ × 67 $\frac{7}{8}$ inches (116.68 × 172.40 cm.). Brigham Young University Museum of Art, Provo, Utah.

Aesthetic Perception

Seeing Like an Artist Look through the window of your classroom. Can you see light values in the hues outside? Where do you see them?

Study

▶ The lightest values in the Wilson painting are below the horizon. The lightest values in the Teichert painting are in the white horses, the rocks, and the man's headdress.

▶ Answers will vary. Students may say that the light values make the subjects seem misty and unreal.

■ For more examples of genre art see *The National Museum of Women in the Arts Collection.*

Art Journal: Exploring

Have students write a list of questions they would ask an artist about light values in the Concepts section of their Art Jouranls.

Aesthetic Perception

Seeing Like an Artist Students should see many light values when looking out the window. Encourage students to share the light values that they find with the rest of the class. Encourage students to identify variations in objects from their environments.   NSAE 2.b, 5.c

Developing Visual Literacy How do these paintings make the students feel?

Art History and Culture

Minerva Teichert

Minerva Teichert (mi nûr´ və tī´ kûrt)(1888–1976) was born in Utah and grew up on a ranch in Idaho. Both parents were prominent Mormons and the influence of those beliefs is often evident in her work. Teichert drew as a child and considered herself to be an artist when she was very young. Later, she traveled east to study art in Chicago. Upon graduation, she returned to Idaho to work on her homestead. Not long after, she moved to New York City to study art. Her mentor, Robert Henri, told her to go back to Idaho and paint. She moved west, married a cowboy and tended their ranch. Her paintings are often large and depict women and Native Americans.

See pp. 24–25 and 16–21 for more about art history and subject matter.

Artist Profiles, p. 60

● Artist Profile ●

Minerva Teichert
1888–1976

Minerva Teichert (mi nûr´ və tī´ kûrt) was born in Utah, the second of ten children, and grew up on a ranch in Idaho. She was encouraged by her parents to read and to appreciate music, literature, drama, and art. She considered herself an artist at the early age of four, when her mother gave her a box of watercolors. Teichert was fascinated with drawing and used her talent to tell the story of her Mormon community. Teichert painted images of western frontier life and interpretations of the scriptures, which are still used today in many Church of Jesus Christ of Latter-day Saints publications.

 Web Connection
Visit http://www.binggallery.com/teichert.asp to see more paintings by Minerva Teichert.

 **each** **Time:** About 35 minutes

"How can you use light values to create a mood?" "¿Cómo pueden usar valores claros para crear un estado de ánimo?"

- Read and discuss the information about light values on page 114.

Practice

Materials: crayons, paper, oil pastels

Alternate Materials: markers

- Distribute materials and have students follow the directions on page 114.

- Have students identify and practice the skills necessary for producing paintings using a variety of materials.

NSAE 1.c, 1.d, 2.c, 3.b

 ### Creative Expression

Materials: paper, white tempera paint, brushes, water dishes, paper plates, colored tempera paint

Alternate Materials: markers

- Distribute the materials and have students follow the directions on page 115.

- Encourage students to express their ideas and feelings in their paintings using a variety of colors.

- Encourage students to create effective compositions using design elements.

- Review the Activity Tips on page 240 for visual examples of the activity if needed.

NSAE 3.a

Art Journal: Listing

Have students write a list of adjectives that they would use to describe the early American West in the Ideas section of their Art Journals. Have them refer to this list when they are coming up with their landscapes.

Using Light Values

Value is how light or dark a color is. To create light values, more white is added to a hue. A light value of a hue is called a **tint.**

Practice

Create a drawing of the American West using tints.

1. Think about the history of the American West. Pick an object that reminds you of the American West.

2. Draw the object on your paper.

3. Use tints of colors to color your picture.

Differentiated Instruction

Reteach

Let each student go on a tint search. Assign them each a hue and encourage them to find tints of that hue around the classroom.

Special Needs

Students with disabilities can achieve the same outcomes in art as other students. Providing opportunities for guided practice is critical to helping students achieve objectives. To ensure students' success, have them practice creating tints prior to beginning the activity.

ELL Tips

Define *tint.* Demonstrate the difference between a hue and a tint by mixing paint for the students.

◀ **Jessie Little.**
Age 6.

Think about how this student used tints to make a landscape.

 Creative Expression

People in the early American West usually lived many miles from their neighbors. What landscape did these people see? Paint the landscape using tints to create a mood picture.

1. Pick three hues. Add small amounts of each hue to white.
2. Think about the scenery that people in the early American West would have seen.
3. Paint your picture using these tints.

 Art Criticism

Describe What objects are in your landscape?

Analyze Which hues did you use to make tints?

Interpret How do the light tints create mood in your painting? What mood do you think they create?

Decide If you were going to use dark values in your landscape, where would you put them?

 **Time:** About 10 minutes

Review and Assess

Can you explain how light values create mood in a painting? *"¿Pueden explicar cómo los valores claros crean un estado de ánimo en una pintura?"*

Think

This student used tints in the tree in her landscape.

- Use *Large Prints 29 Thunderstorm Over Narrangansett Bay* and *30 Exuberance* to have students find tints.
- Have students identify stories and constructions in this lesson's artwork.
- Have students identify ideas of the artists in this lesson's art.

Informal Assessment

Art Journal: Critical Thinking

Have students answer the four art criticism questions—Describe, Analyze, Interpret, and Decide—in the Critical Thinking section of their Art Journals. Have students define their reasons for preferences in their own art. Then have them identify ideas in their peers' artwork.

- For standardized-format test practice using this lesson's art content, see pages 38–39 in *Reading and Writing Test Preparation.*

Art Across the Curriculum

Use these simple ideas to reinforce art concepts across the curriculum

★ **Poetry** Have students write a poem about the history of the American West.

★ **Math** Have students figure out how old these artists are, or would be today.

★ **Science** Have students study the type of vegetation that grows in the American West.

★ **Social Studies** Discuss how the locomotive made it possible for people to travel to and from the West.

★ **Technology** Show students how to research light values on the Internet. Visit **SRAonline.com** to print detailed instructions for this activity.

Lesson 5 Wrap-Up

Light Values

Extra! For the Art Specialist

Time: About 45 minutes

Focus

Study **Large Print 29** and ask the student to describe the objects and colors in the work of art. Are most of the hues light or dark? How do you know? How would you describe the mood of this artwork? What do you have to do to create a light value of a hue?

Teach

Explain to students that they will be creating a flower painting using tints of hues. They will mix white with selected hues and paint a flower scene or vase of flowers. Have students complete the alternate activity.

Reflect

Have students evaluate their work using the four steps of art criticism.

Alternate Activity

Materials:
- 3–5 hues of tempera paint and white tempera paint
- brushes, water dishes, newspapers
- white drawing paper
- paper plates

1. Discuss tints. Mix hues of the tempera you chose with white tempera to create tints.

2. Paint flowers and spread them out over the entire page.

3. Add any details to your painting you wish.

Research in Art Education

Although one examination of nine studies showed only "a positive, moderately-sized relationship between reading improvement and an integrated arts-reading form of instruction," this examination did show that there is a stronger relationship between integrated arts-reading instruction and reading readiness ("Instruction in Visual Art: Can It Help Children to Read?" in *Critical Links*, p. 138).

Assessment

Use the following rubric to evaluate the artwork students make in the Creative Expression activity and to assess students' understanding of light values.

Have students complete page 41 or 42 in their *Assessment* books.

	Art History and Culture	Aesthetic Perception	Creative Expression	Art Criticism
3 POINTS	The student can identify and compare the use of light values and mood in works of art.	The student accurately identifies light values in his or her environment.	The student's painting clearly illustrates a good use of light values.	The student thoughtfully and honestly evaluates his or her own work using the four steps of art criticism.
2 POINTS	The student's identification or comparison is weak or incomplete.	The student shows emerging awareness of light values, but cannot consistently identify them.	The student's painting shows some awareness of light values.	The student attempts to evaluate his or her own work, but shows an incomplete understanding of evaluation criteria.
1 POINT	The student cannot identify or compare the use of light values and mood in different works of art.	The student cannot identify light values.	The student's painting shows no understanding of light values.	The student makes no attempt to evaluate his or her own artwork.

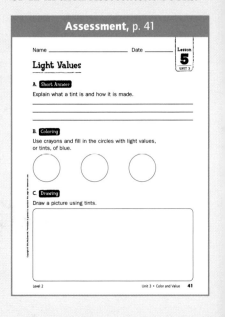

Assessment, p. 41

Name _____ Date _____

Light Values

Lesson **5** UNIT 3

A. Short Answer
Explain what a tint is and how it is made.
_____

B. Coloring
Use crayons and fill in the circles with light values, or tints, of blue.

○   ○   ○

C. Drawing
Draw a picture using tints.

Level 2   Unit 3 • Color and Value   **41**

Lesson 6 explains how artists create and use dark values.

Objectives

 Art History and Culture

To identify and compare the use of dark values to express feelings in two paintings

 Creative Expression

To create a feeling painting using dark values

 Aesthetic Perception

To recognize dark values in students' environments

Art Criticism

To evaluate own work using the four steps of art criticism

Vocabulary ⭐ Vocabulary

Review the following vocabulary words with students before beginning the lesson.

dark values *valores oscuros*—a value that has more black added to it

shade *tono*—dark value of a hue

See page 119B for additional Spanish vocabulary resources.

 Art Journal: Vocabulary

Have students add these words to the Vocabulary section of their Art Journals.

Lesson Materials
- dark paper
- tempera paints
- black tempera paint
- brushes
- water dishes
- paper plates
- white drawing paper
- dark crayons
- dark markers

Alternate Materials:
- dark colored pencils
- dark oil pastels

Program Resources
- *Reading and Writing Test Prep.,* pp. 40–41
- *Transparency 18*
- *Flash Card 10*
- *Artist Profiles,* pp. 21, 62
- *Assessment,* pp. 43–44
- *Large Print 29* Thunderstorm Over Narrangansett Bay
- *The National Museum of Women in the Arts Collection*

Concept Trace
Dark Values
Introduced: Level K, Unit 3, Lesson 6

Reinforced: Level 3, Unit 3, Lesson 1

Lesson 6 Arts Integration

Theatre
Complete Unit 3, Lesson 6, on pages 64–69 of *Theatre Arts Connections.*

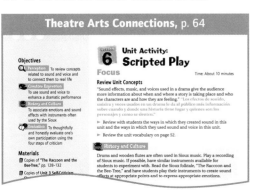

Music
 Listen to *Byldo,* from "Pictures at an Exhibition" by Modest Mussorgsky. The main melody is played by very low woodwind instruments with a background of strings. Sounds of this type are often called dark. What is the feeling of this piece?

Movement and Dance
Ask students to explore creating shapes that have a dark quality. Explore movements that are like shadows falling on the ground—low, contracted, slow. Use the imagery of the sun setting. Have students move for eight counts, then freeze in a dark, hidden, heavy shape for four counts. Have half of the class move and the other half observe.

# Focus

Activate Prior Knowledge

"Have you ever seen a person sitting in the shade or have you ever sat in the shade?"
"¿Alguna vez han visto a una persona sentada bajo la sombra o en la sombra?"

- Discuss student responses. Explain that when they see someone in the shade, they are seeing dark values in that person's clothes because of the shadows.

Using Literature ⭐ Reading

- Read *Alexander and the Terrible, Horrible, No Good, Very Bad Day* by Judith Viorst. Have students look for dark values.

Thematic Connection ⭐ Health

- **Feelings:** Discuss feelings with students and how they have different feelings depending on the situation and mood they are in. How do they think an artist's feelings might effect his or her art?

Introduce the Art

Look NSAE 2.a

"Look closely at the two paintings." "Miren detalladamente las dos pinturas".

- Have students identify value in the artwork and environment.

Comprehension Skills ⭐ Language Arts

- What do students think the artists' purposes were in painting these works of art? Answers will vary depending on what students see in the pictures. However, these are both expressions of the artists' feelings.

NSAE 4.a, 4.b, 4.c, 5.a, 5.b

 Art History and Culture

Possible answer: These artists may be scared, sad, or feel like what they are painting is mysterious.

 Web Connection

Visit http://www.nga.gov/cgi-bin/psearch?Request=S&imageset=1&Person=202030 to see more work by Gottlieb.

---

6 Dark Values

Look at the two paintings on these pages. Both artists used dark values when making their paintings. How do the dark values make you feel?

▲ **Adolph Gottlieb.** (American). *Spectre of the Sea.* 1947.
• •
Oil on canvas. 30 × 38 inches (76.2 × 96.52 cm.). The Montclair Art Museum, Montclair, New Jersey.

 Art History and Culture

What feelings do you think artists express with dark values?

 Art History and Culture

Adolph Gottlieb

Adolph Gottlieb (a´ dolf gät´ léb) (1903–1974) was born in New York in 1903. He moved to France to study art when he was 18. He traveled throughout Europe and studied extensively before returning to New York. He became known as an abstract expressionist and tried to show emotions in art through nontraditional means. He was influenced by the contemporary psychologists Freud and Jung and by the works of primitive, cubist, and surrealist artists. Gottlieb painted in two distinct styles: pictographs and "bursts." Included in his pictograph paintings are images of body parts such as eyes, hands, and heads, as well as birds, fish, dots, and arrows.

See pages 24–25 and 16–21 for more about art history and subject matter.

Artist Profiles, p. 21

◆ Artist Profile ◆
Adolph Gottlieb
1903–1974
The painter Adolph Gottlieb (ä´ dolf gät´ léb) is perhaps best known as an early and outstanding member of the New York School of Abstract Expressionists. Gottlieb, a self-assured native New Yorker, studied at the Art Students League of New York before he ventured to France to study art at the age of 18. He traveled through France, Austria, and Germany before he returned to New York to attend Parsons School of Design, Cooper Union, and the Educational Alliance Art School. Due to health concerns, Gottlieb and his wife lived in Arizona from 1937 to 1938. When he returned to New York, he taught at the Pratt Institute in Brooklyn, New York.

Study the two works of art to find the dark values.

▶ Where are the darkest values in these paintings?

▶ Why do you think these artists used dark values for these subjects?

▶ What do you imagine is happening in these paintings?

◀ **Harold Town.** (Canadian). *The First Aeroplane.* 1956.
Autographic print on woven paper. 25 × 19 inches (63.7 × 48.4 cm.). National Gallery of Canada, Ottawa, Ontario, Canada.

Aesthetic Perception

Design Awareness Look around your room and find three things that are a dark value of red. What are they?

Study

▶ The darkest values in the Gottlieb painting are in the blacks of the grid, face, and eye. In the Town, the darkest values are in the abstract shapes.

▶ Answers will vary, but some students may say so the subjects would look mysterious.

▶ Answers will vary depending on students' imaginations.

■ For more examples of abstract/ nonobjective art, see *The National Museum of Women in the Arts Collection.*

Art Journal: Writing

Encourage students to write their reactions to the dark values used in these paintings in the Concepts section of their Art Journals.

Aesthetic Perception

Design Awareness Have students share three dark red things they find in the classroom. Ask students to find things that are shades of other hues in the room. Encourage students to identify variations in objects from the environment.   NSAE 2.b, 5.c

Developing Visual Literacy Interpret what the artists might have been trying to say in these paintings.

Art History and Culture

Harold Town

Harold Town (hâ rəld toun)(1924–1990) was born in Toronto, Canada, and painted there most of his life. Town is usually called an eclectic artist because he painted in so many styles. Some of his paintings were inspired by the art of Native Americans and Vikings. Other works used imagery from Japanese or Chinese paintings. Many of Town's paintings have decorated designs. He drew simple shapes all over a canvas and painted them with vivid colors, such as bright blue or hot pink. In his collages he glued on colored pieces of paper and often painted them.

See pp. 24–25 and 16–21 for more about art history and subject matter.

Artist Profiles, p. 62

◆ Artist Profile ◆
Harold Town
1924–1990
Harold Town (hâ rəld toun) was born in Toronto, Canada, and painted there almost all his life. He exhibited his work with a group of Canadian painters called the Group of Seven. He had his first one-person show when he was 30 years old. He created paintings and drawings in many styles.

 Web Connection
Visit **http://www.mooregallery.com/Artists/ Town/** to learn more about Town.

Teach

Time: About 35 minutes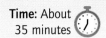

"How can you use dark values to create a mood?" "¿Cómo pueden usar valores oscuros para crear un estado de ánimo?"

- Read and discuss the information about dark values on page 118.

Practice

Materials: white drawing paper, dark crayons, dark markers

Alternate Materials: dark colored pencils

- Distribute materials and have students follow the directions on page 118.

- Have students identify and practice skills necessary for producing paintings using a variety of materials.

NSAE 1.c, 1.d, 2.c, 3.b

 Creative Expression

Materials: dark paper, tempera paints, black tempera paint, brushes, water dishes, paper plates

Alternate Materials: dark oil pastels

- Distribute the materials and have students follow the directions on page 119.

- Encourage students to express their ideas and feelings in their artwork using a variety of colors.

- Encourage students to create effective compositions using design elements.

- Review the Activity Tips on page 240 for visual examples of the activity if needed.

NSAE 3.a

Art Journal: Brainstorming
Have the students make a list of feelings and then list a color or hue they think matches that feeling in the Ideas section of their Art Journals.

Using Dark Values

Artists create dark values by adding more black to a hue. A dark value is called a **shade.** Shades can be used to create moods in a painting that are dark, gloomy, or mysterious. Can you think of other moods you could create by using shades?

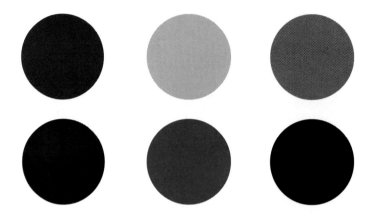

Practice

Use a drawing to express a feeling.

1. Think of different feelings that you want to try to express.

2. Use a crayon or a marker to draw pictures on your paper that represent those feelings to you.

3. Write the name of each feeling under the picture it belongs to.

118 Unit 3 • Lesson 6

Differentiated Instruction

Reteach

Have students look at a neighbor's clothes for dark values. You may wish to have a student wearing obviously dark values stand up so the students have an example.

Special Needs

To reinforce the idea that dark values convey emotions, bring in comic strips or movie posters that show characters experiencing sadness, anger, or gloom. Have students describe the situation the character is in, how he or she might feel, and the colors that the artist used to show these feelings.

ELL Tips

Demonstrate what a dark value is by holding up a paint sample of a shade next to its base hue.

◄ **Yeji Park.**
Age 7

Think about how this student used dark values to express a feeling.

 Creative Expression

How would you represent feelings with pictures? Make a painting using dark values to express feelings.

1. Choose a feeling that you would like to explain using pictures. Pick three colors to use.
2. Mix a small amount of black with each color.
3. Paint your feeling picture using the shades.

Art Criticism

Describe Explain which feeling you showed in your painting.

Analyze Which hues did you use to make the shades?

Interpret How did the shades change the mood of your painting?

Decide If you were to make another painting, what shades would you use?

Review and Assess

"Can you explain how dark values are different from light values?" "¿Pueden explicar en qué se diferencian los valores oscuros de los claros?"

Think

This student showed feelings by using shades to paint the rain and buildings in his picture.

- Use *Large Print 29 Thunderstorm Over Narrangansett Bay* to have students identify dark values.
- Have students identify stories and constructions in this lesson's artwork.
- Have students identify ideas of the artists in this lesson's art.

Informal Assessment

Art Journal: Critical Thinking
Have students answer the four art criticism questions—Describe, Analyze, Interpret, and Decide—in the Critical Thinking section of their Art Journals. Ask students to define their reasons for preferences in their art. Then have them identify ideas in their peers' art.

- For standardized-format test practice using this lesson's art content, see pages 40–41 in *Reading and Writing Test Preparation.*

Art Across the Curriculum   NSAE 6.a, 6.b

Use these simple ideas to reinforce art concepts across the curriculum.

★ **Expository Writing** Have students write a paragraph about how to create dark values.

★ **Math** Have students write math problems using a series of dark values.

★ **Science** Talk about how certain animals have adapted to live in dark environments, such as lantern fish or anglerfish.

★ **Social Studies** Have students find dark values on U.S. currency.

★ **Technology** Show students how to adjust the contrast on the monitor so that the screen is dark. Visit **SRAonline.com** to print detailed instructions for this activity.

Dark Values

For the Art Specialist

Time: About 45 minutes

Focus

Study *Large Print 29* and ask students to describe the objects and colors they see. Do they see dark hues? How would you describe the mood of this artwork? What do you have to do to a hue to darken it?

Teach

Discuss with students what a shade is and explain that they will be creating a dark underwater scene using shades of different hues. Have students complete the alternate activity.

Reflect

Have students evaluate their work using the four steps of art criticism.

Alternate Activity

Materials:
- pencils
- brushes, water dishes, newspapers
- white drawing paper
- colored and black tempera paint
- paper plates

1. Sketch an underwater scene using only a few simple objects.

2. Mix shades of hues by adding black to your selected hues.

3. Paint the scene using shades.

Research
In Art Education

It has been theorized that the reasons arts-involved students tend to excel may be because "the arts serve to broaden access to meaning by offering ways of thinking and representation consistent with the spectrum of intelligences scattered unevenly across our population" ("Involvement in the Arts and Human Development: General Involvement and Intensive Involvement in Music and Theater Arts" in *Champions of Change*, p. 4).

Assessment
Use the following rubric to evaluate the artwork students make in the Creative Expression activity and to assess students' understanding of dark values.

Have students complete page 43 or 44 in their *Assessment* books.

	Art History and Culture	Aesthetic Perception	Creative Expression	Art Criticism
3 POINTS	The student can identify and compare the use of dark values to express feelings in works of art.	The student accurately identifies dark values in his or her environment.	The student's painting clearly illustrates a good use of dark values.	The student thoughtfully and honestly evaluates his or her own work using the four steps of art criticism.
2 POINTS	The student's identification or comparison is weak or incomplete.	The student shows emerging awareness of dark values, but cannot consistently identify them.	The student's painting shows some awareness of dark values.	The student attempts to evaluate his or her own work, but shows an incomplete understanding of evaluation criteria.
1 POINT	The student cannot identify or compare the use of dark values to express feelings in different works of art.	The student cannot identify dark values.	The student's painting shows no understanding of dark values.	The student makes no attempt to evaluate his or her own artwork.

Assessment, p. 43

Name _____ Date _____

Lesson **6** UNIT 3

Dark Values

A.
Explain what a shade is and how it is made.

B.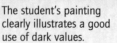
Use crayons and fill in the circles with dark values, or shades, of orange.

○ ○ ○

C. Drawing
Draw a picture using shades.

Level 2   Unit 3 • Color and Value **43**

color—An element of art that includes hue and value. Color refers to all the spectral colors as well as black and white. color—un elemento de arte que incluye matiz y valor. Color se refiere a todos los colores espectral y también a negro y blanco.

color wheel—a way of organizing the colors of the spectrum in a circle círculo cromático—una manera de organizar los colores del espectro en un círculo

cool hues—blue, green, and violet. Cool hues are associated with cool things like snow, water, and grass. matices fríos—azul, verde y violeta. Los matices fríos se asocian con las cosas frías como la nieve, el agua y el pasto.

dark values—a value that has more black added to it valores oscuros—un valor al que se le ha agregado más negro

hue—the colors of the spectrum, or rainbow. All colors excluding black and white. matiz—los colores del espectro, o sea, el arco iris. Todos los colores excluyendo el blanco y el negro.

light value—a value that has more white added to it valor claro—un valor al que se le ha agregado más blanco

photograph—a picture taken using light-sensitive film and a camera fotografía—una imagen tomada con una película sensible a la luz y una cámara

primary hues—cannot be made by mixing other hues. red, blue, and yellow matices primarios—no se pueden hacer al mezclar otros matices. rojo, azul y amarillo

secondary hues—a mixture of two primary hues. Orange, green and purple secundarios—una mezcla de dos matices primarios. Anaranjado, verde y morado

shade—dark value of a hue tono—valor oscuro de un matiz

spectral colors—The hues in the rainbow or spectrum. Red, orange, yellow, green, blue, and violet. colores espectral—los matices en un arco iris o espectro. Rojo, anaranjado, amarillo, verde, azul y violeta.

spectrum—The range of colors that it is possible to see; the rainbow espectro—el rango de colores que es posible de ver; arco iris.

tint—a light value of a hue tinte—un valor claro de un matiz

value—the element of art that describes how light or dark a color is valor—el elemento de arte que describe lo claro u oscuro que es un color

warm hues—red, orange, and yellow. Warm hues are associated with warm things like fire or sunshine. matices cálidos—rojo, anaranjado y amarillo. Los matices cálidos se asocian con las cosas cálidas como el fuego y la luz solar.

Vocabulary Practice

T Display *Transparency 39* to review unit vocabulary words.

Categorizing/Classifying ⭐ Vocabulary
Write the words *color, hue,* and *value* on the board. Ask volunteers to choose a unit vocabulary word, place it under one of these three categories, and explain why it belongs there.

Dictionary Entries ⭐ Vocabulary
Have students look up the definition of *hue* in the dictionary. Is this definition the same as the one that is in the art book? Explain.

Definitions: Demonstrate Meanings ⭐ Vocabulary
Display *Large Print 30*. Have volunteers choose a unit vocabulary word and point out where it is shown in this work of art.

Wrapping Up Unit 3
Color and Value

 Art Criticism

Critical Thinking Art criticism is an organized system for looking at and talking about art. You can criticize art without being an expert. The purpose of art criticism is to get the viewer involved in a perception process that delays judgment until all aspects of the work of art have been studied.

- See pages 28–29 for more about art criticism.

Describe

▶ Possible answer: This woman is wearing a dress with puffy sleeves, a blue blouse with black stripes, and a big skirt covered with flowers. She has a tan hat with feathers and flowers on it. The woman has her arms spread in the air, and her body is bending. She is dancing.

▶ Possible answer: It has black, green, and red squares on the back wall and floor. The floor is slanting toward the viewer. There is a black background with tiny colored dots. There are blue squares. The floor and back wall are filled with orange squares.

Analyze

▶ Possible answer: There is red on the woman's face, hands, dress, and on the floor. Yellow is found in the flowers on her dress and in two feathers on her hat. Blue is the hue of one of her sleeves and the top of her dress. Her hat also has two blue feathers. There is an orange flower in the middle of the dancer's skirt. Orange is also seen on the wall and floor. There are two green feathers in her hat. The floor has green squares. Violet is in the flowers on the dancer's skirt. Her hat has a violet feather.

▶ Possible answer: The white dots in the black background are the lightest values in the painting. The darkest values are the dancer's black shoes and stockings, and the black on the top of her dress and upper sleeve.

▶ Possible answer: Warm hues are the red on the dancer's face, hands, and dress, and

▲ **Miriam Schapiro.** (American). *Personal Appearance.* 1985.

Acrylic, fabric, and paper on canvas. 85 × 77 inches (215.9 × 195.58 cm.). Private Collection.

 Art History and Culture

Miriam Schapiro

Miriam Schapiro (mîr´ ē əm shə pîr´ ō)(1923–) is an American artist who was born in Toronto, Canada. She grew up in the Flatbush section of Brooklyn, New York. Her parents encouraged her interests in art and sent her to art classes at the Museum of Modern Art. She met her husband, Paul Brach, while attending college. In the beginning of Schapiro's career, her work was abstract expressionistic. She became an important leader in the feminist art movement of the early 1970s. In time, Schapiro's work became more geometric and structured. In 1972 Schapiro and other female artists changed an old Hollywood mansion into a totally female environment and called it "Womanhouse."

Artist Profiles, p. 51

Artist Profile

Miriam Schapiro
b. 1923

Miriam Schapiro (mir´ ē am sha pir´ ō) is an American artist who was born in Toronto, Canada. She grew up in the Flatbush section of Brooklyn, New York. Her parents encouraged her pursuit of a career in art and sent her to art classes at the Museum of Modern Art. She met her husband, artist Paul Brach, while attending college. They married in 1946 and have a son who is a writer. Schapiro organizes her home life so that art is woven into it. She can move from baking in the kitchen to painting in her studio and back to the kitchen without feeling interrupted. Her husband says that she has learned to live a "seamless life."

 **Art Criticism** **Critical Thinking**

Describe **What do you see?**

▶ Describe what this person is doing.

▶ Describe the background.

Analyze **How is this work organized?**

▶ Where do you see primary hues?

▶ Where do you see secondary hues?

▶ Where are the lightest values in the painting? The darkest?

▶ Where do you see warm hues? Cool hues?

Interpret **What is the artist trying to say?**

▶ Which hues seem more important, the warm or the cool? How do they affect the mood of the painting?

▶ What music would you hear if you were in this painting?

▶ Pose like the woman in the painting. How does that make you feel?

▶ Where do you think this woman is, and who is watching her?

Decide **What do you think about the work?**

▶ Is this painting successful because it is realistic, well organized, or because it has a strong message? Explain.

Unit 3 **121**

the red squares on the floor. The orange background and the orange squares around the outer edge are also warm hues. Cool hues are the blue in the dress and sleeve, and the blue, green, and violet feathers in her hat. More cool hues are found in the background.

Interpret

▶ Possible answer: Warm colors. They make the painting exciting.

▶ Answers will vary. Students may say the music would be fast, with a strong beat, and perhaps with singing.

▶ Answers will vary.

▶ Answers will vary.

Decide

▶ Possible answer: Most will say the way it is organized. Some may say a strong message.

Art Journal: Writing
Have students write answers to the Aesthetic Perception questions in their Art Journals.

Aesthetic Perception

Seeing Like an Artist Have students look through magazines to find photos of people in action poses. How do these photos compare with *Personal Appearance*?

Describe ▶ List and describe everything you see in the photos of the people.

Analyze ▶ Where do you see color and value in the photos of people?

Interpret ▶ What name would you give the photos of people? Why?

Decide ▶ Do you have strong feelings when you look at the photos? What are they?

"Artists use tints and shades of hues to show us the world and their feelings." "*Artistas usan tintes y sombras de matiz para demostrarnos el mundo y sus sentimientos*".

T Review unit vocabulary with students using *Transparency 39*.

 Art Journal: Writing
Have students answer the questions on page 122 in their Art Journals or on a separate sheet of paper. Answers: 1.C, 2. A, 3. B, 4. C

T For further assessment, have students complete the unit test on *Transparency 45*.

VISIT A MUSEUM
The Museum of Modern Art

► Encourage students to discuss The Museum of Modern Art. What are some of the advantages of collecting modern art? Why would this be important?

■ Have each student put on an exhibition. Have students identify original ideas in their peers' exhibitions.

■ Take students to an artist's exhibition. Have students identify ideas in the artist's exhibition.

"We must never forget that art is not a form of propaganda; it is a form of truth."

—John F. Kennedy

Show What You Know

Choose the best answer to each question and write them on a separate sheet of paper.

❶ A _____ is created by adding white to a hue.
  A. shade
  B. primary hue
  C. tint

❷ Hues are _____.
  A. the colors in the spectrum
  B. the colors in the spectrum plus black and white
  C. shades

❸ Another name for dark values is _____.
  A. tints
  B. shades
  C. spectrum

❹ Red, yellow, and orange are _____.
  A. primary colors
  B. cool hues
  C. warm hues

 VISIT A MUSEUM
The Museum of Modern Art

The Museum of Modern Art in New York City began in 1929 as an educational institution. The creators of the museum wanted a place where people could enjoy art that was being produced at that time. The Museum of Modern Art, or MoMA, has six departments: Architecture and Design, Film and Media, Photography, Painting and Sculpture, Drawings, and Prints and Illustrated Books. MoMA's collection has over 100,000 works of art and is one of the best collections of modern art in the world.

Unit Assessment Options

Aesthetic Perception

Practice Have students select two unit concepts and find examples of these concepts in the classroom.

Creative Expression

Student Portfolio Have students review all the artwork they have created during this unit and select the pieces they wish to keep in their portfolios.

Art Criticism

Activity Have students select a work of art from this unit and study it using the four steps of art criticism. (See pages 28–29 for more information about art criticism.) Have students work alone or in pairs and present their findings orally or in writing.

Color and Value in Dance

▲ Ranganiketan Manipuri Cultural Arts Troupe. "Lai Haraoba."
Photo courtesy of Ranganiketan

Lai Haraoba means 'festival of the gods and goddesses. It is an old folk dance from India that is performed during summer. The dance is accompanied by an ancient, one-stringed instrument called a *pena*. The dancers wear colorful costumes and use expressive hand movements called *mudras*.

What to Do Make up a dance with hand movements.

1. Think of ways you can move your hands to express things. For example, how would you express rain? How would you express fish?

2. Pick words and create movements to express them. Practice your movements. What color would your movements be?

3. Choose two movements to teach a partner. Learn your partner's movements.

4. Perform your movements together for the class.

 Art Criticism

Describe What two words did you pick and what movements did you use to express them?

Analyze What was the hardest thing about learning your partner's movements?

Interpret How did it feel to combine the four movements and perform them with your partner?

Decide Were you able to create movements that expressed an idea or feeling?

Unit 3 **123**

 Art History and Culture

Manipur Indian Dance

The ancient culture of Manipur has been preserved intact for thousands of years. The people believe that everything is divinely inspired; as a symbol of their humility, the performers always touch the floor and then their foreheads before they begin. The dance, art, and music of Manipur are spiritual in nature. From a young age, children commit to an honored and respected relationship with a specific master teacher. The instruments include a variety of percussion, stringed and wind instruments. They dance barefoot, using expressive hand gestures to convey deep meaning. The costumes are elaborate and colorful. In Lai Haraoba, both men and women dance together, ending in a mock tug-of-war.

Color and Value in Dance

Objective: To create original gestures that express specific ideas and feelings

Materials: "Lai Haraoba" performed by Ranganiketan Manipuri Cultural Arts Troupe. Running time: 2:03

Focus

Time: About 5 minutes

- Discuss the information on page 123.

Art History and Culture

- Show the selection and have students discuss and show different ways that gestures can express the meaning or feeling of words.

Teach

Time: About 20 minutes

 **Aesthetic Perception**

- Direct students to create hand gestures that express different words from the list. Ask students to select two words and create a gesture for each.

Creative Expression

- Divide students into partners. Each teach and learn two gestures, combining all four. Ask several sets of partners to perform simultaneously for the class.

- **Informal Assessment** Comment positively on their interpretations.

Reflect

Time: About 10 minutes

 **Art Criticism**

- Have students answer the four art criticism questions on page 123 aloud and in writing.

- Did students create two gestures to express words and then combine and perform them with a partner?

Unit 4 Planning Guide

	Lesson Title	Suggested Pacing	Creative Expression Activity
Lesson 1	Patterns	55 minutes	Create a sponge print pattern to describe students' cultures.
Lesson 2	Patterns in Nature	55 minutes	Create a glue drawing of a natural object that has pattern.
Lesson 3	Rhythm	55 minutes	Create a still life that incorporates rhythm.
Lesson 4	Rhythm and Form	55 minutes	Create a storyteller doll that illustrates rhythm and form.
Lesson 5	Diagonal Movement	55 minutes	Create a drawing of a dance scene on the computer that shows diagonal movement.
Lesson 6	Curving Movement	55 minutes	Create a painting of a journey or place using curving movement.
ART SOURCE ARTSOURCE	Pattern, Rhythm, and Movement in Storytelling	35 minutes	Create a retelling of a myth or legend.

Materials	Program Resources	Fine Art Resources	Literature Resources
6" × 18" white paper strips, liquid tempera, markers, scissors, paper towels, small sponges, paper plates, water dishes	*Reading and Writing Test Preparation*, pp. 42–43 *Flash Card*, 9 *Assessment*, pp. 45–46 *Home and After-School Connections*	*Transparency*, 19 *Artist Profiles*, pp. 72, 81 *Animals Time Line* *Large Prints*, 31 and 32 *Women in the Arts Collection*	*The Seasons Sewn: A Year in Patchwork* by Michael McCurdy
9" × 12" paper, glue, pencils, palettes, water dishes, liquid tempera, small brushes, newspaper, paper towels	*Reading and Writing Test Preparation*, pp. 44–45 *Assessment*, pp. 47–48	*Transparency*, 20 *Artist Profiles*, pp. 5, 38 *Large Print*, 31 *Women in the Arts Collection*	*Lots and Lots of Zebra Stripes: Patterns in Nature* by Stephen Swinburne
large sheets of paper, watercolors, oil pastels, colored chalk, brushes, water dishes, paper towels	*Reading and Writing Test Preparation*, pp. 46–47 *Flash Cards*, 9–11 *Assessment*, pp. 49–50	*Transparency*, 21 *Artist Profiles*, pp. 36, 71 *Large Prints*, 31 and 32 *Art Around the World Collection*	*The Tiny Seed* by Eric Carle
white Longhorn clay, black velvet underglaze, red Longhorn clay that has been thinned to underglaze consistency, pencil, kiln, clay tools, modeling clay	*Reading and Writing Test Preparation*, pp. 48–49 *Assessment*, pp. 51–52	*Transparency*, 22 *Artist Profiles*, pp. 13, 82 *Large Prints*, 31 and 32 *Women in the Arts Collection*	*Painted Words* by Aliki
computer with a drawing program	*Reading and Writing Test Preparation*, pp. 50–51 *Assessment*, pp. 52–53	*Transparency*, 23 *Artist Profiles*, pp. 8, 14 *Large Print*, 32 *Women in the Arts Collection*	*Angelina Ballerina* by Helen Craig
12" × 18" white paper, water dishes, brushes, watercolors, crayons, paper towels, masking tape, oil pastels	*Reading and Writing Test Preparation*, pp. 52–53 *Assessment*, pp. 55–56	*Transparency*, 24 *Artist Profiles*, pp. 24, 64 *Large Print*, 31 *Women in the Arts Collection*	*Paddle-to-the-Sea* by Holling C. Holling
"The Quillwork Girl" by Geri Keams			

Unit Overview

4 Pattern, Rhythm, and Movement

Lesson 1: Patterns are two-dimensional surface designs composed of a motif.

Lesson 2: Patterns in Nature are patterns that are naturally occurring.

Lesson 3: Rhythm is created when an object is repeated throughout a work of art.

Lesson 4: Rhythm and Form is when rhythm is created using forms.

Lesson 5: Diagonal Movement makes viewers' eyes move diagonally through a work of art.

Lesson 6: Curving Movement makes viewers' eyes move on a curving path through a work of art.

Introduce Unit Concepts

"Artists use pattern, rhythm, and movement to create interest and excitement in a work of art." "Los artistas usan el patrón, el ritmo y el movimiento para crear interés y emoción en una obra de arte".

Pattern
- Discuss *pattern* with students. Explain what a surface design is. Have students look at their clothes for patterns.

Rhythm
- Ask students to suggest what they think *rhythm* means. Have students clap a rhythm. Draw lines and shapes on the board to illustrate the rhythm that students clapped.

Movement
- Have students look through their books to find a painting they think shows movement. Discuss the lines the artist chose to use.

Cross-Curricular Projects
- See the *Language Arts and Reading, Mathematics, Science, and Social Studies Art Connections* books for activities that further develop pattern, rhythm, and movement.

124 UNIT 4 • Pattern, Rhythm, and Movement

Pattern, Rhythm, and Movement

Artists use pattern, rhythm, and movement to make their artwork more interesting and exciting.

▲ **Louise Nevelson.** (American). *Dawn.* 1962.
Gold painted wood. 94 $\frac{1}{2}$ × 75 $\frac{1}{2}$ × 7 $\frac{3}{4}$ inches (240.03 × 191.77 × 19.7 cm.). The Pace Wildenstein Gallery, New York, New York.

Pattern, rhythm, and movement make your eyes move around a work of art.

124 Unit 4

Fine Art Prints

Display *Large Prints 31 Only the Children* and *32 Layla and Majnun at School*. Refer to the prints throughout the unit as students learn about pattern, rhythm, and movement.

Large Print 31

Large Print 32

Artists use **pattern** to create a surface design in artwork.

► Are there patterns in *Dawn*?

Artists create **rhythm** by repeating shapes or objects in a work of art.

► What is repeated in this sculpture?

Artists use **movement** to lead your eyes around a work of art.

► What kinds of lines lead your eyes around this sculpture?

► Which direction do your eyes move?

In This Unit you will practice techniques to create pattern, rhythm, and movement. Here are the topics you will study:

► Patterns
► Patterns in Nature
► Rhythm
► Rhythm and Form
► Diagonal Movement
► Curving Movement

Louise Nevelson
(1900–1988)

Louise Nevelson was born in Russia and moved to America when she was five. She was interested in singing and acting, but chose a career in visual arts. Nevelson became famous for her sculptures. She created sculptures by gluing together small pieces of wood that she found and then painting them black, white, or gold. Some of her sculptures are as big as rooms.

Unit 4 **125**

Examine the Artwork

"Let's look closely at the sculpture." "Vamos a mirar detalladamente la escultura".

■ Have students look at Nevelson's *Dawn* and ask them to describe what they see.

■ Have students answer the questions about pattern, rhythm, and movement on page 125.

► There are no patterns in *Dawn*.

► The boxes are repeated. Some forms, such as cylinders, are repeated throughout the sculpture.

► The vertical and horizontal lines lead your eye through the sculpture.

► Vertically and horizontally.
NSAE 1.a; 1.b

■ Discuss with students the differences between materials, techniques, and processes. Ask students to describe how different materials, techniques, and processes cause different viewer responses.

Unit Pretest

T Display *Transparency 46* as a pretest. Answers: 1. A, 2. C, 3. A, 4. A

Home Connection

■ See *Home and After-School Connections* for family newsletters and activities for this unit.

 ## Art History and Culture

Louise Nevelson

Louise Nevelson (lū ēz′ nev′əl sən)(1900–1988) was born in Russia but grew up in America. Considered an innovative sculptor, Nevelson always knew she wanted to be an artist. She's known for her unique wooden sculptures created by arranging collections of posts, spindles, blocks, and trim found at construction sites or lumber yards. The wooden objects are all painted one color to unify the work. Originally, Nevelson painted all of her works black, but she later discovered that the shadows in spaces around the objects she used were also important to the arrangement of forms, so she began to use light colors like white or gold.

Artist Profiles, p. 44

● Artist Profile ●
Louise Nevelson
1900–1988
Louise Nevelson (lōō ēz′ ne′ vəl sən), one of the most important and successful American sculptors of the twentieth century, was born in Kiev, Russia. Her family resettled in Rockland, Maine, when she was five years old. As a child she began assembling wood scraps from her father's contracting business. Her education was rich and varied, including music, theatre, dance, and visual art. She studied in New York, New York and Paris, France. At first she made both paintings and sculptures, but eventually concentrated on sculpture, which she exhibited irregularly from the 1930s onward. It was not until the late 1950s that she began to receive critical acclaim. Before her death, she had received more...

ILLUSTRATOR PROFILE

Carmen Lomas Garza
(1948–)

Growing up as a Mexican American in Kingsville, Texas, Carmen Lomas Garza developed a strong appreciation for her culture and a desire to honor it through art. At the age of 13, she decided to become a professional artist.

The ethnic discrimination Lomas Garza experienced and witnessed as a child and young adult strengthened her resolve to pay tribute to her heritage. She wanted to create images that would instill pride in Mexican Americans and foster understanding among people not familiar with Hispanic culture. Therefore, her paintings portray strong family bonds through scenes of everyday life, such as meals, and rituals, such as ceremonies associated with the Day of the Dead. On this day, Hispanic families remember loved ones who have died.

Lomas Garza's picture books for children include reproductions of her paintings and paper cutouts. She also makes prints and metal cutouts; however, the media for which she is probably best known is gouache, an opaque type of watercolor paint.

Throughout Unit 4, share Lomas Garza's illustrations with the class and discuss the use of pattern, rhythm, and movement in her artwork.

Music

Discuss the contrasts between the straight and zigzag lines of the classroom. Have students think of rhythms to match the two contrasting kinds of lines. For example, zigzag melodies could have wide leaps.

Literature

Show the video or DVD *Song and Dance Man* to introduce the concepts of pattern, rhythm, and movement.

Literature and Art

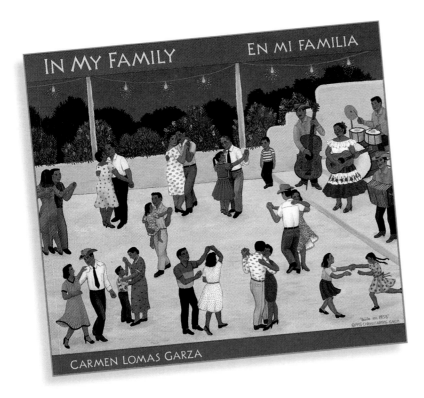

Performing Arts

Show students "The Quillwork Girl," and discuss how the story relates to pattern, rhythm, and movement.

Artsource®

Lesson 1 Patterns

Overview

Lesson 1 introduces the element of pattern. The word *pattern* is commonly used to mean any repetitive sequence. However, in art, pattern has a very specific definition. It is a surface decoration that is always two-dimensional and has a repeating motif. A motif can change color or orientation.

Objectives

 Art History and Culture

To compare how pattern is used in a Delaware bag and American quilt and infer information about the cultures based on the art

 Creative Expression

To create a motif and pattern that describes the student's culture

 Aesthetic Perception

To identify pattern in students' environment

Art Criticism

To evaluate own work using the four steps of art criticism

Vocabulary ★ Vocabulary

Review the following vocabulary words with students before beginning the lesson.

pattern patrón—A decorative surface design. Patterns are two-dimensional.

motif motivo—An image that is duplicated to create a pattern. Motifs can change color or position in a pattern.

See page 149B for additional Spanish vocabulary resources.

 Art Journal: Vocabulary

Have students add these words to the Vocabulary section of their Art Journals.

Lesson Materials

- 6" × 18" white paper strips
- liquid tempera
- markers
- scissors
- paper towels
- small sponges
- paper plates
- water dishes
- different precut colored-paper shapes for students to make a pattern with

Alternate Materials:
- long strips of paper
- precut paper shapes
- scissors
- glue

Program Resources

- *Reading, and Writing Test Prep.*, pp. 42–43
- *Transparency 19*
- *Flash Cards 9*
- *Artist Profiles,* pp 72, 81
- *Animals Through History Time Line*
- *Assessment*, pp. 45–46
- *Large Prints 31 Only the Children* and *32 Layla and Majnun at School*
- *The National Museum of Women in the Arts Collection*

Concept Trace
Patterns
Introduced: Level 1, Unit 5, Lesson 4

Reinforced: Level 3, Unit 5, Lesson 1

Lesson 1 Arts Integration

Theatre

Complete Unit 4, Lesson 1 on pages 72–73 of *Theatre Arts Connections*.

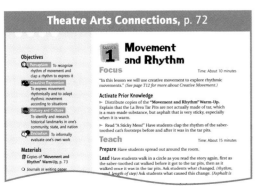

Music

 Listen to *Slavonic Dances* by Antonín Dvořák. The main rhythm pattern always has a falling melody on the first two beats. The most famous combination of rhythm and melody in music is the beginning of Beethoven's *Fifth Symphony*.

Movement & Dance

A motif in dance is an idea or movement that repeats and builds throughout a sequence. Have each student creates a 16 count sequence that is built from a motif. Start with a simple movement, like a bounce, and develop it by performing the movement with a different part of the body or changing the movement speed.

 **Focus**

Time: About 10 minutes

Activate Prior Knowledge

"Have you ever seen a checkerboard?"
"¿Alguna vez han visto un tablero de damas?"

- Discuss student responses. Explain to students that a checkerboard is a pattern and the square is a motif.

Using Literature ⭐ Reading

- Read *The Seasons Sewn: A Year in Patchwork* by Michael McCurdy. Have students look for patterns in the quilts.

Thematic Connection ⭐ Social Studies

- **Cultural Diversity:** Have students discuss what culture is and what kinds of items make up a culture. What do they think cultural diversity is?

Introduce the Art

Look NSAE 2.a

"Let's look at the shoulder bag and quilt."
"Vamos a observar el bolso y la colcha".

- Have students identify pattern in the works of art and the environment.

Main Idea and Details ⭐ Reading

- Ask students to look at both items and talk about what the main use is for each item and then have them describe the details of the items. Students will have many answers. The shoulder bag was used by a Delaware man for carrying things. The quilt was used as decorative bedding. Both of these are functional items that are heavily decorated. When students are describing the details, they should describe the patterns they see.

NSAE 4.a, 4.b, 4.c, 5.a, 5.b

 Art History and Culture

Possible answer: Both cultures valued intricate decoration and were willing to spend a great amount of time to decorate objects that were important to them.

 Web Connection

Visit **http://www.kstrom.net/isk/art/beads/ bando3.html** to see more examples of Native American beaded bags.

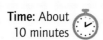 **Lesson 1 Pattern**

Look how these works of art use **pattern.** Pattern is made by repeating a **motif.** The *X* on the bag is one motif. Can you see how it is repeated in a pattern?

◀ **Artist Unknown.** (Delaware).
Delaware Shoulder Bag. c. 1860.
Wool and cotton fabric. 8 ⅗ × 7 ⅘ inches (21.9 × 19.7 cm.). Detroit Institute of Arts, Detroit, Michigan.

 Art History and Culture

Can you guess anything about the cultures that made these works of art by studying the art?

 Art History and Culture

Delaware Shoulder Bags

After the Indian Removal Act of 1830, thousands of Native American people were forced to relocate to reservations in the prairie states of Iowa, Nebraska, Oklahoma, and Kansas. At this time, prairie style beadwork emerged. The Delaware, or Lenape, are believed to be one of the originators of this style of beadwork which involved filling in open areas between designs with bright and contrasting colors. Lenape shoulder bags were often worn by men to intertribal events. Bags like this were used to carry tobacco and other valuable items.

See pages 24–25 and 16–21 for more about art history and subject matter.

Artist Profiles, p. 72

Artist Profile

Delaware Shoulder Bag

The Indian Removal Act of 1830 forced many Native American groups to leave their homelands. The Delaware nation was pushed from homes in the Delaware and Ohio River valleys to land west of the Mississippi River. As in most Native American societies, Delaware women were responsible for caring for children, cooking, housekeeping, gardening, and creating their families' pots, baskets, and clothing.

◀ **Artist unknown** (Delaware, United States).
Delaware Shoulder Bag. c. 1860.

◀ **Artist Unknown.** (American).
*Princess Feather and Rising Sun
Quilt.* c. 1835–1845.

Cotton pieced and appliquéd. 102 × 93 inches
(259.08 × 236.22 cm.). The Newark Museum,
Newark, New Jersey.

Study the two works of art. Find examples
of patterns and motifs.

▶ What motifs do you see in the shoulder bag?

▶ How are the bag motifs different when they
are repeated in the pattern?

▶ What motifs do you see in the quilt?

▶ Are the quilt motifs changed when they are
repeated?

 Aesthetic Perception

Design Awareness Look around your classroom. Can
you find any patterns? Motifs?

Art History and Culture

Princess Feather and Rising Sun Quilt

This American quilt was made in Newark, New Jersey, during the
mid-1800s. Although little is known about the quilter, it may be
assumed that Catherine Fitzgerald was from a relatively prosperous
American family. During the time period when this quilt was made,
nearly all quiltmakers were women. Considering the amount of
time needed to design, cut, assemble, and sew a quilt, the maker
would have to be someone who had significant time to spend on
these tasks.

See pages 24–25 and 16–21
for more about art history
and subject matter.

Artist Profiles, p. 81

◇ Artist Profile ◇

**Princess Feather
and Rising Sun
Quilt**

This American quilt was made in Newark,
New Jersey, during the mid-1800s. Although
little is known about the quilter, it may be
assumed that Catherine Fitzgerald was from
a relatively prosperous American family.
When this quilt was made, nearly all
quiltmakers were women. Considering the
amount of time needed to design, cut,
assemble, and sew a quilt, the maker was
someone who had significant time to spend
on these tasks, free from other work.

Study

▶ There are many motifs in the shoulder
bag. Some of the possible answers are:
triangles on the bag flap, the *X*s on the
right side of the strap, and the leaves on
the left side of the strap.

▶ The colors change, and in the case of the
triangles and leaves on the pouch, they are
oriented in different directions.

▶ The vine with flowers, the pinwheels, and
the sunbursts are all motifs in the quilt.

▶ The flower motif changes by alternating
which side of the vine the flower is on.

■ For more examples of utilitarian art see
***The National Museum of Women in the
Arts Collection.***

Art Journal: Writing
Encourage students to write their
own explanations of pattern in the
Concepts section of their Art Journals.
What questions do they have about
pattern?

 Aesthetic Perception

Design Awareness Discuss student
responses. If they are having difficulty
finding patterns in the classroom, ask them
to look at things like lined paper. Point out to
them that the line is motif, and when it is
repeated on the paper, it creates a pattern.
Encourage students to identify variations in
objects from their environments.

NSAE 2.b, 5.c
Developing Visual Literacy Ask students to
look for and think about patterns and motifs
they see in their everyday lives. Have them
use personal examples to elaborate on the
idea of pattern and motif. For example, if
students have patterned sheets on their bed,
tell them to look for the motif in the sheet.

Web Connection
Visit **http://www.newarkmuseum.org/
quiltmasterpieces/index.htm** to see an
exhibit of quilts.

Teach

Time: About 35 minutes

"Why would you use pattern in a work of art?" "¿Por qué usarían un patrón en una obra de arte?"

■ Read the information about pattern on page 128 and discuss it with the class.

Practice

Materials: different precut colored-paper shapes for students to make a pattern with

■ Distribute the materials and have students follow the directions on page 128.

■ The object of this Practice is for students to work together to create a pattern.

■ Have students identify and practice skills necessary for producing prints using a variety of materials.

NSAE 1.c, 1.d, 2.c, 3.b

Creative Expression

Materials: 6" × 18" white paper strips, liquid tempera, markers, scissors, paper towels, small sponges, paper plates, water dishes

Alternate Materials: long strips of paper, precut paper shapes, scissors, and glue

■ Distribute materials and have students follow the directions on page 129.

■ Encourage students to create effective compositions using design principles.

■ Review the Activity Tips on page 241 for visual examples of the activity if needed.

■ Review the Technique Tips on page 223 for visual examples of sponge prints if needed.

NSAE 3.a

Art Journal: Brainstorming

Have students brainstorm ideas for their motifs in the Ideas section of their Art Journals.

Using Pattern

Pattern is a decorative design on the surface of something. Patterns are two-dimensional. The part of the pattern that repeats is the motif.

Motifs do not always look the same in a pattern. A motif can be turned different ways or be different colors. Look at this pattern. Can you see how the motif repeats and changes?

motif

pattern

Practice

Make a pattern with your classmates.

1. Look at the colors and shapes your teacher has given you.

2. Brainstorm with your classmates about a pattern you can make.

3. Line up the shapes so they are in a pattern. What is the motif?

Differentiated Instruction

Reteach

Have the class plan a colorful motif of shapes, letters, or numbers that could be repeated to make a border around the classroom. Then, let students sketch the repeated motif on long rolls of shelving paper and paint it with bright poster paint.

Special Needs

Some students may have difficulty coming up with ideas for cultural motifs. Enlist the help of parents and family members in identifying and describing motifs that are culturally significant to students in your class.

ELL Tips

Define *pattern* and *motif*. Have students add the words to their vocabulary lists. Show examples of designs and draw a geometric motif on the board.

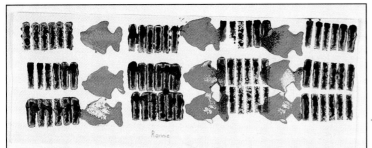

◄ **Ronnie McCullough.** Age 8.

Think about how this student used pattern and motif in his artwork.

 Creative Expression

What kind of patterns could you make that would describe your culture? Design a motif and make a pattern.

1. Think of a motif that describes your culture. Draw the motif and cut it out of a sponge.

2. Dip your sponge into paint. Make prints on the paper using your motif to create a pattern.

3. Fill the paper with your pattern.

 **Art Criticism**

Describe What did you choose for your motif?

Analyze How did you use your motif to make a pattern?

Interpret How does your pattern express your culture?

Decide Did you repeat your motif to make an interesting pattern?

Reflect
Time: About 10 minutes

Review and Assess

"What is the difference between a pattern and a motif?" "¿Cuál es la diferencia entre un patrón y un motivo?"

Think

This student used a fish and line motif to create his pattern.

■ Use **Large Prints 31** *Only the Children* and **32** *Layla and Majnun at School* to have students identify patterns and motifs.

■ Have students identify stories and constructions in this lesson's artwork.

■ Have students identify ideas of the artists in this lesson's art.

Informal Assessment

Art Journal: Critical Thinking

Have students answer the four art criticism questions—Describe, Analyze, Interpret, and Decide—in the Critical Thinking section of their Art Journals. Ask students to define their reasons for preferences in their own art. Then have them identify ideas in their peers' art.

■ For standardized-format test practice using this lesson's art content, see pages 42–43 in **Reading and Writing Test Preparation**.

Art Across the Curriculum
NSAE 6.a, 6.b

Use these simple ideas to reinforce art concepts across the curriculum.

★ **Expository Writing** Have students use the writing process to write a paragraph about their culture.

★ **Math** Discuss tessellations with the students and how they have patterns and motifs.

★ **Science** Discuss the surface pattern of striation found in sedimentary rocks and how it is formed

★ **Social Studies** Discuss what decorative patterns mean in different cultures and how those cultures use decorative patterns.

★ **Technology** Discuss how students could use a patterned background for an e-mail. Visit **SRAonline.com** to print detailed instructions for this activity.

Patterns

<hr>

Extra! For the Art Specialist

Time: About 45 minutes

Focus

Study **Large Prints 31** *Only the Children* and **32** *Layla and Majnun at School* and ask students to point out any patterns they see. Are there patterns on people's clothes? What about in the borders of the art?

Teach

Explain to students that they will be creating glue line prints of shape patterns. They will draw a pattern composed of shapes on tag board and trace it with glue. When dry, they will use the plate to make a print of the pattern. Demonstrate the printmaking process for students. Have students complete the alternate activity.

Reflect

Have students evaluate their work using the four steps of art criticism.

Alternate Activity

Materials:

- glue
- tag board or poster board cut into 6" × 4" pieces
- pencils
- construction paper
- brushers, brayer, water dishes, newspaper
- paints or inks for printing

1. Discuss patterns and how prints are made.

2. Draw a pattern made of shapes on the tag board. Trace the shapes with glue. Make sure your glue lines are thick.

3. When the glue is dry, ink the plate and make a print on the construction paper. Repeat and change colors as many times as you wish.

Research in Art Education

"There is more to learning about art than learning to do it. Most people will not actually seek to make art in their lifetime, but all of us have daily contact with visual stimuli that deliberately (in package design, fashion, or good building) or accidentally (a pattern of leaves on snow or an unexpected bright color against a faded doorway) appeal to our aesthetic sense and offer a bit of visual order in the bustle of the everyday" (Elizabeth Vallance. "Criticism as Subject Matter in Schools and in Art Museums." *Journal of Aesthetic Education* 22 (4). (1988): 69–81).

Assessment
Use the following rubric to evaluate the artwork students make in the Creative Expression activity and to assess students' understanding of pattern.

Have students complete page 45 or 46 in their *Assessment* books.

	Art History and Culture	Aesthetic Perception	Creative Expression	Art Criticism
3 POINTS	The student can identify and compare the use of pattern and infer information about the cultures based on the works of art.	The student accurately identifies pattern and motif in his or her environment.	The student's print clearly illustrates a good use of pattern and motif.	The student thoughtfully and honestly evaluates his or her own work using the four steps of art criticism.
2 POINTS	The student's identification or comparison of pattern and motif is weak or incomplete.	The student shows emerging awareness of pattern and motif, but cannot consistently identify them.	The student's print shows some awareness of pattern and motif.	The student attempts to evaluate his or her own work, but shows an incomplete understanding of evaluation criteria.
1 POINT	The student cannot identify or compare the use of pattern and infer information about the cultures based on the works of art.	The student cannot identify pattern and motif.	The student's print shows no understanding of pattern and motif.	The student makes no attempt to evaluate his or her own artwork.

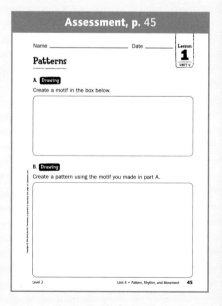

Assessment, p. 45

Name _____ Date _____

Lesson 1 UNIT 4

Patterns

A Drawing
Create a motif in the box below.

B Drawing
Create a pattern using the motif you made in part A.

Level 2   Unit 4 • Pattern, Rhythm, and Movement   **45**

Patterns in Nature

Lesson 2 introduces patterns in nature. Patterns in nature are naturally occurring patterns, that are not made by a human and that are found on plants, animals, and geographical features.

Objectives

Art History and Culture
To recognize how artists often portray realistic depictions of natural objects based on how they feel about nature

Creative Expression
To draw a natural object that has patterns

Aesthetic Perception
To recognize objects in nature that have patterns in students' environments

Art Criticism
To evaluate own work using the four steps of art criticism

Vocabulary Vocabulary

Review the following vocabulary word with students before beginning the lesson.

print grabado—an image created by using a stamp or printing plate. When artists make prints, they can make many identical images.

See page 149B for additional Spanish vocabulary resources.

Art Journal: Vocabulary
Have students add this word to the Vocabulary section of their Art Journals.

Lesson Materials
- 9" × 12" pieces of paper
- glue
- pencils
- palettes
- water dishes
- liquid tempera
- small brushes
- newspaper
- paper towels
- white paper
- crayons

Alternate Materials:
- oil pastels
- black glue

Program Resources
- *Reading and Writing Test Prep.*, pp. 44–45
- *Transparency 20*
- *Artist Profiles*, pp. 5, 38
- *Animals Through History Time Line*
- *Assessment*, pp. 47–48
- *Large Print 31* Only the Children
- *The National Museum of Women in the Arts Collection*

Concept Trace
Patterns in Nature
Introduced: Level 1, Unit 5, Lesson 4

Reinforced: Level 3, Unit 5, Lessons 1–3

Lesson 2 Arts Integration

Theatre
Complete Unit 4, Lesson 2 on pages 74–75 of *Theatre Arts Connections*.

Theatre Arts Connections, p. 74

Music

Putting pulses in units of two (a strong beat plus a weak beat) is called duple meter. A march is in duple meter. Listen to *Walking the Dog* by George Gershwin. Before you even hear the piece can you guess if it is in duple or triple meter? Would it be tricky to walk a dog in three meter time?

Movement & Dance
Have students look at different objects in nature, such as leaves, sea shells, and rocks. Have students identify their patterns and then draw them on a piece of paper. Explore each of the patterns in the body, creating axial movements, such as swinging, twisting, and turning. Select three ideas to work with and organize them into a short sequence.

 **ocus**   Time: About 10 minutes

Activate Prior Knowledge

"Have you ever seen a dalmatian?" "¿Alguna vez han visto un perro dálmata?"

■ Discuss student responses. Explain to students that a dalmatian has spots and those spots are naturally occurring. Spots on a dalmatian are a pattern in nature.

Using Literature 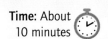 Reading

■ Read *Lots and Lots of Zebra Stripes: Patterns in Nature* by Stephen Swinburne. Have students look for patterns in the natural objects.

Thematic Connection ⭐ Science

■ **Living Things:** Ask students to think of other animals or plants that have patterns on them.

Introduce the Art

Look   NSAE 2.a

"Let's examine these two prints." "Vamos a examinar estos dos grabados".

■ Have students identify pattern in the works of art and the environment.

Finding a Pattern ⭐ Math

■ Have students brainstorm and discuss how they can find patterns on the natural objects in these pictures and in their surroundings. Will these patterns be as easy to see as the humanmade patterns?

NSAE 4.a, 4.b, 4.c, 5.a, 5.b

 Art History and Culture

Possible answer: Both of these artists were interested in nature and liked it very much because they drew such detailed pictures. They wanted to document the things they saw in nature for people to study.

 Web Connection

Visit **http://naturalhistory.mse.jhu.edu/ ChronologicalTour/ChT_Merian.html** to see more of Merian's illustrations.

130 UNIT 4 • Pattern, Rhythm, and Movement

Patterns in Nature

Look at the two pieces of art. Both are realistic illustrations of objects the artists found in nature. Where are patterns in these **prints**?

◀ **Maria Sibylla Merian.** (German). *Plate 2 (from "Dissertation in Insect Generations and Metamorphosis in Surinam").* 1719.

Hand-colored engraving on paper. 18 × 13 ¾ inches (45.72 × 34.93 cm.). National Museum of Women in the Arts, Washington, D.C.

 Art History and Culture

How do you think these two artists felt about nature? Why?

130   Unit 4 • Lesson 2

 **Art History and Culture**

Maria Sibylla Merian

Maria Sibylla Merian (mä rē´ ə si´ bil ə mer´ ē ən) (1647–1717) was born in Frankfurt, Germany. As a child, Merian was always interested in drawing the things she saw around her in nature and as she grew older, she began a career of illustrating nature specimens. Merian raised her own specimens and used living insects as models. At this time, most nature illustrators used preserved specimens. In 1685, Merian moved with her daughters to a Dutch province. At 52, she took a daughter on an unchaperoned trip to Surinam to study wildlife. After returning home, she published the book that includes this illustration.

See pages 24–25 and 16–21 for more about art history and subject matter.

Artist Profiles, p. 38

Artist Profile ◆
Maria Sibylla Merian
1647–1717

Maria Sibylla Merian (mä rē´ ə si´ bil ə mer´ ē ən) grew up in a house full of artists. Her father was an artist and publisher. Her stepfather was a still-life painter, engraver, and art dealer. Merian was surrounded by a large collection of prints, paintings, and books and benefited from her stepfather's artistic instruction. Merian published a number of books on flowers and on the metamorphoses and eating habits of caterpillars. An independent woman, Merian traveled with her daughter to Suriname in South America, where they lived for two years.

Study the two works of art to find examples of patterns in nature.

▶ What patterns do you see in these two pictures?

▶ What are the motifs of the patterns you found?

◀ **John James Audubon.**
(West Indian/American).
Carolina Parakeet. 1832.
....
Aquatint engraving on paper. 33 × 24 inches (83.82 × 60.96 cm). The Morris Museum of Art, Augusta, Georgia.

🔍 Aesthetic Perception

Seeing Like an Artist What patterns can you find on plants and animals in your community?

🏺 Art History and Culture

John James Audubon

John James Audubon (jän jāmz ô´ də bən) (1785–1851) was born in what is now Haiti and was raised in Nantes, France. When he was a young man, he began to draw. In order to avoid being drafted by Napoleon, Audubon moved to America and lived on an estate his father owned. He had little responsibility and spent many days outdoors hunting, riding, and drawing. Audubon was one of the first people to band birds in North America to track their migrations. In order to sketch birds, he would collect them as specimens. He then developed a technique that involved passing wires through their bodies so that he could pose them in lifelike positions.

See pages 24–25 and 16–21 for more about art history and subject matter.

Artist Profiles, p. 5

◆ Artist Profile ◆
John James Audubon
1785-1851

John James Audubon (jän jāmz ô´ də ban) was born in Santo Domingo, now Haiti. His mother died a few months after he was born, so he was raised in France by his father and his father's wife, a kind woman who encouraged his love of the outdoors and art. When he was 18, he left France for America to live on one of his father's plantations in Pennsylvania. Audubon drew birds only as a hobby until he and his family met with hard financial times. Audubon's successful journeys established him as a leading romantic painter and expert on ornithology. Years after his death the National Audubon Society was founded in

Study

▶ In the Merian, the yellow spots on the red leaves are the most obvious pattern. Also, the bugs have striations on their backs that are a pattern. The birds in the Audubon have patterns in the way the feathers are arranged.

▶ Answers will vary depending on what patterns the students find. The spots and feathers are examples of individual motifs.

■ For more examples of genre art see *The National Museum of Women in the Arts Collection.*

📖 Art Journal: Listing

Have students make a list of places in nature where they have seen patterns in the Concepts section of their Art Journals.

🔍 Aesthetic Perception

Seeing Like an Artist Ask students to either look out the window or brainstorm some things they see when they are outside that have patterns. Remind students that pattern is surface design only. Encourage students to look for patterns in natural objects on their way home from school. Encourage students to identify variations in subjects from their environments.   NSAE 2.b, 5.c

Developing Visual Literacy Discuss the careful observation that the two artists put into producing these two illustrations. What kind of preparations would an artist have to make to be able to paint such realistic pictures of living things?

💻 Web Connection

Visit **http://www.mfah.org/exhibition.asp?par1= 1&par2=3&par3=50&par6=3&par4=295&lgc=4& currentPage=1** to see another bird by Audubon.

Teach

Time: About 35 minutes

"How are patterns in nature different from patterns made by a human?" *"¿En qué se diferencian los patrones en la naturaleza de los hechos por los seres humanos?"*

- Read and discuss the information about patterns in nature on page 132.

Practice

Materials: white paper, crayons

Alternate Materials: oil pastels

- Have students identify and practice skills necessary for producing drawings and paintings using a variety of materials.

- Distribute the materials, and have students follow the directions on page 132.

NSAE 1.c, 1.d, 2.c, 3.b

Creative Expression

Materials: 9" × 12" pieces of paper, glue, pencils, palettes, water dishes, glue, liquid tempera, small brushes, newspaper, paper towels

Alternate Materials: oil pastels, black glue

- Distribute the materials and have students follow the directions on page 133.

- Encourage students to create effective compositions using design principles.

- Encourage students to express their ideas and feelings in their fantasy birds using a variety of lines.

- Review the Activity Tips on page 241 for visual examples of the activity if needed.

NSAE 3.a

Art Journal: Brainstorming

Have students make a list of types of patterns that they could put on their natural object in the Ideas section of their Art Journal. Students may wish to sketch examples of the types of patterns they plan to use in the Creative Expression activity.

Using Patterns in Nature

Not all patterns are made by a person. Many patterns are in the plants, animals, and other natural objects around us. Look at the photographs below. Can you see the patterns?

Practice

Draw a leaf with a pattern on it.

1. Draw the outline of a leaf.
2. Think of a pattern to put on the leaf.
3. Draw the pattern on the leaf using crayons or markers. What is your motif?

Differentiated Instruction

Reteach

Have students look through books and magazines to find plants or animals with patterns. Remind students that patterns are surface designs only.

Special Needs

Reinforce the lesson objectives of recognizing and recreating natural patterns by providing students with natural objects they can look at and feel.

ELL Tips

Review the term *free-form* and have students add the word *natural* to their vocabulary lists. Bring in pictures of animals and plants and ask students to describe any naturally occurring patterns they see.

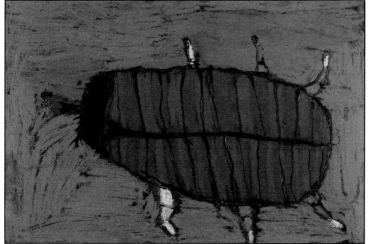

◄ **Mitchell Pettus.**
Age 7.

Think about how this student used pattern on his bug.

 Creative Expression

What kind of patterns have you seen around you? Draw a natural object that has patterns.

1. Think of an animal, plant, or other natural object. Draw a large picture of the object.

2. Add lines and shapes to make natural patterns.

3. Redraw your lines with glue to add texture. Let your drawing dry and fill in the shapes with color.

 **Art Criticism**

Describe What object from nature did you draw?

Analyze What motif did you repeat to create your pattern?

Interpret Give your work a title.

Decide If you were making another natural pattern, how would you change your motif?

Art Across the Curriculum

NSAE 6.a, 6.b

Use these simple ideas to reinforce art concepts across the curriculum.

★ **Poetry** Have students write a poem about a natural object that has a pattern on it.

★ **Math** Discuss with students how they could figure out what percentage of an animal is covered in a pattern.

★ **Science** Discuss with students how different animals have patterns that help them survive in their environments.

★ **Social Studies** Discuss how camouflage is created to mimic nature.

★ **Technology** Show students how to research animals with patterns in an electronic encyclopedia. Visit **SRAonline.com** to print detailed instructions for this activity.

Reflect

Time: About 10 minutes

Review and Assess

"Explain the difference between patterns in nature and humanmade patterns."

"Expliquen la diferencia entre los patrones en la naturaleza y los patrones hechos por los seres humanos".

Think

This student used patterns in the lines on his bug.

■ Use *Large Prints 31 Only the Children* and have students look for natural patterns. Does this picture have any? Why or why not?

■ Have students identify stories and constructions in this lesson's artwork.

■ Have students identify ideas of the artists in this lesson's art.

Informal Assessment

Art Journal: Critical Thinking

Have students answer the four art criticism questions—Describe, Analyze, Interpret, and Decide—in the Critical Thinking section of their Art Journals. Ask students to define their reasons for preferences in their own art. Then have them identify ideas in their peers' art.

■ For standardized-format test practice using this lesson's art content, see pages 44–45 in *Reading and Writing Test Preparation*.

Patterns in Nature

Extra! **For the Art Specialist**   Time: About 45 minutes

Focus

Study **Large Prints 31** *Only the Children* and **32** *Layla and Majnun at School* and ask students to look for patterns.

Teach

Explain to students that they will be creating a pop-up paper plant with a pattern on it. They will use construction paper to make small loops. Have students complete the Alternate Activity.

Reflect

Have students evaluate their work using the four steps of art criticism.

Alternate Activity

Materials:
- construction paper
- scissors
- glue
- pencils
- markers

1. Discuss the types of patterns found in nature.

2. Select a piece of construction paper for your background. Draw several simple plants or flowers and cut them out. Draw patterns on them with markers.

3. Use scrap pieces of construction paper to cut thin 1–2 inch strips. Use a dot of glue to make the strips into loops.

4. Attach your cut flower or plant designs to the background paper using the loops. Repeat until your paper is filled with pop-up plants.

Research in Art Education

Education in the arts aids in "developing worthy citizens, people who enjoy intellectual and emotional control, people with skill and initiative, and people who are aware of their world" (Gaitskell, C. D., and Al Hurwitz. *Children and Their Art: Methods for the Elementary School.* Toronto: Harcourt, 1970).

Assessment

Use the following rubric to evaluate the artwork students make in the Creative Expression activity and to assess students' understanding of patterns in nature.

Have students complete page 47 or 48 in their **Assessment** books.

	Art History and Culture	Aesthetic Perception	Creative Expression	Art Criticism
3 POINTS	The student can identify and compare the use of style and patterns in nature in works of art.	The student accurately identifies patterns in nature in his or her environment.	The student's natural object clearly illustrates a good use of patterns in nature.	The student thoughtfully and honestly evaluates his or her own work using the four steps of art criticism.
2 POINTS	The student's identification or comparison of patterns in nature is weak or incomplete.	The student shows emerging awareness of patterns in nature, but cannot consistently identify them.	The student's natural object shows some awareness of patterns in nature.	The student attempts to evaluate his or her own work, but shows an incomplete understanding of evaluation criteria.
1 POINT	The student cannot identify or compare the use of style and patterns in nature in different works of art.	The student cannot identify patterns in nature.	The student's natural object shows no understanding of patterns in nature.	The student makes no attempt to evaluate his or her own artwork.

Assessment, p. 47

Name _____ Date _____

Lesson
2
UNIT 4

Patterns in Nature

A. Writing
Define *pattern* in your own words.

_____

_____

B. Drawing
In the box below, draw an animal with a pattern on it.

Level 2   Unit 4 • Pattern, Rhythm, and Movement   **47**

Rhythm

Lesson 3 introduces students to rhythm. Rhythm is a principle of design that is created by using repeating elements in a work of art. By repeating the same object in a work of art and separating the objects with negative space, rhythm is created. This draws the eyes through the work of art and creates movement.

Objectives

Art History and Culture

To compare the use of rhythm in two paintings featuring plants and the artists' purpose in depicting plants

Creative Expression

To make a still life that incorporates rhythm

Aesthetic Perception

To recognize rhythm in students' environment

Art Criticism

To evaluate own work using the four steps of art criticism

Vocabulary Vocabulary

Review the following vocabulary words with students before beginning the lesson.

rhythm *ritmo*—the principle of design that is created by repeating objects through a work of art. Rhythm creates movement and is made by using positive and negative space.

positive space *espacio positivo*—any shape or form

negative space *espacio negativo*—the empty space between and surrounding a shape or form

See page 149B for additional Spanish vocabulary resources.

Art Journal: Vocabulary

Have students add these words to the Vocabulary section of their Art Journals.

Lesson Materials
- large sheets of paper
- watercolors
- oil pastels
- colored chalk
- brushes
- water dishes
- paper towels

Alternate Materials:
- crayons
- markers

Program Resources
- *Reading and Writing Test Prep.*, pp. 46–47
- *Transparency 21*
- *Flash Cards, 9, 10, 11*
- *Artist Profiles*, pp. 36, 71
- *Animals Through History Time Line*
- *Assessment*, pp. 49–50
- *Large Prints 31* Only the Children and *32* Layla and Majnun at School
- *Art Around the World Collection*

Concept Trace
Rhythm
Introduced: Level 1, Unit 5, Lesson 6
Reinforced: Level 3, Unit 5, Lessons 4–5

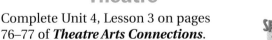

Lesson 3 Arts Integration

Theatre

Complete Unit 4, Lesson 3 on pages 76–77 of *Theatre Arts Connections*.

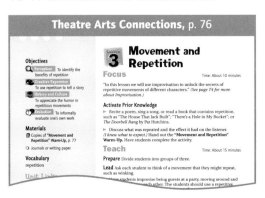

Theatre Arts Connections, p. 76

Music

 Listen to *In the Hall of the Mountain King* from "Peer Gynt Suite No.1, Op. 46" by Edvard Grieg. Clap the rhythm pattern. Grieg does not change this pattern as he makes the music louder or faster. What else changes in the music?

Movement & Dance

Have students hold hands in a line and follow the leader around the classroom on a curved pathway. Both ends of the line will eventually connect, turning it into a circle. Standing in the circle formation, explore different kinds of rhythmic movement such as bouncing for eight counts, clapping hands for eight counts, or swinging arms for eight counts.

ocus

Time: About 10 minutes

Activate Prior Knowledge

"How would you describe a bunch of grapes?"

"¿Cómo describirían un racimo de uvas?".

- Discuss student responses. Explain that a bunch of grapes has rhythm when you look from grape to grape.

Using Literature ⭐ Reading

- Read *The Tiny Seed* by Eric Carle. Discuss where students see rhythm in the book.

Thematic Connection ⭐ Science

- **Plants:** Encourage students to talk about the ways that plants have rhythm. For example, rhythm can be found in the branches on a tree or the petals on a daisy.

Introduce the Art

Look NSAE 2.a

"Look closely at the two paintings."

"Miren detalladamente las dos pinturas".

- Have students identify rhythm in the works of art and the environment.

Similarity ⭐ Math

- Ask students to look for similarities between these two pictures. What do they see? Both are pictures of plants. In both pictures, the plants are separated by negative space.

NSAE 4.a, 4.b, 4.c, 5.a, 5.b

Art History and Culture

Possible answer: This means that plants have been important and interesting to people for a long time, even when other things change.

 **Web Connection**

Visit **http://www.zalucha.com/studio/** to see Peggy Zalucha's website.

134 UNIT 4 • Pattern, Rhythm, and Movement

Lesson 3 Rhythm

Look at the two paintings. Both show objects that are repeated. When an object is repeated, this creates **rhythm.** Rhythm leads your eyes through a work of art.

▲ **Peggy Flora Zalucha.** (American). *Peony Blooms (IX)*. 1992.

Watercolor on paper. 44 × 68 inches (111.76 × 172.27 cm.). Courtesy of Peggy Flora Zalucha.

Art History and Culture

These paintings were made almost 100 years apart. What does this tell you about plants and people?

Art History and Culture

Peggy Flora Zalucha

Peggy Flora Zalucha (peg´ ē flor´ ə zə lōō´ kə) (1948–) was born in Peoria, Illinois. She was raised to appreciate photography and was encouraged to take pictures of the world around her. When Zalucha was in college, women were not advised to obtain studio degrees. Seeing this ideology as a potential obstacle, Zalucha sought a degree in teaching instead. Zalucha has been making and teaching art for over twenty years. Her paintings have been classified as a modern example of genre painting. Genre painting is the art of finding beauty in the everyday objects of life.

See pages 24–25 and 16–21 for more about art history and subject matter.

Artist Profiles, p. 71

Artist Profile

Peggy Flora Zalucha
b. 1948

Peggy Flora Zalucha (peg´ ē flor´ a zə lōō´ kə) was born in Peoria, Illinois. She was raised to appreciate photography and encouraged to take pictures of the world around her. When Zalucha was in college, women were not advised to get studio degrees, so Zalucha got her degree in teaching instead. Her first official job was as an art teacher in a rural Nebraska school. Zalucha has been making and teaching art for more than 20 years.

▲ **William J. McCloskey.**
Wrapped Oranges. 1889.
· ·
Oil on canvas. 12 × 16 inches
(30.48 × 40.64 cm.). Amon Carter
Museum, Fort Worth, Texas.

Study the two paintings to find their rhythm.

▶ What objects are repeated to create the rhythms in the two paintings?

▶ How does the positioning of the objects make your eyes move around the paintings?

Aesthetic Perception

Design Awareness Can you find examples of rhythm in the objects in your classroom? For example, pieces of chalk lined up are an example of rhythm.

Study

▶ The peonies are repeated in the Zalucha painting. The oranges are repeated in the McCloskey painting.

▶ Answers may vary. Most eyes will probably move from left to right and from low to high to low.

■ For more examples of art from North America see the ***Art Around the World Collection.***

Art Journal: Drawing

Have students sketch a picture that illustrates rhythm in the Concepts section of their Art Journals.

Aesthetic Perception

Design Awareness Give students time to look around the classroom to find rhythm. Ask students to share the rhythm that they find or can think of with the rest of the class. Have students identify variations in objects from the environment.

NSAE 2.b, 5.c
Developing Visual Literacy Discuss what each artwork means to the artist and what the artists are trying to say with their artwork. What are the main ideas of these works of art?

Art History and Culture

William J. McCloskey

William McCloskey (wil´ yəm mə kläs´ kē) (1859–1941) was born in Philadelphia, Pennsylvania. He was married to the artist Alberta Binford, who was also a highly regarded realist painter. The two of them set up a portrait studio together and traveled widely across the United States and Europe, earning acclaim for their acutely realistic paintings. McCloskey is best known for his series of still-life paintings of oranges wrapped in paper from 1888 to 1912. This subject matter reflected the great boom of interstate fruit shipments during the time period. McCloskey set up his still lifes in the studio and created sketches and final compositions directly from his arrangements.

See pages 24–25 and 16–21 for more about art history and subject matter.

Artist Profiles, p. 36

● Artist Profile ●
William McCloskey
1859–1941
Realist painter William McCloskey
(wil´ yəm mə kläs´ kē) was born in
Philadelphia, Pennsylvania, where he
studied at the Pennsylvania Academy of
Fine Art. He was married to the artist
Alberta Binford, who was also a highly
regarded realist painter. The two of them
set up a portrait studio together and
traveled widely across the United States
and Europe, earning acclaim for their
acutely realistic paintings.

Web Connection

Visit **http://www.kidsart.com/IS/411.html** to see and learn about another McCloskey orange picture.

each

Time: About 35 minutes

"How can you use rhythm in a work of art?"
"¿Cómo pueden usar el ritmo en una obra de arte?"

- Read and discuss the information about rhythm on page 136.

Practice

- Have students follow the directions on page 136.

- Have students identify and practice skills necessary for producing paintings using a variety of materials.

Creative Expression

Materials: large sheets of paper, watercolors, scissors, oil pastels, colored chalk, brushes, water dishes, paper towels

Alternate Materials: crayons, markers

- Distribute the materials and have students follow the directions on page 137.

- Encourage students to create effective compositions using design principles.

- Review the Activity Tips on page 242 for visual examples of the activity if needed.

NSAE 3.a

Art Journal: Brainstorming

Have students think of and list different plants they could use to create rhythm in the Ideas section of their Art Journals.

Using Rhythm

When an artist draws an object, leaves space, and repeats the object, rhythm is created. The object is **positive space.** The empty space is **negative space.** Rhythm is made when an artist repeats a positive space and separates it with negative space. Can you find the positive space and negative space in this picture?

Practice

Create rhythm with your classmates.

1. Break up into small groups.
2. Arrange your group so you have rhythm.
3. Look at the other groups and their rhythm. Tell the other groups where your positive and negative spaces are.

Differentiated Instruction

Reteach

Have students look through books and magazines to find objects from nature that show rhythm.

Special Needs

Create a multi-sensory learning experience by asking students to sound out the rhythm of their works of art.

ELL Tips

Review *motif* and *rhythm*. Define *visual rhythm*. Use the words in sentence strips. Bring in pictures of different motifs. Have students pick out those they like.

◄ **Alvin Yu.**
Age 8.

Think about how this student used rhythm in his painting.

 Creative Expression

Can you create a still life using plants and rhythm? Paint a still life.

1. Choose and draw a plant. Repeat it several times to create rhythm.
2. Choose another object. Draw and repeat it as well.
3. Paint your composition.

Art Criticism

Describe What plants did you use in your still life?

Analyze Where are the positive and negative spaces in your still life?

Interpret How did you create rhythm in your painting?

Decide How would your painting be different if you hadn't used rhythm?

Reflect

Time: About 10 minutes

Review and Assess

"Can you explain the difference between rhythm and pattern?" "¿Pueden explicar la diferencia entre ritmo y patrón?"

Think

This student created rhythm by separating the leaves and pumpkins with negative space.

■ Use *Large Prints 31 Only the Children* and *32 Layla and Majnun at School* to have students look for rhythm.

■ Have students identify stories and constructions in this lesson's artwork.

■ Have students identify ideas of the artists in this lesson's art.

Informal Assessment

Art Journal: Critical Thinking
Have students answer the four art criticism questions—Describe, Analyze, Interpret, and Decide—in the Critical Thinking section of their Art Journals. Ask students to define their reasons for preferences in their own art. Then have them identify ideas in their peers' art.

■ For standardized-format test practice using this lesson's art content, see pages 46–47 in *Reading and Writing Test Preparation*.

Art Across the Curriculum   NSAE 6.a, 6.b

Use these simple ideas to reinforce art concepts across the curriculum.

★ **Expository Writing** Have students write an expository paragraph comparing the lives of Peggy Flora Zalucha and William J. McCloskey.

★ **Math** Count the number of flowers and the number of oranges and multiply them.

★ **Science** Discuss how plants produce fruit and flowers.

★ **Social Studies** Discuss how plants were brought to new countries from their native regions due to exploration.

★ **Technology** Show students how to use the shape tool to create a drawing that uses rhythm. Visit **SRAonline.com** to print detailed instructions for this activity.

Lesson 3 — Rhythm

Extra! For the Art Specialist

Time: About 45 minutes

Focus

Study **Large Prints 31** *Only the Children* and **32** *Layla and Majnun at School* and ask students to describe any objects that repeat in the works. Discuss rhythm.

Teach

Explain to students that they will be creating a letter design of one of their initials and decorating it in the Art Nouveau style. The focus will be on repeating a floral motif to create rhythm. Discuss Art Nouveau style. Have students complete the Alternate Activity.

Reflect

Have students evaluate their artwork using the four steps of art criticism.

Alternate Activity

Materials:
- white drawing paper
- pencils
- crayons
- watercolors
- brushes, water dishes, and newspaper
- permanent markers in many colors

1. Choose one of your initials and sketch a large bubble or block drawing of it.

2. Fill the letter with a rhythmic floral design.

3. Trace your drawing with markers and color the letter and design using markers and crayons.

4. Paint the background of your design with watercolors.

Research in Art Education

Although it is impossible to prove that arts involvement raises SAT scores, one study did show that "students who take arts classes have higher math, verbal, and composite SAT scores than students who take no arts classes" ("SAT Scores of Students Who Study the Arts: What We Can and Cannot Conclude at the Association" in *Critical Links,* p. 96). This positive correlation is still important.

Assessment

Use the following rubric to evaluate the artwork students make in the Creative Expression activity and to assess students' understanding of rhythm.

Have students complete page 49 or 50 in their *Assessment* books.

	Art History and Culture	Aesthetic Perception	Creative Expression	Art Criticism
3 POINTS	The student can identify and compare the use of rhythm and subject matter in two works of art.	The student accurately identifies rhythm in his or her environment.	The student's still life clearly illustrates a good use of rhythm.	The student thoughtfully and honestly evaluates his or her own work using the four steps of art criticism.
2 POINTS	The student's identification or comparison of the use of rhythm is weak or incomplete.	The student shows emerging awareness of rhythm, but cannot consistently identify them.	The student's still life shows some awareness of rhythm.	The student attempts to evaluate his or her own work, but shows an incomplete understanding of evaluation criteria.
1 POINT	The student cannot identify or compare the use of rhythm and subject matter in different works of art..	The student cannot identify rhythm.	The student's still life shows no understanding of rhythm.	The student makes no attempt to evaluate his or her own artwork.

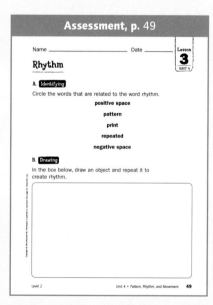

Assessment, p. 49

Name _____ Date _____

Rhythm   Lesson **3** UNIT 4

A. Identifying
Circle the words that are related to the word *rhythm.*

positive space

pattern

print

repeated

negative space

B. Drawing
In the box below, draw an object and repeat it to create rhythm.

Level 2   Unit 4 • Pattern, Rhythm, and Movement   **49**

Rhythm and Form

Lesson 4 explains that rhythm can also be created using forms.

Objectives

 Art History and Culture

To identify and compare the inspiration of two Native American works of art.

 Creative Expression

To create a storyteller doll that illustrates rhythm and form

 Aesthetic Perception

To identify rhythm using forms in students' environments

 Art Criticism

To evaluate own work using the four steps of art criticism

Vocabulary Vocabulary

Review the following vocabulary words with students before beginning the lesson.

storyteller doll muñeca del cuentista—a Native American sculpture that shows one person relating the history of the culture to many children

diorama diorama—a display of a scene using sculpted, miniature figurines

See page 149B for additional Spanish vocabulary resources.

 Art Journal: Vocabulary

Have students add these words to the Vocabulary section of their Art Journals.

Lesson Materials
- white Longhorn clay
- black velvet under glaze
- red Longhorn clay that has been thinned to under glaze consistency
- pencil
- kiln
- clay tools
- modeling clay

Alternate Materials:
- air dry clay

Program Resources
- *Reading and Writing Test Prep.*, pp. 48–49
- *Transparency 22*
- *Artist Profiles*, pp. 13, 82
- *Animals Through History Time Line*
- *Assessment*, pp. 51–52
- *Large Prints 31 Only the Children* and *32 Layla and Majnun at School*
- *The National Museum of Women in the Arts Collection*

Concept Trace
Rhythm and Form
Introduced: Level 1, Unit 5, Lesson 6

Reinforced: Level 3, Unit 5, Lessons 4–6

Lesson 4 Arts Integration

Theatre

Complete Unit 4, Lesson 4 on pages 78–79 of *Theatre Arts Connections*.

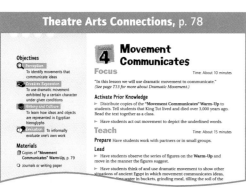
Theatre Arts Connections, p. 78

Music

Listen to *La Raspa*. The rhythm of the first section, suggests movement on beats one, two and three, and no movement on beat four. The rhythm of the second section is even and flowing. Design dance steps for these contrasting sections. How do your movements differ in the different sections?

Movement & Dance

In this activity students will create a moving machine. Have students make a large circle and sit around the edges. Number them in groups of five. Ask one student to enter the circle and create a repetitive movement such as pushing, pulling, swinging, jabbing, lifting, hammering, turning. The next person in their group enters and adds a different repetitive action that in some way rhythmically and action-wise complements or contrasts the first one. Complete with all members of the group.

Focus

Activate Prior Knowledge

"Have you ever seen a group of building blocks?" "¿Alguna vez han visto un grupo de tacos o bloques de construcción?"

■ Discuss student responses. Explain that a group of building blocks has rhythm and form.

Using Literature ⭐ Reading

■ Read *Painted Words* by Aliki. Have students look for rhythm.

Thematic Connection ⭐ Reading

■ **Storytelling:** Encourage students to discuss different reasons that people tell stories. For example, people tell stories for entertainment, or to learn more about other people.

Introduce the Art

Look   NSAE 2.a

"Let's take a close look at the storyteller doll and diorama." "Vamos a mirar detalladamente la muñeca y el diorama".

■ Have students identify rhythm in the works of art and the environment.

■ Have students compare how individuals and families are depicted in the different artwork.

Predicting Outcomes ⭐ Math

■ Ask students to look closely at these two works of art and how the figures are arranged. What do they think the backs of these works of art look like? Students will have many different answers, depending on what they imagine.

NSAE 4.a, 4.b, 4.c, 5.a, 5.b

🏺 Art History and Culture

Possible answer: Both of these works of art were inspired by Native American customs.

Rhythm and Form

◄ **Helen Cordero.** (Pueblo).
Storyteller Doll. 20th century.
....
Museum of International Folk Art, Santa Fe, New Mexico.

Look at the **storyteller doll** and the **diorama.** These pieces of art use forms, are three-dimensional, and have rhythm. Can you see the rhythm in these two sculptures?

🏺 Art History and Culture

What do you think the inspiration was for these two works of art?

🏺 Art History and Culture

Helen Cordero

Helen Cordero (hel´ ən kôr dā´ rō) (1916–)began working with clay when she was 45 years old. Her children were grown, and she wanted to make extra money. When she began, her bowls and jars kept coming out crooked. She was ready to quit when a friend suggested that she try making figures instead. She started to make frogs, birds, and eventually small figures of people. The first time she showed her figures, a folk-art collector bought all her pieces and commissioned her to do a 250-piece nativity scene. She shaped her first storyteller doll in 1963.

See pages 24–25 and 16–21 for more about art history and subject matter.

Artist Profiles, p. 13

● Artist Profile ●

Helen Cordero
b. 1916

Helen Cordero (hel´ ən kôr dēa´ rō) began working with clay when she was 45 years old. After her children were grown, she was looking for a way to make a little extra money. When she began her craft, her bowls and jars kept coming out crooked. She was ready to quit when a friend suggested that she try making figures instead. She started to make frogs, birds, and eventually small figures of people. The first time she showed her figures, a folk art collector bought all her pieces and commissioned her to do a 250-piece nativity scene. Thinking of her *Singing Mother* piece, he also asked her to make a larger seated figure with children. Cordero said she thought about her grandfather who was always surrounded by children as he...

Study the two works of art to find examples of rhythm and form.

► What are the repeating objects in each work of art?

► How does looking at the repeating objects make your eye move through the art?

▲ **Vigil Family.** (Tesuque Pueblo). *Pueblo Scene: Corn Dancers and Church.* 1960.

Painted earthenware. Museum of International Folk Art, Santa Fe, New Mexico.

Aesthetic Perception

Design Awareness How could you arrange the items on your desk to create rhythm?

Study

► The children are the repeated object in the Cordero piece. The sculpted figures in line on the way to the altar are the repeated objects in *Pueblo Scene*.

► The repeating objects lead your eye through the works of art as your eye moves from one to another.

■ For more examples of genre art see *The National Museum of Women in the Arts Collection.*

Art Journal: Brainstorming
Have students brainstorm other ways that forms could be used to create rhythm and write the list in the Concepts section of their Art Journals.

Aesthetic Perception

Design Awareness Have students try to arrange repeating objects on their desk to create rhythm and form. For example, have them arrange their pencils in a pattern that would create rhythm using forms. Can they think of other items they could arrange? Encourage students to identify variations in the objects from their environments.

NSAE 2.b, 5.c
Developing Visual Literacy Ask the students to describe how these two works of art make them feel.

Art History and Culture

Vigil Family
A Pueblo Indian artist from New Mexico created the miniatures that make up *Pueblo Scene: Corn Dancers and Church.* This type of earthenware sculpture work was common in the region where the piece was made. Corn dances are part of Pueblo Indian ceremonies and are performed as prayers or requests for rain and bountiful harvests. The scene depicted in *Pueblo Scene: Corn Dancers and Church* is centered around a feast, with ceremonial corn dancers and masked Kachina dancers in attendance.

See pages 24–25 and 16–21 for more about art history and subject matter.

Artist Profiles, p. 82

⟨ Artist Profile ⟩
Pueblo Scene: Corn Dancers and Church
A Pueblo Indian artist from New Mexico created the miniatures that make up *Pueblo Scene: Corn Dancers and Church.* It is estimated that the piece was made in 1960. This type of earthenware sculpture work was common in the region where the piece was made.

▲ **Vigil Family.** (Pueblo). (United States). *Pueblo Scene: Corn Dancers and Church.* 1960.

Web Connection
Visit **http://www.moifa.org/** to see the website of the Museum of International Folk Art.

 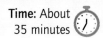

Time: About 35 minutes

"How can you use rhythm and forms in a work of art?" "¿Cómo pueden usar ritmo y formas en una obra de arte?"

- Read and discuss the information about rhythm and form on page 140.

Practice

Materials: modeling clay

- Distribute the materials and have students follow the directions on page 140.

- Have students identify and practice skills necessary for producing modeled forms using a variety of materials.

NSAE 1.c, 1.d, 2.c, 3.b

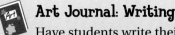 **Creative Expression**

Materials: white Longhorn clay, black velvet underglaze, red Longhorn clay that has been thinned to under glaze consistency, pencil, kiln

Alternate Materials: air dry clay

- Distribute the materials and have students follow the directions on page 141.

- Encourage students to create effective compositions using design principles.

- Review the Activity Tips on page 242 for visual examples of the activity if needed.

NSAE 3.a

Art Journal: Writing
Have students write their experience of making a storyteller doll in the Ideas section of their Art Journals.

Using Rhythm and Form

Rhythm can also be made using forms. Artists who make sculptures or other three-dimensional art might include rhythm in their works to guide the viewer's eyes through their pieces. Like two-dimensional art with rhythm, artists use positive and negative space to create rhythm when using forms. Can you find the positive and negative spaces in the example below?

Practice

Create rhythm in an abstract sculpture.

1. Roll clay into a snake shape.

2. Make several balls of clay.

3. Place them on your snake to create rhythm using forms.

Differentiated Instruction

Reteach
Designate an area of the classroom floor for students to create a still life. Have students place their shoes in an active line. Students can choose how to place their shoes—close together if they are tiptoeing, and wide apart if they are running. Have students use the shoe layout for a painting or drawing illustrating rhythm and form.

Special Needs
If using plasticine clay, ensure that it has been heated so that it is not difficult for students with limited upper body strength to manipulate.

ELL Tips
Define *storyteller* for the students. Have students share some of their favorite stories.

Think about how this student created rhythm in his storyteller doll.

◄ **Christopher Dominque.** Age 7.

 Creative Expression

Who would be your storyteller? Make your own storyteller doll.

1. Think of a person to be your storyteller.

2. Create a clay figure of this person. Add arms, legs, hands, feet, and any details you wish.

3. Make clay children and attach them to your storyteller.

4. Let your doll dry. Paint your doll with glazes to decorate it.

 **Art Criticism**

Describe Who is your storyteller?

Analyze Which forms in your storyteller are used to create rhythm?

Interpret Where are the positive spaces and negative spaces that create rhythm in your work of art?

Decide Do you think it is easier to create rhythm using two- or three-dimensional objects?

Unit 4 • Lesson 4 **141**

 Time: About 10 minutes

Review and Assess

"Can you explain how to create rhythm using forms?" "¿Cómo pueden explicar cómo se puede crear ritmo usando las formas?"

Think

This student created rhythm using forms by placing more than one child on his storyteller doll.

■ Use *Large Prints 31 Only the Children* and *32 Layla and Majnun at School* to have the students find rhythm using forms. Could they find any? Why or why not?

■ Have students identify stories and constructions in this lesson's artwork.

■ Have students identify ideas of the artists in this lesson's art.

Informal Assessment

Art Journal: Critical Thinking
Have students answer the four art criticism questions—Describe, Analyze, Interpret, and Decide—in their Art Journals. Ask students to define their reasons for preferences in their own art. Then have them identify ideas in their peers' art.

■ For standardized-format test practice using this lesson's art content, see pages 48–49 in *Reading and Writing Test Preparation*.

Art Across the Curriculum NSAE 6.a, 6.b

Use these simple ideas to reinforce art concepts across the curriculum.

★ **Narrative Writing** Have students write a story for their storyteller doll to tell.

★ **Math** Have students arrange geometric solids to create rhythm.

★ **Science** Discuss how stalactites and stalagmites show rhythm.

★ **Social Studies** Discuss the ways that different cultures pass on their history through oral traditions.

★ **Technology** Show students how to write a story on the computer and e-mail it to someone. Visit **SRAonline.com** to print detailed instructions for this activity.

Rhythm and Form

Extra! For the Art Specialist

Time: About 45 minutes

Focus

Study **Large Prints 31** *Only the Children* and **32** *Layla and Majnun at School* and ask the students to point out objects that repeat. Can they find any forms in these large prints? If not, can they think of times they have seen repeating forms?

Teach

Explain to students that they will create rhythm using found objects. They will attach various objects to a plate surface and paint the entire plate to unify it. Have students complete the Alternate Activity.

Reflect

Have students evaluate their artwork using the four steps of art criticism.

Alternate Activity

Materials:
- paper plates
- glue
- tempera paint
- brushes, water dishes, newspaper
- small found objects, such as beads, screws, beans, etc.

1. Discuss how artists create rhythm

2. Select found objects and attach them to your plate using glue. Arrange the objects to create rhythm.

3. When the plate is dry, paint the entire work one color.

Research
In Art Education

"Just as culture shapes art, art shapes culture. Our convictions, our technology, and our imagination shape our images, and our images, in turn, shape our perception of the world" (Eisner, Elliot. *The Role of Disciplined-Based Art Education in America's Schools*. The Getty Center for Arts Education in the Arts, 1987).

Assessment

Use the following rubric to evaluate the artwork students make in the Creative Expression activity and to assess students' understanding of rhythm and form.

Have students complete page 51 or 52 in their *Assessment* books.

	Art History and Culture	Aesthetic Perception	Creative Expression	Art Criticism
3 POINTS	The student can identify and compare the inspirations of two works of art.	The student accurately identifies rhythm and form in his or her environment.	The student's storyteller doll clearly illustrates a good use of rhythm and form.	The student thoughtfully and honestly evaluates his or her own work using the four steps of art criticism.
2 POINTS	The student's identification or comparison is weak or incomplete.	The student shows emerging awareness of rhythm and form, but cannot consistently identify them.	The student's storyteller doll shows some awareness of rhythm and form.	The student attempts to evaluate his or her own work, but shows an incomplete understanding of evaluation criteria.
1 POINT	The student cannot identify or compare the inspiration in different works of art.	The student cannot identify rhythm and form.	The student's storyteller doll shows no understanding of rhythm and form.	The student makes no attempt to evaluate his or her own artwork.

Assessment, p. 51

Name _____ Date _____

Lesson **4**
UNIT 4

Rhythm and Form

A. Defining
Write the definition of the word *rhythm* in your own words.

B. Writing
What is a storyteller doll? What is a diorama?

Level 2 — Unit 4 • Pattern, Rhythm, and Movement **51**

Lesson 5 Diagonal Movement

Overview

Lesson 5 explains how artists use diagonal movement to make the viewers' eyes move on a specific path and create the feeling of motion in a work of art.

Objectives

 Art History and Culture

To identify and compare the ways different artists portray dancing

 Creative Expression

To create a drawing of a dance scene on the computer that shows diagonal movement

Aesthetic Perception

To recognize diagonal movement in students' environments

Art Criticism

To evaluate own work using the four steps of art criticism

Vocabulary ☆ Vocabulary

Review the following vocabulary words with students before beginning the lesson.

diagonal movement movimiento diagonal—making the viewer feel that objects in the art are moving along diagonals

movement movimiento—a principle of design that creates the feeling that objects in a work of art are changing position or are active.

See page 149B for additional vocabulary and Spanish vocabulary resources.

 Art Journal: Vocabulary

Have students add these words to the Vocabulary section of their Art Journals.

Lesson Materials
- white paper
- markers
- computer with a drawing program

Alternate Materials:
- oil pastels, crayons

Program Resources
- *Reading and Writing Test Prep.*, pp. 50–51
- *Transparency 23*
- *Artist Profiles*, pp. 8, 14
- *Animals Through History Time Line*
- *Assessment*, pp. 52–53
- *Large Prints 32* Layla and Majnun at School
- *The National Museum of Women in the Arts Collection*

Concept Trace
Diagonal Movement
Introduced: Level K, Unit 6, Lesson 2

Reinforced: Level 3, Unit 5, Lesson 5

Lesson 5 Arts Integration

Theatre

Complete Unit 4, Lesson 5 on pages 80–81 of *Theatre Arts Connections*.

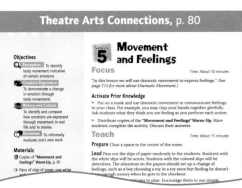
Theatre Arts Connections, p. 80

Music

 Listen to *Vivace* from "Sonata No. 2 in D minor, Op. 14" by Sergei Prokofofiev. Discuss how the melodic line's upward and downward shape combined with the rhythm and tempo suggests movement.

Movement & Dance

Have students spread out and lie on the floor with their feet together and arms above their head. Ask students to reach their arms away from their feet to create a horizontal stretch. Now ask students to separate their arms and feet to create an *X* on the floor. Students reach their right arm and left leg away from each other creating a diagonal stretch. Repeat on the other side.

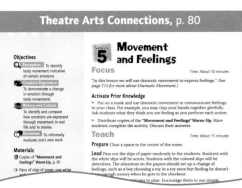

Focus

Time: About 10 minutes

Activate Prior Knowledge

"Have you ever seen a group of people dancing?" "¿Alguna vez han visto a un grupo de personas bailando?"

■ Discuss student responses. Explain to students that dancers often use diagonal movements.

Using Literature ★ Reading

■ Read *Angelina Ballerina* by Helen Craig. Have students look for diagonal movement in the illustrations.

Thematic Connection ★ Social Studies

■ **Dancing:** Discuss the different ways that people dance and what dancing means in different cultures.

Introduce the Art

Look NSAE 2.a

"Look closely at the two paintings."
"Miren detalladamente las dos pinturas".

■ Have students identify movement in the works of art and the environment.

■ Have students compare the ways individuals are depicted in the artwork.

Asking Questions ★ Science

■ Have students look at these two paintings and come up with a list of questions to ask the artists about what is going on. Answers will vary. Allow students to use their imaginations when coming up with questions to ask.

NSAE 4.a, 4.b, 4.c, 5.a, 5.b

 Art History and Culture

Possible answer: The people in the Benton work are dancing to fast music. The ballerinas are dancing to classical music.

 Web Connection

Visit http://www.mostateparks.com/benton.htm to see the studio and home of Thomas Hart Benton.

142 UNIT 4 • Pattern, Rhythm, and Movement

Lesson 5 Diagonal Movement

◀ **Thomas Hart Benton.** (American). *Country Dance.* 1929.

Oil on gessoed canvas. 30 × 25 inches (76.2 × 63.5 cm.). Private Collection.

Look how these works of art use rhythm and **diagonal movement.** The artists wanted viewers to feel the excitement of dancing. The bodies are placed to make your eyes move around the painting.

 Art History and Culture

Look at the way people in the paintings are dressed. What does the music they are dancing to sound like?

142 Unit 4 • Lesson 5

 Art History and Culture

Thomas Hart Benton

Thomas Hart Benton (tom´ əs hart bent´ ən) (1889–1975) was born in Missouri, the son of a congressman. Benton studied at the Art Institute of Chicago and later in Paris. He couldn't support himself on the money he earned selling his near-abstract paintings, so he worked as a set designer in the new motion picture industry in Fort Lee, New Jersey. Benton was the self-appointed leader of the regionalist movement that began in the Midwest between World War I and World War II. Regionalists showed common working men and women in the American heartland, but many Midwesterners didn't enjoy being portrayed in this manner.

See pages 24–25 and 16–21 for more about art history and subject matter.

Artist Profiles, p. 8

Artist Profile

Thomas Hart Benton
1889–1975

Thomas Hart Benton (tom´ as hart bent´ an) was a regional American painter known for his energetic, colorful murals. He was the son of a United States congressional representative and named after his great uncle, a famous pre-American Civil War senator. From his family, Benton developed a strong identity as an American. He studied art in Paris and at the Art Institute of Chicago. Benton believed that American artists should develop their own styles and not just copy French painting styles. Although Benton began his art career as a cartoonist, he was known for his murals depicting scenes from the rural past of the

▲ **Edgar Degas.** (French).
Ballet Scene. 1907.
....
Pastel on cardboard. 30 ¼ × 43 ¾
inches (76.84 × 111.13 cm.). National
Gallery of Art, Washington, D.C.

Study the two works of art to find examples of diagonal movement.

► Where do you see diagonal lines in the two pictures?

► What path do your eyes take as they move around the pictures?

► Which painting has the fastest moving people? Explain.

Aesthetic Perception

Seeing Like an Artist Name a time when people's arms and legs move diagonally.

Unit 4 • Lesson 5   **143**

Study

► There are diagonal lines in the arms and legs of the dancers in the Benton painting as well as in the fiddle bow. The room also feels as though it is set on a diagonal slope. In the Degas, the diagonal lines are in the arms, legs, and tutus of the ballerinas.

► Most students will feel their eyes moving along a diagonal path through the picture.

► Most students will say the people in the Benton painting are moving more quickly.

■ For more examples of portraits see *The National Museum of Women in the Arts Collection.*

Art Journal: Writing
What do students want to learn about diagonal movement? Have them write their questions in the Ideas section of their Art Journals. Encourage students to identify variations in subjects from their environments.

Aesthetic Perception

Seeing Like an Artist Students will have many different answers. If students are having difficulty thinking of times when people's arms and legs are positioned in diagonal ways, encourage them to think of common activities, like running.

NSAE 2.b, 5.c
Developing Visual Literacy What do students think the main ideas of these pictures are?

Art History and Culture

Edgar Degas

Edgar Degas (ed´ gär dā gä´)(1834–1917) was born in Paris to a wealthy family. He studied law for a short time before discovering an interest in painting. He worked at an artist's studio but also traveled widely to study art. His early work was similar to classical painting in subject matter as well as composition. His themes dealt with people and city life, especially dancers at the theatre. After 1909, Degas turned to sculpture due to failing eyesight. Many of his wax models of dancers and horses were cast in bronze after his death. Degas is famous for his portraits, especially of ballet dancers. Unlike other impressionists, he enjoyed painting genre scenes of modern life.

See pages 24–25 and 16–21 for more about art history and subject matter.

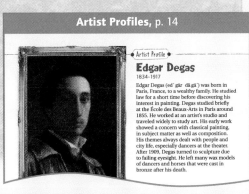

Artist Profiles, p. 14

♦ Artist Profile ♦

Edgar Degas
1834–1917

Edgar Degas (ed´ gär dä gä´) was born in Paris, France, to a wealthy family. He studied law for a short time before discovering his interest in painting. Degas studied briefly at the École des Beaux-Arts in Paris around 1855. He worked at an artist's studio and traveled widely to study art. His early work showed a concern with classical painting, in subject matter as well as composition. His themes always dealt with people and city life, especially dancers at the theater. After 1909, Degas turned to sculpture due to failing eyesight. He left many wax models of dancers and horses that were cast in bronze after his death.

Web Connection
Visit **http://www.artic.edu/artaccess/AA_Impressionist/pages/IMP_5.shtml** to see another work by Degas.

Teach

Time: About 35 minutes

"How can you use diagonal movement to make a picture seem more exciting?" "¿Cómo pueden usar el movimiento diagonal para que una pintura parezca más emocionante?"

- Read and discuss the information about diagonal movement on page 144.

Practice

Materials: white paper, markers

Alternate Materials: oil pastels, crayons

- Distribute the materials and have students follow the directions on page 144.

- Have students identify and practice skills necessary for producing drawings using a variety of materials.

NSAE 1.c, 1.d, 2.c, 3.b

Creative Expression

Materials: a computer with a drawing program

- Have students follow the directions on page 145.

- Encourage students to express their ideas and feelings in their drawings using a variety of lines.

- Encourage students to create effective compositions using design principles.

- Review the Activity Tips on page 243 for visual examples of the activity if needed.

NSAE 3.a

Art Journal: Brainstorming

In the Ideas section of their Art Journals, have students come up with a list of different things they could show dancing.

Using Diagonal Movement

Artists use rhythm to create **movement** in a work of art. Movement helps art seem alive and makes a viewer's eyes follow a path across the art. When artists use diagonal lines, the viewer's eyes follow a diagonal path. Use your finger to trace the path your eye follows while looking at this picture. Are you tracing diagonal lines?

Practice

Draw diagonal lines to match music.

1. Listen to the music that your teacher is playing.

2. Draw diagonal and zigzag lines on your paper to match the music.

3. Look for the diagonal movement in your drawing. How will your viewer's eyes move?

Differentiated Instruction

Reteach

With a marker, trace the outlines of a few people in magazines or newspapers. Have students decide whether the outlines depict movement. Have them identify the lines in the pictures.

Special Needs

Provide motivation for this activity by using available technology. Digital cameras could be used to record students' movement to different types of music. Images can be instantly viewed or printed, allowing students to point out the diagonal lines they observe.

ELL Tips

Review thick, thin, straight, curved, broken, zigzag, and diagonal lines. Ask students which are used to show action.

◀ **Becca Smith.**
Age 7.

Think about how this student made the trees dance in the wind.

 **Creative Expression**

How could you show movement in a dance? Draw a dance scene using the computer.

1. Think about how your arms and legs move when you are dancing. How do objects dance in the wind?

2. Open your computer drawing program.

3. Draw a dance scene that shows lots of diagonal movement. Think about how you want your viewer's eyes to move across your picture.

Art Criticism

Describe Who or what is dancing in your picture?

Analyze Where are the diagonal lines in your picture?

Interpret Where is the diagonal or zigzag path in your drawing?

Decide What other activities would make good drawings for diagonal movement?

eflect Time: About 10 minutes

Review and Assess

"Can you explain how diagonal movement leads your eyes around a painting?" "¿Pueden explicar cómo el movimiento diagonal dirige su vista alrededor de una pintura?"

Think

This student made her trees dance by using diagonal movement.

- Use **Large Print 32** *Layla and Majnun at School* to have students look for diagonal movement.

- Have students identify stories and constructions in this lesson's artwork.

- Have students identify ideas of the artists in this lesson's art.

Informal Assessment

Art Journal: Critical Thinking
Have students answer the four art criticism questions—Describe, Analyze, Interpret, and Decide—in the Critical Thinking section of their Art Journals. Ask students to define their reasons for preferences in their own art. Then have them identify ideas in their peers' art.

- For standardized-format test practice using this lesson's art content, see pages 50–51 in **Reading and Writing Test Preparation**.

Art Across the Curriculum NSAE 6.a, 6.b

Use these simple ideas to reinforce art concepts across the curriculum.

★ **Poetry** Have students write a poem about dancing.

★ **Math** Explain what an angle is, and discuss how angles are composed of diagonal lines.

★ **Science** Discuss with students how animals move. Can they think of animals that move in diagonal lines?

★ **Social Studies** Discuss how specific dances mean very specific things in certain cultures.

★ **Technology** Show students how to use an animated GIF file. Visit **SRAonline.com** to print detailed instructions for this activity.

Lesson 5 Wrap-Up
Diagonal Movement

Extra! For the Art Specialist

Time: About 45 minutes

Focus

Study **Large Print 32** *Layla and Majnun at School* and have students point out the different types of lines. Do these lines make their eyes move slowly or fast? Why?

Teach

Explain to students that they will create a mixed-media project using diagonal and zigzag lines to show movement. They will make a background collage of these lines and then create an animal or person that appears to be moving and attach it to the collage. Have students complete the Alternate Activity.

Reflect

Have students evaluate their artwork using the four steps of art criticism.

Alternate Activity

Materials:

- tempera paint
- brushes, water dishes, newspaper
- scissors
- glue
- white paper
- pencils
- construction paper

1. Draw diagonal and zigzag lines on construction paper and cut them out. Glue them on your white paper.

2. Use another piece of white paper to draw an animal or person in motion.

3. Paint the animal or person, let it dry and cut it out. Glue it to your line background.

Research in Art Education

Research has shown that assessing knowledge through a combination of drawing and writing can lead to higher scores for content knowledge. This applies to native English speakers and limited English speakers alike. This suggests "that drawing may be one way to reveal what students know but cannot put into words" ("The Arts, Language, and Knowing: An Experimental Study of the Potential of the Visual Arts for Assessing Academic Learning by Language Minority Students" in *Critical Links*, p. 141).

Assessment
Use the following rubric to evaluate the artwork students make in the Creative Expression activity and to assess students' understanding of diagonal movement.

Have students complete page 53 or 54 in their *Assessment* books.

	Art History and Culture	Aesthetic Perception	Creative Expression	Art Criticism
3 POINTS	The student can identify and compare the ways artists depict dancing in art.	The student accurately identifies diagonal movement in his or her environment.	The student's computer drawing clearly illustrates a good use of diagonal movement.	The student thoughtfully and honestly evaluates his or her own work using the four steps of art criticism.
2 POINTS	The student's identification or comparison of the use of diagonal movement is weak or incomplete.	The student shows emerging awareness of diagonal movement, but cannot consistently identify them.	The student's computer drawing shows some awareness of diagonal movement.	The student attempts to evaluate his or her own work, but shows an incomplete understanding of evaluation criteria.
1 POINT	The student cannot identify or compare the ways artists depict dancing.	The student cannot identify diagonal movement.	The student's computer drawing shows no understanding of diagonal movement.	The student makes no attempt to evaluate his or her own artwork.

Assessment, p. 53

Name _____ Date _____ Lesson **5** UNIT 4

Diagonal Movement

A. Drawing
Draw a scene that shows diagonal movement in the box below. When you are finished, draw diagonal lines in your picture to show where your diagonal movement is.

B. Writing
Explain what diagonal movement is and how it is created.

Level 2   Unit 4 • Pattern, Rhythm, and Movement   **53**

Curving Movement

Lesson 6 explains how artists use curving movement to make the viewers' eyes move on a specific path and create a sense of motion in a work of art.

Objectives

 Art History and Culture

To identify and compare the use of curving movement and location by van Gogh and Hockney

 Creative Expression

Paint a picture using curving movement of a journey

 Aesthetic Perception

To recognize curving movement in students' environment

Art Criticism

To evaluate own work using the four steps of art criticism

Vocabulary ⭐ Vocabulary

Review the following vocabulary word with students before beginning the lesson.

curving movement movimiento curvo—using curved lines to move the viewer's eyes through a work of art and make the viewer feel that objects in the work of art are moving along curves.

See page 149B for additional vocabulary and Spanish vocabulary resources.

Art Journal: Vocabulary

 Have students add this word to the Vocabulary section of their Art Journals.

Lesson Materials
- 12" × 18" white paper
- water dishes
- brushes
- watercolors
- crayons
- paper towels
- masking tape
- oil pastels

Alternate Materials:
- colored pencils
- pens

Program Resources
- *Reading and Writing Test Prep.*, pp. 52–53
- *Transparency 24*
- *Artist Profiles*, pp. 24, 64
- *Animals Through History Time Line*
- *Assessment*, pp. 55–56
- *Large Print 31* Only the Children
- *The National Museum of Women in the Arts Collection*

Concept Trace
Curving Movement
Introduced: Level K, Unit 6, Lesson 2
Reinforced: Level 3, Unit 5, Lesson 5

Lesson 6 Arts Integration

Theatre

Complete Unit 4, Lesson 6 on pages 82–87 of *Theatre Arts Connections*.

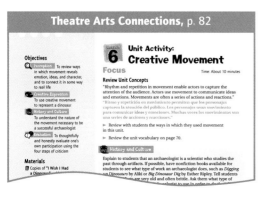

Theatre Arts Connections, p. 82

Music

 Listen to *Morning* from "Peer Gynt" by Edvard Grieg. This piece is in three meter, meaning the beats are in groups of three (the strong beat plus two weak beats.) Use scarves to move to the music. Does it feel natural to move on the strong beat?

Movement & Dance

Look at the van Gogh painting, *The Starry Night*. Identify the spiral, curved, and circular patterns in the painting. In small groups of five to seven, have students hold hands in a line. The student at the top of the line leads their group through the space exploring each of these pathways. Playing classical music in the background will help create the right mood and help the students focus.

Focus

Time: About 10 minutes

Activate Prior Knowledge

"Have you ever seen a roller coaster?"
"¿Alguna vez han visto una montaña rusa?"

■ Discuss student responses. Explain that roller coasters use lots of curving movement.

Using Literature ⭐ Reading

■ Read *Paddle-to-the-Sea* by Holling C. Holling. Have students look for curving movement.

Thematic Connection ⭐ Social Studies

■ **Journeys:** Ask students to talk about all of the different kinds of journeys they have taken or do take. Point out that even coming to school in the morning is a journey.

Introduce the Art

Look NSAE 2.a

"Look closely at the two paintings."
"Miren detalladamente las dos pinturas".

■ Have students identify movement in the works of art and the environment.

Forces and Motion ⭐ Science

■ How do these curving lines make students feel? How do they think that hills and clouds like this would be made? Answers will vary. However, discuss with students how curves like this in nature are the result of forces and motion. For instance, a curving hill would be the result of tectonic movement.

NSAE 4.a, 4.b, 4.c, 5.a, 5.b

 Art History and Culture

Allow the students to use their imaginations and describe the places. Both are real.

💻 **Web Connection**

Visit **www.bewitched.com/m/night.html** where students can design their own starry constellation.

146 UNIT 4 • Pattern, Rhythm, and Movement

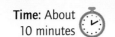
Lesson 6 — Curving Movement

Look at these works of art. These two paintings were made using rhythm and many curving lines. Like diagonal movement, **curving movement** also can make your eyes move across a work of art.

▲ **Vincent van Gogh.** (Dutch). *The Starry Night.* 1889.
Oil on canvas. 29 × 36 3/10 inches (73.7 × 92.1 cm.). Museum of Modern Art, New York, New York.

 Art History and Culture

Look at the two paintings. What do you think these places are like? Do you think they are real or imaginary?

146 Unit 4 • Lesson 6

 Art History and Culture

Vincent van Gogh

Vincent van Gogh (vin´ sənt van gō´) (1853–1890) cared about other people very much. He had many jobs, including being a teacher and a social worker. At 28, van Gogh decided that the best way he could serve others was through art. As he moved from place to place, he left many of his works behind. Some were burned in fireplaces for heat, and some were even used to patch holes in walls. Van Gogh was poor his entire life and often went hungry so that he could buy painting supplies. He died at age 37.

See pages 24–25 and 16–21 for more about art history and subject matter.

 **Artist Profiles, p. 64**

♦ Artist Profile ♦
Vincent van Gogh
1853–1890

Even as a boy in the Netherlands, Vincent van Gogh (vin´ sənt van gō´) cared about other people very much. He tried many jobs, including being a teacher, minister, and social worker. However, he had problems getting along with nearly everyone except his younger brother, Theo. At the age of 28, van Gogh decided that the best way he could serve others was through art. He expressed his deep feelings about people through his paintings. As he moved from place to place, he left many of his works behind. Some were burned in fireplaces for heat, and some were even used to patch holes in walls. Van Gogh was poor his entire life and often went hungry so that he could buy painting supplies. He died at age 37.

Study the two works of art and find examples of curving movement.

▶ Where do you see curving movement in these two paintings?

▶ What paths do your eyes take as they move across the paintings?

▲ **David Hockney.** (English). *Garrowby Hill.* 1998.
....
Oil on canvas. 60 × 76 inches (152.4 × 193.04 cm.). Museum of Fine Arts, Boston, Massachusetts.

Aesthetic Perception

Design Awareness Look at a map and trace several roads. What kind of movement did you find?

Study

▶ There is curving movement everywhere in the van Gogh. Some answers may be the clouds, hills, or moon. There is also a great deal of curving movement in the Hockney. Students will probably notice the curving of the roads, hill, woods, and fields the most.

▶ Students' answers will vary, but they should all feel that their eyes are taken on a curving path.

■ For more examples of landscapes see *The National Museum of Women in the Arts Collection.*

Art Journal: Writing
Have students write their ideas about curving movement in the Concepts section of their Art Journals.

Aesthetic Perception

Design Awareness Have students share the scenes that they can think of that use curving movement. If they have trouble, suggest activities, such as wheels on a bike, or an ice skater. Encourage students to identify variations in objects from the environment.

NSAE 2.b, 5.c
Developing Visual Literacy Interpret what the artists might have been trying to say in these paintings.

Art History and Culture

David Hockney

David Hockney (dā´ vid häk´ nē)(1937–) was born into a working class family in Bradford, England. By the time he was 11 he had decided to become an artist. Hockney first made an impact on the art world in the 1960s as a leader of the English pop art movement in London. In 1961 he made his first trip to the United States. The brightness and light of California was a contrast from the rain and fog of England. He was impressed by the sense of space in Los Angeles, and he moved permanently to the United States in 1978 to become an artist of the California scene.

See pages 24–25 and 16–21 for more about art history and subject matter.

Artist Profiles, p. 24

Artist Profile
David Hockney
b. 1937
David Hockney (dā´ vad häk´ nē) was born in 1937 into a working class family in the northern industrial section of Bradford, England. By the time he was 11, he had decided to become an artist. At 16, he attended the Bradford School of Art, and went on to study at the Royal College of Art. In 1961, he made his first trip to the United States. The brightness and light of California was a sharp contrast with the rain and fog of England. He was impressed by the sense of space in the sprawling city of Los Angeles, and moved permanently to the United States in 1978 to become part of the California art scene.

Web Connection
Visit **http://www.getty.edu/art/collections/bio/ a3283-1.html** to see more art by Hockney.

Teach

Time: About 35 minutes

"How can you use curving movement to create a feeling?" "¿Cómo pueden usar el movimiento curvo para crear un sentimiento?"

- Read and discuss the information about curving movement on page 148.

Practice

Materials: white paper, crayons

Alternate Materials: paper, pens, oil pastels

- Distribute the materials and have students follow the directions on page 148.
- Have students identify and practice skills necessary for producing paintings using a variety of materials.

NSAE 1.c, 1.d, 2.c, 3.b

Creative Expression

Materials: 12" × 18" white paper, water dishes, brushes, watercolors, crayons, paper towels, masking tape, oil pastels

Alternate Materials: pens, colored pencils

- Distribute the materials and have students follow the directions on page 149.
- Encourage students to express their ideas and feelings in their paintings using a variety of lines.
- Encourage students to create effective compositions using design principles.
- Review the Activity Tips on page 243 for visual examples of the activity if needed.

NSAE 3.a

Art Journal: Brainstorming

Have students sketch and brainstorm ideas for their journey pictures in the Ideas section of their Art Journals.

Using Curving Movement

Like diagonal movement, curving movement is made using rhythm. Curving movement draws the viewer's eyes across a work of art in curving lines. Artists use curving movement to make their work feel alive and exciting.

Where is the curving movement in the picture? Trace the curving movement with your fingers.

Practice

Draw a road using curving movement.

1. Think of a road.
2. Draw the road on your paper using curving movement.
3. What path does your road take across your paper? What do you think is at the end of your road?

Differentiated Instruction

Reteach

Draw curving or swirling lines. Have students name ideas, feelings, or things the lines remind them of.

Special Needs

Introduce this lesson with a multi-sensory learning experience for students by going on a walk on the playground that takes a curved route.

ELL Tips

Review *curving movement* by leading students around the room in a curving line.

◄ **Lauren Welch.**
Age 7.

Think about how this student used curving movement in her picture.

 Creative Expression

If you were taking a journey, what kind of road would you take? Where would you go? Paint a picture using curving movement that shows your journey or place.

1. Think of a place you would like to visit or what the road there would look like.
2. Draw your road or place using curving and swirling lines.
3. Paint your place with watercolors.

Art Criticism

Describe What happens at your place or on your trip there?

Analyze Where are the curving lines in your painting?

Interpret What path do your eyes take when you look at your painting?

Decide What other kinds of scenes could you draw using curving movement?

Unit 4 • Lesson 6 **149**

Reflect

Review and Assess

"Can you explain how curving movement makes the viewers' eyes move through a work of art?" "¿Pueden explicar cómo el movimiento curvo hace que la vista de los espectadores se mueva por una obra de arte?"

Think

This student created curving movement in the sky of her picture.

- Use **Large Print 31** *Only the Children* to have students look for curving movement.

- Have students identify stories and constructions in this lesson's artwork.

- Have students identify ideas of the artists in this lesson's art.

Informal Assessment

Art Journal: Critical Thinking
Have students answer the four art criticism questions—Describe, Analyze, Interpret, and Decide—in the Critical Thinking section of their Art Journals. Ask students to define their reasons for preferences in their own art. Then have them identify ideas in their peers' art.

- For standardized-format test practice using this lesson's art content, see pages 52–53 in *Reading and Writing Test Preparation*.

Art Across the Curriculum

NSAE 6.a, 6.b

Use these simple ideas to reinforce art concepts across the curriculum.

★ **Personal Writing** Have students write a letter to their parent or guardian about one of the paintings in this lesson.

★ **Math** Have students count the stars in the van Gogh work.

★ **Science** Discuss how clouds and hills are formed.

★ **Social Studies** Discuss what people believe van Gogh was painting in *The Starry Night*. What could make the sky look that way?

★ **Technology** Have students look for curving lines in different fonts. Visit **SRAonline.com** to print detailed instructions for this activity.

Curving Movement

Extra! For the Art Specialist

Time: About 45 minutes

Focus

Study *Large Print 31* and ask students to describe the lines they see. What do the curving lines in this work of art make your eyes do? Why did this artist want to move the viewer's eyes around the work?

Teach

Explain to students that they will create a colored chalk drawing of a scene that is full of curving and swirling lines. Have students complete the alternate activity.

Reflect

Have students evaluate their artwork using the four steps of art criticism.

Alternate Activity

Materials:
- brown or black construction paper
- newspapers
- colored chalk
- fixative for the finished work

1. Think of a scene that has lots of curving or swirling lines.

2. Draw and color the scene using colored chalk. Focus on creating curving movement in your picture.

Research in Art Education

Research has shown that artistically talented at-risk students make greater gains in reading scores on standardized tests when the arts are integrated into the curriculum ("Using Art Processes to Enhance Academic Self-Regulation" in *Critical Links*, p. 64). The amount of training their teachers received in arts integration predicted how great these gains were.

Assessment

Use the following rubric to evaluate the artwork students make in the Creative Expression activity and to assess students' understanding of curving movement.

Have students complete page 55 or 56 in their *Assessment* books.

	Art History and Culture	Aesthetic Perception	Creative Expression	Art Criticism
3 POINTS	The student can identify and compare the use of curving movement and location in two works of art.	The student accurately identifies curving movement in his or her environment.	The student's painting clearly illustrates a good use of curving movement.	The student thoughtfully and honestly evaluates his or her own work using the four steps of art criticism.
2 POINTS	The student's identification or comparison is weak or incomplete.	The student shows emerging awareness of curving movement, but cannot consistently identify it.	The student's painting shows some awareness of curving movement.	The student attempts to evaluate his or her own work, but shows an incomplete understanding of evaluation criteria.
1 POINT	The student cannot identify or compare the use of curving movement in different works of art.	The student cannot identify curving movement.	The student's painting shows no understanding of curving movement.	The student makes no attempt to evaluate his or her artwork.

Assessment, p. 55

Name _____ Date _____

Curving Movement — Lesson 6 UNIT 4

A. Drawing

Draw a scene in the box below that shows curving movement. When you are finished, draw curving lines in your picture to show where the curving movement is.

B. Writing

Explain what curving movement is, why it is used, and how it is created.

Level 2 — Unit 4 • Pattern, Rhythm, and Movement 55

curving movement—Using curved lines to move the viewer's eyes through a work of art and make the viewer feel that objects in the work of art are moving along curves **movimiento que curva**—usando líneas con curvas para mover los ojos del observador a través de una obra de arte y hacer al observador sentir que los objetos en la obra de arte se mueven a lo largo de curvas

diagonal movement—Using diagonal lines to move the viewer's eyes through a work of art and make the viewer feel that objects in the work of art are moving along diagonals. **movimiento diagonal**—usando líneas diagonales para mover los ojos del obervador a través de una obra de arte y hacer sentir al observador que los objetos en una obra de arte se mueven a lo largo de diagonales

diorama—A display of a scene using sculpted, miniature figurines **diorama**—una exhibición de una escena escultada, figuras miniaturas

motif—An image that is duplicated to create a pattern. Motifs can change color or position in a pattern. **motivo**—un imagen que se duplica para crear un patrón. Los motivos pueden cambiar de color o posición en un patron

movement—A principle of design that creates the feeling that objects in a work of art are changing position or are active. **movimiento**—un principio de diseño que crea la sensación que objetos en una obra de arte cambien de posiciones o estan activos

negative space—The empty space between and surrounding shapes and forms. **espacio negativo**—el espacio vacio entre figuras y formas que los rodean

pattern—A decorative surface design. Patterns are two-dimensional. **patrón**—un diseño decorativo de la superficie. Los patrones son bidimensional

positive space—Any shape or form. **espacio positivo**—cualquier figura o forma

print—An image created by using a stamp or printing plate. When artists make prints, they can make many identical images. **molde**—un imagen creado usando una prensa. Cuando los artistas hacen los moldes, pueden hacer muchos imáganes idénticos

rhythm—A principle of design that is created by repeating objects through a work of art. Rhythm creates movement and is made by using positive and negative space. **ritmo**—un principio de diseño que es creado por objetos que se repiten a través de una obra de arte. El ritmo crea movimiento y se hace usando espacio positivo y negativo

storyteller doll—A Native American sculpture that shows one person relating the history of the culture to many children. **muñeca del cuentista**—una escultura de los americanos nativos que nos enceña a una persona relatando la historia de la cultura a muchos niños

Vocabulary Practice

T   Display *Transparency 40* to review unit vocabulary words.

Definitions:
Visualization Strategies ☆ Vocabulary
Have students select two unit vocabulary words and label places in the classroom where they see those principles.

Analogies ☆ Vocabulary
Have students select three unit vocabulary words and create analogies using those words.

Words and Sounds ☆ Vocabulary
Have students select five unit vocabulary words and make tongue twisters using those words.

Pattern, Rhythm, and Movement

Wrapping Up Unit 4

Pattern, Rhythm, and Movement

 Art Criticism

Critical Thinking Art criticism is an organized system for looking at and talking about art. You can criticize art without being an expert. The purpose of art criticism is to get the viewer involved in a perception process that delays judgment until all aspects of the artwork have been studied.

■ See pages 28–29 for more about art criticism.

Describe

▶ Possible answer: Thirteen people are visible in the painting: four children and one man in the lower left, three people in the lower right, a man and two children in the middle right, and a woman and child near the house. They are wearing winter clothes. They all have on hats and heavy coats and jackets. In the lower left, the children are skating and playing on the ice. The man is watching people arrive in a sleigh. Another sleigh approaches the house, carrying a man and two children. A woman and child walk toward the sleigh.

▶ Possible answer: There are four horses, two pulling each sleigh.

▶ Possible answer: On the left is a blue area that is a frozen river that is bounded by small bushes and weeds. The rest of the ground is covered with white snow. A line of cut logs starts on the right and leads to the blue building. The sky is a gray-blue with dark-gray clouds. On the right, we see a tan house with a chimney and a shed attached in the back. All of the rooftops are covered with snow.

Analyze

▶ Possible answer: The sleigh and the line of logs with bare bushes leads our eye from right to left, upward toward the blue house. The other sleigh leads us back to the right

▲ **Grandma Moses.** (American). *Grand Skating.* c. 1946.

Galerie St. Etienne, New York, New York.

Art History and Culture

Grandma Moses

Anna Mary Robertson Moses (an´ ə mâr´ ē ro´ bərt sən mō´ zəz) (1860–1961) was always interested in art but was too busy raising children and doing farm work to devote much time to her creative talents. It was not until she was in her late 70s that she took up painting. In 1938 her work was discovered when an art collector saw one of her paintings hanging in a drugstore window. Within two years her work was being exhibited at the Museum of Modern Art and the Galerie St. Etienne, both in New York City. In the last 20 years of her life, her popular paintings were in museums and galleries throughout the United States and Europe. She continued to paint until the year she died at age 101.

Artist Profiles, p. 43

Artist Profile

Grandma Moses
1860–1961

Anna Mary Robertson Moses (an´ ə mâr´ ē ro´ bərt sən mō´ zəz) was always interested in art but was too busy raising children and doing farm work to devote much time to her creative talents. It was not until she was in her late 70s that she took up painting. In 1938 her work was discovered when an art collector saw one of her paintings hanging in a drugstore window. Within two years her work was being exhibited at the Museum of Modern Art and the Galerie St. Etienne, both in New York City. In the last 20 years of her life, her paintings appeared in museums and galleries throughout the United States and Europe. She continued to paint until the year she died at age 101.

 **Art Criticism** Critical Thinking

Describe **What do you see?**

▶ How many people do you see? What are they wearing and doing?

▶ What animals do you see?

▶ Describe the rest of the scene.

Analyze **How is this work organized?**

▶ Where do you see curving movement? Diagonal movement?

▶ What shapes are repeated to form patterns?

▶ Where do you see people or objects repeated to create rhythm?

Interpret **What is the artist trying to say?**

▶ How does the rhythm and movement affect the feeling of this work? What is the mood of this work?

▶ Do you think this painting takes place in modern times or long ago? Why?

▶ If you could go into this painting, what sounds would you hear?

Decide **What do you think about the work?**

▶ Is this painting successful because it is realistic, because it is well organized, or because it has a strong message? Explain.

Unit 4 **151**

 Aesthetic Perception

Seeing Like an Artist Have students look at the playground during recess, or have them think about groups of people participating in outdoor recreation. How do these scenes compare with *Grand Skating*?

Describe ▶ Describe everything in your scene. What do you see?

Analyze ▶ Where do you see pattern, rhythm, and movement in your scene?

Interpret ▶ How does this scene make you feel?

Decide ▶ What title would you give this scene?
▶ Does this scene look like one you would want to participate in? Why or why not?

and upward toward the house. There is curving movement up the left side of the painting. The curved line of small trees and grasses at the edge of the ice curves upward toward the blue house. The curve continues over the top of the mill wheel and up the curved line of the snow-covered roof.

▶ Possible answer: Small rectangles are repeated to form stone walls beside the mill and under the blue house. Small squares make the windows in the mill and the house. The wood siding on the buildings is repeated to form a pattern of horizontal lines.

▶ Possible answer: There is a rhythm of logs that pull our eyes to the first group of buildings. There is a rhythm of people that starts with the children skating on the ice. It moves up through the man to the people on the sleds, and ends with the two people near the tan house. The repetition of trees pulls our eyes across the center of the work. The repetition of blue hills in the distance moves our eyes from left to right.

Interpret

▶ Possible answer: Most will say that this is an exciting picture because it is full of movement and rhythm. Most students will say this is a happy painting.

▶ Possible answer: Students will most likely guess it is long ago because horses and sleighs are no longer used for transportation. There are no automobiles or telephone wires in the painting. Mill wheels are no longer used to provide power.

▶ Possible answer: Students may list the sounds of children playing and shouting, the people greeting each other, the horses snorting, the clop-clop of horses' hooves, the hiss of the sleigh runners on snow, or the sound of wind in the bare trees.

Decide

▶ Possible answer: Answers will vary. Some may like the representational quality of the work and cite realism. Others may like the joy expressed by the work and cite a strong message. Others may like the way it is organized. All three theories apply to this work.

Art Journal: Writing
Have students write answers to Aesthetic Perception their Art Journals.

"How do artists create pattern, rhythm, and movement in a work of art?" "¿Cómo crean los artistas patrón, ritmo y movimiento en una obra de arte?"

T Review unit vocabulary with students using *Transparency 40*.

Art Journal: Writing
Have students answer the questions on page 152 in their Art Journals or on a separate sheet of paper. Answers: 1. B, 2. A, 3. B, 4. C

CAREERS IN ART
Movies
► Encourage students to discuss the professions mentioned in this unit. What other jobs do they think people do in movies? Where else would people making movies use art?

"I look out the window sometimes to seek the color of the shadows and the different greens in the trees, but when I get ready to paint I just close my eyes and imagine a scene."

—Grandma Moses

Show What You Know

Select the best answers to these questions. Write your answers on a separate sheet of paper.

❶ A surface design made by repeating a motif is a _____.
A. rhythm
B. pattern
C. curving movement

❷ _____ is the space between objects.
A. Negative space
B. Positive space
C. Motif

❸ Artists use _____ to create movement in a work of art.
A. pattern
B. rhythm
C. positive space

❹ Rhythm can be made using both _____ and _____.
A. motifs; patterns
B. curving movement; diagonal movement
C. shapes; forms

CAREERS IN ART
Movies

Did you know artists work on movies? Everything in a movie is made to look a special way.

CGI Animators draw pictures on a computer and animate them. CGI means *computer generated image.* Many movies are made using computers.

Art Directors help the director of a movie decide how the movie will look. They work with set designers, costumers, and lighting specialists to create the movie setting.

Set Builders build the scenery for a movie. Set builders might build one room or a whole city.

▲ **CGI Animator**

Unit Assessment Options

Aesthetic Perception

Practice Have students list the techniques they learned in this unit and then find examples of each technique in the classroom.

Creative Expression

Student Portfolio Have students review all the artwork they have created during this unit and select the pieces they wish to keep in their portfolios.

Art Criticism

Activity Have students select a work of art from this unit and study it using the four steps of art criticism. (See pages 28–29 for more information about art criticism.) Have students work alone or in pairs and present their findings orally or in writing.

Pattern, Rhythm, and Movement in Storytelling

Geri Keams is a Navajo storyteller. She begins by singing a native song to the rhythm of a drum. *The Quillwork Girl* is a story she tells about a young Navajo girl with a talent for sewing porcupine quills onto buckskin. The adventure she has with her seven brothers is the Navajo legend of the creation of the Big Dipper. Cultures often use legends or myths to explain things in nature.

What to Do Retell a Native American legend or myth in your own words.

1. Work with three other students. Pick a legend and read it together.

2. List the main characters and words to describe them. Describe the setting of the legend.

3. Review the sequence of the legend.

4. Retell the legend. Create rhythm and movement by having one person start the legend, two people tell the middle, and one person tell the end.

▲ Geri Keams. "The Quillwork Girl."

 Art Criticism

Describe Describe your favorite part of the legend.

Analyze How did you decide which was the beginning, middle, and end?

Interpret What feelings or moods were created as you told the legend?

Decide How well do you think your group did retelling the legend?

Unit 4 **153**

 Art History and Culture

Navajo Storytelling

Geri Keams was born in 1951 and raised on the Navajo Nation in the Painted Desert region of Arizona.

Geri's grandmother taught her the importance of passing on the stories of the 'Old Ones.' Her stories come from ones she has heard, or stories she has found in Native American anthologies. After Geri hears or reads a story, she then puts it into her own words. Next, she transcribes her version into a script. She practices telling it until she finds its true voice and natural rhythm. A storyteller uses words to stimulate thoughts and images in our mind. Each person hearing a story will create his own version of the characters, setting and movement. It's different from seeing a movie where the characters, setting and movement are clearly portrayed for all to see.

Pattern, Rhythm, and Movement in Storytelling

Objective: To read a legend or myth and retell it

Materials: "The Quillwork Girl," performed by Geri Keams. Running time 8:17, myths or legends from varied Native American culture

Focus **Time:** About 5 minutes

- Discuss the information on page 153.

 Art History and Culture

- Have students discuss myths and legends to prepare them to retell a story. Have them discuss the relationship of the cultures to the myths that created them.

Teach **Time:** About 20 minutes

 **Aesthetic Perception**

- Have students read some of the myths and legends and discuss oral traditions. What oral traditions do they have in their families?

Creative Expression

- Arrange the students in groups of four. Explain that they will read a story together, discuss it, and retell it with their partners.

- Ask them to list and describe the main characters; recall the setting(s); review the plot and sequence of events; and retell the story.

- Each person tells a portion of the story using his or her own words and style.

- **Informal Assessment** Comment positively on the students' retelling of their myths and legends.

Reflect **Time:** About 10 minutes

 **Art Criticism**

- Have students answer the four art criticism questions on page 153 aloud and in writing.

- Did students successfully understand the story and retell it with their partners creating rhythm and movement?

Unit 5 Planning Guide

	Lesson Title	Suggested Pacing	Creative Expression Activity
Lesson 1	Balance	55 minutes	Create a construction paper jar that has balance.
Lesson 2	Balance in People	55 minutes	Create a drawing of a hero that illustrates balance in people.
Lesson 3	Emphasis	55 minutes	Create a drawing of a group of people in which one is emphasized.
Lesson 4	Emphasis Using Contrast	55 minutes	Create a drawing of a lit building at night and create emphasis using contrast.
Lesson 5	Tactile Texture	55 minutes	Create a needlework piece of a map scene using tactile materials.
Lesson 6	Visual Texture	55 minutes	Create a collage using texture rubbings.
ART SOURCE ARTSOURCE	Balance, Emphasis, and Texture in Dance	40 minutes	Create a sequence of five actions through creative movement.

Materials	Program Resources	Fine Art Resources	Literature Resources
12" × 18" white paper, scissors, pencils, colored construction paper, glue	*Reading and Writing Test Preparation,* pp. 54-55 *Flash Cards,* 12-14 *Assessment,* pp. 57-58 *Home and After-School Connections*	*Transparency,* 25 *Artist Profiles,* pp. 73, 76 *Animals Time Line* *Large Prints,* 33 and 34 *Women in the Arts Collection*	*Let's Fly a Kite* by Stuart J. Murphy
12" × 18" white paper, crayons, black markers	*Reading and Writing Test Preparation,* pp. 56-57 *Assessment,* pp. 59-60	*Transparency,* 26 *Artist Profiles,* pp. 22, 47 *Large Print,* 34 *Women in the Arts Collection*	*He Saves the Day* by Marsha Hayles
12" × 18" white paper, markers	*Reading and Writing Test Preparation,* pp. 58-59 *Flash Card,* 15 *Assessment,* pp. 61-62	*Transparency,* 27 *Artist Profiles,* pp. 6, 54 *Large Prints,* 33 and 34 *Art Around the World Collection*	*Elmer* by David McKee
12" × 18" dark blue or black construction paper, white and yellow oil pastels, other oil pastels	*Reading and Writing Test Preparation,* pp. 60-61 *Flash Card,* 15 *Assessment,* pp. 63-64	*Transparency,* 28 *Artist Profiles,* pp. 35, 66 *Large Print,* 33 *Art Around the World Collection*	*The House in the Meadow* by Shutta Crum
cloth or burlap, tape, sketch paper, scissors, blunt tapestry needles, fabric scraps, yarn, buttons and trims	*Reading and Writing Test Preparation,* pp. 62-63 *Assessment,* pp. 65-66	*Transparency,* 29 *Artist Profiles,* pp. 20, 78 *Large Print,* 33 *Women in the Arts Collection*	*Feely Bugs* by David Carter
12" × 18" white paper, crayons, rubbing paper, scissors, glue, colored construction paper scraps, textured objects, texture plates *"Radio Dance"* by Remy Charlip	*Reading and Writing Test Preparation,* pp. 64-65 *Assessment,* pp. 67-68	*Transparency,* 30 *Artist Profiles,* pp. 10, 68 *Large Print,* 34 *Women in the Arts Collection*	*Is It Rough? Is It Smooth? Is It Shiny?* by Tana Hoban

Balance, Emphasis, and Texture

Lesson 1: **Balance** and symmetry are used to arrange artwork.

Lesson 2: **Balance in People** explains that people can be balanced and symmetrical.

Lesson 3: **Emphasis** makes an object or area in a work of art stand out.

Lesson 4: **Emphasis Using Contrast** is when objects with different properties are next to each other in a work of art.

Lesson 5: **Tactile Texture** is the way that something feels.

Lesson 6: **Visual Texture** is texture that can only be seen. Artists use visual texture to describe the way something would feel if you could touch it.

Introduce Unit Concepts

"Artists use balance, emphasis, and texture to make many different kinds of art." "Los artistas usan el equilibrio, el énfasis y la textura para crear diferentes tipos de arte".

Balance
- Have students talk about what they think balance is. Some students might cite a teeter-totter or a scale.

Emphasis
- Have students look around the room and pick out objects that stand out to them. Then have them try to explain why that object stands out.

Texture
- Ask students to look around the room and outside and describe how they think different objects would feel. Then have the students touch those objects.

Cross-Curricular Projects
- See the *Language Arts and Reading, Mathematics, Science, and Social Studies Art Connections* books for activities that further develop balance, emphasis, and texture.

Balance, Emphasis, and Texture

▲ **Chryssa.** (American). *The Gates to Times Square.* 1966.
Welded stainless steel, neon, and Plexiglas. 120 × 120 × 120 inches (304.8 × 304.8 × 304.8 cm.). Albright-Knox Gallery, Buffalo, New York.

Artists use the principles of balance and emphasis when arranging their work. Texture is an element that can be used to create emphasis.

This artist used **neon** to add emphasis to her art.

154 Unit 5

Fine Art Prints

Display *Large Prints 33 Mask* and *34 Boy with a Tire.* Refer to the prints throughout the unit as students learn about balance, emphasis, and texture.

Large Print 33

Large Print 34

Artists use **balance** when putting together artwork. Balance makes the viewer feel that the work of art is well arranged.

▶ Does this sculpture have balance? Why or why not?

Artists use **emphasis** to call attention to parts of their art they want viewers to notice.

▶ What parts of this sculpture stand out?

Texture can be seen and felt. Texture is how things feel or would feel if they were touched.

▶ What would different parts of this sculpture feel like if you touched them?

In This Unit you will learn about and practice techniques to create balance, emphasis, and texture in your art. Here are the topics you will study:
▶ Balance
▶ Balance in People
▶ Emphasis
▶ Emphasis Using Contrast
▶ Tactile Texture
▶ Visual Texture

Chryssa

(1933–)

Chryssa was born in Athens, Greece, and moved to New York City in 1955. Chryssa loved the bright lights and activity that she saw in New York City. She started using neon in her art to try to capture the feelings she had when she looked at the big bright signs at night. She often uses letters or variations on letters in her art. *The Gates to Times Square* is one of the most important American sculptures.

Unit 5   **155**

Examine the Artwork

"Let's look closely at the sculpture" "Vamos a mirar detalladamente la escultura".

■ Have students look at Chryssa's *The Gates to Times Square*. Ask them to describe what they see.

■ Have students answer the questions about balance, emphasis, and texture on page 155.

▶ Yes, the sculpture is balanced because it is even and both sides of the sculpture have similar features.

▶ The blue neon stands out because it is so bright. The top of the letter *A* stands out since it is a different color.

▶ Most parts would feel smooth. Other parts might feel bumpy.   NSAE 1.a, 1.b

■ Discuss with students the differences between materials, techniques, and processes. Ask students to describe how different materials, techniques, and processes cause different viewer responses.

Unit Pretest

T Display *Transparency 47* as a pretest. Answers: 1.A, 2.C, 3.B, 4.A

Home Connection

■ See *Home and After-School Connections* for family newsletters and activities for this unit.

Art History and Culture

Chryssa

Chryssa (kris´ə) is an artist who works in many mediums, but is best known for her sculptures using bright neon tubing. She began sculpting in New York City in the 1950s and developed a style that incorporated the bright lights that she saw with letters of the alphabet. When she saw the letters of the bright signs in Times Square, she felt that she was seeing a form of art akin to Japanese calligraphy or Byzantine mosaics. Chryssa does all of the metalworking and welding of her sculptures herself.

Artist Profiles, p. 12

● Artist Profile ●
Chryssa
b. 1933
Born and educated in Greece, Chryssa (kris´ə) first studied social work but redirected her career path, because she felt that many relief funds ignored people in need. She studied in Athens, Paris, and California, and began her artistic career as a sculptor in New York during the 1950s. Her exploration of neon light and commercial signs was a new combination of materials to the art scene and opened up many avenues for her public installations. Chryssa does her own metalwork and the physical labor required by her art. She is regarded as highly motivating by her coworkers.

ILLUSTRATOR PROFILE

Donald Crews

(1938–)

Donald Crews was born in 1938 in Newark, New Jersey. He loved to draw as a child and often worked on art projects with his siblings. His family took annual summer trips to his grandparents' home in Florida, where Crews would sit on the porch and watch trains go by.

After studying design in college, Crews worked on the staff of a magazine and later worked as a freelance illustrator. He made his first book, *We Read: A to Z*, as an addition to his portfolio. *Freight Train*, which drew on his childhood trips to Florida, was named a Caldecott Honor Book. Its bold colors, strong shapes, and imaginative use of space show the influence of his design training.

Throughout Unit 5, share Crews's illustrations with the class and discuss the use of balance, emphasis, and texture with the students. Where do students see balance in the illustrations? What about emphasis?

Music

Balance in music is usually associated with symmetrical composition forms such as ABA. Have students sing an example of this by singing *Au Clair de la Lune*. Texture refers to combining melody and harmony to create layers of sound.

Literature

Show the video or DVD *A Chair for My Mother* by Vera B. Williams to help introduce the concept of emphasis. Use the importance of the chair to help define emphasis for the students.

Literature and Art

Performing Arts

Show "Radio Dance." Discuss how Remy Charlip uses balance, emphasis, and texture in his dance.

Artsource®

Lesson 1 Balance

Lesson 1 introduces the students to balance and symmetry. Balance occurs when equal or similar shapes or objects are placed on opposite sides of an axis in a work of art. Symmetry is a special type of balance where two sides of a work of art are mirror images of each other.

Objectives

 Art History and Culture

To recognize that different ancient cultures used jars to store things

 Creative Expression

To create a construction paper jar that has balance

 Aesthetic Perception

To recognize that containers have balance when both sides are similar and symmetry when both sides are the same

Art Criticism

To use the four steps of art criticism to evaluate their own artwork

Vocabulary Vocabulary

Review the following vocabulary words with students before beginning the lesson.

symmetry simetría—a special type of balance where two sides of a work of art are mirror images of each other

axis eje—a real or imaginary line across the center of a work of art

See page 179B for additional vocabulary and Spanish Vocabulary resources.

 Art Journal: Vocabulary

Have students add these words to the Vocabulary section of their Art Journals.

Lesson Materials
- 12" × 18" white paper
- scissors
- pencils
- colored construction paper
- glue
- an assortment of construction paper shapes, some symmetrical, others not

Alternate Materials:
- thin felt
- crayons
- markers

Program Resources
- *Reading and Writing Test Prep.*, pp. 54–55
- *Transparency 25*
- *Flash Cards 12, 13, 14*
- *Artist Profiles*, pp. 73, 76
- *Animals Through History Time Line*
- *Assessment*, pp. 57–58
- *Large Print 33 Mask* and *34 Boy with a Tire*
- *The National Museum of Women in the Arts Collection*

Concept Trace
Balance
Introduced: Level 1, Unit 6, Lesson 1

Reinforced: Level 3, Unit 4, Lessons 1, 3

Lesson 1 Arts Integration

Theatre

Complete Unit 5 Lesson 1 on pages 90–91 of *Theatre Arts Connections.*

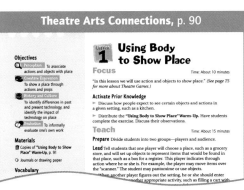

Theatre Arts Connections, p. 90

Music

 Balance in music can describe how evenly different parts are performed at the same time to make the desired blend. Listen to *Akinla*, from *African Suite*, by Fela Sowande. Discuss whether all parts are equal in dynamics at all times.

Movement & Dance

Have students create four different symmetrical designs in the body, working on three different levels. Have students find a way to move from one design to another by turning, jumping, and swinging. Have students teach their designs to a partner and perform their dance together.

Focus

Activate Prior Knowledge

"Are all bowls and cups the same on both halves?" "¿Son iguales en ambas mitades todos los platos hondos y las tazas?"

- Ask students to discuss food containers. Help them understand that cups and mugs are not always symmetrical because some have a handle on only one side.

Using Literature Reading

- Read *Let's Fly a Kite* by Stuart J. Murphy. Discuss the balance and symmetry students see in the book.

Thematic Connection Social Studies

- **Containers:** Encourage students to think about the containers that they use everyday. How and why do they think these containers were developed to suit their purposes?

Introduce the Art

Look NSAE 2.a

"Let's look closely at these two containers." "Vamos a mirar detalladamente estos dos envases".

- Have students identify balance and symmetry in the works of art and the environment.

Human Systems Social Studies

- Have students discuss how humans build civilizations and form settlements. How are these containers a record of human civilization? How do the containers tell us what these ancient civilizations were like?

NSAE 4.a, 4.b, 4.c, 5.a, 5.b

Art History and Culture

Possible answer: The Chinese container was meant to hold food, and the Greek flask was meant to hold oil. Encourage students to think about whether these were everyday storage items.

Web Connection

Visit http://library.thinkquest.org/16325/c-main.html to learn more about the Zhou dynasty.

 Lesson 1 Balance

Look at these two jars. Trace them with your fingers. Are the forms the same on both sides? When things are the same on both sides, they have balance and **symmetry.**

◀ **Artist Unknown.** (China). *Gui Ritual Food Container.* Zhou Dynasty, 11th century B.C.

Bronze. Arthur M. Sackler Gallery, Smithsonian Institution, Washington, D.C.

Art History and Culture

What do you think people stored in these containers?

Art History and Culture

Gui Ritual Food Container

The Chinese food container was created in the eleventh century B.C., during the Zhou Dynasty. Such metal containers were filled with fruit and other foods and placed in tombs for the deceased's afterlife. When this container was made, the artistic influence of the previous rulers, the Shang-Yi Dynasty, was still strong. When important Chinese people died, all their valued possessions were buried with them, along with nourishment for the afterlife. The container pictured is a typical food container cast from a clay mold with a combination of copper, tin, and lead. These metals oxidized and turned the container a greenish color.

See pages 24–25 and 16–21 for more about art history and subject matter.

Artist Profiles, p. 73

Artist Profile

Gui Ritual Food Container

The ancient Chinese used bronze containers during their religious ceremonies or *rituals*. The containers were symbols of political power. The artisans who made them were well respected. Some of the containers were buried with the dead, and others were buried as offerings to the natural spirits of the rivers and mountains. Other containers were carefully hidden. When they were unearthed or found, sometimes generations later, they were treasured as links to the past. These containers now serve as a record of ancient Chinese culture and proof of the skill of its artists.

 Artist unknown. (China). *Gui Ritual Food*

Study the two containers to find the balance.

▶ Describe the shape of each jar.

▶ How are the shapes of the forms the same on both sides of the jars?

◀ **Attributed to the Amasis painter.**
(Greek). *Lekythos (oil flask)*.
c. 550–530 B.C.
·······································
The Metropolitan Museum of Art, New York, New York.

Design Awareness Look at containers in the classroom and at home that you use to store things. Do these containers have balance? Why do you think so?

Art History and Culture

Lekythos (oil flask)

This flask was used in ancient Greece for storing oil. It was painted at a time when the Greeks were keenly interested in studying and portraying the human figure in art. The figures on this vase are women portrayed in a domestic scene. They are spinning, weaving, and preparing wool. This is a black-figure work of art because the characters painted on the vase are black. Alternatively, there is also red-figure style of art where the majority of the vase is black and the characters are painted in terra cotta.

See pages 24–25 and 16–21 for more about art history and subject matter.

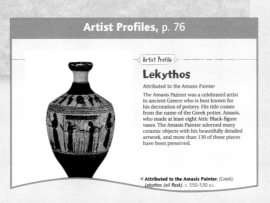

Artist Profiles, p. 76

◇ Artist Profile ◇
Lekythos
Attributed to the Amasis Painter

The Amasis Painter was a celebrated artist in ancient Greece who is best known for his decoration of pottery. His title comes from the name of the Greek potter, Amasis, who made at least eight Attic Black-figure vases. The Amasis Painter adorned many ceramic objects with his beautifully detailed artwork, and more than 130 of these pieces have been preserved.

◀ **Attributed to the Amasis Painter.** (Greek).
Lekythos (oil flask). c. 550-530 B.C.

Study

▶ Student answers will vary. Both jars have narrow tops and become wider. The Chinese container has handles and a square base. The oil flask narrows again at the bottom.

▶ The shapes used to decorate the jars are different, but the forms of the jars are the same on both sides.

■ For more examples of utilitarian art, see *The National Museum of Women in the Arts Collection.*

Art Journal: Writing

Ask students to write a description of what they think balance is in the Concepts section of their Art Journals. Where else have they seen balance?

Aesthetic Perception

Design Awareness Encourage students to look at containers in their classroom and in their homes and think about balance and symmetry. Encourage students to identify the variations in objects from their environments. Why do students think the designers created these containers with balance? One reason is for easy and compact storage.   NSAE 2.b, 5.c

Developing Visual Literacy What do students think the messages of the artists were when they made these containers? Why did they decorate utilitarian objects?

Web Connection

Visit **http://www.bbc.co.uk/schools/ancientgreece/index.shtml** to learn more about Ancient Greece.

Teach

"How can you create balance and symmetry?" "¿Cómo pueden crear equilibrio y simetría?"

■ Read and discuss the information on balance and symmetry on page 158.

Practice

Materials: an assortment of construction paper shapes, some symmetrical, others not

■ Distribute the materials and have students follow the directions on page 158.

■ Give a selection of 3–4 shapes to each group of students. Observe the groups as they come to their conclusions about symmetry.

■ Have students identify and practice skills necessary for producing constructions using a variety of materials.

NSAE 1.c, 1.d, 2.c, 3.b

 ### Creative Expression

Materials: 12" × 18" white paper, scissors, pencils, colored construction paper, glue

Alternate Materials: thin felt, crayons, markers

■ Distribute the materials and have students follow the directions on page 159.

■ Encourage students to create effective compositions using design principles.

■ Review the Activity Tips on page 244 for visual examples of the activity techniques if needed.

NSAE 3.a

Art Journal: Brainstorming

Have students think of and sketch containers that are balanced or symmetrical in the Ideas section of their Art Journals. Have students select their favorite container to use as an idea for the Creative Expression activity.

Using Balance

Balance happens when equal or similar shapes or objects are placed on opposite sides of an **axis.** An axis is a real or imaginary line across the center of the work of art.

Symmetry is a special type of balance. When art has symmetry, the two halves are mirror images of each other. Can you find balance in these pictures? Are they **symmetrical?**

Practice

Can you figure out if shapes are symmetrical?

1. Break into small groups.

2. Look at the selection of shapes your teacher has given you.

3. Find the axis of each shape. Decide if the shape is symmetrical. Share your results with the class.

Differentiated Instruction

Reteach

Hold up symmetrical and asymmetrical objects. Have students tell you which ones are balanced and why.

Special Needs

Students who lack fine motor skills may find it difficult to cut out small shapes for this project. Consider making the jar size larger for the entire class, so that the larger shapes will be scaled to the larger container.

ELL Tips

Define *balance* and *symmetry.* Use each word in a sentence. Bring a two-handled cup to class and ask students if both halves are exactly alike. Does the cup have balance and symmetry? Have students draw the cup.

◀ **Amber Mooney.**
Age 8.

Think about how this student used balance in her jar.

 Creative Expression

Design a symmetrical jar.

1. Think about the jar you want to make.
2. Fold a sheet of paper in half. Draw and cut out your jar shape. Glue your jar to your background paper.
3. Cut out small matching shapes. Arrange the shapes symmetrically around the axis and glue the shapes to the jar.

Art Criticism

Describe What did you design your jar to hold?

Analyze Where is the axis of your jar?

Interpret How would your jar be different if you had not used symmetry?

Decide How could you design your jar so it had balance but not symmetry?

Art Across the Curriculum

NSAE 6.a, 6.b

Use these simple ideas to reinforce art concepts across the curriculum.

★ **Narrative Writing** Have students write a short story pretending they are creating a container in ancient times.

★ **Math** Discuss symmetry. Show students numbers and operational symbols. Which are symmetric?

★ **Science** Have students experiment with a beam balance scale and different weight sets to gather information to extend the senses and their ideas of balance.

★ **Social Studies** Have students compare various interpretations of the same time period using evidence such as photographs and interviews. Explain how this creates a balanced point of view.

★ **Technology** Have students use drawing tools to create symmetrical and asymmetrical shapes. Visit **SRAonline.com** to print detailed instructions for this activity.

eflect

Time: About 10 minutes

Review and Assess

"What makes an object symmetrical? What makes an object balanced?" "¿Qué hace que un objeto sea simétrico? ¿Qué hace que un objeto sea equilibrado?"

Think

The artist created balance by placing similar shapes on opposite sides of the axis of the jar.

■ Use **Large Prints 33** *Mask* and **34** *Boy with a Tire* to have students identify balance and symmetry.

■ Have students identify stories and constructions in this lesson's artwork.

■ Have students identify ideas of the artists in this lesson's art.

Informal Assessment

Art Journal: Critical Thinking
Have students answer the four art criticism questions—Describe, Analyze, Interpret, and Decide—in the Critical Thinking section of their Art Journals. Have students discuss in small groups whether they created symmetry or just balance in their paper jars. Ask students to define their reasons for preferences in their art. Then have them identify ideas in their peers' art.

■ For standardized-format test practice using this lesson's art content, see pages 54–55 in *Reading and Writing Test Preparation.*

Lesson 1

 Wrap-Up

Balance

 Time: About 45 minutes

Extra! For the Art Specialist

Focus

Study **Large Print 33** and ask students to describe the artwork. If the artwork were divided in half, would both sides be the same? Why? Does the artwork look like it is balanced? What makes it appear to have balance? Explain.

Teach

Explain to students that they will create an insect jar using symmetry. They will use chalk and oil pastels to make both halves of their artwork the same. Have students complete the alternate activity.

Reflect

Have students evaluate their art using the four steps of art criticism.

Alternate Activity

Materials:
- black or brown construction paper
- white chalk
- oil pastels
- images of insects

1. Discuss balance and symmetry using the images of bugs. Select a sheet of construction paper and fold it in half.

2. Unfold the paper. Use chalk to draw a large jar. Let the fold line be the line of symmetry.

3. Fold the paper so that you can see only half of your jar. Add bugs to your jar using oil pastels.

4. When the first half is completed, unfold the paper and color the other half so it looks the same.

Research in Art Education

"It seems without a doubt that children do, indeed, respond to and are able to talk about art in meaningful ways." Anderson, Tom. "Talking About Art with Children: From Theory to Practice." *Art Education* 39(1). (1986): 5–8.

Assessment

Use the following rubric to evaluate the artwork students make in the Creative Expression activity and to assess students' understanding of balance and symmetry.

Have students complete page 57 or 58 of their *Assessment* books.

	Art History and Culture	Aesthetic Perception	Creative Expression	Art Criticism
3 POINTS	The student can identify and compare the use of jars in ancient cultures.	The student accurately identifies balance and symmetry in containers.	The student's paper jar clearly illustrates a good use of balance and symmetry.	The student thoughtfully and honestly evaluates his or her own work using the four steps of art criticism.
2 POINTS	The student's identification or comparison is weak or incomplete.	The student shows emerging awareness of balance and symmetry, but cannot consistently identify them.	The student's paper jar shows some awareness of balance and symmetry.	The student attempts to evaluate his or her own work, but shows an incomplete understanding of evaluation criteria.
1 POINT	The student cannot identify or compare the use of jars in ancient cultures.	The student cannot identify balance and symmetry.	The student's paper jar shows no understanding of balance and symmetry.	The student makes no attempt to evaluate his or her own artwork.

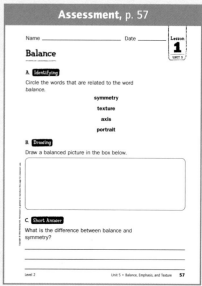

Assessment, p. 57

Lesson 2 Overview

Balance in People

Lesson 2 introduces the students to balance in people. People also have an axis of symmetry. Their poses may be symmetrical or just balanced.

Objectives

 Art History and Culture

To recognize that artists sometimes use cultural heroes as their subjects

 Creative Expression

To create a drawing of a hero that has balance

 Aesthetic Perception

To recognize that human bodies have symmetry and their poses can be balanced or symmetrical

Art Criticism

To use the four steps of art criticism to evaluate their own artwork

Vocabulary ⭐ Vocabulary

Review the following vocabulary word with students before beginning the lesson.

posed (en) pose—arranged in a special way

See page 179B for additional Spanish vocabulary resources.

Art Journal: Vocabulary

Have students add this word to the Vocabulary section of their Art Journals.

Lesson Materials
- 12" × 18" white paper
- crayons
- black markers

Alternate Materials:
- markers
- colored pencils

Program Resources
- *Reading and Writing Test Prep.,* pp. 56–57
- *Transparency 26*
- *Artist Profiles,* pp. 22, 47
- *Animals Through History Time Line*
- *Assessment,* pp. 59–60
- *Large Print 34* Boy with a Tire
- *The National Museum of Women in the Arts Collection*

Concept Trace
Balance in People
Introduced: Level 1, Unit 6, Lesson 2
Reinforced: Level 3, Unit 4, Lessons 2, 4

Lesson 2 Arts Integration

Theatre
Complete Unit 5 Lesson 2 on pages 92–93 of *Theatre Arts Connections.*

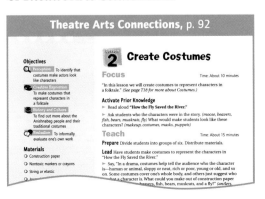

Music
 People have symmetry. Listen to *Contredanse* by Jean-Phillipe Rameau. What form is this piece in? Are the beginning and ending sections exactly the same? How does the orchestration change in the middle section? The rhythm?

Movement & Dance
Have students create four different symmetrical designs with a partner, working on three different levels. In the first design, students must be touching. In the second design, students must be apart. In the third design, students must find a way to move their shape.

 **Focus**   Time: About 10 minutes

Activate Prior Knowledge

"Is your body the same on both the left and right?" "¿Tu cuerpo es igual tanto en el lado derecho como en el izquierdo?"

■ Help students understand that if a line were drawn down the middle of a human body, each half would be a mirror image of the other.

Using Literature ⭐ Reading

■ Read *He Saves the Day* by Marsha Hayles. Have students look for balance in the characters' bodies.

Thematic Connection ⭐ Social Studies

■ **Heroes:** Encourage students to think about what makes a person a hero and who their heroes are.

Introduce the Art

Look NSAE 2.a

"Let's look closely at these two works of art." "Vamos a mirar detalladamente estas dos obras de arte".

■ Have students identify balance in the artwork and their environments.

■ Have students compare the way individuals are depicted in these works of art.

Citizen Responsibility ⭐ Social Studies

■ Have students discuss what the responsibilities of citizens are in a society. Do they think the figures in these works of art meet or exceed these qualities? What makes them think so?

NSAE 4.a, 4.b, 4.c, 5.a, 5.b

 Art History and Culture

Possible answer: The artists felt that these people are heroes. The way the people are posed and dressed tells you that they are heroes.

 Web Connection

Visit **http://museum.oglethorpe.edu/Hanson.htm** to see more of Hanson's work.

Look at these two works of art. Both of these works of art are of people. People have balance.

◀ **Duane Hanson.** (American). *Policeman.* 1992–1994.
....
Bronze polychromed oil, mixed media with accessories. Hanson Collection, Davie, Florida.

 Art History and Culture

Why did the artists make art of these people? What about the art tells you that these people are heroes?

Art History and Culture

Duane Hanson

Duane Hanson (dwān han´ sən) (1925–1996) once carved little figures out of logs. Later, his life-size sculptures of ordinary people were an immediate success with the public. Hanson's super-realistic style is so successful that people try to start conversations with his sculptures. One time a museum visitor dialed 911 to get help for an "unconscious" Hanson sculpture. Hanson created more than 100 sculptures during his career. His subjects were real people, ranging from janitors to sunbathers to athletes. Hanson's aim was to make viewers more aware of themselves and others.

See pages 24–25 and 16–21 for more about art history and subject matter.

 **Artist Profiles, p. 22**

▸ Artist Profile ◂
Duane Hanson
1925–1996

Duane Hanson (dwān han´ sən) carved little figures out of logs using kitchen knives as a boy in his native Minnesota. Later he attended art school and taught art in Atlanta, Georgia and Miami, Florida. The same art dealer who discovered Andy Warhol arranged for Hanson's first solo exhibition. His life-size sculptures of ordinary people were an immediate success with the public. People could identify with his work. Hanson married and had five children. He continued to plan and create sculpture until the end of his life.

Study the two works of art of heroes to find balance in people.

▶ Can you find the axis in each person in each work of art?

▶ What body parts are repeated on both sides of the bodies?

◀ **James Peale.** (American). *George Washington.* c. 1782.

Oil on canvas. 36 × 27 inches (91.4 × 68.6 cm.). The Metropolitan Museum of Art, New York, New York.

Aesthetic Perception

Seeing Like an Artist Look closely at how people stand and sit. Do people tend to be in symmetrical or nonsymmetrical positions?

Study

▶ The axis is down the middle of each person.

▶ Ears, arms, legs, hands, eyes, feet, and so on.

▪ For more examples of portraits, see *The National Museum of Women in the Arts Collection.*

Art Journal: Writing

Have students write explanations of the difference between *balance* and *symmetry* in the Concepts section of their Art Journals.

Aesthetic Perception

Seeing Like an Artist Encourage students to look at people they see everyday in the community. How do these people stand and sit? Many people in casual situations will be in nonsymmetrical poses more often than symmetrical ones. Encourage students to identify variations in subjects from their environments.

NSAE 2.b, 5.c

Developing Visual Literacy Have students look carefully at the two images and look at the surrounding areas. How is the Hanson work positioned? What is in the background of the Peale work? How do students think these settings contribute to the messages the artists are trying to convey?

Art History and Culture

James Peale

James Peale (jāmz pēl) (1749–1831) was born in Chestertown, Maryland. When his older brother Charles returned from London as a trained artist in 1769, Peale became his assistant and student and earned a reputation for his detailed, realistic paintings. By the late 1780s he had established himself as a successful painter of miniature portraits and landscapes. Peale served during the American Revolution as a first lieutenant until 1779. During this time, he painted two full-length portraits of George Washington at Yorktown. When Peale's eyesight began to fail in 1810, he discontinued his miniatures and turned to large landscapes and still lifes.

See pages 24–25 and 16–21 for more about art history and subject matter.

Artist Profiles, p. 47

Artist Profile ▶
James Peale
1749–1831
James Peale (jāmz pēl) was born in Chestertown, Maryland, in 1749. When he was 13, he worked in his brother's saddlery, and several years later he became an apprentice to a cabinetmaker. When his older brother Charles returned from London as a trained artist in 1769, Peale became his assistant and student and earned a reputation for his detailed, realistic paintings. Peale served during the American Revolution as a first lieutenant until 1779, and then resided in Philadelphia with Charles until 1782. His popularity as a romantic artist eventually grew and earned him a respectable following of patrons and collectors. His three daughters continued the "Peale Dynasty" and became successful

Web Connection

Visit **http://www.umfa.utah.edu/index.php?id= MjE&collection_id=29** to see another Revolutionary War painting by James Peale.

# Teach

"Can you and a partner move your bodies like mirror images of each other?" "¿Pueden ustedes junto con un compañero mover sus cuerpos como si cada uno fueran la imagen del otro al mirarse en un espejo?"

- Read and discuss the information on balance in people on page 162.

Practice

Materials: 12" × 18" white paper, crayons

Alternate Materials: markers, colored pencils

- Distribute the materials and have students follow the directions on page 162.

- If students are having difficulty thinking of poses, encourage them to think of activities and the way people move when doing those activities.

- Have students identify and practice skills necessary for producing drawings using a variety of materials.

NSAE 1.c, 1.d, 2.c, 3.b

 ## Creative Expression

Materials: 12" × 18" white paper, crayons, black markers

Alternate Materials: markers, colored pencils

- Distribute the materials and have students follow the directions on page 163.

- Encourage students to create effective compositions using design principles.

- Review the Activity Tips on page 244 for visual examples of the activity techniques if needed.

NSAE 3.a

Art Journal: Sketching
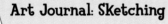
Have students sketch possibilities for their hero pose in the Ideas section of their Art Journals. Have them pick a favorite sketch for their Creative Expression drawing.

# Using Balance in People

Art is not the only place you can find balance. People also have balance and symmetry. This means people also have an axis. Many body parts are mirrored on both sides of the body. Even though people have symmetry, they can be **posed** in ways so they are not symmetrical. Look at the pictures. Are both people symmetrical? Are both people balanced?

Practice

Can you draw people in symmetrical and nonsymmetrical poses?

1. Think of some poses.
2. Draw people in those poses.
3. Are all the poses symmetrical? Are all your people balanced?

Differentiated Instruction

Reteach

Have students stand up and strike symmetrical and asymmetrical poses. Encourage the class to guess which activity each pose represents.

Special Needs

Consider allowing this project to be a culminating activity for a unit on heroes. Provide students choices of heroes to research, and cultivate disability awareness by including persons with disabilities among the choices.

ELL Tips

Help students understand how bodies have balance and symmetry. Point out parts of the body that come in pairs.

Think about how this student used balance and symmetry in his hero picture.

◀ **Trent Abbey.**
Age 7.

Creative Expression

Who are some of your heroes? Draw your hero using balance and symmetry.

1. Think of a real or imaginary hero to draw.

2. Sketch your hero on your paper.

3. Use a black marker to outline your drawing. Add details using crayons, colored pencils, or markers.

Art Criticism

Describe Who did you select for your hero drawing?

Analyze Where is the axis in your hero drawing?

Interpret Why did you pick this person to be your hero?

Decide Do you like symmetrical or nonsymmetrical poses better for your hero drawing?

 **Reflect**   Time: About 10 minutes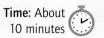

Review and Assess

"What makes a body symmetrical? What makes a body balanced?" "¿Qué hace que un cuerpo sea simétrico? ¿Qué hace que un cuerpo sea equilibrado?"

Think

The artist created strong balance and symmetry in his hero drawing by placing the soldier in this pose.

- Use *Large Print 34* *Boy with a Tire* to have students identify balance in people.

- Have students identify stories and constructions in this lesson's artwork.

- Have students identify ideas of the artists in this lesson's art.

Informal Assessment

Art Journal: Critical Thinking
Have students answer the four art criticism questions—Describe, Analyze, Interpret, and Decide—in the Critical Thinking section of their Art Journals. Have students discuss in small groups whether they created symmetry or just balance in the poses in their hero pictures. Ask students to define their reasons for preferences in their own art. Then have them identify ideas in their peers' art.

- For standardized-format test practice using this lesson's art content, see pages 56–57 in *Reading and Writing Test Preparation*.

Art Across the Curriculum

NSAE 6.a, 6.b

Use these simple ideas to reinforce art concepts across the curriculum.

★ **Expository Writing** Have students write a paragraph about their favorite heroes.

★ **Math** Have students count the pairs of things that give a human body balance, such as eyes or hands.

★ **Science** Have students discuss why human and animal bodies are balanced so there is more than one of an object. Have them also identify the external characteristics of different kinds of animals that allow their needs to be met.

★ **Social Studies** Discuss with students local and national figures who have exhibited a love of individualism, inventiveness, and an influence on history.

★ **Technology** Show students how to use drawing tools to draw a balanced person. Visit **SRAonline.com** to print detailed instructions for this activity.

Balance in People

Extra! For the Art Specialist

Time: About 45 minutes

Focus

Study *Large Print 34* and ask students to describe the artwork. Is it balanced? Where is the line of symmetry? Do human bodies have balance? Explain.

Teach

Explain to students that they will create a self-portrait using balance and symmetry. They will draw with pencils and markers, and paint it using tempera cakes. Have the students complete the Alternate Activity.

Reflect

Have students evaluate their art using the four steps of art criticism.

Alternate Activity

Materials:

- 12" × 18" white drawing paper
- pencils and black markers
- brushes, buckets, and newspapers
- tempera cake palettes with all colors
- self-portraits by Master artists

1. Discuss balance and symmetry and how it applies to the body. Talk about various self-portraits by Master artists.

2. On the drawing paper, sketch a large self-portrait (from the shoulders up). Keep it symmetrical and balanced.

3. When finished, trace your work with a marker and add patterns and details.

4. Paint the portrait with the tempera cakes to finish it.

Research in Art Education

"If perception is basic to all learning, if selective viewing is a desirable kind of behavior, and if conceptualization comes after sensory experiences, then it becomes imperative that teachers provide paths for numerous visual and tactile explorations so as to keep all of the child's senses alive and active." Herberholz, Barbara, and Lee Hanson. *Early Childhood Art.* New York: McGraw-Hill, 1994.

Assessment

Use the following rubric to evaluate the artwork students make in the Creative Expression activity and to assess students' understanding of balance and symmetry in people.

Have students complete page 59 or 60 of their *Assessment* books.

	Art History and Culture	Aesthetic Perception	Creative Expression	Art Criticism
3 POINTS	The student can identify and compare the use of heroes in a work of art.	The student accurately identifies balance in people in his or her environment.	The student's hero drawing clearly illustrates a good use of balance in people.	The student thoughtfully and honestly evaluates his or her own work using the four steps of art criticism.
2 POINTS	The student's identification or comparison is weak or incomplete.	The student shows emerging awareness of balance in people, but cannot consistently identify it.	The student's hero drawing shows some awareness of balance in people.	The student attempts to evaluate his or her own work, but shows an incomplete understanding of evaluation criteria.
1 POINT	The student cannot identify or compare the use of heroes in different works of art.	The student cannot identify balance in people.	The student's hero drawing shows no understanding of balance in people.	The student makes no attempt to evaluate his or her own artwork.

Assessment, p. 59

Name _____ Date _____ Lesson **2** UNIT 5

Balance in People

A. Writing

Define *symmetry* in your own words.

_____

B. Drawing

Draw a person in a balanced pose in the box below.

Level 2 — Unit 5 • Balance, Emphasis, and Texture **59**

Lesson 3 Overview — Emphasis

Lesson 3 introduces the students to emphasis. Emphasis is used to make one part or area of a work of art stand out from the rest of the piece.

Objectives

 Art History and Culture

To recognize that groups of people portrayed in art usually have a relationship that is significant to the artist

Creative Expression

To create a drawing of a group of people in which one is emphasized

 Aesthetic Perception

To recognize that one person can be emphasized, or stressed, in a group of people

Art Criticism

To use the four steps of art criticism to evaluate their own artwork

Vocabulary Vocabulary

Review the following vocabulary words with students before beginning the lesson.

point of view *punto de vista*— the position from which the viewer sees an object or work of art

dominant *dominante*— the part of the work of art that seems more important to the viewer. Dominant elements have been emphasized.

See page 179B for additional vocabulary and Spanish vocabulary resources.

 Art Journal: Vocabulary

Have students add these words to the Vocabulary section of their Art Journals.

Lesson Materials

- 12" × 18" white paper
- markers
- one sentence on a piece of paper for each student

Alternate Materials:
- crayons
- colored pencils

Program Resources

- *Reading and Writing Test Prep.*, pp. 58–59
- *Transparency 27*
- *Flash Card 15*
- *Artist Profiles,* pp. 6, 54
- *Animals Through History Time Line*
- *Assessment,* pp. 61–62
- *Large Prints 33* Mask and *34* Boy with a Tire
- *Art Around the World Collection*

Concept Trace

Emphasis

Introduced: Level 1, Unit 6, Lessons 3–4

Reinforced: Level 3, Unit 6, Lessons 3–4

Lesson 3 Arts Integration

Theatre

Complete Unit 5 Lesson 3 on pages 94–95 of *Theatre Arts Connections.*

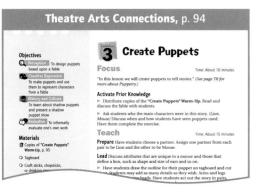

Music

 Various musical devices create emphasis in music. One way is with dynamics. To create meter in music, a strong beat is combined with weak beats to create duple or triple meter, as in "boom-chick boom-chick" or "boom-chick-chick boom-chick-chick." The most famous dance in triple meter is the waltz. Listen to *Waltz of the Flowers* by Peter Ilyich Tchaikovsky. Step to the beat of the music. Do you notice how the strong beat changes from the right foot to the left?

Movement & Dance

Dancers use accents in movement when they want to emphasize a particular idea. Students can accent a movement by making it stronger, bigger, repeating it several times, or adding in sudden stops and starts. Ask students to create three different movements and find a way to build accents into each one.

Focus

Activate Prior Knowledge

"Why do you think that street signs are often bright colors?" "¿Por qué creen que las señales de tránsito a menudo son de colores vivos?"

■ Help students understand that bright colors are often used to emphasize objects. Ask them to think of other ways to get people to notice things.

Using Literature Reading

■ Read *Elmer* by David McKee. Discuss the emphasis that students see in the book.

Thematic Connection Social Studies

■ **Groups:** Encourage students to think about different groups they have encountered such as families, friends, or teachers and principles. Do some people tend to stand out in these groups?

Introduce the Art

Look NSAE 2.a

"Let's look closely at these two works of art." "Vamos a mirar detalladamente estas dos obras de arte".

■ Have students identify emphasis in the works of art and their environments.

■ Have students compare the way individuals and families are depicted in the different works of art.

Author's Point of View Reading

■ Discuss with students how an artist is like an author in that they tell a story with their art. Ask students to discuss the artist's point of view in these two paintings. Where do they think the artists are? What relationships do they think the artists have to the subjects?

NSAE 4.a, 4.b, 4.c, 5.b

Art History and Culture

Possible answer: The first painting is of sisters. The second group is a child with her nanny.

 Web Connection

Visit http://www.folkart.org/ to learn more about folk art and folk artists.

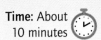 **Lesson**  Emphasis

▲ **Lorenzo Scott.** (American). *Ballet Dancers.*

Oil on canvas. 50 × 30 inches (127 × 76.2 cm.). Collection of Ann and Ted Oliver.

Look at these paintings. In both paintings, one person stands out from the other subjects. This is called emphasis. Artists have many ways to emphasize an object, including making it larger than other objects, using a different color, or using an unusual **point of view.**

Art History and Culture

Look at the titles of these works. What do you think the relationships are among the people in these paintings?

Art History and Culture

Lorenzo Scott

Folk artist Lorenzo Scott (lor´ n zō skät) (1934–) was born and raised in Georgia and began drawing when he was five years old. He has been a construction worker and house painter throughout his adult life, yet he has also made a name for himself as an artist. He still paints houses for a living and works on his personal paintings in his spare time. Large canvases and bright colors typify his work, and his subjects tend to be at the front of the composition without expansive depth.

See pages 24–25 and 16–21 for more about art history and subject matter.

Artist Profiles, p. 54

◆ Artist Profile ◆

Lorenzo Scott
b. 1934

Folk artist Lorenzo Scott (lor´ n zō skät) was born and raised in Georgia and began drawing when he was five years old. He has been a construction worker and house painter, yet he has also made a name for himself as a talented fine artist. In 1968 he traveled to New York and was so inspired by artists painting in the streets that he went home determined to do the same thing. Without any formal training, Scott taught himself to paint by studying oil paintings of the old masters in Atlanta museums.

▲ **Lorenzo Scott.** (American). *Ballet Dancers.* 2001.
Oil on canvas.

Study the two paintings and look for emphasis.

- ▶ Which parts of the paintings look most important?
- ▶ How did the artists make parts of the paintings look more important?
- ▶ When you look at these paintings, what do your eyes move to first?

◀ **Cecelia Beaux.** (American). *Ernesta (Child with Nurse).* 1894.

Oil on canvas. 50 $\frac{1}{2}$ × 38 $\frac{1}{8}$ inches (128.27 × 96.84 cm.). The Metropolitan Museum of Art, New York, New York.

 Aesthetic Perception

Seeing Like an Artist Look at groups of people you see together. Does one person seem to stand out from the others?

Study

- ▶ The middle girl is most important in the Scott painting. The child is most important in the Beaux painting.
- ▶ In the Scott painting, the middle girl is larger. In the Beaux painting, the artist made the girl seem most important by composing the picture using an unusual point of view.
- ▶ The middle girl in the Scott painting and the child in the Beaux painting.
- ■ For more examples of art from America, see the *Art Around the World Collection.*

Art Journal: Defining

Have students write their own definitions and explanations of *point of view* in the Concepts section of their Art Journals. In what other context have they heard of point of view?

Aesthetic Perception

Seeing Like an Artist Encourage students to examine the groups they see around them in the community. Have students identify variations in subjects from their environments. Although groups will often have a common theme, one person may be dominant and stand out from the rest of the group.

NSAE 2.b, 5.c

Developing Visual Literacy Have students discuss how these paintings make them feel. Do the points of view used have any effect on how they feel?

Art History and Culture

Cecilia Beaux

Cecilia Beaux (sə sēl′ yə bō) (1855–1942) was born in Philadelphia, Pennsylvania. At age 16, she began art training with a relative, Catherine A. Drinker. By the time she was 18, Beaux earned income from her artistic ability by teaching art and creating portraits of children. *Ernesta with Nurse* is a painting of one of Beaux's favorite nieces, Ernesta Drinker. Ernesta was the daughter of Catherine Drinker's brother and Cecilia's sister. Ernesta appeared in many of Beaux's compositions. Beaux herself never married or had children, although she received many offers. She instead chose to focus on her art.

See pages 24–25 and 16–21 for more about art history and subject matter.

Artist Profiles, p. 6

◆ Artist Profile ◆
Cecilia Beaux
1855–1942

Cecilia Beaux (sə sēl′ yə bō) was born in Philadelphia, Pennsylvania. When she wasn't working, Beaux studied at the Pennsylvania Academy where she later taught. In 1887, one of Beaux's paintings was accepted into the Paris Salon. This inspired her to travel overseas to continue her studies. For a year and a half Beaux studied in Paris at the Academie Julian and Colarossi. Returning to Philadelphia in 1889, Beaux's reputation quickly spread, with commissions from clients in Philadelphia, Boston, New York, and Washington D.C. Throughout her lifetime Beaux won awards for her work and received praise from her peers.

Web Connection

Visit **http://www.metmuseum.org/collections/ view1.asp?dep=2&full=1&item=15%2E82** to see a portrait Beaux painted of Ernesta 20 years later.

Teach

"Can you think of situations in which an object seems to be emphasized?" "¿Pueden pensar en situaciones en las que un objeto pareciera ser enfatizado?"

- Read and discuss the information on emphasis on page 166.

Practice

Materials: one sentence on a piece of paper for each student

- Distribute the materials and have students follow the directions on page 166.

- Have students identify and practice skills necessary for producing drawings using a variety of materials.

NSAE 1.c, 1.d, 2.c, 3.b

Creative Expression

Materials: 12 × 18 inch white paper, markers

Alternate Materials: Crayons, colored pencils

- Distribute the materials and have students follow the directions on page 167.

- Encourage students to create effective compositions using design principles.

- Review the Activity Tips on page 245 for visual examples of the activity techniques if needed.

NSAE 3.a

Art Journal: Make a List

Have students make a list of groups of people that they could make a drawing of in the Ideas section of their Art Journals. Have them select their favorite idea for use in the Creative Expression activity.

Using Emphasis

Emphasis makes one part of a work of art seem more important than the rest of the work. The part that is important is called **dominant.** The parts of a work of art that are not emphasized are **subordinate.** If artists emphasize an entire area instead of an object, they create a **focal point.**

Practice

Read a sentence aloud and give a word emphasis.

1. Look at the sentence your teacher gives you.

2. Pick a word to emphasize. When it is your turn, read your sentence aloud.

3. Have your classmates tell you which word you emphasized.

Differentiated Instruction

Reteach
Encourage students to look around the classroom and pick out objects that stand out to them.

Special Needs
Create charts for students to refer to as they complete work for this unit. The charts should list and illustrate the elements and principles of art for this unit.

ELL Tips
Review emphasis and define stress. Ask students what creates emphasis in outfits they wear. Then ask them to give examples of color emphasis, shape emphasis, and pattern emphasis.

◄ **Ryan Spell.**
Age 7.

Think about how this student created emphasis in his drawing.

 Creative Expression

Can you draw a group of people and give one person emphasis? Draw a picture of a group of people.

1. Think of a scene that shows people working or playing.

2. Draw the scene using markers. Give one person in the scene emphasis.

3. Color your picture and add details.

Art Criticism

Describe What are the people in your scene doing?

Analyze Who in your scene has emphasis?

Interpret How did you emphasize the person in your scene?

Decide What would your scene look like if there were no emphasis?

Reflect

Time: About 10 minutes

Review and Assess

"How do artists emphasize the most important part of their artwork?" "¿Cómo enfatizan los artistas la parte más importante de sus obras de arte?"

Think

The artist created emphasis by placing one player in a position ahead of the others and by varying the size of the players.

■ Use *Large Print 33 Mask* and *34 Boy with a Tire* to have students look for emphasis.

■ Have students identify stories and constructions in this lesson's artwork.

■ Have students identify ideas of the artists in this lesson's art.

Informal Assessment

Art Journal: Critical Thinking
Have students answer the four art criticism questions—Describe, Analyze, Interpret, and Decide—in the Critical Thinking section of their Art Journals. Ask students to define their reasons for preferences in their own art. Then have them identify ideas in their peers' art.

■ For standardized-format test practice using this lesson's art content, see pages 58–59 in *Reading and Writing Test Preparation.*

Art Across the Curriculum

NSAE 6.a, 6.b

Use these simple ideas to reinforce art concepts across the curriculum.

★ **Poetry** Have students write a poem and repeat a word in it several times to add emphasis.

★ **Math** Have students write the numbers 1–50 and emphasize the multiples of 10.

★ **Science** Discuss how the dominant animal of a group is usually emphasized physically in some way. For example, a male silverback mountain gorilla is the leader of the group, and a queen honey bee is the largest bee in the hive.

★ **Social Studies** Discuss national and state holidays and why emphasis is placed on certain days.

★ **Technology** Show students how to highlight a word in a document to give the word emphasis. Visit **SRAonline.com** to print detailed instructions for this activity.

Extra! For the Art Specialist

Time: About 45 minutes

Focus

Study **Large Print 33** and ask students to describe what part or parts of the work stand out the most. Why? Would this work look any different if another part were emphasized? Why? Are there any other ways to emphasize something in a work of art? Explain.

Teach

Explain to students that they will create a vase drawing in pencil and focus attention to their design using a patterned background. They will view a variety of vase styles and draw three to five of their own using colored pencils. To emphasize one of the vases, the students will leave it blank while adding patterns to the others and the background. Have the students complete the Alternate Activity.

Reflect

Have students evaluate their art using the four steps of art criticism.

Alternate Activity

Materials:
- pencils
- colored pencils
- 12" × 18" white paper
- vases and containers of varying shapes and sizes

1. Discuss emphasis by looking at the various types of vases and pointing out the similarities and differences among them.

2. Use a pencil and lightly sketch 3–5 vases of your own. The teacher should point out how to overlap the vases.

3. Use the colored pencils and fill in the background with small patterns of lines or shapes. Finally, fill all your vases except one with larger patterns. Discuss how the blank vase is emphasized.

Research in Art Education

"The making of art is an essential activity for elementary children. They need and want hands-on experiences in this 'other language.' Art lessons must include cycles of experiences with basic media and techniques, allowing students to acquire and then build upon skills fundamental to creative expression." Kay Alexander, "Art Curricula by and for Art Educators," in *Art Education: Elementary* ed. Andra Johnson (1992).

Assessment

Use the following rubric to evaluate the artwork students make in the Creative Expression activity and to assess students' understanding of emphasis.

Have students complete page 61 or 62 of their *Assessment* books.

	Art History and Culture	Aesthetic Perception	Creative Expression	Art Criticism
3 POINTS	The student can identify that groups of people portrayed in a work of art often have a significant meaning to the artist.	The student accurately identifies emphasis in his or her environment.	The student's drawing clearly illustrates a good use of emphasis.	The student thoughtfully and honestly evaluates his or her own work using the four steps of art criticism.
2 POINTS	The student's identification is weak or incomplete.	The student shows emerging awareness of emphasis, but cannot consistently identify it.	The student's drawing shows some awareness of emphasis.	The student attempts to evaluate his or her own work, but shows an incomplete understanding of evaluation criteria.
1 POINT	The students cannot identify that groups of people portrayed in a work of art often have a significant meaning to the artist.	The student cannot identify emphasis.	The student's drawing shows no understanding of emphasis.	The student makes no attempt to evaluate his or her own artwork.

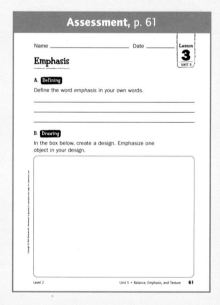

Assessment, p. 61

Name _____ Date _____ Lesson **3** UNIT 5

Emphasis

A. Defining
Define the word *emphasis* in your own words.

_____

B. Drawing
In the box below, create a design. Emphasize one object in your design.

Level 2   Unit 5 • Balance, Emphasis, and Texture   **61**

Emphasis Using Contrast

Lesson 4 introduces the students to emphasis using contrast. Contrast is another way to create emphasis in a work of art.

Objectives

Art History and Culture

To recognize that artists painted pictures of buildings they saw and that people used those buildings for specific purposes

Creative Expression

To create a drawing of a building at night and create emphasis using contrast

Aesthetic Perception

To recognize that objects in students' environments may have contrast.

Art Criticism

To use the four steps of art criticism to evaluate their own artwork

Vocabulary Vocabulary

Review the following vocabulary word with students before beginning the lesson.

contrast contraste—a way of creating a focal point. Contrast occurs when different elements are placed next to each other in a work of art.

See page 179B for additional Spanish vocabulary resources.

Art Journal: Vocabulary

Have students add this word to the Vocabulary section of their Art Journals.

Lesson Materials

- 12" × 18" white paper
- markers
- 12" × 18" dark blue or black construction paper
- white and yellow oil pastels
- various colored oil pastels

Alternate Materials:
- colored chalk
- crayons
- colored pencils

Program Resources

- *Reading and Writing Test Prep.*, pp. 60–61
- *Transparency 28*
- *Flash Card 15*
- *Artist Profiles*, pp. 35, 66
- *Animals Through History Time Line*
- *Assessment,* pp. 63–64
- *Large Print 33 Mask*
- *Art Around the World Collection*

Concept Trace
Emphasis Using Contrast
Introduced: Level 1, Unit 6, Lessons 3–4

Reinforced: Level 3, Unit 6, Lessons 3–4

Lesson 4 Arts Integration

Theatre

Complete Unit 5 Lesson 4 on pages 96–97 of *Theatre Arts Connections.*

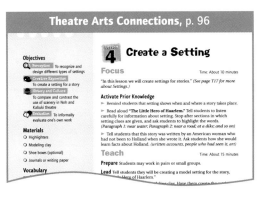

Music

 As we look back in music history, one of the biggest changes is how the composers group sounds of the instruments. Richard Gill is a composer from Australia. He combines the very large and very small in *Dance for Piccolo, Oboe, Bassoon and Side Drum.* Listen to the humor created by the contrasts of sound. Notice that he demands flexibility from the bassoon you would normally attribute to a small piccolo.

Movement & Dance

Students can use contrasting movement energies to build simple but dynamic sequences. For example, moving for eight counts in a locomotor movement and ending in a shape which is held for two counts. The locomotor movement (skip, gallop, slide) should be made with a light energy. The shape should be made with a strong, forceful energy.

Emphasis Using Contrast

▲ **Rembrandt van Rijn.**
(Dutch). *The Mill.* c. 1650.
Oil on canvas. $34\frac{1}{2} \times 38\frac{1}{8}$ inches
(87.63 × 96.84 cm.). The National
Gallery of Art, Washington, D.C.

Look at these two paintings. The artists used **contrast** to create emphasis and focal points in these paintings. Contrast occurs when two objects that are different are placed together. For example, a light color is placed next to a dark color.

Art History and Culture

What kind of people do you think would live in these buildings?

Focus

Activate Prior Knowledge

"Have you ever noticed streetlights on a street at night?" "¿Alguna vez han notado las luces de una calle durante la noche?"

■ Help students understand that areas of light in the dark are a way of creating contrast.

Using Literature ☆ Reading

■ Read *The House in the Meadow* by Shutta Crum. Discuss the emphasis using contrast students find in the book.

Thematic Connection ☆ Social Studies

■ **Buildings:** Encourage students to think about different buildings in the community and what those buildings are used for. How does their purpose affect their design?

Introduce the Art

Look NSAE 2.a

"Let's look closely at these two works of art." "Vamos a mirar detalladamente estas dos obras de arte".

■ Have students identify emphasis in the works of art and the environment.

Making Connections ☆ Reading

■ Have students study the two paintings and make connections between the building style and setting and who they think might inhabit the building. Also discuss the connection between light and dark in the Magritte painting. If students look closely at the painting, they will see that Magritte used visual tricks to create the appearance of a night scene when the sky is in actuality light.

NSAE 4.a, 4.b, 4.c, 5.b

Art History and Culture

Possible answer: A miller probably lived in the mill. A family probably lived in the house.

Web Connection

Visit **http://www.mfa.org/exhibitions/ rembrandt/onlinepreview.htm** to tour other Rembrandt images.

Art History and Culture

Rembrandt van Rijn

Rembrandt van Rijn (rem´ bränt vän rīn´) (1606–1669) was an influential Dutch artist. Rembrandt showed talent early in life, and his parents took great interest in providing him with an education despite their modest income. Rembrandt learned how to create dramatic accents using light and shadow, and composition. Rembrandt created more than 600 paintings. Rembrandt used a technique called *chiaroscuro,* meaning "light and dark." He used light to focus on areas that contained details. He left other parts in shadows using dark colors.

See pages 24–25 and 16–21 for more about art history and subject matter.

Artist Profiles, p. 66

Artist Profile

Rembrandt van Rijn
1606–1669

Rembrandt van Rijn (rem´ brandt vän rin´) was the most influential Dutch artist of the seventeenth century. The seventh of nine children born to a miller and his wife, Rembrandt showed talent early in life. His parents took great interest in providing him with an education despite their modest income. Rembrandt studied a short time at the Leiden Latin School in the Netherlands to prepare for a profession as a city administrator. His parents eventually removed him from school and placed him in apprenticeships with painters. After moving to Amsterdam in 1631, he gained the commissions of several wealthy patrons and achieved great success. Rembrandt spent a large portion of the money he

◀ **Rene Magritte.** (Belgian). *The Empire of Lights.* 1954.

Oil on canvas. 18 $\frac{1}{2}$ × 24 $\frac{1}{8}$ inches (46.99 × 61.28 cm.). Musees d'Art Moderne, Brussels, Belgium.

Study these two paintings to find emphasis, focal points, and contrast.

▶ What areas of these paintings do you notice first?

▶ Which areas of the paintings are alike?

Aesthetic Perception

Design Awareness Look for things that stand out in your classroom because of contrast. For example, a shiny glass clock against a dull wall creates contrast.

Study

▶ The light part of the sky is most noticeable in the Rembrandt. The windows and porch light are most noticeable in the Magritte.

▶ The dark parts of the sky and background are alike in both paintings.

■ For more examples of art from Europe, see the *Art Around the World Collection.*

Art Journal: Writing

Have students write about ways to create contrast in the Concepts section of their Art Journals. Why do they think artists use contrast?

Aesthetic Perception

Design Awareness Encourage students to look around the classroom and find objects that contrast with each other. Encourage students to identify variations in the objects from their environments. Ask students if they can also find things that contrast with each other in their homes. NSAE 2.b, 5.c

Developing Visual Literacy Have students discuss personal examples of contrast that remind them of the images in the paintings. Where were they when they saw this contrast? How did it make them feel?

Art History and Culture

René Magritte

René Magritte (rə nē´ mə grēt´) (1898–1967) was born in Belgium at the end of the nineteenth century. After studying art in Brussels, he worked briefly in a wallpaper factory. The influence of his time at this factory is sometimes evident in his patterned paintings. Magritte's surrealist artwork had a mischievous attitude and displayed an avant-garde, poetic energy. Surrealists valued fantastic, absurd, and poetic images. They also valued the artwork of children, the insane, or the untrained amateur artist, because these people were thought to create from pure impulse and to be free from convention.

See pages 24–25 and 16–21 for more about art history and subject matter.

Artist Profiles, p. 35

◆ Artist Profile ◆

René Magritte
1898-1967

René Magritte (rə nē´ ma grēt´) was born in Belgium at the end of the nineteenth century. After studying art in Brussels, he worked briefly in a wallpaper factory. The influence of his time at this factory is sometimes evident in his patterned paintings. Magritte had a mischievous attitude, and displayed an avant-garde, poetic energy. He directed this energy into numerous creations and was honored with retrospective exhibitions in both Europe and the United States.

Web Connection

Visit **http://www.guggenheimcollection.org/ site/artist_work_md_92_2.html** to view another Magritte painting.

each

Time: About 35 minutes

"Can you think of ways to create contrast?"
"¿Pueden pensar en maneras de crear contraste?"

■ Read and discuss the information on emphasis using contrast on page 170.

Materials: 12 × 18 inch white paper, markers

Alternate Materials: colored pencils, crayons

■ Distribute the materials and have students follow the directions on page 170.

■ Have students identify and practice skills necessary for producing drawings using a variety of materials.

NSAE 1.c, 1.d, 2.c, 3.b

 Creative Expression

Materials: dark blue or black 12 × 18 inch construction paper, white and yellow oil pastels, various colored oil pastels

Alternate Materials: colored chalk

■ Distribute the materials and have students follow the directions on page 171.

■ Encourage students to create effective compositions using design principles.

■ Review the Activity Tips on page 245 for visual examples of the activity techniques if needed.

NSAE 3.a

Art Journal: Brainstorming
Have students brainstorm ideas for their night scene in the Ideas section of their Art Journals. Have them select their favorite idea for use in the Creative Expression activity.

Using Emphasis Using Contrast

Contrast is a way to create a focal point. When an artist uses an object that is different from the other objects in an area, this creates contrast. Artists can create contrast by varying sizes of objects, types of shapes they use, hues of objects, or values of areas. What is creating contrast in the pictures below?

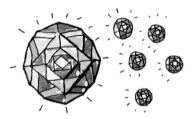

Practice
Draw two objects that contrast with each other.

1. Choose a way to create contrast. Think of two objects to draw.

2. Draw the objects on your paper so they create contrast.

3. Explain to the class how you created contrast in your drawing.

Differentiated Instruction

Reteach
Say an adjective to the class and have them call out a contrasting adjective.

Special Needs
If students have difficulty visualizing a night scene, provide them with pictures from magazines or photographs as visual prompts.

ELL Tips
Define the word *contrast* for students and demonstrate it by showing them several contrasting objects. For example, a loud noise and a quiet noise, or a soft object and a hard object.

◀ **Caleb Hudson.**
Age 7.

Think about how this student used contrast in his night scene.

 Creative Expression

Can you use contrast in a nighttime scene? Draw a building at night using contrast.

1. Think of a night scene to draw. Draw the scene on dark construction paper.

2. Add the contrast of lights in the dark by using yellow and white oil pastels.

3. Add details to your drawing and name it.

Art Criticism

Describe What is happening in your nighttime scene?

Analyze Where are the focal points in your drawing?

Interpret Would your drawing still have contrast if you used light paper and dark pastels?

Decide How else could you have created contrast in your drawing?

 **Time:** About 10 minutes

Review and Assess

"How and why do artists create contrast in their artwork?" "¿Cómo y por qué los artistas crean contraste en sus obras de arte?"

Think

The artist created contrast in his night scene by making lit windows on a dark house.

■ Use *Large Print 33 Mask* to have students identify emphasis created using contrast.

■ Have students identify stories and constructions in this lesson's artwork.

■ Have students identify ideas of the artists in this lesson's art.

Informal Assessment

Art Journal: Critical Thinking
Have students answer the four art criticism questions—Describe, Analyze, Interpret, and Decide—in the Critical Thinking section of their Art Journals. Ask students to define their reasons for preferences in their own art. Then have them identify ideas in their peers' art.

■ For standardized-format test practice using this lesson's art content, see pages 60–61 in *Reading and Writing Test Preparation.*

Art Across the Curriculum   NSAE 6.a, 6.b

Use these simple ideas to reinforce art concepts across the curriculum.

★ **Persuasive Writing** Have students write a letter to an artist to convince the artist that he or she should utilize emphasis using contrast in his or her next work of art.

★ **Math** Have students create flashcards of math problems and use contrast to emphasize the answers.

★ **Science** Discuss how scientists sometimes add stains to cell specimens and emphasize them in order to see the cells better under microscopes.

★ **Social Studies** Show students a map. Discuss how countries are emphasized by using contrasting colors.

★ **Technology** Show students how to change the contrast settings on the monitor. Visit **SRAonline.com** to print detailed instructions for this activity.

Emphasis Using Contrast

Extra! For the Art Specialist

Focus

Study **Large Print 33** and ask students to describe what part or parts of the work stand out the most. Why? How could other parts of this work be emphasized? Are there any other ways that artists can create contrast and emphasize things? Explain.

Teach

Explain to students that they will create an aquarium scene using crayon resist and stamping. They will color aquarium or fish tank objects like plants, rocks, and decorations using crayons. Next they will paint their scene using only cool-hued watercolors. To finish their piece, they will create a simple stamp using tagboard and stamp a school of fish in contrasting warm hues. Have the students complete the Alternate Activity.

Reflect

Have students evaluate their art using the four steps of art criticism.

Alternate Activity

Materials:
- pencils
- cool-hued watercolor paints
- brushes, buckets, and newspapers
- crayons, scissors
- tagboard
- tape
- 12" × 18" white drawing paper
- warm-hued tempera paint

1. Discuss emphasis using contrast by talking about how warm and cool hues contrast.

2. Draw an aquarium bottom in pencil including many things. You can cut their paper into a bowl shape first, if desired.

3. Color the drawn objects with crayons, being sure to make them dark and waxy.

4. Paint the aquarium using cool watercolors.

5. Create a fish stamp from tagboard. Stamp a school of fish using warm hues. Discuss the contrast you created.

Research
In Art Education

It has been proven that "at the level of neuro-function, learning experiences unequivocally impact future learning experiences." While more research is still needed on exactly how the reorganization of neural pathways and receptors impacts student's transfer of skills from the arts to reading and math, it is reasonable to assume that experiences with the arts may "enhance performance in related skills" ("The Arts and the Transfer of Learning" in *Critical Links,* p. 152).

Assessment
Use the following rubric to evaluate the artwork students make in the Creative Expression activity and to assess students' understanding of emphasis using contrast.

Have students complete page 63 or 64 of their *Assessment* books.

	Art History and Culture	Aesthetic Perception	Creative Expression	Art Criticism
3 POINTS	The student can identify that artists often paint buildings they are familiar with and that the buildings often have a purpose.	The student accurately identifies emphasis using contrast in his or her environment.	The student's night scene clearly illustrates a good use of emphasis using contrast.	The student thoughtfully and honestly evaluates his or her own work using the four steps of art criticism.
2 POINTS	The student's identification is weak or incomplete.	The student shows emerging awareness of emphasis using contrast, but cannot consistently identify it.	The student's night scene shows some awareness of emphasis using contrast.	The student attempts to evaluate his or her own work, but shows an incomplete understanding of evaluation criteria.
1 POINT	The students cannot identify that artists often paint buildings they are familiar with and that the buildings often have a purpose.	The student cannot identify emphasis using contrast.	The student's night scene shows no understanding of emphasis using contrast.	The student makes no attempt to evaluate his or her own artwork.

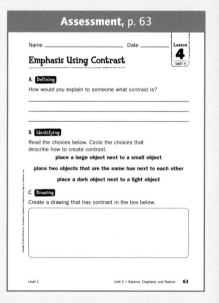

Assessment, p. 63

Name _____ Date _____

Lesson **4** UNIT 5

Emphasis Using Contrast

A. Defining
How would you explain to someone what *contrast* is?

_____

B. Identifying
Read the choices below. Circle the choices that describe how to create contrast.

place a large object next to a small object

place two objects that are the same hue next to each other

place a dark object next to a light object

C. Drawing
Create a drawing that has contrast in the box below.

Level 2

Unit 5 • Balance, Emphasis, and Texture   **63**

Lesson 5 Overview

Tactile Texture

Lesson 5 introduces the students to tactile texture. Tactile texture can be used to create emphasis and refers to how something feels when it is touched.

Objectives

Art History and Culture
To recognize that artists sometimes incorporate maps into their art

Creative Expression
To create needlework of a scene that could be used to decorate a map using yarn and other tactile materials

Aesthetic Perception
To understand that tactile texture is texture you can feel and that it is incorporated in everyday objects

Art Criticism
To use the four steps of art criticism to evaluate their own artwork

Vocabulary Reading

Review the following vocabulary words with students before beginning the lesson.

carving *tallar o esculpir*—art made by cutting into the surface of the medium

stitchery *bordado*—technique for decorating fabric by sewing threads and fibers on it

tactile texture *textura táctil*—a texture that can be felt

See page 179B for additional vocabulary and Spanish vocabulary resources.

Art Journal: Vocabulary

Have students add these words to the Vocabulary section of their Art Journals.

Lesson Materials
- cloth or burlap
- tape
- sketch paper
- scissors
- blunt tapestry needles
- fabric scraps
- yarn
- buttons and trims
- markers and pencils
- a variety of objects with different tactile textures

Alternate Materials:
- embroidery floss

Program Resources
- *Reading and Writing Test Prep.,* pp. 62-63
- *Transparency 29*
- *Artist Profiles,* pp. 20, 78
- *Animals Through History Time Line*
- *Assessment,* pp. 65-66
- *Large Print 33* Mask
- *The National Museum of Women in the Arts Collection*

Concept Trace
Tactile Texture
Introduced: Level 1, Unit 5, Lesson 1
Reinforced: Level 3, Unit 4, Lesson 6

Lesson 5 Arts Integration

Theatre
Complete Unit 5 Lesson 5 on pages 98–99 of *Theatre Arts Connections.*

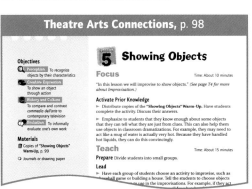

Music
 Texture in music describes whether one melody is alone or with other contrasting melodies (Polyphony), or with harmonic accompaniment. Listen to *The Moldau* by Bedrich Smetana. The Moldau is a river in his native Czechoslovakia. The piece starts with a small flow of melody from two flutes depicting two streams coming out of the mountains. Listen how the texture changes as goes on and instruments are added.

Movement & Dance
Have students work in pairs to build sculptures that express emotion. Number the students 1 and 2. 1 takes a neutral position standing, 2 then moves 1 into a shape by respectfully bending and placing parts of 1's body in specific positions, demonstrating how emotion in still life can be expressed. Each person (sculptor) makes three separate sculptures on their partner and then changes role.

Focus

Activate Prior Knowledge

"Do you have a blanket, pillow, quilt, or chair covering that was sewn by hand?" "¿Tienen una cobija, una almohada, una colcha o un forro para silla cosido a mano?"

- As students tell about hand-sewn items around their homes, stress that people who make such items are craft artisans.

Using Literature ⭐ Reading

- Read *Feely Bugs* by David Carter. Discuss the different textures in the book.

Thematic Connection ⭐ Social Studies

- **Maps:** Encourage students to think about different maps that they have seen and why artists might choose to decorate a map.

Introduce the Art

Look NSAE 2.a

"Let's look closely at these two maps."
"Vamos a mirar detalladamente estos dos mapas".

- Have students identify texture in the works of art and the environment.

Map Scales ⭐ Math

- Discuss map scales with the students. What scale do they think these works of art were made using? Art they realistic scales, or not?

NSAE 4.a, 4.b, 4.c, 5.a, 5.b

🏺 Art History and Culture

Possible answer: These artists used maps as decorations because the places on the maps were important to them.

 Web Connection
Visit http://www.loc.gov/exhibits/treasures/trm003.html to see another Revolutionary War powder horn.

Tactile Texture

▲ **Jacob Gay.** (American). *Powder Horn.* 1759.
....
Cow horn. 15 ½ inches (39.97 cm.). The Metropolitan Museum of Art, New York, New York.

Look at these two works of art. Notice the **carving** on the horn and the **stitchery** on the quilt. How do you think the quilt and the carved horn would feel if you touched them? The way things feel is called texture.

🏺 Art History and Culture

Why do you think these artists used maps in their art?

🏺 Art History and Culture

Jacob Gay

Jacob Gay (jā´ kəb gā) was a professional engraver living in the Great Lakes region of North America during the mid-eighteenth century. It is believed that Gay engraved this powder horn in New York in 1759. This horn was carried by a British soldier during the American Revolution, as is indicated by the engraving of the British coat of arms on its surface. Gay used sharp hand tools to engrave this powder horn with a map of the Hudson Valley and the locations of forts from Albany, New York, to the Great Lakes. Also engraved into the surface of the horn is the name of its owner, Jotham Bemus.

See pages 24–25 and 16–21 for more about art history and subject matter.

Artist Profiles, p. 20

● Artist Profile ●
Jacob Gay
Jacob Gay (jā´ kəb gā) was a professional engraver living in the Great Lakes region of North America during the mid-eighteenth century. It is believed that Gay engraved this powder horn in New York in 1759.

▲ **Jacob Gay.** (American). *Engraved Powderhorn.* 1759.

Study the two works of art and look for tactile texture.

▶ What do you think the horn would feel like if you touched it?

▶ What do you think the quilt would feel like if you touched it?

▲ **Artist Unknown.**
(American). *Map Quilt.*
1886.
. . . .
Silk and cotton with silk embroidery.
78 $\frac{3}{4}$ × 82 $\frac{1}{4}$ inches (200.03 ×
208.92 cm.). American Museum of
Folk Art, New York, New York.

Aesthetic Perception

Design Awareness Why do you think some maps are designed with tactile texture? How would that help someone looking at the map?

Study

▶ The horn would feel smooth and the carved parts would feel rough and bumpy.

▶ The quilt would feel soft and some areas of the stitching would feel rough and bumpy.

■ For more examples of utilitarian art, see *The National Museum of Women in the Arts Collection.*

Art Journal: Writing
Have students write a paragraph about the sensations they remember from touching items with tactile textures in the Concepts section of their Art Journals.

Aesthetic Perception

Design Awareness Discuss with students how some maps have tactile texture so people can feel geographical features like mountain ranges. Encourage students to identify variations in textured objects from their environments.   NSAE 2.b, 5.c

Developing Visual Literacy Discuss with students how the artist's choice of style and media adds to the meaning of the map art. Why do they think these artists created these maps in the ways they did?

Art History and Culture

Map Quilt

This quilt was made in 1886 by an unidentified American artist. Although it is not known who created the quilt, it is believed that the artist was a woman. This quilt was made during the Victorian era when nearly all quilt makers were women. Although the quilt may have been made by a group of women, such as a quilting bee or quilting party, the process of completing the piece would have been quite time consuming. This quilt was probably made to serve as a bedspread. Quilts featuring elaborate designs and beautiful stitching and embroidery were often made as wedding gifts, baby gifts, or as friendship quilts to be given to friends or family as a remembrance in the event of their relocation to a new area.

See pages 24–25 and 16–21 for more about art history and subject matter.

Artist Profiles, p. 78

◇ Artist Profile ◇

Map Quilt

This quilt was made by an unidentified American artist in 1886. Although it is not known who created the quilt, it is believed the quilt may have been made by a group of women at a quilting bee or quilting party, the process of completing the piece would have been quite time consuming.

Web Connection
Visit **http://www.womenfolk.com/historyofquilts/** to learn about the history of quilting.

Teach

Time: About 35 minutes

"Find objects in this room that have texture."
"Busquen objetos en este salón que tengan textura".

- Read and discuss the information on tactile texture on page 174.

Practice

Materials: variety of objects that have tactile texture

- Distribute the materials and have students follow the directions on page 174.

- Have students identify and practice skills necessary for producing constructions using a variety of materials.

- Give each group a texture word and allow them to pick out objects that match that word.

NSAE 1.c, 1.d, 2.c, 3.b

Creative Expression

Materials: cloth or burlap, tape, sketch paper, scissors, blunt tapestry needles, fabric scraps, yarn, buttons and trims, markers and pencils

Alternate Materials: embroidery floss

- Distribute the materials and have students follow the directions on page 175.

- Some students may wish to sketch their ideas before starting to cut fabric.

- Students will most likely need help threading their needles.

- Encourage students to create effective compositions using design elements.

- Review the Activity Tips on page 246 for visual examples of the activity techniques if needed.

NSAE 3.a

Art Journal: Brainstorming

Encourage students to think about maps and common features in the area as they decide what to make a stitchery of. Have them keep a list in the Ideas section of their Art Journals.

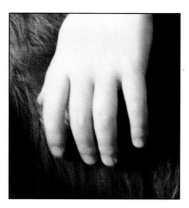

Using Tactile Texture

One way we identify texture is by touching it. Texture you can touch and feel is called **tactile texture.** Tactile texture can be **rough** or **smooth.** What are some words you would use to describe tactile textures?

Practice

Gather objects that have tactile texture.

1. Break into small groups.

2. Gather objects from the pile that are good examples of the tactile texture word your teacher gives you.

3. Share your word and objects with the rest of the class.

Differentiated Instruction

Reteach

Show students a group of textured items and then place them all in a bag. Have students close their eyes, reach in the bag, and tell you which object they are holding based on its texture.

Special Needs

Larger needles and thread would benefit all students at this age level, including students with low vision or low fine motor skills.

ELL Tips

Bring in a quilt, patent-leather shoe, shoestring, and a teddy bear. Help students understand that if a work of art contained bits of these materials, it would have *tactile texture,* or texture that can be felt.

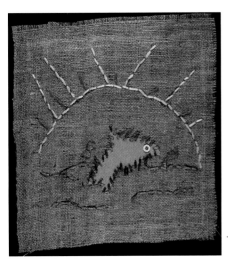

◀ **Veeda Mashayekh.**
Age 7.

Think about how this student used texture in her map decoration.

 Creative Expression

How would you decorate a map? Sew a work of art to decorate a map using texture.

1. Think about a design you could make with fabric to decorate a map. Draw your ideas on fabric scraps.

2. Cut them out and stitch them onto your fabric background.

3. Add more details with stitches and buttons.

Art Criticism

Describe How did you construct your stitchery?

Analyze What textures does your stitchery project have?

Interpret How would your stitchery be different if you used materials with different textures?

Decide If you were going to make a stitchery map decoration again, what other items would you sew?

Art Across the Curriculum   NSAE 6.a, 6.b

Use these simple ideas to reinforce art concepts across the curriculum.

★ **Descriptive Writing** Have students write a descriptive paragraph about a tactile texture word, such as *soft*.

★ **Math** Have students feel carpet samples of several different piles. Then have them measure the thickness of the carpet to see how the measurement correlates to the tactile texture.

★ **Science** Discuss the tactile textures of different plants and animals and the correlation to the environment the plants and animals live in.

★ **Social Studies** Have students feel a piece of silk. Discuss the role of silk in global development.

★ **Technology** Have students find and describe different tactile textures on the computer. Visit **SRAonline.com** to print detailed instructions for this activity.

**eflect**   Time: About 10 minutes

Review and Assess

"Why do artists put tactile texture in their artwork?" "¿Por qué los artistas ponen una textura táctil en sus obras de arte?"

Think

The artist used texture by adding buttons and fabric to her map scene.

■ Use *Large Print 33 Mask* to have students identify tactile texture. Although students cannot touch the mask, they should be able to identify the areas of tactile texture on the actual mask.

■ Have students identify stories and constructions in this lesson's artwork.

■ Have students identify ideas in the art by this lesson's artists.

Informal Assessment

Art Journal: Critical Thinking
Have students answer the four art criticism questions—Describe, Analyze, Interpret, and Decide—in the Critical Thinking section of their Art Journals. Have students define reasons for preferences in their personal artwork. Then have them identify ideas in their peers' artwork.

■ For standardized-format test practice using this lesson's art content, see pages 62–63 in *Reading and Writing Test Preparation*.

Lesson 5

Tactile Texture

Wrap-Up

Extra! For the Art Specialist

 Time: About 45 minutes

Focus

Study **Large Print 33** and ask students to point out the textures they see. If you were holding the object, could you feel the texture? What would it feel like? What other tactile textures can you think of? Would the objects look different if they had different tactile textures?

Teach

Explain to students that they will create a texture tile out of clay. They will use a ball of clay to form a tile to work on. Tactile texture will be added using a variety of tools to carve or stamp the clay. The students will paint their work after it's fired. Discuss tactile texture with the class using the example items. Demonstrate how to roll the clay into a ball and flatten it.

Reflect

Have students evaluate their art using the four steps of art criticism.

Alternate Activity

Materials:
- clay
- mats to work on
- clay tools
- tempera paint
- brushes, buckets, and newspapers
- samples of various tactile textures (fur, sandpaper, marble, etc.)

1. Either form the clay tile or use the tools to cut out the shape you want.

2. Using the tools, create tactile texture on your tile. Include a variety of textures.

3. When fired, paint your tile with tempera paints.

Research

In Art Education

It is important that arts education not only be present, but "rich and continuous" in order to receive the full benefits it can add to "learning and instruction that is critical to healthy development." These benefits include higher levels of cooperation, creativity, and problem-solving skills ("Learning in and Through the Arts: Curriculum Implications" in *Champions of Change*, p. 36).

Assessment

Use the following rubric to evaluate the artwork students make in the Creative Expression activity and to assess students' understanding of tactile texture.

Have students complete page 65 or 66 of their *Assessment* books

	Art History and Culture	Aesthetic Perception	Creative Expression	Art Criticism
3 POINTS	The student can identify and compare the use of tactile texture in maps created by artists.	The student accurately identifies tactile texture in his or her environment.	The student's stitchery clearly illustrates a good use of tactile texture.	The student thoughtfully and honestly evaluates his or her own work using the four steps of art criticism.
2 POINTS	The student's identification or comparison is weak or incomplete.	The student shows emerging awareness of tactile texture, but cannot consistently identify it.	The student's stitchery shows some awareness of tactile texture.	The student attempts to evaluate his or her own work, but shows an incomplete understanding of evaluation criteria.
1 POINT	The student cannot identify or compare the use of tactile texture in maps created by artists.	The student cannot identify tactile texture.	The student's stitchery shows no understanding of tactile texture.	The student makes no attempt to evaluate his or her own artwork.

Assessment, p. 65

Name _____ Date _____ | Lesson **5** UNIT 5

Tactile Texture

A. Short Answer
What is *tactile texture*? How would you define *smooth*? How would you define *rough*?

B. Short Answer
Write a word describing how each object feels on the blank next to the object's name.

feathers _____
desktop _____
brick _____
basketball _____
quilt _____
branch _____
glass _____

Level 2 | Unit 5 • Balance, Emphasis, and Texture **65**

Lesson 6 Overview

Visual Texture

Lesson 6 introduces the students to visual texture. Visual texture can be used to create emphasis and refers to how something looks like it would feel if you could touch it.

Objectives

 Art History and Culture

To recognize that when artists paint portraits, they portray the subjects in clothing that is representative of the subjects

 Creative Expression

To create a collage of people using texture rubbings as clothing to create visual texture

 Aesthetic Perception

To observe visual texture in the environment

 Art Criticism

To use the four steps of art criticism to evaluate their own artwork

Vocabulary Reading

Review the following vocabulary words with students before beginning the lesson.

portrait retrato—an image of a person, especially the face

visual texture textura visual—texture that can not be felt, but can be seen. Visual texture is often used in paintings

shiny brillante—a visual texture that reflects light well

See page 179B for additional vocabulary and Spanish vocabulary resources.

 Art Journal: Vocabulary

Have students add these words to the Vocabulary section of their Art Journals.

Lesson Materials
- crayons
- rubbing paper
- 12" × 18" white paper
- scissors
- glue
- colored construction paper scraps
- textured objects
- texture plates

Alternate Materials:
- markers
- colored pencils

Program Resources
- *Reading and Writing Test Prep.*, pp. 64–65
- *Transparency 30*
- *Artist Profiles*, pp. 10, 68
- *Animals Through History Time Line*
- *Assessment*, pp. 67–68
- *Large Print 34* Boy with a Tire
- *The National Museum of Women in the Arts Collection*

Concept Trace
Visual Texture
Introduced: Level 1, Unit 5, Lesson 2
Reinforced: Level 3, Unit 4, Lesson 5

Lesson 6 Arts Integration

Theatre

Complete Unit 5 Lesson 6 on pages 100–105 of *Theatre Arts Connections.*

Theatre Arts Connections, p. 100

Music

An American composer who created sounds and textures that were purely his own was Aaron Copeland. Listen to his "Variations on Simple Gifts" from *Appalachian Spring*. He created the ballet Appalachian Spring for the dancer Martha Graham in 1944. His textures are open and transparent. One of the ways he creates this open sound is grouping few instruments together, sometimes very high instruments with low pitched instruments.

Movement & Dance

Have students create expressive sculptures with a partner. Number each student 1 or 2. 1 takes a neutral position standing. 2 moves 1 into an expressive sculpture by placing parts of that body in specific positions. 2 observes the sculpture and then places himself in the same design as 1 to see how it feels. 1 then leaves the sculptural shape and observes 2 to see what the sculpture looked like. Partners repeat, changing roles.

Focus

Time: About 10 minutes

Activate Prior Knowledge

"How do you think an elephant would feel if you touched it?" "¿Cómo creen que se sentiría un elefante si lo tocaran?"

- Help students understand that some textures can be seen, but not felt. Artists try to copy the way a texture looks so the viewer can understand more about what the artist has created.

Using Literature ⭐ Reading

- Read *Is It Rough? Is It Smooth? Is It Shiny?* by Tana Hoban. Discuss the visual textures in the book.

Thematic Connection ⭐ Social Studies

- **Communication:** Encourage students to think about how the artists who painted these portraits used communication to show what the people in them were like.

Introduce the Art

Look NSAE 2.a

"Let's look closely at these two portraits." "Vamos a mirar detalladamente estos dos retratos".

- Have students identify texture in the works of art and the environment.

- Have students compare the ways individuals are depicted in this lesson's artwork.

Environment and Society ⭐ Social Studies

- Have students examine and discuss the two portraits. What kind of society do they think these people lived in? How can they tell?

NSAE 4.a, 4.b, 4.c, 5.b

Art History and Culture

Possible answer: These people lived a long time ago because their clothes are old-fashioned. It is hard to tell what they did, but they were probably important because they both have on elaborate clothing.

 Web Connection

Visit **http://www.cacr.caltech.edu/~roy/vermeer/ thumb.html** to see the 35 known Vermeer images.

 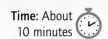 # Visual Texture

Look at these two **portraits.** These artists used texture to paint their subjects' clothing. You can't touch the paintings and feel the texture of the clothes. What do you think the subjects' clothes would feel like if you could touch them?

◄ **Jan Vermeer.** (Dutch). *The Girl With the Red Hat.* c. 1665.

Oil on panel. $9\frac{1}{2} \times 7\frac{1}{8}$ inches (24.13 × 18.10 cm.). The National Gallery of Art, Washington, D.C.

 ## Art History and Culture

Look at the clothing in these paintings. When do you think these people lived? What do you think they did? Why?

 ## Art History and Culture

Jan Vermeer

Jan Vermeer (yän vər mer´) (1632–1675) was a Dutch painter. Although little is known about his life, we know he made a modest living as an art dealer. No records have been found to show that he sold any of his own works. Forgotten for almost 200 years, Vermeer is regarded as one of the greatest painters. Only 35 of his paintings are known to exist. The textures of his painted objects are so realistic that viewers are tempted to touch the surface.

See pages 24–25 and 16–21 for more about art history and subject matter.

 **Artist Profiles,** p. 68

Artist Profile

Jan Vermeer
1632-1675

Jan Vermeer (yän var mer´) was a Dutch painter born in Delft. Little is known about his life; he married at the age of 21 and was the father of 11 children. Vermeer served a six-year apprenticeship and was admitted to the Delft painters guild in 1653. He made a modest living as an art dealer running a business that was left to him by his father. No records have been found to show that he sold any of his own works. Forgotten for almost 200 years, Vermeer is now regarded as one of the greatest painters of all time. This is remarkable because only 35 of his paintings are known to exist. This small number of works is attributed to his deliberate, methodical work habits, his short life, and the disappearance of many

◄ **George Catlin.**
(American). *NO-HO-MUN-YA, One Who Gives No Attention.* 1844.

Oil on canvas. 29 × 24 inches (73.66 × 60.96 cm.). Smithsonian American Art Museum, Washington, D.C.

Study the two portraits to find examples of visual texture.

► What would the girl's hat feel like?

► What would the man's necklace feel like?

 **Aesthetic Perception**

Seeing Like an Artist Look around at the different textures in the room. How does light reflect off of the different textures?

Study

► The girl's hat would feel soft. The feathers would feel tickly.

► The claws on the necklace would feel smooth, hard, and sharp.

■ For more examples of portraits, see *The National Museum of Women in the Arts Collection*.

Art Journal: Writing
Have students write about their experiences with visual texture in the Concepts section of their Art Journals.

Aesthetic Perception

Seeing Like an Artist Discuss with students the different textures that they see and how the light reflects differently off different objects. Encourage students to identify variations in the objects from their environments. Talk about how light reflects off different materials in different ways. For example, objects that reflect a lot of light tend to feel smooth.   NSAE 2.b, 5.c

Developing Visual Literacy Discuss with students how these pictures make them feel. Are they happy or sad portraits? What do they think happened to the people in the portraits?

 Art History and Culture

George Catlin

George Catlin (jorj kat´ lən) (1796–1872) was born in Pennsylvania. While painting miniatures in Philadelphia, he happened to meet a visiting group of Native Americans, and became fascinated by their culture. He visited Native American territory and studied groups that had not yet been influenced by European culture. Catlin created more than 500 paintings and wrote several books about Native American customs and ceremonies. He tried to sell his paintings to the United States government but was unsuccessful.

See pages 24–25 and 16–21 for more about art history and subject matter.

Artist Profiles, p. 10

● Artist Profile ●
George Catlin
1796-1872

George Catlin (jorj kat´ lən) was born in Pennsylvania. He first became a lawyer, but painting lured him away from a law career. While painting miniatures in Philadelphia, he happened to meet a visiting group of Native Americans, and Catlin became fascinated by Native American culture. He made many trips into Native American territory and spent weeks studying groups that had not yet been influenced by European culture. He spent his own money to exhibit his paintings in England and France, where they were much admired. Living on a small income, Catlin traveled to South America to paint genre paintings of indigenous groups. Catlin has had more paintings displayed in the Louvre in Paris.

Web Connection
Visit **http://catlinclassroom.si.edu/cl.html** to view an interactive website about George Catlin.

Teach

Time: About 35 minutes

"Let's try and create some visual textures."
"Vamos a intentar y crear algunas texturas visuales".

■ Read and discuss the information on visual texture on page 178.

Practice

Materials: crayons, rubbing paper, textured objects, texture plates

Alternate Materials: colored pencils

■ Distribute the materials and have students follow the directions on page 178.

■ Review with students the proper way to make their rubbings. Students should only rub away from themselves, not back and forth.

■ Have students save their texture rubbings for use in the Creative Expression activity.

■ Have students identify and practice skills necessary for producing constructions using a variety of materials.

NSAE 1.c, 1.d, 2.c, 3.b

Creative Expression

Materials: crayons, 12 × 18 inch white paper, scissors, glue, colored construction paper scraps

Alternate Materials:
• markers
• colored pencils

■ Encourage students to create effective compositions using design elements.

■ Distribute the materials and have students follow the directions on page 179.

■ Review the Activity Tips on page 246 for visual examples of the activity techniques if needed.

NSAE 3.a

Art Journal: Making a List

Have students make a list of items that would make good texture rubbings in the Ideas section of their Art Journals.

Using Visual Texture

Visual texture is texture you see. Artists use visual texture to describe how something feels when the viewer can't touch the object. Visual texture is created by copying the way light reflects off of different surfaces. Surfaces can be **shiny** or **matte.** Look at the picture. Even though you cannot touch the object, you can describe how it would feel.

Practice

Can you capture visual textures? Make rubbings of visual textures.

1. Choose several different textures from the selection your teacher has.

2. Place your paper on top of a textured surface. Use the long side of your crayon to make a rubbing.

3. Look at the different rubbings you made. Save them for later use.

Differentiated Instruction

Reteach
Compare objects to pictures of the same objects. Have students describe the differences between what they see and what they feel.

Special Needs
Students with unsteady hands or a lack of fine motor skills may benefit from having the object and the paper taped down as they create a rubbing.

ELL Tips
Define *visual texture* and show examples of pictures with textures drawn or painted on them. Have students identify the textured items and describe how each would feel. Did the artists capture the texture of each item?

◀ **Clayton Beahr.**
Age 7.

Think about how this student used visual textures in his collage.

 Creative Expression

How would you use visual textures to design clothing? Create a collage.

1. Draw items of clothing on the visual textures you collected.
2. Cut out the clothes and glue them onto your paper.
3. Use markers to draw people wearing the clothes.

Art Criticism

Describe What kind of clothes are the people in your collage wearing?

Analyze What different visual textures did you use for your clothing?

Interpret How do you want your viewers to feel about the clothes you created?

Decide Would you like to wear clothes that feel the way your textures do?

Reflect

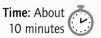 **Time:** About 10 minutes

Review and Assess

"What is visual texture?" "¿Qué es la textura visual?"

Think

The artist created visual texture to show how the clothes of the person and the fur of the dog would feel.

■ Use *Large Print 34 Boy with a Tire* to have students identify visual texture.

■ Have students identify stories and constructions in this lesson's artwork.

■ Have students identify ideas in the art by this lesson's artists.

Informal Assessment

Art Journal: Critical Thinking

Have students answer the four art criticism questions—Describe, Analyze, Interpret, and Decide—in the Critical Thinking section of their Art Journals. Have students define reasons for preferences in their personal artwork. Then have them identify ideas in their peers' artwork.

■ For standardized-format test practice using this lesson's art content, see pages 64–65 in *Reading and Writing Test Preparation.*

Art Across the Curriculum   NSAE 6.a, 6.b

Use these simple ideas to reinforce art concepts across the curriculum.

★ **Personal Writing** Have students pretend to be a person writing to an artist to have a portrait commissioned. What will they tell the artist about how they want their portrait to look?

★ **Math** Have students find visual textures in magazines then cut out numbers from the textures.

★ **Science** Discuss how some animals use visual textures to communicate. For example, a porcupine fish when it is in danger.

★ **Social Studies** Show students photos of Native American clothing and have then identify visual textures.

★ **Technology** Show students how to use texture fills in their drawings. Visit **SRAonline.com** to print detailed instructions for this activity.

 **Visual Texture**

Extra! ## For the Art Specialist

Time: About 45 minutes

Focus

Study **Large Print 34** and ask students to describe the textures of the objects. Could they really feel this texture? Why or why not?

Teach

Explain to students that they will design a new piece of clothing using a variety of patterns to create visual texture. They will sketch several ideas first and then choose the best one to transfer to large paper. After drawing their clothing, they will choose a texture for it. Using patterns, they will give their piece visual texture and trace their work with permanent markers. They will finish their design by painting it with watercolors. Have students complete the Alternate Activity.

Reflect

Have students evaluate their art using the four steps of art criticism.

Alternate Activity

Materials:

- permanent markers (all colors)
- pencils
- practice paper and 12" × 18" white drawing paper
- examples of different visual textures
- brushes, buckets, and newspapers
- watercolor paints

1. Discuss visual texture with the class. Think of a new piece of clothing you would like to design.

2. Sketch 3–5 ideas on the practice paper. Select your favorite one and transfer it to the drawing paper. Make your drawing large so you can create visual texture.

3. Create visual texture on your clothing by using small patterns. Trace your pencil lines with the markers when you are done.

4. Paint your finished piece with watercolors.

Research
In Art Education

"Art is a biological phenomenon that has been present as a characteristic of the human race ever since Homo sapiens emerged from prehistory. Since art is the skill man uses to give meaningful form to his intuitions and perceptions, art was one of the chief agencies of man's emergence." Herbert Read, *Education Through Art.* Random House, 1974.

Assessment
Use the following rubric to evaluate the artwork students make in the Creative Expression activity and to assess students' understanding of visual texture.

Have students complete page 67 or 68 of their *Assessment* books.

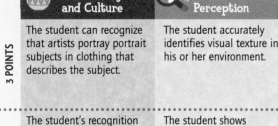

	Art History and Culture	Aesthetic Perception	Creative Expression	Art Criticism
3 POINTS	The student can recognize that artists portray portrait subjects in clothing that describes the subject.	The student accurately identifies visual texture in his or her environment.	The student's texture rubbing collage clearly illustrates a good use of visual texture.	The student thoughtfully and honestly evaluates his or her own work using the four steps of art criticism.
2 POINTS	The student's recognition is weak or incomplete.	The student shows emerging awareness of visual texture, but cannot consistently identify it.	The student's texture rubbing collage shows some awareness of visual texture.	The student attempts to evaluate his or her own work, but shows an incomplete understanding of evaluation criteria.
1 POINT	The students cannot recognize that artists portray portrait subjects in clothing that describes the subject.	The student cannot identify visual texture.	The student's texture rubbing collage shows no understanding of visual texture.	The student makes no attempt to evaluate his or her own artwork.

Assessment, p. 67

---

axis—A real or imaginary line across the center of a work of art. **eje**—una línea real o imaginaria a través del centro de una obra de arte

balance—A principle of design that deals with arranging art. Balance occurs when equal or similar shapes or objects are placed on opposite sides of an axis in a work of art **equilibrio**—un principio de diseño que trata sobre arte ordenado. Equilibrio ocurre cuando figuras iguales o parecidas u objetos son puestos en lados opuestos en un eje de una obra de arte

carving—Art made by cutting into the surface of the medium. **tallar**—El arte que se hace cortando en la superficie del medio

contrast—A way of creating a focal point. Contrast occurs when elements that are different are placed next to each other in a work of art. **contraste**—una manera de crear un punto focal. Contraste ocurre cuando los elementos que son diferentes son puestos adyacentes en una obra de arte.

dominant—The part of the work of art that seems more important to the viewer. Dominant elements have been emphasized. **dominante**—La parte de la obra de arte que parece ser más importante para el observador

emphasis—A principle of design that makes one part of a work of art seem more important than the rest. **énfasis**—un principio de diseño que hace una parte de la obra de arte aparesca más importante que el resto

focal point—An area of an artwork that has been emphasized. **punto focal**—un área de la obra de arte que está enfatizada

matte—A visual texture that does not reflect much light. **mate**—una textura visual que no refleja mucha luz

neon—A special kind of light that can be made to be many bright colors. **neón**—un tipo de luz especial que se puede hacer a muchos colores brillantes

point of view—The position from which the viewer sees an object or work of art. **punto de vista**—la posición en que un observador ve un objeto u obra de arte

portrait—The image of a person, especially the face. **retrato**—la imagen de una persona, especialmente la cara

posed—Arranged in a special way. **pose**—ordenado en una manera especial

rough—Tactile texture that feels uneven. **áspero**—textura táctil que se siente irregular

shiny—A visual texture that reflects light well. **brillante**—una textura visual que refleja bien la luz

smooth—Tactile texture that feels even. **suave**—textura táctil que se siente liso

stitchery—Technique for decorating fabric by sewing threads on it. **bordado**—técnica para decorar tela cosiendo hilo en ella

subordinate—The parts of the artwork that seem less important. Subordinate objects are not emphasized. **subordinado**—las partes de la obra de arte que parecen ser menos importantes. Objetos subordinados no están enfatizados

symmetrical—When two sides of a work of art are mirror images of each other. **simétrico**—cuando los dos lados de una obra de arte se reflejan uno al otro

symmetry—A special type of balance where two sides of a work of art are mirror images of each other. **simetría**—un tipo especial de equilibrio donde los dos lados de una obra de arte se reflejan uno al otro

tactile texture—A texture that can be felt. **textura táctil**—una textura que se siente

texture—An element of art that refers to how things feel or would feel if they were touched. **textura**—un elemento artístico que se refiere a cómo las cosas se sienten si fueran tocadas

visual texture—Texture that can not be felt, but can be seen. Visual texture is often used in paintings. **textura visual**—textura que no se puede sentir, pero se puede ver. Textura visual se usa a menudo en pinturas

Vocabulary Practice

T Display *Transparency 41* to review unit vocabulary words.

Definitions: ☆ Vocabulary
Entire Definitions vs. Brief Definitions
Have students select four unit vocabulary words and read their complete definitions. Have students write their own brief definitions of the words.

Context Clues ☆ Vocabulary
Have students select three unit vocabulary words and create sentences in which the reader could infer the words' meanings by the context.

Other References ☆ Vocabulary
Have students look up two unit vocabulary words using an electronic encyclopedia.

Wrapping Up Unit **5**

Balance, Emphasis, and Texture

Wrapping Up Unit 5
Balance, Emphasis, and Texture

▲ **Rosalind Ragans.** (American). *Teacher.* 1988.

Batik dyes and wax on cotton fabric. 27 × 23 inches (68.58 × 58.42 cm.). Private Collection.

 Art Criticism

Critical Thinking Art criticism is an organized system for looking at and talking about art. You can criticize art without being an expert. The purpose of art criticism is to get the viewer involved in a perception process that delays judgment until all aspects of the artwork have been studied.

■ See page 28–29 for more about art criticism.

Describe

► Possible answer: A blue head and shoulder fill the painting. The eyes are staring straight ahead, and the mouth is straight; it is not smiling or frowning. There are long swirling lines of hair. There are eighteen swirling people with obvious arms and heads in the hair and in the background. There are more partial figures all over the painting. There are wiggly lines that look like plants on the face and in the corner. They are green and yellow in the left area above the head and in the bottom right corner. There are three butterflies.

Analyze

► Possible answer: The face shows balance. The bodies of some of the dancers show balance.

► Possible answer: All the texture is visual because the surface of the fabric is smooth. The large areas of blue look smooth. The areas with the wiggly lines look rough.

► Possible answer: The turquoise blue face against the black background shows emphasis through contrast. The eye on the left with the flower in its pupil is the focal point of the work. The wiggly red, yellow, and white lines spread out from that eye.

Art History and Culture

Rosalind Ragans

Rosalind Ragans (roz´ ə lind rā´ gənz) (1933–) was born and raised in New York City. When she was 11, polio paralyzed the right side of her body. Fortunately two years of therapy helped her regain nearly all the movement she had lost. Ragans works in a style of her own that approaches abstraction. All of Ragans's batik paintings have dancers and plants in them—either as the main subject or hidden in the background. Ragans has always loved music and dancing. She also is fascinated by plants because she saw so few of them as a child in New York City.

Artist Profiles, p. 48

Artist Profile

Rosalind Ragans
b. 1933

Rosalind Ragans (ro´ zo lind rā´ gənz) was born and grew up in New York City. When she was 11, polio paralyzed the right side of her body. Fortunately two years of therapy helped her regain nearly all the movement she had lost. Ragans had planned to be a stage designer but discovered that she loved teaching art. She began teaching in New Jersey in 1956. She earned a doctoral degree in education. While teaching art in Georgia in 1975, she began developing *ArtTalk.* This art education program presents art as a language, or way of communicating. Published in 1987, it has been well received by art teachers across the nation. Since then Ragans has created *Art Connections,* which you are using now. She still finds time to

 **Art Criticism** **Critical Thinking**

Describe **What do you see?**
▶ What do you see in this painting?

Analyze **How is this work organized?**
▶ Which part of this work shows balance?
▶ Is the texture in this art visual or tactile? Describe it.
▶ What part of this work shows emphasis?

Interpret **What is the artist trying to say?**
▶ Whose face is this?
▶ What is happening in this picture? Tell the story you see.

Decide **What do you think about the work?**
▶ Is this painting successful because it is realistic, because it is well organized, or because it has a strong message? Explain your answer.

Interpret

▶ Possible answer: Answers will vary. Since the title is *Teacher* many will say this is the face of a teacher. Many other answers are possible including parents and fantasy figures.

▶ Possible answer: Answers will vary. Some may say that the person with the blue face is thinking. The long curved lines coming from the head represent ideas. The little people could be her students or her ideas about teaching. The butterflies are her ideas flying out. The wiggly lines that look like plants could be her ideas growing.

Decide

▶ Possible answer: Answers will vary. Most will not cite realism, even though the face is realistic. Some will cite composition and most will talk about the message being communicated.

Art Journal: Writing
Have students write answers to Aesthetic Perception in the Critical Thinking section of their Art Journals.

 Aesthetic Perception

Seeing Like an Artist Have students look at the faces of their family members. How do these faces compare with the one in *Teacher*?

Describe ▶ List everything you can about the faces in your family.

Analyze ▶ Where do you see balance, emphasis, and texture in your family faces?

Interpret ▶ How do the faces make you feel?

Decide ▶ Are the faces in your family more realistic or less realistic than the face in *Teacher*? Why?

"How do artists create balance, emphasis, and texture in their art?" "¿Como crean los artistas el equilibrio, el énfasis y la textura en su arte?"

Art Journal: Writing
Have students answer the questions on page 182 in their Art Journals or on a separate sheet of paper. Answers: 1. A, 2. C, 3. B, 4. C

T For further assessment, have students complete the unit test on *Transparency 47*.

VISIT A MUSEUM
The National Gallery of Canada

► Encourage students to think about what kind of objects they might find in a museum. Why would a museum collect these objects?

- Take students to an artist's exhibition. Have students identify ideas in the artist's exhibition.

- Invite an artist to share his or her portfolio with the class. Have students identify ideas in this artist's portfolio.

"The function of the creative artist consists of making laws, not in following laws already made."

—Ferruccio Busoni

Show What You Know

Answer these questions on a separate sheet of paper.

1 Visual texture is texture you _____.
A. see
B. touch
C. balance

2 _____ occurs when two sides of a work of art are mirror images.
A. Visual texture
B. Emphasis
C. Symmetry

3 _____ makes one part of a work of art stand out.
A. Balance
B. Emphasis
C. Symmetry

4 _____ occurs when two different objects are placed next to each other.
A. Tactile texture
B. Balance
C. Contrast

Unit Assessment Options

Aesthetic Perception
Practice Have students list the unit concepts and then find examples of the unit concepts in the classroom.

Creative Expression
Student Portfolio Have students review all the artwork they have created during this unit and select the pieces they wish to keep in their portfolios. Then have students look at peers' portfolios and identify ideas.

Art Criticism
Activity Have students select a work of art from this unit and study it using the four steps of art criticism. (See pages 28–29 for more about Art Criticism.) Have students work alone or in pairs and present their findings orally or in writing.

VISIT A MUSEUM
The National Gallery of Canada

The National Gallery of Canada was started in 1880 when members of the Royal Canadian Academy agreed to donate art to make a collection. At first the collection was in the same building as the Canadian Supreme Court. Soon the collection grew, and art was purchased for the museum. Today the collection has a permanent home in Ottawa, and the museum occupies over 500,000 square feet.

Balance, Emphasis, and Texture in Dance

▲ Remy Charlip. "Radio Dance."

Remy Charlip is a choreographer who finds new and interesting ways to create dances. Instead of making up specific dance steps, he thinks of everyday movements and changes them to fit into the dance. When people dance, they emphasize the way they are moving and the rhythm of their movements. Remy Charlip makes up his dances by emphasizing everyday movements.

What to Do Create a Radio Dance using contrasting movements.

1. Make up a Radio Dance with a small group. Brainstorm and select five or seven common action words and place them in an order. Examples of some action words are *stretch, turn, toss, jump,* and *swing.* Decide which movements will have more emphasis.

2. Select an announcer to call out the words while the rest of the group improvises ways to change an ordinary movement into a dance. The announcer should call "freeze" at the end of each movement.

3. Practice your Radio Dance several times. Perform it for the rest of the class.

 Art Criticism

Describe What did you do to turn a simple movement into a dance?

Analyze How did you give emphasis to one of your action words?

Interpret What feelings or ideas were you thinking of as you performed your dance?

Decide How well do you think your group did when you created a Radio Dance?

Unit 5 **183**

 Art History and Culture

Contemporary American Dance

Remy Charlip is a man of many talents. He designs unusual ways to make up dances. His "Radio Dance" uses words such as *stretch, swing,* and *slide* to inspire the listening audience to dance in their own ways. Each time the sequence of words is repeated, it is accompanied by a different style of music.

Balance, Emphasis, and Texture in Dance

Objective: to create a sequence of five actions through creative movement

Materials: Radio Dance, performed by Remy Charlip. Running time: 6:16

Focus

Time: About 10 minutes

■ Discuss the information on page 183.

Art History and Culture

■ Have students brainstorm a list of common action words to select their actions from.

Teach

Time: About 20 minutes

Aesthetic Perception

■ Direct all students to interpret several words using movement. Encourage them to think about how this is an emphasized common movement.

Creative Expression

■ Have students each select five words to explore, four counts each.

■ Encourage them to vary the levels, space, energy, rhythm and tempo.

■ Have them perform their sequences in small groups.

■ **Informal Assessment** Comment positively on their interpretations.

Reflect

Time: About 10 minutes

Art Criticism

■ Have students answer the four art criticism questions on page 183 aloud or in writing.

■ Did students create emphasized and balanced movements in their dance?

Unit 6 Planning Guide

	Lesson Title	Suggested Pacing	Creative Expression Activity
Lesson 1	Harmony of Color	55 minutes	Create a class mural using harmony of color.
Lesson 2	Harmony of Shape and Form	55 minutes	Create a computer drawing of an animal family using harmony of shape.
Lesson 3	Variety of Color	55 minutes	Create a print of an underwater scene using variety of color.
Lesson 4	Variety of Shape and Form	55 minutes	Create a drawing of a fantasy bird.
Lesson 5	Unity in Sculpture	55 minutes	Create a stuffed paper carousel animal and class carousel.
Lesson 6	Unity in Architecture	55 minutes	Create a cityscape using a computer drawing program.
ART SOURCE	Harmony, Variety, and Unity in Dance	40 minutes	Create a circle dance to a drum beat.

Materials	Program Resources	Fine Art Resources	Literature Resources
4" × 4" tiles, tile paints, brushes, water containers	*Reading and Writing Test Preparation*, pp. 66–67 *Flash Card*, 17 *Assessment*, pp. 69–70 *Home and After-School Connections*	*Transparency*, 31 *Artist Profiles*, pp. 19, 30 *Animals Through History Time Line* *Large Prints*, 35 and 36 *Women in the Arts Collection*	*The Buffalo Jump* by Peter Roop
computer with a drawing program	*Reading and Writing Test Preparation*, pp. 68–69 *Flash Cards*, 17–18 *Assessment*, pp. 71–72	*Transparency*, 32 *Artist Profiles*, pp. 9, 45 *Large Print*, 35 *Art Around the World Collection*	*Solo* by Paul Geraghty
12" × 18" white paper, 2 laminated posterboards, crayons, easel brushes, blue, red, and green tempera paints, spray bottle, paper scraps	*Reading and Writing Test Preparation*, pp. 70–71 *Flash Card*, 16 *Assessment*, pp. 73–74	*Transparency*, 33 *Artist Profiles*, pp. 33, 40 *Large Print*, 36 *Art Around the World Collection*	*To the Depths of the Ocean* by Nicholas Harris
12" × 18" white paper, black permanent markers, colored pencils, watercolors, brushes, water containers	*Reading and Writing Test Preparation*, pp. 72–73 *Flash Card*, 16 *Assessment*, pp. 75–76	*Transparency*, 34 *Artist Profiles*, pp. 5, 52 *Large Print*, 36 *Art Around the World Collection*	*Stellaluna* by Janell Cannon
12" × 18" white drawing paper, oil pastels, watercolors, brushes, water dishes, newspaper, cardboard tubes, white school glue	*Reading and Writing Test Preparation*, pp. 74–75 *Flash Card*, 18 *Assessment*, pp. 77–78	*Transparency*, 35 *Artist Profile*, p. 16 *Large Prints*, 35 and 36 *Women in the Arts Collection*	*Carousel* by Donald Crews
computer with a drawing program	*Reading and Writing Test Preparation*, pp. 76–77 *Flash Card*, 18 *Assessment*, pp. 79–80	*Transparency*, 36 *Artist Profiles*, pp. 50, 77 *Large Prints*, 35 and 36 *Art Around the World Collection*	*A Picnic in October* by Eve Bunting
"Korean Classical Music and Dance ArtSource Video", a bell, gong, or drum to provide a beat for the dance			

Unit Overview

6 Harmony, Variety, and Unity

Lesson 1: Harmony of Color is using similar colors and hues in a work of art.

Lesson 2: Harmony of Shape and Form is using similar shapes and forms in a work of art.

Lesson 3: Variety of Color is using contrasting colors in a work of art.

Lesson 4: Variety of Shape and Form is using contrasting shapes and forms in a work of art.

Lesson 5: Unity in Sculpture is using different sculptures to create one unit.

Lesson 6: Unity in Architecture is using different elements of a building to create a feeling of wholeness.

Introduce Unit Concepts

"Artists use harmony, variety, and unity to make many different kinds of art." "Los artistas usan armonía, variedad y unidad para crear diferentes tipos de arte".

Harmony
- Ask students to think of an event at which people wear the same outfit to create harmony.

Variety
- Ask students to collect objects of similar colors, then add an object of a different color and describe what happens to their groups.

Unity
- Give each student a small sheet of matching paper. Have them use a crayon to draw a letter. Put the papers together to make a quilt and show unity.

Cross-Curricular Projects
- See the *Language Arts and Reading, Mathematics, Science,* and *Social Studies Art Connections* books for activities that further develop harmony, variety, and unity.

184 UNIT 6 • Harmony, Variety, and Unity

Unit 6

Harmony, Variety, and Unity

▲ **Diego Velázquez.** (Spanish). *Las Meninas (The Maids of Honor).* 1656.

Oil on canvas. 10 feet 5 $\frac{1}{4}$ × 9 feet $\frac{3}{4}$ inches (3.18 × 2.76 meters). Museo Nacional del Prado, Madrid, Spain.

Artists use harmony, variety, and unity to organize the elements of art.

When used correctly, harmony, variety, and unity make a work of art more interesting and pleasing to the viewer.

184   Unit 6

Fine Art Prints

Display *Large Prints 35 Still Music* and *36 Quilting Time.* Refer to the prints throughout the unit as students learn about harmony, variety, and unity.

Large Print 35

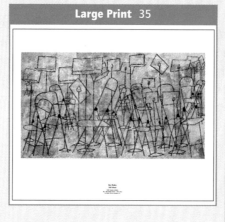

Large Print 36

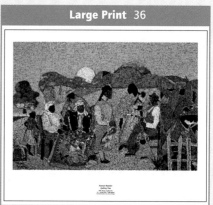

Harmony is the use of similar and related objects.

▶ Where are objects that are alike in this painting?

Variety is the use of different objects.

▶ Where are two objects that are different in this painting?

Unity occurs when artists balance harmony and variety.

▶ How do you feel when you look at this scene?

In This Unit you will learn about and practice creating harmony, variety, and unity. Here are the topics you will study:

▶ Harmony of Color
▶ Harmony of Shape and Form
▶ Variety of Color
▶ Variety of Shape and Form
▶ Unity in Sculpture
▶ Unity in Architecture

Detail from Las Meninas

Diego Velázquez

(1599–1660)

Diego Velázquez was the court painter for King Philip IV of Spain. He was famous for creating art that had unity. *Las Meninas* is one of Velázquez's most famous paintings. As court painter, it was his job to paint the scenes and people of the court. This painting shows the daughter of the king of Spain. If you look carefully, you can see her parents reflected in a mirror at the back of the painting.

NSAE 1.a, 1.b

Examine the Artwork

"Let's look closely at the painting." "Vamos a mirar detalladamente la pintura".

■ Have students look at *Las Meninas*. Ask them to describe what they see.

■ Have students answer the questions about harmony, variety, and unity on page 185.

▶ The ladies-in-waiting attending to the girl all look similar.

▶ The man standing in the doorway and the dog on the floor are different.

▶ Like everyone in the painting belongs together.

■ Discuss the differences between materials, techniques, and processes. Have students describe how different materials, techniques, and processes cause different responses.

Unit Pretest

T Display *Transparency 48* as a pretest. Answers: 1. A, 2. C, 3. C, 4. B

Home Connection

■ See *Home and After-School Connections* for family newsletters and activities for this unit.

Art History and Culture

Diego Velázquez

Diego Velázquez (dē ā´ gō və las´ kwiz) (1599–1660), was born in Seville, Spain. At age 11 he was apprenticed to the painter Francisco Pacheco, and by 18 he was an independent painter. In 1623 Velázquez moved to Madrid, where he became court painter to King Philip IV. This was a comfortable position that he held until his death. This occupation in court required him to paint many portraits, and Velázquez used his position to redefine the traditional portrait. Instead of the stiff poses and distant attitudes of conventional subjects, his richly colored portraits concentrated on the psychology of his subjects.

Artist Profiles, p. 67

Artist Profile

Diego Velázquez
1599–1660

Diego Velázquez (dē ā´ gō və las´ kwiz) was born in Seville, Spain, in 1599. At the young age of 11, he was apprenticed to the painter Francisco Pacheco, and by the time he was 18 he was an independent painter. In 1623, Velázquez moved to Madrid where he became court painter to King Philip IV, a comfortable position that Velázquez held until his death. Velázquez eventually became a knight of the Military Order of Santiago and a friend of the king. This occupation in court required him to paint many portraits, and his richly colored portraits captured the personalities of his subjects.

◀ **Diego Velázquez.** (Spanish). *Las Meninas (The Maids of Honor).* 1656.

Unit 6 Arts Integration

ILLUSTRATOR PROFILE
Kevin Henkes
(1960-)

As a child growing up in Wisconsin, Kevin Henkes seldom left home without one of his prized possessions, his favorite books. Henkes explored his books from cover to cover, carefully examining each page and wondering about the authors and illustrators who created them.

Henkes's affinity for books, coupled with an artistic talent he developed at a young age, brought an early start to his career. When he was only 19, Henkes secured a contract with Greenwillow Books and began working on his first picture book, *All Alone* (1981).

Drawing from personal experiences, Henkes writes about common childhood situations, such as starting school, with uncommon insight and tenderness. In addition to his numerous picture books, Henkes has written several novels for older children. Henkes said, "I like the variety of trying new ways to fill the pages between two covers. Experimenting with words and paint and ink keeps my job interesting." Henkes's evolving style is evidence of his experimentation. While his first picture books included realistic drawings of children, his later illustrations have a cartoon-like quality.

Throughout Unit 6, share Henkes's illustrations with students as they learn about harmony, variety, and unity. Can they find these concepts in Henkes's illustrations?

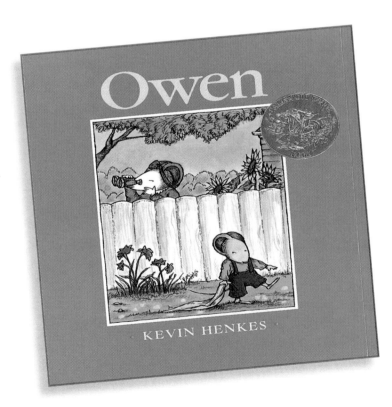

Music

Harmony in music refers to different pitches played or sung at the same time to produce chords. Variety gives a composition interest. Have students sing a song and identify variety.

Literature

Show the video or DVD *It Could Always Be Worse* by Harve and Margot Zemach to help introduce harmony, variety, and unity and discuss how the illustrator demonstrated each concept.

Literature and Art

Performing Arts

 Show "Kahng Gang Sool Le." Point out instances of harmony, variety, and unity in the Korean dance.

ArtSource®

Harmony of Color

Lesson 1 introduces the students to harmony of color. Artists can create harmony in a work of art by using similar colors and hues throughout the entire work.

Objectives

Art History and Culture

To recognize that different colors have different symbolic meanings in different cultures

Creative Expression

To use harmony of color to create a class mural

Aesthetic Perception

To identify harmony of color in students' environments

Art Criticism

To evaluate own work using the four steps of art criticism

Vocabulary ⭐ Vocabulary

Review the following vocabulary word with students before beginning the lesson.

harmony armonía—a principle of design that helps create unity by showing how objects in a work of art are similar

See page 209B for additional Spanish vocabulary resources.

Art Journal: Vocabulary

Have students add this word to the Vocabulary section of their Art Journals.

Lesson Materials

- 4" × 4" tiles
- tile paints
- pencils
- brushes
- water containers
- assortment of crayons

Alternate Materials:
- assortment of markers
- 6" × 6" paper squares
- construction paper scraps
- scissors
- glue

Program Resources

- *Reading and Writing Test Prep.*, pp. 66–67
- *Transparency 31*
- *Flash Card 17*
- *Artist Profiles*, pp. 19, 30
- *Animals Through History Time Line*
- *Assessment*, pp. 69–70
- *Large Prints 35 Still Music* and *36 Quilting Time*
- *The National Museum of Women in the Arts Collection*

Concept Trace
Harmony of Color
Introduced: Level 2, Unit 6, Lesson 1

Reinforced: Level 3, Unit 6, Lesson 1

Lesson 1 Arts Integration

Theatre

Complete Unit 6 Lesson 1 on pages 108–109 of *Theatre Arts Connections*.

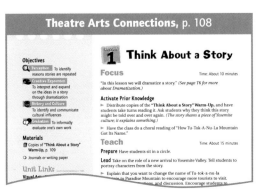

Theatre Arts Connections, p. 108

Music

The colors of the orchestra are heard in a traditional context in classical orchestral music. Contemporary composers use new ways of combining instruments to create different colors. Listen to *Estancia Battel Suite Op.8a First Movement* "Los trabadores agricolas" by Alberto Ginnestera. Do you hear any interesting combinations of instruments?

Movement & Dance

Dancers can create harmony in movement by building smooth transitions. Ask students to create three axial movements (for example: push, pull, twist). Now have them find a way to transition smoothly from one axial movement to another, taking four counts for each transition. Some transitional movements are turning, melting, or reaching.

Activate Prior Knowledge

"Do you have a special place you like to go to think?" "¿Tienen un sitio especial donde les gusta ir para pensar?"

■ Let students describe their special places. Why is it a special place?

Using Literature Reading

■ Read *The Buffalo Jump* by Peter Roop. Have the students find harmony of color in the illustrations.

Thematic Connection ⭐ Reading

■ **Sharing Stories:** Encourage students to discuss how they can share stories with people. Why do people share stories? What stories are the artists sharing with these paintings?

Introduce the Art NSAE 2.a

Look

"Let's look closely at the two paintings." "Vamos a mirar detalladamente las dos pinturas".

■ Have students identify harmony in the works of art and the environment.

Environment ⭐ Science

■ Discuss what *environment* means with the students. Do students think the environments in these paintings are real or imaginary? How do they think the environments in these paintings would effect things living in them?

NSAE 4.a, 4.c, 5.a, 5.b

Art History and Culture

Possible answer: These artists picked colors that mattered to them. Green is often seen as a sign of growth and life. In some ancient cultures, red was used to protect against illness and ward off evil.

 Web Connection

Visit **www.artsmia.org/collection/search/ art.cfm?id=1318** to see another painting by Paul Klee.

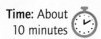

Harmony of Color

Look at the two paintings. In each painting, one hue has been used to make many objects. By using the same hue for the different objects, the artists have made the viewer feel like these different objects belong together.

◀ **Paul Klee.** (Swiss). *The Tree of Houses.* 1918.
....
Watercolor and ink on chalk-primed gauze on papers, mounted on painted board. Norton Simon Museum, Pasadena, California.

Art History and Culture

Colors represent different things in different cultures. Why do you think these artists chose red and green for their paintings?

Art History and Culture

Paul Klee

Paul Klee (paul klā) (1879–1940) was born into a musical Swiss family that hoped he also would become a musician. At age five his grandmother gave him his first box of pencils. He thought of himself as an artist from then on, but he kept an interest in music. Klee believed that childlike drawings were the most creative and original. Color was very important to Klee. He once said, "Color and I are one; I am a painter." In his watercolors Klee used thin layers of pale color. This technique added a gentle shimmer to his pictures. Klee used color the way a musician uses sound. He tried to touch the feelings of his viewers.

See pages 24–25 and 16–21 for more about art history and subject matter.

Artist Profiles, p. 30

Artist Profile ✦
Paul Klee
1879–1940
Paul Klee (paul klā) was born into a musical Swiss family. His family hoped he also would become a musician. At age five his grandmother gave him his first box of pencils. He thought of himself as an artist from then on, but he continued to have an interest in music. Klee played his violin for an hour nearly every morning of his life. He married a pianist. As an adult Klee still drew in a childlike way. Klee believed that childlike drawings were the most creative and original. He was not trying to share his ideas through his work. He just wanted to explore his imagination. Klee could use either hand proficiently when painting.

Study the two works of art to find examples of harmony of color.

▶ What is the main hue in each painting?

▶ Which objects in each painting are shades or tints of the main hue?

▶ How does the artists' use of a main hue make you feel about the scenes?

▲ **Ivan Eyre.** (Canadian).
Valleyridge. 1974.
....
Acrylic on canvas. 50 $\frac{1}{10}$ × 64 inches
(142.4 × 162.6 cm.). National Gallery
of Canada, Ottawa, Canada.

⚲ Aesthetic Perception

Seeing Like an Artist Look around the room and find objects that are in the same color family. Do these similar color groups create pleasant relationships?

🏺 Art History and Culture

Ivan Eyre

Ivan Eyre (ī´ vən ēr) (1935–) was born in rural Saskatchewan, a province in Canada. His family was extremely poor, and they moved from place to place throughout Canada as his father looked for work. When Eyre was in fifth grade, he won a prize for painting. His teachers encouraged him to continue making art. Eyre's work is difficult to categorize, since he often crosses boundaries of styles, themes, and media. He paints many landscapes of wooded forests. Some of these appear to be seen through frames, as if the viewer is looking out a window. He uses analogous colors, usually all from one color family.

See pages 24–25 and 16–21 for more about art history and subject matter.

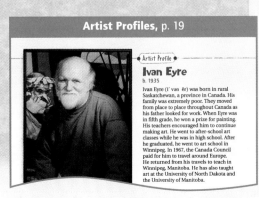

Artist Profiles, p. 19

◆ Artist Profile ◆
Ivan Eyre
b. 1935

Ivan Eyre (ī´ vən ēr) was born in rural Saskatchewan, a province in Canada. His family was extremely poor. They moved from place to place throughout Canada as his father looked for work. When Eyre was in fifth grade, he won a prize for painting. His teachers encouraged him to continue making art. He went to after-school art classes while he was in high school. After he graduated, he went to art school in Winnipeg. In 1967, the Canada Council paid for him to travel around Europe. He returned from his travels to teach in Winnipeg, Manitoba. He has also taught art at the University of North Dakota and the University of Manitoba.

Study

▶ In the Klee painting, the main hue is red. In the Eyre painting, the main hue is green.

▶ The trees and vegetation in the Eyre painting are all shades and tints of green. The tree, sky, some houses, and other details are shades and tints of red in the Klee painting.

▶ Answers will vary. Some students will say the green calms them and the red makes them feel warm.

■ For more examples of genre art, see *The National Museum of Women in the Arts Collection.*

📔 Art Journal: Writing

Ask students to write an explanation of why they think artists use harmony of color in the Concepts section of their Art Journals.

⚲ Aesthetic Perception

Seeing Like an Artist Have students discuss what items in the room are from the same color family and how the combination of harmony using color makes them feel. Encourage them to find objects in their homes and community that are in the same color families. Encourage students to identify variations in objects from the environment.
NSAE 2.b, 5.c

Developing Visual Literacy What do students think the messages of the artists were when they made these paintings? Why did they use so much of the same color in their work?

💻 Web Connection

Visit **http://collections.ic.gc.ca/bank_art/ eyrei.htm** to see another landscape by Eyre.

Teach

Time: About 35 minutes

"What would be the mood if we all wore the same-colored shirt today?" "¿Cuál sería el estado de ánimo de hoy si todos nos vistiéramos con una camisa del mismo color?"

- Read and discuss the information on harmony of color on page 188.

Practice

Materials: assortment of crayons in many colors

Alternate Materials: assortment of markers in many colors

- Distribute the materials and have students follow the directions on page 188.
- Have students identify and practice the skills necessary for producing constructions using a variety of materials.

Creative Expression

NSAE 1.c, 1.d, 2.c, 3.b

Materials: 4" × 4" tiles, tile paints, pencils, brushes, water containers

Alternate Materials: 6" × 6" paper squares, construction paper scraps, scissors, glue

- Distribute the materials and have students follow the directions on page 189.
- Regular glazed tiles can be purchased at most hardware stores. If you do not want students to use tiles for this mural project, have them use the paper squares and make a collage using construction paper.
- Review the Activity Tips on page 247 for visual examples of the activity techniques if needed.
- Encourage students to express their ideas and feelings in their artwork using a variety of colors.
- Encourage students to create effective compositions using design principles.

NSAE 3.a
Art Journal: Brainstorming

Have students brainstorm subjects that would make a good class mural in the Ideas section of their Art Journals. Have students present their favorite ideas to the class and vote on a mural subject for the Creative Expression activity.

Using Harmony of Color

Artists create **harmony** by making separate objects in a work of art look pleasing together. One way to create harmony is with color. When the same color is used for different objects or parts in a work of art, the viewer feels like the objects belong together. Look at the pictures. Which is more harmonious?

Practice

Group objects to create harmony of color.

1. Look at the crayons your teacher has given you.
2. Place the crayons in groups according to color families.
3. Can you see the harmony of color between the different crayons in each family?

188 Unit 6 • Lesson 1

Differentiated Instruction

Reteach
Have students sort themselves into color groups by clothes. Have students arrange themselves according to the color of their shirts.

Special Needs
Students may be passive during group activities. There could be many reasons for this, ranging from painful prior experiences to personality. Be sensitive to these issues and provide supports such as modeling of group norms and carefully assigning individual roles in the group.

ELL Tips
Define *harmony* for students. Use the word in a sentence. Review cool and warm hues and how they are harmonious, including their position on the color wheel.

Think about how these students used harmony of color in their tile mural.

◀ **Duncan Creek Second Grade.** Ages 6–8.

Creative Expression

Can you use color to create harmony? Use color to harmonize a class mural.

1. As a group, decide on a theme and color for your class mural.

2. Paint the basic shapes of your design on your tile and let it dry. Remember to use the color your class selected.

3. Add details to your design. When the tiles are all dry, arrange them as a class.

Art Criticism

Describe What is the theme of your mural?

Analyze How did you create harmony of color in your mural?

Interpret How does your color choice help communicate your mural theme?

Decide Did you successfully create harmony using color in your mural?

Review and Assess

"How can you create harmony of color in a work of art?" "¿Cómo pueden crear armonía de color en una obre de arte?"

Think

These artists created harmony of color using the same background color for each tile in their mural.

- Use *Large Prints 35 Still Music* and *36 Quilting Time* to have students identify harmony of color.

- Have students identify stories and constructions in this lesson's artwork.

- Have students identify ideas of the artists in this lesson's art.

Informal Assessment

Art Journal: Critical Thinking

Have students answer the four art criticism questions—Describe, Analyze, Interpret, and Decide—in the Critical Thinking section of their Art Journals. Ask students to define their reasons for preferences in their own art. Then have them identify ideas in their peers' art.

- For standardized-format test practice using this lesson's art content, see pages 66–67 in *Reading and Writing Test Preparation.*

• Art Across the Curriculum •

NSAE 6.a, 6.b

Use these simple ideas to reinforce art concepts across the curriculum.

★ **Personal Writing** Have students write a letter to a friend explaining harmony of color.

★ **Math** Have students write three math problems using one color for odd numbers and another color for even numbers.

★ **Science** Discuss how different colors are made of different wave lengths. Explain that similar colors have similar wave lengths.

★ **Social Studies** Have students look through flags of the world to find countries whose flags have harmony of color with each other.

★ **Technology** Show students how to mix colors in the painting program to create colors that have harmony with each other. Visit **SRAonline.com** to print detailed instructions for this activity.

Harmony of Color

Extra! For the Art Specialist

Time: About 45 minutes

Focus

Study *Large Print 36* and ask students to describe the colors they see. Are any colors repeated? Where are they repeated? Why do you think the artist used the same colors throughout this work? Would the print look the same without the harmony of color? Explain.

Teach

Explain to students that they will create a weaving from painted paper strips. These strips will be painted either in warm or cool hues and woven into a paper background. The warp cuts in the background paper and the weft paper strips will be cut using various line directions. The color of the strips will create harmony in the work. Explain the process of weaving paper. Have students complete the Alternate Activity.

Reflect

Have students evaluate their artwork using the four steps of art criticism.

Alternate Activity

Materials:

- 12" × 18" heavy-weight white drawing paper
- 12" × 18" construction paper (all colors)
- brushes, buckets, and newspapers
- tempera paints
- scissors
- glue

1. Use warm or cool hues to paint the entire sheet of white drawing paper.

2. Select a piece of colored construction paper for the background and fold it in half. Cutting from the fold, make the warp slots. Cut using different line directions.

3. Cut the painted paper into thin strips and use different line styles when you cut.

4. Weave your painted strips into the background until it is full. Glue the tips down at both ends. How did you create harmony using color?

Research in Art Education

"Enriched and stimulated in art classes by a teacher's varied and challenging motivations, children learn to see more, sense more, and recall more . . . Some people, however, think that anything a child draws, paints, or constructs is art . . . It may indeed be a child's visual statement, but it is not necessarily a quality work of art. To have quality, it must, as much as possible, be expressed in the language, structure, and form of art" (Wachowiak, Frank, and Robert Clements, *Emphasis Art: A Qualitative Art Program for Elementary and Middle Schools* (7th ed.). New York: Longman, 2001).

Assessment

Use the following rubric to evaluate the artwork students make in the Creative Expression activity and to assess students' understanding of harmony of color.

Have students complete page 69 or 70 of their *Assessment* books.

	Art History and Culture	Aesthetic Perception	Creative Expression	Art Criticism
3 POINTS	The student can identify that different colors have special meanings in different cultures.	The student accurately identifies harmony of color in his or her environment.	The student's tile clearly illustrates a good use of harmony of color.	The student thoughtfully and honestly evaluates his or her own work using the four steps of art criticism.
2 POINTS	The student's identification is weak or incomplete.	The student shows emerging awareness of harmony of color, but cannot consistently identify them.	The student's tile shows some awareness of harmony of color.	The student attempts to evaluate his or her own work, but shows an incomplete understanding of evaluation criteria.
1 POINT	The student cannot identify that different colors have special meanings in different cultures.	The student cannot identify harmony of color.	The student's tile shows no understanding of harmony of color.	The student makes no attempt to evaluate his or her own artwork.

Assessment, p. 69

Name _____ Date _____ **Lesson 1 UNIT 6**

Harmony of Color

A. Identifying
Circle the descriptions of pictures that would have harmony of color.

a green house in a forest of green trees

a blue beetle on a red flower

a man dressed in orange looking at a sunset

a purple bat in a red room

B. Drawing
In the box below, draw a picture that has harmony of color.

C. Short Answer
What is *harmony*?

Level 2   Unit 6 • Harmony, Variety, and Unity   **69**

Harmony of Shape and Form

Lesson 2 introduces the students to harmony of shape and form. Artists can also create harmony by repeating similar shapes and forms in a work of art.

Objectives

Art History and Culture

To recognize that artists often portray animals that are significant to them because of their culture or location

Aesthetic Perception

To recognize harmony of shape or form in animals in students' environments

Creative Expression

To create a computer drawing of an animal group using harmony of shape

Art Criticism

To evaluate own work using the four steps of art criticism

Vocabulary Vocabulary

Review the following vocabulary word with students before beginning the lesson.

proportions *proporciones*—the relationship of the size of different objects to each other

See page 209B for additional Spanish vocabulary resources.

Art Journal: Vocabulary

Have students add this word to the Vocabulary section of their Art Journals.

Lesson Materials
- 12" × 18" white paper
- crayons
- computer

Alternate Materials:
- markers
- colored pencils

Program Resources
- *Reading and Writing Test Prep.*, pp. 68–69
- *Transparency 32*
- *Flash Cards 17* and *18*
- *Artist Profiles*, pp. 9, 45
- *Animals Through History Time Line*
- *Assessment*, pp. 71–72
- *Large Print 35 Still Music*
- *Art Around the World Collection*

Concept Trace
Harmony of Shape and Form
Introduced: Level 2, Unit 6, Lesson 2

Reinforced: Level 3, Unit 6, Lesson 1

Lesson 2 Arts Integration

Theatre

Complete Unit 6 Lesson 2 on pages 110–111 of *Theatre Arts Connections*.

Theatre Arts Connections, p. 110

Objectives

Lesson 2 What Is This Story About?

Focus Time: About 15 minutes

"In this lesson we will improvise a story to dramatize its subject." *(See page T4 for more about Improvisation.)*

Activate Prior Knowledge

▶ Hand out the **"What Is This Story About?" Warm-Up.** Read the stories with students. Discuss students' answers. More than one answer is appropriate for each question, so encourage students to defend their answers with reasons.

▶ Give each student a sheet of white construction paper. Have students choose one subject word from the **Warm-Up** and write it on an index card. Then have students illustrate the word they chose.

Teach Time: About 15 minutes

Prepare Divide the class into small groups of five or six students.

Lead Write these idea words on the board: *truth, right and wrong, courage,* and *love.* Discuss with the class what image comes to mind when they hear each word. Using a web, jot their ideas on the board or ... as a reminder for later. Ask each group to choose ...

Music

Music in the Western tradition is often composed according to forms that create harmony throughout the piece. Rondo form takes one main musical idea and repeats it several times while adding contrasting sections between. Listen to *Rondo* from "Rage over a Lost Penny" by Ludwig van Beethoven. How many times is the *A* section played?

Movement & Dance

A sense of harmony in movement is created by building smooth transitions. Ask students to create three shapes: one high, one middle, and one low. Have them transition smoothly from one shape to another, taking four counts for the transitions. Some good transitional movements are contracting, expanding, and jumping.

Focus

Time: About 10 minutes

Activate Prior Knowledge

"Are there certain animals that you see more than others?" "¿Hay ciertos animales que ustedes ven más que otros?"

- Encourage students to discuss the kinds of animals they have encountered. Ask them if they have ever seen a family of animals.

Using Literature ⭐ Reading

- Read *Solo* by Paul Geraghty. Discuss the harmony of shape students see in the book.

Thematic Connection ⭐ Science

- **Animals:** Discuss with students what some of their favorite animals are. Why do they like those animals?

Introduce the Art NSAE 2.a

Look

"Let's look closely at these two works of art." "Vamos a mirar detalladamente estas dos obras de arte".

- Have students identify harmony in the artwork and environment.

- Have students compare the way families are depicted in the artwork.

Similar Figures ⭐ Math

- Have students discuss how animal families are often composed of similar figures. How are their figures similar to the members of their families?

NSAE 4.a, 4.b, 4.c, 5.a, 5.b

🏺 Art History and Culture

Possible answer: The artists wanted to show animals together. Taqialuk is Inuit, so he would see polar bears since they live in the northern Arctic. Brach has lived in the Southwest and worked on a ranch, so he is familiar with horses.

💻 Web Connection

Visit http://www.civilization.ca/aborig/iqqaipaa/home-e.html to learn more about Inuit art.

190 UNIT 6 • Harmony, Variety, and Unity

Lesson 2 Harmony of Shape and Form

Look at these works of art. One is a sculpture and one is a painting. Both works of art create harmony using either shape or form.

▲ **Taqialuk Nuna.** (Inuit). *Polar Bears and Cubs.*

7 × 12 × 9 inches (17.78 × 30.48 × 22.86 cm.). Burdick Gallery, Washington, D.C.

🏺 Art History and Culture

Why do you think these artists chose to create art using groups of animals? Why these animals?

190 Unit 6 • Lesson 2

🏺 Art History and Culture

Taqialuk Nuna

Taqialuk Nuna (tah kē´ ə lŭk nōōnə) (1958–) was born and raised in an Inuit community. Taqialuk works in an outdoor studio while the climate drops to temperatures in the negative forties. His serpentine sculptures reflect the natural life of his Arctic environment and portray a respect for the power, beauty, and intelligence of other living creatures. In addition to being a successful artist, Taqialuk is also a good hunter. His hunting skills provide him with further inspiration and understanding of the animals he carves. This helps him portray the behaviors of his subjects in addition to their appearance.

See pages 24–25 and 16–21 for more about art history and subject matter.

Artist Profiles, p. 45

Artist Profile

Taqialuk Nuna
b. 1958

Taqialuk Nuna (tah kē´ ə lŭk nōōnə) was born and raised in Cape Dorset, a rapidly growing Inuit community located on the southwest coast of Baffin Island in the Canadian territory of Nunavut. The son of Inuit artist Sharky Nuna, Nuna is a self-taught carver and a member of the West Baffin Eskimo Cooperative. Nuna works in an outdoor studio even when the temperature drops to the negative forties. His serpentine sculptures reflect the natural life of his arctic environment and portray a respect for the power, beauty, and intelligence of other living creatures. He also uses his art to express the sense of fear, awe, and mystery people have about the forces that shape our lives.

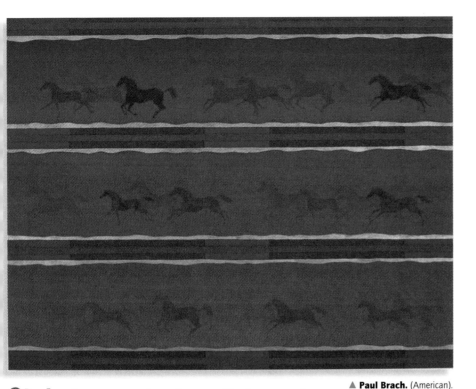

Study the two works of art to find examples of harmony using shape and form.

▶ How many of each animal do you see in each work of art?

▶ How are the animals in each work of art similar?

Aesthetic Perception

Seeing Like an Artist Can you think of times when you have seen groups of animals? Why might animals be in a group together?

▲ **Paul Brach.** (American).
Red Horse Frieze. 1983.

Oil on canvas. 54 × 72 inches
(137.16 × 182.88 cm.). Collection
of the artist.

Study

▶ There are three polar bears and twenty-three horses.

▶ In the Brach piece, the horses are almost identical. In the Taqialuk sculpture, the adult polar bear is larger than the child bears, but they are similar forms.

▪ For more examples of art from North America, see the *Art Around the World Collection.*

Art Journal: Writing
Have students write their own definitions of *harmony of shape and form* in the Concepts section of their Art Journals.

Aesthetic Perception

Seeing Like an Artist Encourage students to discuss times that they have encountered groups of animals together. Animals might be together because they live in packs or herds. Some animals stay in family groups to raise their young. Encourage students to identify variations in the subjects from the environment.
NSAE 2.b, 5.c

Developing Visual Literacy Have students evaluate the different ways the two artists portrayed groups of animals. Which way do students feel is more successful? Why did each artist work with a different medium?

Art History and Culture

Paul Brach

Paul Brach (pôl brak) (1924–) was born and raised in New York City. Even though Brach grew up during the Depression, his family was not hit hard financially, and he was afforded a privileged education in his youth. As a teenager he spent his summers working on ranches in Arizona. He developed an appreciation for the freedom and space of the West, and this experience continued to appear in his paintings throughout his career. In the 1980s, Brach became interested in the patterns he saw in the Navajo blankets of the American Southwest. His paintings combined the patterns of the blankets with the monumental landscapes in which the weavers live.

See pages 24–25 and 16–21 for more about art history and subject matter.

Artist Profiles, p. 9

Artist Profile
Paul Brach
b. 1924

Paul Brach (pôl brâk) was born and raised in New York City. Even though Brach grew up during the Great Depression, his family was not hit hard financially, and he was afforded a privileged education. As a teenager he spent his summers working on ranches in Arizona. He developed an appreciation for the freedom and space of the West, and evidence of this experience continues to appear in his paintings. He attended the University of Iowa, one of the first schools to offer a degree in creative work. After serving in World War II, Paul returned to the United States and married Miriam Shapiro, a widely respected painter whom he had met in Iowa. Today, Brach lives in New York and continues to ride his

Web Connection

Visit http://www.polkmuseumofart.org/content/inteior.asp?section=collections&body=paintings.htm to see two paintings by Paul Brach.

Teach

Time: About 35 minutes

"Can you think of a way to create harmony using shape and form?" "¿Pueden pensar en una manera de crear armonía usando la figura y la forma?"

- Read and discuss the information on harmony of shape and form on page 192.

Practice

Materials: 12 × 18 inch white paper, crayons

Alternate Materials: markers, colored pencils

- Have students identify and practice the skills necessary for producing drawings using a variety of materials.

- Distribute the materials and have students follow the directions on page 192.

Creative Expression

NSAE 1.c, 1.d, 2.c, 3.b

Materials: computer with a drawing or painting program

- Have students follow the directions on page 193.

- Help students with computer basics if they are having difficulty.

- Encourage students to create effective compositions using design principles.

- Review the Activity Tips on page 247 for visual examples of the activity techniques if needed.

NSAE 3.a
Art Journal: Brainstorming

Have students sketch possibilities for their animal family in the Ideas section of their Art Journals. Have students pick a favorite sketch to render on the computer in the Creative Expression activity.

Using Harmony of Shape and Form

Harmony can also be created in a work of art using similar shapes and forms. When artists repeat shapes and forms that are related, they create harmony in their art. The shapes and forms may have different **proportions** and still create harmony. Look at the pictures. Which is more harmonious? Why?

Practice

Draw a group of animals that has harmony.

1. Think of a group of animals to draw.
2. Draw them on your paper.
3. Why does your group have harmony?

Differentiated Instruction

Reteach

Have students look around the classroom to find objects that could be grouped together to create harmony of shape and form.

Special Needs

Provide visual cues for students as they complete this project, such as illustrated directions displayed near the computer.

ELL Tips

Show examples of harmonious designs and ask students what makes each design harmonious.

◀ **Penny Levine.**
Age 7.

Think about how this student used shapes to create harmony.

 Creative Expression

Can you create a family of animals? Use the computer to draw an animal family.

1. Draw the adult animal or animals using the drawing tool.
2. Select and copy the adult animal several times. Resize the copies to create child animals.
3. Use the fill tool or drawing tool to add details to your animals.

 **Art Criticism**

Describe What animal did you use to create your animal family?

Analyze Why does your animal family have harmony?

Interpret What does the animal family that you created mean to you?

Decide If you were making another animal family, how else could you create harmony?

Art Across the Curriculum

Use these simple ideas to reinforce art concepts across the curriculum.

★ **Expository Writing** Have students write a paragraph about why animals live in groups.

★ **Math** Show students the family of four conic sections and ask them to describe how they have harmony of shape.

★ **Science** Discuss how the planets in the Solar System exhibit harmony of form.

★ **Social Studies** Have students look at patriotic symbols and try to find harmony of shape between and within them.

★ **Technology** Have students find objects on the computer that have harmony of form, for example, the keys on the keyboard. Visit **SRAonline.com** to print out detailed instructions for this activity.

Reflect

Time: About 10 minutes

Review and Assess

"How can you create harmony using shape and form?" "¿Cómo pueden crear armonía usando la figura y la forma?"

Think

The artist used similar shapes and varied the sizes to create harmony of shape in her art.

■ Use **Large Print 35** *Still Music* to have students identify harmony of shape.

■ Have students identify stories and constructions in this lesson's artwork.

■ Have students identify ideas of the artists in this lesson's art.

Informal Assessment

Art Journal: Critical Thinking
Have students answer the four art criticism questions—Describe, Analyze, Interpret, and Decide—in the Critical Thinking section of their Art Journals. Ask students to define their reasons for preferences in their art. Then have them identify ideas in their peers' art.

■ For standardized-format test practice using this lesson's art content, see pages 68–69 in **Reading and Writing Test Preparation.**

Harmony of Shape and Form

Extra! For the Art Specialist

Time: About 45 minutes

Focus

Study **Large Print 35** and ask students to describe what they see. Do they see anything that is repeated? How many different elements of parts are used more than once? Would the artwork have harmony if there were no repetition? Why would an artist want to create harmony in his or her art?

Teach

Explain to students that they will create a cut paper collage using organic shapes to create harmony. They will begin by selecting a background and a variety of colored paper to cut shapes from. They will also develop a theme. Have students complete the Alternate Activity.

Reflect

Have students evaluate their artwork using the four steps of art criticism.

Alternate Activity

Materials:
- 12" × 18" white and black construction paper
- pencils
- glue
- scissors
- colored construction paper

1. Select either black or white paper for your background and think of a theme for your work.

2. Begin cutting your organic shapes using colored construction paper and glue them down. Be sure to create harmony among your shapes.

Research in Art Education

Another benefit of fine arts curricula is that it gives "minority cultures an opportunity to express themselves fully, thereby promoting cross-cultural understanding and the elimination of prejudice." One noted gang expert suggests that certain art forms may be "a successful intervention for gang members" ("The Fourth R: The Arts and Learning" in *Schools, Communities, and the Arts: A Research Compendium*).

Assessment

Use the following rubric to evaluate the artwork students make in the Creative Expression activity and to assess students' understanding of harmony using shape and form.

	Art History and Culture	Aesthetic Perception	Creative Expression	Art Criticism
3 POINTS	The student can identify and compare the use of animals based on the artist's location.	The student accurately identifies harmony of shape and form in his or her environment.	The student's animal family clearly illustrates a good use of harmony of shape and form.	The student thoughtfully and honestly evaluates his or her own work using the four steps of art criticism.
2 POINTS	The student's identification or comparison is weak or incomplete.	The student shows emerging awareness of harmony of shape and form, but cannot consistently identify it.	The student's animal family shows some awareness of harmony of shape and form.	The student attempts to evaluate his or her own work, but shows an incomplete understanding of evaluation criteria.
1 POINT	The student cannot identify or compare the use of animals based on the artist's location.	The student cannot identify harmony of shape and form.	The student's animal family shows no understanding of harmony of shape and form.	The student makes no attempt to evaluate his or her own artwork.

Have students complete page 71 or 72 of their *Assessment* books.

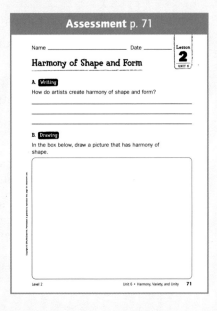

Assessment p. 71

Name _____ Date _____

Harmony of Shape and Form

Lesson 2 UNIT 6

A. Writing
How do artists create harmony of shape and form?

B. Drawing
In the box below, draw a picture that has harmony of shape.

Level 2   Unit 6 • Harmony, Variety, and Unity   71

Variety of Color

Lesson 3 introduces the students to variety of color. Artists create variety using color to create contrast and interest in their art.

Objectives

 Art History and Culture

To recognize how Monet and Lionni's ocean scenes both portray variety of color

 Creative Expression

To create a print of an ocean scene using variety of color

 Aesthetic Perception

To discover that variety of color creates a contrast that keeps viewers interested in a work of art

 Art Criticism

To evaluate own work using the four steps of art criticism

Vocabulary Vocabulary

Review the following vocabulary word with students before beginning the lesson.

variety *variedad*—the use of different lines, shapes, and hues in artwork to create complicated relationships

See page 209B for additional Spanish vocabulary resources.

Art Journal: Vocabulary

Have students add this word to the Vocabulary section of their Art Journals.

Lesson Materials
- 2 laminated posterboards
- 12" × 18" white paper
- crayons
- easel brushes
- blue and green tempera paints
- water spray bottle
- drying rack
- fluorescent or bright red tempera paint
- construction paper scraps
- scissors
- glue
- photo of a squid

Alternate Materials:
- markers
- colored pencils

Program Resources
- *Reading and Writing Test Prep.*, pp. 70–71
- *Transparency 33*
- *Flash Card 16*
- *Artist Profiles*, pp. 33, 40
- *Animals Through History Time Line*
- *Assessment*, pp. 73–74
- *Large Print 36* Quilting Time
- *Art Around the World Collection*

Concept Trace
Variety of Color
Introduced: Level 2, Unit 6, Lesson 3
Reinforced: Level 3, Unit 6, Lesson 2

Lesson 3 Arts Integration

Theatre
Complete Unit 6 Lesson 3 on pages 112–113 of *Theatre Arts Connections*.

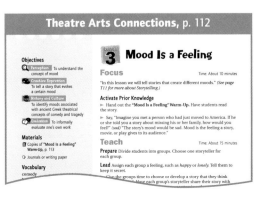

Music
 The contrast of tonal colors in music keeps our interest and also helps us identify the form. Listen to *Hornpipe* from "Water Music Suite" by George Frederic Handel. The strings introduce a melody that is repeated by the oboe and bassoon. What orchestral family do the oboe and bassoon belong to? How does having different instruments play the same melody create variety?

Movement & Dance
Have students identify effort actions that demonstrate contrasting quality and force. Some examples of these movements are: thrust, float, slash, flick, wring, and press. Explore each of these ideas by calling out each word as students improvise with movement. Then create a short movement study that combines three effort actions; take eight counts for each action.

Focus

Time: About 10 minutes

Activate Prior Knowledge

"What do you think of when you think of the ocean?" "¿Qué les viene a la mente cuando piensan en el océano?"

- Listen to student answers about their perceptions of the ocean and encourage class discussion.

Using Literature ⭐ Reading

- Read *To the Depths of the Ocean* by Nicholas Harris. Have students find variety of color.

Thematic Connection ⭐ Science

- **Ocean Life:** Encourage students to think about the ocean and how varied life in the ocean is. Discuss how different sea creatures live in different oceans just as different animals live in different parts of the world.

Introduce the Art

Look NSAE 2.a

"Let's look closely at these two works of art."
"Vamos a mirar detalladamente estas dos obras de arte".

- Have students identify variety in the artwork and their environment.

Fact and Opinion ⭐ Reading

- Discuss with students whether they think these are factual paintings. Why or why not? The Monet work is an actual place that Monet vacationed at and painted many times. Is the Lionni painting factual?

NSAE 4.a, 4.b, 4.c, 5.a, 5.b, 5.c

 Art History and Culture

Possible answer: The ocean was important to Monet and Lionni. Monet painted this particular area of the sea many times. Lionni wrote several books that take place underwater.

 Web Connection

Visit http://www.randomhouse.com/kids/lionni/index.html to learn more about Leo Lionni.

 # Variety of Color

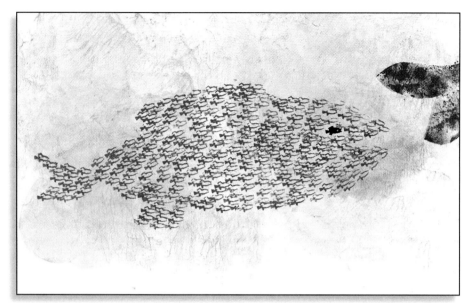

▲ **Leo Lionni.** (Dutch). *Selection from* Swimmy. 1963.

Look at the two works of art. Both are scenes of the sea and use many different colors. These artists used different colors to add interest to their works of art. In the *Swimmy* painting, one fish is a different color. In the Monet painting, the ocean is made of many different colors.

 Art History and Culture

Why did these artists paint pictures of the ocean? What do you think the ocean meant to them?

Art History and Culture

Leo Lionni

Leo Lionni (lē´ ō lē ō´ nē) (1910–1999) was born in Holland. He grew up during social and political revolution and appreciated art at a young age. Without formal experience in children's literature, Lionni began authorship by chance. In 1959 he found himself responsible for entertaining his two grandchildren on a dull train ride. He tore blue and yellow shapes from the pages of a magazine, made his briefcase into a stage, and improvised a story about the two colors. The result was his first book. The bright illustrations in *Swimmy* are created with watercolors, torn paper, and textured crayon collages.

See pages 24–25 and 16–21 for more about art history and subject matter.

Artist Profiles, p. 33

◆ Artist Profile ◆

Leo Lionni
1910–1999

Leo Lionni (lē´ ō lē ō´ nē) was an illustrator, author, critic, art director, painter, sculptor, printmaker, cartoonist, and teacher. Born in the Netherlands, he grew up in an atmosphere of social and political revolution and came to appreciate art at a young age through his uncles' art collections. Without formal training in children's literature, Lionni began writing by chance. In 1959, he found himself responsible for entertaining his two grandchildren on a long and boring train ride. He tore blue and yellow shapes from the pages of a magazine, made his briefcase into a stage, and improvised a story about the two colors. The result was his first book, *Little Blue and Little Yellow*, which was soon

▲ **Claude Monet.** (French).
The Cliff, Etretat, Sunset.
1883.

Oil on canvas. 21 ⅜ × 31 ¾ inches
(55.3 × 80.7 cm.). North Carolina
Museum of Art, Raleigh, North
Carolina.

Study both works of art to find examples of variety of color.

▶ How many different colors do you see in these works of art?

▶ How did Lionni and Monet use colors to create difference and interest?

Aesthetic Perception

Design Awareness What would your classroom look like if everything in it were the same color? How would that make you feel?

Art History and Culture

Claude Monet

Claude Monet (klōd mō nā´)(1840–1926) did not want to be a painter as a young man in France. He already was well paid for drawing caricatures of tourists. Painter Eugene Boudin saw talent in Monet's exaggerated drawings and encouraged him to paint. Monet made a large contribution to the development of impressionism through his ideas and paintings. Monet painted landscapes and people but especially loved scenes that included water. At one time he had a floating studio. He filled a rowboat with art supplies and painted in the shade of a striped awning.

See pages 24–25 and 16–21 for more about art history and subject matter.

Artist Profiles, p. 40

◆ Artist Profile ◆
Claude Monet
1840–1926
Claude Monet (klōd mō nā´) did not want to be a painter as a young man in France. He was already well paid for drawing caricatures of tourists. Painter Eugene Boudin saw talent in Monet's exaggerated drawings and encouraged him to paint. Although artists were "supposed" to paint in studios, Boudin urged Monet to paint outside in the open air. There Monet learned to capture his first impressions on canvas. He recorded these impressions during a long and productive life. His greatest wish was to "mingle more closely with nature."

Study

▶ Answers will vary. Encourage students to name as many colors and hues as they can.

▶ The red fish in the Lionni illustration creates interest. The variation in the water color and the contrast of the dark cliff against the light sky create interest in the Monet painting.

■ For more examples of art from Europe, see the ***Art Around the World Collection.***

Art Journal: Writing

Have students write their own definitions and explanations of *variety of color* in the Concepts section of their Art Journals. Can they name some color groupings that would have variety of color?

Aesthetic Perception

Design Awareness Encourage students to visualize what the classroom would look like if everything in the room were the same color. Have them verbalize their feelings about this. Encourage students to identify variations in objects from their environment.
NSAE 2.b, 5.c
Developing Visual Literacy Have students discuss how the artists' choices of style and media help extend the meaning of the art. How did the style choices of Monet and Lionni add meaning to these works of art? What are they saying?

Web Connection

Visit **http://www.artic.edu/artaccess/AA_Impressionist/pages/IMP_2.shtml** to see more paintings by Monet.

Teach

Time: About 35 minutes

"What makes a picture boring?" "¿Qué hace que una pintura sea aburrida?"

- Read and discuss the information on variety of color on page 196.

Practice

Materials: colored construction paper, scissors, glue, photo of a squid

Alternate Materials: markers, colored pencils

- Distribute the materials and have students follow the directions on page 196.

- Have students identify and practice skills necessary for producing prints using a variety of materials.

NSAE 1.c, 1.d, 2.c, 3.b

Creative Expression

Materials: 2 laminated posterboards, 12" × 18" white paper, crayons, easel brushes, blue and green tempera paints, water spray bottle, drying rack, fluorescent or bright red tempera paint, scraps of construction paper, scissors, glue

Alternate Materials: markers, colored pencils

- Help students wet the laminated posterboard and make their prints. You should demonstrate this technique first.

- Encourage students to express their ideas and feelings in their prints using a variety of colors.

- Encourage students to create effective compositions using design principles.

- Distribute the materials and have students follow the directions on page 197.

- Review the Activity Tips on page 248 for visual examples of the activity techniques if needed.

NSAE 3.a

Art Journal: Brainstorming

Have students sketch creatures they could include in their ocean scene in the Ideas section of their Art Journals. Have them select their favorite idea for use in the Creative Expression activity.

Using Variety of Color

Artists use contrast to create **variety** in their art. Variety makes art more interesting. One way artists can create variety is by using different colors in a work of art. Look at the groupings. Which one has variety because of color?

Practice

Create a construction paper squid using variety of color.

1. Look at the picture of the squid your teacher has.

2. Draw a squid on construction paper. Cut your squid out.

3. Select an eye that will give your squid variety of color. Glue the eye on your squid.

Differentiated Instruction

Reteach
Have students look around the room for things with the same shape but different colors. List their findings on the board.

Special Needs
Engage the multiple senses of students by showing them a video clip of ocean creatures as motivation for this activity.

ELL Tips
Define *variety* and use it in a sentence. Bring different shapes of paper in a variety of colors and sizes to class. Have the students paste them on a paper to create a design.

◄ **Mitchell Pettus.**
Age 7.

Think about how this student used variety of color in his underwater scene.

 **Creative Expression**

What do you think lives in the ocean? Make a print about ocean life.

1. Use crayons and draw the ocean floor on your paper.
2. To create the ocean, lightly apply paint to wet posterboard. Place your paper face down on the paint and rub your paper. Peel the paper away quickly.
3. Let your paper dry. Cut out construction paper sea creatures and glue them to your paper using variety of color.

Art Criticism

Describe What animals live in your ocean?

Analyze Where did you create variety using color?

Interpret How does the variety of color make your ocean more interesting?

Decide What other scenes could you make using variety of color?

Unit 6 • Lesson 3 **197**

 **Reflect** Time: About 10 minutes

Review and Assess

"Is artwork with variety more interesting? Why?" "¿Es más interesante una obra de arte con variedad? ¿Por qué?"

Think

The artist created variety of color by making a red fish.

- Use *Large Print 36* *Quilting Time* to have students look for variety of color.
- Have students identify stories and constructions in this lesson's artwork.
- Have students identify ideas of the artists in this lesson's art.

Informal Assessment

Art Journal: Critical Thinking
Have students answer the four art criticism questions—Describe, Analyze, Interpret, and Decide—in the Critical Thinking section of their Art Journals. Ask students to define their reasons for preferences in their own art. Then have them identify ideas in their peers' art.

- For standardized-format test practice using this lesson's art content, see pages 70–71 in *Reading and Writing Test Preparation.*

NSAE 6.a, 6.b

Art Across the Curriculum

Use these simple ideas to reinforce art concepts across the curriculum.

★ **Descriptive Writing** Have students write a paragraph describing a red boat on a blue sea.

★ **Math** Teach students about the Four Color Theorem.

★ **Science** Discuss how poisonous animals and insects are often a bright color that is different from their environment. Some examples are Poison Dart frogs and Monarch butterflies.

★ **Social Studies** Discuss how money from other countries often has variety of color.

★ **Technology** Show students how to change the color of their text to create variety of color. Visit **SRAonline.com** to print detailed instructions for this activity.

Extra! For the Art Specialist

Time: About 45 minutes

Focus

Study *Large Print 36* and ask students to describe the colors they see. How many colors can they find? Would this image look different if it were only one or two colors? Explain.

Teach

Explain to students that they will create a crayon resist painting of an animal using the spectrum hue order as a background. The spectral hues will provide variety of color. Have students complete the Alternate Activity.

Reflect

Have students evaluate their artwork using the four steps of art criticism.

Alternate Activity

Materials:
- 12" × 18" white drawing paper
- watercolors
- brushes, buckets, and newspapers
- pencils
- permanent black markers
- crayons

1. Discuss variety of color and the order of colors in the spectrum.

2. Sketch an animal on the drawing paper. Add other things in the background and foreground, but keep your picture simple.

3. Trace your drawing with a marker and color it using crayons. Press hard so the drawing looks waxy. Leave the sky white.

4. Paint your sky using watercolor and the order of colors in the spectrum. How does this work display variety of color?

Research in Art Education

"In the role of aesthetic observer, the appreciator functions in a manner which is almost the reverse of the artist's function. For example, the artist has certain emotions which are infused into the work. The appreciator looks at the artist's work and tries to extract those emotions which are inherent in the work. This is not to imply that the emotional state of the contemplative viewer would or should duplicate that of the artist at work. In appreciating artwork the viewer savors what is enjoyed" (Squires, William. *Art Experience and Criticism.* Needham Heights, MA: Ginn Press, 1991).

Assessment
Use the following rubric to evaluate the artwork students make in the Creative Expression activity and to assess students' understanding of variety of color.

Have students complete page 73 or 74 of their *Assessment* books.

	Art History and Culture	Aesthetic Perception	Creative Expression	Art Criticism
3 POINTS	The student can identify and compare the use of variety of color in Monet and Lionni's work.	The student accurately identifies the purpose of variety of color in a work of art.	The student's underwater print clearly illustrates a good use of variety of color.	The student thoughtfully and honestly evaluates his or her own work using the four steps of art criticism.
2 POINTS	The student's identification or comparison is weak or incomplete.	The student shows emerging awareness of variety of color, but cannot consistently identify it.	The student's underwater print shows some awareness of variety of color.	The student attempts to evaluate his or her own work, but shows an incomplete understanding of evaluation criteria.
1 POINT	The student cannot identify or compare the use of variety of color in the different works of art.	The student cannot identify variety of color.	The student's underwater print shows no understanding of variety of color.	The student makes no attempt to evaluate his or her own artwork.

Assessment, p. 73

Name _____ Date _____

Lesson **3** UNIT 6

Variety of Color

A. Defining
Explain what *variety of color* is in your own words.

_____

_____

B. Drawing
In the box below, create a picture that has variety of color.

Level 2   Unit 6 • Harmony, Variety, and Unity   **73**

Lesson 4 Overview

Variety of Shape and Form

Lesson 4 introduces the students to variety of shape and form. Artists can also create variety by varying the shapes and forms used in their art.

Objectives

 Art History and Culture

To recognize that some artists portray things realistically and others use more abstract methods

 Creative Expression

To create a drawing of a fantasy bird using different shapes and forms

Aesthetic Perception

To discover that variety can be created using shapes and forms in everyday objects

Art Criticism

To evaluate own work using the four steps of art criticism

Vocabulary Vocabulary

Review the following vocabulary word with students before beginning the lesson.

monotonous monótono—lack of variety; boring

See page 209B for additional vocabulary and Spanish vocabulary resources.

 Art Journal: Vocabulary

Have students add this word to the Vocabulary section of their Art Journals.

Lesson Materials

- 12 × 18 inch white paper
- black permanent markers
- colored pencils
- watercolors
- brushes
- water containers
- newspapers

Alternate Materials:
- oil pastels
- crayons
- colored markers

Program Resources

- *Reading and Writing Test Prep.*, pp. 72–73
- *Transparency 34*
- *Flash Card 16*
- *Artist Profiles*, pp. 5, 52
- *Animals Through History Time Line*
- *Assessment*, pp. 75–76
- *Large Print 36* Quilting Time
- *Art Around the World Collection*

Concept Trace
Variety of Shape and Form
Introduced: Level 2, Unit 6, Lesson 4
Reinforced: Level 3, Unit 6, Lesson 2

Lesson 4 Arts Integration

Theatre

Complete Unit 6 Lesson 4 on pages 114–115 of *Theatre Arts Connections*.

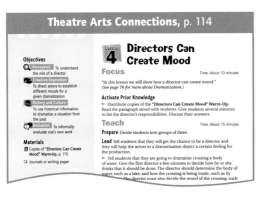

Theatre Arts Connections, p. 114

Music

 In music, form is how the sections of a composition relate to each other, and can be outlined by using a different letter for each new section. For example, *A* is the first section, *B* a contrasting section, and so on. Listen to *Los Mariachis* and note how many times *A* is repeated.

Movement & Dance

Working in groups of five, have students collaborate to create three shapes together using three different levels. Discuss different lines that can be created in the shapes to help build variety.

For example: curved lines that contract, straight lines that stretch, or diagonal lines that pierce through space.

Focus

Activate Prior Knowledge

"Have you ever seen a set of building blocks?"
"¿Alguna vez han visto un conjunto de tacos de madera?"

■ Ask students to think about all of the different shapes of building blocks there are in a set.

Using Literature ⭐ Reading

■ Read *Stellaluna* by Janell Cannon. Discuss the variety of shape in the book.

Thematic Connection ⭐ Science

■ **Birds:** Encourage students to think about different birds and how different types of birds live in different parts of the country.

Introduce the Art

Look NSAE 2.a

"Let's look closely at these two birds." "Vamos a mirar detelladamente estos dos pájaros".

■ Have students identify variety in the artwork and their environment.

Spatial Visualization ⭐ Math

Ask students to visualize what the Schimmel work would look like if it were two-dimensional and what the Audubon work would look like if it were three-dimensional?

NSAE 4.a, 4.b, 4.c, 5.a, 5.b

🏺 Art History and Culture

Possible answer: Every artist has his own style. Audubon traveled the country and painted realistic pictures of birds to document them. Schimmel was a folk artist who was more interested in the idea of making an eagle.

 Web Connection

Visit http://www.audubon.org/ to see the homepage of the National Audubon Society.

 Lesson 4 Variety of Shape and Form

Look at these two birds. These artists used many different shapes and forms to make their works of art interesting. The swan is made of many different shapes. The eagle feathers are many different forms.

▲ **John James Audubon.**
(West Indian/American).
Tundra Swan. 1838.

Historical Museum of Southern Florida.

🏺 Art History and Culture

One bird is realistic, the other is not. Why do you think each artist made his bird in a different way?

🏺 Art History and Culture

John James Audubon

John James Audubon (jän jāmz ô´ də bən) (1785–1851) was born in Santo Domingo, the son of a French sea merchant. His mother died a few months after he was born, so he was raised in France by his father and his wife, who encouraged his love of the outdoors and art. When he was 18, Audubon left France for America and lived on one of his father's plantations in Pennsylvania. Audubon drew birds as a hobby until he and his family met with hard financial times, prompting him to draw and paint America's birds. He would spend weeks painting some of his compositions, painstakingly rendering each feather or nuance of form.

See pages 24–25 and 16–21 for more about art history and subject matter.

Artist Profiles, p. 5

◆ Artist Profile ◆

John James Audubon
1785-1851

John James Audubon (jän jāmz ô´ də bən) was born in Santo Domingo, now Haiti. His mother died a few months after he was born, so he was raised in France by his father and his father's wife, a kind woman who encouraged his love of the outdoors and art. When he was 18, he left France for America to live on one of his father's plantations in Pennsylvania. Audubon drew birds only as a hobby until he and his family met with hard financial times. Audubon's successful journeys established him as a leading romantic painter and expert on ornithology. Years after his death the National Audubon Society was founded in

▲ **Wilhelm Schimmel.**
(American). *Large Eagle.*
....
Paint on pine. 21 $\frac{3}{8}$ × 37 $\frac{3}{4}$ inches
(54.29 × 95.89 cm.). American
Folk Art Museum, New York,
New York.

Study the two works of art to find examples of variety of shape and form.

▶ What different shapes do you see in *Tundra Swan*?

▶ What different forms do you see in *Large Eagle*?

Aesthetic Perception

Design Awareness Look at the art supplies in your room. Where do you see variety of shape and form?

Study

▶ The flowers, shapes of the feathers, lily pads, and parts of the bird are all different shapes in *Tundra Swan*.

▶ The different feathers in the Schimmel eagle all are different forms.

■ For more examples of art from North America, see the *Art Around the World Collection.*

Art Journal: Writing
Have students write about ways to create variety using shape and form in the Concepts section of their Art Journals.

Aesthetic Perception

Design Awareness Encourage students to look closely at the art supplies in the room. Let them share their ideas about how the shapes and forms of the supplies are different. Have students identify variations in objects from the environment.
NSAE 2.b, 5.c
Developing Visual Literacy Have students interpret and evaluate the ways these artists represented the meanings of their work. How do Audubon's detailed drawings and Schimmel's rough carvings tell the viewer what the meanings are behind the works?

Art History and Culture

Wilhelm Schimmel

Wilhelm Schimmel (wil´ helm shim´ məl) (1817–1890) was born in Hesse-Darmstadt, Germany, and moved to Pennsylvania, just after the Civil War. He earned a living by carving birds and animals to sell or to trade for food and a place to sleep. His carvings were not successful, but they are now regarded as some of America's finest folk art. These small carvings were often set aside in attics or storage closets and were not discovered until nearly a century later. The most famous of Schimmel's works are his eagles painted in bright colors and a few inches to a few feet. Schimmel traveled with few possessions, so his works were painted with whatever paint he could find.

See pages 24–25 and 16–21 for more about art history and subject matter.

Artist Profiles, p. 52

♦ Artist Profile ♦
Wilhelm Schimmel
1817–1890
Wilhelm Schimmel (wil´ helm shim´ məl) was born in Hesse-Darmstadt, Germany, and moved to the Cumberland Valley near Carlisle, Pennsylvania, just after the Civil War. He earned a living by carving birds and animals to sell or to trade for food and a place to sleep. At the time of his travels his carvings were not seen as successful works of art, but they are now regarded as some of America's finest folk art pieces and are sold at auctions for thousands of dollars. One characteristic of Schimmel's work is a lack of signature; he never signed his name on his carvings. Because he traded small carvings for meals, they were often set aside in attics or storage closets and were not discovered until nearly a century later.

Web Connection
Visit http://www.artnet.com/magazine/features/karlins/karlins7-11-10.asp to see another Schimmel eagle.

Teach

Time: About 35 minutes

"How many different kinds of circles can you make?" "¿Cuántos tipos diferentes de círculos pueden hacer?"

- Read and discuss the information on variety of shape and form on page 200.

Materials: 12" × 18" white paper, colored pencils

Alternate Materials: markers, crayons

- Distribute the materials and have students follow the directions on page 200.

- Have students identify and practice the skills necessary for producing paintings using a variety of materials.

NSAE 1.c, 1.d, 2.c, 3.b

Creative Expression

Materials: 12" × 18" white paper, black permanent markers, colored pencils, watercolors, brushes, water containers, newspapers

Alternate Materials: oil pastels, crayons, colored markers

- Distribute the materials and have students follow the directions on page 201.

- Encourage students to create effective compositions using design principles.

- Review the Activity Tips on page 248 for visual examples of the activity techniques if needed.

NSAE 3.a

Art Journal: Brainstorming

Have students write a list of qualities they want to incorporate in their fantasy birds in the Ideas section of their Art Journals. Have them select their favorite ideas for use in the Creative Expression activity.

Using Variety of Shape and Form

Artists can create variety by using different shapes and forms in a work of art. By creating variety, artists can make their art more interesting to the viewer. If everything in a work of art were the same shape, the art would be **monotonous** and boring. Look at the pictures. Which one has more variety of shape?

Practice

Draw the wing of a bird using variety of shapes.

1. Draw the wing of a bird.
2. Add feathers to the wing using different shapes.
3. Where are the different shapes on your wing? Did you create variety?

200 Unit 6 • Lesson 4

Differentiated Instruction

Reteach

Have students use modeling clay to create a grouping of objects that has variety of form. They may wish to etch lines on the objects that would also give them variety of shape.

Special Needs

Ensure student success in this project by providing a brief visual review of different shapes at the beginning of the lesson. Keep these shapes displayed for students to refer to as needed.

ELL Tips

Use the word *variety* in a sentence. Show students a range of red circles and then a range of red rectangles. Ask them how the shapes are different.

200 UNIT 6 • Harmony, Variety, and Unity

◀ **Rachel Yates.**
Age 7.

Think about how this student used variety of shape in her bird.

 Creative Expression

What kind of bird would you make? Create a fantasy bird using variety of shape.

1. Draw a fantasy bird. Make it large.
2. Outline your bird with black marker. Add pattern to your bird using black marker.
3. Use colored pencils to color the bird. Paint the background using watercolors.

Art Criticism

Describe What does your fantasy bird look like?

Analyze How did you use different shapes to create variety on your bird?

Interpret How would your bird be different if you had not used variety of shape?

Decide Did the variety of shapes you used make your bird more interesting?

Unit 6 • Lesson 4 **201**

 **Reflect**

Review and Assess

"How can you create variety using shapes and forms?" "Cómo pueden crear variedad usando las figuras y las formas?"

Think

The artist created variety by decorating her swan's neck with different shapes.

- Use *Large Print 36* Quilting Time to have students identify variety of shape.
- Have students identify stories and constructions in this lesson's artwork.
- Have students identify ideas of the artists in this lesson's art.

Informal Assessment

Art Journal: Critical Thinking
Have students answer the four art criticism questions—Describe, Analyze, Interpret, and Decide—in the Critical Thinking section of their Art Journals. Ask students to define their reasons for preferences in their own art. Then have them identify ideas in their peers' art.

- For standardized-format test practice using this lesson's art content, see pages 72–73 in *Reading and Writing Test Preparation.*

Art Across the Curriculum   NSAE 6.a, 6.b

Use these simple ideas to reinforce art concepts across the curriculum.

★ **Narrative Writing** Have students retell the story of *The Ugly Duckling* in their own words and emphasize the variety of form.

★ **Math** Have students look at Arabic numbers compared to other numbering systems. Which has more variety of shape?

★ **Science** Discuss how body parts on animals are adapted to fit their environments and functions so that there is variety of form in a family of animals. For example, the mammal family.

★ **Social Studies** Have students examine objects that are significant to the community and look for variety of shape and form.

★ **Technology** Show students how to change the fonts they use within a document. Visit **SRAonline.com** to print detailed instructions for this activity.

Variety of Shape and Form

Extra! For the Art Specialist

 Time: About 45 minutes

Focus

Study **Large Print 36** and ask students to point out and name the shapes they see. Are all of the shapes the same? How would this image look if only two shapes had been used? Why would an artist choose to use a variety of shapes and forms in his or her work?

Teach

Explain to students that they will create a mobile. The moving sculptures will be made by forming and joining wire and will include a variety of shapes and forms. Have the students complete the Alternate Activity.

Reflect

Have students evaluate their artwork using the four steps of art criticism.

Alternate Activity

Materials:
- thin and thick wire
- string
- wire snips (for the teacher only)
- images of Alexander Calder's mobiles

1. Study the images of mobiles and discuss mobiles as an art form.

2. Demonstrate how to form shapes with the wire by bending and twisting it.

3. Place containers at each table containing wire, scissors and string. Begin by making the top of your mobile and joining strings to suspend smaller shapes.

4. Create smaller shapes and attach them to the strings. Use a variety of shapes.

Research in Art Education

"Only through a multifaceted education program that develops divergent as well as convergent thinking—that encourages intuitive as well as rational thought processes—can today's young learner begin to be prepared to cope with the rapidly changing aspects of a technology-oriented world" (Herberholz, Barbara, and Lee Hanson. *Early Childhood Art*. New York: McGraw-Hill, 1994).

Assessment

Use the following rubric to evaluate the artwork students make in the Creative Expression activity and to assess students' understanding of variety of shape and form.

Have students complete page 75 or 76 of their *Assessment* books.

	Art History and Culture	Aesthetic Perception	Creative Expression	Art Criticism
3 POINTS	The student can identify and compare the style of two works of art.	The student accurately identifies variety of shape and form in everyday objects.	The student's fantasy bird clearly illustrates a good use of variety of shape and form.	The student thoughtfully and honestly evaluates his or her own work using the four steps of art criticism.
2 POINTS	The student's identification or comparison is weak or incomplete.	The student shows emerging awareness of variety of shape and form, but cannot consistently identify it.	The student's fantasy bird shows some awareness of variety of shape and form.	The student attempts to evaluate his or her own work, but shows an incomplete understanding of evaluation criteria.
1 POINT	The student cannot identify or compare the style of two works of art.	The student cannot identify variety of shape and form.	The student's fantasy bird shows no understanding of variety of shape and form.	The student makes no attempt to evaluate his or her own artwork.

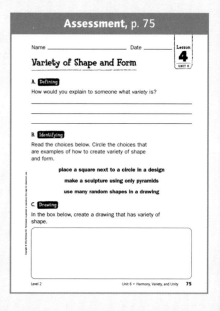

Assessment, p. 75

Name _____ Date _____
Lesson **4** UNIT 6

Variety of Shape and Form

A Defining
How would you explain to someone what *variety* is?

B Identifying
Read the choices below. Circle the choices that are examples of how to create variety of shape and form.

place a square next to a circle in a design

make a sculpture using only pyramids

use many random shapes in a drawing

C Drawing
In the box below, create a drawing that has variety of shape.

Level 2   Unit 6 • Harmony, Variety, and Unity   **75**

 **Lesson 5**

Unity in Sculpture

Overview

Lesson 5 introduces the students to unity in sculpture. Unity in sculpture can be used to make many smaller sculptures into a larger work of art.

Objectives

 Art History and Culture

To learn that some carousels feature exotic animals, and not horses

 Creative Expression

To create a stuffed paper carousel animal and create a class carousel

 Aesthetic Perception

To find unity in objects in students' environments

 Art Criticism

To evaluate own work using the four steps of art criticism

Vocabulary ⭐ Vocabulary

Review the following vocabulary word with students before beginning the lesson.

unity unidad—the feeling that parts of a work of art belong together. Unity is created by balancing harmony and variety

See page 209B for additional Spanish vocabulary resources.

Art Journal: Vocabulary

Have students add this word to the Vocabulary section of their Art Journals.

Lesson Materials
- 12 × 18 inch white drawing paper
- oil pastels
- watercolors
- brushes
- water dishes
- newspaper
- cardboard tubes
- white school glue

Alternate Materials:
- markers
- crayons

Program Resources
- *Reading and Writing Test Prep.*, pp. 74–75
- *Transparency 35*
- *Flash Card 18*
- *Artist Profiles*, p. 16
- *Animals Through History Time Line*
- *Assessment*, pp. 77–78
- *Large Prints 35* Still Music and *36* Quilting Time
- *The National Museum of Women in the Arts Collection*

Concept Trace
Unity in sculpture
Introduced: Level 1, Unit 6, Lessons 5–6
Reinforced: Level 3, Unit 6, Lessons 5–6

Lesson 5 Arts Integration

Theatre

Complete Unit 6 Lesson 5 on pages 116–117 of *Theatre Arts Connections*.

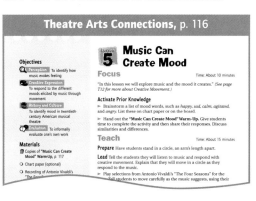

Theatre Arts Connections, p. 116

Music

SPOTLIGHT on MUSIC

Listen to *Canon in D Major* by Pachebel. The three high voices are playing the same melodic material but entering at different times, therefore creating the *canon*. Singing a round is similar to a canon, except in a canon everyone stops together. The bass line of the canon, or *continuo* is supposed to create unity in the composition. Is the continuo successful?

Movement & Dance

In small groups, have students create a dynamic sculpture that shows unity. Each person in the group finds a separate place at the edge of the room to begin. Take eight counts to travel to the center and make the unified group sculpture. How does it feel to begin in separation from the group and end up in unity? Try it in reverse, beginning in unity and then peeling off one by one to each exit in a different way and direction.

 **Focus**

Time: About 10 minutes

Activate Prior Knowledge

"Have you ever seen a carousel?" "¿Alguna vez han visto un carrusel?"

■ Ask students to talk about carousels and their experiences riding them.

Using Literature 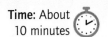 Reading

■ Read *Carousel* by Donald Crews. Have students find examples of unity in the book.

Thematic Connection Science

■ **Recreation:** Encourage students to think about the ways that people have entertained themselves throughout history and how that has changed.

Introduce the Art

Look NSAE 2.a

"Let's look closely at the carousel art."
"Vamos a mirar detalladamente la obra de un carrusel".

■ Have students identify unity in the works of art and the environment.

Making Connections Reading

■ Discuss how these two pieces of art are related. What kind of connections can the students make between the two works of art?

NSAE 4.a, 4.b, 4.c, 5.a, 5.b

 Art History and Culture

This carousel was made at a time when carousels were very popular throughout the country. The artist made his carousel elaborate so that it would stand apart from other carousels.

 Web Connection

Visit **http://www.castlepark.com/carousel2.html** for a history of the Dentzel Company.

 Lesson **5** Unity in Sculpture

◄ **Dentzel Company.** (American). *Carousel.* c. 1905.

Ontario Beach, Rochester, New York.

Look at these two works of art. One is a carousel. The other is a carousel animal. There are many different animals on the carousel, but when they are put together, they create one unified carousel.

 Art History and Culture

Many carousels were made using only horses. Why do you think this artist used so many different animals?

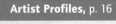 **Art History and Culture**

Dentzel Company

Carousels became popular in America during the early 1900s. Although they were invented in Europe, the rotating carnival rides were redesigned and improved upon in the United States, becoming more grand and elaborate as their popularity increased. After the turn of the twentieth century, the majority of large, ornate carousels were located in the states of New York and California, although by the 1920s, industrious craftsmen began building them in cities all over the United States. The Dentzel Company carved their carousel animals from wood. The animals were painted with realistic detail and were sometimes given real horsehair tails.

See pages 24–25 and 16–21 for more about art history and subject matter.

Artist Profiles, p. 16

Artist Profile

The Dentzel Company

The Dentzel Company was started by Gustav A. Dentzel, a woodcarver who immigrated to America from Europe and settled in Philadelphia in 1860. Gustav Dentzel had already begun his career carving carousel horses in his native Germany, where he had learned the trade from his father. After arriving in America soon after his twentieth birthday Dentzel opened a cabinet making shop. Within seven years' time he succeeded in shifting the focus of his business to building steam- and horse-powered carousels.

◄ **Dentzel Company, Philadelphia.** (American).

◀ **Dentzel Company, Philadelphia.**
(American). *Carousel Rabbit*. 1915.
....
Paint on wood with glass. 57 $\frac{1}{4}$ × 49 × 12 $\frac{1}{2}$
inches (145.42 × 124.46 × 31.75 cm.).
American Folk Art Museum, New York, New York.

Study the two works of art to find examples
of unity in sculpture.

▶ What kind of animals do you see on the
carousel? Are they all the same?

▶ How do the animals on the carousel work
together to make one object?

 Aesthetic Perception

Design Awareness Look at a box of crayons. There
are many crayons, but when put together they make
one set. What other items do you see that make a set?

Study

▶ Horses, giraffes, pigs, cats, ostriches, and
so on. There are many different animals.

▶ Even though the animals are different,
they work together to create one carousel.

■ For more examples of utilitarian art, see
*The National Museum of Women in the
Arts Collection.*

Art Journal: Writing
Have students write their own
definitions of *unity* in the Concepts
section of their Art Journals.

Aesthetic Perception

Design Awareness Encourage students to
brainstorm how individual items can make
up a set. Some examples are textbooks on a
shelf and milk cartons in the cooler.
Encourage students to identify variations in
the objects from their environments.
NSAE 2.a, 5.c
Developing Visual Literacy Discuss with
students how the artist's choice of style
and media adds to the meaning of the
carousel art.

Art History and Culture

Dentzel Company

The Dentzel Company was started by Gustav A. Dentzel, a woodcarver who immigrated to America from Europe and settled in
Philadelphia in 1860. After arriving in America soon after his
twentieth birthday, Dentzel opened a cabinet-making shop. Within
seven years' time, he succeeded in shifting the focus of his business
to building carousels. Designing and perfecting the carousels
themselves and carving the magnificently detailed and beautiful
animals became Dentzel's life work. His son, William, continued
what had become the family
tradition, building carousels
and their horses, and running
the Dentzel Company until
his death in 1928. At that
time, the company was sold
outside the Dentzel family.

See pages 24–25 and 16–21
for more about art history
and subject matter.

Artist Profiles, p. 16

◀ Artist Profile ◦

**The Dentzel
Company**

The Dentzel Company was started by
Gustav A. Dentzel, a woodcarver who
immigrated to America from Europe and
settled in Philadelphia in 1860. Gustav
Dentzel had already begun his career
carving carousel horses in his native
Germany, where he had learned the trade
from his father. After arriving in America
soon after his twentieth birthday Dentzel
opened a cabinet making shop. Within
seven years' time he succeeded in shifting
the focus of his business to building steam-
and horse-powered carousels.

◀ **Dentzel Company, Philadelphia.** (American).

Web Connection
Visit **http://www.ggw.org/frc/index.htm** to learn
more about the Dentzel carousel at Ontario Beach.

Teach

"How many different parts do you think a washing machine has?" "¿Cúantos partes diferentes creen que tiene una lavadora?"

- Read and discuss the information on unity in sculpture on page 204.

Practice

Materials: 12" × 18" white drawing paper, oil pastels

Alternate Materials: markers, crayons

- Distribute the materials and have students follow the directions on page 204.

- Have students identify and practice the skills necessary for producing constructions using a variety of materials.

NSAE 1.c, 1.d, 2.c, 3.b

 ## Creative Expression

Materials: 12" × 18" inch white drawing paper, oil pastels, watercolors, brushes, water dishes, newspaper, cardboard tubes, white school glue

Alternate Materials: markers, crayons

- Distribute the materials and have students follow the directions on page 205.

- Students will need help placing their cardboard tubes and stuffing their animals.

- Encourage students to create effective compositions using design principles.

- Review the Activity Tips for visual examples of the activity techniques if needed.

NSAE 3.a

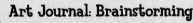

Art Journal: Brainstorming

Encourage students to keep a list of their favorite animals and sketch a plan for the class carousel. Have them keep a list in the Ideas section of their Art Journals.

Using Unity in Sculpture

Artists balance variety and harmony to create **unity.** When a work of art has unity, the viewer feels like everything in the work of art belongs together and that nothing could be removed without changing the work of art. Unity brings all the elements in a work of art together. Look at the pictures. Which one has more unity?

Practice

Sketch objects that have unity.

1. Think of items that have unity, like a block of buildings, or a chest of toys.

2. Sketch one of these items on your paper.

3. What parts in your drawing come together to create unity?

Differentiated Instruction

Reteach

In small groups have students role-play their ideas for unity.

Special Needs

Sequence instruction for students with disabilities by breaking down the project into concise steps. Show students the ways that the project will look at various stages and keep these examples displayed until the lesson is complete.

ELL Tips

Define the word *unity* and ask for students to volunteer using the word in a sentence.

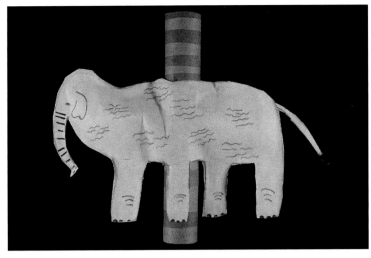

◀ **Rosemary Ankerich.**
Age 7.

Think about how this student's animal could be used to create unity in a carousel.

Creative Expression

How would you create a class carousel? Create a carousel animal.

1. Draw an animal. Add details and paint the animal.

2. Cut the animal out and glue it to a sheet of paper. Do not put glue where the pole will go.

3. Stuff the animal with paper. Insert the pole into the space left for it and glue it in place.

4. Arrange your animals with your class to create a carousel.

Art Criticism

Describe What type of animal did you choose and why?

Analyze What lines and shapes did you use on your animal?

Interpret What unifies your class carousel?

Decide What other things could you have done to give your carousel unity?

Unit 6 • Lesson 5 **205**

**eflect** Time: About 10 minutes

Review and Assess

"How do you create unity in art?" "¿Cómo crean unidad en una obra de arte?"

Think

The artist's animal could be arranged with the rest of her class to create unity.

■ Use **Large Prints 35** *Still Music* and **36** *Quilting Time* to have students identify unity.

■ Have students identify stories and constructions in this lesson's artwork.

■ Have students identify ideas of the artists in this lesson's art.

Informal Assessment

Art Journal: Critical Thinking
Have students answer the four art criticism questions—Describe, Analyze, Interpret, and Decide—in the Critical Thinking section of their Art Journals. Have students define their reasons for preferences in their own art. Then have them identify ideas in their peers' art.

■ For standardized-format test practice using this lesson's art content, see pages 74–75 in **Reading and Writing Test Preparation.**

NSAE 6.a, 6.b
• Art Across the Curriculum •

Use these simple ideas to reinforce art concepts across the curriculum.

★ **Poetry** Have students write a poem about a carousel.

★ **Math** Show students different number families, such as even numbers, multiples of five, and multiples of ten, and ask them to find unity.

★ **Science** Discuss how different groups of animals are united by common properties, for instance, the traits of mammals.

★ **Social Studies** Discuss how several states are unified to make a country.

★ **Technology** Ask students to name the parts of a computer that joined together, create unity in the computer. For example, the keyboard, monitor, and hard drive. Visit **SRAonline.com** to print detailed instructions for this activity.

Unity in Sculpture

Extra! For the Art Specialist

Time: About 45 minutes

Focus

Show students *Large Prints 35* and *36* and have them look for unity. How would they explain unity?

Teach

Explain to students that they will create an original miniature mask from clay. They will form the mask by pinching a shape and then create a design. The masks will then be arranged as a class to create unity in sculpture. Have the students complete the Alternate Activity.

Reflect

Have students evaluate their artwork using the four steps of art criticism.

Alternate Activity

Materials:
- clay
- mats to work on
- clay tools
- tempera paint
- brushes, buckets, and newspapers

1. Discuss unity in sculpture and talk about making masks. Demonstrate how to roll the clay into a ball and flatten it. Either form the clay mask or use the tools to cut out the shape you want.

2. Create a mask by pinching and joining clay. When the mask is fired, paint it one color.

3. Arrange your mask with your classmates' to create unity in sculpture.

Research in Art Education

Arts involvement increases student self-image. Students involved in the arts are "far more likely that their low-arts counterparts to think of themselves as competent in academics" ("Learning in and Through the Arts: Curriculum Implications" in *Champions of Change*, p. 40).

Assessment

Use the following rubric to evaluate the artwork students make in the Creative Expression activity and to assess students' understanding of unity in sculpture.

Have students complete page 77 or 78 of their *Assessment* books.

	Art History and Culture	Aesthetic Perception	Creative Expression	Art Criticism
3 POINTS	The student can identify that some carousels feature animals other than horses.	The student accurately identifies unity in his or her environment.	The student's stuffed paper animal clearly illustrates a good use of unity in sculpture.	The student thoughtfully and honestly evaluates his or her own work using the four steps of art criticism.
2 POINTS	The student's identification is weak or incomplete.	The student shows emerging awareness of unity, but cannot consistently identify it.	The student's stuffed paper animal shows some awareness of unity in sculpture.	The student attempts to evaluate his or her own work, but shows an incomplete understanding of evaluation criteria.
1 POINT	The student cannot identify that some carousels feature animals other than horses.	The student cannot identify unity.	The student's stuffed paper animal shows no understanding of unity in sculpture.	The student makes no attempt to evaluate his or her own artwork.

Assessment, p. 77

Name _____ Date _____ Lesson **5** UNIT 6

Unity in Sculpture

A. Short Answer
What is *unity*?
_____
_____

B. Drawing
In the box below, create and sketch a plan for a sculpture that has unity.

Level 2   Unit 6 • Harmony, Variety, and Unity **77**

Lesson 6 Unity in Architecture

Overview

Lesson 6 introduces the students to unity in architecture. Unity in architecture occurs when buildings are designed so that different elements come together to create a feeling of continuity in the building.

Objectives

 Art History and Culture

To recognize that unity in architecture can be seen in ancient and modern buildings

 Creative Expression

To design a cityscape on the computer that shows unity in architecture

 Aesthetic Perception

To recognize that unity in buildings in students' environments

Art Criticism

To evaluate own work using the four steps of art criticism

Vocabulary  Vocabulary

Review the following vocabulary words with students before beginning the lesson.

column columna—a supporting pillar on a building

architecture arquitectura—the study of buildings

architects arquitectos—highly trained artists and engineers who design buildings

See page 209B for additional Spanish vocabulary resources.

 Art Journal: Vocabulary

Have students add these words to the Vocabulary section of their Art Journals.

Lesson Materials
- crayons
- 12 × 18 inch white paper
- computer with a drawing or painting program

Alternate Materials:
- markers
- colored pencils

Program Resources
- *Reading and Writing Test Prep.,* pp. 76–77
- *Transparency 36*
- *Flash Card 18*
- *Artist Profiles,* pp. 50, 77
- *Animals Through History Time Line*
- *Assessment,* pp. 79–80
- *Large Prints 35 Still Music* and *36 Quilting Time*
- *Art Around the World Collection*

Concept Trace
Unity in Architecture
Introduced: Level 1, Unit 6, Lessons 5–6

Reinforced: Level 3, Unit 6, Lessons 5–6

Lesson 6 Arts Integration

Theatre

Complete Unit 6, Lesson 6, on pages 118–123 of *Theatre Arts Connections.*

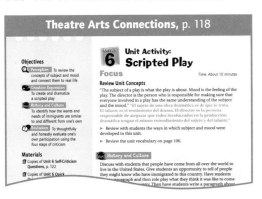

Music

 Listen to *Russian Sailors' Dance* from The Red Poppy by Reinhold Gliere. Different instruments repeat the same theme to give the piece unity despite changes in tempo and register. Have students listen to the piece and describe how the contrasting instruments are working together to create unity.

Movement & Dance

In groups of five, create a collaborative, dynamic shape showing unity. Choose three line patterns to work with, finding a way to connect and overlap them to give a sense of unity. Each person in the group should find a separate place at the edge of the room to begin. Using one of the line patterns as a pathway, each group travels to the center to make the unified group shape.

Activate Prior Knowledge

"Have you ever noticed how some buildings seem to stand out and others blend in with their settings?" "¿Alguna vez han notado cómo algunos edificios parecen resaltar y otros parecen mezclarse con sus alrededores?"

- Discuss the difference between a house or office building that sticks out and one that harmonizes with the other buildings in the area.

Using Literature Reading

- Read *A Picnic in October* by Eve Bunting. Have students discuss the importance of monuments.

Thematic Connection ⭐ Social Studies

- **Society:** Encourage students to think about why buildings are created and how different buildings are used

Introduce the Art

Look NSAE 2.a

"Let's look closely at these two buildings." "Vamos a mirar detalladamente estos dos edificios".

- Have students identify unity in the artwork and their environment.

Human Settlement ⭐ Social Studies

- Have students examine these two buildings and discuss their possible uses. Why do they think they were designed? What were they used for?

NSAE 4.a, 4.b, 4.c, 5.a, 5.b

🏺 Art History and Culture

Possible answer: The temple was probably used for official business or important events. The tower is more decorative than useful.

💻 **Web Connection**

Visit **http://harpy.uccs.edu/roman/temples.htm** to see other examples of Roman temples.

▲ **Artist Unknown.** (Roman). *Maison Carrée.* 1st century B.C.

Nimes, France.

Look at these two buildings. **Columns** go around the Roman temple to give it unity. Rodia combined many small towers and found objects to create unity in *Watts Tower.*

🏺 Art History and Culture

What do you think these buildings were used for?

🏺 Art History and Culture

Maison Carrée

The large, stone temple Maison Carrée was built during the first century, B.C., under the direction of Marcus Vipsanius Agrippa, the son-in-law of the Roman emperor Augustus. Maison Carrée means "square house" in French. He established impressive urban centers in the Roman provinces. The city of Nimes, located in southern France, was under Roman control when Maison Carrée was built. Stonemasons cut precisely measured stones to build Maison Carrée. The methods used to build the temple were technologically advanced for the time, and are still impressive today.

See pages 24–25 and 16–21 for more about art history and subject matter.

Artist Profiles, p. 77

Artist Profile

Maison Carrée

The large stone temple *Maison Carrée* was built during the first century, B.C. under the direction of Marcus Vipsanius Agrippa, the son-in-law of the Roman emperor Augustus. *Maison Carree* means "square house" in French.

◄ **Artist unknown.** (France). *Maison Carrée.* c. First century B.C.

Limestone. Nimes, France.

is characteristic of Roman architecture. The frieze

◀ **Simon Rodia.** *Watts Tower.*
1921–1954.
· ·
Steel rods, wire mesh, concrete, and found
objects. Watts, Los Angeles, California.

Study both works of art to find examples of
unity in architecture.

▶ What parts of each building are repeated?

▶ What similarities do you see in the forms in
these buildings?

Aesthetic Perception

Seeing Like an Artist Think of buildings that you
see in your community. What parts on the buildings
work together to create unity?

Study

▶ The towers are repeated in *Watts Tower*.
The columns and steps are repeated in the
temple.

▶ The towers and the columns look similar
because they are long and tall.

■ For more examples of art from Europe, see
the ***Art Around the World Collection.***

Art Journal: Writing

Have students write about times
they saw buildings with unity in the
Concepts section of their Art Journals.

Aesthetic Perception

Seeing Like an Artist Encourage students to
think of different buildings in the
community. It might be helpful to have them
name buildings, such as post office,
courthouse, etc. Encourage students to
identify variations in objects from their
environments.   NSAE 2.b, 5.c

Developing Visual Literacy Have students
make a careful observation of the
surroundings of these buildings. What can
they tell about the buildings based on the
surrounds? What can they tell about the
buildings based on the materials used to
create them?

Art History and Culture

Simon Rodia

Simon Rodia (sē´ mōn rō dē´ ä) (1875–1965) was born in Italy.
He moved to the United States when he was 14 years old. Every
evening, weekend, and holiday, he built towers and sculptures
in his yard in Los Angeles. He worked for 33 years to build his
fantastic towers. By the age of 75, Rodia had grown tired of his
neighbors laughing at him for making his art. He completed all
the sculptures in his yard and moved away from Los Angeles.
Rodia collected more than 70,000 seashells to create his work.

He disassembled many pipe
structures and steel bed
frames. He salvaged
truckloads of ceramic tiles
and glass bottles from other
people's trash.

See pages 24–25 and 16–21
for more about art history
and subject matter.

Artist Profiles, p. 50

◆ Artist Profile ◆
Simon Rodia
c. 1875–1965
Simon Rodia (sē´ mōn rō dē´ ä) was born in
Avelino, Italy. He moved to the United States
when he was 14 years old. He lived with his
brother in Pittsburgh for a few years and
then moved to California. He worked during
the day as a tile setter for a construction
company. Every evening, weekend, and
holiday he built towers and sculptures in his
yard in Los Angeles. He liked to read about
heroes in history, such as Marco Polo,
Christopher Columbus, and Galileo. Rodia
once said that a person has to do "good
good" or "bad bad" to be remembered. He
worked for 33 years to build his fantastic
Watts Towers. By the age of 75, Rodia had
grown tired of his neighbors laughing at him
for making his art. He completed all the…

Web Connection

Visit **http://www.arts.ufl.edu/art/rt_room/
watts/tower.html** to learn more about the
Watts Towers.

each

Time: About 35 minutes

"How many different shapes can we find in our classroom?" "¿Cuántos figuras diferentes podemos encontrar en nuestro salón de clases?"

- Read and discuss the information on unity in architecture on page 208.

Practice

Materials: crayons, 12 × 18 inch white paper

Alternate Materials: markers, colored pencils

Alternate Materials: colored pencils

- Distribute the materials and have students follow the directions on page 208.

- Have students identify and practice skills necessary for producing drawings using a variety of materials.

NSAE 1.c, 1.d, 2.c, 3.b

Creative Expression

Materials: computer with a drawing or painting program

- Have students follow the directions on page 209.

- Encourage students to create effective compositions using design principles.

- Review the Activity Tips on page 249 for visual examples of the activity techniques if needed.

 Art Journal: Listing

Have students make a list of items that would help create unity in their cityscape in the Ideas section of their Art Journals.

Using Unity in Architecture

Architecture is the study of buildings. When buildings are designed, **architects** decide how the parts of a building will work together to create one building. This gives the building unity. Look at this building. What parts work together to create unity?

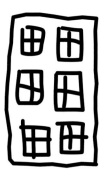

Practice

Draw a building that has unity.

1. Think of different objects that you see on buildings.
2. Choose an object, and draw a building by repeating that object.
3. How does your building have unity?

Differentiated Instruction

Reteach
Have students use connecting blocks to create a building that has unity.

Special Needs
Encourage the development of students' expressive language skills by asking them to describe what is inside each building they created.

ELL Tips
Ask students how a building can be harmonious. What adds textures to a building? What unifies a structure?

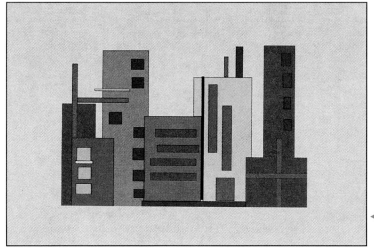

◄ **Andrew Neesmith.** Age 7.

Think about how this student created unity in his buildings.

 Creative Expression

How would you design a city? Draw a city that has unity using the computer.

1. Think of what your cityscape would look like.

2. Use the drawing tool and shape tools to make your buildings.

3. Add any details you wish.

Art Criticism

Describe Explain the design of your cityscape.

Analyze What parts of each building did you repeat?

Interpret How did you create unity in your cityscape?

Decide If you were going to design another cityscape, would you use unity?

Unit 6 • Lesson 6 **209**

Art Across the Curriculum NSAE 6.a, 6.b

Use these simple ideas to reinforce art concepts across the curriculum.

★ **Personal Writing** Have students pretend to be an architect designing a major structure. Have them write a letter to the town planning committee explaining how they will create unity in their structure.

★ **Math** Practice basic operations using the number of visible columns on Maison Carrée and the number of Rodia's towers.

★ **Science** Discuss the different properties of materials that are used for construction.

★ **Social Studies** Discuss the reasons why human beings build monuments.

★ **Technology** Discuss how architects could use computers to design buildings and create 3-D models. Visit **SRAonline.com** to print detailed instructions for this activity.

 **Reflect** Time: About 10 minutes

Review and Assess

"What elements can architects use to unify buildings?" "¿Qué elementos pueden usar los arquitectos para unificar los edificios?"

Think

The artist created unity in architecture by making his buildings all squares and rectangles and using many windows.

▪ Use *Large Prints 35 Still Music* and *36 Quilting Time* to have students identify unity.

▪ Have students search for and identify stories and constructions in this lesson's artwork.

▪ Have students identify ideas of the artists in this lesson's art.

Informal Assessment

Art Journal: Critical Thinking
Have students answer the four art criticism questions—Describe, Analyze, Interpret, and Decide—in the Critical Thinking section of their Art Journals. Ask students to define their reasons for preferences in their art. Then have them identify ideas in their peers' art.

▪ For standardized-format test practice using this lesson's art content, see pages 76–77 in *Reading and Writing Test Preparation*.

Unity in Architecture

Time: About 45 minutes

Focus

Show students *Large Prints 35* and *36* to have students look for unity. Where do they see unity in these prints? What elements are repeated?

Teach

Explain to students that they will create a city scene using found objects. They will choose what kind of a city to make. The students will use repeating shapes and objects to create unity in their work. Have students complete the Alternate Activity.

Reflect

Have students evaluate their artwork using the four steps of art criticism.

Alternate Activity

Materials:

- cardboard for a city base
- found objects like raw pasta, buttons, and so on
- small cardboard boxes
- construction paper
- glue
- scissors
- brushes, buckets, and newspapers
- tempera paints

1. Brainstorm different kinds of cities.

2. Select materials. Glue, cut, and organize the materials on the cardboard base to create a city.

3. When the glue is dry, paint your city. How did you create unity in architecture?

Research
in Art Education

"The purposes of Art Education are to build awareness of the aesthetic components in human experience: the feeling of kinship between the young 'artist-analyst' and the traditions of artistic creation and comprehension of the language of visual form as embodied and as experienced through the visual impact of everyday objects" (*Report of the Commission on Art Education*, 1965, NAEA).

Assessment

Use the following rubric to evaluate the artwork students make in the Creative Expression activity and to assess students' understanding of unity in architecture.

	Art History and Culture	Aesthetic Perception	Creative Expression	Art Criticism
3 POINTS	The student can identify and compare the use of unity in architecture in two buildings from different periods.	The student accurately identifies unity in architecture in his or her environment.	The student's cityscape clearly illustrates a good use of unity in architecture.	The student thoughtfully and honestly evaluates his or her own work using the four steps of art criticism.
2 POINTS	The student's identification or comparison is weak or incomplete.	The student shows emerging awareness of unity in architecture, but cannot consistently identify it.	The student's cityscape shows some awareness of unity in architecture.	The student attempts to evaluate his or her own work, but shows an incomplete understanding of evaluation criteria.
1 POINT	The student cannot identify or compare the use of unity in architecture in two buildings from different periods.	The student cannot identify unity in architecture.	The student's cityscape shows no understanding of unity in architecture.	The student makes no attempt to evaluate his or her own artwork.

Have students complete page 79 or 80 of their *Assessment* books.

Assessment, p. 79

Name _____ Date _____

Unity in Architecture

Lesson **6** UNIT 6

A. Short Answer

What is *architecture*? What is an *architect*?

_____

B. Drawing

In the box below, draw a picture of a building that has unity.

Level 2   Unit 6 • Harmony, Variety, and Unity   **79**

architects—Highly trained artists and engineers who design buildings. **arquitectos**—artistas sumamente entrenados e ingenieros que diseñan edificios

architecture—The study of buildings. **arquitectura**—el studio de edificios

column—A supporting pillar on a building. **columna**—una columna de soporte en un edificio

harmony—A principle of design that helps create unity by showing how objects in a work of art are similar. **armonía**—un principio de diseño que ayuda a crear unidad enseñando como objetos en una obra de arte son parecidos

monotonous—Lack of variety; boring. **monotóno**—falta de variedad; aburrido

proportions—Size relationships between parts. **proporciones**—la relacion de tamaño entre partes

unity— The feeling that parts of a work of art belong together. Unity is created by balancing harmony and variety. **unidad**—la sensación de que partes de una obra de arte pertenecen juntas. La unidad es creada equilibrando la armonía y la variedad

variety—The use of different lines, shapes, and hues in art to create complicated relationships. **variedad**—el uso de líneas, figuras y colores diferentes en obras artísticas para crear relaciones comlejas

Vocabulary Practice

T Display **Transparency 42** to review unit vocabulary words.

Alphabetizing ☆ Vocabulary
Have students select four unit vocabulary words and alphabetize them.

Examples ☆ Vocabulary
Have students select three unit vocabulary words and create picture examples to illustrate the definitions.

Word Walls ☆ Vocabulary
Have students create a word wall using the unit vocabulary words.

Wrapping Up Unit 6

Harmony, Variety, and Unity

 Art Criticism

Critical Thinking Art criticism is an organized system for looking at and talking about art. You can criticize art without being an expert. The purpose of art criticism is to get the viewer involved in a perception process that delays judgment until all aspects of the work of art have been studied.

■ See pages 28–29 for more about art criticism.

Describe

▶ Possible answer: The cars, trucks, and buses on the road are moving. They have been painted with blurry edges to show movement. There is a parking lot with cars and trucks. In the parking lot, at the bottom of the painting, there is a yellow tractor with a forklift.

▶ Possible answer: At the top of the painting, there are houses and a city hall with a white cupola on top. Along the road there are buildings with flat roofs. At the edge of the water there is a large, red brick building with many sections. At the curve in the road there is an office building with many windows. Next door is a white church. Between the road and the water there is a red brick building with a black roof. Behind it there is a long, yellow building with a light, blue-green roof built over the water. In the lower right there is a white building with a flat black roof and small windows. At the lower left there is a small white house.

▶ Possible answer: The road was built by people. The large dam and the small dam were also built by people. There are trees in the painting. The water begins in the upper left, then comes to a "T" shape in the lower part of the painting.

▲ **Yvonne Jacquette.** (American). *Town of Skowhegan, Maine.* 1988.

Oil on canvas. 78 $\frac{3}{16}$ × 64 $\frac{3}{16}$ inches (198.60 × 163.04 cm). Brooke Alexander Gallery, New York, New York.

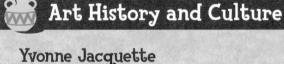 **Art History and Culture**

Yvonne Jacquette

Yvonne Jacquette (e´ von ja´ ket)(1934–)was born in Pittsburgh, Pennsylvania. She studied at the Rhode Island School of Design and then moved to New York City. Her first exhibition was in 1965 at the age of thirty-one. She has taught art in colleges and art schools. She is married to filmmaker Rudy Burckhardt and has designed sets for his movies. Jacquette and her husband often vacation in Maine, and many of her paintings are Maine landscapes. Jacquette often works from a penthouse window or a small, circling plane. When she flies in airplanes, she sketches quickly during takeoffs and landings. Sometimes she takes photographs during a flight. She uses them to jog her memory when she returns to her studio and finishes a painting.

Artist Profiles, p. 26

Artist Profile

Yvonne Jacquette
b. 1934

Yvonne Jacquette (e´ von ja´ ket) was born in Pittsburgh, Pennsylvania. She studied at the Rhode Island School of Design, and then moved to New York City. Her first exhibition was held in 1965. Jacquette has taught art in colleges and art schools. She is married to filmmaker Rudy Burckhardt and has designed sets for his movies. Jacquette and her husband often vacation in Maine; many of her paintings portray Maine landscapes.

 **Art Criticism** Critical Thinking

Describe What do you see?
- ▶ What kind of transportation do you see in this painting?
- ▶ What buildings do you see?
- ▶ Where else do you see objects made by people? What else do you see?

Analyze How is this work organized?
- ▶ Where did the artist create harmony using color and shape?
- ▶ Where did the artist create variety using color and shape?
- ▶ How did the artist create unity?

Interpret What is the artist trying to say?
- ▶ What part of town is shown?
- ▶ What is the difference between the cars close to the viewer and the cars at the top of the painting? Why are they different?
- ▶ Where do you think the artist was when she saw this scene?

Decide What do you think about the work?
- ▶ Is this painting successful because it is realistic, because it is well organized, or because it has a strong message?

Unit 6   **211**

Aesthetic Perception

Seeing Like an Artist Have students go to the top floor of a building and look out a window. How does this scene compare with *Town of Skowhegan, Maine?*

Describe ▶ List everything you see from the window.

Analyze ▶ Where do you see harmony, variety, and unity in the scene below?

Interpret ▶ How does this scene make you feel?

Decide ▶ Do you enjoy looking at scenes from this perspective?

Analyze
- ▶ Possible answer: The artist used yellow and green on the trees. The green trees are harmonious with the blue water. The buildings all have rectangle shapes. The cars, trucks and buses are also rectangles
- ▶ Possible answer: The white buildings and the white parts of buildings contrast with the red-brown color of the brick. The curved shapes of the road, the water's edge, and the large dam contrast with the square shapes of the buildings.
- ▶ Possible answer: All of the buildings are rectangles. Except for the yellow building in the center, the colors used for all of the buildings are red-brown and white. All of the buildings have a pattern of rough lines on their roofs. The curved road ties both parts of the painting together. The curve of the road is repeated by the curve of the dam. All three sections of land have the same kinds of trees.

Interpret
- ▶ Answers will vary. Some will say this looks like the edge of town with warehouses. It looks like the town is at the top of the painting.
- ▶ Possible answer: The cars close to the viewer have been painted with streaks to indicate that they are moving quickly. The cars on the other side of the water have been painted with sharp outlines. They seem to be moving more slowly. When cars get into town they have to slow down.
- ▶ Answers will vary. Most will guess that she is up in the air in a plane.

Decide
- ▶ Answers will vary. Most will cite realism and composition.

Art Journal: Writing
Have students write answers to Aesthetic Perception in their Art Journals.

"Artists make artwork more interesting and satisfying by using common elements but adding something that is different." "Los artistas hacen que la obra artistica sea más interesante y satisfaciente usando elemetes comunes pero añadiendo algo diferente".

T Review unit vocabulary with students using *Transparency 42.*

Art Journal: Writing
Have students answer the questions on page 212 in their Art Journals or on a separate sheet of paper. Answers: 1. A, 2. C, 3. B, 4. A

T For further assessment, have students complete the unit test on *Transparency 48.*

CAREERS IN ART
Architecture

► Encourage students to think about what objects in their lives are influenced and designed by architects and interior designers. What are some of these objects?

■ Have each student in the class put on an exhibition. Have students identify ideas in peers' exhibitions.

■ Take students to an exhibition. Have them identify ideas in the exhibition by the artist.

"My business is to paint not what I know, but what I see.

—Joseph Turner

Harmony, Variety, and Unity, continued

Show What You Know

Write the best answers to these questions on a separate sheet of paper.

❶ Artists create _____ by making different parts of a work of art pleasing to look at together.
A. harmony
B. variety
C. monotonous

❷ Adding _____ makes art more interesting to look at.
A. paint
B. harmony
C. variety

❸ Artists create _____ by balancing harmony and variety.
A. architecture
B. unity
C. columns

❹ _____ is the study of buildings.
A. Architecture
B. Variety
C. Unity

212 Unit 6

CAREERS IN ART
Architecture

Have you ever wondered why buildings look different? This is because of architecture.

Architects design all kinds of buildings. Architects think about how buildings will be used and what they will be made from.

Interior Designers design the inside of buildings. Interior designers select paint colors, furniture, fabrics, and the layout of the rooms.

▲ **Interior Designer**

Unit Assessment Options

🔍 Aesthetic Perception

Practice Have students list the unit concepts and then find examples of the unit concepts in the classroom.

🎨 Creative Expression

Student Portfolio Have students review all the artwork they have created during this unit and select the pieces they wish to keep in their portfolios. Ask an artist to come in and share his or her portfolio. Have students identify ideas in the artist's portfolio.

❓ Art Criticism

Activity Have students select a work of art from this unit and study it using the four steps of art criticism. (See pages 28–29 for more about Art Criticism.) Have students work alone or in pairs and present their findings orally or in writing.

Harmony, Variety, and Unity in Dance

▲ Korean Classical Music and Dance Company. "Korean Classical Music and Dance" and "Kahng Gang Sool Le."

The tradition of Korean folk music and dancing is very old. The music is played on stringed instruments, flutes, and different drums. The dancers wear bright costumes. The music and dancing show harmony and variety. When put together, they create unity.

What to Do Create a circle dance to a drum beat.

1. Stand in a circle with your classmates.

2. Create a dance by swaying and walking.

3. Add head movements, walking in a different direction, and raising and lowering your arms.

4. Perform your dance twice.

 Art Criticism

Describe Name the movements for your circle dance.

Analyze How is this dance similar or different to others you have done?

Interpret What feelings did you have as you performed your dance with others?

Decide How well do you think you did in performing a circle dance?

Unit 6 **213**

 Art History and Culture

Contemporary Dance

The Korean Classical Music and Dance Company, directed by Don Kim, keeps ancient traditions alive. Many of the songs praise and glorify the beauty and wonders of nature. Many Korean dances emphasize graceful movement of the shoulders, arms, and head, uniting with the harmonious flow of the melody in Korean music. Sometimes the dancers dance with a drum or play stationary drums. Korean folk music and dance have been traced back more than 2000. They were passed on through the oral tradition, rather than being written down. The two categories of Korean music are traditional music, which includes court and folk, and music of the West. Some instruments and court compositions were imported from China and adapted over time. Other court music and instruments originated in Korea. Court music was provided for religious ceremonies, memorials for ancestors, military occasions, and special royal events.

Harmony, Variety, and Unity in Dance

Objective: To create a circle dance to a drum beat

Materials: Korean Classical Music and Dance Artsource video, running time 3 minutes 8 seconds, a bell, gong or drum to provide a basic 4/4 meter for the dance

Focus
 Time: About 10 minutes

- Discuss the information on page 213.

Art History and Culture

- Have students discuss Korean music and dance and the movements that will be combined for their dance. Discuss how they can perform with variety and harmony.

Teach
Time: About 20 minutes

Aesthetic Perception

- Ask students to form one circle or one large circle with a smaller one inside. Use a bell, claves, and a gong or drum to keep a steady 4/4 meter to accompany the dance. Encourage students to think about music they are familiar with and compare the two.

Creative Expression

- Teach students the movements and sequence of the dance.

- Have them perform the dance twice.

- **Informal Assessment** Comment positively on their efforts.

Reflect
 Time: About 10 minutes

 **Art Criticism**

- Have students answer the four art criticism questions on page 213 aloud or in writing.

- Did students create harmony, variety, and unity in their dance?

Drawing

It is important to allow the students to experiment with the drawing media. Use gentle guidance to show them how to properly hold the drawing media. Prior to use, demonstrate the techniques as they are illustrated here. Proper handling and use will increase success and establish good habits for the future. It will also make the media last longer.

Pencil

- Primary pencils with medium-soft lead should be used.

- When making thin lines, the students should hold the pencil as in writing.

- For thick lines, hold the pencil on its side near the point between the thumb and fingertips.

Colored Pencils

- When blending colors with colored pencils, it is important to color the lighter color before the darker one. A color can be darkened easily, but it is almost impossible to lighten a color.

- To create shadows, blend complementary colors. This will create browns and darker colors.

Technique Tips
Drawing

Pencil Basics

For darker values, use the side of your pencil lead, press harder, and go over areas more than once. You can add form to your objects using shading.

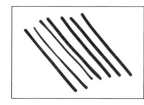

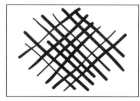

Colored Pencils

You can blend colors with colored pencils. Color with the lighter hue first. Gently go over the light hue with the darker hue until you get the hue you want.

You can create shadows by blending complementary colors.

Technique Tips

Crayon Basics

Crayons can be used to make thick and thin lines and dots. You can use both ends of a crayon.

You can color in large areas by using the long side of a crayon.

Marker Basics

You can use the point of a marker to create thin lines and small dots.

You can use the side of a marker tip to make thick lines.

Always replace the cap of a marker when you are finished using it.

Crayon

- Thin lines and small dots can be created with the sharpened end of the crayon.
- Thick lines and large dots can be made with the flat end. Large areas can be colored in with the side of an unwrapped crayon.
- Students may become concerned over broken crayons. Reassure them that these pieces are still useful for drawing and coloring in areas.

Marker

- To avoid damage, students should not press hard on the marker tip. Tell them to handle the marker gently for better control.
- For thin lines and dots, a conical-tipped marker can be used.
- The side of the tip can be used to make wider lines and color in areas.
- Remind students to replace the cap to prevent drying.

Oil Pastels

- Oil pastels are pigments that are mixed with oil and compressed into sticks. They are used like crayons. By pressing with gentle force and coloring over an area several times, students can create the effect of paint.

- Students can create lines by drawing with the tip. Textures can be created by making marks such as dots and lines. Textures can also be made by layering colors and scratching through with a paper clip straightened out at one end.

- Colors can be mixed or blended by smearing them with a paper towel wrapped around a finger.

- Oil pastels break easily. Reassure the students that these pieces can still be used like new ones. If the oil pastels become dirty from use, instruct the students to mark on a paper towel until the colors are clean again.

Colored Chalk

- Colored chalks are used to make colorful, soft designs. The use of dustless chalk is recommended for elementary classrooms. The tip of the chalk is used much like an oil pastel to make lines. To fill a space or shape with solid color, use gentle force and color over an area more than once.

- Colors can be mixed or blended by smearing them together with a paper towel wrapped around a finger.

- Like oil pastels, colored chalks break easily. Reassure the students that these pieces can still be used like new ones. Colored chalks also become dirty from use. Instruct students to mark on a paper towel until the colors are clean.

Technique Tips

Oil Pastels

Oil pastels can be used like crayons. When you press down hard on oil pastels, your picture will look painted. Oil pastels are soft and break easily. They can also be messy. Wash your hands with soap and water after using them.

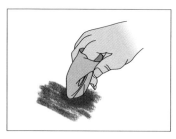

Colors can be mixed or blended by smearing them using a tissue or your finger.

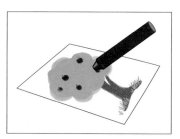

You can use oil pastels to draw over other media, such as tempera and crayon.

Colored Chalk

Colored chalks can be used to make colorful, soft designs. Colored chalk is soft and breaks easily. Reuse broken pieces.

Make bolder colors by going over an area more than once.

Blend colors by using a soft tissue or your finger.

Technique Tips
Painting
Brush Care

Rinse your brush in water between colors.
Blot the brush dry on a paper towel.

Clean the brush when you are finished painting.

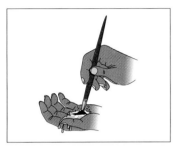

1. Rinse the brush in clean water. Wash the brush with soap.

2. Rinse the brush well again and blot it dry.

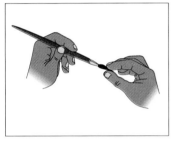

3. Shape the bristles.

4. Store brushes with bristles up.

Painting
Brush Care

- Taking proper care of a paintbrush will increase its time in use. By teaching students the rules for proper care, good habits will be established in the beginning.

- Students should always thoroughly rinse their brush tips between colors of paint. Next, they should gently blot the brush on a paper towel to test for missed paint. If paint appears on the towel, it should be rinsed and tested again. Sometimes paint gets deep inside the bristles and the brush needs more rinsing.

- To properly wash and store the brush when finished, students should:

  1. Rinse the brush under gently flowing water. Do not use hot water. Place a small amount of soap in the palm of one hand. Gently rub the bristles of the brush in their soapy palms. This will remove stubborn paint from deep inside the bristles.

  2. Rinse the brush under gently running water to remove all of the soap.

  3. Reshape the bristles into a point.

  4. Store the brushes in a container with the bristles up so their shape will be kept when the brush dries.

- When these habits are established early in the school year, the students will be more likely to respect the importance of proper care of the art media and tools.

Tempera

- For best results, it is recommended that quality liquid tempera paint is used.

- To remove excess water from the brush, gently wipe the end of the brush on the inside edge of the container. This will allow the water to run back into the container. Discourage students from tapping their brushes on the rim of the container. This will prevent paint splatters.

- When mixing paints on a palette, always mix the darker color into the lighter color a little at a time until the desired color is reached. This reduces wasted paint. Paper plates work well as palettes and reduce cleanup.

- Use a thin brush for details.

- Use a wide brush for large spaces.

Technique Tips

Tempera

Wet your brush in a water container. Wipe off extra water using the inside wall of the container and blot the brush on a paper towel.

Mix colors on a palette. Put some of each color that you want to mix on the palette. Add darker colors a little at a time to lighter colors. To create a tint, mix a small amount of a hue into white. To create a shade, mix a small amount of black into a hue.

Use a thin, pointed brush to paint thin lines and details.

Use a wide brush to paint large areas.

Technique Tips

Watercolors

Wet your brush in a water container. Wipe off extra water using the inside wall of the container and blot the brush on a paper towel. Add a drop of water to each watercolor cake. Rinse your brush between colors.

Mix colors on a palette. Put some of each color that you want to mix on the palette. Add darker colors a little at a time to lighter colors. To create a tint, add more water to a hue. To create a shade, mix a small amount of black into a hue.

Paint on damp paper to create soft lines and edges. Tape your paper to the table, brush clean water over the paper, and allow the water to soak in.

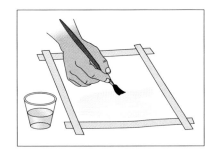

Paint on dry paper and use very little water to create sharp lines and shapes.

Watercolors

- School watercolors come in semimoist cakes. Moisten each cake that is going to be used by dripping a little water from the brush onto the cake and gently stirring the water on the surface of the paint.

- Create thick lines by gently pressing down on the brush.

- Create thin lines by lightly touching the surface of the paper with the tip of the brush.

Watercolor Resists

- By drawing on the paper first with crayons and/or oil pastels, students can achieve a resist effect. Because of their waxy or oily compositions, crayons and oil pastels show through watercolors. Best results are achieved when cool-colored drawings are painted over with warm colors, or vice versa.

Collage

Scissors

- It is important to teach students safety when they use scissors. They should always cut away from their bodies. Of course they should never point their scissors at others, spin them on the table, or walk around the room with them.

- There are scissors specially made to spring open for students who are physically challenged, or who are not yet developmentally ready to use standard school scissors. Many scissors on the market today can be used with the right or left hand. If these are not available, keep a supply of "lefty" scissors for students who need them.

- To cut thick yarn or fabric, encourage students to work in pairs. While one cuts, the other can stretch the yarn or fabric. This makes cutting easier and encourages cooperation.

Technique Tips

Watercolor Resists

Certain materials will show through watercolors. Crayons and oil pastels both show through watercolors. To make a watercolor resist, make a drawing using crayons or oil pastels. Then paint over the drawing using watercolors. The watercolors will cover the blank parts of the paper. The watercolors will not be visible on the parts of the paper covered with crayon or oil pastels.

Collage

Scissors

Always cut away from your body.

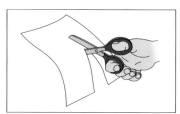

Ask a classmate to stretch yarn or fabric as you cut.

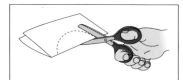

Use folded paper to cut symmetrical shapes. Fold a sheet of paper in half. Cut a shape using the folded edge as the axis.

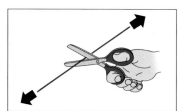

Technique Tips

Arranging a Design

When creating a collage, it is important to plan your design. Take into consideration the size of shapes and spaces, placement of shapes and spaces, color schemes, and textures. When you have made an arrangement you like, glue the shapes in place.

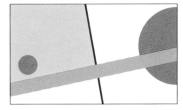

Glue

Squeeze a line of glue onto the paper. You can smooth the line with the tip of the glue bottle.

Close the glue bottle and clean the top when you are finished using it.

Arranging a Design

- Provide a variety of textured and colored papers, yarns, fabrics, and found objects for students to use. Hard-to-cut materials should be precut for students.

- When using paper, students may choose to tear and/or cut their shapes.

- Encourage students to arrange the design first. They should pay as much attention to the negative spaces as the positive ones.

- Glue only after the final colors, shapes, ad textures have been chosen and arranged. White glue will attach most porous items to the background surface.

Glue

- To attach two pieces of fabric or paper, use only a few drops of glue and smooth them with the tip of the bottle.

- When finished, students should wipe the bottle clean with a paper towel, close the top, and store upright.

Texture Rubbing

- When rubbing textures have the student hold the uncovered crayon so that he is rubbing with the side and not the tip.

- With one hand hold the paper and the edges of the material being rubbed. Then rub away from the holding hand for every stroke. If the student rubs back and forth the paper will wrinkle up and a smooth rubbing will not be made.

- Rubbings can be made with the side of a pencil point, an uncovered wax crayon, or an uncovered oil pastel.

- It is better to use dark colors to make the rubbing so that the texture impression shows up. Red, green, blue, and violet are good colors to use.

- Some materials that make good rubbings are burlap, lace, weeds, shoe bottoms, and commercial rubbing plates.

Technique Tips

Texture Rubbing

Place a texture plate or textured surface underneath your paper.

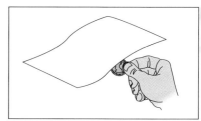

Hold the paper and object down firmly so they do not slip.

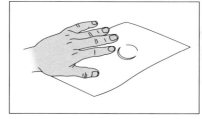

Use the long side of your crayon and rub away from you only. Do not move the crayon back and forth.

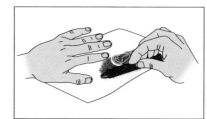

Technique Tips
Printmaking
Making Stamps

You can cut sponges into shapes to make stamps.

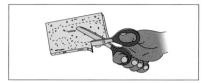

You can carve shapes into potatoes to make stamps.

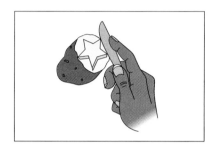

Making a Sponge Print

Use a different sponge for each color. Dip a sponge into paint. Press the sponge onto paper.

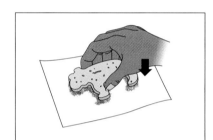

Printmaking
Making Stamps

- If students wish to cut a sponge into a specific shape, use thin sponges. Draw the shape on the sponge with a marker and use scissors to cut it out.

- To make a potato print the teacher should pre-cut potatoes in half with a sharp knife to make sure that the printing surface is smooth. To keep the potatoes for any length of time put them in a container of water. When you are ready to use them be sure to blot them dry.

  1. Have the students use a pencil or ballpoint pen to draw a shape on the potato surface.

  2. Then using a plastic knife or a metal spoon, the child can outline the shape first and then carve away the area that is not to be printed. Remember that the print will be the opposite of the stamp. If the child is making a letter of the alphabet the letter must be backwards on the potato so that it will be correct in the print.

  3. The best way to apply paint to the stamp is to brush on tempera using a flat, broad brush making sure that the paint is only applied to the raised surface. The potato can be rinsed in water and blotted so that another color can be used.

- Oil-based modeling clay can also be used to make a stamp. This is done by drawing or sculpting a design on a flat piece of modeling clay. There are a variety of tools manufactured for carving clay. Some classroom items that will work just as well include plastic eating utensils, craft sticks, and paper clips. The straightened end of a paper clip can be used to draw in the clay. The rounded end can be used as a gouge to carve clay away. To create a raised stamp, simply add pieces of clay to the bottom of the clay stamp.

Printing a Sponge Print

- Dispense colors onto individual palettes, or spread out on a surface large enough to avoid mixing. Lightly press the sponge into the paint, being careful not to get too much paint on it. Lift the sponge and lightly press it into place on the paper. The sponge should be thoroughly rinsed between colors.

More about Making Prints

■ Below is the procedure for using a brayer, which is a soft roller, to make prints.

1. Pour a small amount of water-based printing ink or paint onto a flat, solid surface. Roll the brayer in the ink or paint until there is an even coating on the surface and brayer.

2. Roll the brayer over the top of the stamp. The ink should cover the stamp evenly without getting into the grooves of the design.

3. Apply the stamp carefully to the paper, rubbing the back of the stamp with the side of the fist.

4. Peel the paper and stamp apart.

5. Reink the stamp as needed if you wish to make more than one print.

6. When finished, wash the brayer, surface, and stamp.

■ Another method for making prints calls for a paintbrush to apply the ink or paint. This method works better than the brayer with a raised stamp that the brayer would flatten out. Brush the ink or paint onto the stamping surface. Then follow the steps above, ending with thoroughly cleaning the brush.

Technique Tips

Printing Stamps

Put a small amount of ink or paint on a flat solid surface. Roll a brayer back and forth in the ink until there is an even coating of ink on the surface and the brayer.

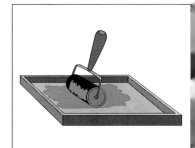

Roll the brayer over your stamp.

Apply the stamp carefully to your paper.

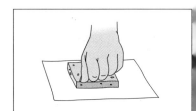

Sculpture

Clay Basics

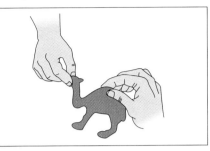

Clay can be pinched, pulled, and squeezed into the desired shape.

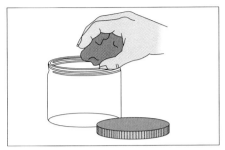

Store clay in an airtight container to keep it from drying out.

Pinch Pots

Push your thumb into your clay up to the first joint. Turn the clay on your thumb to create an opening.

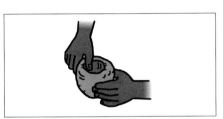

Keeping your thumb in the hole, place your fingers on the outside of the clay and gently squeeze as you turn. Repeat until you have formed a bowl.

Gently tap the bottom of your bowl on your table so that it sits flat.

Sculpting

Working with Clay

- Always protect the work area with a cloth or newspaper. Clay dust is messy. Always wash the tables after working with clay.

- To help prevent earth clay from drying and cracking, students should not overhandle the clay. Keep damp paper towels nearby for students to keep their hands moist.

- The following steps are for modeling a person or animal from clay:
  1. Roll the piece of clay into an oval-shaped form. Describe this to the students as a "potato" shape.
  2. Pinch a head shape on one end.
  3. Pinch and pull out arms and legs.
  4. Leave some, but not too much, clay for the body.
  5. Squeeze the head, arms, legs, and body into the desired shapes.

- Clay is often sold in 25 pound bags. The bags are usually strong enough to keep the clay damp, but be sure to close the bag tightly with a twist tie or some other device to keep it sealed. It is a good idea to place the bag inside a second bag, like a heavy duty garbage bag, for long time storage.

Making a Pinch Pot

- It is important that the students gently squeeze the clay to form the pot. If they pinch the clay quickly the walls will be uneven. If they pinch the clay too hard they might make a hole in the wall of the bowl. If a student makes a hole, you might have him or her start over, or you can repair the hole by adding a small piece of clay using slip and scoring.

- The walls of the pinch pot should be the same width all around the bowl. To do this, have students hold their bowls with one thumb inside the bowl and their fingers held flat on the outside of the bowl. Then have students squeeze gently while constantly turning the bowl with their other hand. As the bowl opens up, both hands can be used to shape the walls.

- If the students are going to press designs into the walls of the bowl make sure that they have their fingers together inside the bowl to keep the bowl from collapsing.

Joining Clay

- Clay is joined by using **slip,** a creamy mixture of clay and water. Slip can be made by putting a few dry pieces of clay in a container and covering them with water. When the clay dissolves, stir to achieve a creamy consistency.

- Joining clay also requires a scoring tool such as a straightened paper clip. The steps below are called the four S's–score, slip, smooth, and squeeze.

  1. **Score** the two pieces to be joined.
  2. Apply **slip** to one of the surfaces.
  3. **Smooth** the seam.
  4. **Squeeze** the two surfaces together.

Carving Clay

There are a variety of tools manufactured for carving clay. Some classroom items that will work just as well are plastic eating utensils, craft sticks, and paper clips. The straightened end of a paper clip can be used to draw in the clay. The rounded end can be used as a gouge to carve clay away.

Painting Clay

- Once clay has been properly fired in a kiln it can be painted with tempera or acrylic paints. It can be glazed and refired.

- The biggest problem with firing student work is that the clay must be thoroughly dried before firing. This can be achieved in an old kiln by stacking everything that is ready to be fired in the kiln and then leaving the lid cracked open. Turn on only one heating coil to dry out the ware for a few hours before closing the lid and firing it up to the desired temperature.

Technique Tips

Joining Clay

Two pieces of clay can be joined together by using slip and scoring.

Score both pieces to help them stick together.

Apply slip to one of the pieces using a brush.

Squeeze together the two pieces of clay. Smooth the edges where they are joined.

Painting Clay

Clay can be painted and decorated with glazes once it is dry or fired.

Technique Tips

Paper Sculpture

You can curl, fold, and bend paper strips to make paper sculptures.

 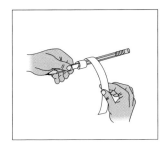

Papier-Mâché

Create a supporting form, if needed. Forms can be made of almost anything. Masking tape can be used to hold the form together.

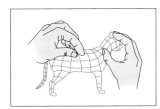

Tear paper into strips. Dip the strips into paste, or rub the paste onto the strips using your fingers. Use wide strips for wide forms and small strips for small forms.

Apply several layers of strips, applying each layer in a different direction. Smooth over rough edges with your fingers. When your sculpture dries, you can paint it.

Paper Sculpture

Making Strip Forms

Paper strips can be folded, curved, twisted, and then glued to create many different forms. A few basic forms are described here. Students will create many more.

1. Prepare by precutting enough paper strips for class use. This can be done on a paper cutter. The strips should be one to three inches wide in a variety of lengths.

2. Make a circle by curving the strip around to its beginning and gluing the ends together.

3. Make a box by folding a strip into four equal sections, leaving a small section for a tab. Bend the tab over its matching end and glue.

4. Make a triangle form by folding a strip into three sections plus a tab. Glue together.

5. Make a cone by cutting out a circle, cutting along its radius, overlapping the side of the cut, and gluing into a cone shape.

Papier-Mâché

Papier-Mâché is a French term that means "mashed paper." It refers to sculpting methods that use paper and liquid paste. The wet paper and paste material is molded over supporting structures such as wadded dry paper or crumpled foil. The molded paper dries to a hard finish.

▪ Below are three common papier-mâché solutions:

1. Mix one part white glue to one part water by adding one half the amount of water to a glue bottle that is half full. Close the lid. Shake vigorously. Add second half of the water. Close the lid and shake until mixed.

2. Make a creamy mixture of wheat paste and water. To mix wheat paste, wear a dust mask and pour dry paste into a large mixing bowl. Add water and stir until the mixture is creamy. Mash lumps with a spoon or your hands.

3. Use liquid starch.

Aluminum Foil

- Before making a finished product, give students a small piece of foil to experiment with so that they can see how the foil holds its shape.

- Use thin foil so that it can be easily manipulated.

- To add something like a tail, use a pencil to poke a hole into a form, insert the tail, and then press the foil form around the tail to hold it in place.

- Two separate pieces can be joined by wrapping them with thin strips of foil which are then pressed into the form to make them "disappear."

Building with Forms

- To join two cardboard forms, it is best to put the tape on one piece and then place it against the second before pressing the tape firmly in place.

- Tacky glue can also be used to join two forms. Apply a small amount of tacky glue to one surface, spread it thin with the bottle tip, and then gently press the two pieces together and hold them for a count of ten.

Technique Tips

Aluminum Foil

Foil can be pinched and squeezed to make sculptures.

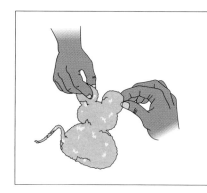

Building with Forms

To make sculptures with paper or cardboard forms, place the forms together and use masking tape to join them.

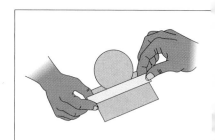

Technique Tips

Puppets

Cut out the pieces for your puppet from paper.

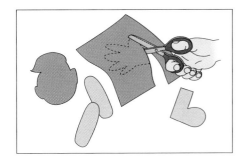

Use a hole punch to make holes at the joints where two pieces go together.

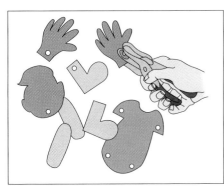

Use a brad to join the pieces. Stick a brad through both holes, and then unfold the metal clamps.

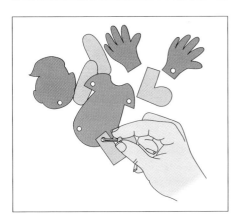

Puppets

- Have students draw the parts of the puppet before they cut them out. Check to make sure the arms and legs are wide enough to have holes punched in them.

- Use poster board or tag board to make the puppets so that the parts are strong enough to work together without tearing.

Needlewok

- Large tapestry needles purchased at fabric stores, craft shops, or from art supply catalogs are appropriate for embroidery. They have blunt points and large eyes for easier threading.

- For threading the needle, discourage students from moistening the end of the yarn or thread. It doesn't work and spreads germs. Below are two alternate methods. Either of them will require some patience to master.

  1. Demonstrate twisting the end of the yarn or thread to make a point. Then push it through the eye of the needle.

  2. Another method is to bend the end of the yarn or thread back against itself and then push the looped end through the eye of the needle. This method keeps the frayed end from blocking the opening of the eye of the needle.

- Pull about one fourth of the length of the yarn or thread through the needle. The students can grasp this in their stitching hand as they embroider to keep the yarn or thread from pulling out of the needle. Do not encourage them to tie knots.

- The running stitch is made by simply pulling the needle and yarn or thread up through the fabric and pushing it back through the front in a path. When finished, let the loose ends hang out the back. Trim them.

Needlework

Thread your needle, or get help threading your needle. Tie a knot in the end of the thread.

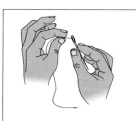

Carefully push the needle up from the bottom through the fabric where you want your stitch to start. Pull the needle through until the knot catches.

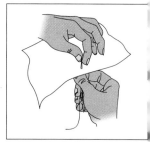

Carefully push the needle down through the fabric where you want your stitch to end. Repeat.

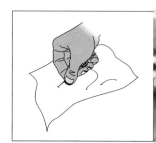

Technique Tips

Sewing a Book

1. Find the center of the fold and make a mark. Measure 1″ above and below the center mark.

2. Use a tapestry needle and poke holes through your marks.

3. Thread your needle and go through the top hole from the outside of your book and back through the center hole. Cut your thread so that you can tie both ends together.

4. Repeat for the bottom of your book.

Sewing a Book

- Choose a strong yarn or embroidery thread for sewing a book.

Activity Tips

Line Direction

 **Creative Expression**

1. Think of a playground you would like to create.

2. Twist, curl, and fold strips of paper to make different line directions.

3. Fold the ends of the strips for tabs and glue them onto the base paper to make your playground.

Types of Lines

 **Creative Expression**

1. Draw the lines for your tree with a pencil. Fill the page.

2. Glue the line collage materials over the lines.

3. Add objects you like to the branches of the tree. Name your piece.

232   Activity Tips

Activity Tips

Unit 1 · Lesson 3   Calm Lines

 Creative Expression

1. Think of a calm water scene. What would you see there?

2. Paint your scene. Fill the paper using vertical and horizontal brush strokes.

3. Use markers to add details to your painting after it is dry.

Unit 1 · Lesson 4   Active Lines

 Creative Expression

1. Think about which lines could describe an exciting event.

2. Draw different active lines with black paint to show the activity in your event.

3. Choose some bright colors and paint the spaces between the black lines.

Activity Tips

Unit 1 · Lesson 5 — Geometric Shapes

 **Creative Expression**

1. Think of a picture you would like to make.
2. Cut out geometric shapes using the colored construction paper.
3. Glue them onto the white paper to create your picture.

Unit 1 · Lesson 6 — Free-Form Shapes

 **Creative Expression**

1. Think of a puppet you would like to create.
2. Draw it and cut out the parts. Add any details to the parts that you wish.
3. Attach moving parts. Tape the puppet to a stick. Add a costume to the puppet using fabric and ribbon.
4. Hold the puppet in front of a light to make a shadow.

234 Activity Tips

Activity Tips

Geometric Forms

 **Creative Expression**

1. Look at your teacher's selection of geometric forms. Think about how you would stack the forms. Plan your design.

2. Select three forms you want to work with. Stack and tape the forms.

Free-Form Forms

 **Creative Expression**

1. Think about things you like or that describe you. What free-form forms will you use to show these things?

2. Paint a background on tagboard.

3. Draw your forms on cardboard, decorate them, and cut them out.

4. Glue your free-form forms onto the background.

Activity Tips

Body Forms

🎨 Creative Expression

1. Decide how your body form will represent your culture.

2. Make the parts of your body form from the clay your teacher gives you. Join the pieces together using slip and scoring.

3. Add details to your body form by using a pencil to etch lines and shapes.

Animal Forms

🎨 Creative Expression

1. Think about a four-legged animal form you would like to make.

2. Create your animal form. Score your clay and use slip when joining two pieces.

3. Carve details in the clay.

236 Activity Tips

Activity Tips

Unit 2 · Lesson 5 — People and Space

 **Creative Expression**

1. Think about the way your body moves when you play.

2. Use construction paper and draw a family playing. Cut out the shapes.

3. Arrange and overlap your family on white paper. Move them around until you like the way they look. Glue the shapes onto the paper.

Unit 2 · Lesson 6 — Objects and Space

Creative Expression

1. Think of some objects and foods you would like to draw.

2. Arrange your objects so some overlap.

3. Start by drawing the objects closest to you. Then draw the objects that are farther away.

4. Paint your still life.

Activity Tips

Color and Hue

 **Creative Expression**

1. Think of a scene or picture that you would like to draw.

2. Draw the scene on your paper using a black marker. Make your lines very bold.

3. Paint your picture using spectral colors in the correct order.

Warm Hues

Creative Expression

1. Think of an object that reminds you of summer.

2. Draw that item with warm oil pastels.

3. Paint over the drawing using black tempera.

Activity Tips

Cool Hues

 Creative Expression

1. Think about your perfect backyard. What would it look like? What would be there?

2. Paint the background for your landscape using cool watercolors.

3. Add details to your painting using cool oil pastels or tempera paints.

Value

 Creative Expression

1. Think of an object that you see often in your neighborhood. Paint that object using white paint.

2. Mix black and white paint to create a gray value. Make a gray outline around your object.

3. Mix darker values and continue outlining your object until you make a black line.

Activity Tips

Light Values

 Creative Expression

1. Pick three hues. Add small amounts of each hue to white to make tints.

2. Think about the scenery that people in the early American West would have seen.

3. Paint your picture using these tints.

Unit 3 · Lesson 6 **Dark Values**

  Creative Expression

1. Choose a feeling that you would like to explain using pictures. Pick three hues to use.

2. Mix a small amount of black with each hue.

3. Paint your feeling picture using the shades.

Activity Tips

Patterns

Creative Expression

1. Think of a motif that describes your culture. Draw the motif and cut it out of a sponge.

2. Dip your sponge into paint. Make prints on the paper using your motif to create a pattern.

3. Fill the paper with your pattern.

Patterns in Nature

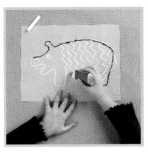

Creative Expression

1. Think of an animal, plant, or other natural object. Draw a large picture of the object.

2. Add lines and shapes to make natural patterns.

3. Redraw your lines with glue to add texture. Let your drawing dry and fill in the shapes with color.

Activity Tips

Rhythm

Creative Expression

1. Choose and draw a plant. Repeat it several times to create rhythm.

2. Choose another object. Draw and repeat it as well.

3. Paint your composition.

Rhythm and Form

Creative Expression

1. Think of a person to be your storyteller.

2. Create a clay figure of this person. Add arms, legs, hands, feet, and any details you wish.

3. Make clay children and attach them to your storyteller.

4. Let your doll dry. Paint your doll with glazes to decorate it.

242 Activity Tips

Activity Tips

Unit 4 · Lesson 5   Diagonal Movement

 **Creative Expression**

1. Think about how your arms and legs move when you are dancing. How do objects dance in the wind?

2. Draw a dance scene that shows lots of diagonal movement. Think about how you want your viewer's eyes to move across your picture.

Unit 4 · Lesson 6   Curving Movement

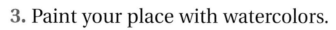 **Creative Expression**

1. Think of a place you would like to visit and what the road there would look like.

2. Draw your road or place using curving and swirling lines.

3. Paint your place with watercolors.

Activity Tips

Balance

 Creative Expression

1. Think about the jar you want to make.

2. Fold a sheet of paper in half. Draw and cut out your jar shape. Glue your jar to your background paper.

3. Cut out small matching shapes. Arrange the shapes symmetrically around the axis and glue the shapes to the jar.

- -

Balance in People

Creative Expression

1. Think of a real or imaginary hero to draw.

2. Sketch your hero on your paper.

3. Use a black marker to outline your drawing. Add details using crayons, colored pencils, or markers.

Activity Tips

 Unit 5 · Lesson 3 **Emphasis**

Creative Expression

1. Think of a scene that shows people working or playing.

2. Draw the scene using markers. Give one person in the scene emphasis.

3. Color your picture and add details.

 Unit 5 · Lesson 4 **Emphasis Using Contrast**

Creative Expression

1. Think of a night scene to draw. Draw the scene on dark construction paper.

2. Add the contrast of lights in the dark by using yellow and white oil pastels.

3. Add details to your drawing and name it.

Activity Tips

Tactile Texture

 Creative Expression

1. Think about a design you could make with fabric to decorate a map. Draw your ideas on fabric scraps.

2. Cut them out and stitch them onto your fabric background.

3. Add more details with stitches and buttons.

Visual Texture

 Creative Expression

1. Draw items of clothing on the visual textures you collected.

2. Cut out the clothes and glue them onto your paper.

3. Use markers to draw people wearing the clothes.

Activity Tips

Unit 6 · Lesson 1   Harmony of Color

 **Creative Expression**

1. As a group, decide on a theme and color for your class mural.

2. Paint the basic shapes of your design on your tile and let it dry. Remember to use the color your class selected.

3. Add details to your design. When the tiles are all dry, arrange them as a class.

Unit 6 · Lesson 2   Harmony of Shape and Form

 Creative Expression

1. Draw the adult animal or animals using the drawing tool.

2. Select and copy the adult animal several times. Resize the copies to create child animals.

3. Use the fill tool or drawing tool to add details to your animals.

Activity Tips

Variety of Color

 Creative Expression

1. Use crayons and draw the ocean floor on your paper.

2. To create the ocean, lightly apply paint to wet posterboard. Place your paper face down on the paint and rub your paper. Peel the paper away quickly.

3. Let your paper dry. Cut out construction paper sea creatures and glue them to your paper using variety of color.

Variety of Shape and Form

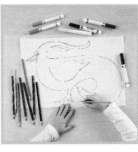

 Creative Expression

1. Draw a fantasy bird. Make it large.

2. Outline your bird with black marker. Add pattern to your bird using black marker.

3. Use colored pencils to color the bird. Paint the background using watercolors.

Activity Tips

Unit 6 · Lesson 5 **Unity in Sculpture**

🎨 Creative Expression

1. Draw your animal on paper. Add details using oil pastels. Paint your animal using watercolors.

2. Cut your animal out and glue it to a sheet of paper. Do not put any glue at the places where the pole will go.

3. Stuff your animal with paper. Insert the pole into the space you have left for it and glue it in place.

4. Arrange your animals with your class to create a carousel.

Unit 6 · Lesson 6 **Unity in Architecture**

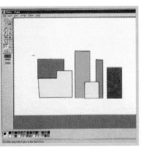

🎨 Creative Expression

1. Think of what your cityscape would look like.

2. Use the drawing tool and shape tools to make your buildings.

3. Add any details you wish.

Visual Index

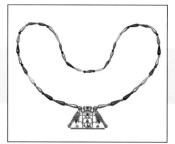

Artist Unknown
*Pectoral with the Name
of Senwosret II*
c. 1897–1878 B.C.
(page 71)

Artist Unknown
Gui Ritual Food Container
11th century B.C. (page 156)

**Attributed to the
Amasis Painter**
Lekythos (oil flask)
c. 550–530 B.C.
(page 157)

Artist Unknown
*Maison Carrée,
Nîmes, France*
1st century B.C. (page 206)

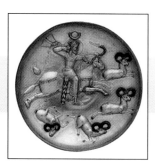

Artist Unknown
*Plate with King
Hunting Rams*
late 5th century A.D.
(page 70)

Artist Unknown
Leopard Aquamanile
16th–19th century.
(page 79)

Louise Moillon
*Still Life with Cherries,
Strawberries, and Gooseberries*
1630. (page 86)

Rembrandt van Rijn
The Mill
c. 1650. (page 168)

Diego Velázquez
*Las Meninas (The
Maids of Honor)*
1656. (page 184)

Jan Vermeer
The Girl With the Red Hat
c. 1665. (page 176)

Maria Sibylla Merian
Plate 2 from "Dissertation in Insect Generations and Metamorphosis in Surinam"
1719. (page 130)

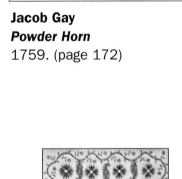

Jacob Gay
Powder Horn
1759. (page 172)

James Peale
George Washington
c. 1782. (page 161)

John James Audubon
Carolina Parakeet
1832. (page 131)

George Catlin
NO-HO-MUN-YA, One Who Gives No Attention
1832. (page 177)

John James Audubon
Tundra Swan
1844. (page 198)

Artist Unknown
Princess Feather and Rising Sun
c. 1835–1845.
(page 127)

John Frederick Kensett
A View of Mansfield Mountain
1849. (page 105)

John Bell (attributed)
Figure of a Lion
c. 1850–1860. (page 78)

Artist Unknown
Delaware Shoulder Bag
c. 1860. (page 126)

Wilhelm Schimmel
Large Eagle
c. 1860–1890. (page 199)

Auguste Renoir
Two Sisters (On the Terrace)
1881. (page 83)

Claude Monet
The Cliff, Etretat, Sunset
1883. (page 195)

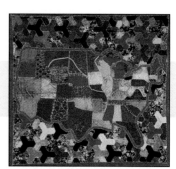

Artist Unknown
Map Quilt
1886. (page 173)

William H. McCloskey
Wrapped Oranges
1889. (page 135)

Vincent van Gogh
The Starry Night
1889. (page 146)

Cecilia Beaux
Ernesta (Child with Nurse)
1894. (page 165)

James J. Shannon
Jungle Tales
1895. (page 82)

Paul Cézanne
Still Life With Apples
1895–1898. (page 87)

Yoruba People
Headdress for Epa Masquerade
early 20th century. (page 90)

Kiawak Ashoona
Seal Hunter
20th century. (page 75)

Helen Cordero
Storyteller Doll
20th century. (page 138)

Taqialuk Nuna
Polar Bears and Cubs
20th century.
(page 190)

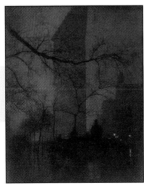

Edward Steichen
The Flatiron
1904 (printed 1909).
(page 108)

Dentzel Company
Carousel
1905. (page 202)

Edgar Degas
Ballet Scene
1907. (page 143)

Claude Monet
Palazzo da Mula, Venice
1908. (page 45)

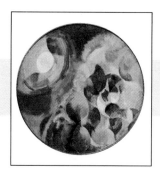

Robert Delaunay
Simultaneous Contrasts:
Sun and Moon
1913. (page 97)

Wassily Kandinsky
Composition VI
1913. (page 48)

Dentzel Company
Carousel Rabbit
c. 1915. (page 203)

Tom Thomson
Spring Ice
1916. (page 104)

Paul Klee
The Tree of Houses
1918. (page 186)

Joseph Stella
The Voice of the City of
New York Interpreted/ The
Great White Way Leaving
the Subway (White Way 1)
c. 1920–1922. (page 37)

Simon Rodia
Watts Tower
1921–1954. (page 207)

Georgia O'Keeffe
The Red Poppy
1927. (page 94)

Thomas Hart Benton
Country Dance
1929. (page 142)

Edward Hopper
Early Sunday Morning
1930. (page 53)

**Beatrice Whitney
Van Ness**
Summer's Sunlight
c. 1932–1934.
(page 101)

Minerva Teichert
Night Raid
c. 1935. (page 113)

Willam H. Johnson
Jitterbugs (II)
c. 1941. (page 60)

**Grandma Moses (Anna
Mary Robertson Moses)**
Grand Skating
c. 1946. (page 150)

Adolph Gottlieb
Spectre of the Sea
1947. (page 116)

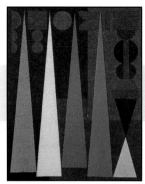

Auguste Herbin
Amour
1948. (page 52)

Henry Moore
Family Group
1948–1949 (cast 1950).
(page 64)

Artist Unknown
*Indonesian Shadow
Puppet*
c. 1950. (page 56)

Ansel Adams
*Early Sunday Morning,
Merced River, Yosemite
Valley, CA*
c. 1950 (print c. 1978).
(page 109)

René Magritte
The Empire of Lights
1954. (page 169)

Harold Town
The First Aeroplane
1956. (page 117)

Franz Kline
Blueberry Eyes
c. 1959–1960.
(page 41)

Herón Martínez Mendóza
Church
c. 1960. (page 36)

Vigil Family
Pueblo Scene: Corn Dancers and Church
c. 1960. (page 139)

Jacob Lawrence
Street Scene (Boy with Kite)
1962. (page 34)

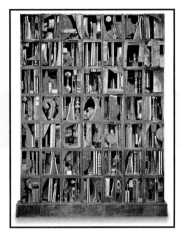

Louise Nevelson
Dawn
1962. (page 124)

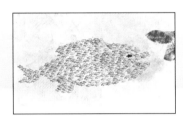

Leo Lionni
Selection from Swimmy
1963. (page 194)

David Smith
Cubi XVIII
1964. (page 66)

Artist Unknown
Thai Shadow Puppet
c. 1965. (page 57)

Chryssa
The Gates to Times Square
1966. (page 154)

Patrick DesJarlait
Gathering Wild Rice
1972. (page 100)

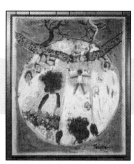

Leo Twiggs
At Four and a Half
1972. (page 49)

Ivan Eyre
Valleyridge
1974. (page 187)

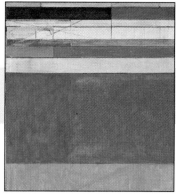

Richard Diebenkorn
Ocean Park #105
1978. (page 44)

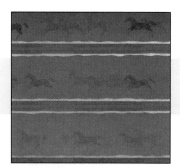

Paul Branch
Red Horse Frieze
1983. (page 191)

Robert Lostutter
Baird Trogon
1985. (page 96)

Miriam Schapiro
Personal Appearance
1985. (page 120)

John T. Scott
Alanda's Dream Tree
1985. (page 40)

Yvonne Jacquette
Town of Skowhegan, Maine
1988. (page 210)

Rosalind Ragans
Teacher
1988. (page 180)

Roxanne Swentzell
The Emergence of the Clowns
1988. (page 74)

Jane Wilson
Solstice
1991. (page 112)

Peggy Flora Zalucha
Peony Blooms IX
1992. (page 134)

Duane Hanson
Policeman
1992–1994. (page 160)

David Hockney
Garrowby Hill
1998. (page 147)

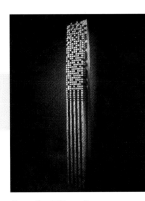

Jesús Moroles
Georgia Stele
1999. (page 67)

Lorenzo Scott
Ballet Dancers
2001. (page 164)

Glossary

A

active lines   Lines that show action and add energy and movement to a work of art. Diagonal, zigzag, and curved lines are examples of active lines.

angle   A shape formed when two lines extend in different directions from the same point

animal forms   A three-dimensional representation of an animal

arc   Any portion of a curved line from a circle

architect   Highly trained artists and engineers who design buildings

architecture   The study of buildings

axis   A real or imaginary line across the center of a work of art

B

balance   A principle of design that deals with arranging art. Balance occurs when equal or similar shapes or objects are placed on opposite sides of an axis in a work of art.

blob   A type of free-form shape

body forms   Three-dimensional representations of a person

brass   A metal made by combining copper and zinc

broken (line)   A line that is made of a series of dashes, not solid

C

calm lines   Lines that give a work of art a quiet and peaceful mood. Horizontal and vertical lines are calm lines.

carving   Art made by cutting into the surface of the medium.

circle   A round, geometric shape made when all points are placed the same distance from a center point.

coil   A long roll of clay joined into a circle or spiral. Clay coils are used to make pottery.

color wheel   A way of organizing the spectral colors in a circle

contrast   A way of creating a focal point. Contrast occurs when elements that are different are placed next to each other in a work of art.

collage   A work of art made of found objects, paper, or other things, glued on a surface

color   An element of art that includes hue and value. Color refers to all the spectral colors as well as black and white.

column   A supporting pillar on a building

cool hues   Blue, green, and violet. Cool hues are associated with cool things like snow, water, and grass.

curved (line)   A line that changes directions slowly and bends in arcs

curving movement   Using curved lines to move the viewer's eyes through a work of art and make the viewer feel that objects in the work of art are moving along curves

D

dark value   A value that has more black added to it

depth   A front to back measurement, or how far back something goes

diagonal (line)   A line that is oriented or moving on a slant

diagonal movement   Using diagonal lines to move the viewer's eyes through a work of art and make the viewer feel that objects in the work of art are moving along diagonals

dimension   A measurement of the amount of space an object takes up in one direction

diorama   A display of a scene using sculpted, miniature, figurines

dominant   The part of the work of art that seems more important to the viewer. Dominant elements have been emphasized.

E

earthenware   Ceramics made out of clay and fired at a low heat

emphasis   A principle of design that makes one part of a work of art seem more important than the rest

F

focal point   An area of an artwork that has been emphasized

form   Any object that has three dimensions: height, width, and depth

free-form form   An irregular, three dimensional object

free-form shapes   Irregular shapes. Splashes, blobs, and sails are all free-form shapes.

G

geometric forms   A three dimensional object whose corresponding shape is geometric.

geometric shapes   Common shapes that are regular, have specific names, and can be created using mathematical formulas. Circles, squares, triangles, and rectangles are all geometric shapes.

H

hand tools   Simple instruments for carving or sculpting

harmony   A principle of design that helps create unity by showing how objects in a work of art are similar

height   A vertical measurement, or how tall something is

horizontal (line)   Lines that are oriented or move from left to right.

hues   The spectral colors, or colors of the rainbow. Hues do not include black or white. Hues are red, orange, yellow, green, blue, and violet.

I

irregular   Does not follow a rule or pattern

L

light value   A value that has more white added to it

line   A mark made by a tool, such as a pen, pencil, or crayon as it moves across a surface

M

matte   A visual texture that does not reflect much light

medium   The supply an artist uses to create art. Some mediums are clay, paint, or wood.

monotonous   Lack of variety; boring

motif   An image that is duplicated to create a pattern. Motifs can change color or position in a pattern.

movement   A principle of design that creates the feeling that objects in a work of art are changing position or are active

N

negative space   The empty space between and surrounding shapes and forms

neon   A special kind of light that can be made to be many bright colors

O

overlap   To place one object on top of another object and partially cover the first object up

P

painting   A picture or scene that an artist has created on canvas or another surface using paint

pattern   A decorative surface design. Patterns are two-dimensional. The part of the pattern that repeats is the motif.

photograph   A picture taken using light-sensitive film and a camera

point of view   The position from which the viewer sees an object or work of art

portrait   The image of a person, especially the face

posed Arranged in a special way

positive space Any shape or form

primary hues Red, blue, and yellow. Two primary hues mixed together make a secondary hue. No two colors can be mixed to make a primary hue.

print An image created by using a stamp or printing plate. When artists make prints, they can make many identical images.

proportion The relationship of the size of different objects to each other

proportions Size relationships between parts

R

rectangle A four-sided geometric shape made of all right angles and whose opposite sides are equal in length

relief A type of sculpture where forms project from a flat background

rhythm A principle of design that is created by repeating objects through a work of art. Rhythm creates movement and is made by using positive and negative space.

rough Tactile texture that feels uneven

rough (line) A line that has jagged, uneven edges

S

sail A type of free-form shape

sculpture Three–dimensional art that is not a body form

secondary hues Orange, green, and violet. Two primary hues mixed together make a secondary hue.

shade Dark value of a hue

shapes A flat, two-dimensional figure. Shapes can only be measured by height and width.

shiny A visual texture that reflects light well

smooth Tactile texture that feels even

smooth (line) A line that has even edges

solid (line) A line that has no breaks, gaps, or holes

space An element of art that is the area in, around, and between objects. Shapes and forms are defined by the space around them.

spectral colors The hues in the rainbow or spectrum. Red, orange, yellow, green, blue, and violet.

spectrum The range of colors that it is possible to see; the rainbow

splash A type of free-form shape

square A four-sided geometric shape where all sides are the same length and all angles are right angles

statue Three-dimensional art that is a body form

still life A painting or drawing of a collection of objects that cannot move

stitchery Technique for decorating fabric by sewing threads on it

storyteller doll A Native American sculpture that shows one person relating the history of the culture to many children

style A unique quality of an object

subordinate The parts of the artwork that seem less important. Subordinate objects are not emphasized.

symmetrical When two sides of a work of art are mirror images of each other

symmetry A special type of balance where two sides of a work of art are mirror images of each other

T

tactile texture The texture that can be felt

texture An element of art that refers to how things feel or would feel if they were touched

thick (line) Wide

thin (line) Narrow

three-dimensional Has measurements in three directions: height, width, and depth

tint A light value of a hue

triangle A three-sided geometric shape

two-dimensional Has measurements in two directions: height and width

U

unity   The feeling that parts of an artwork belong together. Unity is created by balancing harmony and variety.

V

value   How light or dark a color is

variety   The use of different lines, shapes, and hues in artwork to create complicated relationships

vertical (line)   Lines that are oriented or move up and down

visual texture   Texture that can not be felt, but can be seen. Visual texture is often used in paintings.

W

warm hues   Red, orange, and yellow. Warm hues are associated with warm things such as fire or sunshine.

width   A horizontal measurement, or how long across something is

Z

zigzag (line)   Diagonal lines that connect at their ends and change direction sharply

Index

A

Adams, Ansel, 109
Alanda's Dream Tree (Scott), 40
Amour (Herbin), 52
animals, 78–81
animators, CGI, 152
architects, 208, 212
architecture, 206–209
art directors, 152
Ashoona, Kiawak, 75
Audubon, John James, 131, 198
axis, 158, 162

B

Baird Trogon (Lostutter), 96
balance, 155–163
Ballet Dancers (Scott), 164
Ballet Scene (Degas), 143
Beaux, Cecilia, 165
Bell, John, 78
Benton, Thomas Hart, 142
Blueberry Eyes (Kline), 40, 41
body forms, 74–77
Brach, Paul, 191

C

careers, 92, 152, 208, 212
Carolina Parakeet
   (Audubon), 131
Carousel Rabbit (Dentzel
   Company), 203
carving, 172
Catlin, George, 177

Cézanne, Paul, 87
CGI animators, 152
Charlip, Remy, 183
Chryssa, 154, 155
Church (Mendoza), 36
The Cliff, Etretat, Sunset
   (Monet), 195
colors, 94–107, 186–189
color wheel, 98, 102, 106
columns, 206
Composition VI (Kandinsky), 48
contrast, 168–171
Cordero, Helen, 138
Country Dance (Benton), 142
Cubi XVIII (Smith), 66
curators, 92

D

dance, 212
Dawn (Nevelson), 124
Degas, Edgar, 143
Delaunay, Robert, 97
Delaware Shoulder Bag
   (Unknown), 126
Dentzel Company, 203
depth, 88–89
DesJarlait, Patrick, 100
Diebenkorn, Richard, 44
dominant part, 166

E

Early Sunday Morning
   (Hopper), 53
Early Sunday Morning, Merced

River, Yosemite Valley, CA (Adams), 108, 109
earthenware, 78
The Emergence of the Clowns (Swentzell), 74
emphasis, 164–171
The Empire of Lights (Magritte), 169
Ernesta (Child with Nurse) (Beaux), 165
Eth-Noh-Tec, 93
Eyre, Ivan, 187

F

Family Group (Moore), 64
Figure of a Lion (Bell), 78
The First Aeroplane (Town), 117
The Flatiron (Steichen), 108
florists, 92
focal point, 166, 170
form
    and animals, 78–81
    body, 74–77
    defined, 64–65
    geometric, 66–69
    and harmony, 192–193
    and rhythm, 138–142
    and theater, 93
    three-dimensional, 68
    and variety, 198–201
At Four and a Half (Twiggs), 49
free-form forms, 70–73
free-form shapes, 56–59

G

Garrowby Hill (Hockney), 147

The Gates to Times Square (Chryssa), 154, 155
Gathering Wild Rice (DesJarlait), 100
Gay, Jacob, 172
geometric forms, 66–69
geometric shapes, 52–55
George Washington (Peale), 161
Georgia Stele (Moroles), 67
Girl With the Red Hat (Vermeer), 176
Gottlieb, Adolph, 116
Grand Skating (Moses), 150
Gui Ritual Food Container, 156

H

Hanson, Duane, 160
harmony
    of color, 186–189
    in dance, 212
    defined, 185
    of shape and form, 192–193
Headdress for Epa Masquerade (Yoruba People), 90
Herbin, Auguste, 52
Hockney, David, 147
Hopper, Edward, 53
hues, 94, 96–99, 100–107, 114, 186–189

I

Indonesian Shadow Puppet (Unknown), 56
interior designers, 212

J

Jacquette, Yvonne, 210
Jitterbugs [II] (Johnson), 60
Johnson, Willam H., 60
Jungle Tales (Shannon), 82

K

Kandinsky, Wassily, 48
Kensett, John Frederick, 105
Klee, Paul, 186
Kline, Franz, 41

L

Large Eagle (Schimmel), 199
Las Meninas (The Maids of Honor)
    (Velazquez), 184, 185
Lawrence, Jacob, 35
Lekythos (oil flask), 157
Leopard Aquamanile
    (Unknown), 79
light, 178
lines
        active, 48–51
        calm, 44–47
        and movement, 48–51
        types of, 40–43
        using, 34–39
Lionni, Leo, 194
Lostutter, Robert, 96

M

Magritte, Rene, 169
Maison Carree, Nimes, France
    (Unknown), 206
Map Quilt (Unknown), 173
matte surface, 178

McCloskey, William J., 135
Mendoza, Heron Martínez, 36
Merian, Maria Sibylla, 130
The Mill (van Rijn), 168
Moillon, Louise, 86
Monet, Claude, 45, 195
Moore, Henry, 64, 65
Moroles, Jesús, 67
Moses, Grandma, 150
motif(s), 126–129
movement, 48–51, 125, 142–149
The Museum of Modern Art, 122
museums, 62, 122, 182

N

National Gallery of Canada, 182
nature, 130–133
negative space, 136
neon, 154
Nevelson, Louise, 124, 125
Night Raid (Teichert), 113
*NO-HO-MUN-YA, One Who Gives
    No Attention* (Catlin), 177

O

Ocean Park #105 (Diebenkorn), 44
O'Keeffe, Georgia, 94, 95
overlapping, 82–85, 87

P

Palazzo da Mula, Venice
    (Monet), 45
pattern, 125–133
Peale, James, 161

Pectoral with the Name of Senwosret II (Unknown), 71
Peony Blooms IX (Zalucha), 134
people, 74–77, 82–85, 160–163
Personal Appearance (Schapiro), 120
photographs, 108–109
Plate 2 (from "Dissertation in Insect Generations and Metamorphosis in Surinam (Merian), 130
Plate with Rams (Unknown), 70
point of view, 164
Polar Bears and Cubs (Taqialuk), 190
Policeman (Hanson), 160
portraits, 176
positive space, 136
Powder Horn (Gay), 172
primary hues, 98
Princess Feather and Rising Sun Quilt, 127
proportion, 192
Pueblo Scene Corn Dancers and Church (Vigil Family), 139
puppets, 56–59

R

Ragans, Rosalind, 180
rainbow colors, 94
Red Horse Frieze (Branch), 191
The Red Poppy (O'Keeffe), 94
reliefs, 70, 73
Rembrandt (van Rijn), 168
Renoir, Pierre Auguste, 83
rhythm, 125, 134–142
Rodia, Simon, 207

S

Schapiro, Miriam, 120
Schimmel, Wilhelm, 199
Scott, John T., 40
Scott, Lorenzo, 164
sculpture, 66–69, 78, 140, 202–205
Seal Hunter (Ashoona), 74, 75
secondary hues, 98
Selection from Swimmy (Lionni), 194
set builders, 152
shade, 118
Shannon, James J., 82
shape(s). *See also* form
    free-form, 56–59
    geometric, 52–55
    and harmony, 192–193
    irregular, 58
    two-dimensional, 68, 128
    and variety, 198–201
shiny surface, 178
Simultaneous Contrasts: Sun and Moon (Delaunay), 97
Smith, David, 66
The Smithsonian Museum of American Art, 62
Solstice (Wilson), 112
space, 82–89, 93, 136
Spectre of the Sea (Gottlieb), 116
spectrum, 94–95
Spring Ice (Thomson), 104
The Starry Night (van Gogh), 146
statues, 74–75
Steichen, Edward, 108
Stieglitz, Alfred, 95
Stella, Joseph, 37

still lifes, 86–89
Still Life with Apples
    (Cézanne), 87
Still Life with Cherries,
    Strawberries, and Gooseberries
    (Moillon), 86
stitchery, 172, 175
Storyteller Doll (Cordero), 138
Street Scene (Boy with Kite)
    (Lawrence), 34
subordinate part, 166
Summer's Sunlight
    (Van Ness), 101
Swentzell, Roxanne, 74
symmetry, 156, 158, 162

T

tactile texture, 173–174
Taqialuk, Nuna, 190
Teacher (Ragans), 180
Teichert, Minerva, 113
texture, 155, 172–179
Thai Shadow Puppet
    (Unknown), 57
theatre, 93
Thomson, Tom, 104
three-dimensional forms, 68, 140
tint, 114
Town, Harold, 117
Town of Skowhegan, Maine
    (Jacquette), 210
The Tree of Houses (Klee), 186
Tundra Swan (Audubon), 198
Twiggs, Leo, 49

two-dimensional shape, 68, 128
Two Sisters (On the Terrace)
    (Renoir), 83

U

unity, 185, 202–209, 212

V

Valleyridge (Eyre), 187
value, 108–109, 110–119
van Gogh, Vincent, 146
Van Ness, Beatrice Whitney, 101
van Rijn, Rembrandt, 168
variety, 185, 194–201, 212
Velásquez, Diego, 184, 185
Vermeer, Jan, 176
A View of Mansfield Mountain
    (Kensett), 104, 105
Vigil Family, 139
visual texture, 176–179
The Voice of the City of New York
    Interpreted... (Stella), 37

W

Watts Tower (Rodia), 207
Wilson, Jane, 112
Wrapped Oranges
    (McCloskey), 135

Z

Zalucha, Peggy Flora, 134

Acknowledgments

Grateful acknowledgment is given to the following publishers and copyright owners for permissions granted to reprint selections from their publications. All possible care has been taken to trace ownership and secure permission for each selection included. In case of any errors or omissions, the Publisher will be pleased to make suitable acknowledgments in future editions. Cover from MIKE MULLIGAN AND HIS STEAM SHOVEL by Virginia Lee Burton. Copyright © 1939 by Virginia Lee Burton, © renewed 1967 by Virginia Lee Demetrios. Reprinted by permission of Houghton Mifflin Company. All rights reserved. PARADE by DONALD CREWS. Copyright © Donald Crews. Used by permission of HarperCollins Publishers. From THE BERENSTAIN BEARS' NEW BABY by Stan and Jan Berenstain, copyright © 1974 by Stanley Berenstain and Janice Berenstain. Used by permission of Random House Children's Books, a division of Random House, Inc. From HORTON HATCHES THE EGG by Dr. Seuss, copyright TM & Copyright © by Dr. Seuss Enterprises, L.P. 1940, renewed 1968. Used by permission of Random House Children's Books, a division of Random House. OWEN by KEVIN HENKES. COPYRIGHT © 1993 BY KEVIN HENKES. Used by permission of HarperCollins Publishers. IN MY FAMILY/EN MI FAMILIA. Reprinted with the permission of the publisher, Children's Book Press, San Francisco. Art copyright © 1990 by Carmen Lomas Garza.

Photo Credits

Cover Collection American Folk Art Museum, New York. Promised gift of Ralph Esmerian. P.1.2001.156 Photo © 2000 John Bigelow Taylor, New York; 5 © Jacob and Gwendolyn Lawrence Foundation. Photograph Courtesy of Gwendolyn Knight Lawrence/Art Resource, NY; 6 © Digital Image © The Museum of Modern Art/Licensed by Scala/Art Resource, NY. © Henry Moore Foundation; 7 Art Resource, NY. © 2004 The Georgia O'Keeffe Foundation/Artists Rights Society (ARS), New York; 8 © 2004 Artists Rights Society (ARS), New York/ADAGP, Paris; 9 Albright-Knox Art Gallery; 10 © Erich Lessing/Art Resource, NY; 12 (tl) Collection of Whitney Museum of American Art, New York. Photography Copyright © 1998: Whitney Museum of American Art, New York, (tr) The Baltimore Museum of Art: The Cone Collection formed by Dr. Claribel Cone and Miss Etta Cone of Baltimore, Maryland. © 2004 Estate of Pablo Picasso/Artists Rights Society (ARS), New York, (bl) Home and Away Gallery, (br) © Archivo Iconografico, S.A./Corbis; 13 (tl) National Museum of Women in the Arts. Gift of Wallace and Wilhelmina Holladay, (tr) The Asia Society, New York, Mr. and Mrs. John D. Rockefeller III Collection/Photo by Lynton Gardiner, (bl) Photography by Ansel Adams. Used with permission of the Trustees of the Ansel Adams Publishing Rights Trust. All Rights Reserved. © Digital Image © The Museum of Modern Art/Licensed by Scala/Art Resource, NY, (br) The Metropolitan Museum of Art, the Michael C. Rockefeller Collection, Purchase, Nelson A. Rockefeller Gift, 1964. (1978.412.489) Photograph by Schecter Lee. Photograph © 1986 The Metropolitan Museum of Art; 15 (tl) Photograph Oliver Folk Art, (tr) Collection of The Newark Museum, Newark, New Jersey. Purchased 1937 Felix Fund Bequest Fund, (bl) © Digital Image © The Museum of Modern Art/Licensed by Scala/Art Resource, NY. © Henry Moore Foundation, (br) The Metropolitan Museum of Art, Gift of Mrs. J. Insley Blair, 1950. Photograph © 1981 The Metropolitan Museum of Art; 16 Erich Lessing/Art Resource, NY; 17 The Metropolitan Museum of Art, H.O. Havemeyer Collection, Bequest of Mrs. H.O. Havemeyer, 1929. (29.100.113) Photograph © 1996 The Metropolitan Museum of Art; 18 © Jacob and Gwendolyn Lawrence Foundation. Photograph Courtesy of Gwendolyn Knight Lawrence/Art Resource, NY; 19 Collection of The Newark Museum, Newark, New Jersey. Purchased 1937 Felix Fund Bequest Fund. Art Resource, NY; 20 San Francisco Museum of Modern Art, Bequest of Elise S. Hass. Photo by Ben Blackwell; 21 The Metropolitan Museum of Art, New York, New York; 22 (t, tcl, tcr, br, bcr) © Photodisc/Getty Images, Inc, (bcl, bl) © Digital Vision/Getty Images, Inc; 23 (t) © Corbis, (tcl, tcr, bl, bcl, bc) © Photodisc/Getty Images, Inc, (br) © Index Stock Inc; 22 (bl) © Digital Vision/Getty Images, Inc; 24, 26, 28, 30 The Metropolitan Museum of Art, Arthur Hoppock Hearn Fund, 1958. (58.26) Photograph © 1992 The Metropolitan Museum of Art; 32, 33 © Aaron Haupt; 34 © Jacob and Gwendolyn Lawrence Foundation. Photograph Courtesy of Gwendolyn Knight Lawrence/Art Resource, NY; 35 Black Images; 36 From the Girard Foundation Collection, in The Museum of International Folk Art, a unit of the Museum of New Mexico, Santa Fe, New Mexico. Photographer: Michel Montraux; 37 Collection of The Newark Museum, Newark, New Jersey. Purchased 1937 Felix Fund Bequest Fund; 38 © Eclipse Studios; 39 Frank Fortune; 40 John T. Scott; 41 © Smithsonian American Art Museum, Washington, DC/Art Resource, NY. © 2004 The Franz Kline Estate/Artists Rights Society (ARS), New York; 42 © Eclipse Studios; 43 Randy Ellett; 44 Collection of the Modern Art Museum of Fort Worth, Museum Purchase, Sid W. Richardson Foundation Endowment Fund and The Burnett Foundation; 45 National Gallery of Art, Washington, D.C. Chester Dale Collection, Image © 2003 Board of Trustees, National Gallery of Art, Washington; 47 Frank Fortune; 48 Erich Lessing/Art Resource, NY. © 2004 Artists Rights Society (ARS), New York/ADAGP, Paris; 49 Leo Twiggs; 50 © Eclipse Studios; 51 Frank Fortune; 52 Musee departmental Matisse, Le Cateau-Cambresis. Photo Glaude Gaspari. © 2004 Artists Rights Society (ARS), New York/ADAGP, Paris; 53 Collection of Whitney Museum of American Art, New York. Photography Copyright © 1998: Whitney Museum of American Art, New York; 54 © Eclipse Studios; 55 Randy Ellett; 56 Frank Fortune; 57 Photo by Ko Yoshida; 58 © Eclipse Studios; 59 Randy Ellett; 60 © Art Resource, NY/Smithsonian Museum of American Art; 62 Michael Ventura/FOLIO; 63 Gary Gunderson; © 1993; 64 © Digital Image © The Museum of Modern Art/Licensed by Scala/Art Resource, NY. © Henry Moore Foundation; 65 © David Lees/Corbis; 66 Museum of Fine Arts Boston, Boston, Massachusetts. Art © Estate of David Smith/Licensed by VAGA, New York, New York; 67 Smithsonian American Art Museum/ Art Resource, NY; 68 © Eclipse Studios; 69 Randy Ellett; 70 The Metropolitan Museum of Art, Fletcher Fund, 1934. Photograph © 1995 The Metropolitan Museum of Art; 71 The Metropolitan Museum of Art, Rogers Fund and Henry Walters Gift, 1916. Photograph © 1983 The Metropolitan Museum of Art; 72 © Eclipse Studios; 73 Randy Ellett; 74 Heard Museum, Phoenix, Arizona; 75 Home and Away Gallery; 76 © Eclipse Studios; 77 Frank Fortune; 78 Collection American Folk Art Museum, New York. Promised gift of Ralph Esmerian. P1.2001.156 Photo © 2000 John Bigelow Taylor, New York; 79 The Metropolitan Museum of Art, New York, New York; 80 © Eclipse Studios; 81 Randy Ellett; 82 The Metropolitan Museum of Art, Arthur Hoppock Hearn Fund, 1913. Photograph © 1988 The Metropolitan Museum of Art; 83 The Art Institute of Chicago, Mr. and Mrs. Lewis Larned Coburn Memorial Collection, 1933.455 Image © The Art Institute of Chicago; 84 © Eclipse Studios; 85 Randy Ellett; 86 The Norton Simon Foundation, Pasadena, California; 87 Erich Lessing/Art Resource, NY; 88 © Eclipse Studios; 89 Randy Ellett; 90 Birmingham Museum of Art, Birmingham, Alabama; 92 © Tom Stewart/Corbis; 93 Allen Nomura; 94 Art Resource, NY. © 2004 The Georgia O'Keeffe Foundation/Artists Rights Society (ARS), New York; 95 © Getty Images; 96 Art Institute of Chicago. Restricted Gift of the Illinois Arts Council, Logan Fund, 1985.348; 97 © Digital Image The Museum of Modern Art/Licensed by Scala / Art Resource, NY; 98 © Eclipse Studios; 99 Roz Ragans; 100 Heard Museum, Phoenix, Arizona; 101 National Museum of Women in the Arts. Gift of Wallace and Wilhelmina Holladay; 103 Randy Ellett; 104 National Gallery of Canada, Ottawa, Canada; 105 Museum of Fine Arts; Museum purchase with funds provided by Hogg Brothers Collection, gift of Miss Ima Hogg by Exchange; the Houston Friends of Art and Mrs. William Stamps Farish, by exchange; and the General Accessions Fund; 108 The Metropolitan Museum of Art, Alfred Stieglitz Collection, 1933. (33.43.39) Photograph © 1998 The Metropolitan Museum of Art; 109 Photography by Ansel Adams. Used with permission of the Trustees of the Ansel Adams Publishing Rights Trust. All Rights Reserved. © Digital Image © The Museum of Modern Art/Licensed by Scala/Art Resource, NY; 110 © Eclipse Studios; 112 Courtesy DC Moore Gallery, NY; 113 Courtesy of Brigham Young University Museum of Art. Photo by David W. Hawkinson; 115 Frank Fortune; 116 The Montclair Art Museum. © Adolph and Esther Gottlieb Foundation/Licensed by VAGA, New York, New York; 117 National Gallery of Canada, Ottawa, Ontario, Canada; 119 Randy Ellett; 120 Courtesy of Miriam Schapiro; 122 © Michael S. Yamashita/Corbis; 123 Photo courtesy of Ranganiketan; © 1992; 124 Pace Wildenstein Gallery, New York. © 2004 Estate of Louise Nevelson/Artists Rights Society (ARS), New York; 125 © Bettmann/Corbis; 126 Photograph © 1996 Detroit Institute of Arts, Founders Society Purchase; 127 The Newark Museum / Art Resource, NY; 128 © Eclipse Studios; 129 Frank Fortune; 130 National Museum of Women in the Arts. Gift of Wallace and Wilhelmina Holladay; 131 Morris Museum of Art, Augusta, Georgia; 132 (tl, tr) Digital Vision/Getty Images, Inc, (tc) Photodisc/Getty Images, Inc; 133 Randy Ellett; 134 © Peggy Flora Zalucha; 135 Amon Carter Museum, Fort Worth, Texas. Acquisition in memory of Katrine Deakins, Trustee, Amon Carter Museum, 1961.1985; 136 © Eclipse Studios; 137 Photo by Ko Yoshida; 138 From the Girard Foundation Collection in the Museum of International Folk Art, a unit of the Museum of New Mexico, Santa Fe, New Mexico. Photographer: Michel Monteaux; 139 International Folk Art Foundation Collection. Museum of International Folk Art. Santa Fe, New Mexico. Photo by: Michel Monteaux; 140 (t) © Photodisc/Getty Images Inc, (b) © Eclipse Studios; 141 Randy Ellett; 142 © T.H. Benton and R.P. Benton Testamentary Trusts/Licensed by VAGA, New York, New York; 143 National Gallery of Art, Washington, D.C. Chester Dale Collection, Image © 2003 Board of Trustees, National Gallery of Art, Washington; 145 Randy Ellett; 146 Digital Image © The Museum of Modern Art/Licensed by Scala/Art Resource, NY; 147 Museum of Fine Arts, Boston; 149 Randy Ellett; 150 © Grandma Moses Properties; 152 Corbis Images; 153 Craig Schwartz; © 1990; 154 Albright-Knox Art Gallery; 155 © Chryssa; 156 Arthur M. Sackler Gallery, Smithsonian Institution. Washington, DC; 157 The Metropolitan Museum of Art, Fletcher Fund, 1931. Photography © 1999 The Metropolitan Museum of Art; 158 © Eclipse Studios; 159 Frank Fortune; 160 Collection of Mrs. Duane Hanson, Davie, Florida. Art © Estate of Duane Hanson/Licensed by VAGA New York, New York; 161 The Metropolitan Museum of Art, Bequest of William H. Huntington 1885; 163 Randy Ellett; 164 Photograph Oliver Folk Art; 165 The Metropolitan Museum of Art, Maria DeWitt Jesup Fund, 1965. Photograph © 1993 The Metropolitan Museum of Art; 166 © Eclipse Studio; 167 Randy Ellett; 168 National Gallery of Art, Washington, D.C. Widener Collection, Image © 2003 Board of Trustees, National Gallery of Art, Washington; 169 © 2004 C. Herscovici, Brussels/Artists Rights Society (ARS), New York. Photo © Herscovici/Art Resource, NY; 171 Mike Ramsey; 172 The Metropolitan Museum of Art, The Collection of J. H. Grenville Gilbert, of Ware, Massachusetts, Gift of Mrs. Grenville, 1937. Photograph © 1991 The Metropolitan Museum of Art; 173 Collection American Folk Art Museum, New York. Gift of Dr. and Mrs. C. David McLaughlin 1987.1.1. Photo by Schecter Lee; 174 (t) Alan Abramowitz/Getty Images, Inc, (b) © Eclipse Studios; 175 Randy Ellett; 176 © 1996 Board of Trustees, National Gallery of Art, Washington, DC. Andrew W. Mellon Collection; 177 Smithsonian American Art Museum, Washington, DC / Art Resource, NY; 178 © Eclipse Studios; 179, 180 Randy Ellett; 182 © Wolfgang Kaehler/Corbis; 183 Photo courtesy of Remy Charlip; 184, 185 © Erich Lessing/Art Resource, NY; 186 Norton Simon Museum, Pasadena, California. © 2004 Artists Rights Society (ARS), New York/VG Bild-Kunst, Bonn; 187 National Gallery of Canada; 188 © Eclipse Studios; 189 Randy Ellett; 190 Burdick Gallery, Washington, DC; 191 © Paul Brach; 193 Randy Ellett; 195 North Carolina Museum of Art, Purchased with funds from the state of North Carolina; 196 © Eclipse Studios; 197 Randy Ellett; 198 Historical Museum of Southern Florida; 199 Collection American Folk Art Museum, New York. Promised gift of Ralph Esmerian. Photo © 2000 John Bigelow Taylor; 201 Randy Ellett; 202 Photograph by Steve Shanker; 203 Collection American Folk Art Museum, New York. Promised gift of Ralph Esmerian. Photo © 2000 John Bigelow Taylor; 205 Randy Ellett; 206 © Archivo Iconografico, S.A./Corbis; 207 (l) © Jian Chen/Art Resource, NY, (r) © Bettman/Corbis; 208 © Mark E. Gibson/Corbis; 209 Randy Ellett; 210 Brooke Alexander Gallery, New York; 212 © Chabruken/Getty Images, Inc; 213 Craig Schwartz; 232 (t) Aaron Haupt, (b) © Eclipse Studios; 233 (t) © Eclipse Studios, (b) Aaron Haupt; 234 (t) Aaron Haupt, (b) © Eclipse Studios; 235, 236 © Eclipse Studios; 237 Aaron Haupt; 239 © Eclipse Studios; 240 Aaron Haupt; 241 Eclipse Studios; 243 (t) © Matt Meadows, (b) © Aaron Haupt; 244 (t) Aaron Haupt, (b) © Eclipse Studios; 245 © Eclipse Studios; 246 (t) Aaron Haupt, (b) © Eclipse Studios; 247 (t) © Eclipse Studios, (b) © Matt Meadows; 248 © Eclipse Studios; 249 (t) © Eclipse Studios, (b) © Matt Meadows.

Table of Contents

The Elementary Art Curriculum T2

About Aesthetic Perception T3

Introduction to Art History T4

Art Criticism T6

Meeting National and State Standards for Art Education T7

The Development of Children's Art T8

Brain-Based Learning T9

Classroom Management and Motivation
Strategies for Teaching Elementary Art T10

Art Instruction for Students with Disabilities T11

Safe Use of Art Materials T12

The Community as a Resource for Art Materials T13

Displaying Students' Art T14

Art Assessments T15

Art and Cross-Curricular Connections T16

Integrating the Four Art Forms T17

The Creative Process and Problem Solving T18

Using Writing to Enhance Your Art Curriculum T19

The Importance of Cultural Diversity Through
Art in the Elementary Classroom T20

Museum Education T21

United States Museum Resources T22

World Museum Resources T26

Program Scope and Sequence T30

Program Glossary T34

Program Index T40

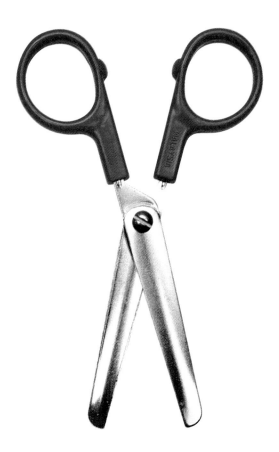

The Elementary Art Curriculum

Rosalind Ragans, Ph.D., Associate Professor Emerita, Georgia Southern University

Art education is for all students. It provides learning opportunities for the artistically talented few, as well as the many students who may never produce art outside the classroom.

A strong elementary visual arts curriculum teaches students that they can communicate a variety of ideas and emotions in many different ways. Students learn that some problems have many different solutions, and they will not be afraid to use divergent-thinking strategies. They will learn concepts and techniques that will give them control of the visual images they produce.

A strong elementary art curriculum also enables students to expand their perceptive, interpretive, and analytical abilities. They learn to find meaning in visual images, and they learn to identify aesthetic qualities in a variety of works of art and in the environment. They begin to develop the ability to make aesthetic judgments.

The visual arts have always been an integral component in the history of humanity, and through the study of art history, students will develop a better understanding of beliefs and ideas that are different from their own.

The four components of a quality art program are Aesthetic Perception, Art Criticism, Art History and Culture, and Art Production and Creative Expression.

Aesthetic Perception

Aesthetics is a branch of philosophy. In visual art, aesthetics becomes the study of the nature of beauty and art. Aesthetics is concerned with the question "What is art?" In the past, aesthetics was defined as the study of beauty because the creation of beauty was thought to be the purpose of art. Today, some aestheticians still believe that the purpose of art is to create beauty or beautifully organized arrangements of the elements of art. Some believe that art must imitate reality. Others think of art as a strong means to communicate ideas and emotions.

Aesthetic concepts are the core of the *Art Connections* curriculum. They are the framework upon which all aspects of art learning are constructed. The **About Aesthetic Perception** section in the *Student Edition* and *Teacher Edition* offers concrete methods for introducing students to aesthetics.

 Art Criticism

Works of art are the focus of every lesson. Art criticism is the sequential process used in this textbook to guide students through the procedures needed to learn from these works of art. Art criticism enables students to learn from works of art that have been created by artists from many cultures and time periods. Art criticism also provides a procedure that students can use to objectively study their own art products.

The four-step process of art criticism will help students expand their perceptive, analytical, interpretive, and aesthetic valuing abilities. The sequential steps of art criticism are similar to those used in the scientific method. During the first two steps, **Describe** and **Analyze,** students are asked to collect data objectively. During the third step, **Interpret,** students speculate about the meaning of the work based on the data collected: they make a hypothesis abut the idea, emotion, or mood expressed by the artist. During the fourth step, **Decide,** or aesthetic judgment, the students offer their conclusions about the work of art.

Art criticism helps students study a work of art before making an aesthetic judgment. Too often, beginners look at a work of art briefly and immediately make a value judgment. The sequential procedures in art criticism force the students to postpone judgment while becoming immersed in the image.

In this program art criticism is used as a higher-level method of thinking about the concepts taught in each unit. One work of art has been selected that emphasizes the elements or principles that were the focus of the lesson. Art criticism is also used to help students make a personal assessment of the artwork produced during the Creative Expression activities. The questions offered are neutral and avoid judgments involving likes and dislikes. This avoids embarrassing moments when discussing works in front of peers.

Art History and Culture

Art Connections is not an art history text, but any study of art should begin with learning something about the history of world art and the people who created it. Information about art history related to the featured work of art in each lesson is provided for the students throughout the text. The **About Art History and Culture** section provides an overview of how to include art history information in classroom instruction. Additional information is provided for the teacher in each lesson and in ancillary materials such as the *Artist Profiles* books and on the backs of the *Large Prints.* The *Art Around the World* collection and *The National Museum of Women in the Arts Collection* contain works of art from many countries and provide additional historical and cultural information.

Art Production and  Creative Expression

Each lesson includes an art production activity identified as **Practice** and **Creative Expression** in the *Student Edition.* This is the place for each student to creatively explore the lesson concept. Hands-on activities are often the most enjoyable aspect of art learning. The student integrates and internalizes the verbal and visual concepts of the lesson during the creative manipulation of art materials. While every component in the art program is equally important, every component does not need equal time. Art production requires the longest amount of time.

Do not skip the self-assessment section of the lesson. Most students would be embarrassed to offer subjective statements about their own work or the work of classmates. The four steps of art criticism offer an objective procedure for thinking about the concepts and technical procedures used during the creation of art.

Art Magazine Resources for Teachers

American Artist	*ARTnews*	*Crayola Kids*
Art Education	*Arts and Activities*	*Scholastic Art*
Art to Zoo	*Arts Education Policy Review*	*School Arts*

About Aesthetic Perception

Richard W. Burrows , Executive Director, Institute for Arts Education, San Diego, California

> *The Association of Institutes for Aesthetic Education promotes and fosters aesthetic education principles and practices through professional and institutional development. The Association provides policy and program leadership to the arts and education field at the national, state, and local levels.*

Aesthetics has been defined as the branch of philosophy that focuses on the nature of beauty, the nature and value of art, and the inquiry processes and human responses associated with those topics.

Aesthetic perception can be most simply defined as an educational approach designed to enhance understanding of artistic expression. Aesthetic perception requires two primary elements to exist: a work of art and a viewer to perceive it. An aesthetic perception approach to viewing works of art is predicated on the belief that the arts can be studied in an active, experiential way. The focus is on developing skills of perception by using works of art as a "textbook" or a focus for study. The instruction delivered by teachers is in partnership with the work of art.

Aesthetic perception provides opportunities to heighten perception and understanding through direct encounters with a broad spectrum of works of art. Students and teachers become actively involved with the artwork—observing, listening to and discussing works of art, and exploring their perceptions of these works through participatory activities. The focus is on developing skills of perception through greater understanding of art forms, of how artists make aesthetic choices, and of how these understandings relate to other aspects of life.

Misconceptions About Aesthetic Perception

As aesthetic perception approaches have become more widely used, a number of misconceptions have developed about the purpose of aesthetic perception education in the understanding of works of art.

Multidisciplinary Versus Interdisciplinary

The purpose of aesthetic perception is not to explore the commonalities among works of art. Each work of art must be studied separately first; connections should be made after an in-depth understanding of that particular work. Every work of art has a separate intention and

different meaning. If aesthetic perception is to develop a thinking- or meaning-based understanding of the work of art, then activities must reflect that point of view.

You Cannot Teach What You Do Not Like

A strong "personal" negative reaction to a work of art does not invalidate it as an object of study for students.

Arts Integration

While arts experiences must integrate with all other areas of the curriculum, it is important to understand the separate language that the arts have and acknowledge the connections with other cross-curricular areas as they arise.

The Therapeutic Value of Aesthetic Perception

Very often students and teachers will comment on the therapeutic value of aesthetic perception—it seems separate from the actual art-making processes. This is often a side effect of active engagement in artistic creation and perception. This is not the purpose of aesthetic perception, which should be seen as an alternative way of viewing the work of art and the world in which it is created.

Using Aesthetic Perception

Below are some guidelines for using an aesthetic-perception approach to education.

Deciding What to Teach

It would not be appropriate to teach the same elements over and over in connection with each work of art. Instead, knowledge of all of the elements within a given art discipline should provide the background knowledge for making a decision about what aesthetic perception experiences to design. These decisions should be based on the most predominant elements in the work of art—the responses and the backgrounds of the students.

Creating a Safe Space and Adopting a Critical Stance

It is important to create a working and learning environment with both students and teachers in which they feel comfortable taking risks and trying out new ideas. This does not mean, however, that everything that occurs in aesthetic perception has to be met with uncritical approval. Instead, experiences can be structured so that participants receive feedback on their aesthetic choices and are given an opportunity to revise and improve their solutions to problems.

Documenting the Experience

Various types of documentation serve as a way of recording the aesthetic perception events as they occur or are revisited. This documentation should include written observations, interviews, journals, and student projects. It is important in any case to record this work in order to be able to see the "habits of mind" that reveal themselves in this complex and rich way of thinking and knowing.

Aesthetic perception is a long-term undertaking and requires a patient conviction that the arts and aesthetic perception should be a part of the learning experience of young people. It requires flexibility, stamina, ingenuity, and perseverance. The rewards are astronomical in terms of student response, content understanding, and classroom relationships.

Introduction to Art History

Gene A. Mittler, Ph.D., Professor Emeritus, Texas Tech University

> *"The art of the Greeks, of the Egyptians, of the great painters who lived in other times, is not an art of the past; perhaps it is more alive today than it ever was. Art does not evolve by itself; the ideas of people change and with them their mode of expression."* —Pablo Picasso

One of the primary goals of education in the visual arts is to prepare students to make and support intelligent and sensitive decisions about works of art. In order to make those kinds of decisions students can employ two ways of examining and responding knowledgeably to visual art forms. One of these ways, art criticism, involves them in learning *from* works of art. Another approach is art history, which enables students to learn *about* works of art and the artists who created them.

The Art History Approach to Learning about Art and Artists

Art historians contend that no work of art can be fully understood unless it is viewed in relation to the circumstances in which it was created. Every artwork is created in a particular place at a particular time in history and to some degree is bound to reflect the prevailing conditions of that time and place. For example, an art history approach to the study of a painting by Rembrandt would include an examination of seventeenth century Holland—the time and place in which that particular artist lived and worked. Adhering to this approach would require that students focus attention on the social, religious, and economic conditions that existed in the republic at that time in history before focusing attention on the painter and his work. All these conditions would have impacted Rembrandt's choice of subject matter, medium, his way of handling materials, and the visual language he chose to use in expressing his ideas and feelings.

Art history, then, involves a study of the visual arts in relation to the times and places from which they sprang. This study will provide students with a richer, broader, and deeper understanding of the specific art objects selected for study and the world as it existed when those art objects were created. However, to determine the significance of the place of a particular work, such as a picture by Rembrandt, involves more than just an examination of the world conditions at the time that artist lived. It also requires a study of what went on in the world *before* and *after* Rembrandt painted his picture. A study of this kind will show students that Rembrandt, like all artists, took into account the works of other artists, selecting some ideas and techniques to use in his own painting while rejecting other ideas and techniques. This is a valuable lesson that students can apply to their own efforts to create art.

Consequently, a historical examination of a painting by Rembrandt would include the identification of any artists who may have influenced his style of painting. The most important of these artists was the Italian painter Caravaggio, whose paintings Rembrandt never saw, but without which his own work would not have taken on certain stylistic innovations. However, to understand Caravaggio, students would have to become acquainted with the artists *he* admired as well as the ones he rejected while arriving at his own revolutionary painting style. Thus, students adhering to an art history approach will find themselves involved in a fascinating learning process not unlike a game of dominoes, in which an entire row of game pieces is seen to collapse by upsetting the first domino in that row. The very last "domino" to fall in this comparison of art history to dominoes would be the very first visual image ever created—perhaps an image scratched on the rough wall of a cave by the very first prehistoric artist.

The Use of Historical Periods

For convenience, art historians divide the history of art into more or less artificial periods such as Medieval, Renaissance, Baroque, and Rococo. Doing so does no harm as long as students are reminded that the changes in art history identified by these labels, like changes of the seasons, are gradual. Each historical period passes into the next as smoothly as spring passes into summer.

If it can be assumed that an understanding of the present can be illuminated by a study of the past, then a chronological ordering of art history periods can be most helpful. By beginning at the beginning and observing the changes in art created from one year, decade, or century to the next, students will find it easier to understand how the art produced today has its roots in the art produced in the past. If students are to gain an understanding of art history, they should be afforded opportunities to see and learn about art examples from every corner of the world representing every historical period, not just those created by Western artists.

In every art history period students will encounter artists whose works preserve the traditional values of earlier artists, artists who chose to build upon current art trends, and still other artists who opted to explore revolutionary ways of expressing themselves through their art. Art history is filled with the stories of artists who accepted or rejected, endorsed or protested, conformed or reformed, contrasted or destroyed, dreamed of the past or conjured up visions of the future—but every one of those artists did so from the springboard of his or her own time and place, be that tenth-century China or twentieth-century America.

Art History as a Means of Understanding Each Other

Through art history students learn that a painting, a statue, or a temple is a consequence of how imaginative, sensitive members of any given society viewed and responded to the world around them. Art history also encourages students to regard works of art as more than objects that are pleasing to the eye, more than splendid and original products of human skill and inventiveness. Works of art also represent springboards for learning, revealing how differently people thought and acted at different times and in different geographical locations throughout the long history of humankind. A work of art reveals not only the customs, social habits, architecture, and technical achievements of its time and place; it also reflects the prevailing fears, beliefs, superstitions, desires, and values of people living in different ages at different geographic locations. Art history, then, is a vital part of the history of the human race.

Art History and Changing Tastes

As they study art history, students will discover that, over time, works of art do not always look the same to the people viewing them. This happens because people from different times and places look at art from different points of view. Cultures vary and change and so do tastes. Take any great artist or any great work of art from a bygone era and note how there have been periods in which that artist or work has been highly regarded, treated with indifference, or even ridiculed. For example, few today would venture a negative judgment of a painting created by Rembrandt, who is universally regarded as one of the greatest artists of all time. Yet, over the years, this Dutch master has not always been understood or appreciated. Indeed, when Italian artists first viewed a painting by Rembrandt they were puzzled and disappointed. They failed to understand why this artist was so highly regarded. His style, they concluded, was most peculiar because it made use of large areas of dark values and made no use of outlines favored by Italian artists.

Students must learn that art is a two-way process involving *both* artist and viewer. If students are to grasp more than the superficial appearance of a work of art, they must be prepared to learn its purpose, its *contemporary* meaning within the society in which it was produced, and its place in the historical process. No work of art is created in a vacuum. If students are to share in the ideas and feelings that contributed to the creation of a work of art, they must recognize the concepts, desires, and expectations of the person expressing those ideas and feelings at a particular point in time. This will result in a richer, broader, deeper understanding of both the artwork and the culture that witnessed its creation.

The Art History Operations

The study of art history is made easier for students if a plan of action is offered. One such plan makes use of four steps, or operations, that bear the same labels used to describe the four steps used in art criticism. These operations are description, analysis, interpretation, and decision. However, while these operations enable students to gain information from works of art during art criticism, they also are used to help students gather information about those works during art history. Briefly, the four art history operations are:

Description During this first operation, students seek to discover when, where, and by whom the work was created. In other words, they determine the period in which the work was created, the place where the artist lived, and, assuming it is known, the name of the artist.

Analysis This operation requires students to identify the unique features in a work of art that determine its artistic style. In the visual arts, style has come to mean the personal and unique way in which the artist uses the elements and principles of art to express ideas and feelings. For example, one artist may choose to delineate shapes in his painting by surrounding them with a heavy dark outline. Another painter might ignore the use of an outline and suggest shapes by creating areas of bright hues that contrast with the dull hues surrounding them.

> "Art historians contend that no work of art can be fully understood unless it is viewed in relation to the circumstances in which it was created."

Interpretation When interpreting a work of art, students take into account the impact of time and place upon the artist. It is during this operation that they learn that pictures of the same subject painted at the same time but in different geographic locations typically differ in appearance because they reflect different traditions and values. A landscape painted in fifteenth-century Italy will differ dramatically from a landscape painted at the same time in Japan. Moreover, a work of art created in the same country but at different times may also bear few stylistic similarities. A landscape painted by a French artist living and working in the late nineteenth century would have little in common with a landscape done by a French artist living and working at the beginning of the same century.

In an effort to express themselves in visual terms, artists make use of the materials and processes placed in their hands by the circumstances of time and place. Thus, a nineteenth-century African artist might have carved a figure from a piece of wood to serve as a dwelling place for a departed spirit, while a seventeenth-century artist applied his brush to canvas to paint a lifelike portrait of his king. In the spotlight of history, the efforts of both artists are magnified or diminished, honored or dismissed by forces that neither could predict or control but that had little to do with the values the artists sought to express in their work. It is the desire to discover those values that motivates students when interpreting artists' works.

Decision The final art history operation requires that students make a decision about the historical importance of a work of art. They will discover that some works are more important than others because they were the first examples of a new, revolutionary style. Others are found to be significant because they are the most accomplished and successful examples of a particular style. As their knowledge and understanding of art grows, students will find themselves liking a great many more works of art than they thought possible at the start. Gradually they will gain confidence in their historical judgments and exercise skill in defending those judgments.

Art history is a fascinating, provocative learning experience affording students the opportunity to travel through time and space. It provides them with access to the inner lives of many kinds of people and offers clues to where we come from and who we are. Finally, art history reveals that artists and their art have succeeded in helping people communicate with each other in a manner we cannot express in any other way.

Art Criticism

Rosalind Ragans, Ph.D., Associate Professor Emerita, Georgia Southern University

Art criticism is organized discussion about art. The art criticism procedures used in this program were developed by Edmund B. Feldman based on his analysis of the writings of professional art critics. He organized the elaborate procedures followed by critics and summarized them into four steps. The purpose of these four steps is to delay impulse judgments of visual images and to involve the viewer in a complex interaction with the image that can result in a truly aesthetic experience.

Art criticism involves the use of high-level thinking skills. The viewer translates the visual language of the image created by an artist into everyday words. To have a truly aesthetic experience the viewer must go beyond simple identification and recognition to the types of thinking required to analyze, interpret, and judge visual clues.

Anyone can do art criticism. All that is needed are eyes to see the image and a brain to think about what is seen. Art criticism gives a viewer of any age the confidence to discuss a work of art without worrying about what other people have said about it. One does not need to know anything about the artist, the style, or the time when the work was made to get involved with the work. After the steps of art criticism have been followed in a school setting, students are usually so interested in the art that they want to know more about the who, what, where, when, and how of the work. In other words, the students are ready to learn about art history and culture.

Description

The first step of art criticism is a clue-collecting step. The purpose of this step is to get to know the work as intimately and deeply as one can. All the information from the credit line should be noted. It is important for the viewer to know whether the artwork is 20 × 30 inches or 20 × 30 feet. The medium with which the work is made is also important. Whether a piece of sculpture is modeled with clay or carved from stone affects the viewer's impression. Then the observer names everything that is seen in the image. During description the observer must remain objective. All the descriptive terms must be neutral, value-free words.

Analysis

This is an advanced form of description. It is also an objective, clue-collecting step. During this stage the viewer studies the elements of art and the principles that have been used to organize those elements. It is during this step that the viewer begins to discover how the artist has organized the formal qualities of the work to create the content or meaning. In this program you will see how the art criticism lesson at the end of each unit is used to reinforce the concepts taught during each unit. Works of art have been selected that will help the student comprehend the artist's use of the specific elements or principles that were introduced in that unit.

Interpretation

This is the most important part of art criticism. It is during this step that the viewer pulls together all the descriptive and analytical observations to make sense of the work. The viewer makes inferences about the mood, meaning, or message being conveyed by the work. This step goes beyond narration to a generalization about life. The viewer makes guesses, but these ideas must be supported by the clues collected during the first two steps. This can be the most difficult step because it requires imagination and courage. Every interpretation can be different because each is based on the feelings and life experiences of the viewer. No one individual has done or seen exactly the same things as the next person. The viewer may see ideas in a work of art that were never dreamed of by the artist. That is not wrong. It simply means that the work is so powerful that it carries special meanings for everyone.

A good interpretation goes beyond answering "What is happening?" to answering "What does it mean?"

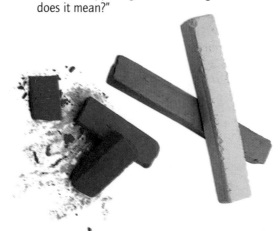

Decision (Judgment)

This is the step where a professional critic will decide the quality of a work. Is this as good as the rest of the works by this artist? How does it measure up to the works of other artists in the same group? The students who are using this program do not have enough experience to make that level of decision, so the works of art in *Art Connections* have been selected because they have already been judged to be outstanding examples of art.

The students are asked to make personal decisions. There are two levels of judgment to be made. The first is "Do you like the work?" This opinion may be embarrassing for students to share in front of classmates, and it is best left unspoken. No one can ever tell someone else what they should like or dislike.

The second level of judgment is also subjective. We ask the student to decide why the work is successful, and we use aesthetic theories to help each individual make decisions about the work. The three aesthetic theories that we employ are the most common theories: imitationalism/realism, formalism/composition, and emotionalism/expressionism. More than one theory can be used to judge a work of art.

- Some critics think the most important thing about a work of art is the realistic presentations of the subject matter. People with this point of view think that an artwork should imitate life. This theory, called **imitationalism** or **realism,** focuses on realistic representation.
- Other critics think that composition is the most important factor in a work of art. This aesthetic theory, called **formalism** or **composition,** places emphasis on the design qualities, the arrangement of the elements of art using the principles of art.
- **Emotionalism** or **expressionism** is the theory concerned with the content or meaning of the work. This theory requires that a work of art convey a message. It must arouse a response of feelings, moods, or emotions in the viewer.

In this program we provide leading questions to help the teacher and student delve into a work of art by using the steps of art criticism. These are not all the questions that can be addressed in viewing a work, and teachers are encouraged to go beyond what is presented on the pages of these books.

Meeting National and State Standards for Art Education

Nan Yoshida

Art Connections has been carefully designed to help educators meet the standards of state and national art curriculum guidelines.

The *National Standards for Arts Education* are part of Goals 2000, the overarching plan for improving American education. Approved by the United States Congress in 1994, the standards describe what every young American student should know and be able to do in the arts.

In addition to the national standards, individual states have curriculum documents that set forth guidelines and requirements in subject areas. For example, both the *Texas Essential Knowledge and Skills for Art* and the *Visual and Performing Arts Framework for California Public Schools, Kindergarten through Grade Twelve* discuss four components of visual arts education common to most other state guidelines.

Placing the national standards side by side with the Texas and California standards, one can readily see that the documents match in their expectations of what students should know and be able to do in the visual arts.

Art Connections has been developed with these national and state expectations in mind. Every lesson in the program was designed to address the components of art education in Aesthetic Perception, Art History and Culture, Creative Expression, and Art Criticism.

Aesthetic Perception
(Artistic Perception)

Each lesson begins with Activate Prior Knowledge, which asks students to recall and visualize an image from personal experience that will help them take a purposeful look at the artwork.

Introduce the Art focuses students' attention on specific attributes of the artwork, design elements and principles, underlying structures, and functions. As students answer the questions about the work of art, they develop critical *observation* skills.

Aesthetic Perception directs students to extend their artistic perception to their environment and objects in the environment. The transition is made to use keen visual and tactile perception of formal art objects in everyday life (lifelong learning).

> "In **Art Connections** students are exposed to a variety of types and styles of art from many cultures and historical periods."

Art History and Culture
(Cultural Context)

In *Art Connections* students are exposed to a variety of types and styles of art from many cultures and historical periods. Students study art from Africa; Asia; Australia; Europe; and North, Central, and South America. They learn about the role of the artist in societies. They develop appreciation for paintings, drawings, prints, photographs, sculptures, textiles, and architecture. They relate to folk, decorative, functional, and formal arts.

While information about the works of art and the artist is necessarily brief in the *Student Edition,* teachers are encouraged to use the Art History and Culture feature of the *Teacher Edition* and the *Artist Profiles* books to provide students with enriching information about the artists, the periods of art history, and cultural perspectives.

Creative Expression
(Art Production)

Creative expression is fundamental to every art lesson. The Practice activity provides a structure for students to apply lesson concepts in meaningful practice. In the Creative Expression activity, students refine their new knowledge and skills by producing original artwork based on their personal visions. The lessons throughout the program introduce a variety of art media and techniques.

Art Criticism
(Aesthetic Valuing)

Reflection and self-assessment are inherent in the art-making process. Upon completion of the Creative Expression activity, students

evaluate their own work using the four steps of art criticism: Describe, Analyze, Interpret, and Decide. These four steps of art criticism are a method for making an informed critique of others' artwork as well.

Arts Integration

In addition to the high priority placed on teaching the visual arts as a unique discipline, both national and state standards recommend the appropriate integration or interrelation of the visual arts with the other arts disciplines of music, dance, and theatre. Toward this goal, every unit in *Art Connections* culminates with a lesson integrating one of these performing arts. In addition, connections are made to music and movement/dance in every lesson of the *Teacher Edition.*

Curriculum Integration

The *Teacher Edition* has an Art Across the Curriculum section that ties art concepts to other curriculum areas. Every lesson has a connection to Reading/Language Arts, Math, Science, Social Studies, and Technology.

> ### National Standards for Arts Education © 1994
> 1. Understand and apply media, techniques, and processes.
> 2. Use knowledge of structures and functions.
> 3. Choose and evaluate a range of subject matter, symbols, and ideas.
> 4. Understand the visual arts in relation to history and cultures.
> 5. Reflect upon and assess the characteristics and merits of their work and the work of others.
> 6. Make connections between the visual arts and other disciplines.

The Development of Children's Art

Rosalind Ragans, Ph.D.

A child's ability to make and understand art develops along with his or her cognitive, social, emotional, and physical development. In 1947 Victor Lowenfeld was the first to identify and label the sequential stages that students move through as they create images. Since then many others have continued to study the development of children's visual images.

Understanding these stages will help you recognize what your students are doing; however, you must also understand that these stages describe untutored progression through the making of images. There are many outside influences on students, and these will show in their work. A well-meaning adult might teach a child to make stick figures, and because they are so easy to make, the child adopts this symbol.

Just as reading levels vary widely within one class, so do art abilities. Just as you teach students to appreciate differences in ability in other subject areas, you must help them understand that not everyone will have the same art abilities at the same time.

There are many different versions of the developmental stages; here we present a three-step version of art development. The stages of artistic development are useful norms that can help you, but they are **not** rules that must be followed.

The Manipulative Stage

Ages 2–5 (Grade K)

This has been called the scribble stage, and it is usually seen in children from two to five years old. During the early part of this stage, the child makes random, disordered scribbles. Making art at this stage is such a sensory experience that the child may hold crayons in both hands. Children who have opportunities to scribble produce a wide variety of lines, marks, dots, and shapes. The child who develops a variety of graphic marks during the scribble years will use them to produce complex symbolic drawings as he or she matures. Children who rarely scribble will have a more limited range of expression, and they will need a great deal of encouragement to continue drawing.

As the random scribbles become more controlled, the child starts to pull the marks into circular patterns until a mandala, or rough circle, is created. Rhoda Kellogg, who

studied thousands of children's drawings from all over the world, found that the mandala appears as the final stage between random scribbling and representation. This controlled scribble becomes a named scribble. Expressive concepts develop as children recognize the relationship between their marks and the visual outcome.

The Symbol-Making Stage

Ages 4–9 (Grades 1–4)

When a child makes the connection between images and an idea, a shape becomes a symbol. During this stage children develop a series of distinct images that stand for objects in their experiences. These symbols are eventually related to an environment within the drawing. The first representation of a person is a mandala. This can represent anyone the child wants it to be. Although this shape appears to be just a head, it represents the entire person. Soon the child adds a line and two marks, which represent a person with a mouth and two eyes. Then two lines are added to the shape to represent legs, two lines for arms, and a scribble for hair. The child is drawing what he or she knows, not what he or she sees. As children develop from the early symbolic stage into the symbol-making stage, they start to add more details and develop a symbol that includes all the body parts.

At first, space is not a consideration, and the size of symbols in a work is related to importance. Objects and people seem to float. Eventually the child wants to make people and objects stand up and will line things up on the bottom of the paper or on a baseline. Along with a baseline, the child starts to represent the sky with a strip of color across the top of the paper that includes a round symbol with radiating lines for the sun. As far as the child is concerned, the space between the sky and the baseline is air. The sky will not touch the earth until the child develops a more mature sense of perception, usually the result of sensitive art instruction.

Another spatial problem is overlap. Children realize that two objects cannot occupy the same space at the same time, and they avoid overlapping. As the environments they depict become more complex, children may use a bird's-eye view, a foldover view, or multiple views to represent space.

Children in this stage develop their own schema, or image, that resembles an actual object. Once a schema has been invented it will be used over and over. As the child continues to make art, the schema will become more detailed and sophisticated.

Giving a child this age coloring books may lead to self-doubt because of the conflict between the child's schema and the adult image. After coloring a seated dog in a coloring book, the child may become frustrated when his or her own drawing of a dog does not measure up to his or her memory of the adult image. Because children are exposed to so many adult images, many of which have low artistic quality, it is helpful for the teacher to expose children to the many high-quality works of art available in this program.

The Preadolescent Stage

Ages 8–13 (Grades 3–8)

Preadolescent children are still naturally inquisitive and creative, but they have learned to be more cautious. They have become very sensitive to peer opinion. They have reached a "crisis of confidence" regarding the images they make. If a work doesn't look exactly the way they think it should, or if it looks childlike, they reject the art product. This is the time when many children become frustrated and stop making art.

This is a critical time in students' visual development. They need to be taught to work slowly and with patience. They need to be taught drawing skills such as perspective and human proportions. They need to master the language of art and the use of design principles. They need the technical skills to master the various media such as painting, printmaking, ceramics, and sculpture.

Students need to see how different artists in the past have solved problems, and to observe what contemporary artists are doing today. Artists solve problems differently, and young people need to be exposed to many different ideas as they try to create their own solutions to visual problems.

The strong art teacher will lead students over this perilous bridge of doubt by gently stretching their minds to help them see more so that they can do more. At every stage in the child's visual development, a strong, understanding teacher can help the child move forward.

Brain-Based Learning

Jamye Ivey, K–12 Art Supervisor, Dougherty County School System, Georgia

At the end of the school day, teachers often face many unanswered questions concerning the young people whose education is their responsibility. Educators cannot help but wonder why students fail to respond to instructional strategies that were successful in their own experiences. Why is today's student so different?

Brain Research

Neuroscientists are now able to supply some of the answers that have plagued educators for years. The amazing, constantly changing world of technology has unlocked for researchers a new realm of understanding of the human brain. With the aid of advanced medical techniques and strategies using equipment such as MRI, FMRI, CAT, and PET scans, the working brain can be observed. Translating these new and often startling medical findings into the educational arena has provided the classroom teacher with practical methodologies and a better understanding of how, why, and when students learn best.

The brain is the most powerful organ in the body. Researchers have discovered that today's brains grow better in the real world than in artificial learning environments. Students must be able to connect their learning to previous experience in order for new learning to occur. For years teachers have designed and taught units with the activities culminating in field trips. When we consider these recent findings, we realize this procedure should be reversed. The field trip provides the student relevance that would facilitate learning. Without a related experience in the memory bank of past experiences, the learner finds no significance in the new material.

It is also important to note that synapses in the brain are formed, strengthened, and maintained by interaction with experience. The stronger the synapses, the faster the messaging travels and the greater the number of neural pathways that are created in the brain. This enables a person to be capable of creating more flexible thought processing and better memory.

Research confirms that environments shape brains. Teachers should create an environment that provides the best opportunities for this generation of young people to learn. Students of today need to move, talk, and touch more than previous learners did. Eric Jensen explains that the part of the brain that processes movement is the same part that processes learning. Thus, there needs to be movement in the classroom.

Today, we know that lecturing is the poorest way to present new learning. Only about fifty percent of the audience is actively listening in any given oral presentation. Students learn the most at the beginning of a presentation, the second-most at the end, and the least in the middle. Learners need breaks during teacher talk sessions. The attention span of a preadolescent is ten to twelve minutes.

This generation of children has more trouble organizing thoughts and learns on a more global scale. Expect students to want to understand the big picture before dealing with the details. One way to accomplish this is to let the class spend a few minutes looking through the whole chapter before focusing on the first page.

We know now that students cannot learn if they feel threatened or stressed. If a teacher shouts at a student, it takes fifteen minutes for the adrenaline levels to subside in all the students in the class. The glucose needed for cognitive functioning is redirected to combat stress, so all learning is governed to some extent by emotions. The constant threat of failure needs to be removed and recognition should be placed on individual performance, experience, and interest. Pressure, tension, and stress slow down or eliminate learning.

Brain-Based Learning and the Arts

Art teachers are known for using creative methods to capture the imaginations of their students. Need, novelty, meaning, and emotion are four ways to gain a student's attention, and using humor during instruction increases attention by fifty percent. A happy classroom is a more brain-compatible classroom.

The arts are an important part of effective teaching and an essential component of brain-compatible instruction. There is evidence that art-making has been around for over one million years. Brain research documents the arts as basic to the brain. Every culture in human history has one common thread: all had the arts. Stable art, music, and dance experiences not only enhance the aesthetic life of the learner, but they also provide important activity for the growing neurological system.

For both teacher and student, the most encouraging summation from recent research is that we continue to grow brain cells regardless of our age. Noted neuroscientist

Marion Diamond explains that it is best to keep the brain curious and active. In her opinion the most significant finding of her career has been that the brain can learn at any age. Be a lifelong learner and engage in physical activitites, which also helps build brain cells. Stay curious and stay active. How affirming this is for art educators because the successful teaching of art daily demands both creative curiosity and physical endurance.

References

Sousa, David A. (2002). *How the Brain Learns, Second Edition.* Corwin Press.

Sylwester, Robert (1995). *A Celebration of Neurons, an Educator's Guide to the Brain.* Alexandria, VA: Association for Supervision and Curriculum Development.

Eric Jensen (2001). *Arts With the Brain in Mind.* Alexandria, VA: Association for Supervision and Curriculum Development.

Sprenger, Marilee (1999). *Learning & Memory-The Brain in Action.* Alexandria, VA: Association for Supervision and Curriculum Development.

Armstrong, Thomas (1987). *In Their Own Way.* G.P. Putnam's Sons.

Armstrong, Thomas (1991). *Awakening Your Child's Natural Genius.* G.P. Putnam's Sons.

Classroom Management and Motivation Strategies for Teaching Elementary Art

Bunyan Morris, Art Teacher, Effingham County School System, Georgia

While motivating students to express themselves visually through creative means, the elementary art teacher is challenged with the task of maintaining proper classroom management. The purpose of this article is to provide some practical methods of motivating creative thought and action under the guidance of successful classroom management. Combine these methods with your own to give students the best learning experience possible.

Be Prepared. Begin the lesson excited and ready. Students will pick up on your mood the moment they walk into the room. If you set the tone at the beginning and grasp immediate control, it will be much easier to keep it throughout the lesson. It is important to have art prints and demonstration materials ready and in place for the initial focus. Practice an activity before demonstrating it if it is the first time that it has been taught. Something might happen that could not be foreseen; prepare for the best and the worst. Also, it might be a good idea to practice a concept or an activity that has not been taught in a long time. Even classroom veterans forget things.

Focus. For the initial focus of the lesson, gather the students into a group on the floor, in chairs, or on benches in an area of the room that is ready for discussion and demonstration. By gathering the students into a compact group, it is easier to make eye contact and to keep the attention of all learners. If there is no room for a separate demonstration and discussion spot, gather the tables or desks into a closer group so that no one is "out of reach."

Introduce the Art. Always introduce a lesson with a work of art that relates to what the students will be learning. Students get excited playing detective. Finding clues and ideas in a painting or sculpture allows them to make their own interpretations and assessments about art. They will in turn learn to apply this to their own work. The students don't have to know that this activity has a lofty term called *art criticism* to gain from its purpose. Encouraging them to ask questions and share ideas about a master work will give the students motivation and fresh ideas to take into the Creative Expression portion of the lesson.

Moving to Art Production. Always control the manner in which students move to the Creative Expression area from the Demonstration/Discussion center. Release students in a manner that will keep order but not quell their enthusiasm about the lesson. Use positive reinforcement by complimenting those who are sitting quietly, and send them first. It will not take long for the others to catch on. After time most of the students will become conditioned to this expectation. Even if they've been involved in a lively discussion, they will automatically become settled as this transitional period approaches.

Classroom Design. Not only should the students be orderly, but the classroom must also be organized and conducive to the movement of the teacher and students. The Creative Expression stations should have enough space between them for the teacher to reach every student. There should be enough space in traffic areas for student movement. Children need easy access to supply shelves and sinks, and should be able to move from one Creative Expression station to another unencumbered. The supplies should be organized on leveled shelves so that the students will return them to their proper places. If the teacher keeps the room and supplies organized, hopefully the students will too.

As well as keeping the room and supplies organized, the rest of the room should be visually pleasing. Display student art with master prints. This builds self-esteem. When possible, display every child's work. Make learning centers organized and interesting. Keep interesting objects around the room for visual reference. These objects might include plants, pottery, old bottles, discarded sports equipment, old toys, or anything that might capture the attention and interest of your students. Use these objects in still lifes and as objects of visual reference for lines, shapes, and other elements and principles of art.

When moving about the room assisting students, it is important to keep the senses alive and be aware of what is happening with the other students. See and hear what they think you can't.

Closing the Lesson. Normally one should try to close the class with a review of the lesson's objectives. This should be short and interesting. This is also the time to reward the students for good behavior. The art teacher must set the criteria for earning the award. Do not give the award if it is not earned. Of course, the students must be aware of the opportunity to earn an award ahead of time.

One method that works is to award the students with a "Super Behavior Card." This is simply a colorful card that can be given to the class to take back to their classroom teacher for having good behavior during art. This requires the cooperation of the classroom teacher to award the students in some manner for collecting a certain number of Super Behavior Cards. Awards might include a popcorn party or extra time at recess. If the classroom teacher is unwilling, you will have to provide the award in your class. Awarding of the Super Behavior Card can be coordinated with cleanup at the end of the period. Choose one student at the table who cleans up most thoroughly and quietly to carry the Super Behavior Card back to the classroom teacher. The students at each table will work together to earn the Super Behavior Card.

Hopefully these ideas and suggestions will reduce the challenge of maintaining classroom control and motivating students. The individual teacher must decide what works best for each situation. All of the motivation and management techniques suggested here have been tried and have been proven to work. Combined with each teacher's individual strategies, they will increase the probability of success in the art classroom.

A Sampling of Art Games for Home or School

Art Lotto: National Gallery of Art. Safari Limited, Miami, Florida.

ARTDECK. Aristoplay, Ann Arbor, Michigan.

The Fine Art Game. Piatnik, Wiener Spielkartenfabrik, Ferd. PIATNIK & Söhne.

Where Art Thou? WJ Fantasy, Inc., Bridgeport, Connecticut.

Art Instruction for Students with Disabilities

Mandy Yeager, Art Educator, Ph.D. Student, The University of North Texas, Denton, Texas

Art education empowers all students to look at, respond to, create, and enjoy works of art. Students who are disabled are no exception to this privilege. The arts have often been understood as an equalizing force in the education of students with disabilities; often these students experience discrimination from peers and adults because of their disability. This discrimination often manifests itself in avoidance of or lowered expectations for these students. Stereotypes of persons with disabilities cast them as helpless, unintelligent, dangerous, or contemptible. These stereotypes are maintained by a lack of knowledge or personal experiences with persons who are disabled.

The visual arts, because they use images to express ideas about the human experience, play a vital role in challenging and eliminating many of these stereotypes. The current emphasis of art education upon visual literacy allows students to examine and transform stereotypes that exist in the media regarding all types of differences (including age, race, class, gender, and ability). Artists throughout time have engaged in this process of recording and seeking to transform societal injustices through visual imagery.

The benefits of art for students with disabilities cannot be underestimated. The skills gained in visual arts often result in increased confidence and ability in other academic subjects. Arts-based learning is often effective because of the ways it engages the multiple senses and abilities of students.

The arts also give students opportunities to explore, express, and celebrate their identities. Teachers who include the work of artists with disabilities in their art curriculum help all students realize that disability is a part of the human experience and does not prevent anyone from being a creator of art.

Resources to Assist Art Educators

The first step to developing competence is to develop an understanding of the child's disability. There are a number of resources to assist the art teacher in this regard.

Resources at the School Level

Resources at the school level include special-education staff and related service providers who have contact with the child such as occupational and physical therapists. All of these staff members can provide the art teacher with insight into the child's learning strengths and needs and his or her physical and emotional development. They can also provide helpful suggestions for how a particular art medium or tool can be made accessible to a particular student.

Another valuable resource for the art teacher is the student's Individualized Education Plan (IEP). This plan exists for every student receiving special education services and provides information about learning styles, needs, and modifications. The *Individuals with Disabilities Education Act* (IDEA) requires that all regular education teachers of students with disabilities have access to the child's IEP and are provided support in implementing modifications to the general curriculum.

Art educators can design their art curricula to meet students' annual IEP goals. For instance, art criticism activities have the potential to enhance students' expressive language skills. Cooperative learning activities such as mural painting can foster social skills. Art production often produces self-efficacy in students with disabilities as they learn to trust their ability to achieve success. Art teachers who engage in this process of reviewing a child's IEP and delineating the ways that art curricula can address annual goals become more confident in their abilities to successfully instruct students with disabilities.

Art Education and Disability Organizations

VSA arts has been designated by the U.S. Congress as the National Coordinating Agency of Arts in Learning for Persons with Disabilities. The agency fulfills this role through a vast network of state affiliates. VSA arts produces art and disability awareness curricula and showcases the work of students with disabilities by regularly sponsoring national calls for art. It also provides access to the work of artists with disabilities.

The Special Needs Interest Group of the National Art Education Association (NAEA) meets annually at the NAEA convention to discuss best practices in art education and disability. This group publishes a column in the bimonthly publication *NAEA News*.

Adapting the Art Experience for Students with Disabilities

It is often necessary to adapt some aspect of the art experience for students with disabilities. Adaptations ensure that learning is accessible to every child; as such, adaptation is a principle of good instruction.

Adapting the art experience is essentially a creative activity, as many different combinations of students, media, and processes coalesce in one semester of art instruction. Accordingly, effective adaptations are individualized and begin with knowledge of a particular student's learning strengths and needs. Teachers may choose to adapt art media, instructional strategies, and/or physical space, depending upon the situation. This process of adaptation often begins by observation of students in an introductory art-making experience. If a student is having difficulty with an art task, try to determine the source of the difficulty. Consult with other school staff and use some of the resources listed below to determine what is most appropriate for the student and situation.

The adaptations accompanying every lesson in this text are provided as suggestions only, because learning needs and strengths vary with each child, medium, and project. It is hoped that art educators, upon reading this article, will feel equipped to utilize available resources to design and implement empowering learning experiences for all students.

Resources

Disability Education Organizations

National Dissemination Center for Children with Disabilities (NICHCY), www.nichy.org/index.html

The Council for Exceptional Children, www.cec.sped.org/

ERIC Clearinghouse on Disability and Gifted Education, http://ericec.org

Art and Disability Organizations and Resources

VSA arts, www.vsarts.org

Art, Disability and Expression Online Exhibit, www.vsarts.org/showcase/exhibits/disability/index.html

The National Art Education Association Special Needs Interest Group

EDGE: Education for Disability and Gender Equity, www.disabilityhistory.org/dwa/edge/curriculum/index-netscape.htm

National Arts and Disability Center (NADC), http://nadc.ucla.edu/

Safe Use of Art Materials

Mary Ann Boykin, Director, The Art School for Children and Young Adults
University of Houston—Clear Lake, Texas

Elementary art teachers need to be aware of safety issues that can affect the well-being of the children they teach, as well as themselves. Follow the guidelines established by the Center for Safety in the Arts to assure that neither students nor teachers are injured by the unsafe use of art materials.

Elementary teachers should do two things to prevent problems. The first is to keep all toxic and hazardous substances out of the classroom. The second is to know how to use the materials safely, because any materials can become hazardous when used inappropriately.

Toxic Substances

A toxic substance is defined by the Center for Occupational Hazards as "a poison which can damage your body's organ systems when you are overexposed to it." This harm can be immediate or can be the result of repeated exposure over time. Toxic substances can enter the body in three ways:

1. absorption through the skin
2. inhalation through the nose or mouth
3. ingestion through eating or drinking in the area where toxic materials are being used

It is up to the teacher to make sure toxic substances do not enter the classroom and that all materials are used safely to avoid problems.

Pregnant women and those who are nursing must be especially careful to prevent exposure to toxic substances. Fumes, sprays, dusts, and powders present a real hazard to the fetus, can be transferred to the infant through the mother's milk, and can be carried home to the infant or young child through dusts and residue picked up by clothing and hair. The safe path is to completely avoid exposure to any toxin by carefully reading labels and applying common sense to the situation. For example, if you plan to mix powdered tempera paint or work with chalks or clay, the safe method would include use of a respirator mask, which would prevent inhalation of these substances.

Children and Safe Art Materials

Preschool and elementary children are particularly vulnerable to unsafe art materials for a variety of reasons. Their lower body weight allows a toxic substance to become more concentrated in their bodies. Because children have a more rapid metabolism than adults, toxic substances are more quickly absorbed into their bodies. Children also tend to have more hand-to-mouth contact than adults, which allows ingestion of toxic materials. Furthermore, children are easily distracted from safety warnings regarding materials as they become involved in the art process. The tendency of children to have cuts and scratches also allows for ready entry of toxins into their bodies.

What the Labels Mean

Since 1990 our government has required the labeling of all hazardous materials. Any product labeled as hazardous is totally inappropriate for the elementary school. Safe art materials carry the statement that the material "Conforms to ASTMD-4236." A simple "nontoxic" statement on a product is not adequate.

The Arts and Crafts Materials institute developed a voluntary program to provide a safe standard for materials used by children. Products bearing the labels AP (Approved Product) or CP (Certified Product) have been tested by toxicologists in major universities and have been deemed safe for children to use. The HL (Health Label) on art products indicates that these products are appropriate to use with children 12 years old or older under the supervision of an art teacher. Products with HL labels are not safe for elementary children.

Safe Art Materials

The following are guidelines for choosing and using basic art materials in a safe manner.

Drawing Materials

- Use only water-soluble AP- or CP-designated markers. Permanent markers are extremely dangerous and can cause lung and liver damage if inhaled. Never use permanent markers in the elementary classroom.
- Do not use scented markers. This teaches children to sniff or smell materials.
- Use only dustless chalk. The amount of dust created in a classroom by twenty children wiping and blowing chalk can be irritating to those who suffer from allergies, asthma, and other respiratory problems.
- Use oil pastels; the colors are richer than crayons and the satisfaction is greater! Crayons should also bear the AP or CP label to ensure that no lead is present in these materials.

Painting Materials

- Use only liquid tempera and/or watercolor paints. If you must use powdered tempera paints, mix these outside and have the paints ready before children enter the classroom. Avoid inhaling the powders of tempera paints.
- Do not use any spray paints or fixatives. These are extremely dangerous.

Printmaking Materials

- Use only water-soluble printers' inks. Do not use any solvent-based inks.
- Use pencils to carve into unused foam trays for printing blocks. Do not use mat knives or other sharp instruments.

Collage Materials

- Sharp scissors should not be used by young children; blunt points are safe. Fourth- and fifth-graders may use rounded points with teacher supervision.
- Use only school paste or white glue for adhering papers. Do not use rubber cement unless it bears the AP or CP label. Do not use any solvent-based glues.

Sculpture and Three-Dimensional Materials

- Use premixed, moist clay for sculpture and pottery. Do not allow students to take home any unfired clay.
- Remind students to wash their hands thoroughly after using clay. The residual dust can be harmful and irritating if inhaled.
- Paint clay pieces with tempera or watercolor paints. Do not use glazes. Some have the approved labels, but they are not recommended for elementary use.
- Use pencils, craft sticks, or other blunt tools to carve clay. Soapstone should not be used for carving in a closed environment.
- Read labels carefully on pastes used for papier-mâché, because some pastes contain pesticides or preservatives that are extremely harmful.

Stitchery, Weaving, and Fiber Materials

- Use blunt plastic needles and loosely woven fabrics such as burlap for stitchery. Blunt metal tapestry needles are safe if their use is supervised.
- Young children will have trouble cutting fabric and yarn with their scissors. Precut lengths of fabric and yarn prior to introducing a task.

The Community as a Resource for Art Materials

Willis "Bing" Davis, Associate Professor Emeritus, Central State University, Ohio
President and Founder of SHANGO: The Center for the Study of African American Art & Culture

Ingenuity, resourcefulness, and creative survival have always been important to most successful art and classroom teachers when it comes to providing meaningful arts experiences for students. We are known as collectors who almost never throw anything away. Some art and classroom teachers will need to acquire the skill of always being on the lookout for resources, materials, and supplies that can supplement art materials in the classroom. It can be fun; plus, it stimulates the imagination and creative impulse. This is also a great way to build bridges and advocates for arts education.

Think of all the things you use in the art room. How many can be found locally? Safe, usable materials or supplies that can be found free or reduced in price leave more of the art budget to buy the things that have to be purchased. There are different forms of searching for inexpensive and free materials for art activities. The following are a few tried and proven ways to acquire materials, supplies, and resources that can be used for art and other educational activities.

Materials in the School Building

- Leftover wood or metal from a shop class
- Clean, empty food containers from the food-service area
- Cardboard tubes from the food-service area or copy machine
- Scrap paper from copy machines

Annual Open-House Night Resources

Open house is a great time to post a small list of hand tools needed for the art program. You would be surprised by how many extra hammers, pliers, screwdrivers, bent forks, and so on are in garages and basements. Many parents or caregivers also work at places that have by-products that could supplement the art materials in the art program.

Local Business Material Sources

- *Wood* Lumberyards are usually willing to let teachers collect boxes of scrap wood for art production. Some lumberyards will even let you leave a box with your school's name on it.
- *Wallpaper* Ask for discontinued wallpaper design sample books from paint stores.
- *Paper* Large quantities of damaged paper may be available from local paper or paper distribution companies.

> "Many local service organizations have an interest and commitment to youth and the arts."

Community Resources

- Many communities participate in the popular "Take a Child to Work" programs that allow children to see and experience where their parents or caregivers work. Almost every school also has a career day when many professional individuals visit schools to talk to students about potential careers. Both programs put schools, students, and teachers into direct contact with local businesses.
- Teachers may find that companies with national headquarters in their communities often have a strong commitment to those communities and their educational systems. Teachers can assist these companies in reaching their community commitment goals by suggesting ways to assist the school art program. Local businesses may want to sponsor the visit of a local artist or donate materials.
- Many local service organizations have an interest and commitment to youth and the arts. They often look for art and cultural events and activities to which they can contribute. Find out how they want to contribute and help them reach their goal. These events could be funding an exhibit, hosting an art reception, donating materials and supplies, framing student artwork for display in the hallways, sponsoring a local or major art field trip, and so on.

Artist Resources

- Local and regional emerging artists live in every community and can make meaningful contributions to the school art program. Artists from the community or region offer a "realness" to the program from knowing and living in the area.
- Some artists do a good job at demonstrating, some do a good slide lecture, some are more effective in large or small groups, some do great critique sessions, and some may be better mentoring one-on-one. Each individual teacher or school district can develop an annotated artist directory listing the artists' strong points for reference.
- Most communities also have one or more local arts groups or arts organizations that can assist schools in identifying and securing the services of local artists. A local arts group may be willing to do a series of Member Art Demos over the course of the year in your school.
- Another great source of local and regional artists can be found in the colleges and universities in your area. The college or university art program can show your students some of the quality art teachers students might be working with in the future. This is a great source of judges for student competitions.

Art Agencies at Local and State Levels

While everyone is aware of the existence of the National Endowment for the Arts in Washington, D.C., many may not be aware that there are state arts agencies and many community-based arts councils that can be an important resource for your art program. Find ways to let everyone in the community help your art program to be the best it can be.

Displaying Students' Art

Jackie Ellett

"My picture is hanging in the hall!" exclaims an excited second-grader. Yes, having one's work displayed is exciting. When you display a child's artwork, you are communicating two things to that child: you value what he or she has created *and* you value the child.

Why Display Students' Art?

Students are intrigued by the work their peers produce and are eager to join in any discussion that arises from the shared experiences of the work. They often compare what they have created to the work made by their peers. A natural aesthetic experience occurs, and questions and comparisons arise. These are either verbalized or internalized, depending on the circumstance of the viewing. "Why did Erin paint that flower large and the others small?" "I like the details of the seeds that Galvin added to his painting; I'll do more details next time." These are examples of questions, comments, or thoughts that may arise when students are viewing a display. Not only do displays allow students to appreciate their completed projects, but they also allow students to aspire to better art endeavors.

A class display allows students the opportunity to stand back and critique their work. A teacher-led critique is best. Students are able to evaluate their work, gain insight into things they may not have thought about, and may learn a new solution to a problem they have encountered. Discussing their works as you would a fine-art print validates the importance of what they have created. Art is so personal that a discussion can become quite insightful.

Preschool and early elementary-aged students are eager to take their works of art home to show their parents what they have created. You should ask permission of all students to display their work. By asking permission you are showing respect for their work, and for those students as individuals.

Displays are also a good way to show administrators, parents, and the community what students are learning.

Where to Display Students' Art

Many art educators believe that the farther away from the classroom the display, the more selective the images need to be. In the classroom, every student's art may be displayed.

This area can be controlled by the teacher, students, or both. Students can be allowed to change their own work when they decide to.

Outside of the classroom there is usually an assigned area for each class to display its work. Bulletin boards made of composition board are the most desirable of all surfaces for two-dimensional art. Artwork is easily attached using staples, and the walls are protected from any damage.

Setting up a school gallery of permanent or rotating student art is wonderful for promoting the art program within a school. This should be housed in a high-traffic area where parents, administrators, and visitors can view students' art. In "Leadership and the Elementary Art Specialist: Twenty Ways to Improve Your Program's Position in the Educational System," Phillip Dunn recommends establishing a "Principal's Permanent Art Collection." Having a gallery within the school with professionally matted and framed student art communicates that students' works and the art program are valued. In an era where budget cuts are customary, promoting the work of students is very important to the survival of art programs.

Displays in local businesses, civic centers, or art centers help educate the public about the work being done within their schools. These exhibits contain a mix of student art that has gone through a selection process. Depending on the guidelines and formality of the display, the works can be mounted, matted, or framed, with three-dimensional works displayed in sculpture cases or on sculpture stands.

How to Display Students' Art

Student art can be displayed in a variety of ways. Some teachers take digital photos of their students in the process of creating a work of art and critiquing their work, and then take a photo of the finished art itself. These images can be posted on a school Web site with descriptions of the activity. Digital images are sometimes used as screen savers on the school's computer system and highlighted on closed-circuit TVs in the classrooms. The most common method of display, however, is the bulletin board. These have evolved from simple displays to elaborate descriptions of the process and documentation of student learning. Teacher-focused bulletin boards have given way to student-focused displays that often include student reflections

and interpretations. Including descriptions of the process and background information adds to better understanding of the learning that has taken place.

Two-dimensional works of art should be mounted on larger contrasting or neutral-toned paper. The top and sides are usually of equal width with the bottom larger, unless the work is square, in which case all four sides are equal in width. When matting art, a two- to three-inch mat is standard, with the bottom being an inch wider than the top and sides. The mat acts as a resting place, so when arranging mounted or matted art, the works should not overlap.

A sheet of butcher paper or bulletin-board paper can be attached to a wall to define a display area and unify the works of art. Poster board or construction paper cut wider on all sides than the largest paper used by a class can be attached to the wall as an area for mounting individual students' work. Glue a clothespin to the top of the mounted paper so students can easily change their artwork. The background papers are usually in neutral colors, although primary colors may be used in classrooms for younger children. Each background paper is individually identified by placing the child's name in large print on a label.

Three-dimensional works look best in sculpture cases or on sculpture stands. Not every school can afford these. Arranging sturdy boxes of varying heights and covering them with complementary cloths allow sculptures to be equally viewed. If sculptures are of varying sizes, the largest should always be placed toward the back and the small works in front. Arranging works in odd numbers creates interest as well.

Mobiles and kites are best displayed from the ceiling. Make certain that all materials are well attached and that the items hung from the ceiling are secure so they do not fall or set off sensor alarms. As with all displays, it is important to know your school's policies about the types of adhesives allowed. Hot glue has a tendency to peel paint, low-temperature glue guns may not work on some surfaces, and double-sided tape can leave a residue. Humidity and the wall's surface both affect what will and will not work. Reusable tacky putty sticks to most surfaces and leaves few marks.

Displays do much to enhance and rejuvenate students' spirits and allow students to communicate in a way that is neither mathematical nor verbal. The art that students make is very personal and deserves careful attention when being displayed.

Art Assessments

Assessment in art can be problematic for a variety of reasons. Many educators are reluctant to evaluate a student's creative expression as good or bad. Because there are often no right or wrong answers, students and their parents could challenge a teacher's subjective opinion of a work if it is reflected in a letter grade. Furthermore, many teachers without a strong art background do not feel qualified to grade student artwork. In addition, teachers do not want to discourage creative expression by giving a low grade or an undeserved grade. Many people also often feel that talented students have the advantage in art class and that students should not be evaluated on how talented they are, but rather on how much effort they put into their work and how much progress they make.

All of these assessment difficulties stem from the focus on art production in the art classroom, rather than a reflection of art history and culture, aesthetics, or art criticism. A broader focus in the art classroom and a variety of assessment options may help in more effective art assessment.

Assessment of Lesson Objectives

Instead of subjective opinions of whether or not one likes a student's artwork, students can be evaluated on whether or not they meet the art lesson objectives or demonstrate the knowledge and skills introduced in the lesson. In a quality art program, there are objectives for aesthetic perception, art history, and art criticism, as well as for demonstrating understanding of the elements and principles of art in art production.

In *Art Connections,* every lesson has four clear, measurable objectives. At the end of each lesson, a rubric provides evaluation criteria for each objective.

Art Production: Evaluating Student Artwork

Art teachers frequently evaluate student artwork on the basis of how well it reflects the elements and principles of art that are being stressed in the lesson and how well the student meets the criteria for the artwork. Some teachers can construct rubrics or standards for the artwork beforehand and tell students how their work will be evaluated at the time it is assigned. Other teachers use written or mental checklists of their standards as they look at student artwork. Teachers may use this form of evaluation as an opportunity to discuss the work with a student and find out whether the student thought he or she met the objectives for the artwork.

In *Art Connections,* teachers can also use the Assessment Masters in the *Assessment* book to get an idea of whether a student understands the elements or principle of art for a lesson.

Art Criticism and Aesthetic Perception: Self- and Peer-Assessment

The four-step process of art criticism (Describe, Analyze, Interpret, Decide) provides a procedure that students can use to objectively study their own art products, as well as the works of others. The sequential steps of art criticism are similar to those used in the scientific method. During the first two steps, Describe and Analyze, students are asked to collect data objectively. During the third step, Interpret, students speculate about the meaning of the work based on the data collected: they make a hypothesis about the idea, emotion, or mood expressed by the artist. During the fourth step, Decide, students offer their aesthetic judgment about the work of art. The sequential procedures in art criticism force students to postpone judgment while becoming immersed in the image. It forces them to have a fully funded visual experience before drawing conclusions about a work.

Art Connections includes art criticism questions for every Creative Expression activity. Additionally, the Aesthetic Perception feature in every lesson of the *Student Edition* provides students with an opportunity to evaluate their developing aesthetic perception.

Art History and Culture

Art is a visual record of history and diverse cultures. The goals for elementary art education are that students understand and appreciate different historical periods, cultures, and artistic styles and develop respect for the traditions and contributions of diverse societies.

In *Art Connections* every lesson introduces a work of art from a particular culture, time, and style. In the Introduce the Art strategies, teachers are encouraged to compare, contrast, and share the Art History and Culture information as well as the information provided in *Artist Profiles* to help students develop an understanding of the visual arts in relation to history and cultures. Through discussion and elements in students' own artwork, teachers can evaluate students' awareness in this area.

Portfolio Assessment

Art educators could claim to have inspired the growing use of portfolio assessment in other subject areas. Many art teachers collect the best examples of a student's work and look at the progress over time. They display it and discuss it with students and parents. Student art journals with ideas, drawings, and sketches also provide an opportunity for portfolio assessment.

In *Art Connections* students are encouraged to keep their best work in a Student Portfolio and to maintain an Art Journal. Reminders of these types of portfolio assessments appear in the *Teacher Edition.*

Performance Assessment

Unlike other subject areas, art education has a long tradition of performance assessment. In art class students make things to demonstrate what they can do. In quality art programs, teachers use performance descriptions not only for art production, but also for art criticism, art history and culture, and aesthetic perception to aid them in evaluating student demonstrations of their knowledge and skills in art.

In *Art Connections,* every work of art a student produces can be considered for performance assessment of the lesson concept. Performance assessments can also involve discussions about the works of art to introduce the lesson concept and art criticism questions.

Art not only enables teachers to evaluate student knowledge and skills in art each year, but it also provides a wonderful opportunity to assess students' growth and development over time. Students and parents are often reluctant to discard artwork and fondly review it from time to time to see how children's ideas and skills have changed. Schools often keep examples of student artwork in student portfolios from year to year.

A thoughtful and fair art assessment program enables teachers to really see how much their students are capable of accomplishing.

Art and Cross-Curricular Connections

Tina Farrell

The study and production of artwork enhances learning in all areas of the curriculum. When teachers and students connect art to other subjects, learning occurs in the natural and interrelated way that it exists in the real world. We know from experience that learning is most meaningful when it is interconnected, not isolated. Therefore, making the natural connections that exist within each discipline of study, art including, enhances total understanding and brings meaning to fragmented information.

Below are a few of the ways that art education can impact the study of other subjects.

Reading/Language Arts In the viewing and analysis of a work of art, students develop oral and written communication skills. Teachers can enhance the language process by writing art terms and concepts on the board, having students generate lists of adjectives and adverbs to describe works of art, encouraging reflective inquiry into art, having students read about art and artists, and having students use works of art as stimuli for all forms of writing.

Mathematics Mathematics concepts are enhanced through art. When math concepts are presented or expressed in a visual or manipulative manner, students can more easily grasp them. The comparison and development of shapes and forms, visual-spatial relationships, measurement, proportion, estimation, and grids and graphs, for example, all are best explained through art.

> "We know from experience that learning is most meaningful when it is interconnected—not isolated."

Science In the art-making process, children learn that multiple ways to solve problems exist. They learn to discover, imagine, try new materials and techniques, experiment, develop and test hypotheses, and observe and record visual data. These are many of the skills, objectives, and habits of mind taught in science.

Social Studies The history of the world is reflected in the functional and aesthetic works of art produced by the peoples of the world. Children can gain great insights about near and distant cultures through the study of art, artifacts, and architecture.

The Arts The arts all complement each other in the skills, elements, principles, and beliefs that are emphasized in each one. Each discipline presents a unique way to express ideas and transform emotions into song, dance, interactions, words, or images. Visual artists research, develop rough drafts

(sketches), plan, develop ideas, produce completed visual ideas, and sign and title their works. These are the processes that authors, writers, dancers, composers, actors, and poets also employ.

Life Skills In art, children develop craftsmanship, self-discipline, dedication to a task, skills for working both individually and cooperatively, and pride in one's work. These skills are necessary for success in all areas of their lives.

Critical-Thinking Skills Studying the visual arts develops higher-level thinking skills as studenst analyze, compare, interpret, synthesize, and make inferences and judgments about works of art.

Art is a great integrating subject because art, first and foremost, is a form of human communication. Art is one of the first forms of communication for children. Children often express complex ideas through visual symbols that represent their beginning language systems. Art is a vehicle for children to learn about the world around them and to organize the information in a comprehensive format. As young children draw, they take textures, shapes, and colors from a complex world and form them into coherent visual images. This visual cognition, a powerful way for children to process information, is the basis for learning in and through art.

A Sampling of Art Program Resources for Schools

The California Arts Project
  (http://www.ucop.edu/tcap/aeol.html)
Getty Education Institute for the Arts
  (http://www.artsednet.getty.edu)
The Kennedy Center ArtsEdge
  (http://artsedge.kennedy-center.org)

The Metropolitan Museum of Art
  (http://www.metmuseum.org/explore/index.asp)
The Educator's Reference Desk
  (http://www.eduref.org/cgi-bin/res.cgi/Subjects/Arts)

Integrating the Four Art Forms

Susan Cambigue-Tracey, Education Division, The Music Center of Los Angeles County

Albert Einstein said, "Imagination is more important than knowledge." Without exercising the imagination, knowledge is stored in the individual containers of the mind, but connections are not made. When students are taught to use the elements, skills, and content of the visual and performing arts the possibilities for synthesizing and applying what they know are multiplied. Teachers need to ensure that imagination and creativity are always nourishing the roots of learning.

The importance of artistic activity for all students goes beyond the intrinsic value of each art form in itself. Real arts investigation requires the rigor of being able to focus, make decisions, develop discipline, promote originality, and undertake research, study, and practice. Helping students to experience new ways of thinking and seeing allows them to construct personal meaning from what they experience and to build confidence and motivation.

Each art form is a discrete discipline with its own elements, vocabulary, and strategies. However, it is interesting to see connections among them where there are fundamental concepts shared across the arts and other subjects. For example, lines in art are the marks used to create images. Line in dance is the path of gestures and traveling movements, as well as body design. Line in music is a melody and also the lyrics of a song, while lines in theatre are the words that the actors speak.

A common core of knowledge is built through the arts. The principles of visual art, such as emphasis, variety, harmony, unity, and contrast, are the underlying principles used to creating anything—an architectural structure, a musical composition, a piece of literature, a dance, or a play.

It is easy to find ways to integrate one or more of the art forms and still make connections that are viable and authentic. For example, when viewing and discussing a work of art from a particular time period or culture, select music from that same time period or culture. Aztec art will have more relevance when Aztec-inspired music is played or students can view an Aztec dance and see the colors and design of the costumes. A style of music might also inspire art. Matisse did a jazz series that begs for jazz music and dance. Students can then see and hear the structural and improvisational aspects of this style in three different art forms.

When viewing or painting family scenes in art, challenge students to think of family activities that can be portrayed in a tableau, or live, frozen picture. When viewing or creating sculpture, pair students and have one person become the "clay" and the other the "sculptor" who shapes the clay with respect and cooperation. This can extend into dance by directing the sculpted person (clay) to develop a movement idea lasting eight counts that starts and ends with the sculpted pose or form. Two people in contrasting sculptural poses can have eight counts to slowly transform from one into the other.

Three-dimensional forms in art can inspire counterbalanced (push, pull, leaning) designs made by small groups. A story, such as "The Two Skyscrapers Who Wanted to Have a Child" by Carl Sandburg, could be retold using story theatre or be portrayed in tableaux or as dramatized scenes. Students could also research musical selections to accompany their work.

> "Imagination is more important than knowledge."
> —Albert Einstein

Students will be better able to express emotions in their visual artwork if they first work with them through drama, music, and dance. Students can begin by showing a variety of emotions in the face, hands, and feet and then move toward portraying these emotions in postures such as sitting, standing, and walking. Everyday activities such as cooking or brushing teeth can be done with different emotional motivations. Students can also create short musical pieces depicting an emotion or mood or find music that expresses specific feelings or moods.

All four performing arts can become a powerful component of integrated learning. For example, during a fifth-grade project focused on the Lewis and Clark expedition, students did research in books and on the Internet to collect historical, scientific, geographical, and cultural content. This information served as the basis for group projects in music, dance, theatre, visual arts, technology, and language.

Challenged by well-designed tasks, students discussed what they knew and selected different aspects to explore through dance, music, theatre, and visual art. They learned songs of the times, listened to traditional fiddle music, and learned a rhythmic chant that was used to measure the depth of rivers. In dances, they captured the sense of traveling through "boundless space"; portrayed animals encountered during the expedition; created weather conditions such as storms; and showed the struggles in navigating rivers, waterfalls, and mountains. In theatre, students drew upon the historical characters, interpreted various scenarios, and read journal entries of Lewis and Clark. Visual art classes focused on observation drawings of plants and wild animals.

Students also created journals in which they recorded their feelings, observations, sketches, and discoveries. They were able to make connections between their own journeys and that of the Corps of Discovery. Finally, the students shared what they had learned about this epic journey in a multi-arts culmination.

The arts bring accessibility and vitality to learning, empowering students to construct meaning that has relevance for their lives. When children learn to draw, they learn to see. When children learn to act, they learn how it feels to be in different roles, cultures, and circumstances. When children learn to dance, they learn to feel comfortable in their bodies and to use movement expressively. When children learn to play an instrument, they learn perseverance and the rewards of expression through music. When children learn to sing, they release their voices and are empowered to harmonize. When children learn to write a play, they learn to observe life by thinking, reflecting, and writing. When creativity and imagination are nurtured, children learn how to use all of their resources to solve problems, to dream, and build on the ideas of others.

The Creative Process and Problem Solving

Bunyan Morris, Art Teacher, Effingham County School System, Georgia

There is great reward in watching the artistic growth of a child. Simply providing the media and the time for creating is not enough. The student's natural curiosity and desire to create must be nurtured, encouraged, and challenged. Even the brightest and most talented students need a teacher's guidance in developing the critical-thinking skills necessary for creative problem solving. The intention of this article is to provide ideas and methods for fostering creativity by developing and encouraging divergent problem solving and critical-thinking skills in elementary school art students.

Classroom Management

Fostering creativity in the art classroom is possibly an art teacher's most important skill. In order to encourage creativity, a teacher must be able to relate to students at their thinking level and then guide them to a higher level of cognitive reasoning. Classroom and behavior management are essential. There cannot be an atmosphere of creativity in a room with chaos. That is not to say that one must be a firm authoritarian. A good art teacher will learn how to walk the fine line between maintaining order and maximizing creative energy among students. Although some may not admit it, all students prefer an educational environment that is free from annoying distractions created by other students. Therefore, good behavior management is a must for maintaining a creative environment.

Visual References

Introducing a lesson with a work of art and going through the art criticism process is a tried and true method of encouraging creativity. It is important to discuss works of art that are related to the objectives of the lesson. Working strictly from imagination and memory is usually not effective. Students must have visual references from which to gather ideas.

Picture files, reference books, and the Internet are just a few sources for visual images. Photographs of people and various natural and humanmade objects provide ideas and references for drawing. Images can be collected from magazines and calendars or unwanted photographs. The image file should be organized according to subject matter or theme.

Reference books filled with images related to the lesson should be available to students. They may be checked out of the media center and kept in the room, or they may belong to the classroom. Some media specialists are willing to search for and reserve books that a teacher may need for an upcoming lesson.

An image search on the Internet is one method to help students access a visual reference that may not be available in the classroom's image file, reference books, or the school's media center.

Art Journals

Students who keep art journals maintain handy reference tools. An art journal is the best way to record ideas through sketching and writing. If art journals and writing tools are kept handy, students can jot down ideas or make sketches to save for future use. Ideas can come to mind any place or any time such as in the cafeteria, on the playground, or at the bus stop. The method or tool doesn't really matter that much. It is just important that students have a way of practicing and recording creative ideas.

Exercising the Brain

Reading should be encouraged. Students who like to read perform better in all subjects. Descriptive language stimulates the imagination. Reading a passage about the beauty of a tree or the sound of a waterfall creates a visual image in the brain. This visual image can be stored in the sketchbook and later rendered as a sculpture, painting, or drawing. Encouraging reading encourages creativity. Teachers and schools should encourage parents to limit their children's time watching television because this takes away from reading and creative play time.

Resting the Brain

Teachers should be tolerant of students taking small breaks. Sometimes students need down time to regenerate their mental energy. This down time can take the form of daydreaming or play. Both are important to the creative process. Common sense and good judgment is used to determine when a student is using time for thinking as opposed to just wasting time. Students should be reminded to get a

> "Fostering creativity in the art classroom is possibly an art teacher's most important skill."

good night's sleep every night. This is not something teachers can control, but it should be encouraged. We all know that brains function better after a good night's rest.

Enriching Observation Skills

Enriched observation skills lead to more focused experimentation in art. Artists are naturally observant, but teachers know that most students are not born with natural talent. Through practice, all students can enrich their observation and critical-thinking skills. It is important to get students to slow down and see what they might not otherwise observe. One way to do this is to play an observation game. With the students' help, the teacher can set up a still life in the room. A fun game similar to "I Spy" can be played once the still life is ready. The students describe textures, lines, shapes, colors, and other elements and principles of art found within the real-life objects. The teacher writes the observations and descriptions on the board. Once the game is over and students move to the project portion of the lesson, they will be better equipped with enriched observation skills and more focused critical-thinking skills as they create.

In order to gain more focused and creative experimentation from students, an important goal of every art teacher should be to encourage creativity and divergent problem solving and critical thinking. Hopefully, teachers will find value in the ideas shared in this article and combine them with their own ideas to encourage creativity in their students.

Using Writing to Enhance Your Art Curriculum

Mary Lazzari, Ed.S., Elementary Art Teacher, Clarke County School District, Athens, Georgia

In recent decades, art teachers have expanded their area of expertise from art production to lessons that include art criticism, art history, and aesthetics. Art is being used as a vehicle not only for increasing creativity but also for developing thinking skills. One way to broaden the art experience and enhance these skills is through guided, interactive writing techniques. Writing about art is an essential component of a well-rounded art curriculum because it provides students with the opportunity to transform thoughts and feelings into words and images. It can also provide the art teacher a more personalized format for communicating with a large student population and assist art teachers in meeting the increased demand to qualify and quantify their students' learning.

> "Art is being used as a vehicle not only for increasing creativity but also for developing thinking skills."

A visual arts curriculum rich in written language activities can facilitate the development of higher-order thinking skills, such as the ability to analyze, defend, and interpret. The use of written statements can help students slow down and refine their thoughts about their own art and the art of others. Words can become the voice for a shy or inarticulate student. With writing as a means of self-expression, art educators can be more in tune with their students' inner thoughts. Some art teachers may be reluctant to incorporate writing into their curriculum because they fear a less than enthusiastic response from their students. Here are a variety of suggestions that can help motivate elementary students to write about art.

Journals

Whether it is a few sheets of paper stapled together or a spiral notebook, students enjoy having a place to write their private thoughts and feelings. Journals can be used to record the thought process from the beginning to the end of a project. It can also be a place to brainstorm ideas or vent frustrations. Art teachers can give written feedback and encouragement to each student in his or her journal.

Titles

Materials: Selected works of art, pencil and paper

At the completion of a project, students can write descriptive titles for their works of art. A title can inform, challenge, or even surprise a viewer. Younger children or students with a language deficit can dictate the title as the teacher writes. Include the student's title when displaying the artwork. Students can also think of a new title for a famous work of art. Compare it to the artist's original title and discuss the similarities and differences.

Acrostic Poems

Materials: Selected works of art, pencil and paper (for individual writings), or dry/wipe board (for group writing)

Select an artist's name or art topic and write the letters vertically. Instruct students to think of words that describe the artist or topic. Students should think of a decriptive word for each letter in the artist's name or art topic. Descriptive words can start, end, or have the letter anywhere in the selected word. Display acrostic poems with the art work that inspired them.

Venn Diagrams

Materials: Individual sheets of Venn diagrams (or draw a large diagram on the board for a whole group discussion); a set of art postcards

Place an image in each of the two outer circles of the Venn diagram. Students describe qualities they see in each of the two works of art. Qualities that are unique to each image are written in the circle that contains the image. Qualities that they have in common are written in the center of the diagram where the two circles overlap. Invite individuals or groups to share their observations. Mount and display Venn diagrams with student artwork.

Artist Statements

Materials: Pencil and paper

Direct students to write three to five sentences about their artwork. Have the students consider these questions: What did I study? What did I create? What did I learn? Display the artist statements with the completed artwork.

Writing Buddies

If you have students who are reluctant or unmotivated to write during art class, have them work in groups. Ask for a student volunteer to be the group secretary. This student is responsible for writing down the group's thoughts and ideas. Students who are not strong in written expression will still feel success in sharing their ideas and opinions.

Brainstorming Ideas

Incorporate writing at the beginning of a lesson by having students use writing devices such as webs. The main topic is placed on the center of the page and ideas that support or expand it are written on the sides.

Vocabulary

Incorporate vocabulary into the art room. Post the "Word of the Day" on a chart or bulletin board display. Build a "Word Wall" with art vocabulary that is added throughout the year. Use word labels on art materials and equipment around the room. Create art flash cards with art words or concepts printed on them. Use the flash cards to find elements such as line, shape, and color in works of art or to review these concepts at the beginning or end of a lesson.

Try writing yourself!

Post statements about projects when displaying your students' works of art. Describe the learning objects and concepts in your statement. Use the display to inform parents, teachers and administrators about the rich and interesting learning that is taking place in your art class. Include articles about lessons, projects, and student achievements in your school or district newsletter.

Writing is an important means of creative expression. It is as valid and essential to the art curriculum as drawing or painting. Using writing to augment the art curriculum not only improves the students' ability to express ideas, it helps the art teacher communicate more effectively with every student. When art teachers integrate art instruction and writing about art, the entire curriculum is enhanced. By pairing art production, a realization of students' thoughts and ideas, with writing, a reflective way to understand and validate their opinions and feelings, art teachers can broaden the scope of the art experience. At the same time, the art teacher will develop a critical means to record and assess student learning.

The Importance of Cultural Diversity Through Art in the Elementary Classroom

Jane Rhoades Hudak, Ph.D., Professor of Art, Georgia Southern University

Culture is learned. People acquire information about the world and how to deal with it as members of a society. Individuals do not learn about their culture by themselves. Children learn about the art of their own culture and other cultures through family and friends, through the mass media, and through the Internet. The information learned this way is often valuable, but it cannot be relied upon to always give adequate and correct information. Schools are often the most effective place for giving students the opportunity to learn about the art of their culture and other cultures.

Our view of the nature of the world and our place in it is expressed and communicated culturally. Every society has institutions that teach culture—family and school are two of the best examples in our society. All societies have religions, which are bodies of cultural knowledge and practices. We also have rituals for birth and death. All cultures have objects that are used for everyday living. We express our world and views through dance, drama, music, and art. We decorate our world and our bodies. We paint our faces and the walls of our houses. We make music with instruments and our voices. All this activity is shaped by our participation in a cultural tradition.

A quality elementary art program provides a wonderful opportunity for teachers to expose students to a variety of cultures as well as their own and to help them to become culturally aware. Following are several of the areas such a program can enhance.

Art Promotes Intracultural Understanding

Through a culturally diverse art program, students begin to understand the role and function that art and artists play in society. Through learning about the art of other cultures, they have the opportunity to identify similarities and differences among their culture and others. They learn that art reflects the religion, politics, economics, and other aspects of a culture.

Through a quality art program, students can address issues of ethnocentrism, bias, stereotyping, prejudice, discrimination, and racism. Students can learn that no one racial, cultural, or national group is superior to another and that no one group's art is better than another.

Art Teaches Self-Esteem Through Diversity

Through a quality art program, students learn to recognize, acknowledge, and celebrate racial and cultural diversity through art within their own society. A good program helps promote the enhancement and affirmation of their self-esteem and encourages pride in their heritage. Personal expression is encouraged, and the result is often a statement in visual form that is both inventive and filled with personal meaning.

Art Teaches Effective Communication

When a quality art program is implemented, students are encouraged to increase their visual literacy skills. Students begin to understand that artists transmit information that cannot be disclosed through other modes of communication. Students learn visual literacy by looking, understanding, talking, writing, and making images. They learn that each society has its own way of communicating through image. Through a culturally sensitive art program, students will be able to discuss and compare art from other societies.

Art Teaches about the Past

Through a quality art program, students develop sensitivity and understanding for the history of humankind. For many periods in history, it is only through visual remains or material culture that societies' cultures can be pieced together. Experiences that students have with these art objects from the past teach them respect for others, challenge their minds, and stimulate not only their intellect but also their imagination.

Art Teaches Critical Thinking

A culturally sensitive art program encourages a variety of critical thinking skills. When students look at art from other cultures, they make critical judgments and develop their own opinions. Students are asked to identify and recall information; to organize selected facts and ideas; to use particular facts, rules, and principles; to figure out component parts or to classify; and to combine ideas and form a new whole.

Art Teaches Perceptual Sensitivity and Aesthetic Awareness

As a result of a quality art program, students develop a keen sense of awareness and an appreciation for beauty. They learn that each culture has its own criteria for beauty. Art experiences help cultivate an aesthetic sensitivity and respect for the natural and humanmade environment. Art classes are the only place in the school curriculum where students learn about what constitutes quality visual design—about harmony, order, organization, and specific design qualities such as balance, movement, and unity.

Art Teaches Creativity

When a culturally sensitive art program is implemented, creativity in all students is stimulated and nurtured. Students learn to solve problems creatively. They learn that every society has some form of creative expression. In some societies, no one special person is called an artist—everyone in the culture makes "art" objects.

Teachers can help prevent students from having a simplistic view of other cultures and help them understand the cultural context of how and why works of art are created. *Art Connections* has been carefully constructed so that students will be exposed to works of art that represent a wide variety of cultures. Questions and strategies are designed to help teachers put art in a cultural context for students. The Art History and Culture feature in the *Teacher Edition* and the *Artist Profiles* book provide additional information about the works of art and the artists.

As a teacher, you are a cultural transmitter. A quality art program taught by a culturally sensitive teacher benefits every student. When educators teach in a systematic, meaningful way, students acquire knowledge about art and cultures that will benefit them throughout their lives.

Museum Education

Marilyn J.S. Goodman, Director of Education, Solomon R. Guggenheim Museum

Museums are truly magnificent places. In recent years, these bastions of culture have taken tremendous strides toward making their collections accessible to a broader audience. Museum educators are usually eager to share new information and ideas and are delighted to assist school educators with programs and materials that can easily be incorporated into the classroom. Museums contain a wealth of treasures that offer extraordinary resources for teachers and students, and which will undoubtedly enrich the overall classroom experience.

Getting acquainted with museums in your region can be a real eye-opener. Museums collect objects that document human achievement, both in our own and in other cultures. A local historical society or farm museum might contain a variety of clothing and tools that can bring history to life. A science museum may offer interactive exhibits about phenomena in the natural or physical sciences, sensory perception, new technologies, or space exploration. A children's museum will offer hands-on displays specially designed to motivate young children to learn by doing. Art museums contain visually stunning works that reflect the diversity of human thought and experience.

Museums do not supplant classroom instruction. They enhance and reinforce what is taught by providing raw materials in the forms of objects, artifacts, and exhibits. Museums give students the chance to see and sometimes handle the real thing. It is one thing to talk about Egypt's role in the history of civilization; it is another thing entirely to see the wrappings on a cat mummy, discover hieroglyphs on a sarcophagus, or be overwhelmed by the power and grandeur of large stone sculptures of kings and queens.

When students have the chance to look at portraits, still lifes, landscapes, genre scenes, furniture, clothing, and artifacts, they learn more than by just seeing a picture of a person, place, or thing. They learn how to "read" a culture. Perhaps more importantly, they learn to develop their own process of investigation and critical inquiry. What was this person's life really like? What can one learn about the class structure of this society? What can we tell about craftspeople, available materials, or the objects this society valued? What does the clothing tell us about the climate of the region? What can we learn about the geography, topography, and vegetation? What did people eat? How did they spend leisure time? What were their religious beliefs? Is there any evidence of trade and communication with other regions? What scientific inventions were present at the time? Can one tell if they communicated through language or by writing? Because children are naturally curious, objects will motivate them to think, research, and learn.

> "A visit to a museum will make the curriculum come alive as students begin to explore objects and learn about their meanings."

A visit to a museum will make the curriculum come alive as students begin to explore objects and learn about their meanings. Museum objects give us information in a way that is very different from reading about the objects. Students must think critically to determine both the questions and answers for themselves. A first-hand, visual investigation of an object's style, material, subject matter, and physical characteristics offers preliminary clues to deciphering its meaning. When the exploration is combined with other knowledge, such as the geography and natural resources of a region; the historical context; the social, political, and economic structure of a culture; or even advances in science and technology, students can be engaged in a type of learning that is truly multidisciplinary and may lead them into other areas of study. Moreover, methods for gathering information go far beyond what people see. Exploring objects and works of art allows students to use all of their senses, combining intellect with intuition. The opportunity for experiential, emotional, and intellectual learning is always present.

Museum objects present different historical and cultural perspectives. Students can gather information about people, culture, belief systems, values, and the ways people lived in the past. Museum visits encourage students to see things from broader global and intellectual points of view, developing respect for the work, lives, and points of view of others. Students are encouraged to respond in a variety of ways and on different levels. Most importantly, students are invited to formulate and express their ideas and then discuss them with others.

To learn about museum resources, teachers can contact the education departments of museums in their region. If teachers explain the level of their students, the subjects they are studying, and the specific aspects of the curriculum they would like to supplement, the museum's education department can help to tailor the resources to the class. In addition to guided tours and workshops, the museum education department may offer materials for loan, including slides, pamphlets, posters, postcards, kits, and other printed materials. Some museums have teacher resource rooms filled with books, films, videos, CD-ROMs, and computer databases geared toward educators. Trained staff is available to answer questions or to help teachers develop a complete learning unit that can integrate museum objects with classroom studies.

Using museums is an excellent way to enrich and enliven the classroom experience. Educators can take the first step by learning all they can about the rich and diverse resources available to them and their students.

U.S. Museum Resources

Alabama

1 Birmingham Museum of Art
*2000 8th Avenue North,
Birmingham*
http://www.ARTSbma.org

2 Mobile Museum of Art
4850 Museum Drive, Mobile
http://www.mobilemuseum
ofart.com

3 Montgomery Museum
of Fine Arts
1 Museum Drive, Montgomery
http://www.mmfa.org

Alaska

4 Alaska State Museum
395 Whittier Street, Juneau
http://www.museums.
state.ak.us/asmhome.html

5 Anchorage Heritage Library
Museum
*301 West Northern Lights
Boulevard, Anchorage*
http://www.wellsfargohistory.
com/museums/alaska.ht

6 Anchorage Museum
of History and Art
*121 West 7th Avenue,
Anchorage*
http://www.anchorage
museum.org

Arizona

7 Heard Museum
2301 N Central Avenue, Phoenix
http://www.heard.org/

8 Phoenix Art Museum
*1625 North Central Avenue,
Phoenix*
http://www.phxart.org

9 Scottsdale Museum
of Contemporary Art - (SMOCA)
7380 E 2nd St, Scottsdale
http://www.scottsdalearts.org

Arkansas

10 Arkansas State
University Museum
Jonesboro, AR 72467
http://museumastate.edu

11 Historic Arkansas Museum
*200 East 3rd Street,
Little Rock*
http://www.arkansashistory.
com/

12 Old State House Museum
*300 West Markham Street,
Little Rock*
http://www.oldstatehouse.com

California

13 Asian Art Museum
of San Francisco
Golden Gate Park, San Francisco
http://www.asianart.org

14 Berkeley Art Museum
and Pacific Film Archive
2625 Durant Avenue, Berkeley
http://www.bampfa.berkeley.
edu

15 El Museo Mexicano -
Mexican Museum
*Fort Mason Center,
Building D, San Francisco*
http://www.mexican
museum.org

16 J Paul Getty
Center Museum
*1200 Getty Center Drive,
Los Angeles, CA*
http://www.getty.edu

17 Japanese American
National Museum
*369 East 1st Street,
Los Angeles*
http://www.janm.org

18 Korean American Museum
*3780 Wilshire Boulevard
220, Los Angeles*
http://www.kamuseum.org

19 L A County Museum
of Art
*5905 Wilshire Boulevard,
Los Angeles*
http://www.lacma.org

20 San Francisco Museum
of Modern Art
*151 3rd Street Building A,
San Francisco*
http://www.sfmoma.org/

21 Santa Barbara
Museum of Art
1130 State Street, Santa Barbara
http://www.sbmuseart.org

22 Southwest Museum
234 Museum Drive, Los Angeles
http://www.southwest
museum.org/

Colorado

23 Aspen Art Museum
590 North Mill Street, Aspen
http://www.aspenart
museum.org

24 Boulder Museum
of Contemporary Art
1750 Thirteenth Street, Boulder
http://www.bmoca.org/

25 Denver Art Museum
100 West 14th Avenue, Denver
http://www.denverart
museum.org

Connecticut

26 New Britain Museum
of American Art
*56 Lexington Street,
New Britain*
http://www.nbmaa.org

27 Norwalk Museum
41 North Main Street, Norwalk
http://www.norwalkct.org/
norwalkmuseum/index.htm

28 Wadsworth Atheneum
Museum of Art
600 Main Street, Hartford
http://www.wadsworth
atheneum.org/

Delaware

29 Delaware Art Museum
*800 S Madison Street
Suite B, Wilmington*
http://www.delart.org

30 Sewell C Biggs Museum
of American Art
406 Federal Street, Dover
http://www.biggsmuseum.
org

31 Winterthur Museum
Route 52, Winterthur
http://www.winterthur.org/

Florida

32 Bass Museum of Art
2121 Park Ave, Miami
http://www.bassmuseum.org/

33 Key West Art and
Historical Society
281 Front Street, Key West
http://www.kwahs.com

34 Lowe Art Museum
1301 Stanford Drive, Miami
http://www.lowemuseum.
com/

35 Miami Art Museum
101 West Flagler Street, Miami
http://www.miamiart
museum.org/

36 Museum of Fine Arts,
St Petersburg
*255 Beach Drive Northeast, St
Petersburg*
http://www.fine-arts.org

37 Salvador Dali Museum
*1000 3rd Street South,
St Petersburg*
http://www.salvadordali
museum.org

Georgia

38 Albany Museum of Art
311 Meadowlark Drive, Albany
http://www.albany
museum.com/

39 High Museum of Art
*1280 Peachtree Street
Northeast, Atlanta, GA*
http://www.high.org

40 Morris Museum of Art
1 10th Street, Augusta
http://www.themorris.org

Hawaii

41 Contemporary Museum,
Honolulu
*2411 Makiki Heights Drive,
Honolulu*
http://www.tcmhi.org

42 Kauai Museum
4428 Rice Street, Lihue
http://www.kauaimuseum.org

43 University of Hawaii
at Manoa Art Gallery
*University of Hawaii at Manoa,
Honolulu*
http://www.hawaii.edu/
artgallery

Idaho

44 Boise Art Museum

670 Julia Davis Drive, Boise
http://www.boiseart
museum.org

45 Eagle Rock Art Museum
and Education Center, Inc.
*300 S Capital Avenue,
Idaho Falls*
http://www.eaglerockart
museum.org

Illinois

46 Art Institute of Chicago
*111 South Michigan Avenue,
Chicago*
http://www.artic.edu/aic/

47 Krannert Art Museum
*500 East Peabody Drive,
Champaign*
http://www.kam.uiuc.edu

48 Martin D'Arcy
Museum of Art
*6525 N Sheridan Road,
Chicago*
http://darcy.luc.edu

49 Mitchell Museum
of the American Indian
*2600 Central Park Ave,
Evanston*
http://www.mitchell
museum.org/

50 Museum of
Contemporary Art
*220 East Chicago Avenue,
Chicago*
http://www.mcachicago.org

51 Smart Museum of Art
*5550 South Greenwood Avenue,
Chicago*
http://smartmuseum.
uchicago.edu/

Indiana

52 Brauer Museum of Art
*Valparaiso University Center
for the Arts, Valparaiso*
http://wwwstage.valpo.edu/
artmuseum/index.html

53 Eiteljorg Museum
of American Indian
and Western Art
*500 West Washington Street,
Indianapolis*
http://www.eiteljorg.org

54 Indianapolis
Museum of Art
*1200 West 38th Street,
Indianapolis*
http://www.ima-art.org

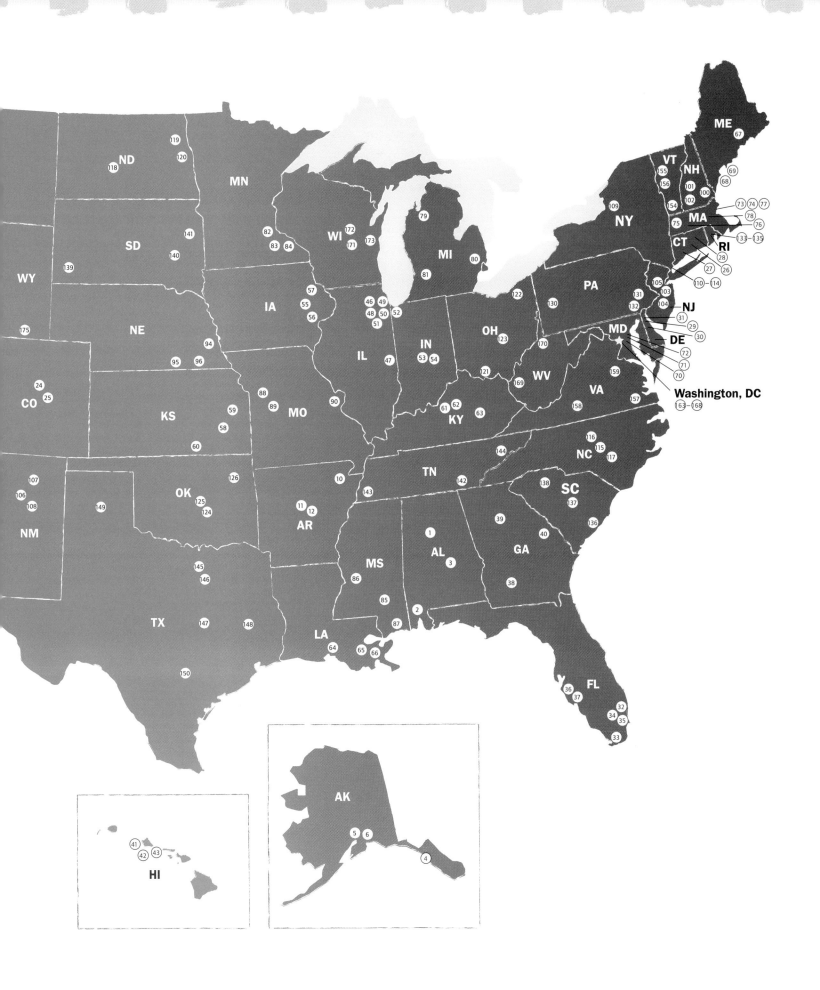

U.S. Museum Resources (continued)

Iowa

55 Cedar Rapids
Museum of Art
*410 3rd Avenue Southeast,
Cedar Rapids*
http://www.crma.org

56 Davenport Museum of Art
*1737 West 12th Street,
Davenport*
http://www.art-dma.org

57 Dubuque Museum of Art
36 East 8th Street, Dubuque
http://www.dbqart.com

Kansas

58 Coutts Memorial Museum
*110 North Main Street,
El Dorado*
http://skyways.lib.ks.us/
kansas/museums/coutts/ind

59 Spencer Museum of Art
*1301 Mississippi Street,
Lawrence*
http://www.ukans.edu/~sma/

60 Wichita Art Museum
*West Museum Boulevard,
Wichita*
http://www.wichitaart
museum.org

Kentucky

61 Kentucky Museum
of Arts + Design
609 West Main Street, Louisville
http://www.kentuckycrafts.org

62 Speed Art Museum, the
2035 South Third St., Louisville
http://www.speedmuseum.org

63 University of Kentucky
Art Museum
*Rose and Euclid Avenue,
Lexington*
http://www.uky.edu/Art
Museum/

Louisiana

64 African-American Museum
*125 New Market Street,
St Martinville*
http://stmartinparish-
la.org/tourism_africanmuseum

65 Louisiana State Museum
751 Chartres Street, New Orleans
http://lsm.crt.state.la.us/

66 New Orleans
Museum of Art
*City Park 1 Collins Diboll Circle,
New Orleans*
http://www.noma.org

Maine

67 Farnsworth Art Museum
*352 Main Street, Box 466,
Rockland*
http://farnsworthmuseum.org/

68 Ogunquit Museum
of American Art
Shore Road, Ogunquit
http://www.ogunquit
museum.org

69 Portland
Museum of Art
7 Congress Square, Portland
http://www.portlandmuseum.
org

Maryland

70 African Art
Museum of Maryland
*5430 Vantage Point Road,
Columbia*
http://www.Africanart
museum.org

71 Baltimore
Museum of Art
10 Art Museum Drive, Baltimore
http://www.artbma.org/

72 Walters Art Museum
*600 North Charles Street,
Baltimore*
http://www.thewalters.org

Massachusetts

73 Harvard University
Art Museums
32 Quincy Street, Cambridge
http://www.artmuseums.
harvard.edu/

74 Institute of Contemporary
Art
955 Boylston Street, Boston
http://www.icaboston.org

75 MASS MoCA -
Massachusetts Museum
of Contemporary Art
87 Marshall Street, North Adams
http://www.massmoca.org

76 Mead Art Museum
*Amherst College, PO Box 5000,
Amherst*
http://www.amherst.edu/
~mead/

77 Museum of Fine Arts
Boston
465 Huntington Avenue, Boston
http://www.mfa.org/

78 Worcester Art Museum
55 Salisbury Street, Worcester
http://www.worcesterart.org

Michigan

79 Cranbrook Art Museum
*39221 Woodward Avenue,
PO Box 801, Bloomfield Hills*
http://www.cranbrook.
edu/art/museum/

80 Detroit Institute of Arts
*5200 Woodward Avenue,
Detroit*
http://www.dia.org

81 Grand Rapids
Art Museum
55 Division Ave N, Grand Rapids
http://www.gramonline.org

Minnesota

82 Frederick R Weisman
Art Museum
*333 East River Road # 200,
Minneapolis*
http://hudson.acad.umn.edu/

83 Minnesota Museum
of American Art
*Landmark Center 75 West 5th
Street West, St Paul*
http://www.mmaa.org

84 Walker Art Center
*725 Vineland Place,
Minneapolis*
http://www.walkerart.org

Mississippi

85 Lauren Rogers
Museum of Art
*5th Avenue and 7th Street,
Laurel*
http://www.lrma.org/

86 Mississippi Museum
of Art
*201 E Pascagoula St
Ste 103, Jackson*
http://www.msmuseumart.
org/

87 Walter Anderson
Museum of Art
*510 Washington Avenue,
Ocean Springs*
http://www.walteranderson
museum.org/

Missouri

88 Albrecht-Kemper Art Museum
2818 Frederick Avenue, St Joseph
http://www.albrecht-
kemper.org/

89 Nelson-Atkins
Museum of Art
4525 Oak Street, Kansas City
http://www.nelson-
atkins.org/

90 St Louis Art Museum
1 Fine Arts Drive, St Louis
http://www.slam.org

Montana

91 Art Museum of Missoula
*335 North Pattee Street,
Missoula*
http://www.artmissoula.org/

92 Hockaday Museum
of Art
*2nd Avenue East at
Third Street, Kalispell*
http://www.hockadayart
museum.org/

93 Montana Museum
of Art and Culture
University of Montana, Missoula
http://www.umt.edu/partv/
famus/

Nebraska

94 Joslyn Art Museum
2200 Dodge St., Omaha
http://www.joslyn.org

95 Museum of Nebraska Art
(MONA)
2401 Central Avenue, Kearney
http://monet.unk.edu/mona/

96 Sheldon Memorial
Art Gallery and
Sculpture Garden
*University of Nebraska-Lincoln,
12th and R Streets, Lincoln*
http://sheldon.unl.edu/

Nevada

97 Las Vegas Art Museum
*9600 West Sahara Avenue,
Las Vegas*
http://www.lvam.com

98 Nevada Museum of Art
160 West Liberty Street, Reno
http://www.nevadaart.org

99 Walker African-American
Museum and Research Center
*705 W Van Buren Ave,
Las Vegas*
http://members.aol.com/
Bigbrwnsis/

New Hampshire

100 Currier Museum of Art
201 Myrtle Way, Manchester
http://www.currier.org

101 Hood Museum of Art
Wheelock Street, Hanover
http://web.dartmouth.
edu/~hood/

102 Mariposa Museum
26 Main Street, Peterborough
http://www.mariposa
museum.org

New Jersey

103 Jane Voorhees
Zimmerli Art Museum
*71 Hamilton St, Rutgers
University, New Brunswick*
http://www.zimmerlimuseum.
rutgers.edu

104 Jersey City Museum
*350 Montgomery Street,
Jersey City*
http://www.jerseycity
museum.org/

105 Princeton University
Art Museum
Princeton University, Princeton
http://www.princetonart
museum.org/

New Mexico

106 Georgia O'Keeffe Museum
217 Johnson Street, Santa Fe
http://www.okeeffe
museum.org

107 Harwood Museum of Art
*238 Ledoux Street, 4080
NDCBU, Taos*
http://www.harwood
museum.org

108 Institute of American
Indian Arts Museum
Cathedral Place, Santa Fe
http://www.iaiancad.org

New York

109 Albright-Knox
Art Gallery
1285 Elmwood Avenue, Buffalo
http://www.albrightknox.org

110 Metropolitan Museum
of Art
*6626 Metropolitan Avenue
FL 2, Flushing*
http://www.Metmuseum.org/

111 Museum of Modern Art
MoMA
11 West 53 Street , New York
http://www.moma.org/

112 New Museum
of Contemporary Art
583 Broadway, New York
http://www.newmuseum.org/

113 Solomon R Guggenheim
Museum, New York
1071 5th Ave at 89th, New York
http://www.guggenheim.org
/new_york_index.html

114 Whitney Museum
of American Art
*945 Madison Avenue FL 5,
New York*
http://www.whitney.org

North Carolina

115 Ackland Art Museum
*Columbia and Franklin Street,
Chapel Hill*
http://www.ackland.org

116 Duke University
Museum of Art
*Buchanan Blvd-Trinity Avenue,
Durham*
http://www.duke.edu/web/
duma/

117 North Carolina Museum
of Art
2110 Blue Ridge Road, Raleigh
http://www.ncartmuseum.org/

North Dakota

118 *North Heritage Center of
the State Historical Society of
North Dakota, Bismarck*
http://www.state.nd.us/hist/
index.html

119 North Dakota
Museum of Art
Centennial Drive, Grand Forks
http://www.ndmoa.com

120 Plains Art Museum
219 7th Street South, Fargo
http://www.plainsart.org/

Ohio

121 Cincinnati Art Museum
953 Eden Park Drive, Cincinnati
http://www.cincinnatiart
museum.com/

122 Cleveland Museum of Art
11150 East Boulevard, Cleveland
http://www.clemusart.com/

123 Columbus Museum of Art
480 East Broad Street, Columbus
http://www.columbusmuseum.
org

Oklahoma

124 Fred Jones Jr
Museum of Art
*410 West Boyd Street,
University of Oklahoma, Norman*
http://www.ou.edu/fjjma/

125 Oklahoma City
Art Museum
*3113 Pershing Boulevard,
Oklahoma City*
http://www.okcartmuseum.
com/

126 Philbrook Museum of Art
*2727 South Rockford Road,
Tulsa, OK*
http://www.philbrook.org/

Oregon

127 Coos Art Museum
235 Anderson Avenue, Coos Bay
http://www.coosart.org

128 Portland Art Museum
1219 SW Park Ave., Portland
http://www.pam.org

129 University of Oregon
Museum of Art
*1223 University of Oregon,
Eugene*
http://uoma.uoregon.edu/

Pennsylvania

130 The Andy Warhol
Museum
117 Sandusky Street, Pittsburgh
http://www.clpgh.org/warhol/

131 The Palmer
Museum of Art
*Curtin Rd, The Pennsylvania
State University, University Park*
http://www.psu.edu/dept/
palmermuseum/

132 Philadelphia
Museum of Art
*26th Street and the Benjamin
Franklin Parkway, Philadelphia*
http://pma.libertynet.org/

Rhode Island

133 Museum of Art,
Rhode Island School of Design
224 Benefit Street, Providence
http://www.risd.edu/

134 Museum Of Primitive
Art & Culture
*1058 Kingstown Road,
South Kingstown*

135 National Museum
of American Illustration
*Vernon Court 492 Bellevue
Avenue , Newport*
http://www.american
illustration.org

South Carolina

136 Gibbes Museum of Art
135 Meeting Street, Charleston
http://www.gibbes.com/

137 Columbia Museum of Art
*Main and Hampton Streets,
Columbia*
http://www.colmusart.org/

138 The Spartanburg County
Museum of Art
385 S Spring St., Spartanburg
http://www.sparklenet.com/
museumofart

South Dakota

139 Journey Museum
222 New York Street, Rapid City
http://www.journeymuseum.org

140 Oscar Howe Art Center
and Middle Border Museum
*1300 E University Street P.O
Box 1071 Mitchell*
http://www.oscarhowe.com/
index.htm

141 South Dakota Art Museum
P.O Box 2250, Brookings
http://web.sdstate.edu/sites/
artmuseum/

Tennessee

142 Hunter Museum of Art
10 Bluff View, Chattanooga
http://www.huntermuseum.
org/

143 Institute of Egyptian
Art and Archaeology
*The University of Memphis,
Memphis*
http://www.memst.edu/
egypt/about.html

144 Knoxville Museum of Art
*1050 Worlds Fair Park Drive,
Knoxville*
http://www.knoxart.org

Texas

145 Dallas Museum of Art
1717 North Harwood, Dallas
http://dm-art.org/

146 Kimbell Art Museum
*3333 Camp Bowie Blvd.,
Fort Worth*
http://kimbellart.org/

147 Mexic-Arte Museum
419 Congress Avenue, Austin
http://www.mexic-arte
museum.org

148 The Museum of Fine Arts
1001 Bissonnet, Houston
http://mfah.org/

149 Panhandle-Plains
Historical Museum,
West Texas A&M University
2401 4th Ave., Canyon
http://www.wtamu.edu/
museum/

150 San Antonio Museum
of Art
*200 West Jones Avenue,
San Antonio*
http://www.sa-museum.org

Utah

151 BYU Museum of Art
*Brigham Young University,
Provo*
http://www.byu.edu/moa/

152 St George Art Museum
175 East 200 North, St George
http://www.ci.st-george.ut.us/
arts/artmuseum.php

153 Utah Museum of Fine
Arts, University of Utah
*370 South 1530 East
University of Utah , Salt Lake City*
http://www.utah.edu/umfa/

Vermont

154 The Bennington Museum
West Main St., Bennington
http://www.bennington
museum.com

155 Robert Hull
Fleming Museum
Colchester Avenue, Burlington
http://www.uvm.edu/
~fleming/home/

156 Shelburne Museum
*US Route 7, PO Box 10,
Shelburne*
http://www.shelburne
museum.org

Virginia

157 Chrysler Museum of Art
245 West Olney Rd., Norfolk
http://www.chrysler.org/

158 Maier Museum of Art
*2500 Rivermont Avenue,
Lynchburg*
http://www.rmwc.edu/
Maier/

159 Virginia Museum
of Fine Arts
2800 Grove Ave., Richmond
http://www.vmfa.state.va.us/

Washington

160 Frye Art Museum
704 Terry Ave., Seattle
http://fryeart.org/

161 Jundt Art Museum
*502 East Boone Avenue,
Spokane*
http://www.gonzaga.edu/
Campus+Resources/Museums
+an

162 Seattle Art Museum
100 University St., Seattle
http://seattleartmuseum.
org/

Washington, D.C.

163 Arthur M Sackler Gallery
and the Freer Gallery of Art
1050 Independence Avenue, SW
http://www.asia.si.edu/
default.htm

164 Corcoran Gallery of Art
500 17th Street Northwest
http://www.corcoran.org/

165 Hirshhorn Museum
and Sculpture Garden
*Independence Avenue
and 7th Street Southwest*
http://hirshhorn.si.edu/

166 National Gallery of Art
http://www.nga.gov/

167 The National Museum
of Women in the Arts
1250 New York Ave., NW
http://www.nmwa.org/

168 Smithsonian Museums
Smithsonian Institution
http://www.si.edu/

West Virginia

169 Huntington Museum
of Art
2033 McCoy Rd., Huntington
http://www.hmoa.org/

170 Oglebay Institute:
Mansion Museum and
Glass Museum
Burton Center, Wheeling
http://www.oionline.com/

Wisconsin

171 Elvehjem Museum of Art
*800 University Avenue,
Madison*
http://www.lvm.wisc.edu

172 Leigh Yawkey Woodson
Art Museum
700 North Twelfth St, Wausau
http://www.lywam.org/

173 Milwaukee Art Museum
*750 North Lincoln Memorial
Dr., Milwaukee*
http://www.mam.org/

Wyoming

174 National Museum
of Wildlife Art
2820 Rungius Road, Jackson
http://www.wildlifeart.org

175 University of Wyoming
Art Museum
2111 Willett Dr., Laramie
http://uwadmnweb.uwyo.
edu/artmuseum/

World Museum Resources

Argentina

1 Fundacion Federico Klemm
Buenos Aires, Argentina
www.fundacionfjklemm.org

Australia

2 Art Gallery of New South Wales
Sydney, Australia
www.artgallery.nsw.gov.au/

3 Australian National Art Gallery
Canberra, Australia
www.nga.gov.au/Home/index.cfm

4 Museum of Contemporary Art
Sydney, Australia
www.mca.com.au/

Austria

5 Kunsthistorisches Museum Wien
Vienna, Austria
www.khm.at/

Bahrain

6 Al Hayat Museum
Manama, Bahrain
www.beitalquran.com/

Brazil

7 Museu Historico Nacional
Rio de Janeiro, Brazil
www.museuhistoriconacional.com.br/ingles/index.htm

Canada

8 Art Gallery of Calgary
Calgary, Canada
www.artgallerycalgary.com/

9 Morris and Helen Belkin Art Gallery, University of British Columbia
Vancouver, Canada
www.belkin-gallery.ubc.ca/

10 Art Gallery of Newfoundland and Labrador
St. Johns, Canada
www.mun.ca/agnl/main.html

11 Art Gallery of Nova Scotia
Halifax, Canada
www.agns.ns.ca/

12 Art Gallery of Ontario
Toronto, Canada
www.ago.net/navigation/flash/index.cfm

13 National Gallery of Canada
Ottawa, Canada
www.national.gallery.ca/

14 The Montreal Museum of Fine Arts
Quebec, Canada
www.mmfa.qc.ca/en/index.html

15 McMichael Canadian Art Collection
Toronto, Canada
www.mcmichael.com/

16 Winnipeg Art Gallery
Winnipeg, Canada
www.wag.mb.ca/

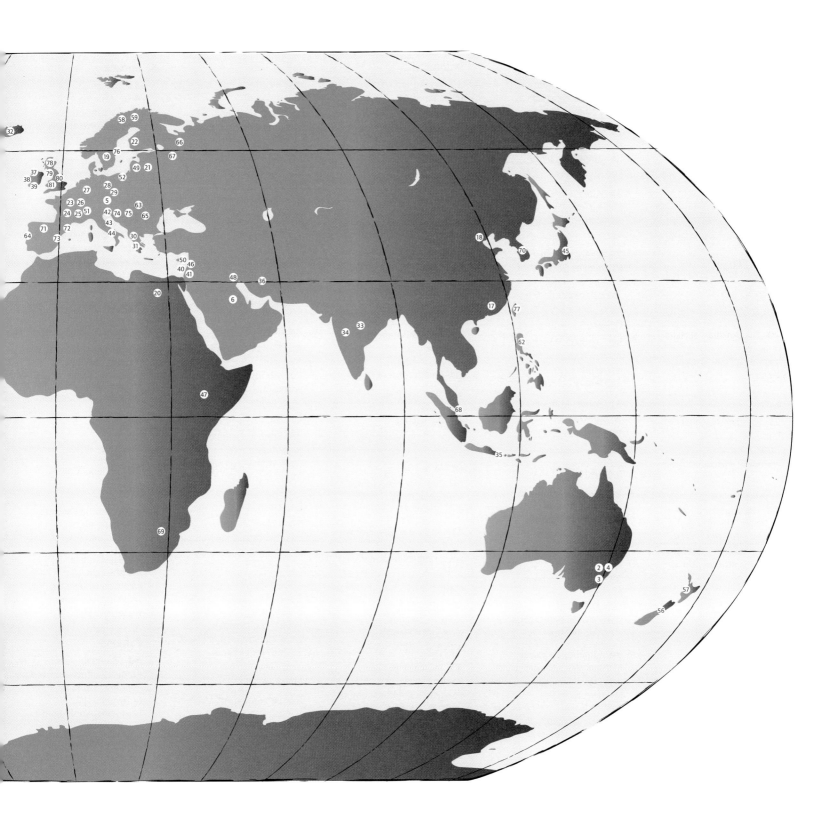

World Museum Resources

China

17 Hong Kong
Museum of Art
Hong Kong, China
www.lcsd.gov.hk/CE/Mus
eum/Arts/english/intro/
eintro.html

18 Palace Museum
Beijing, China
www.dpm.org.cn/

Denmark

19 National Museum
Copenhagen, Denmark
www.natmus.dk/sw1413.
asp

Egypt

20 The Egyptian Museum
Cairo, Egypt
www.egyptianmuseum.
gov.eg/

Estonia

21 Estonian National
Museum
Tartu, Estonia
www.erm.ee/?lang=ENG

Finland

22 The Finnish
National Gallery
Helsinki, Finland
www.fng.fi/fng/rootnew/
en/vtm/etusivu.htm

France

23 The Louvre
Paris, France
www.louvre.fr/louvrea.htm

24 Musee d'Orsay,
Paris, France
www.musee-orsay.fr/

25 Centre Georges
Pompidou
Paris, France
www.cnac-gp.fr/Pompidou/
Accueil.nsf/tunnel?
OpenForm

Germany

26 Neues Museum
Nuremberg, Germany
www.nmn.de/

27 Hamburg Kunsthalle
Hamburg, Germany
www.hamburger-
kunsthalle.de/

28 Alte National Galerie
Berlin, Germany
www.alte-nationalgalerie.
de/

29 Bauhaus Archiv
Museum of Design
Berlin, Germany
www.bauhaus.de/english/

Greece

30 Acropolis Museum
Athens, Greece
www.culture.gr/2/21/211/
21101m/e211am01.html

31 Benaki Museum
Athens, Greece
www.benaki.gr/index-
en.htm

Iceland

32 Living Art Museum
Reykjavik, Iceland
www.nylo.is/English/
index.html

India

33 National Museum
of India
New Delhi, India
www.nationalmuseumindia
.org/index.html

34 Chhatrapati Shivaji
Maharaj Vastu Sangrahalaya
(Formerly the Prince of Wales
Museum of
Western India)
Mumbai (Bombay), India
www.bombaymuseum.org/

Indonesia

35 Agung Rai
Museum of Art
Ubud, Bali, Indonesia
www.nusantara.com/
arma/

Iran

36 National
Museum of Iran
Tehran, Iran
www.nationalmuseumofira
n.com/

Ireland

37 Hunt Museum
Limerick, Ireland
www.huntmuseum.com/

38 Irish Museum
of Modern Art
Dublin, Ireland
www.modernart.ie/

39 National Gallery
of Ireland
Dublin, Ireland
www.nationalgallery.ie/

Israel

40 The Israel Museum
Jerusalem, Israel
www.imj.org.il/

41 Tel Aviv Museum of Art
Tel Aviv, Israel
www.tamuseum.com/

Italy

42 Uffizi Gallery
Florence, Italy
www.uffizi.firenze.it/
welcomeE.html

43 Museo di Roma
Rome, Italy
www.museodiroma.comune
.roma.it/PalazzoBraschi/
inizio.mostra

44 Vatican Museum
Vatican City
http://mv.vatican.va/
3_EN/pages/MV_Home.
html

Japan

45 Kyoto National Museum
Tokyo, Japan
www.kyohaku.go.jp/index
e.htm

Jordan

46 Darat al Funun
Home for the Arts
Amman, Jordan
www.daratalfunun.org/

Kenya

47 National Museum
of Kenya
Nairobi, Kenya
www.museums.or.ke/

Kuwait

48 Kuwait National
Museum
Kuwait City, Kuwait
www.kmia.org.kw

Latvia

49 State Museum of Art
Riga, Latvia
www.vmm.lv/en/muzejs.
html

Lebanon

50 American University of
Beirut Archaeology Museum
Beirut, Lebanon

Liechtenstein

51 Kunstmuseum
Liechtenstein
Vaduz, Liechtenstein
www.kunstmuseum.li/web
2306e/index.html

Lithuania

52 Lithuanian Art Museum
Vilnius, Lithuania
www.ldm.lt/ldm_en.htm

Mexico

53 Museo de
Arte Moderno
Mexico City, Mexico
www.arts-history.mx/
museos/mam/home2.html

54 National Museum
of Anthropology
Mexico City, Mexico
www.mna.inah.gob.mx/

55 Museo de Arte
Contemporaneo de Oaxaca
Oaxaca, Mexico
www.arts-history.mx/
museos/maco/home.html

New Zealand

56 Centre of
Contemporary Art
Christchurch, New Zealand
www.coca.org.nz/

57 Auckland Art Gallery
Auckland, New Zealand
www.aucklandartgallery.
govt.nz/

Norway

58 National Gallery
of Norway
Oslo, Norway
www.museumsnett.no/
nasjonalgalleriet/flash_
versjon_engelsk/

59 Lillehammer
Art Museum
Lillehammer, Norway
www.lillehammerart
museum.com/

Panama

60 Museo de Arte
Contemporaneo de Panama
*Panama, Republic
of Panama*
www.macpanama.org/

Peru

61 Museo Arqueologico
Rafael Larco Herrera
Lima, Peru
museolarco.perucultural.
org.pe/

Philippines

62 Philippine National
Museum
Manila, Philippines
http://nmuseum.tripod.
com/

Poland

63 Polish National Museum
Warsaw, Poland
www.mnw.art.pl/

Portugal

64 Museu Calouste
Gulbenkian
Lisbon, Portugal
www.gulbenkian.pt/

Romania

65 The National Museum
of Art of Romania
Bucharest, Romania
http://art.museum.ro/
museum.html

Russia

66 The State Hermitage
Museum
St. Petersburg, Russia
www.hermitagemuseum.
org/

67 Pushkin Museum
of Fine Arts
Moscow, Russia
www.museum.ru/gmii/

Singapore

68 Singapore Art Museum
*Singapore, Republic of
Singapore*
www.nhb.gov.sg/SAM/
sam.shtml

South Africa

69 Pretoria Art Museum
Pretoria, South Africa
www.pretoriaartmuseum.
co.za/

South Korea

70 Seoul Metropolitan
Museum of Art
Seoul, South Korea
www.metro.seoul.kr/
muse/eng/

Spain

71 Guggenheim
Bilbao Museum
Bilbao, Spain
www.guggenheim-
bilbao.es/idioma.htm

72 Museu d'Art
Contemporani
Barcelona, Spain
www.macba.es/home.php

73 Valencian Institute
of Modern Art
Valencia, Spain
www.ivam.es/

Switzerland

74 Kunstmuseum Basel
Basel, Switzerland
www.kunstmuseumbasel.
ch/de/

75 Kunsthaus
Zurich, Switzerland
www.kunsthaus.ch/

Sweden

76 National Museum
Stockholm, Sweden
www.nationalmuseum.se/

Taiwan

77 National Palace Museum
T'aipei, Taiwan
www.npm.gov.tw/english/
index-e.htm

United Kingdom

78 National Gallery
of London
London, England
www.nationalgallery.
org.uk/

79 British Museum
London, England
www.thebritishmuseum.
ac.uk/

80 Tate Gallery
London, England
www.tate.org.uk/home/
default.htm

81 Victoria and
Albert Museum
London, England
www.vam.ac.uk/

Uruguay

82 Museo Nacianal
de Artes Visuales
Montevideo, Uruguay
www.mnav.gub.uy/

Elements and Principles of Art

Scope and Sequence

Elements of Art	Level K						Level 1						Level 2						Level 3					
	U1	U2	U3	U4	U5	U6	U1	U2	U3	U4	U5	U6	U1	U2	U3	U4	U5	U6	U1	U2	U3	U4	U5	U6
Line	1–6						1–6	1					1–4							1–2				
Shape		1–6			6			1–6		1			5–6					2, 4	3–6					
Color			1–6						1–6						1–3			1, 3			1–6			
Value															4–6						1			
Space				1, 3						2, 5, 6				5–6						1–3				
Form			2–6	5						1–4		4	1–4				2, 4		4–6					
Texture					1–6					1–3							5–6						5–6	

Principles of Art	Level K						Level 1						Level 2						Level 3					
	U1	U2	U3	U4	U5	U6	U1	U2	U3	U4	U5	U6	U1	U2	U3	U4	U5	U6	U1	U2	U3	U4	U5	U6
Pattern						1				4–5					1–2								1–3	
Rhythm						2					6				3–6								4–6	
Balance				3–4								1–2				1–2						1–4		
Proportion																								
Emphasis										3–4						3–4								3–4
Variety																3–4								2
Harmony																1–2								1
Unity						5–6						5–6						5–6						5–6

*Numbers indicate lesson numbers within a given unit.

Top table

Level 4						Level 5						Level 6						Level 7 — Exploring Art	Level 8 — Understanding Art
U1	U2	U3	U4	U5	U6	U1	U2	U3	U4	U5	U6	U1	U2	U3	U4	U5	U6		
1-6						1-2						1						Chapter 2, 6, 7, 8, 9, 10, 11	Chapter 2, 6, 8, 9, 12, 15, 16
	1-2					3	1					2						Chapter 2, 6, 8, 9, 10, 11	Chapter 2, 3, 5, 8, 9, 13, 14, 16, 17
		1-4						1-4				1-4						Chapter 2, 4, 8, 9, 11, 13	Chapter 2, 3, 4, 8, 11, 12, 14-17
		5-6				4-6							2-3					Chapter 14	Chapter 13, 14, 15
				1-3			1-3							5-6				Chapter 2, 4, 10, 12	Chapter 6, 7, 13, 15
		1-3						4-6					3-4					Chapter 2, 6, 11, 12, 13	Chapter 6, 14, 15
			4-5							1				5-6				Chapter 2, 14	Chapter 3, 5, 6, 11-16

Bottom table

Level 4						Level 5						Level 6						Level 7 — Exploring Art	Level 8 — Understanding Art
U1	U2	U3	U4	U5	U6	U1	U2	U3	U4	U5	U6	U1	U2	U3	U4	U5	U6		
	3							5-6					1-3					Chapter 3, 6	Chapter 7, 8, 10, 15, 17
	4-6								2-3				4-6					Chapter 3, 4, 7	
		1-3							4-6						1-4			Chapter 3, 11, 12	Chapter 5, 7, 9, 10, 11, 13
			4-6					1-6									1-6	Chapter 3, 11, 14	Chapter 5, 11, 12
			6								5			3-4	5-6			Chapter 3, 11	Chapter 5, 10, 11, 12, 16
											5			2				Chapter 3, 6, 13	Chapter 3, 4, 5, 10, 15
											4			1			1-2	Chapter 3, 6, 7	Chapter 4, 5, 7, 12, 16
											6			5-6			5-6	Chapter 3	Chapter 7

Media

Scope and Sequence

Media	Level K						Level 1						Level 2						Level 3					
	U1	U2	U3	U4	U5	U6	U1	U2	U3	U4	U5	U6	U1	U2	U3	U4	U5	U6	U1	U2	U3	U4	U5	U6
Collage	6	2	2, 3		1	3	3		5			3, 4	5	5					4					
Drawing	2, 4, 5	4, 5	1, 4, 5	1	2	1, 2	1	1–3, 5	1, 4		2, 6	1, 5				2, 3	2–4, 6	4	1, 2, 5, 6	3	1	1	3, 5	6
Fiber Arts					4, 6						5						5					6		2
Mixed Media		6		3, 4	3			5		5	1	2	2, 6	2	2, 3	6				6	4, 6			4
Painting	1		6					1, 2, 4	4	3, 6	6		3, 4	6	1, 4–6			1, 3	3	2	2, 3, 5	4		
Photography																								
Printmaking		3									4					1				1				1
Three-Dimensional Forms				2, 5, 6	5	4, 6			1–4	3		6	1	1, 3, 4		4	1	5		4, 5		2, 3	4, 6	1, 5
Technology	3	1				5	6	6	2							5		2, 6				5	2	3

*Numbers indicate lesson numbers within a given unit.

Level 4 U1	U2	U3	U4	U5	U6	Level 5 U1	U2	U3	U4	U5	U6	Level 6 U1	U2	U3	U4	U5	U6	Level 7 Exploring Art	Level 8 Understanding Art
	6	3				1		4	2		5	6					1	Chapter 1, 6, 10	Chapter 10
1-6	3, 4	2		1, 2, 4, 5		2, 4, 5	1, 4	1, 5	1, 4	3	2	1	3	1, 2, 4	3-5	1, 2, 5		Chapter 2, 7, 11, 14	Chapter 3, 15, 16
					3, 6					2	4	2					3, 5	Chapter 1, 2, 3, 13	Chapter 7, 8, 10, 12
	1, 5		4, 5		1, 4					1			6			6	4	Chapter 5, 13	Chapter 2, 3
		4-6			2, 5		2, 3	3	3	4, 5	1	5	1, 2, 4		5	1		Chapter 2, 3, 4, 5, 6, 9, 11, 14	Chapter 1-8, 10, 11, 13-17
			3			6											2	Chapter 10	Chapter 1, 17
											3							Chapter 3, 4, 8	Chapter 1, 3, 6, 8, 14-17
		1-3					5, 6	6	5, 6		6	3, 4		3, 6	6	3	6	Chapter 2, 3, 4, 5, 7, 12, 13	Chapter 1, 2, 3, 5-13, 15-17
	2	1	6	6		3		2			6	5				2	4	Chapter 4, 11, 15	Chapter 3, 17

Program Glossary

A

active lines *noun* Lines that show action and add energy and movement to a work of art. Diagonal, zigzag, and curved lines are examples of active lines.

additive sculpture *noun* When something is added to either relief or freestanding sculpture

alternating pattern *noun* Can repeat a motif, but change position; alter spacing between motifs or add a second motif

analogous color scheme *noun* Uses colors that are side by side on the color wheel and have a common color

analogous colors *noun* Colors that sit side by side on the color wheel and have a common hue. Violet, blue-violet, blue, blue-green are examples of analogous colors.

angle *noun* A shape formed when two lines extend in different directions from the same point

animal forms *noun* A three-dimensional representation of an animal

ant's view *noun* Viewers feel they are looking up, toward an object or figure.

appliqué *noun* An art form in which cutout fabrics are attached to a larger surface

approximate symmetry *noun* A special kind of formal balance where both sides of a design are almost exactly the same. One example is the human face: each side is almost the same as the other.

arc *noun* Any portion of a curved line from a circle

architects *noun* Artists who design buildings, cities, and bridges using three-dimensional forms

architecture *noun* The art of designing and planning buildings, cities, and bridges

armature *noun* A framework for supporting material used in sculpting

art form *noun* A type of art

assemblage *noun* A sculpture technique in which a variety of objects is assembled to create one complete piece

asymmetrical balance *noun* Another name for informal balance

asymmetry *noun* Another name for informal balance. Something asymmetrical looks balanced even if it is not the same on both sides.

atmospheric perspective *noun* The effects air and light have on how we perceive an object

axis *noun* A real or imaginary line across the center of a work of art

B

background *noun* The area of the picture plane farthest from the viewer

balance *noun* The principle of design that deals with visual weight in an artwork

bird's-eye view *noun* Or aerial view; viewers feel they are looking down on a scene.

black ▪

blending *noun* A shading technique that creates a gradual change from light to dark or dark to light

blind contour drawing *noun* A drawing that is made by looking at the object being drawn, not at the paper.

blob *noun* A type of free-form shape

body forms *noun* Three-dimensional representations of a person

body proportions *noun* The size relationship of one part of the body to another

brass *noun* A metal made by combining copper and zinc

bright colors *noun* colors that appear to reflect light

broken (line) *noun* A line that is made of a series of dashes, not solid

building *noun* a structure where we live, work, meet, or play

C

calm lines *noun* Lines that give a work of art a quiet and peaceful mood. Horizontal and vertical lines are calm lines.

carving *noun* Art made by cutting into the surface of the medium.

central axis *noun* A real or imaginary dividing line that can run in two directions, vertically and horizontally

circle *noun* A round, geometric shape made when all points are placed the same distance from a center point.

close-up view *noun* Viewers feel they are right next to an object, or are a part of the action in a picture.

coil *noun* A long roll of clay joined into a circle or spiral. Clay coils are used to make pottery.

collage *noun* A two-dimensional work of art made up of pieces of paper and/or fabric to create the image.

collograph *noun* A printmaking technique where cut papers or thin boards are arranged to create an image on a stiff printing plate.

color *noun* 1. The art element that is created from reflected light; 2. In balance: a brighter color has more visual weight than a dull color; 3. In perspective: bright-colored objects seem closer, while dull or pale objects appear farther away.

color intensity *noun* The brightness or dullness of a color

color scheme *noun* A plan for organizing the colors used in an artwork

color spectrum *noun* The effect that occurs when light passes through a prism and separates into a band of colors in the order of red, orange, yellow, green, blue, and violet.

color wheel *noun* Shows the color spectrum bent into a circle

column *noun* A supporting pillar on a building

complementary color scheme *noun*   Uses one set of complementary colors; for example, red and green, blue and orange, and yellow and violet

complementary colors *noun*   Colors that are opposite each other on the color wheel

complex geometric shapes *noun*   Shapes made by combining simple geometric shapes such as triangles, squares, and rectangles. Some examples of complex geometric shapes are diamonds, pentagons, trapezoids, hexagons, parallelograms, and octagons.

contour *noun*   The edges and surface ridges of an object

contour hatching *noun*   A shading technique that follows the form of an object

contour lines *noun*   Continuous, unbroken lines that show the edges and surface ridges of an object or figure

contrast *noun*   1. A technique for creating a focal point or area of interest in a work of art using differences in elements; 2. In emphasis: contrast occurs when one element stands out from the rest of the work; 3. showing differences between things

converging *adj.* (*verb*) Coming together at one point or place

converging lines *noun*   One of the six perspective techniques. Parallel lines seem to converge or move toward the same point as they move away from you.

cool colors *noun*   Green, violet, and blue. They suggest coolness and move away from the viewer.

cool hues *noun*   Blue, green, and violet. Cool hues are associated with cool things like snow, water, and grass.

cross-hatching *noun*   A shading technique created when sets of parallel lines cross or intersect

culture *noun*   Another word for custom

curling *verb*   Hold one end of a long strip of paper. Grip the middle of the paper strip next to the side of a pencil. With a quick motion, pull the strip firmly across the pencil.

curved *adj.*   Lines that bend and change gradually or turn inward to form spirals

curved (line) *noun*   A line that changes directions slowly and bends in arcs

curving movement *verb*   Using curved lines to move the viewer's eyes through a work of art and make the viewer feel that objects in the work of art are moving along curves

D

dark lines *noun*   Created by using less water for watercolor paints

dark value *noun*   A value that has more black added to it

decorative *adj.*   Serving to make more beautiful; to adorn with ornaments

depth *noun*   1. The appearance of distance; 2. How far something extends toward or away from the viewer.

detail *noun*   One of the six perspective techniques. Objects with fuzzy, blurred edges appear farther away than those with clear sharp edges.

diagonal *noun* (*adj.*) Lines that are slanted. They look as if they are falling or rising. They make things look active.

diagonal movement *verb*   Using diagonal lines to move the viewer's eyes through a work of art and make the viewer feel that objects in the work of art are moving along diagonals

dimension *noun*   A measurement of the amount of space an object takes up in one direction

diorama *noun*   A display of a scene using sculpted, miniature figurines

directional lines *noun*   How a line moves: diagonally, vertically, or horizontally

distortion *noun*   A deviation from normal or expected proportions

dominant *noun* (*adj.*) The part of the work of art that seems more important to the viewer. Dominant elements have been emphasized.

dominant element *noun*   The element in a work of art that is noticed first.

dull colors Colors that are not bright

E

earthenware *noun*   Ceramics made out of clay and fired at a low heat

elongate *verb*   To stretch out or make long

embroidery *noun*   The art of decorating designs with needle and thread

emphasis *noun*   The principle of design that stresses one area in an art work over another area

even balance *adj.*   Both halves are equal. Left side and right side are the same.

exaggerate *verb*   To make much larger than actual size

exaggeration *noun*   To increase or enlarge beyond what is expected or normal

F

facial proportions *noun*   The relationship of one feature of a face to another feature

faraway view *noun*   Or eye-level view; viewers feel they are standing far away from the scene.

fiber *noun*   A material used to make baskets and cloth. Grass, yarn, and straw are kinds of fibers.

flowing lines *noun*   Create a feeling of calm and gracefulness. Flowing lines are fluid; they change direction and size.

flowing rhythm *noun*   Created when curved lines or shapes are repeated

focal point *noun*   The point where the receding lines meet. It is the first part of a composition to attract the viewer's attention.

foreground *noun*   The area of the picture plane that is closest to the viewer

form *noun*   A three-dimensional object that is measured by height, width, and depth

formal balance *noun*   Occurs when equal or similar elements are placed on opposite sides of a central axis

Program Glossary (continued)

free-form forms *noun* Three-dimensional forms with irregular edges often found in nature

free-form shapes *noun* Two-dimensional images made of straight or curved lines or a combination of both

freestanding *noun* Forms that can be seen from all around

freestanding sculpture *noun* A three-dimensional work of art that can be viewed on all sides because it is surrounded by space

fringing *verb* Make parallel straight cuts along the edge of a piece of paper to create a ruffled look.

frontal proportions *noun* A front view of the head that is divided by three horizontal lines across the central axis

futurists *noun* A group of Italian artists during the early twentieth-century who repeated and overlapped shapes and lines to create the illusion of movement

G

geometric forms *noun* Mathematically precise forms based on geometric shapes

geometric shapes *noun* Mathematically precise shapes: circle, square, and triangle

gesture *noun* An expressive movement

gesture drawings *noun* Quick drawings used to capture the position or pose of the body

gesture lines *noun* Lines drawn to capture the movement of a person, an animal, or an object in a painting or drawing

gesture sketch *noun* Quick drawings used to capture the position or movement of the body

guide lines *noun* Lines used by artists to create both full-face and profile portraits more accurately

H

hand tools *noun* Simple instruments for carving or sculpting

harmony *noun* The principle of art that creates unity by stressing similarities of separate but related parts

hatching *noun* A shading technique that looks like a series of parallel lines

height *noun* A vertical measurement, or how tall something is

high-intensity color *noun* A pure hue such as red

highlights *noun* Small areas of white or light value to show the brightest spots

horizon line *noun* The point at which the earth and sky meet. The horizon line is always at the viewer's eye level.

horizontal *noun* (*adj.*) A line that moves from side to side

hues *noun* The spectral colors, or colors of the rainbow. Hues do not include black or white. Hues are red, orange, yellow, green, blue, and violet.

I

informal balance *noun* A way of organizing parts of a design so that unlike objects have equal visual weight

installation *noun* An artwork that was created for a specific place, such as a gallery or outdoor location

intensity *noun* The brightness or dullness of a color

interior designers *noun* Artists who decorate the inside of a building

intermediate colors *noun* Colors made by mixing a primary color and a secondary color. There are six intermediate colors—red-orange, yellow-orange, yellow-green, blue-green, blue-violet, and red-violet.

intermediate hues *noun* Yellow-green, red-orange, blue-green, made by combining a primary hue with either of the secondary hues that are adjacent on the color wheel

invented texture *noun* Created when an artist uses lines or other elements to make a textural look without any specific texture in mind

irregular *adj.* Does not follow a rule or pattern

isolation *noun* An object is emphasized by its placement apart from other objects.

J

jeweler *noun* An artist who designs and makes jewelry

jewelry *noun* Three-dimensional artwork that is made for people to wear

K

kinetic movement *noun* Actual or real movement

kinetic sculpture *noun* A three-dimensional form that actually moves in space

L

landscape *noun* a picture of the outdoors

light lines *noun* Created by adding more water to watercolor paints

light value *noun* A value that has more white added to it

line *noun* A mark drawn by a tool such as a pencil, pen, or paintbrush as it moves across a surface

line variety *noun* The different possibilities in the character of lines. For example, lines can be long or short, thick or thin, rough or smooth, and broken or solid.

linear perspective *noun* A system used to create the illusion of depth on a flat surface

lines *noun* One of the six perspective techniques. Parallel lines seem to converge or move toward the same point as they move away from the viewer.

location *noun* Artists can emphasize an object by placing it closer to the center of the piece.

low-intensity color *noun* A dull hue made by mixing a color with its complement

M

mandala *noun* A radial design divided into sections or wedges, each of which contains a different image

maquette *noun* A small model for a larger sculpture

mask *noun* A three-dimensional art form of sculpted faces

matte *noun* A dull, sometimes rough finish

medium *noun* The supply an artist uses to create art. Some media are clay, paint, or wood.

middle ground *noun* The area of the picture plane that is usually toward the center

minimal details *noun* Used in gesture sketches to complete the drawing

mix a neutral color *verb* Mix a neutral color with another color to change its value

mixed-media *noun* An art object that has been created from an assortment of media or materials

mobile *noun* A moving sculpture in which shapes are balanced and arranged on wire arms and suspended from the ceiling to move freely in the air currents

monochromatic *adj.* A color scheme that is made up of one color and the tints and shade of that color

monochromatic color scheme *noun* Uses only one color and the values of that color

monotonous *adj.* Lack of variety; boring

monumental sculptures *noun* Sculptures that are larger than human forms

motif *noun* A unit that is made up of objects or art elements that can be repeated

movement *noun* The principle of art that leads a viewer's eyes throughout a work of art

mural *noun* A painting done on a wall

N

negative space *noun* The empty space that surrounds objects, shapes, and forms

neon *noun* A special kind of light that can be made to be many bright colors

neutral color scheme *noun* Uses black, white, and a variety of grays

neutral colors *noun* Black, white, and gray; give hues a range of values

nonobjective *adj.* Art that has no recognizable subject matter

O

one-point linear perspective *noun* A system used to create the illusion of depth on a flat surface where all receding lines meet at one point

opaque *adj.* Does not let light through

outline *noun* a line drawn around the edge of an object

overlap *verb* To place one object on top of another object and partially cover the first object up

overlapping *noun* 1. One object covers a portion of another object. 2. In perspective: one of the six perspective techniques; the object covering another will appear closer to the viewer, creating a feeling of depth.

P

painting *noun* An art form using paint on a flat surface

paper sculpting techniques *noun* Six different techniques used to create paper sculptures: scoring a straight line, scoring a curve, pleating, curling, fringing, tab and slot.

parallel lines *noun* Lines that move in the same direction and always stay the same distance apart

pattern *noun* A repeated surface decoration

perception drawing *verb* Looking at something carefully and thinking deeply about what you see as you draw

perspective *noun* The method used to create the illusion of depth in two-dimensional art: overlapping, size, placement, detail, color, converging lines

perspective techniques *noun* The six techniques an artist uses to create the illusion of depth in two-dimensional art: overlapping, size, placement, detail, color, converging lines

photograph *noun* A picture taken using light-sensitive film and a camera

picture plane *noun* The surface of a drawing or painting

placement *noun* One of the six perspective techniques. Objects placed lower in the picture appear to be closer than those placed near eye level. There are three areas on a picture plane: foreground, middle ground, and background.

pleating *verb* Fold piece of paper from edge to edge. Then fold the same amount of paper in the other direction. Continue folding the paper back and forth in this manner.

point of view *noun* The angle at which the viewer sees an object

portrait *noun* A two- or three-dimensional artwork created in the image of a person or animal

posed *verb* Arranged in a special way

position *noun* In balance: a larger, positive shape and a small, negative space can be balanced by a small, positive shape and a large, negative space.

positive space *noun* Refers to any object, shape, or form in two- and three-dimensional art

primary colors *noun* Red, yellow, and blue. They cannot be made by mixing colors.

primary hues *noun* Red, yellow, and blue, used to mix the other hues on the color wheel

print *noun* An image created by using a stamp or printing plate. When artists make prints, they can make many identical images.

printing *verb* Pressing a shape from one thing to another many times

printing plate *noun* A plate that holds the image that will be used to create a print

prism *noun* A wedge-shaped piece of glass that bends light as it passes through

profile *noun* A side view of a person or animal

profile proportions *noun* A side view of the head that is divided by three horizontal lines

proportion *noun* The principle of art that is concerned with the size relationship of one part to another

Program Glossary (continued)

R

radial balance *noun* A type of balance that occurs when the art elements come out, or radiate, from a central point

rainbow *noun* An arc of spectral colors, usually identified as red, orange, yellow, green, blue, indigo, and violet, that appears in the sky opposite the sun

random pattern *noun* Occurs when the motif is repeated in no apparent order

ratio *noun* A comparison of size between two things

real texture *noun* Texture you can feel

realistic scale *noun* When an artist creates a work of art where everything fits together and makes sense in size relation

rectangle *noun* A four-sided geometric shape made of all right angles and whose opposite sides are equal in length.

regular pattern *noun* Occurs when identical motifs are repeated with an equal amount of space between them

relief *noun* A type of sculpture where forms project from a flat background

relief sculpture *noun* A sculpture in which objects stick out from a flat surface

repeated lines *noun* Used to give the feeling of movement or motion in a gesture drawing

repetition *noun* Lines, shapes, colors, or textures that are repeated throughout an artwork

rest *noun* The negative space between repetitions of the motif

rhythm *noun* The principle of design that organizes the elements in a work of art by repeating elements and/or objects

rough *noun* (*adj.*) A surface that has ridges; not smooth

rough (line) *noun* A line that has jagged, uneven edges

S

sail *noun* A type of free-form shape

scale *noun* Size as measured against a standard reference

score *verb* The repeated scratching of the clay surface at the area that another scored piece will be attached

scoring a curve *verb* Gradually cut bending curves in the paper with the point of the scissors

scoring a straight line *verb* Hold a ruler in the center of a piece of paper. Run the point of the scissors along the edge of the ruler to cut the paper in a straight line.

sculpture *noun* Three-dimensional art

sculpture model *noun* The study or detailed example of what the sculpture will look like when completed

secondary colors *noun* Orange, green, and violet. These colors are made by mixing two primary colors.

secondary hues *noun* Orange, green, and violet; the result of mixing two primary hues

self-portrait *noun* A two- or three-dimensional artwork that an artist makes of him or herself

sets of complementary colors *noun* There are three sets on the color wheel: red and green, blue and orange, and yellow and violet.

shade *noun* Any hue blended with black

shading *noun* A technique for creating dark values or darkening an area by repeating marks such as lines or dots

shadows *noun* Shaded areas in a painting or drawing

shape *noun* A two-dimensional area that is measured by height and width

shape reversal *noun* Occurs when an object, shape, or form is positive space in one image and then in another image becomes negative space

shiny *noun* Bright from reflected light

silhouette *noun* The shape of a shadow

simulated texture *noun* Imitates real texture, see also visual texture

size *noun* 1. in perspective: objects that are closer look larger than objects that are farther away; 2. In balance: a large shape or form will appear to be heavier than a small shape, and several small shapes can balance one large shape.

slip *noun* A mixture of clay and water that is creamy to the touch and is used to attach two scored pieces of clay together

smooth *noun* A surface free from roughness; even

smooth (line) *noun* A line that has even edges

solid (line) *noun* A line that has no breaks, gaps, or holes

space *noun* The art element that refers to the areas above, below, between, within, and around an object

spectral color scheme *noun* Uses all the colors of the rainbow: red, orange, yellow, green, blue, and violet

spectral colors *noun* The colors of the light spectrum: red, orange, yellow, green, blue, and violet

spectrum *noun* The range of colors that it is possible to see; the rainbow

splash *noun* A type of free-form shape

square *noun* A four-sided geometric shape where all sides are the same length and all angles are right angles

statue *noun* Three-dimensional art that is a body form

still life *noun* The arrangement of common inanimate objects from which artists draw or paint

stippling *noun* A shading technique using dots to show value

stitchery *noun* Art made with yarn on cloth

storyteller doll *noun* A Native American sculpture that shows one person relating the history of the culture to many children

style *noun* A unique quality of an object

subordinate *noun* The parts of the artwork that seem less important. Subordinate objects are not emphasized.

subtractive sculpture *noun* When an artist carves pieces away from a form

surrealism *noun* An art movement that emphasized art in which dreams, fantasy, and the subconscious served as inspiration for artists

symmetrical When two sides of a work of art are mirror images of each other

symmetry *noun* A type of formal balance in which two halves of a balanced artwork are identical, mirror images of each other

T

tactile texture *noun* The texture that can be felt

texture *noun* 1. The art element that refers to the way something feels; 2. In balance: a rough texture has an uneven pattern of highlights and shadows. For this reason, a rough surface attracts the viewer's eyes more easily than a smooth, even surface.

thick (line) *adj.* Wide

thick line *noun* Created by beginning with a thin line and gradually pressing the brush down

thin (line) *adj.* Narrow

thin line *noun* Created when a brush is held vertically to paper and touched lightly with the tip of the brush

three-dimensional *adj.* Has measurements in three directions: height, width, and depth

three-dimensional patterns *noun* Patterns that have depth and are formed on the surface of a sculptural form

three-dimensional rhythm *noun* A principle of design that indicates movement by the repetition of elements in a form

tint *noun* Any hue blended with white

transparent *adj.* Allows light to pass through so objects on the other side can be seen

triangle *noun* A three-sided geometric shape

two-dimensional *adj.* Shapes that are flat and can be measured by length and width

two-dimensional decoration *noun* Flat decoration produced on the surface of a work of art

U

unity *noun* The feeling of wholeness in a work of art. Artists use repetition and grouping to show that different parts of a work belong together.

unrealistic scale *noun* When an artist makes size relationships that do not make sense

V

value *noun* The lightness or darkness of a hue

value contrast *noun* The lightness or darkness stands out from the value that surrounds it

vanishing point *noun* The point on the horizon line where all parallel receding lines meet

variety *noun* The principle of art which is concerned with difference or contrast

vertical *noun* (*adj.*) Lines that move straight up and down. They make things look tall, steady, and calm.

visual movement *noun* Occurs when the eye is pulled through a work of art by a rhythm of beats and rests

visual rhythm *noun* The feeling of movement created when artists repeat colors, shapes, lines, and textures to lead the viewer's eyes through a work of art

visual texture *noun* Or simulated texture, imitates real texture. It is the illusion of a three-dimensional surface.

visual weight *noun* cannot be measured on a scale; it is measured by which objects the viewer's eyes see first.

W

warm colors *noun* Red, yellow, and orange. They suggest warmth and come toward the viewer.

warm hues *noun* Red, orange, and yellow. Warm hues are associated with warm things such as fire or sunshine.

weave *verb* To interlace or interweave strips or strands of material

width *noun* A horizontal measurement, or how long across something is

Z

zigzag *noun* (*adj.*) A line that is made by joining diagonal lines

Program Index

A

About Me, **L3** 138; **L4** 74
Abrasha, **L3** 169
abstract art, **L1** 36, 82; **L3** 96, 97; **L4** 34, 71
Abstract Art in Five Tones and Complementaries (Torres Garcia), **L4** 67
Adams, Ansel, **L2** 109; **L5** 57
additive sculpture, **L4** 130–133
advertisers, **L3** 62
advertising photographers, **L4** 92
Aesthetic Perception
  balance, **LK** 195, 199; **L1** 187, 191; **L2** 157, 161; **L3** 127, 131; **L4** 187, 191, 195; **L5** 169, 177, **L6** 135, 139
  blending, **L5** 53
  buildings, **L1** 143
  colors, **LK** 97, 101, 105, 109, 113, 117; **L1** 97, 101, 105, 109, 113, 117; **L2** 97, 101, 105, 187; **L3** 97, 101, 105, 109, 113, 117; **L4** 97, 101, 105, 109, 117; **L5** 97, 101, 105, 109, 117; **L6** 79
  contrast, **L5** 57
  depth, **L3** 71
  distortion, **L4** 177; **L5** 139, 143, **L6** 165, 169
  emphasis, **L1** 195, 199; **L2** 165, 169; **L3** 195, 199; **L4** 145B; **L5** 196, 199; **L6** 143, 147
  foreground, middle ground, and background, **L4** 157
  form, **L1** 131, 135, 139; **L2** 67, 71, 75, 79, **L3** 79; **L4** 125B; **L5** 83, 87; **L6** 45, 49
  harmony, **L2** 191; **L3** 187; **L4** 199; **L5** 187; **L6** 195, 199
  hatching, **L5** 49
  hues, **L6** 67
  intensity, **L6** 75
  lines, **LK** 37, 41, 45, 49, 53, 57, 60; **L1** 37, 41, 45, 49, 53, 57, 61; **L2** 37, 41, 45, 49; **L3** 37, 41; **L4** 37, 41, 49, 53; **L5** 37; **L6** 37
  motif, **L6** 97
  movement, **L2** 143, 147; **L6** 113, 117
  observation drawings, **L4** 45
  overlapping, **L3** 75
  pattern, **LK** 187; **L1** 169, 173; **L2** 127, 131; **L3** 157, 161, 165; **L4** 75; **L5** 113, 117; **L6** 101, 105
  perception drawing, **L5** 41
  perspective, **L4** 161; **L5** 75; **L6** 53
  point of view, **L4** 165
  proportion, **L4** 169, 173; **L5** 127, 135, 147; **L6** 157, 161

rhythm, **LK** 191; **L1** 177; **L2** 135, 139; **L3** 169, 173, 177; **L4** 79, 82, 87; **L5** 161, 165; **L6** 109
scale, **L5** 131; **L6** 173, 177
sculpture, **L3** 83; **L4** 131, 135
shading, **L4** 57, 113; **L5** 79
shapes, **LK** 67, 71, 75, 79, 83, 87; **L1** 67, 71, 75, 79, 83, 87, 91, 127; **L2** 53, 57; **L3** 45, 49, 53, 57; **L4** 67, 71; **L5** 45, 67, 71; **L6** 41
space, **L1** 147, **L2** 83, 87, **L3** 67, **L6** 57
symmetry, **L3** 135, 139; **L6** 127, 131
texture, **L1** 157, 161, 165; **L2** 173, 177, **L3** 143, 147; **L4** 139, 143; **L5** 157; **L6** 83, 87
three-dimensional art, **L3** 87
unity, **LK** 203, 207; **L1** 203, 207; **L2** 203, 207; **L3** 203, 207; **L4** 207; **L5** 201B, 207; **L6** 203, 207
value, **L2** 109, 113, 117; **L6** 71
variety, **L2** 195, 199; **L3** 191; **L4** 203; **L5** 191; **L6** 187, 191
African American art, **L6** 164, 165
African American Dance Ensemble, **L3** 123; **L6** 123
African Americans, **LK** 82–83
akrafokonmu, **L6** 138
Akrafokonmu (Soul Discs) (Unknown), **L6** 139
Alanda's Dream Tree (Scott), **L2** 40
Aliki, **L3** 125A
'Ali, Mir Sayyid, **L3** 180
alternating pattern, **L3** 164–167; **L4** 76; **L5** 118; **L6** 102, 106
AMAN International Folk Ensemble, **LK** 93; **L4** 63
America
  demographics, **L5** 193
  economics, **L5** 43
  Harlem Renaissance, **L5** 189
  history and culture, **LK** 111, 198; **L1** 116; **L5** 51, 96
  Native Americans, **LK** 36; **L1** 156; **L2** 74
  patriotism, **L5** 209
  society, **L4** 206
American Collectors (Hockney), **LK** 41
American Express Train (Currier and Ives), **LK** 91
American Gothic (Wood), **LK** 64
American Indian Dance Theatre, **L3** 63
Americanoom (Chyrssa), **L4** 143
Amour (Herbin), **L2** 52
analogous color scheme, **L4** 118; **L5** 100–103; **L6** 80
Ancestral Spirit Dance #187 (Davis Bing), **L5** 105

Ancestral Spirit Dance (Davis), **L3** 206
Ancient Civilizations, **L2** 70; **L5** 179; **L6** 86, 103
Ancient Egyptian Hippo "William" (Unknown), **LK** 142–145
Anderson, N., **L5** 177
Andrews, Benny, **L4** 48; **L6** 210
Anguissola, Sofonisba, **L5** 172
animals
  in art, **L5** 206
  and balance, **LK** 194–97
  body shapes, **LK** 89
  coloration, **LK** 103
  ecology, **L1** 77
  and form, **LK** 142–145; **L2** 78–81
  habitats, **LK** 119
  and harmony, **L2** 190
  and lines, **LK** 47; **L1** 66–68
  in Native American art, **L3** 63
  and pattern, **L2** 130
  and texture, **LK** 52
  and variety, **L2** 198
Animals in a Landscape (Marc), **L6** 108
animation, **L3** 93; **L6** 62
animators, **LK** 152; **L2** 152
Anna and David (Schapiro), **L6** 66
Anno, Mitsumasa, **LK** 125A
Apollinaire, Guillaume, **L6** 56, 57
Appalachian Basket (Unknown), **LK** 168
Appalachian Big Circle Dance, **LK** 93; **L4** 63
Appalachian Folk Music and Dance, **LK** 93
appliqué, **L3** 66, 148
appraisers, **L5** 152
approximate symmetry, **L3** 138–141; **L6** 130–133
Arapaho Man's Shirt, **L1** 187
Archaeology, **L1** 164; **L4** 137; **L6** 103
architects, **LK** 138, 186; **L1** 152; **L2** 208, 212; **L3** 54, 92, 148
architectural graphic designers, **L3** 182
Architecture, **L2** 206–209; **L3** 52–55; **L4** 186; **L5** 86–89, 126; **L6** 126
archivists, **L6** 119A, 122
area, **L6** 146–149
Armor of George Clifford, Third Earl of Cumberland (Royal Workshops), **L6** 160
Around the Cake (Thiebaud), **L4** 112
art directors, **L3** 62
The Art Institute of Chicago, **L5** 62
Artist's Sisters Playing Chess and Their Governess (Anguissola), **L5** 172
art photography, **L4** 92
art teachers, **L1** 212
Art Teacher (Surowiec), **L5** 190

Aruego, José, **L1** 185A
Asante Paramount Chief Nana Akyanfuo Akowuah Dateh II, Akwamuhene of Kumase (Elisofon), **L4** 75
Asante people, **L6** 138
Ashanti people, **LK** 172; **L1** 172
Ashoona, Kiawak, **L2** 75
Aspens, Northern New Mexico (Adams), **L5** 57
assemblages, **L4** 200; **L6** 200
Astronomy, **L1** 69, 130; **L3** 39; **L5** 69, 78, 81; **L6** 81
asymmetry, **L4** 192
atmospheric perspective, **L6** 54
Audubon, John James, **L2** 131, 198; **L3** 154, 155
Au Printemps, Springtime (Hofmann), **L1** 120
Autumn Leaves-Lake George (O'Keeffe), **LK** 75
Avery, Milton, **L3** 108, 109; **L4** 100
axis, **L2** 158, 162; **L3** 136; **L5** 170; **L6** 128, 158

B

background, **L3** 72; **L4** 158; **L6** 54
back view, **L4** 166
Bactrian Camel (Unknown), **LK** 142–145
Baird Trogon (Lostutter), **L2** 96
Bakula, Stanistawa, **L3** 67
balance
  creating, **L4** 185
  in dance, **L6** 153
  defined, **LK** 194–197; **L1** 185–189; **L5** 155
  formal, **L3** 126–129; **L4** 186–189; **L5** 168–171; **L6** 126–129
  informal, **L4** 190–193; **L5** 172–175; **L6** 134–137
  in masks, **L1** 190–193
  and people, **L2** 155–163
  radial, **L4** 194–197; **L5** 176–179; **L6** 138–141
  and sculpture, **LK** 198–201
  in stories, **L1** 213
  and symmetry, **L3** 134–137
  and texture, **L3** 124–125
Baliker, Paul A., **L6** 48
Ballerinas (Degas), **L5** 40
Ballet Dancers (Scott), **L2** 164
Ballet Folklórico de México, **L4** 213
Ballet Scene (Degas), **L2** 143
Bang, Molly, **LK** 155A
Baranoff-Rossine, Vladimir, **L4** 198
Bareback Riders (Brown), **LK** 42
Bartlett, Jennifer, **L5** 164
Basket (Keyser), **L6** 202
baskets, **LK** 168–171; **L4** 206

Basket (Unknown), **L4** 207
Bates, David, **L6** 56
Bearden, Romare, **LK** 87; **L4** 138
Beaux, Cecilia, **L2** 165
Begay, Harrison, **L1** 56, 57
Bell, John, **L2** 78
Bellows, George Wesley, **L6** 60
Bennion, Lee, **L6** 187
Benton, Thomas Hart, **L1** 116; **L2** 142; **L5** 186
Berenstain, Stan and Jan, **L2** 65A
Bernadita (Henri), **L4** 169
Berry, Martha, **L1** 173
Between the Clock and the Bed (Johns), **L1** 44
Bible Quilt, Detail: Dark Day of May 19, 1817 (Powers), **LK** 176
The Bicycle Race (Ruíz), **L4** 161
Big Blues Man II (Twiggs), **LK** 90
Biggers, John, **L4** 66, 90
Billy the Kid, **L3** 213; **L5** 183
Bird Watchers (Tooker), **L5** 127
Birthday (Chagall), **L1** 195
The Birthplace of Herbert Hoover, West Branch, Iowa (Wood), **L4** 160
Bishop, Isabel, **L1** 79; **L5** 210; **L6** 156
Black Bear Storyteller figurine with Six Cubs (Naranjo), **L2** 138
Blake, William, **LK** 48
Blanco, Teodora, **L4** 131; **L6** 104
The Blank Signature [Carte Blanc] (Magritte), **L3** 90
blending, **L5** 52–55, 80; **L6** 72
blind contour drawing, **L4** 50
Blue and Green Music (O'Keeffe), **L4** 116
Blueberry Eyes (Kline), **L2** 40, 41
Blue Dome-House Blessing (Anderson), **L5** 177
Bo Bo Festival Series #30 (Bustion), **L6** 186
body forms, **L2** 74–77
body proportions, **L5** 138–141
Bonheur, Rosa, **L3** 168
Bonnard, Pierre, **L1** 90
book designers, **L6** 182
Borofsky, Jonathan, **L3** 41
Botero, Fernando, **L5** 138; **L6** 168, 169
Bottom of the Ravine (Cézanne), **L6** 113
Bouguereau, William Adolphe, **L5** 71
Bowl (Unknown), **LK** 147; **L5** 116
Boy Juggling Shells (Hokusai), **LK** 49
Boy's day (Russell), **L3** 96
The Boy Who Wanted to Talk to Whales, **L6** 63
The Boy Who Wnated to Talk to Whales, **L4** 123

Boy with a Flute (Hokusai), **L4** 53
Brach, Paul, **L6** 191
Branch, Paul, **L2** 191
Braque, Georges, **L5** 44; **L6** 78, 79, 94
The Brass Ring, **L6** 153
The Breakfast Room (Bonnard), **L1** 90
Brett, Jan, **L5** 125A
Bridal Bed Cover (Unknown), **L1** 48, 49
Brilliant as the Sun Upon the World (Jones), **L3** 105
British Museum Memoir (Spitzmueller), **L3** 198, 199
Broadway Boogie Woogie (Piet), **L1** 100
The Brooding Woman (Gauguin), **L6** 184
The Brooklyn Bridge: Variations on an Old Theme (Stella), **LK** 210
Brosen, Frederick, **L5** 75
Brother Sun, Sister Moon, **LK** 213
Brown, Roger, **L5** 78
Brown, W. H., **LK** 42, 44
Bruegel, Pieter (the Elder), **L4** 44
Bryan, Ashley, **L1** 35A
Builders No. 1 (Lawrence), **L3** 60
Builders Red and Green Ball (Lawrence), **L1** 82
buildings. *See also*
   Architecture
   and form, **LK** 138–141
   and formal balance, **L6** 126–129
   and lines, **L1** 52–55
   and pattern, **LK** 186–189
   and shapes, **L3** 52–55
   and space, **L1** 142–145
Bull's Eye Quilt (Herb), **L6** 138
Burton, Virginia Lee, **L2** 95A
Bustion, Nathaniel, **L6** 186
Butterfield, Deborah, **L1** 66, 67; **L4** 199
Butterfly (Unknown), **LK** 194
Button Robe-Orca Whale Design (Yeiltatzie), **LK** 195

C

Cabin Fever (Rothenberg), **L6** 142
Café Terrace at Night (van Gogh), **L6** 53
Caged Pie (Thiebaud), **LK** 71
Cai, Lily, **L1** 123
Caillebotte, Gustave, **L3** 142
Calder, Alexander, **L1** 126; **L6** 116, 118
Camillus (Unknown), **LK** 131
Canal, Giovanni Antonio, **L3** 53
Candelabra (Flores), **L3** 134, 135
Canister (Unknown), **L4** 105
careers
   advertisers, **L3** 62
   animators, **LK** 152; **L6** 62
   architects, **LK** 138, 186; **L1** 152; **L2** 208; **L3** 148
   in architecture, **L3** 92, 182; **L5** 92

in art history, **L6** 122
in art photography, **L4** 92
art teachers, **L2** 212
botanical curators, **L2** 92
in computers, **L4** 152
designers, **L6** 182
fabric and fashion designers, **L1** 92
illustrators, **LK** 74, 92; **L4** 212
interior designers, **L3** 148
in jewelry making, **L3** 88; **L5** 152
make-up artists, **LK** 152
in movies, **L2** 152
museum guides, **L1** 212
painters, **LK** 212
sculptors, **LK** 212
toy designers, **L5** 212
Carle, Eric, **L1** 95A
Carolina Parrot (Audubon), **L2** 131
Carousel Rabbit (Dentzel Company), **L2** 203
Carr, Emily, **L4** 60
Carved Animals (Unknown), **L6** 105
carving, **L1** 166; **L2** 172
Case with Five Balusters (Nevelson), **L3** 176, 177
Cassatt, Mary, **L1** 94, 95; **L6** 90, 134, 135
Catlett, Elizabeth, **L5** 48, 134
Catlin, George, **L2** 177; **L5** 157
Cattleya Orchid and Three Brazilian Hummingbirds (Heade), **L4** 202, 203
central axis, **L3** 136; **L5** 170; **L6** 128, 158
Ceramic Figures (Blanco), **L6** 104
Ceremonial Hanging (Unknown), **L6** 203
Ceremonial Shield (Unknown), **L4** 108
Ceremonial Skirt (Unknown), **L6** 37
Cézanne, Paul, **L1** 86; **L2** 87; **L5** 45, 120; **L6** 112, 113
CGI animators, **L2** 152
Chagall, Marc, **LK** 57, 104; **L1** 195; **L4** 177; **L5** 150
Chapelle de Notre-Dame du Haut (Le Corbusier), **L5** 86
Chardin, Jean-Baptiste Simeon, **L6** 82, 83
Charlip, Remy, **L2** 183
Cherry, Lynne, **L4** 125A
chiaroscuro, **L6** 124
Chicago Picasso (Picasso), **L6** 177
Chief Black Hawk, **L4** 78
Children at Play (Lawrence), **L1** 56
Children's Games (Bruegel), **L4** 44
Children's Theatre Company, **L1** 93; **L3** 123
Child's Beaded Shirt (Unknown), **L3** 190
Child with Ball (Münter), **LK** 160
Chinese Children's Slippers (Unkown), **L1** 198
Chinese Restaurant (Weber), **L6** 94
chromolithography, **L6** 142
Chryssa, **L2** 154, 155; **L4** 143
Church (Mendoza), **L2** 36
Chuska (Brach), **L6** 191

cinematographers, **L2** 152
circle, **LK** 72; **L1** 72; **L3** 46; **L4** 68, 128; **L5** 88; **L6** 46
The City (Hopper), **L3** 52
city planners, **L3** 92
City Square (Glacometti), **L6** 168
Classic Serape Style Wearing Blanket (Unknown), **LK** 36
Cliff Dwellers (Bellows), **L6** 60
The Cliff, Etretat, Sunset (Monet), **L2** 195
The Clock Tower in the Piazza San Marco (Canaletto), **L3** 53
cloth, **LK** 176–179
The Cocktail Party (Skoglund), **L4** 142
coiling, **L6** 202
Cole, Allen E., **L3** 56
collages, **LK** 107, 159; **L5** 39
Collar (Unknown), **L3** 164, 165
colors
   analogous, **L5** 100–103; **L6** 80
   and balance, **L3** 127; **L5** 174
   complementary, **L4** 104–107; **L5** 104–107; **L6** 76, 78
   and contrast, **L3** 116–119; **L4** 106
   cool, **L3** 108–111, 118; **L5** 108–111; **L6** 80
   and dance, **L1** 123; **L4** 123; **L6** 93
   and feelings, **LK** 112–115
   green, **L1** 108–111
   and harmony, **L2** 186–189; **L3** 188; **L4** 200; **L5** 188
   and hues, **L2** 96–107
   and informal balance, **L6** 136
   intermediate, **L3** 100–103, 118
   light and dark, **LK** 116–119
   low-intensity, **L4** 108–111
   monochromatic, **L5** 96–99
   and mood, **L4** 116–119
   neutral, **L4** 100–103; **L6** 72
   of objects, **LK** 100–105
   orange, **L1** 104–107
   and pattern, **L5** 94–95
   and perspective, **L4** 162; **L5** 72; **L6** 54
   primary, **L1** 100–103; **L3** 98, 102; **LK** 108–111
   of the rainbow, **L1** 96–99
   secondary, **L1** 106, 110, 114; **L3** 98, 102
   spectrum, **L3** 106
   and texture, **L6** 64–65
   in theater, **L5** 123
   tint and shade, **L4** 112–115
   and unity, **LK** 208; **L3** 202–205
   using, **LK** 106; **L6** 66–69
   and value, **L3** 94–95, 123; **L4** 94–95, 102, 114
   and variety, **L3** 192; **L6** 186–189
   variety of, **LK** 96–99
   violet, **L1** 112–115
   and visual weight, **L4** 192
   warm, **L3** 112–115, 118; **L5** 108–111; **L6** 80
color schemes, **L4** 118; **L5** 102; **L6** 78–81
color wheel, **L1** 98; **L2** 98, 102, 106; **L3** 102, 104–107; **L4** 96–99; **L5** 102
columns, **L2** 206

Coming of Age Hat (Unknown), **L6** 86, 87
Coming of Age (Houser), **L4** 86
Communication
   in art, **L4** 70
   cooperation, **L1** 82
   feelings, **LK** 82, 112; **L2** 116; **L5** 48; **L6** 74, 190
   masks, **L3** 130
   portraits, **L2** 176
   types of, **L5** 134
complementary colors, **L4** 104–107; **L5** 104–107; **L6** 76, 78
complementary color scheme, **L4** 118
Composition 8 (Wassily), **L1** 37
Composition (Davis), **L4** 64
Composition on the Word "Vie" 2 (Herbin), **LK** 70
Composition VI (Kandinsky), **L2** 48
Composition V (Piet), **L1** 41
Composition (Vytlacil), **L3** 45
computer game developers, **L4** 152
computer graphics designers, **L4** 152
Conception Synchromy (Stanton), **L6** 67
The Concert (Leyster), **L4** 184
The Concert (Vermeer), **L5** 64
Conchero Pull Toys (Unknown), **LK** 164–167
cone, **L3** 80–81; **L5** 88; **L6** 46
conservators, **L6** 122
contour hatching, **L4** 58
contour lines, **L4** 48–51, 53, 192; **L5** 42; **L6** 38
contrast, **L2** 168–171; **L3** 116–119, 196; **L4** 106; **L5** 56–59; **L6** 148, 190–193
Control Chair (Greenblat), **LK** 120
Convergence (Pollock), **L5** 36, 37
converging lines, **L5** 72; **L6** 54
Conversation Piece (Muñoz), **L6** 147
cool hues, **L5** 108–111
Cooney, Barbara, **L1** 125A
Cooperation
   and colors, **L5** 52, 108
   communication, **L1** 82
   community, **LK** 206; **L1** 36
   competition, **L4** 78; **L5** 36
   harmony, **L4** 198; **L6** 198
   and pattern, **L5** 112
   in school, **LK** 44
Cooper, Floyd, **L3** 65A
Copley, John Singleton, **L1** 160; **L4** 154, 155; **L6** 157
Le Corbusier, **L5** 86
Corn Palace (Unknown), **L1** 142–145
Cote d'Ivoire (Unknown), **L3** 87
Cottingham, Robert, **L3** 195
Country Dance (Benton), **L2** 142
Country Life, **L4** 141, 156; **L5** 129
Courage, **L6** 176
Covered Jar (Unknown), **L3** 116, 117
Cover of Armenian Book (Unknown), **L3** 198
Cow's Skull: Red White and Blue (O'Keefe), **L6** 130

Coyote Koshare (Fonseca), **L1** 176
Crews, Donald, **L2** 155A
Crite, Allan Rohan, **LK** 78
cropping, **L6** 134
cross hatching, **L4** 58; **L5** 50, 58, 80; **L6** 72
Crow Men in Ceremonial Dress (Chief Black Hawk), **L4** 78
cube, **L4** 128; **L5** 88; **L6** 46
cubism, **L3** 35; **L6** 78, 94
Cubi XVIII (Smith), **L2** 66; **L6** 44
Cultural Diversity
   discuss, **L2** 126; **L3** 66; **L5** 104
   families, **LK** 86
   history, **L4** 104
   Native Americans, **LK** 36; **L1** 156; **L2** 74; **L3** 146
   and student experience, **LK** 89
culture, **L3** 132
Cups 4 Picasso (Johns), **L5** 66, 67
curators, **L2** 92; **L6** 122
curling, **L5** 84
Currier and Ives, **LK** 53, 191
Curry, John Steuart, **L5** 126
cylinder, **L3** 80–81

D

Dali, Salvador, **L4** 176
Dali, Salvador, **L6** 176
Dallas Museum of Art, **L6** 212
dance, **LK** 183; **L1** 123, 183; **L2** 212; **L4** 63, 123; **L6** 93, 153, 183, 213
Dance at El Jardin (Garza), **LK** 203
Dance By Numbers Bandolier Bag (Berry), **L1** 173
Dancing in Colombia (Botero), **L6** 169
Dancing Lady (Unknown), **L6** 160, 161
Danza de Reata & Jarabe del Amor Ranchero, **L4** 213
Dark Snapper (Warren), **L6** 48, 49
The Daughters of Edward Darley Boit (Sargent), **L4** 191
David (del Verrocchio), **L4** 172
da Vinci, Leonardo, **L1** 184, 185; **L6** 180
Davis, Stuart, **L1** 202, **L4** 64, 65, 97
Davis, Willis Bing, **L3** 206
Davis, Willis Bing, **L5** 105
Dawn (Nevelson), **L2** 124
On the Day You Were Born, **L5** 123
Dead as a Dodo & Save the Forests, Save the Trees, **L1** 63; **L5** 93
decoration, **L3** 200–201; **L5** 116–119
Deep Dish/Spain/from Valencia (Unknown), **L5** 176
Degas, Edgar, **L2** 143; **L3** 64, 65; **L5** 40
degikup, **L6** 202
Delaunay, Robert, **L2** 97
Delaware Shoulder Bag (Unknown), **L2** 126
del Verrocchio, Andrea, **L4** 172

Program Index (continued)

Dentzel Company, **L2** 203
depth, **L2** 88–89; **L3** 70–77; **L4** 155; **L6** 53
Derain, André, **L6** 74
design, **LK** 164–167
Design Made at Airlie Gardens (Evans), **L4** 70
DesJarlait, Patrick, **L2** 100
detail, **L4** 162; **L5** 72
Dhon Dholak Cholam, **L5** 213; **LK** 153
diamond, **L3** 50
Díaz, David, **LK** 95A
Dick, Beau, **LK** 154, 155
Dido (Hartigan), **L1** 112
Diebenkorn, Richard, **L2** 44
Die Brücke, **L6** 75
Die Erfüllung (Fulfillment) (Klimt), **L6** 34
digital filmmakers, **L4** 152
Dillon, Diane and Leo, **L3** 155A
The Diner (Segal), **LK** 150
Display Rows (Thiebaud), **L3** 120
distortion, **L4** 176–179; **L5** 124–125, 138–145; **L6** 155, 164–171, 183
Djanbazian Dance Company, **L6** 93
Djukulul, Dorothy, **L3** 161
dominant element, **L2** 166; **L4** 204
Double Pan Swoosh (Rose), **L6** 116, 117
Double Saddlebag (Unknown), **L3** 48
Dove, Arthur, **L5** 194
Down Eighteenth Street (Thiebaud), **L6** 120
Drouet (Whistler), **L4** 56
Dr. Seuss, **L2** 35A
Dufy, Raoul, **LK** 126; **L5** 60, 108
Duke, Jerry, **LK** 93; **L4** 63
Dürer, Albrecht, **L1** 34, 35
The Dwell House (Central Office of Architecture, LA, CA), **L1** 143

E

Eagle and Salmon (Hoover), **LK** 157
Eagle Dance, **L3** 63
Eagle Eye (Paik), **L6** 206
Eagle's Song (Naranjo), **L4** 164–165
Early Sunday Morning (Hopper), **L2** 53
Early Sunday Morning, Merced River, Yosemite Valley, CA (Adams), **L2** 108, 109
earthenware, **L2** 78
Earth Song (Houser), **LK** 124
Easy Chair (Gardner), **L3** 157
Ecology
  animals, **L1** 77
  economics, **L1** 103
  environment, **LK** 116; **L1** 108, 197; **L4** 100
  form, **L1** 134
  fossils, **L1** 164
  habitats, **LK** 119
  insects, **L1** 168
  lines, **L1** 44

and the outdoors, **L5** 70
  plants, **LK** 96, 99; **L1** 74; **L2** 134; **L4** 202
  recycling, **L1** 159
Edenshaw, Charles, **L4** 187
Egungun from Ogbomoso (Unknown), **L6** 96, 97
Egyptian Cat (Unknown), **L4** 135
Eiffel Tower (Eiffel), **L6** 126, 127
  element, **L5** 194–197
The Elephants (Dali), **L4** 176
Elevator Grill (Sullivan), **L5** 117
Elisofon, Eliot, **L4** 75
Ellett, Randy, **L6** 198, 199
The Elm Tree (Summer) (Mangold), **L1** 45
Embroidered Pillow (Unknown), **LK** 176
embroidery, **L6** 36
The Emergence of the Clowns (Swentzell), **L2** 74
Emperor Shah Jahan, **L5** 130
Emperor Shah Jahan and His Son, Suja (Nanha), **L5** 131
emphasis
  of area, **L6** 146–149
  creating, **L2** 164–171; **L3** 196–197; **L4** 146–149; **L5** 195
  and decoration, **L3** 200–201
  defined, **L1** 185; **L3** 185
  of an element, **L5** 194–197; **L6** 142–145
  in forms, **L1** 198–201
  in paintings, **L1** 194–197
  through placement, **L5** 198–201
  and variety, **L4** 202–205
The Empire of Lights (Magritte), **L2** 169
Endangered Species (Goodnight), **L4** 44, 45
Energy Apples (Flack), **LK** 100
Ensor, James, **L6** 78
The Equatorial Jungle (Rousseau), **L1** 74
Ernesta (Child with Nurse) (Beaux), **L2** 165
Escobar, Marisol, **L5** 90
Esquisse for Ode to Kinshasa (Jones), **L1** 64
Estes, Richard, **L3** 142, 143
Eth-Noh-Tec, **L2** 92, 93; **L4** 93
Evans, Minnie, **L4** 70; **L6** 100, 101
even balance, **LK** 196–197
Evergood, Philip, **L3** 139
Every Picture Tells a Story, **L3** 93; **L6** 213
exaggerated features, **L3** 132; **L5** 144; **L6** 170
Exotic Landscape (Rousseau), **L6** 112
expression, **L5** 36–39
Eyre, Ivan, **L1** 108; **L2** 187

F

Faaturuma [Melancholic] (Gauguin), **L4** 120
fabric designers, **L1** 92
face distortion, **L6** 164–167
Face Jugs (Unknown), **L6** 165
Face Mask of Kumugwe'

(Unknown), **L6** 96
face proportions, **L5** 134–137, 142–145; **L6** 156–159
False Face Mask (Webster), **L5** 142
Families, **L5** 130
Family (Bearden), **LK** 87
The Family (Escobar), **L5** 90
Family Group (Moore), **L2** 64
Family Portrait (Frey), **L4** 210
fashion designers, **L1** 92
fashion photographers, **L4** 92
Father and Daughter (Schapiro), **LK** 86
Faust, Robert, **L2** 63; **L3** 153; **L5** 63; **L6** 183
Fauves, **L1** 112
Featherwork Neckpiece (Unknown), **L5** 104
Feeding Caitlin (Fish), **LK** 112
Feline Felicity (Sheeler), **L5** 52
Fenetre Ouverte Devant la Mer (Dufy), **L5** 108
fiber textures, **L5** 168–171
fiber works of art, **L4** 74
Figure: Churinga (Hepworth), **L1** 135
figure distortion, **L6** 168–171
Figure from House Post (Unknown), **L4** 186
Figure (Lipchitz), **L1** 131
Figure of a Lion (Bell), **L2** 78
figure proportion, **L6** 160–163
Fireworks (Ensor), **L6** 78
The First Aeroplane (Town), **L2** 117
Fish, Gold Weight (Unknown), **LK** 172
Fishing Boats (Braque), **L6** 79
Fish, Janet, **LK** 112; **L1** 82; **L3** 44
Fish Story (Baliker), **L6** 48
Flack, Audrey, **LK** 100; **L3** 124, 125; **L4** 40
The Flatiron (Steichen), **L2** 108
Flores, Aurelio and Francisco, **L3** 135
florists, **L2** 92
Flower Day (Rivera), **L5** 169
Flowers (Warhol), **L3** 202
flowing contour lines, **L4** 53
The Fly (Blake), **LK** 48
Flying Goddess, **L1** 123
focal point, **L2** 166, 170; **L3** 196; **L4** 148; **L5** 200; **L6** 140, 148
folk art, **L6** 104
Fonseca, Harry, **L1** 176
Fontana, Lavinia, **L5** 94, 95
font designers, **L6** 182
Football Player (Hanson), **L5** 147
The Football Players (Rousseau), **L2** 150; **L3** 150
foreground, **L3** 72; **L4** 158; **L6** 54
form
  and animals, **LK** 142–145; **L2** 78–81
  in animation, **L3** 93
  in architecture, **L5** 86–89
  body, **L2** 74–77
  and buildings, **LK** 138–141
  defined, **L2** 64–65
  and emphasis, **L1** 198–201
  free form, **L6** 48–51
  geometric, **L1** 136;

L2 66–69; **L6** 44–47
  and harmony, **L2** 192–193
  in music, **LK** 153; **L6** 62
  and people, **L1** 138–141
  and real texture, **LK** 172–175
  and rhythm, **L2** 138–142
  and sculpture, **LK** 130–137, 144; **L4** 130–133
  and shapes, **L1** 126–129; **L3** 78–81; **L4** 128
  in song writing, **L5** 93
  and space, **LK** 124–125, 134–138; **L1** 125, 130–133; **L3** 64–65; **L5** 64–65
  and theater, **L2** 93
  three-dimensional, **L2** 68
  and unity, **LK** 208
  using, **LK** 146–149; **L5** 82–85
  and variety, **L2** 198–201
formal balance, **L3** 126–137; **L4** 186–189; **L5** 168–171; **L6** 126–129
La Fortune (Ray), **L3** 104
At Four and a Half (Twiggs), **L2** 49
Four by Four (Loeser), **L3** 160
Four Ladies of the Court Playing Polo (Unknown), **LK** 207
The Four Seasons (Chagall), **LK** 57
Francesco Sasetti and His Son Teodoro (Ghirlandaio), **L5** 130
Frances Lehman Loeb Art Center, **L1** 122
Free Fall (Wiesner), **LK** 74
free-form forms, **L2** 70–73; **L6** 48–51
free-form shapes, **LK** 74–81, 83–84; **L1** 74–77, 85, 88, 134–137; **L2** 56–59; **L3** 46, 54, 58, 80; **L4** 70–73, 128; **L5** 44–47, 88; **L6** 40–43
freestanding sculpture, **L3** 84; **L4** 132
Frey, Viola, **L4** 210; **L5** 124, 125
Frieda y Diego Rivera (Kahlo), **L6** 154
Friendship, **L6** 156
Friesen, Eugene, **L3** 153; **L5** 63
fringing, **L5** 84
frontal proportion, **L6** 158
front view, **L4** 166
Full Fathoms Five, Turbo Power, Spirit of the Landscape, **L3** 93; **L6** 213
futurists, **L6** 118

G

Gainsborough, Thomas, **L3** 57
Games, **LK** 48; **L1** 56, 186; **L2** 202; **L3** 96; **L5** 172
Garden at Vaucresson (Vuillard), **LK** 97
In the Garden (Cassatt), **L1** 94
Garden Landscape and Fountain (Tiffany), **LK** 56
Gardner, Caleb, **L3** 157
Garrison, Elizabeth, **L5** 203
Garrowby Hill (Hockney), **L2** 147
Garza, Carmen Lomas, **LK** 203; **L1** 78; **L2** 125A

The Gates to Times Square (Chryssa), **L2** 154, 155
Gathering Wild Rice (DesJarlait), **L2** 100
Gauguin, Paul, **L4** 120; **L5** 160; **L6** 184, 185
Gay, Jacob, **L2** 172
Geisel, Theodore Seuss, **L2** 35A
genre paintings, **L1** 116
geometric forms, **L1** 136; **L2** 66–69; **L6** 44–47, 50
geometric shapes, **LK** 70–73, 78–81; **L1** 70–73, 88; **L2** 52–55; **L3** 46, 48–51, 58; **L4** 66–69; **L5** 44–47; **L6** 40–43, 40–43
Georgia (Garrison), **L5** 203
Georgia Stele (Moroles), **L2** 67
gesture art, **L5** 42
gesture drawings, **L4** 40–44
Ghirlandaio, Domenico, **L5** 130
Gift Basket (Unknown), **LK** 168–171
Gile, Seldon Conner, **L1** 101
Gilles, Joseph-Jean, **L3** 74, 75
Ginevra de' Benci (da Vinci), **L6** 180
Gin Matsuba (Kudo), **L3** 202, 203
Girl in a Boat with Geese (Morisot), **L4** 157
The Girl on the Rock, **LK** 123
The Girl With the Red Hat (Vermeer), **L2** 176
Glacometti, Alberto, **L6** 168
A Glimpse of Notre Dame in the Late Afternoon (Matisse), **L1** 113
Going West, **L2** 112; **L5** 100
goldsmiths, **L5** 152
Goncharova, Natalia, **L4** 34, 35
Goodnight, Paul, **L4** 45
Gottlieb, Adolph, **L2** 116
Gracehoper (Smith), **L5** 83
Graham, Martha, **L5** 153
Grandma Moses [Anna Mary Robertson Moses], **L6** 194
Grandmother's Dinner (Andrews), **L6** 210
Grandmother Series: July Cone Hat (Frey), **L5** 124
Granite Weaving (Moroles), **L1** 154
graphic designers, **L3** 182
Great Blue Heron (Audubon), **L3** 154
Great Water Lily of America (Sharp), **L6** 143
The Great Wave Off Kanagawa (Hokusai), **LK** 34
green, **L1** 108–111
Greenblat, Rodney Alan, **LK** 120
The Green House (Skoglund), **LK** 206
Guevara, Susan, **L4** 65A
guide lines, **L5** 136
Gui Ritual Food Container, **L2** 156

H

Habitat (Safdie), **L6** 172
Hairdresser's Window (Sloan), **L3** 194

Haitian Landscape (Jean Gilles), **L3** 74, 75
Hand Puppets (Unknown), **LK** 164
Hannukka Menorah (Abrasha), **L3** 168, 169
Hanson, Duane, **LK** 135; **L2** 160; **L4** 173; **L5** 147
harmony
 of color, **L2** 186–189
 creating, **L3** 188–189; **L4** 185, 198–201; **L5** 185–189; **L6** 185
 in dance, **L2** 212; **L6** 213
 defined, **L2** 185; **L3** 185
 of shape and form, **L2** 192–193
 in three-dimensional art, **L6** 198–201
 in two-dimensional art, **L6** 194–197
Harriet Tubman Series #4 (Lawrence), **LK** 83
Harris, Lawren S., **L1** 52
Hart, George, **L6** 45
Hartigan, Grace, **L1** 112
Hartley, Marsden, **L6** 100
Hartmann, William, **L6** 176
Hassam, Childe, **L5** 74
Hat: Birds and Geometric Patterns (Unknown), **L3** 100
hatching, **L4** 58; **L5** 48–51, 58, 80; **L6** 72
Headdress for Epa Masquerade (Yoruba People), **L2** 90
Heade, Martin Johnson, **L4** 203
Health
 human body, **LK** 69, 73, 85; **L1** 78, 137, 190; **L4** 172; **L6** 168
 nutrition, **LK** 100; **L1** 86; **L2** 86; **L3** 44; **L4** 112
 safety, **LK** 47, 81; **L1** 70, 85, 194
In the Heart of the Beast Puppet and Mask Theatre, **L1** 153; **L5** 123
Held, Al, **L3** 97
Helder, Z. Vanessa, **L4** 101
Henkes, Kevin, **L2** 185A
Henri, Robert, **L4** 169; **L5** 135
Henry Pelham (Boy with a Squirrel) (Copley), **L6** 157
Hepworth, Barbara, **L1** 135
Herb, Alverda, **L6** 138
Herbin, Auguste, **LK** 70; **L1** 70; **L2** 52
Here Look at Mine (Robinson), **L5** 191
The Hermitage at Pontoise (Pissaro), **L4** 156
Heroes, **L2** 160
hexagon, **L3** 50; **L5** 46; **L6** 42
highlights, **L3** 144
High School Student (Hanson), **L4** 173
Hirondelle/Amour (Miro), **L5** 161
Hmong Story Cloth (Unknown), **L1** 180
Hoban, Tana, **LK** 65A
Hockney, David, **LK** 41; **L1** 97; **L2** 147; **L4** 96
Hodges, Margaret, **LK** 35A
Hodler, Ferdinand, **L6** 130, 131
Hofmann, Hans, **L1** 120
Hokusai, Katsushika, **LK** 34,

35, 49, 117; **L4** 53, 87; **L6** 134
Holidays, **L3** 134
Hollywood Hills House (Hockney), **L1** 97
Homer, Winslow, **L1** 161; **L5** 70
Homes
 buildings, **L1** 142
 families, **LK** 86; **L1** 48; **L2** 82
 geography, **L3** 55
 imagination, **L3** 160
 location, **L2** 104
 objects in, **L1** 146; **L5** 176; **L6** 172
Homesick Proof Space Station (Brown), **L5** 78
Hong Shancha: Red Camellia (Liu), **L1** 75
Hoop Dance, **L3** 63
Hoover, John, **LK** 157; **L3** 176
Hopper, Edward, **LK** 126, 127; **L2** 53; **L3** 52
house posts, **LK** 198, 201
House Post (Unknown), **LK** 199
Houser, Allan, **LK** 124, 125; **L4** 86
Houses at Auvers (van Gogh), **L5** 154
Hudson River Quilters, **L5** 202
The Hudson River Quilt (Miller), **L5** 202
hues, **L2** 94, 96–99, 100–107, 114, 186–189; **L3** 98; **L4** 98; **L5** 98; **L6** 66–69. *See also* colors
Huichol Bead Mask (Unknown), **L5** 199
Huipil Weaving (Unknown), **L5** 36
Humpty Dumpty Circus (Schoenhut), **LK** 44, 45
Hunting Scene on Handle from a Large Bowl (Unknown), **L3** 83
Hyman, Trina Schart, **L3** 35A

I

Ice Cream Cones (Bishop), **L1** 79
illustrators, **LK** 35A, 65A, 74, 92, 95A, 125A, 155A, 185A; **L1** 35A, 65A, 95A, 125A, 155A, 185A; **L2** 35A, 65A, 95A, 125A, 155A, 185A; **L3** 35A, 65A, 95A, 125A, 155A, 185A; **L4** 35A, 65A, 95A, 125A, 155A, 185A, 212; **L5** 35A, 65A, 95A, 125A; **L6** 35A, 65A, 95A, 125A, 155A, 185A
Imagination
 artists, **L3** 40; **L4** 116
 communication, **L5** 138
 creativity, **L6** 56
 homes, **L3** 160
 inventions, **L1** 129
 lines, **L2** 40
 stories, **LK** 66; **L3** 82
 texture, **L1** 160
impressionism, **L6** 112, 134
Impressions #2, **LK** 63
Improvisation No. 27 (Kandinsky), **L3** 40
Indian Fantasy (Hartley), **L6** 100
Indonesian Shadow Puppet (Unknown, **L2** 56
informal balance, **L4** 190–193; **L5** 172–175; **L6** 134–137

intensity, **L4** 108–111; **L6** 74–77
interior designers, **L2** 212; **L3** 148; **L5** 92
intermediate colors, **L3** 100–103, 118; **L4** 98; **L5** 102; **L6** 68
invented texture, **L4** 140
Isa, Ustad, **LK** 139
Isicathulo, **L3** 123; **L6** 123
isolation, **L5** 200; **L6** 148

J

Jackson, Mary A., **L4** 206
Jacquette, Yvonne, **L2** 210
Jaguar (Unknown), **L4** 134
James, Charlie, **L5** 142
James Vilbert, Sculptor (Hodler), **L6** 131
Jane's Remington (Cottingham), **L3** 194, 195
Japanese Bridge over a Pool of Water Lilies (Monet), **L3** 36
Japanese prints, **LK** 116
Jar (Unknown), **L3** 126, 127, 186
jewelers, **L3** 88
jewelry, **L3** 86–89; **L5** 152; **L6** 206–207
Jitterbugs [II] (Johnson), **L2** 60
Joffrey Ballet, **L1** 183
The Joffrey Ballet of Chicago, **L4** 153
John, Isabel, **L3** 191
Johns, Jasper, **L1** 44; **L5** 66, 67, 97
Johnson, Joshua, **L4** 190
Johnson, Willam H., **LK** 82; **L2** 60
Johnson, William, **L4** 195
Jonathan Buttall: The Blue Boy (Gainsbough), **L3** 57
Jones, Ben, **L5** 96
Jones, Calvin, **L3** 104, 105
Jones, Loïs Mailou, **L1** 64, 65
Joropo Azul, **L4** 183
Journeys, **L2** 146, 172; **L5** 198; **L6** 146, 160, 186
July Hay (Benton), **L1** 116
Jump (Fish), **L1** 83
Jungle Tales (Shannon), **L2** 82

K

Kabotie, Fred, **L3** 173
Kahlo, Frida, **L5** 180; **L6** 154, 155
Kahng-Gang-Sool-Le, **L2** 213
Kahn, Wolf, **L1** 40
Kandinsky, Wassily, **L1** 37; **L2** 48; **L3** 40; **L4** 36, 37
Keams, Geri, **L2** 153
Keats, Ezra Jack, **L3** 95A
Kelly, Ellsworth, **L1** 96
Kensett, John Frederick, **L2** 105
Kente Cloth (Unknown), **L1** 172
Keyser, Louisa (Dat So La Lee), **L6** 202
Kimbell Art Museum, **L1** 182
kinetic movement, **L6** 116–119
King (Evans), **L6** 101
King Family (Jones), **L5** 96
King's Crown (Unknown), **L6** 86
*Kirifuri Waterfall on Mount Kurokami in Shimotsuke

Province* (Hokusai), **LK** 117
Klee, Paul, **L2** 186; **L3** 112; **L4** 108, 109
Klimt, Gustav, **L6** 34, 35
Kline, Franz, **L2** 41
Kneeling Child on Yellow Background (Rivera), **L3** 94
Kohlmeyer, Ida, **L1** 202, 203
Korean Classical Music and Dance Company, **LK** 183; **L2** 213
Krasle, Elizabeth Paulos, **L5** 207
Krasner, Lee, **L4** 138, 139
Kudo, Lundin, **L3** 203
Kurelek, William, **L2** 180
Kwele Face Mask (Unknown), **L5** 143

L

Lai Haraoba, **L2** 123
Lamentation, **L5** 153
landscape architects, **L1** 152; **L3** 92
landscape paintings, **L4** 100, 101, 156–157
landscapes, **L1** 108
Language Arts and Reading Art Connections
 Descriptive Writing, **LK** 39, 69, 103, 107, 193; **L1** 43, 69, 115, 133, 159, 201; **L2** 43, 55, 89, 99, 175, 197; **L4** 47, 73, 99, 133, 159, 205; **L5** 47, 51, 59, 77, 145, 171, 175; **L6** 59, 77, 85, 89, 115, 145, 167, 189;
 Expository Writing, **LK** 59, 81, 99, 201; **L1** 39, 89, 107, 129, 175, 193; **L2** 51, 77, 107, 119, 129, 137, 163, 193; **L4** 55, 69, 111, 129, 179, 197; **L5** 85, 103, 129, 209; **L6** 47, 73, 99, 141, 171, 197;
 Narrative Writing, **LK** 47, 77, 89, 115, 197, 209; **L1** 59, 85, 99, 137, 167, 189; **L2** 59, 73, 103, 141, 159, 201; **L3** 39, 43, 47, 51, 55, 59, 69, 73, 77, 81, 85, 89, 99, 107, 133, 137, 141, 145; **L4** 43, 85, 119, 145, 163, 193, 209; **L5** 39, 69, 99, 115, 119, 137, 149, 205; **L6** 39, 43, 51, 107, 133, 137, 159, 209
 Personal Writing and Poetry, **LK** 51, 119, 189, 205; **L1** 47, 55, 73, 77, 103, 111, 141, 145, 163, 171, 197, 209; **L2** 39, 47, 69, 81, 85, 111, 115, 133, 145, 149, 167, 189, 209; **L4** 51, 59, 77, 81, 103, 115, 137, 149, 167, 171, 189; **L5** 43, 55, 81, 107, 133, 141, 159, 167, 179, 189, 197, 201; **L6** 69, 103, 111, 129, 149, 175, 179, 193, 205
 Persuasive Writing, **LK** 43, 55, 73, 85, 111; **L1** 51, 81, 119, 149, 179, 205; **L2** 171; **L4** 39, 89, 107, 141, 175, 201; **L5** 73, 89, 111, 163, 193; **L6** 55, 81, 119,

163, 201
Large Eagle (Schimmel), **L2** 199
Large Interior Los Angeles (Hockney), **L4** 96
Las Meninas (The Maids of Honor) (Velazquez), **L2** 184, 185
Lawrence, Jacob, **LK** 83, 101; **L1** 56, 82; **L2** 35; **L3** 60,172; **L4** 180
layout artists, **L3** 62; **L6** 62
Lazzell, Blanche, **L1** 53
Leger, Fernand, **L3** 78
Lemon, Christina, **L6** 206, 207
Leonardo da Vinci Chair (Russell), **L6** 173
Leopard Aquamanile (Unknown), **L2** 79
Letter Holder or Book Cover (Mimac People, Nova Scotia) (Unknown), **L1** 157
Let Them Eat Books, **L1** 213
LeVan, Susan, **L6** 82
Lewitzky Dance Company, **LK** 63
Leyster, Judith, **L4** 184, 185
L'Hiver: Chat sur un Coussin (Winter: Cat on a Cushion) (Steinlen), **L4** 52
Li Bai (Hokusai), **L6** 134
light, **LK** 40; **L2** 178
Lighted City (Thiebaud), **L3** 108
The Lighthouse at Two Lights (Hopper), **LK** 127
Lilac-colored Landscape (Kahn), **L1** 40
Li'l Sis (Johnson), **LK** 82
linear perspective, **L5** 74–77; **L6** 54
lines
 active, **L2** 48–51
 broken, **LK** 56–59
 in buildings, **L1** 52–55
 calm, **L1** 40–43; **L2** 44–47
 contour, **L4** 48–51
 converging, **L5** 72; **L6** 54
 curved, **LK** 48–50; **L1** 48–51, 58
 in dance, **L4** 63
 diagonal, **LK** 45–47; **L1** 44–47, 58
 expressive, **L3** 34–39; **L5** 36–39
 finding, **L1** 34–39
 flowing, **L4** 52–55
 and harmony, **L3** 188; **L5** 188
 horizontal, **LK** 40–43; **L5** 76
 and movement, **L1** 56–59; **L2** 48–51; **L4** 41–43
 in music, **L6** 62
 perspective, **L4** 162
 qualities of, **L6** 36–39
 rough, **LK** 52–55
 and shape, **L1** 65
 smooth, **LK** 52–55
 in song writing, **L1** 63
 in theatre, **L5** 63
 thick, **LK** 36–39
 thin, **LK** 36–39
 types of, **L2** 40–43; **L3** 40–43; **L4** 36–39
 using, **L2** 34–39; **L6** 35
 and variety, **L3** 192; **L6** 186–189
 vertical, **LK** 40–43
 and visual weight, **L4** 192
 zigzag, **LK** 45–47; **L1** 46, 58
Lionni, Leo, **LK** 185A; **L2** 194

Program Index (continued)

The Lion on the Path, **LK** 123
Liotard, Jean Etienne, **LK** 161
Lipchitz, Jacques, **L1** 131; **L4** 126, 127
Lismer, Arthur, **L3** 37
Literature, **LK** 35A
Literature and Art Video
Abeula, **L3** 155A
Bridge to Terabithia (Paterson), **L6** 65A
Call it Courage (Sperry), **L6** 35A
A Chair for My Mother (Williams), **L2** 155A
At the Crossroads, **L4** 155A
The Dancing Skeleton, **L4** 35A
Diego, **L3** 95A
Ernst, **L1** 95A
Eskimo Art, **L4** 125A
Follow the Drinking Gourd, **L5** 185A
The Forest Dwellers: Native American Arts of the Pacific Northwest, **L3** 125A
Free Fall (Wiesner), **LK** 65A
The Girl Who Loved Wild Horses (Goble), **L6** 95A
The Great Kapok Tree (Cherry), **LK** 95A
The Grey Lady and the Strawberry Snatcher (Bang), **L6** 155A
Heckedy Peg (Wood), **L2** 65A
Henry and Mudge Under the Yellow Moon (Rylant), **LK** 125A
Hiawatha's Childhood, **L4** 95A
The Hundred Penny Box (Mathis), **L6** 185A
It Could Always Be Worse (Zemach), **L2** 185A
Jumanji, **L5** 35A
Kachina Spirit, **L4** 65A
King Bidgood's in the Bathtub, **L4** 185A
The Little Band, **L1** 185A
The Maestro Plays (Martin), **LK** 185A
Mama Don't Allow, **L1** 35A
Meet Leo Lionni, **L3** 185A
Meet the Caldecott Illustrator: Jerry Pinkney, **L5** 95A
Monster Mama, **L1** 155A
Narrative Writing, **L3** 129
Old Henry, **L3** 35A
Paper Crane, **L1** 125A
The Pig's Picnic (Kasza), **LK** 155A
The Polar Express (Van Allsburg), **L2** 95A
The Relatives Came, **L1** 65A
Rumpelstiltskin, **L5** 155A
Saint George and the Dragon (Hodges), **LK** 35A
Song and Dance Man (Ackerman), **L2** 125A
The Talking Eggs (San Souci), **L2** 65A
Tuesday (Weisner), **L6** 125A
When I Was Young in the Mountains, **L3** 65A
Yonder, **L5** 65A
lithography, **L6** 142
Little Dancer, Aged Fourteen (Degas), **L3** 64

Little Painting with Yellow (Improvisation) (Kandinsky), **L4** 37
Liu, Hung, **L1** 75
Lobel, Arnold, **L3** 185A
Lobster Trap and Fish Tail (Calder), **L6** 116
location, **L5** 200; **L6** 148
The Locust Trees with Maple (Mangold), **L3** 74
Loeser, Tom, **L3** 160
Loneliness (Neel), **L6** 150
Long Haired Girl, **L2** 92; **L4** 93
Long, Sylvia, **LK** 37
Look Again, **L2** 48; **L5** 116; **L6** 82, 130
The Lookout—"All's Well" (Homer), **L1** 161
Loomings 3X (Stella), **L1** 127
Looner Eclipse (Hoover), **L3** 176
Loring, Eugene, **L3** 213; **L5** 183
Lostutter, Robert, **L2** 96
Lovebird Token (Johnson), **L4** 195
Low Basket with Handle (Jackson), **L4** 206
Lower Manhattan (View Down Broad Street) (Hassam), **L5** 74
low-intensity colors, **L4** 108–111
Lyons, Mitch, **L5** 195

M

Mabe, Manabu, **L5** 109
Macaulay, David, **L6** 65A
MacDonald-Wright, Stanton, **L6** 67
Madame Thadée Natanson at the Theater, **L5** 41
The Magic Room (Valdez), **L4** 82
Magritte, Rene, **L1** 194; **L2** 169; **L3** 90
Mah-To-Toh-Pa, Four Bears, Second Chief (Catlin), **L5** 157
Maison Carree, Nimes, France (Unknown), **L2** 206
"Ma Jolie" (Woman with a Zither or Guitar) (Picasso), **L5** 165
make-up artists, **LK** 152
Mangold, Sylvia Plimack, **L1** 45; **L3** 74
Manguin, Henri-Charles, **LK** 60
Manitoba Party (Kurelek), **L2** 180
Man's Headband of Toucan Feathers (Unknown), **L1** 104
Man (Trujillo), **LK** 130
Map (Johns), **L5** 96, 97
Map Quilt (Unknown), **L2** 173
Maquillage (Goncharova), **L4** 34
Marc, Franz, **L6** 108
marine architects, **L5** 92
marine illustrators, **L4** 212
Marquet, Albert, **L1** 71
Martínez, Maria, **LK** 184, 185
Mask Brooch (Lemon), **L6** 207
Mask Communion

(Mazloomi), **L4** 74
The Mask Messenger, **L2** 63; **L6** 183
Mask of Fear (Klee), **L4** 109
Mask of the Moon (Seaweed), **L1** 191
masks, **L1** 190–193; **L2** 63; **L3** 130–133
Masks: A World of Diversity, **L5** 125A
Mask (Unknown), **L5** 143
Mask with Seal or Sea Otter Spirit (Unknown), **L3** 130, 131
materials, **L2** 66
Mathematics Art Connections
Geometry, **LK** 43, 47, 59, 73, 89, 189, 197, 201, 209; **L1** 39, 43, 51, 73, 129, 137, 145, 159, 197; **L2** 47, 51, 55, 59, 69, 73, 141, 145, 159, 163; **L3** 39, 47, 51, 55, 77, 99, 137, 145; **L4** 39, 43, 47, 51, 55, 69, 73, 163, 167, 171, 201, 205; **L5** 47, 51, 55, 59, 69, 73, 81, 85, 89, 115, 141, 145, 171; **L6** 39, 43, 47, 55, 73, 77, 119, 149, 193, 197, 201
Measurement, **LK** 55, 99; **L1** 111, 141, 149, 167, 209; **L2** 43, 107, 175, 193; **L3** 43, 141; **L4** 89, 103, 111, 129, 179, 197; **L5** 129, 197; **L6** 51, 59, 103, 115, 141, 167, 179, 205
Numbers and Operations, **LK** 51, 69, 77, 81, 85, 103, 107, 111, 115, 119, 193, 205; **L1** 47, 55, 59, 69, 77, 81, 85, 89, 99, 103, 107, 115, 119, 133, 163, 171, 175, 179, 189, 193, 201, 205; **L2** 39, 77, 81, 85, 89, 99, 103, 111, 129, 137, 201, 209; **L3** 59, 69, 81, 89, 107; **L4** 59, 77, 81, 85, 99, 107, 115, 119, 133, 137, 141, 145, 149, 159, 175, 193, 209; **L5** 39, 43, 77, 99, 103, 107, 111, 119, 137, 149, 159, 163, 167, 175, 179, 189, 201, 205, 209; **L6** 69, 81, 89, 99, 107, 111, 129, 133, 145, 159, 163, 171
Problem Solving, Reasoning, and Proof, **L3** 85; **L4** 189; **L5** 133, 193; **L6** 85, 137, 175, 189, 209
Matisse, Henri, **LK** 94, 95, 108; **L1** 112, 113; **L3** 207; **L4** 49; **L6** 36
matte surface, **L2** 178; **L6** 88
Mayer, Mercer, **LK** 67
Mazloomi, Carolyn, **L4** 74
McCall, Robert, **L5** 79
McCloskey, Robert, **L4** 35A
McCloskey, William H., **L2** 135
McIntosh, Harrison, **L1** 168
McIntyre, Chuna, **LK** 213
McKissack, Patricia C., **L5** 95A
media, **L5** 202–205
medical illustrators, **L4** 212
The Meeting of David and Abigail (Rubens), **L4** 146, 147
Mei, Gu, **L4** 52

Melancholy Metropolis (Mabe), **L5** 109
Memory Jar (Unknown), **L5** 156
Mendoza, Heron Martínez, **L2** 36
Merian, Maria Sibylla, **L2** 130
The Metropolitan Museum of Art, **L5** 122
Michelangelo, **L4** 124, 125
middle ground, **L4** 158; **L6** 54
Mihrab (Unknown), **L3** 49
Milkweed (Krasner), **L4** 139
Miller, Irene Preston, **L5** 202
The Mill (van Rijn), **L2** 168
Miró, Joan, **L5** 161
Miró, Joan, **L4** 79
Miss Liberty Celebration (Zeldis), **L4** 116, 117
mixed-media collages, **L5** 39
Miyawaki, Ayako, **L3** 146
mobiles, **L1** 126, 129; **L3** 81; **L6** 116–117, 119
Model Totem Pole (Edenshaw), **L4** 187
Modigliani, Amedeo, **L5** 139
Moillon, Louise, **L2** 86
Mola (Unknown), **L1** 186
Mona Lisa (da Vinci), **L1** 184
Mondrian, Piet, **L1** 41, 100
Monet, Claude, **LK** 40; **L2** 45, 195; **L3** 36
Money, **L1** 99, 167, 201; **L5** 56; **L6** 202, 206
monochromatic color scheme, **L4** 118; **L5** 96–99
The Monongahela at Morgantown (Lazzell), **L1** 53
Monument (Snowden), **L1** 206
mood, **L4** 116–119
Moore, Henry, **LK** 134; **L1** 208; **L2** 64, 65; **L4** 126
Morandi, Giorgio, **L4** 56, 57
Morisot, Berthe, **L4** 157; **L5** 184, 185
Moroles, Jesús, **L1** 154, 155
Mortlake Terrace (Turner), **L3** 71
mosaic, **LK** 56
Moses, Anna Mary Robertson, **L6** 194
Mother and Child (Cassatt), **L6** 90
Mother and Child (Picasso), **L3** 34
Mother of the Eagles (Unknown), **L5** 198
motif(s)
and alternating pattern, **L3** 166
and pattern, **L1** 174, 176–179; **L2** 126–129; **L3** 162; **L4** 76; **L5** 114; **L6** 96–99, 106
and regular pattern, **L3** 155–159
motion pictures, **LK** 152
Moulthrop, Philip, **L3** 156
Mountain Man (Remington), **L3** 184
movement
curving, **L2** 146–149
defined, **L2** 125, **L3** 155
diagonal, **L2** 142–145
kinetic, **L6** 116–119
and lines, **LK** 47–50;

L1 56–59; **L2** 48–51; **L4** 41–43
and observation drawings, **L4** 45
and rhythm, **LK** 190–193; **L4** 82–85; **L5** 164–167
and shape, **L1** 82–85
and theatre, **L4** 93
using, **L5** 155
visual, **L6** 112–115
and visual rhythm, **L3** 174
Movement and Dance Arts Integration
balance, **LK** 193B, 197B; **L1** 185B, 189B; **L2** 155B, 159B; **L3** 125B, 129B; **L4** 185B, 189B, 193B; **L5** 167B, 171B, 175B; **L6** 137B
blending, **L5** 51B
buildings, **L1** 141B
colors, **LK** 95B, 99B, 103B, 107B, 111B, 115B ; **L1** 95B, 99B, 103B, 107B, 111B, 115B; **L2** 95, 99B, 103B, 185B; **L3** 95B, 99B, 103B, 107B, 111B, 115B; **L4** 95B, 99B, 103B, 107B, 115B; **L5** 95B, 99B, 103B, 107B; **L6** 77B
contrast, **L5** 55B
depth, **L3** 69B
distortion, **L4** 175B; **L5** 137B, 141B; **L6** 163B, 167B
emphasis, **L1** 193B, 197B; **L2** 163B, 167B; **L3** 193B, 197B; **L4** 145B; **L5** 193B, 197B; **L6** 141B, 145B
foreground, middle ground, and background, **L4** 155B
form, **L1** 129B, 133B, 137B; **L2** 65B, 69B, 73B, 77B; **L3** 77B; **L4** 125B; **L5** 81B, 85B; **L6** 43B, 47B
harmony, **L2** 189B; **L4** 197B; **L5** 185B; **L6** 193B, 197B
hatching, **L5** 47B
hues, **L6** 65B
intensity, **L6** 73B
lines, **LK** 35B, 39B, 43B, 47B, 51B, 55B ; **L1** 35B, 39B, 43B, 47B, 51B, 55B; **L2** 35B, 39B, 43B, 47B; **L3** 35B, 39B; **L4** 35B, 39B, 47B, 51B; **L5** 35B; **L6** 35B
motif, **L6** 95B
movement, **L2** 141B, 145B; **L6** 111B, 115B
observation drawings, **L4** 43B
overlapping, **L3** 73B
pattern, **LK** 185B; **L1** 167B, 171B; **L2** 125B, 129B; **L3** 155B, 159B, 163B; **L4** 73B; **L5** 111B, 115B; **L6** 99B, 103B
perception drawing, **L5** 39B
perspective, **L4** 159B; **L5** 73B; **L6** 51B
point of view, **L4** 163B
proportion, **L4** 167B, 171B; **L5** 125B, 133B, 145B; **L6** 155B, 159B
rhythm, **LK** 189B; **L1** 175B; **L2** 133B, 137B; **L3** 167B, 171B, 175B; **L4** 77B, 81B, 85B; **L5** 159B, 163B;

L6 107B
scale, L5 129B; L6 171B, 175B
sculpture, L3 81B; L4 129B, 133B
shading, L4 55B, 111B; L5 77B
shapes, LK 65B, 69B, 73B, 77B, 81B, 85B ; L1 65B, 69B, 73B, 77B, 81B, 125B; L2 51B, 55B; L3 43B, 47B, 51B, 55B; L4 65B, 69B; L5 43B, 65B, 69B; L6 39B
space, L1 145B; L2 81B, 85B; L3 65B; L6 55B
symmetry, L3 133B, 137B; L6 125B, 129B
texture, L1 155B, 159B, 163B; L2 171B, 175B; L3 141B, 145B; L4 137B, 141B; L5 155B; L6 81B, 85B
three-dimensional art, L3 85B
unity, LK 201B, 205B; L1 201B, 205B; L2 201B, 205B; L3 201B, 205B; L4 205B; L5 201B, 205B; L6 201B, 205B
value, L2 107B, 111B, 115B; L6 69B
variety, L3 193B, 197B; L3 189B; L4 201B; L5 189B; L6 185B, 189B
Mrs. Ezekiel Goldthwait (Copley), L1 160
Mt. Nebo on the Hill (Moses), L6 194
Munch, Edvard, L6 164
Muniti Red Snapper (Puruntatameri), L1 66
Muñoz, Juan, L6 147
Münter, Gabriele, LK 160; L1 147
Murray, Elizabeth, L4 70, 71
museum guides, L1 212
The Museum of Fine Arts, Houston, Tx., LK 62; L3 122
The Museum of Modern Art, L2 122
museums, LK 62, 182; L1 62, 122, 182; L2 62, 122, 182; L3 122, 152, 212; L4 62, 122, 182; L5 62, 122, 182; L6 92, 152, 212
music
dancing, L2 142
harmony, L5 186, 189
lines, L4 63; L6 62
sharing, LK 108
space, LK 153, 183; L4 183;
Music Arts Integration
balance, LK 193B, 197B; L1 185B, 189B; L2 155B, 159B; L3 125B, 129B; L4 185B, 189B, 193B; L5 167B, 171B, 175B; L6 137B
blending, L5 51B
buildings, L1 141B
colors, LK 95B, 99B, 103B, 107B, 111B, 115B; L1 95B, 99B, 103B, 107B, 111B, 115B; L2 95, 99B, 103B, 185B; L3 95B, 99B, 103B, 107B, 111B, 115B; L4 95B, 99B, 103B, 107B, 115B; L5 95B, 99B, 103B, 107B; L6 77B
contrast, L5 55B
depth, L3 69B

distortion, L4 175B; L5 137B, 141B; L6 163B, 167B
emphasis, L1 193B, 197B; L2 163B, 167B; L3 193B, 197B; L4 145B; L5 193B, 197B; L6 141B, 145B
foreground, middle ground, and background, L4 155B
form, L1 129B, 133B, 137B; L2 65B, 69B, 73B, 77B; L3 77B; L4 125B; L5 81B, 85B; L6 43B, 47B
harmony, L2 189B; L4 197B; L5 185B; L6 193B, 197B
hatching, L5 47B
hues, L6 65B
intensity, L6 73B
lines, LK 35B, 39B, 43B, 47B, 51B, 55B; L1 35B, 39B, 43B, 47B, 51B, 55B; L2 35B, 39B, 43B, 47B; L3 35B, 39B; L4 35B, 39B, 47B, 51B; L5 35B; L6 35B;
motif, L6 95B
movement, L2 141B, 145B; L6 111B, 115B
observation drawings, L4 43B
overlapping, L3 73B
pattern, LK 185B; L1 167B, 171B; L2 125B, 129B; L3 155B, 159B, 163B; L4 73B; L5 111B, 115B; L6 99B, 103B
perception drawing, L5 39B
perspective, L4 159B, L5 73B; L6 51B
point of view, L4 163B
proportion, L4 167B, 171B; L5 125B, 133B, 145B; L6 155B, 159B
rhythm, LK 189B; L1 175B; L2 133B, 137B; L3 167B, 171B, 175B; L4 77B, 81B, 85B; L5 159B, 163B; L6 107B
scale, L5 129B; L6 171B, 175B
sculpture, L3 81B; L4 129B, 133B
shading, L4 55B, 111B; L5 77B
shapes, LK 65B, 69B, 73B, 77B, 81B, 85B; L1 65B, 69B, 73B, 77B, 81B,125B; L2 51B, 55B; L3 43B, 47B, 51B, 55B; L4 65B, 69B; L5 43B, 65B, 69B; L6 39B
space, L1 145B; L2 81B, 85B; L3 65B; L6 55B
symmetry, L3 133B, 137B; L6 125B, 129B
texture, L1 155B, 159B, 163B; L2 171B, 175B; L3 141B, 145B; L4 137B, 141B; L5 155B; L6 81B, 85B
three-dimensional art, L3 85B
unity, LK 201B, 205B; L1 201B, 205B; L2 201B, 205B; L3 201B, 205B; L4 205B; L5 201B, 205B; L6 201B, 205B
value, L2 107B, 111B, 115B; L6 69B
variety, L2 193B, 197B; L3 189B; L4 201B; L5 189B; L6 185B, 189B
Music (Matisse), LK 108

My Dad's Violin (Zalucha), LK 180
My Little White Kittens into Mischief (Currier and Ives), LK 53

N

Nanha, L5 131
Naranjas (Oranges) (Garza), L1 78
Naranjo, Michael, L4 164–165
Naranjo, Virginia, L2 138
narrative painting, L1 176
National Gallery of Canada, L2 182
The National Museum of Women in the Arts, L5 182
National Parts (Ellett), L6 199
Native American art, LK 36; L3 63; L4 206
Native Americans, L1 156; L2 74; L3 146
nature, LK 36, 75; L2 130–133. *See also* Ecology
Navajo Blanket Eye Dazzler (Unknown), L5 101
Necklace (Unknown), L3 86
Neel, Alice, L6 150
negative space, L2 136; L3 66–70, 178; L4 136; L5 68; L6 56–59
Neighborhoods
buildings, L2 168; L3 48, 52; L5 86
community, LK 186; L6 194
ecology, L2 108
economy, LK 202; L5 74
rhythm, L1 176
The Nelson Atkins Museum, LK 182
neon, L2 154
neutral colors, L4 100–103
neutral color scheme, L4 118; L6 72
Nevelson, Louise, L2 124, 125; L3 177; L6 198
New York City—Bird's-Eye View (Torres-García), L1 36
Ngady Ammmwaash (Mweel) Mask (Unknown), L1 190
Night Chant Ceremonial Hunt (Begay), L1 57
Night Raid (Teichert), L2 113
Nighttime in a Palace ('Ali), L3 180
Noah, Third Day (Bearden), L4 138
NO-HO-MUN-YA, One Who Gives No Attention (Catlin), L2 177
Nooning (Homer), L5 70
Norman, Joseph, L1 60
Norton Simon Museum, L6 152
The Nutcracker, "Waltz of the Flowers", L4 153
The Nut Gatherers (Bouguereau), L5 71

O

Oaxacan sculpture, L6 104
observation drawings, L4 44–47

Ocean Park #105 (Diebenkorn), L2 44
Oceans, L1 66; L2 44, 194; L4 197; L6 36, 48, 99
octagon, L3 50; L5 46; L6 42
Octopus Bag (Unknown), LK 108, 109
Offering (Shapiro), L1 210
O'Keeffe, Georgia, LK 75; L1 109; L2 94, 95; L3 113; L4 116, 202; L5 100; L6 130
Old Couple on a Bench (Hanson), LK 135
Oldenburg, Claes, L1 124, 125
Open Window (Dufy), L5 60
Opera House (Utzon), L5 87
orange, L1 104–107
Orchids and Rocks (Mei), L4 52
Ortiz, Alfredo Rolando, L4 183
outline, LK 66–69; L1 66–68
oval, L3 46; L4 68
Oval with Points (Moore), L4 126
overhead view, L4 166
overlapping, L2 82–85, 87; L3 74–77; L4 162; L5 72; L6 54

P

packaging designers, L6 182
Paik, Nam June, L6 206
Painted Storage Jar (Unknown), LK 146
painters, LK 212
Palazzo da Mula, Venice (Monet), L2 45
palepai, L6 202
Pannini, Giovanni Paolo, L6 52
Le Pantheon et Saint-Etienne-du-Mont (Dufy), LK 126
Papaw Tree (O'Keeffe), L1 109
paper designs, LK 194; L3 67
Parade (Lawrence), L3 172
parallelogram, L3 50; L5 46; L6 42
Paris Street, Rainy Day (Caillebotte), L3 142
Paris Through the Window (Chagall), L1 177
Parsons, Betty, LK 156
Pas de Deux (Ragans), L6 190
Pas de Deux (Schapiro), L4 94
Patriots (Andrews), L4 48
pattern
alternating, L3 164–167
and buildings, LK 186–189
changing, L1 172–175
and color, L5 94–95
decorative, L5 112–119
defined, L1 154; L4 65
and motif, L2 126–129; L3 162; L6 96–99
in nature, L2 130–133
random, L3 158
regular, L3 160–163
and repetition, L4 74–78
in theatre, L5 123
three-dimensional, L6 104–107
two-dimensional, L6 100–103
using, L1 168–171
Peale, James, L2 161
Pectoral with the Name of

Senwosret II (Unknown), L2 71
Peeters, Clara, L4 113
pentagon, L3 50; L5 46; L6 42
Peony Blooms IX (Zalucha), L2 134
people
and approximate symmetry, L3 140
in art, LK 86–89
and balance, L2 160–163
body proportion, L4 172–175; L5 128
face proportion, L4 168–171; L5 134–137
and form, L2 74–77
and shape, L1 78–81; L3 56–59
and space, L2 82–85
perception drawing, L5 40–43
Persistence of Memory (Dali), L6 176
Personal Apperance (Schapiro), L2 120
perspective, L4 158–163; L5 72, 74–77; L6 52–55
The Philadelphia Museum of Art, L3 212
photographers, L4 92
photographs, L2 108–109
photojournalists, L4 92
Picasso, Pablo, LK 112, 113; L1 87; L3 34, 35; L5 165; L6 56, 57, 94, L6 109, 176, 177
Pictorial Quilt (Powers), L6 41
Pictorial Tapestry (John), L3 191
The Picture Gallery of Cardinal Silvio Valenti Gonzaga (Pannini), L6 52
picture plane, L4 158
Piero's Piazza (Held), L3 97
Pierrot and Harlequin (Cézanne), L5 120
Pietà (Michelangelo), L4 124
Pilobolus Dance Company, L6 153
Pinkney, Jerry, LK 92
Pippin, Horace, L3 126
Pissaro, Camille, L4 156
Pistia Kew (Weber), L3 116
placement, L4 162; L5 72, 198–201; L6 54
Plaque (Unknown), L1 164
Plate 24 from Poésies (Matisse), L6 36
Plate 2 (from "Dissertation in Insect Generations and Metamorphosis in Surinam (Merian), L2 130
Plate with Rams (Unknown), L2 70
pleating, L5 84
Plowing in Nivernais Region (Bonheur), L3 168
point of view, L2 164; L4 46, 164–167
Polacco, Patricia, L4 185A
Polar Bears and Cubs (Taqialuk), L2 190
Policeman (Hanson), L2 160
Pollock, Jackson, L5 36, 37
Le Pont Saint-Michel in Paris (Marquet), L1 70, 71
Poplars (Monet), LK 40
Portrait of a Boy (Unknown), L3 138
Portrait of a Noblewoman (Fontana), L5 94

Portrait of a Polish Woman (Modigliani), **L5** 139
Portrait of a Woman with a Hood (Matisse), **L4** 49
Portrait of a Young Boy (Andre Berard) (Renoir), **L4** 168
Portrait of a Young Girl in Black (Derain), **L6** 74
Portrait of Dora Maar (Picasso), **L6** 109
Portrait of Emy (Schmidt-Rottluff), **L6** 74, 75
Portrait of Joseph Roulin (van Gogh), **L6** 70
Portrait of Marthe Marie Tronchin (Liotard), **LK** 161
Portrait of Rembrandt (van Rijn), **L6** 124
portraits, **L1** 160; **L2** 176; **L3** 140
Port Saint Tropez, le 14 Juillet (Manguin), **LK** 60
position, **L1** 84; **L6** 136
positive space, **L2** 136; **L3** 66–70; **L4** 136; **L5** 68; **L6** 56–59
Potawatomi Turban (Wisconsin, CIS 3146) (Unknown), **L1** 156
Potter, Beatrix, **LK** 35A
Pottery Vessels (Youngblood), **L3** 186, 187
Pousette-Dart, Richard, **L4** 83
Powder Horn (Gay), **L2** 172
Powers, Harriet, **LK** 176; **L6** 41
Prendergast, Maurice, **L1** 117
Presentation of Captives to a Maya Ruler (Unknown), **L3** 82
primary colors, **LK** 108–111; **L1** 100–103, 116–119; **L3** 98, 102; **L4** 98; **L5** 98; **L6** 68
primary hues, **L2** 98
prism, **L6** 68
profile proportion, **L6** 158
proportion, **L2** 192; **L4** 168–175, 183; **L5** 124–129, 132, 134–149; **L6** 155–163, 183
Proposal for a Monument to Apollinaire (Picasso), **L6** 57
Pueblo Scene Corn Dance, Hopi (Kabotie), **L3** 172, 173
Pueblo Scene Corn Dancers and Church (Vigil Family), **L2** 139
Puff (Krasle), **L5** 207
puppets, **LK** 164–165; **L2** 56–59
Puruntatameri, Francesca, **L1** 66
pyramid, **L3** 80–81; **L4** 128; **L6** 46

Q

quilting, **LK** 176; **L5** 202–204
Quilt (Unknown), **L6** 40
The Quiltwork Girl, **L2** 153

R

radial balance, **L4** 194–197; **L5** 176–179; **L6** 138–141
Radio Dance, **L2** 183

Ragans, Rosalind, **L6** 190
rainbow colors, **L1** 96–99; **L2** 94
Rainbow (Smith), **L4** 36
raised texture, **L1** 164–167
Ramirez, John, **L3** 93; **L6** 213
random pattern, **L3** 158; **L4** 76; **L5** 114, 118; **L6** 102, 106
Ranganiketan Manipuri Cultural Arts, **LK** 153; **L2** 123, **L5** 213
ratio, **L5** 148; **L6** 162
Ray, Man, **L3** 104
realistic art, **L1** 82
realistic scale, **L5** 132; **L6** 172–175
real texture, **LK** 158–159, 172–175; **L1** 156–159
Reclining Figure (Moore), **LK** 134
Reclining Figure with Guitar (Lipchitz), **L4** 126, 127
rectangle, **LK** 72; **L1** 72; **L3** 46; **L4** 68; **L5** 88
Red and Pink Rocks and Teeth (O'Keeffe), **L5** 100
Red Canna (O'Keeffe), **L3** 113
The Red Foulard (Picasso), **L1** 87
The Red Horse (Chagall), **L5** 150
Red Horse Frieze (Branch), **L2** 191
The Red Poppy (O'Keeffe), **L2** 94
Red Rudder in the Air (Calder), **L1** 126
regular pattern, **L3** 160–163; **L4** 76; **L5** 118; **L6** 102, 106
relief art, **L3** 82–85; **L4** 132
reliefs, **L2** 70, 73
Rembrandt (van Rijn), **L2** 168; **L4** 146; **L6** 124, 125
Remedial Archaeology (Wiley), **L3** 101
Remington, Fredric, **L3** 184
Renoir, Pierre Auguste, **L2** 83; **L4** 168; **L6** 64, 65
repetition, **LK** 184–185; **L3** 206–209; **L4** 74–78
Report from Rockport (Davis), **L4** 97
rest, **L3** 170
Return from Bohemia (Wood), **LK** 65
Rex (Butterfield), **L1** 67
Rhinoceros (Dürer), **L1** 130
rhythm
	creating, **L5** 160–163
	and dance, **L1** 183
	defined, **L1** 154; **L2** 125; **L3** 155; **L4** 65
	flowing, **L4** 86–89
	and form, **L2** 138–142
	and motif, **L1** 176–179
	and movement, **LK** 190–193; **L4** 82–85; **L5** 164–167
	and repetition, **L2** 134–137
	and space, **L3** 168–171
	in theatre, **L4** 93
	three-dimensional, **L3** 176–179
	using, **L6** 95, 108–111
	visual, **L3** 172–175
Ringgold, Faith, **L3** 210; **L6** 95A
Riot (Butterfield), **L4** 199

Ritual Bell (Unknown), **LK** 198
Ritual Figure (Unknown), **L1** 138
Ritual Wine Container (Unknown), **LK** 173
Rivera, Diego, **LK** 202; **L3** 94, 95; **L5** 53, 169
Riverbank (Murray), **L4** 71
Roads Untaken (Hart), **L6** 45
The Robert Minden Ensemble, **L4** 123; **L6** 63
Robinson, John, **L5** 191
Rocks and Concrete (Helder), **L4** 101
Rodilla, Simon, **L2** 207
Within the Room (Pousette Dart), **L4** 82, 83
Rose, Timothy, **L6** 116, 117
Rotes Hause (Klee), **L3** 112
Rothenberg, Susan, **L6** 142
Rousseau, Henri, **L1** 74; **L2** 150; **L3** 150; **L6** 112
Royal Workshops, **L6** 160
Rubens, Peter Paul, **L4** 147
Ruben's Wife (Botero), **L5** 138
Ruíz, Antonio, **L1** 177; **L4** 161
Russell, Julia, **L6** 172, 173
Russell, Shirley Hopper Ximena, **L3** 96

S

Safdie, Mosche, **L6** 172
Saint George and the Dragon (Hodges), **LK** 35A
de Saint Phalle, Niki, **L3** 79
Sandburg, Carl, **L1** 213
The San Francisco Museum of Modern Art, **L4** 122
Sargent, John Singer, **L4** 191
Sarve Kashmir, **L6** 93
Satyric Festival Song, **L5** 153
Savitsky, Jack, **LK** 190
Savoy: Heel and Toe (Yard), **L5** 187
Say, Allen, **L6** 185A
scale, **L5** 130–133, 146–149; **L6** 155, 172–179, 183
Schapiro, Miriam, **LK** 86; **L1** 210; **L2** 120; **L6** 66
Schimmel, Wilhelm, **L2** 199
Schmidt-Rottluff, Karl, **L6** 74, 75
Schoenhut, Albert, **LK** 45
Scholl, John, **L4** 194
School, **L4** 171; **LK** 78
School Children on Parade (Ruíz), **L1** 177
School's Out (Crite), **LK** 78
Science Art Connections
	Earth Science, **LK** 81, 115; **L1** 69, 85, 119, 141, 145, 159, 175, 201; **L2** 43, 47, 55, 77, 89, 99, 103, 149; **L3** 39, 43, 89; **L4** 51, 89, 99, 103, 111, 119; **L5** 47, 69, 81, 111, 159, 179; **L6** 47, 59, 73, 77, 81, 89, 107, 129, 137, 163, 189
	Health, **LK** 43, 69, 73, 85; **L1** 137; **L3** 85; **L4** 43; **L5** 73, 209; **L6** 175
	Life Science, **LK** 47, 51, 55, 59, 77, 89, 99, 103, 111, 119, 189, 197, 205, 209; **L1** 43, 51, 59, 77, 89, 103, 111, 115, 149, 171, 179, 193, 197, 201, 209; **L2** 51, 73, 81, 85, 111, 115, 119, 133, 137, 163, 167, 171, 175, 197, 201; **L3** 47, 77; **L4** 39, 47, 55, 69, 73, 77, 81, 115, 133, 137, 141, 149, 159, 163, 167, 171, 179, 189, 197, 205; **L5** 39, 43, 59, 89, 99, 107, 115, 119, 129, 133, 141, 171, 189, 205; **L6** 39, 43, 51, 85, 99, 103, 115, 133, 145, 159, 167, 171, 193, 201, 205
	Physical Science, **LK** 107; **L1** 39, 47, 55, 73, 99, 107, 129, 133, 163, 189, 193, 205; **L2** 59, 69, 107, 159, 189; **L3** 51, 55, 59, 69, 73, 81, 137, 141; **L4** 59, 85, 107, 129, 145, 175, 193, 201, 209; **L5** 55, 77, 85, 103, 137, 145, 149, 163, 167, 175, 193; **L6** 55, 69, 119, 141, 149, 179, 197, 209
Scientific Method, **L2** 39; **L5** 51, 197
scoring, **L5** 84
Scott, John T., **L2** 40
Scott, Lorenzo, **L2** 164
The Scream (Munch), **L6** 164
sculptors, **LK** 212
sculpture
	additive, **L4** 130–133
	and balance, **LK** 198–201
	earthenware, **L2** 78
	and form, **LK** 130–137, 144; **L3** 78–79
	and geometric form, **L2** 66–69
	positive and negative space, **L4** 136
	reliefs, **L3** 82–85
	and rhythm, **L2** 140
	and space, **L1** 131
	subtractive, **L4** 134–137
	techniques, **L5** 84
	and unity, **LK** 206–209; **L1** 206–209; **L2** 202–205
Sea Grasses and Blue Sea (Avery), **L3** 109
Seal Hunter (Ashoona), **L2** 74, 75
Seated Arhat (Unknown), **L1** 139
Seated Man #4 (Bates), **L6** 56
Seaweed, Joe, **L1** 191
secondary colors, **L1** 106, 110, 114, 116–119; **L3** 98, 102; **L4** 98; **L5** 98; **L6** 68
secondary hues, **L2** 98
Segal, George, **LK** 150; **L5** 146; **L6** 146
Selection from Swimmy (Lionni), **L2** 194
Self-Portrait (Carr), **L4** 60
Self-Portrait Dedicated to Leon Trotsky (Kahlo), **L5** 180
Self Portrait (Hokusai), **LK** 35
Self-Portrait (the Memory) (Flack), **L4** 40
Self Portrait with Big Ears (Learning to Be Free) (Borofsky), **L3** 41
Sendak, Maurice, **LK** 66;

L4 155A
Senufo Face Mask (Unknown), **L3** 130
September Gale, Georgian Bay (Lismer), **L3** 37
set builders, **L2** 152
Sewell, Leo, **L4** 150
Shacks (Harris), **L1** 52
shade, **L2** 118; **L3** 98; **L4** 112–115; **L5** 98; **L6** 72
shading, **L4** 56–59; **L5** 78–81
shadows, **L2** 56
Shadows, **L5** 66; 70
Shahn, Ben, **LK** 79
Shannon, James J., **L2** 82
shape reversal, **L5** 68
shape(s). *See also* form
	and action, **L1** 82–85
	in architecture, **L3** 52–55
	body, **LK** 82–83
	characteristics, **L1** 128
	free-form, **LK** 74–77, 78–81, 83–84; **L1** 74–77, 134–137; **L2** 56–59; **L3** 46, 54, 58; **L4** 70–73; **L6** 40–43
	geometric, **LK** 70–73, 78–81; **L1** 70–73; **L2** 52–55; **L3** 46, 48–51, 58; **L4** 66–69; **L5** 44–47; **L6** 40–43
	and harmony, **L2** 192–193; **L3** 188; **L5** 188
	irregular, **L2** 58
	and lines, **L1** 65; **L3** 34–39
	in music, **L6** 62
	and outline, **LK** 66–69; **L1** 66–68
	and people, **LK** 86–89; **L1** 78–81; **L6** 56–59
	and rhythm, **L6** 110
	in song writing, **L5** 93
	and space, **LK** 126–129; **L6** 95
	still life, **L1** 86–89
	and texture, **L6** 176–179
	in theatre, **L1** 93; **L4** 93; **L5** 63
	two-dimensional, **L2** 68, 128; **L3** 80; **L4** 68
	using, **L3** 44–47
	and variety, **L2** 198–201; **L3** 192; **L6** 186–189
	and visual weight, **L4** 192
Shapiro, Miriam, **L4** 94, 95
Sharecropper (Catlett), **L5** 48
Sharing Stories
	About Me, **L3** 138; **L4** 74
	families, **L5** 156
	feelings, **L4** 108, 168
	imagination, **L3** 82; **L5** 190
	journeys, **L5** 198
	music, **L5** 160
	storytelling, **L2** 138; **L3** 70; **L4** 66; **L5** 142
	Taking a Stand, **L4** 176
Sharp, William, **L6** 143
Sheeler, Charles, **L5** 52
Sheet of Studies for "The Martyrdom of Saint George" (Veronese), **L4** 40, 41
shiny surface, **L2** 178; **L6** 88
Shoestring Potatoes Spilling from a Bag (Oldenburg), **L1** 124
Shotguns Fourth Ward (Biggers), **L4** 66
side view, **L4** 166
Silas Johnson (Cole), **L3** 56

silversmiths, **L5** 152
simplicity, **L3** 204; **L4** 204
simulated texture, **L4** 140; **L6** 84
Simultaneous Contrasts: Sun and Moon (Delaunay), **L2** 97
Singing Their Songs (Catlett), **L5** 134
Sioux Moccasins (Unknown), **L1** 199
Sir William Pepperrell and His Family (Copley), **L4** 154
The Sisters (Morisot), **L5** 184
size, **L4** 162; **L5** 72, 174; **L6** 54, 136
Skating in Central Park (Tait), **L1** 48
Skoglund, Sandy, **L4** 142; **LK** 206
Sleeveless Shirt (Unknown), **L3** 66
Slip Trail (Lyons), **L5** 195
Sloan, John, **L3** 194
Smith, David, **L2** 66; **L6** 44
Smith, Jaune Quick to See, **L4** 36; **L5** 34, 35
The Smithsonian Institution, **L4** 182
The Smithsonian Museum of American Art, **L2** 62
Smith, Tony, **L5** 83
Snowden, Gilda, **L1** 206
Snow Queen, Portrait of Adah (Bennion), **L6** 187
Snow Scene (Twachtman), **L6** 70, 71
Social Studies Art Connections
  Civics and Government, **LK** 43, 55, 73, 81, 103, 107, 189, 193, 197, 205, 209; **L1** 39, 51, 55, 85, 107, 115, 119, 145, 167, 171, 175, 197, 209; **L2** 47, 99, 111, 133, 167, 189, 193, 209; **L3** 39, 43, 51, 55, 69, 73, 81, 99, 133; **L4** 51, 77, 81, 103, 115, 119, 145, 167, 171, 201; **L5** 47, 59, 73, 77, 129, 171, 175, 209; **L6** 47, 69, 73, 77, 111, 129, 163, 171, 201, 209
  Economics, **LK** 99; **L1** 103, 189; **L5** 43, 119, 133, 197
  Geography, **LK** 39, 69, 77, 115, 119; **L1** 43, 47, 69, 77, 111, 133, 149, 159, 201; **L2** 39, 43, 55, 59, 69, 103, 107; **L3** 47, 89, 137; **L4** 39, 99, 159, 205; **L5** 39, 55, 69, 99, 103, 115, 141, 201, 205; **L6** 55, 59, 81, 141, 193, 205
  History and Culture, **LK** 36, 37, 40, 44, 45, 48, 49, 52, 56, 59, 60, 63, 85, 89, 111, 201; **L1** 59, 73, 81, 89, 99, 129, 141, 163, 179, 193, 205; **L2** 51, 73, 77, 81, 85, 89, 115, 129, 141, 145, 159, 163; **L3** 59, 77, 85, 129, 141; **L4** 43, 47, 55, 59, 69, 73, 85, 89, 107, 111, 129, 133, 137, 141, 149, 163, 175, 179, 189, 193, 197, 209; **L5** 51, 81, 85, 89, 107, 111, 145, 149, 159, 163, 167, 179, 189, 193; **L6** 39, 43, 51, 85, 89, 99, 103, 107, 115, 119, 133, 137, 145,

149, 159, 167, 175, 179, 189, 197
Solstice (Wilson), **L2** 112
song writing, **L1** 63; **L5** 93
The Sources of Country Music (Benton), **L5** 186
space
  in animation, **L3** 93
  and buildings, **L1** 142–145
  and depth, **L4** 155
  and form, **LK** 124–129, 134–138; **L1** 125, 130–133; **L3** 64–65; **L5** 64–65
  in music, **LK** 153; **L6** 62
  overlapping, **L2** 82–87
  and perspective, **L6** 52–55
  positive and negative, **L3** 66–70; **L5** 66–69
  and rhythm, **L2** 136; **L3** 168–171; **L6** 110
  and shape, **L6** 95
  in song writing, **L5** 93
  and still lifes, **L1** 146–149; **L2** 86–89
  and theatre, **L2** 93
  in three-dimensional art, **L6** 58
  in two-dimensional art, **L5** 70–73
  using, **L6** 35
Space Station #1 (McCall), **L5** 79
Spam (Smith), **L5** 34
Spanish Garden #IV (Norman), **L1** 60
special-effects technicians, **L6** 62
spectral color scheme, **L4** 118
Spectre of the Sea (Gottlieb), **L2** 116
spectrum, **L2** 94–95; **L3** 106; **L4** 98; **L6** 68
Spectrum III (Kelly), **L1** 96
Spectrum II (Kelly), **L1** 96
sphere, **L3** 80–81; **L4** 128; **L5** 88; **L6** 46
Spitzmueller, Pamela, **L3** 199
Spring Ice (Thomson), **L2** 104
Sprinkler Garden (Zalucha), **LK** 96
square, **LK** 72; **L1** 72; **L3** 46; **L4** 68, 128; **L5** 88; **L6** 46
Standing Ruler (Unknown), **L4** 130
Standing Youth (Unknown), **L1** 134
Starry Crown (Biggers), **L4** 90
The Starry Night (van Gogh), **LK** 63; **L2** 146
statues, **L2** 74–75
Stegosaurus (Sewell), **L4** 150
Steichen, Edward, **L2** 108
Steiglitz, Alfred, **L2** 95
Steig, William, **L6** 35A
Steinlen, Theophile-Alexandre, **LK** 52
Stella, Frank, **L1** 127; **L5** 82
Stella, Joseph, **LK** 210; **L2** 37
Steptoe, John, **L4** 95A
Still Life of Fish and Cat (Peeters), **L4** 113
Still Life on Red Tablecloth (Braque), **L5** 44
still lifes, **L1** 86–89, 146–149; **L2** 86–89; **L3** 44–45, 47
Still Life (Walker), **L1** 146
Still Life with Apples and Peaches (Cézanne), **L1** 86
Still Life with Apples and

Peaches (Lawrence), **LK** 101
Still Life with Apples (Cézanne), **L2** 87
Still Life with Basket of Apples (Cézanne), **L5** 45
Still Life with Cherries, Strawberries, and Gooseberries (Moillon), **L2** 86
Still Life with Coffee Pot (Morandi), **L4** 57
Still Life with Porcelain Dog (Münter), **L1** 147
Still Life with the Attributes of the Arts (Chardin), **L6** 82, 83
Still Life with Three Puppies (Gauguin), **L5** 160
stippling, **L5** 58, 80; **L6** 72
stitchery, **LK** 177; **L2** 172, 175
St. Michaels Counterguard (Frank), **L5** 82
Stockman House (Wright), **LK** 138
Stoneware Vase #661 (McIntosh), **L1** 168
stories, **L1** 213
storyboard artists, **L6** 62
The Story of Babar, the Little Elephant, **L1** 93
The Story ofo Babar, the Little Elephant, **L3** 123
The Story of the Nutcracker Ballet, **L4** 153
storytelling, **LK** 48; **L3** 132; **L6** 62
Strand, Paul, **L5** 56
Strawberry Tart Supreme (Flack), **L3** 124
Study for the Munich Olympic Games Poster (Lawrence), **L4** 180
Study for Time-Life Frieze (Moore), **L1** 208
Study of a Sleeping Woman (Rivera), **L5** 53
style, **LK** 96
subordinate part, **L2** 166
subtractive sculpture, **L4** 134–137
Subway Scene (Bishop), **L5** 210
Sugarman, George, **L1** 134
Suite of Appalachian Music & Dance, **LK** 93; **L4** 63
Sullivan Building (TK), **LK** 186
Sullivan, Louis, **L5** 117
Summer, New England (Prendergast), **L1** 134
Summer's Sunlight (Van Ness), **L2** 101
Sunburst (Scholl), **L4** 194
Sun (Dove), **L5** 194
The Sunflower Quilting Bee at Arles (Ringgold), **L3** 210
Sun God (de Saint Phalle), **L3** 78, 79
Sun Transformation Mask (James), **L5** 142
Surowiec, Judith, **L5** 190
Swentzell, Roxanne, **L2** 74
Swimmer Lost at Night (Bartlett), **L5** 164
symbols, **L1** 202–205
Symbols and Love Constellations of a Woman (Miró), **L4** 79
Symbols (Kohlmeyer), **L1** 203
Symmetrical View of a Totem Pole (Unknown), **L3** 134
symmetry, **L2** 156, 158, 162; **L3** 134–141; **L4** 188;

L6 126–133
Symphony Number 1 (Baranoff-Rossine), **L4** 198
synchromy, **L6** 66

T

tab and slot, **L5** 84
tactile texture, **L2** 173–174; **L3** 146–149; **L4** 142–145; **L5** 158; **L6** 86–89
Tait, Agnes, **L1** 48
Taj Mahal, **L5** 130
Taj Mahal (Isa), **LK** 139
Taking a Stand, **L4** 176; **L5** 82
The Tale of Peter Rabbit (Potter), **LK** 35A
Tamayo, Rufino, **L1** 104, 105
Taqialuk, Nuna, **L2** 190
The Tea (Cassatt), **L6** 134, 135
teachers, **L1** 212
technical illustrators, **L4** 212
Technology Art Connections
  balance, **L1** 189, 193; **L3** 129, 133; **L4** 189, 193, 197; **L5** 171, 175, 179; **L6** 137, 141
  blending, **L5** 55
  buildings, **L1** 145
  colors, **LK** 99, 103, 107, 111, 115, 119; **L1** 99, 103, 107, 111, 115, 119; **L2** 99, 103, 107; **L3** 99; **L4** 99, 103, 107, 111, 119; **L5** 99, 103, 107, 111; **L6** 81
  contrast, **L5** 59
  depth, **L3** 73
  distortion, **L4** 179; **L5** 141, 145; **L6** 167, 171
  emphasis, **L1** 197, 201; **L4** 149; **L5** 197, 201; **L6** 145, 149
  foreground, middle ground, and background, **L4** 159
  form, **L1** 129, 133, 137, 141; **L2** 69, 73, 77, 81; **L3** 81; **L4** 129; **L5** 85, 89; **L6** 51
  harmony, **L4** 201; **L5** 189; **L6** 197, 201
  hatching, **L5** 51
  hues, **L6** 69
  intensity, **L6** 77
  lines, **LK** 39, 47, 51, 55, 59; **L1** 39, 43, 47, 51, 55, 59; **L2** 39, 43, 47, 51; **L3** 39, 43; **L4** 39, 43, 51, 55; **L5** 39; **L6** 39, 43, 47
  motif, **L6** 99
  movement, **L2** 145, 149; **L6** 115, 119
  observation drawings, **L4** 47
  overlapping, **L3** 77
  pattern, **L1** 171, 175; **L2** 129, 133; **L4** 77; **L5** 115, 119; **L6** 103
  perception drawing, **L5** 43
  perspective, **L4** 163; **L5** 77; **L6** 55
  point of view, **L4** 167
  proportion, **L4** 171, 175; **L5** 129, 137, 149; **L6** 159, 163
  rhythm, **L1** 179; **L2** 137, 141; **L4** 81, 85, 89; **L5** 163, 167; **L6** 111
  scale, **L5** 133; **L6** 175, 179
  sculpture, **L3** 85; **L4** 133, 137

shading, **L4** 59, 115; **L5** 81
shapes, **LK** 69, 73, 77, 81, 85, 89; **L1** 69, 73, 77, 81, 85, 89; **L2** 55, 59; **L3** 47, 51, 55, 59; **L4** 69, 73; **L5** 47, 69, 73
space, **L1** 149; **L2** 85, 89; **L3** 69; **L6** 59
symmetry, **L3** 137, 141; **L6** 129, 133
texture, **L1** 159, 163, 167; **L3** 145; **L4** 141, 145; **L5** 159; **L6** 85, 89
three-dimensional art, **L3** 89
unity, **L1** 205, 209; **L4** 209; **L5** 205, 209; **L6** 205, 209
value, **L2** 111, 115, 119; **L6** 73
variety, **L4** 205; **L5** 193; **L6** 189, 193
Teichert, Minerva, **L2** 113
Telfair Museum of Art, **L1** 62
Ten Little Rabbits (Long), **LK** 37
textiles, **L6** 194
texture
  and balance, **L3** 124–125; **L5** 174
  and color, **L6** 64–65
  creating, **L5** 155–159
  in dance, **LK** 154–155; **L1** 183; **L6** 93
  defined, **LK** 154–155; **L1** 154; **L2** 155
  and design, **LK** 164–167
  and fibers, **LK** 168–171
  and form, **LK** 172–175
  and informal balance, **L6** 136
  in music, **LK** 183
  real, **LK** 158–159, 172–175; **L1** 156–167
  and shape, **LK** 176–179
  tactile, **L2** 172–175; **L3** 146–149; **L4** 142–145; **L6** 86–89
  and touch, **LK** 156–159
  and variety, **L3** 192
  visual, **LK** 162–163; **L2** 176–179; **L3** 142–145; **L4** 138–141; **L6** 82–85
Thai Shadow Puppet (Unknown), **L2** 57
theatre, **L1** 93; **L2** 63, 93; **L4** 93; **L5** 63, 123
Theatre Arts Integration
  balance, **LK** 193B, 197B; **L1** 185B, 189B; **L2** 155B, 159B; **L3** 125B, 129B; **L4** 185B, 189B, 193B; **L5** 167B, 171B, 175B; **L6** 133B, 137B
  blending, **L5** 51B
  buildings, **L1** 141B
  colors, **LK** 95B, 99B, 103B, 107B, 111B, 115B; **L1** 95B, 99B, 103B, 107B, 111B, 115B; **L2** 95, 99B, 103B, 185B; **L3** 95B, 99B, 103B, 107B, 111B, 115B; **L4** 95B, 99B, 103B, 107B, 115B; **L5** 95B, 99B, 103B, 107B; **L6** 77B
  contrast, **L5** 55B
  depth, **L3** 69B
  distortion, **L4** 175B; **L5** 137B, 141B; **L6** 163B, 167B
  emphasis, **L1** 193B, 197B; **L2** 163B, 167B; **L3** 193B, 197B; **L4** 145B; **L5** 193B, 197B; **L6** 141B, 145B
  foreground, middle ground,

and background, **L4** 155B
form, **L1** 129B, 133B, 137B;
  L2 65B, 69B, 73B, 77B; **L3**
  77B; **L4** 125B; **L5** 81B,
  85B; **L6** 43B, 47B
harmony, **L2** 189B; **L3**
  185B; **L4** 197B; **L5** 185B,
  L6 193B, 197B
hatching, **L5** 47B
hues, **L6** 65B
intensity, **L6** 73B
lines, **LK** 35B, 39B, 43B,
  47B, 51B, 55B; **L1** 35B,
  39B, 43B, 47B, 51B, 55B;
  L2 35B, 39B, 43B, 47B; **L3**
  35B, 39B; **L4** 35B, 39B,
  47B, 51B; **L5** 35B; **L6** 35B
motif, **L6** 95B
movement, **L2** 141B, 145B;
  L6 111B, 115B
observation drawings,
  L4 43B
overlapping, **L3** 73B
pattern, **LK** 185B; **L1** 167B,
  171B; **L2** 125B, 129B; **L3**
  155B, 159B, 163B; **L4** 73B;
  L5 111B, 115B; **L6** 99B,
  103B
perception drawing, **L5** 39B
perspective, **L4** 159B; **L5**
  73B; **L6** 51B
point of view, **L4** 163B
proportion, **L4** 167B, 171B;
  L5 125B, 133B, 145B;
  L6 155B, 159B
rhythm, **LK** 189B; **L1** 175B;
  L2 133B, 137B; **L3** 167B,
  171B, 175B; **L4** 77B, 81B,
  85B; **L5** 159B, 163B;
  L6 107B
scale, **L5** 129B; **L6** 171B, 175B
sculpture, **L3** 81B;
  L4 129B, 133B
shading, **L4** 55B, 111B;
  L5 77B
shapes, **LK** 65B, 69B, 73B,
  77B, 81B, 85B; **L1** 65B,
  69B, 73B, 77B, 81B, 125B;
  L2 51B, 55B; **L3** 43B, 47B,
  51B, 55B; **L4** 65B, 69B; **L5**
  43B, 65B, 69B; **L6** 39B
space, **L1** 145B; **L2** 81B,
  85B; **L3** 65B; **L6** 55B
symmetry, **L3** 133B, 137B;
  L6 125B, 129B
texture, **L1** 155B, 159B, 163B;
  L2 171B, 175B; **L3** 141B,
  145B; **L4** 137B, 141B; **L5**
  155B; **L6** 81B, 85B
three-dimensional art,
  L3 85B
unity, **LK** 201B, 205B; **L1**
  201B, 205B; **L2** 201B, 205B;
  L3 201B, 205B; **L4** 205B; **L5**
  201B, 205B; **L6** 201B, 205B
value, **L2** 107B, 111B,
  115B; **L6** 69B
variety, **L2** 193B, 197B; **L3**
  189B; **L4** 201B; **L5** 189B;
  L6 185B, 189B
theme, **L5** 206–209
*There's a Nightmare in My
  Closet* (Mayer), **LK** 67
Thiebaud, Wayne, **LK** 71, 104;
  L3 108, 120; **L4** 112; **L6** 120
The Thinker (Unknown), **L1** 150

Thomson, Tom, **L2** 104
three-dimensional art,
  L6 198–201, 206–209
three-dimensional forms,
  L1 138–141; **L2** 68, 140; **L3**
  80–81, 86–89; **L4** 128
three-dimensional rhythm,
  L3 176–179
three-dimensional shapes,
  L4 200
three-dimensional space,
  L6 58
Three Machines (Thiebaud),
  LK 104
*Three People on Four Park
  Benches* (Segal), **L6** 146
Thunderbird Shield
  (Unknown), **L3** 146, 147
Tiffany, Louis Comfort, **LK** 56
Tilly (Henri), **L5** 135
Time Transfixed (Magritte),
  L1 194
tint, **L2** 114; **L3** 98; **L4**
  112–115; **L5** 98; **L6** 72
Tissot, James, **L5** 173
Tlingit society, **L4** 104
Toast to the Sun (Tamayo),
  L1 105
Tooker, George, **L5** 127
Toraji Taryong **LK** 183
Tornado Over Kansas
  (Curry), **L5** 126
Torres-García, Joaquín, **L1** 36;
  L4 67
Tortilla Molds (Unknown),
  L1 165
Touchwood Hills (Eyre), **L1** 108
Toulouse-Lautrec, Henri de,
  L5 41
Town, Harold, **L2** 117
Town of Skowhegan, Maine
  (Jacquette), **L2** 210
Toy Banks (Unknown), **L5** 206
toy designers, **L5** 212
Tracey, Paul, **LK** 123; **L1** 63;
  L3 93; **L5** 93; **L6** 213
The Tragedy (Picasso), **LK** 113
Train in Coal Town
  (Savitsky), **LK** 190
trains, **LK** 190–193
Transportation, **LK** 190;
  L1 100; **L3** 39, 51
trapezoid, **L3** 50; **L5** 46; **L6** 42
The Tree of Houses (Klee),
  L2 186
Tree of Life (Bakula), **L3** 66, 67
triangle, **LK** 72; **L1** 72; **L3** 46;
  L4 68, 128; **L5** 88; **L6** 46
Trujillo, Felipa, **LK** 130
Tudor, Tasha, **L1** 155A
Tundra Swan (Audubon),
  L2 198
Tunic (Unknown), **L3** 164
Turner, Joseph Mallord
  William, **L3** 71
Twachtman, John Henry,
  LK 116; **L6** 70, 71
Twiggs, Leo, **LK** 90; **L2** 49
Two Birds in Hand (LeVan),
  L6 82
Two Black-on-Black Pots
  (Martínez), **LK** 184
two-dimensional art,
  L6 194–197
two-dimensional forms,
  L4 128

two-dimensional shapes,
  L2 68, 28; **L3** 80, **L4** 68
two-dimensional space,
  L5 70–73
Two Fishermen and a Boat
  (Gile), **L1** 101
Two Girls (Bishop), **L6** 156
Two Sisters (On the Terrace)
  (Renoir), **L2** 83

U

United States Capitol, **L6** 126
unity
  in architecture, **L2** 202–209
  and color, **L3** 202–205
  creating, **L4** 185, 206–209;
    L5 185; **L6** 185
  in dance, **L2** 212; **L6** 213
  defined, **LK** 202–209;
    L1 185; **L2** 185; **L3** 185
  and media, **L5** 202–205
  and repetition, **L3** 206–209
  in sculpture, **L1** 206–209
  in stories, **L1** 202–205, 213
  and theme, **L5** 206–209
  in three-dimensional art,
    L6 206–209
  in weaving, **L6** 202–205
unrealistic scale, **L5** 132;
  L6 176–179
urban design, **L5** 92
*Urban Raven/Urban Indian
  Transformation Mask*
  (Dick), **LK** 154
Utzon, Jørn Oberg, **L5** 87

V

Valdez, Patssi, **L4** 82
Valleyridge (Eyre), **L2** 187
value
  and blending, **L5** 52–55
  and color, **L3** 94–95, 123;
    L4 94–95, 102, 114
  and contrast, **L5** 56–59
  and dance, **L4** 123
  dark, **L2** 116–119
  defined, **L3** 98
  and hatching, **L5** 48–51
  light, **L2** 112–115
  in photographs, **L2** 108–109
  and shading, **L4** 58
  in theatre, **L5** 63
  using, **L6** 70–73
Van Allsburg, Chris, **L6** 155A
van Gogh, Vincent, **LK** 63;
  L2 146; **L5** 154, 155; **L6** 53, 70
vanishing point, **L5** 76
Van Ness, Beatrice Whitney,
  L2 101
van Rijn, Rembrandt, **L2**
  168; **L4** 146; **L6** 124, 125
variety
  of color, **L2** 194–197
  and contrast, **L6** 190–193
  creating, **L3** 190–193;
    L4 185; **L5** 185, 190–193;
    L6 185–189
  in dance, **L2** 212; **L6** 213
  defined, **L2** 185; **L3** 185
  and emphasis, **L4** 202–205
  of shape and form,

  L2 198–201
Various Fish (Miyawaki),
  L3 146
Velásquez, Diego, **L2** 184, 185
Vermeer, Jan, **L2** 176; **L5** 64, 65
Veronese, Paolo, **L4** 41
From the Viaduct, 125th St.
  (Strand), **L5** 56
Victorian Parlor (Pippin),
  L3 126
Vie No. 1 (Life No. 1)
  (Herbin), **L1** 70
A View of Mansfield Mountain
  (Kensett), **L2** 104, 105
Vigil Family, **L2** 139
violet, **L1** 112–115
Visa (Davis), **L1** 202
The Visitation (Rembrandt),
  L4 146
visual movement, **L4** 84;
  L5 166; **L6** 112–115
visual rhythm, **L3** 172–175;
  L4 78–81; **L5** 155, 162
visual texture, **LK** 162–163;
  L1 160–163; **L2** 176–179;
  L3 142–145; **L4** 138–141;
  L5 158; **L6** 82–85
visual weight, **L4** 192
*The Voice of the City of New
  York Interpreted…* (Stella),
  L2 37
Voice of the Wood, **L3** 153;
  L5 63
Vuillard, Edouard, **LK** 97
Vytlacil, Vaclav, **L3** 45

W

The Wadsworth Atheneum,
  L4 62
Walk Don't Walk (Segal),
  L5 146
The Walker Art Center, **L3** 152
Walker, Patricia, **L1** 146
The Walking Flower (Leger),
  L3 78
Warhol, Andy, **L3** 202
warm hues, **L5** 108–111
Warnyu (flying boxes)
  (Djukulul), **L3** 160, 161
Warren, John, **L6** 49
Washington at Yorktown
  (Peale), **L2** 161
Washington's Headquarters
  (Unknown), **L3** 70
watercolor, **L4** 54
Waterfall Blue Brook
  (Twachtman), **LK** 116
Watts Street (Brosen), **L5** 75
Watts Tower (Rodilla), **L2** 207
Weary (Whistler), **L5** 49
Weather
  changes, **L3** 36
  rainbow colors, **L1** 96
  seasons, **LK** 56; **L1** 40, 119; **L2**
    100; **L3** 74, 104; **L4** 99, 160
  shadows, **L5** 66; **L6** 70
  temperature, **LK** 40
  time, **L1** 112
  wind, **LK** 74; **L4** 86
weaving, **LK** 36, 170; **L1** 172;
  L6 202–205
Weber, Idelle, **L3** 116
Weber, Max, **L6** 94, 95
Webster, Elon, **L5** 142

Wells, Rosemary, **L1** 65A
The Westwood Children
  (Johnson), **L4** 190
We Tell Stories, **L1** 213
Where the Wild Things Are
  (Sendak), **LK** 66
Whistler, James McNeill,
  L4 56; **L5** 49
White Pine Mosaic
  (Moulthrop), **L3** 156
White Vertical Water
  (Nevelson), **L6** 198
The White Wave (Avery), **L4** 100
The Whitney Museum, **L6** 92
Wiesner, David, **LK** 74; **L5** 185A
Wiley T, William, **L3** 101
Williams, Garth, **L5** 35A
Williams, Vera B., **L5** 155A
Wilson, Jane, **L2** 112
Winged Frog (Parsons), **LK** 156
Winter Loneliness (Hokusai),
  L4 87
Winxiang, Prince Yi
  (Unknown), **L5** 168
Woman (Blanco), **L4** 131
Woman in a Purple Coat
  (Matisse), **LK** 94
Woman in Blue (Matisse),
  L3 207
Woman's Headcloth
  (Unknown), **L6** 195
*Women of Paris: The Circus
  Lover* (Tissot), **L5** 173
Wood, Grant, **LK** 64, 65; **L4** 160
words, **L1** 202–205
Her World (Evergood),
  L3 138, 139
World's Greatest Comics
  (Shahn), **LK** 79
Wrapped Oranges
  (McCloskey), **L2** 135
Wright, Frank Lloyd, **LK** 138
Wyeth, N. C., **L6** 125A

Y

The Yale University Gallery,
  LK 122
Yard, Richard, **L5** 187
Yeihl Nax'in Raven Screen
  (Unknown), **L4** 104
Yeiltatzie, John, **LK** 195
*Yellow Hickory Leaves with
  Daisy* (O'Keefe), **L4** 202
Yellow Pad (Fish), **L3** 44
Yellow Top (Sugarman), **L1** 130
Young, Ed, **L5** 65A
Youngblood, Nancy, **L3** 187
*Young Spanish Woman with
  a Guitar* (Renoir), **L6** 64

Z

Zalucha, Peggy Flora, **LK** 96,
  180; **L2** 134
*Zandunga Tehuantepec
  Dance* (Rivera), **LK** 202
Zeldis, Malcah, **L4** 117
zigzag lines, **L1** 46, 58